The MODERNIZATION
of CHINA

CONTRIBUTING AUTHORS

Thomas P. Bernstein

Cyril E. Black

Sally Borthwick

Marius B. Jansen

Marion J. Levy, Jr.

F. W. Mote

Ramon H. Myers

Gilbert Rozman

Lynn T. White III

Written under the auspices of the
Center of International Studies,
Princeton University

The MODERNIZATION of CHINA

Edited by Gilbert Rozman

THE FREE PRESS
A Division of Macmillan Publishing Co., Inc.
NEW YORK

Collier Macmillan Publishers
LONDON

The Free Press
A Division of Macmillan Publishing Co., Inc.
866 Third Avenue, New York, N.Y. 10022

Collier Macmillan Canada, Inc.

First Free Press Paperback Edition 1982

Library of Congress Catalog Card Number: 81-66985

Printed in the United States of America

printing number hardcover

1 2 3 4 5 6 7 8 9 10

printing number paperback

1 2 3 4 5 6 7 8 9 10

Library of Congress Cataloging in Publication Data

Main entry under title:

The modernization of China.

    Bibliography: p.
    Includes index.
    1. China—History—19th century. 2. China—History—
20th century. I. Rozman, Gilbert. II. Black, Cyril
Edwin
DS755.M63   951   81-66985
ISBN 0-02-927480-X
ISBN 0-02-927360-9 pbk.

Maps 1 and 2, "China Proper in the Nineteenth Century" and
"Growth of the Treaty Port System," are from *The Cambridge
History of China,* volume 10, part 1, pp. 7 and 512, respectively,
and are reprinted here with the permission of Cambridge
University Press.
Map 3, "Japanese-occupied Areas of China, 1937–1945," first
appeared in *The Rise of Modern China* by Immanuel C. Y. Hsu
(New York: Oxford University Press, 1970). Copyright © 1970 by
Oxford University Press, Inc. It is reprinted here with
permission of the publisher.
Map 4, "People's Republic of China," first appeared in *Chinese
Civilization and Society* by Patricia Buckley Ebrey (New York: Free
Press, 1980) and is reprinted here with the permission of the
author.
Table 10.2 was originally compiled from data appearing in *The
Economic Growth of Nations* by Simon Kuznets (Cambridge, Mass.:
Belknap Press, 1971) and was published in *The Chinese Economy
Past and Present* (Belmont, Calif.: Wadsworth, 1980). It has been
adapted and is reprinted here with the permission of the
publisher.

Contents

Part One: THE LEGACY OF THE PAST
The Eighteenth and Nineteenth Centuries

Contents

Contents

Contents

LIST OF MAPS

Preface

THIS STUDY WAS WRITTEN UNDER THE AUSPICES of the Center of International Studies, Princeton University, with the support of grants from the National Science Foundation and the National Endowment of the Humanities. The views expressed in this study are those of the authors, and do not necessarily represent those of the Center, the Foundation, or the Endowment.

In no conventional sense is this an edited volume. Over a five-year period the authors collaborated closely, jointly planning the contents and organization, continuously coordinating their interpretations and conclusions, and taking an active role in revising all chapters regardless of primary authorship. Individually or in pairs, authors did take separate charge of initial drafts of chapters: Marius B. Jansen prepared Chapters 2 and 8; F. W. Mote wrote Chapter 3 and, together with Lynn T. White III, Chapter 9; Ramon H. Myers drafted Chapter 4 and, together with Lynn T. White III, Chapter 10; Gilbert Rozman prepared Chapters 5, 11, and 14; Sally Borthwick wrote Chapter 6 and, together with Thomas P. Bernstein, Chapter 12; and, working along with Gilbert Rozman, Cyril E. Black and Marion J. Levy, Jr. gave their primary attention to Chapters 1 and 15. Bernstein's participation was largely limited to Chapter 12, and neither Borthwick nor Myers was close enough at hand to take more than an intermittent role in the revising of chapters other than their own. While there has been a division of labor, we want to emphasize that the findings of this manuscript represent the collective work of the authors.

Inherent in the controversial nature of the subject of China's modernization is the inevitability that what we have written represents only our views. Even among this group of authors there are differences of emphasis and viewpoint reflected in the individual chapters. On the basis of each chapter's findings we have drawn general conclusions that are supported by the group as a whole, but not all authors necessarily subscribe to every set of conclusions.

Preface

The gratitude of the authors is extended to others who participated in the preparation of this volume. Barbara Westergaard made an important contribution to clarity and consistency with her professional editing. As research assistants knowledgeable about China, Elizabeth Allan and Janis Michael made numerous suggestions pertaining to every chapter. Ms. Allan also prepared portions of the bibliography and chronology. In the early stages of the project C. T. Hu took part in shaping the chapters on knowledge and education. D. Eleanor Westney wrote down her thoughts about the conclusions, which played a part in the revisions of Chapter 15. Gary Hamilton, William L. Parish, Evelyn S. Rawski, Thomas Rawski, and Denis Twitchett served as an advisory group and each scrutinized early drafts of chapters. No fewer than forty others attended one or more of the conferences for this project, commenting on drafts and contributing to the general understanding of the subject.

A preparatory conference was held in December 1974, before the project got under way, and subsequent consultations were held in February and November 1977, April and September 1978, and May and October 1979.

There is insufficient space to thank each individual in Chinese and comparative studies who participated in these conferences or in some other manner assisted this project. The many revisions we have made in an effort to respond to their suggestions should testify to our appreciation.

Our thanks are also due to Jane G. McDowall, Administrative Officer of the Center of International Studies, and her staff for their valuable role in the preparation of this volume. Theresa Kuzianik of the Sociology Department and Carol MacKinnon have also helped importantly in the production.

In 1975 four of the present group of authors, along with four other specialists on the countries involved, wrote a book entitled *The Modernization of Japan and Russia.* In the preparation of this volume, as in that prior project, the collaborative effort extended for many years and required the close cooperation of area specialists with diverse interests among which is the general study of modernization. Altogether many of us have been involved in these studies for ten years. The process has been continuous, and the two books are parallel and complementary in most respects, facilitating the comparisons essential for research on the topics introduced.

As this book was being written, the People's Republic of China changed course from the tumultuous rule of Mao Tse-tung (Mao Zedong) and the so-called Gang of Four, who had led the Chinese through the Cultural Revolution, to the pragmatic leadership of Teng Hsiao-p'ing (Deng Xiaoping) and fellow supporters of the newly proclaimed four modernizations. Both of these communist-led approaches to social change can be interpreted in the context of our perspective on modernization, but clearly the latter is more consistent with the long-term patterns that we anticipate in this volume.

Chinese history since 1949 is not singled out for separate attention in most of this volume. Thus Chapter 14 stands apart by making this period the explicit focus. It does so by drawing primarily on information introduced earlier and reinterpreting this from the point of view of comparative communism.

Chinese policies are in considerable flux. Leadership struggles at the highest levels continue, and the realization of a highly modernized society is not yet within sight. Our perspective is not to emphasize the most recent initiatives, but to look at the basic problems and responses that have shaped the entire course of modernization and that continue to form the background for contemporary developments.

GILBERT ROZMAN

Chronology

960–1279	Sung (Song) dynasty.
1280–1368	Yuan/Mongol dynasty.
1368–1644	Ming dynasty.
1644–1912	Ch'ing (Qing) dynasty.
1839–1860	Period of Opium Wars and unequal treaties: the "opening of China" (1842 Treaty of Nanking ending Opium War; 1858 Tientsin treaties; 1860 occupation of Peking by British and French forces).
1850–1881	Period of revolts and rebellions (1850–1864 Taiping rebellion; 1853–1868 Nien rebellion; also Shanghai, Moslem, and Miao revolts).
1877–1878	Establishment of Chinese legations in western capitals and Tokyo.
1894–1895	China defeated by Japan.
1897–1898	Scramble for concessions by Germany, England, Russia, and France.
1898	Hundred Days reform.
1900	Boxer uprising.
1901–1911	The Decade of Conservative Reform: abolition of the examination system (1905); program instituted to send thousands of students abroad to study; preparation for constitutional monarchy.
1904–1905	Russo-Japanese War, fought on Chinese territory.
1905	Sun Yat-sen organizes T'ung-meng hui (Revolutionary League) among Chinese students in Tokyo.
1911–1912	Republican revolution, abdication of the Manchus, and establishment of the Republic of China.
1915	Japan presents Twenty-One Demands. "New Culture Movement" founded to promote values of science and democracy.
1916–1926	Warlord period; failure of republicanism.
1919	May Fourth Movement. Paris Peace Conference.
1921	Founding of the Chinese Communist Party.

Chronology

1923–1927	Nationalist-communist united front.
1925	May 30th antiforeign movement.
1927	Chiang Kai-shek crushes communists in Shanghai and Nanking; beginning of ten-year Nanking phase of Nationalist government.
1931	Kiangsi Soviet (Chinese Soviet Republic) established by Communist Party.
1934	Chinese communists forced by Nationalists to flee Kiangsi area; beginning of Long March.
1935	New communist base set up in Shensi, at Yenan.
1937	War with Japan begins; second Nationalist-communist united front.
1945	End of war with Japan.
1946	Beginning of civil war.
1949	Establishment of People's Republic of China.
1950	Sino-Soviet Pact of Friendship and Alliance. Land reform and marriage laws.
1953	First five-year plan.
1956	Nationalization of enterprises and collectivization of land.
1957	Hundred Flowers period, followed by antirightist campaign.
1958–1960	Great Leap Forward.
1966–1968	Great Proletarian Cultural Revolution.
1976	Mao Tse-tung dies. Gang of Four arrested.
1977	Four modernizations (agriculture, industry, science, and defense) set as urgent priorities.

The MODERNIZATION
of CHINA

CHAPTER ONE

Introduction

CHINA HAS LONG OCCUPIED A CONSPICUOUS PLACE in the general awareness of how modernization varies throughout the world. Opinions about, interest in, and affection for China's extraordinary nature abound, but solid information and extended analyses remain scant. Perhaps because of its enormous population, its unparalleled historical continuity, and its awesome cultural creativity and depth, China has continued to fascinate all manner of people, yet the country has been persistently neglected in the specialized literature that contributes to our understanding of modernization.

Popular perceptions of China have oscillated widely over the years. At the dawn of the modern era it appeared likely that if any country apart from the European nations and their offshoots was to modernize—to achieve a massive transformation from an agrarian-based society with low per capita income to an urbanized, industrialized one oriented to the application of science and technology—it would be China. By practically any standard of sophistication and development, China seemed to have been, if not *the* leading, one of the leading civilizations for at least two millennia. In the governance of a society large in both extent and population, the Chinese knew neither peers nor superiors. They had in the past shown themselves flexible in absorbing peoples and ideas from other quarters. Yet, when the patterns associated with modernization began to appear in the world, not only did China not emerge among the first-comers, for over a century it did not even show any signs of becoming what will be called here a "successful" latecomer. The expectations of this early period were not sustained. Indeed, the optimism of eighteenth-century admirers was already being eclipsed in the early nineteenth century, when modernization in Europe was still in its first stages.

1

A second perception—of a country hopelessly impoverished and misman-aged—prevailed during most of the years between 1840 and 1949, the pessimism doubtless reinforced by the devastating Taiping rebellion in the 1850s and 1860s. Overcoming the inertia of a venerable and enduring civilization and setting so great a mass of humanity on a strikingly new path appeared to be beyond the capacities of any Chinese government.

During this period, a brief interlude of rising hopes and expectations accompanied the end of the Ch'ing dynasty and the birth of the Chinese republic in 1911. The doctrines of Sun Yat-sen, which certainly constituted the leitmotif of the republican period, promised economic development and were, to a substantial extent, republican and democratic. The new China was to be based on the Enlightenment, which had given birth to the radical new forms of the American and French revolutions. This optimism briefly flickered again when the Kuomintang established a national government in 1927 and perhaps again in 1937 when China's adverse circumstances seemed for a bit to have effectively reunited the Chinese in their opposition to Japan. But these rising hopes were dashed by the consequences of domestic disunity and foreign intervention.

Again the pendulum swung after 1949, as a new image spread, an image of a communist state able to modernize by entering the Soviet orbit. This perception, shared by the eastern and western blocs, forecast Chinese modernization as a socialist society according to an already tested model. Although observers disagreed on the costs of Soviet-style forced industrialization for the Chinese people and their traditions, they widely anticipated the results of rapid modernization.

Another impression took center stage after the Sino-Soviet alliance was abruptly terminated and, shortly thereafter, the Cultural Revolution became China's all-consuming motif. China would modernize in a radically new way without many effects—especially inequalities—often deemed essential to modernization. Some proposed that China's divergence from what was presumed to be the necessary path to modernization would demonstrate the ideological bankruptcy of this term as a defense of hierarchy, specialization, bureaucracy, and orderly evolution. According to this version, the universality of a process called modernization would be disproved by a divergent course designed by China's revolutionary leader Mao Tse-tung (Mao Zedong) that achieved economic growth on a strikingly different social foundation.

Finally, when the Cultural Revolution was repudiated by a new leadership in favor of a more conventional path explicitly designed to achieve modernization, China suddenly emerged in the limelight as a test case of a more usual sort. Its experience would help answer standard questions about the conditions conducive to modernization. Individuals around the world are watching with special interest to see how successful the post-Mao leadership will be in realizing its oft-repeated goals for modernization.

Despite the continued fascination with China that has accompanied these exaggerated swings in popular perceptions, the scholarly literature either explicitly or implicitly concerned with the modernization of China is meager and unsystematic. Little is known about China's actual chances for modernization or about the barriers that stood in the way during the nineteenth and twentieth centuries. The authors of this volume believe that an analysis of China's experience with modernization has a great deal to offer: it can focus attention on important questions in the social sciences; it can merge the resources of several academic disciplines, showing, as has seldom been done for China, how each sheds light on different aspects of the same problems. A study of modernization must also delve into the relations between periods that are normally treated separately in Chinese studies. Furthermore, it promises an avowedly comparative perspective on a country so often studied in isolation.

What Is Modernization?

We view modernization as the process by which societies have been and are being transformed under the impact of the scientific and technological revolution. The experience of already modernized societies indicates that modernization is best considered as a process affecting all aspects of society. Some social elements are changed directly, but others are changed, perhaps even more significantly, because the introduction of new, even of apparently unconnected elements, changes the context in which historical elements operate. Throughout this volume we refer to elements of social change commonly associated with modernization and often regarded as essential features or even as the defining elements of that process, such as increased international dependence; relative growth in nonagricultural production, especially manufactures and services; a movement from high birth and death rates to low ones; sustained economic growth; more even distribution of income; specialization and proliferation of organizations and skills; bureaucratization; mass political participation (whether democratic or not); and an expansion of education at all levels. The list could be greatly enlarged. No consensus exists on the items to be included or the relative rates of change of various indicators. But there is a widespread impression, which we share, that in the long run one can more or less predict what magnitude of change in various indicators corresponds to increasing modernization.* The accuracy of that im-

---

* For the reader who prefers a parsimonious index of modernization, we would define the degree of modernization by the ratio of inanimate to animate sources of power. When that ratio reaches a point such that relatively small decreases in inanimate power cannot be compensated for by increases in animate (which for most human history has meant human) power without far-reaching social changes, a society or country may be considered modernized—and the higher that ratio the more highly modernized. "High modernization" is characterized by mass markets for heavy consumer goods.

pression must be ascertained by research; it is not a matter of definition, and it should not be left to unsupported intuition.

We regard modernization as one of the most dramatic, far-reaching, and apparently ineluctable examples of social change in human history. Whether for good or for ill, the influence of these changes spreads to all peoples who come in contact with those already possessed of these patterns. Invariably, existing social patterns are undermined, and modernization becomes a goal, however qualified the commitment to it may be. It is universal in having effects and in some of its effects, although this does not mean that all countries become modernized. It may be that some areas will never reach a point of no return, and it is certain that many will not do so for a long time. Resources may not be plentiful enough to support all societies at a high level of modernization. Many societies, perhaps all to some degree, will experience fundamentalist reactions. It is also certain, however, that no peoples will ever go back to what they were before contact with modernization.

Our major aims are to identify the elements in Chinese society that are or have been conducive to modernization as well as those that hinder it and to assess the rate and pattern of modernization that occurred. The elements that affect modernization in China, whether indigenous premodern conditions, aspects of international relations, or policies promoted by modernizing leaders, are never exact duplicates of elements elsewhere. Above all, these elements fit into a different social context, a specifically Chinese context. Yet the numerous similar features of successfully modernizing societies suggest that it is useful to search for a common set of conditions that make modernization possible. By examining the course of modernization in China, we hope to determine in what respects it follows the basic routes of other modernizing countries and in what respects it diverges along a path of its own.

The most spectacular differences among modernizing societies have been those between the early modernizing countries we refer to as first-comers (primarily England, France, and the United States) and successful latecomers (such as Japan and Russia). The former gradually transformed indigenous elements over a long period, while the latter relied more heavily on borrowing from foreign models and on rapidly adding to or replacing existing structures. Since China is also a latecomer, the focus of our comparative attention is on the path followed by the latecomers.

It is assumed here that once modernization developed anywhere in the world, it was inevitable that its influences would spread to other parts of the globe, whether by force of arms, by people's preferences, or by combinations of the two. Thus all countries that were not first-comers became latecomers, and all latecomers found that major elements in their social structure were subverted by the enormous appeal and pressure of elements connected with modernization. The subversiveness of the process did not need to be a function of the direct revolutionizing of existing social structures, though often enough it was. Even under more benign or indigenously controlled leadership, the introduction of new patterns radically changed the context in which the stability of former patterns had been achieved. The peculiar interdependence of the patterns of modernization with other social structures dooms self-conscious attempts, however well intended, to combine "the best of the old with the best of the new." Experience with modernization generally moves some members of society, even some leaders, to fundamentalist reactions—attempts to go back to the good old days in real or idealized form—but such attempts are never successful. Elements of the old society persist and influence the course of modernization, but many other elements are subverted, and many new elements are introduced.

Obviously, both indigenous and exogenous factors contribute to the way in which modernization develops in a country. The exogenous patterns are more likely to be similar to those of other latecomers, the indigenous to reflect a country's distinctive historical background. The relation between these factors is one of the important themes to be investigated in this study.

As we use the terms, "modernization" is not equivalent to "industrialization" or "westernization." Industrialization signifies to us the development of the manufacturing sector, including both heavy and light manufacturing, certainly one of the processes that occur in modernizing societies, but only one of many. We believe that by spreading our net more widely, by examining the interaction of different elements in a society over time, the modern transformation of societies can be more fully understood. Of course, the term "industrialization" may also be given a broader meaning. The tendency to equate industrialization with modernization may stem from the use of one element of the process to name the whole; in conventional usage the term sometimes refers to the same range of changes we mean by modernization. Its weakness for our purposes lies in its connotative distinction from agrarian processes. For the world in which we live the exponential increases in agrarian productivity per hectare and per worker have proved at least as significant as increases in factory-based productivity.

The term "westernization," on the other hand, is based on the association of patterns of modernization with the countries in which they first developed. These patterns are, however, by no means exclusively associated with the West, nor are all western countries highly modernized. Some of the most important twentieth-century variations on the pattern of modernization developed in Japan and others may now be developing in countries around the periphery of China and in China itself. Indeed, Japan may well become *the* most modernized society for reasons that have more to do with Japan's indigenous background than with the elements of modernization itself. Westernization signifies to us the adoption of distinctively western characteristics. It is a misnomer for modernization, but it is sometimes used by others with that broader significance.

We use such terms as "successful" and "latecomer," which both imply comparisons with other societies, in a value-neutral sense—as descriptive

5

terms, not evaluative ones. The only relevance the value of modernization has to this volume lies in the fact that the Chinese participants in the modernization process have often equated early modernization with success and late-coming with failure, a belief that has had important consequences for modernization in China. No judgment on a society's wisdom or worth is implicit in calling it successful or lagging in modernization. Indeed, perhaps as many people would assign negative as positive values to the process, especially when it is viewed from a distance and does not directly affect the observer's life style.

In short, using the modernization approach to study China is a device, not a goal, a tool to be used as long as it proves useful, not an ideology. We do not seek to pass judgment on the phenomena we are studying. We only wish to understand more fully recent social change in China and to improve the general understanding of social change elsewhere on the basis of findings about China. Our choice of this approach does not rule out the desirability of using other approaches to study China and modern change elsewhere.

The Long-term Course of Modernization

No single book can pretend to close the large gap in our knowledge of modern social change in China. By taking an interdisciplinary, multifaceted approach and examining in an integrated way historical periods usually treated in isolation, we seek to build on recent beginnings in Chinese studies and to explore fresh perspectives. This book is divided into two parts. The first and last chapters stand apart, but Part One (Chapters 2–7) focuses primarily on the eighteenth and nineteenth centuries, and Part Two (Chapters 8–13) on the twentieth.

Several decisions underlay our choice of periods. First, the decision to encompass the historical basis from which change took place as well as the full course of modernization to date requires that we examine a long time span. One has to reach back to the middle of the Ch'ing dynasty, even back into the late Ming dynasty in some political aspects, to gain a relatively clear impression of both stable premodern conditions and the pattern of change prior to contact with modernized countries. To the extent that we can demonstrate that much of the variation in the rate and pattern of modernization is likely to be accounted for by internal conditions already present when that process began, it becomes imperative to delve into the historical background out of which the changes emerged. Furthermore, it behooves us to consider the impression that China early possessed many modern features by looking at the historical record. The nature of Chinese society during the final centuries before the foreign challenge that led to modernization is a major concern of this study.

Second, we bridge two dates that are rightly regarded as watersheds in

Chinese history, 1840 and 1949. The decision not to start Part Two around 1840, when the Opium War opened China to ever-widening foreign influences, was based on evidence that the major reforms launching a massive transformation were not promulgated until many decades later. Each of the chapters of Part One distinguishes the premodern setting of the middle Ch'ing dynasty from the gradually changing setting in the late Ch'ing, but in no case do we regard the changes of the mid-nineteenth century as a decisive break with the past for internal conditions, however much they may foreshadow it.

The year 1949 obviously does represent a sharp break with the past along many dimensions. We decided to bridge that year in Part Two so that we could observe the continuities in problems of modernization and compare responses to them. By not limiting ourselves to the widespread practice of treating post-1949 separately (apart from Chapter 14), we seek a broader context for understanding the contemporary era. Modernization, including the abandonment of many longstanding pillars of Chinese social structure, began before 1949. Indeed, with a broader time frame, it should be easier to ascertain in what respects 1949 was a turning point in China's modernization: like so many others, we certainly do find that that year is a major turning point, especially with regard to coordination and control.

The years between 1895 and 1911 are widely regarded as the period in which the impetus to modernize took on a new urgency. Popular demands for major policy changes resounded. Reforms dismantled many basic features of the dynastic era, and revolution toppled the vestiges of the imperial order. Although the chapters in this book do not rigidly adhere to a single year as the dividing line between Parts One and Two, we do stick fairly closely to the year 1900, a point on the eve of major reforms.

For China after 1900, our attention shifts from the conditions affecting the country's capacity to respond to external forces of modernization to the policies directed at its modernization. How effective were they? How rapidly did modernization proceed in successive periods? Were there factors that quickened modernization in the short run but could not be reconciled with it in the long run? In what ways was the process uneven? Which dimensions led and which lagged? We also consider in Part Two how the legacy of the past discussed in Part One relates to the policies of the twentieth century.

The Multifaceted Nature of Modernization

Each social science has areas of interest that are linked to the concept of modernization, but the changes that take place during the modernization of a society do not respect disciplinary boundaries. As the leaders of China and other nations have discovered, it is impossible to adopt desired aspects of modernization, such as industrial development, without experiencing profound and often unanticipated repercussions in other areas. It is for this reason that we have selected an interdisciplinary approach. By examining the changes in five areas—international context, political structure, economic structure and growth, social integration, and knowledge and education—we try to approximate a complete picture of this interrelated, multifaceted transformation.

We begin with the international context (Chapters 2 and 8). For a late-comer, modernization always involves a response to a foreign challenge. The latecomer faces a changing international environment and must agree, or be forced to agree, on the importance of a massive program of change based heavily on borrowing from abroad. To be successful it must borrow without undermining, or must largely create, the internal conditions conducive to modernization. Yet for well over a millennium, the Chinese, without substantial challenge, saw themselves in a sinocentric world. They were able to persist in this general view of China as the "middle country" even in the face of the Mongol and Manchu conquests. Starting in the nineteenth century, however, the non-Chinese world impinged much more deeply on Chinese perceptions and behavior. What was the nature of the various pressures brought to bear on China? Was the external environment the Chinese faced at this critical juncture different in important respects—perhaps harsher—than that faced by others at similar points in their development? Was the foreign challenge of such a nature that it left a less compelling impression of the power of modernization than that made on people of other nations? Does the timing of China's most meaningful contacts with the modernizing powers help explain its course of modern transformation?

Another set of question directs attention at the historical factors affecting the Chinese response. Did China's particular legacy of perceiving and dealing with foreigners limit its capacity to borrow effectively? Was the Chinese world view an important factor in its reaction to a changing world? Was modernization thwarted because of a special habit of mind? Did preoccupation with an ideal past inhibit efforts to respond to opportunities for creating a different future? Positive answers to these questions would point to limitations the legacy of the past, particularly its intellectual aspects, places on modernization.

We also ask how leaders adjusted China's alliances, trade, investment, and borrowing in general in the pursuit of modernization. Was borrowing well suited to domestic needs or was it misguided, unnecessarily rootless and traumatic? How did successive strategies of isolation and alliance affect the desire and ability to modernize?

The examination of the external setting is followed by an inquiry into four internal areas. Chapters 3 and 9 consider China's political structure. Here we are concerned with the increasing ability of the members of a society to use public and private institutions to control and allocate resources with a view to realizing the possibilities implicit in the advancement of knowlege that results initially from foreign contacts. Attention centers primarily on the national government, the level at which leaders select policies and engineer changes. Our concern with political structure, however, also extends to regional and local distributions of power and responsibility, involving units as scattered as community and kinship organizations. These units are often critical in determining the success or failure of policies desired and promulgated centrally. Political structure is of great importance to modernization because it affects decision making and the coordination and control that determine whether policies are carried out and which options are viable. It involves not just power but the mobilization of will.

The most pervasive theme in the treatment of political structure is the coordination and control of people and goods. Were existing patterns of coordination and control adaptable to conditions of initial modernization? Can we identify changes in the quality and effectiveness of political structure during the Ch'ing dynasty that affected the controls necessary for modernization? Could the relative fullness and perfection of the early Chinese political ideal have acted as a stumbling block? Were the stabilizing forces of tradition difficult to dislodge? Did the longstanding bases of coordination and control depend on other structures highly vulnerable to the social changes associated with modernization? Once dislodged, could these structures be readily replaced? How did successive modernizing leaderships, including the various communist leaderships after 1949, act to increase coordination and control?

From time to time in the chapters on political structure we seek to answer questions about the extent to which state actions could have accelerated the course of modernization. To what extent was inadequate leadership a drawback? How did national decisions, such as the campaign methods of popular mobilization after 1949, affect modernization? With reference to the twentieth century, we probe the importance for modernization of popular participation, the extension of rights and freedoms, and opportunities for interest groups to form and express their views. Was political leadership the prime determinant of the main contours of modernization, or were other factors equally decisive?

In Chapters 4 and 10 we look at economic structure and growth. A massive increase in production (accompanied by a shift away from agricultural predominance) is essential for other modernizing changes. The sequence of change for a successful latecomer can be described rather simplistically as consisting of the following steps: first, a sharp stimulus to action from threatening and, at the same time, in some ways appealing foreign contacts; second, the emergence of a new modernizing leadership committed to extensive changes; third, an avid pursuit of economic growth, which brings a major structural change in the balance of economic sectors; and fourth, a transformation in the conditions of life which accompanies occupational shifts and the growing specialization of labor. Economic performance emerges as the primary test of the leadership's success in achieving modernization and as the basic predictor of other kinds of social change for two reasons: (1) it is the easiest to measure, and the meaning of the measures is most easily interpreted; and (2) if economic growth—the special lure of modernization—cannot be achieved, no other policies of development can be either since none rests on free goods alone.

Many questions about the Chinese economy center on problems of raising adequate funds for investment and balancing various types of activities and development. How did population growth in a densely settled country affect the capacity to save? Did the flow of goods lead to a distribution of resources conducive to economic growth? Was the structure of rewards suitable for allocating scarce resources to activities that promote growth? Could the economic vitality of local systems provide a sufficient base for national growth? What are the consequences of uneven development favoring heavy industry, or of economic growth without a large shift of labor to cities or a large increase in consumption? What are the consequences of growth that results almost exclusively from increases in the supply of labor and other resources? Other questions pertain to the balance between public and private sectors. During the Ch'ing dynasty were the limited role of the state (compared to other premodern countries) and the weak perception of the need for an activist state barriers to modern growth? In the economics chapters we seek to determine whether historical conditions were favorable to growth, how rapidly growth occurred, and what the effects of policies directed at growth were.

The fourth area, social integration, deals with the processes leading to greater unity and interaction within a society. Chapters 5 and 11 raise general social questions about modernization. These questions concern the quantity and quality of human resources and their spatial distribution and organization, processes of redistribution, and aspects of personal relationships. A long list of elements is considered, each a possible index of modernization as well as a possible factor contributing to the process.

To a large extent the questions raised in the social integration chapters refer to general patterns of human interaction. Had occupations and skills become differentiated in a manner suited to modernization? Had settlement patterns and social organizations developed sufficiently and effectively for promoting modernization? How effective over the short and long run were the incentives the Chinese Communist Party (CCP) used to mobilize resources? To the extent that the patterns of social integration significantly impaired the mobilization of resources, one must conclude that even an activist leadership would have faced formidable obstacles and that problems of economic growth must be seen in the context of problems of general social structure.

In the chapters on social integration we seek above all to answer questions about the means and incentives for mobilizing and channeling resources. Were the human and material resources scattered in local communities adequate to the needs of modernization? Were they deeply embedded locally, or had the Chinese developed mechanisms for reallocating them to the cities either through a concentrated elite, or through taxation and commerce? Were the patterns of control for mobilizing resources adaptable to a modernized setting? Families, merchant and state organizations, elites and many other social matters are examined in the search for answers to these questions.

Our final area is knowledge and education. In Chapters 6 and 12 we recognize the importance for modernization of the advance of knowledge and its dissemination through education. Any modernizing society must give high priority to absorbing and expanding modern knowledge and technology; they are necessary for borrowing and for building a new society. As a minimum, literacy must be extended to the general public. Education has been given considerable attention in the literature on China, from the suggestion that the Confucian system of education accompanied by the national examination system long delayed the acceptance of modern knowledge, to the idea that the educational policies under the so-called Gang of Four severely set back modernization.

Like the people of other premodern societies, most Chinese were not educated in school, but unlike the situation nearly everywhere else, schooling in China had a venerable tradition and commanded enormous respect. What was the relationship between this heritage and China's capacity to modernize? In what ways was intellectual life conducive or detrimental to modernization? What were the implications of the examination system? What have been the implications of more recent policies aimed at combining ''redness'' and expertise? At combining mental and manual labor? With even tentative answers to these questions we can consider whether aspects of knowledge and education have, as some suggest, been decisive in shaping the course of China's modernization.

It is obvious that a single study cannot cover comprehensively all the subjects commonly considered in the disciplines represented in this volume. This range of topics, however, provides a framework within which we can examine many of the important issues that come up in the literature on modernization in a broad yet systematic way.

Other Approaches

We are, of course, aware that ours is not the only approach to such changes and that some of the literature on China makes use of one or another of the various Marxist approaches. Some approaches influenced by Marx claim that Asian societies did not have an indigenous capacity to modernize and that consequently European penetration was a first step toward modern development. Condemning colonialism as much as capitalism, they nonetheless see foreign penetration as a prerequisite to the eventual realization of socialism in countries that did not share the characteristics of European feudalism. Many others influenced by Marx and Lenin argue that indigenous "sprouts of capitalism" would have grown more rapidly in the absence of colonialism and of neocolonialist forms of exploitation associated with the international division of labor. From this perspective, ties to capitalist countries are seen as continuous barriers to the operation of internal forces of development. Still others argue that the Asiatic mode of production forces countries like China into a peculiar pattern of development under extensive state control. One version holds that communist leaders must pursue careful policies to alleviate the consequences of Asiatic despotism, while another identifies the communist party as the logical heir to this tradition of despotism.

Marxist-Leninist interpretations have been diverse and at times contradictory, but their common theme has been the need for Asian and other less-developed countries to free themselves from colonial control. The correct timing of revolutionary action varies from one interpretation to another. It was long popular to proclaim that a country had to develop politically and economically under bourgeois leadership over an extended period before it could reach a level at which the introduction of socialism would be possible.

In recent years, many writers interested in problems of national development have interpreted the relations of the more modernized societies to the latecomers as a global extension of the class struggle, in which the advanced societies exploit the less advanced. In this view, although some nonwestern countries, notably Japan, may share the attributes of the imperialists, most will be subjected to a dependence from which they can escape only through a socialist revolution.

What these various Marxist approaches have in common is the belief that the motor of history is the class struggle provoked by the exploitation inherent in feudal and capitalist patterns of the ownership of the means of production. In this view relations within and between countries should be interpreted essentially in terms of exploiters and exploited until such time as the introduction of socialism leads to the disappearance of exploitation. The slowness of China to modernize is thus attributed primarily to exploitation by imperialists, Japanese as well as European and American, and its history in the twentieth century is seen as a struggle against imperialism, which finally met with success in 1949.

We do not deny that some patterns of dependency fostered by local elites as well as by foreign interests must be overcome before national will and resources can be mobilized adequately for purposes of modernization. In some countries such patterns have become so entrenched that they operate as the primary immediate impediment to modernization. Yet, once even this impediment is removed, the basic problems of modernization remain. Analysis of these remaining problems requires, above all, an understanding of domestic conditions. We argue that dependency was not, except during the Japanese occupation, the basic impediment in China.

The approach that informs our study sees the unprecedented growth of knowledge in the modern era as the motor of history and considers the resulting levels of political development, economic growth, and social welfare to be the critical variables in relations within and between societies. Two lines of interpretation following from this view distinguish modernization studies from the various Marxist approaches. The first is that the process of modernization in both early modernizers and latecomers is essentially one of domestic transformation. The principal questions that students of modernization ask about premodern societies are concerned with the capacity of the leaders of a society to accept modern knowledge and to establish the institutions and policies required for economic growth and social welfare. Premodern societies vary greatly in such capacities, and latecomers normally find it necessary to supplement the adaptation of their own heritage of institutions with extensive borrowing from more modern societies. The influence of colonial rule in this process is important but limited, and has generally had significant positive as well as negative features.

The second line of interpretation distinguishing modernization studies holds that the level of development of a society should be measured by the best available indicators—political, economic, demographic and others (none of which is entirely satisfactory)—and not by the extent of public ownership of the means of production or any other institutional norm. As our earlier study, *The Modernization of Japan and Russia,* has indicated, rather similar levels of development can be achieved under both "capitalist" and "socialist" policies. One is led to put the two terms in quotation marks because the relation between the public and private sectors varies so greatly from country to country that reality can be described better in terms of the relative roles of markets and planning than by the two ideologies. The role of the public sector, as of other institutional arrangements, is related more to the political history of a society and to the contingencies of leadership and ideology than to levels of development. So far as the available evidence permits us to judge, many combinations of market and central planning have provided serviceable frameworks for modernization. As responsible citizens, adherents of modernization studies are no less concerned than those of Marxist studies with exploitation and related injustices, but they have not found that countries under Marxist leadership have been characterized by more benevolent domestic or international policies than those with market economies. Studies of income distribution, for example, suggest that level of development is the principal factor in social equity—although societies at the same level of development may vary somewhat depending on government policies.

It is important to note the differences between the approaches taken by modernization studies and Marxist studies, but one should also recognize that they are dealing with a common subject, share many conclusions, and have much to learn from each other. While adherents of one approach may think that adherents of the other are asking the wrong questions, empirical research may lead to valuable insights regardless of the world view of the questioner.

It is significant in this context that the dominant trend in post-Stalin and post-Mao thinking about recent domestic change, as distinct from earlier historical development, stresses the importance of the scientific and technological revolution rather than the class struggle. In its emphasis on evaluating the capacity to take advantage of the opportunities offered by contemporary knowledge for political development, economic growth, and social welfare, this view closely resembles that of modernization studies.

The Comparative Context of Modernization

Scholarship on China has been more isolated from the currents of comparative social science research than that of any other major country. The prevailing world view in scholarship on China is hardly less sinocentric than that traditionally held by the Chinese themselves. Nor can one find much solace in the parochialism of the opposite extreme—in losing China in supposedly universal statements based on other areas of the world, without bothering to check how closely they apply. In place of these extremes we seek to demonstrate that the vastly expanded, yet only nascent, knowledge of Chinese history derived in recent decades from direct use of original Chinese sources provides a satisfactory foundation for building anew in Chinese studies using comparative materials, and that findings on modernization elsewhere, although in many cases still inconclusive, offer a useful basis for extending comparisons to China. This study seeks in the characteristics China shares with others the very basis for discovering its distinctive attributes.

Which countries should be included for comparative purposes and how should the comparative orientation be integrated with the substantive treatment centered on China? The possible benefits of introducing a long list of countries are outweighed by the fact that we are unlikely to possess a comprehensive view of all of them. We prefer to return repeatedly to the same countries with which the reader can gain familiarity as the authors have already done. Guiding the choice is the sequence of China's experience as an extraordinarily highly developed premodern society, as a latecomer, and as a socialist society. Our criteria also include a country's scale, its historical continuity, its premodern development, the timing and nature of its transformation, its success in rapid modernization, its experience with socialism, and the extent of available knowledge of both the premodern and the modernizing periods. The list of countries that generally satisfy even half of these criteria is extremely short. Obviously no country fully corresponds to the ideal historical laboratory for comparisons with China, but two countries, Russia and Japan, provide probably the closest approximations.

Clearly, these are appropriate choices for this group of authors, because with the completion of *The Modernization of Japan and Russia,* much of the relevant information about these two countries is at our fingertips and available to readers, albeit with all our biases and crotchets. But the choice can also be defended on grounds other than convenience. By the standards of population size and area, only India has consistently exceeded even one-third of the Chinese totals over the past two centuries. Yet India long remained a decentralized congeries of states, its premodern development along the dimensions we are considering appears to us to have been both problematic and inadequately recorded, and its slow transformation does not offer many lessons on what might have been done in China to accelerate modernization.

In contrast, Russia not only occupied a vast area and was relatively populous, it meets all our other criteria. Japan, although small, has supported a population consistently among the largest and densest in the world. In the eighteenth century it was probably the only country apart from India to maintain more than one-tenth of the Chinese total. Unlike China and Russia, Japan has not experienced communist leadership, but in other respects, it appears to present more close parallels to the Chinese historical record and more instructive alternatives than any other country.

Japan and Russia also stand out for their continuity of government at the national level. Their transformation began in the mid-nineteenth century, and they avoided direct colonial rule by more modernized countries. Russia more than Japan offers an example of a strong government-guided transformation; the strong governmental influences in Japan were exerted in a generally capitalist context. Japan more than Russia duplicates the timing of exposure to the external impetus for modernization. These two are perhaps the only cases of large countries that modernized rapidly as latecomers.

In making our comparisons we draw on *The Modernization of Japan and Russia* and on the background of some of our authors in Japanese and Russian studies in three ways. First, comparisons are interspersed with the treatment of China in many sections of Chapters 2–6 and 8–12. The titles of these chapters and some of their sections follow the form of the earlier volume, facilitating direct and frequent comparisons. Second, each of these chapters concludes with a section on international comparisons. The primary focus is on Japan and Russia, but other countries appear as well. Third, Chapters 14 and 15 develop the conclusions of this study in an explicitly comparative manner. In these concluding chapters we give some, necessarily brief, attention to the implications the experiences of China, Russia, and Japan hold for a general approach to (1) the conditions in premodern societies conducive to modernization, (2) the modernization of countries led by communist parties, and (3) contemporary latecomers to modernization. Each of these major areas of scholarly inquiry stands to benefit from further scrutiny of China.

Much of the comparison between China, on the one hand, and Japan and Russia, on the other, emphasizes China's relatively slow modernization. Throughout this study we search for contrasts, conditions that distinguish China from the other two countries. Yet is is not sufficient to make a case for what apparently relegated China to a course of slow modernization while

Japan and Russia pushed more briskly ahead—we also seek to explain China's more rapid modernization after 1949 and to find early similarities to Japan and Russia that advanced China's prospects for modernization. Comparisons are central to the entire book.

Throughout most of world history, China was for the whole of East Asian society a cultural colossus, a role that combined features of the western cultural attitudes to the classical antiquity of Greece and Rome and to France as the modern center of civilization in Europe. For well over two thousand years the Chinese have proved that they possessed cultural values of an extremely high, varied, and sophisticated order; the ability to control, coordinate, and manage a very large and populous country; and the organizational talent to make effective use of available technology for the expansion of production and the support of populations many times larger than those of the nineteenth-century European states. The living standards of the Chinese people more than matched those achieved by populations elsewhere.

The Chinese had also achieved very high levels in some characteristics we associate with modern societies. Most notably they developed a bureaucracy overwhelmingly based on merit, which until the nineteenth century was also a model of efficiency and effectiveness. It may still be something of a model in terms of the efficiency with which relatively small numbers of highly trained individuals managed large-scale problems. Well over a thousand years ago the Chinese proved themselves capable of marshaling capital, labor, and the necessary planning resources for the creation of public works on a scale unapproached anywhere else in the world until the twentieth century. For over two thousand years China had what was at least ideally an open-class system, in which advancement depended primarily on education and merit. While it is true that the system was badly abused again and again during that two thousand years, nothing even approaching it existed anywhere else. Whatever one may mean by terms like "high civilization," China had certainly achieved it at least as early as people we call European or western today. Indeed, future students of the world may hold that prior to the sixteenth or seventeenth century, and perhaps for some time thereafter, only European ethnocentrism and a disinclination to learn difficult and subtle languages could account for the impression that European civilization was the equal, let alone the superior, of China's. China had shown enormous flexibility in learning from and absorbing others, even conquerors. For a nonmodern society, literacy rates were extraordinarily high, and commerce, industry, and marketing were generally highly developed. Finally, pragmatism, in John Dewey's view the critical underlying philosophy of western modernization, had in many, if not most, of its aspects been taken for granted in China for two thousand years.

And yet as the Chinese attempted to cope with foreigners and the foreign patterns brought on by modernization, things seemed to go from bad to worse. From the beginning of the nineteenth century until the middle of the twentieth, substantial parts of the world surpassed China in their capacity to

16

cope with elements of modernization. Alone among the Asian complex, the Japanese, considered by the Chinese as hardly worthy of notice, a people to whom they had given literacy, Buddhism, and Confucianism and for whom they had served as a cultural model for well over a millennium, proved themselves superlatively equipped to cope with these new onslaughts. Even after the middle of the twentieth century, certain other latecomers managed at least as well as China.

Does the record that so surprises us and so challenges our curiosity rest on the international setting of these events, on the curious nature of the modernization process itself, or on certain strategic aspects of that civilization, which is surely one of humankind's best claims to be, culturally at least, but little lower than the angels? Elements of all three no doubt, but we think it is primarily elements of the process and the civilization, and we hope here to lay bare our reading of these matters.

PART ONE

The Legacy of the Past

The Eighteenth and Nineteenth Centuries

CHAPTER TWO

The International Context

For most of the world and for all of Asia, the process of modernization has required adjustment to and adaptation of technological and institutional patterns that first took form in a small number of western countries. Whether accepted voluntarily or imposed by arms, the patterns of organization and production modern knowledge made possible became a force in the course of the nineteenth century. Consideration of the historical development of late-comers to modernization consequently begins with questions about their access to modern knowledge and their willingness to import and adapt to their own needs the products of that knowledge. The question is not, moreover, one of volition alone. Encounters with modern arms and technology under unfavorable conditions can result in limitations on sovereignty and cultural resistance that limit the ability to respond to new challenges effectively. The manner, as well as the fact, of modern China's contact with the non-Chinese world requires comment. This discussion therefore begins with an examination of the way in which China's world view and world order prepared it for the challenge of modern times, and it continues with a discussion of the way in which that challenge came and of how the international system imposed on China during the nineteenth century acted to speed, impede, or channel the Chinese response.

Modernization and International Relations

The above-mentioned questions are central to a large body of historical scholarship that deals with nineteenth- and early twentieth-century China. The study of modern Chinese history in the West began as a byproduct of the diplomatic and military clash between China and the western world. The standard work of Hosea Ballou Morse, *The International Relations of the Chinese Empire* (1910–1918), is an early monument. The work of Morse's most distinguished successor, John K. Fairbank (1953), opens with a section entitled "China's Unpreparedness for Western Contact," and states that "the British (*Ying-i*) were the unwitting inheritors of the status which had been reserved for barbarians (*i*) in Chinese society since time immemorial. Age-old stereotypes took the place of a creative response. The first step in understanding the Western influence on China, is, therefore, to understand the traditional role of the barbarians in Chinese society" (p. 7). In 1978 Fairbank concluded that "the underlying weakness was intellectual-institutional; that is, an habituated ignorance of foreign realities and a wilful refusal to take them into account. This was evidenced most signally in the purblind adherence to an imperial policy of asserted supremacy over all foreign sovereigns. Peking refused intercourse on equal terms until it was perforce extorted on unequal terms" (*Cambridge History of China,* vol. 10, pt. 1, p. 260).

The initial focus of this discussion is therefore on the first half of the intellectual-institutional weakness of which Fairbank speaks. The issue of intellectual weakness is important, if only because it comes so immediately and automatically to the fore in most western discussions of the problem. Nevertheless, it should also be noted that the study of modern Chinese history is changing as a result of a vigorous debate in which internal and political differences rooted in regional differentiation are beginning to add color and even to overshadow the non-Chinese historians' earlier monochromatic disdain for the Chinese inability to adapt. That writing took form in the full knowledge of the tragedies of failure in nineteenth- and twentieth-century China.

It is important to remember that Chinese views about the centrality of their civilization lost cogency only because of the dramatic changes in industrial and military technology in nineteenth-century Europe. A full and famous statement of the Chinese world view on the eve of those changes, one beloved of historians, can be found in the words in which the Ch'ien-lung emperor responded to the request of George III's Ambassador Macartney for regular diplomatic relations in 1793. The emperor pointed out that the English could not possibly play a role at his court, as their "language will be unintelligible. Moreover the territory under the control of the Celestial Court is very large and wide. . . . The Celestial Court has pacified and possessed the territory within the four seas. Its sole aim is to do its utmost to achieve good government and to manage political affairs, attaching no value to strange jewels and precious objects. . . . As a matter of fact, the virtue and prestige of the Celestial Dynasty having spread far and wide, the kings of the myriad nations come by land and sea with all sorts of precious things. Consequently there is nothing we lack. . . . We have never set much store on strange or ingenious objects, nor do we need any more of your country's manufactures" (quoted in S. Y. Teng and J. K. Fairbank, 1954, p. 19).

The emperor's description was not far from the way things had been until then. As Bertrand Russell once wrote of this response, "No one has begun to understand China until this document has ceased to seem absurd." If not absurd, it was nevertheless anachronistic. At the beginning of Ch'ien-lung's long reign (1736–1795) it might well have stood as fact. At the end of his life, it was sufficiently wide of the mark to raise doubts about the conviction that lay behind it. What made it so was the difference between the earlier threats to China and those posed by the power of the industrializing West. Before discussing that challenge it is necessary to examine the Chinese world view and world order that were challenged.

The World Order

Within decades of Ch'ien-lung's response to George III, Great Britain began the assault on Chinese sovereignty. Within a century of that response the emperor's disdain was fully matched by the tone assumed by representatives of Queen Victoria when they addressed Peking. Was China's disastrous course a product of its assumptions of cultural and political centrality? Were those assumptions particularly important at the Manchu court?

THE WORLD VIEW

Fairbank's work has made us familiar with the concept of China as middle country, ruled by the Son of Heaven and surrounded by less civilized and barbarian states. It was an order that "did not use concepts corresponding to the Western ideas of nation, or sovereignty, or equality of states," as "non-Chinese rulers participated in the Chinese world order by observing the appropriate forms and ceremonies (*li*) in their contact with the Son of Heaven. . . . It became established in the Chinese view that the mystical influence of the all-wise example and virtue (*te*) of the Son of Heaven not only reached throughout China proper but continued outward beyond the borders of China to all mankind and gave them order and peace, albeit with decreasing efficacy, as parts of a concentric hierarchy" (1968, pp. 5–10). China's ascendancy was more than political; it was based upon normative and moral considerations inherent in the power of civilization over noncivilization. There could be no real equality in any relations between China and another country, since that would call into question the most fundamental premises that underlay a structured and consistent universe.

This was an ideal view invoked in memorials addressed to the throne and imperial edicts addressed to lesser breeds without the law. Actual patterns were a good deal more varied, and dynasties were often ready to sacrifice theory for security and gain. It remains true, however, that ''China's political structures possess[ed] unmatched continuity of development without having been threatened or challenged *in the eyes of the Chinese themselves*'' (Chapter 3, italics added). Although the Chinese were continually in touch with other centers of early civilization through the trade routes of Central Asia, no sustained, purposeful burst of cultural borrowing, comparable to those experienced by Japan and Russia, ever took place. Awareness of cultural imports was further weakened by the great distances those imports had to travel, by the fact that they were brought by intermediaries and did not result from direct contact with the centers that produced them, and by the fact that they entered over long periods and not, as in Japan, in concentrated programs that alternated with periods of relative isolation. Nor were such imports at any time recognized as the products of higher civilizations, as had been the case for Japan and Russia, where literacy itself had to wait for the adaptation of externally derived systems of transcription.

Three implants from outside the Chinese culture sphere stand as partial modifications of this statement. The first is Indian Buddhism, which entered China from India during the later Han dynasty (A.D. 25–200) and profoundly transformed Chinese religion and thought. At the time of its entry Buddhism was deplored as an expression of barbarian values. It soon took on strongly Chinese characteristics and, controlled and used by the state, seemed less of an import. By the eighth century its thrust was again deplored by many Confucian thinkers (and their successors) as an unfortunate aberration from the humanistic pattern of indigenous values. A second import was Islam, which took firm root in border provinces of the west, where it was accepted as indigenous to racial minorities. Islam also spread throughout China as a pervasive Chinese minority religion and culture, without, however, impinging seriously on dominant patterns of high culture. The third came in the seventeenth century when European missionaries and learning quickened the interest of Chinese intellectuals in the progress of physical science in the non-Chinese world. Their bridge to this interest did not, however, require that they abandon major tenets of Chinese values. Scientific principles were seen to be universal and not culturally bound to the men who transmitted them, and their application could be shown to have utility for Chinese life, especially for astronomy and a calendar that was set by the throne as a function of its mediation between heaven and man. Islamic astronomy had previously proved acceptable in the same way. Moreover, although interest in European science continued for a time at the capital and in the court, the curiosity about western learning, like the earlier growth of Buddhism, came during a period of political and social disunity and decline. With the return of stability and a heightened concern for social order and moral certainty, and with the awareness of the possibility that an externally derived, papal, authority could rival the moral primacy of imperial standards, western influence declined and western missionaries were restricted, confined to a few bases, and eventually removed.

The final millennium of imperial China saw a progressive expansion of Chinese assertions of ascendancy over the border areas around China and greater emphasis on the centrality of the imperial role in the governance of intramural China. The two were related. With the exception of Sung and Ming rule, China was governed in whole or in part during those thousand years by outsiders from the north. The conquerors required and developed strong instruments of central control and maintained effective military strength through most of their rule. By using a Chinese political philosophy, the neo-Confucian synthesis codified by the twelfth-century scholar Chu Hsi, whose era was dominated by struggle with the barbarians to the north, they acknowledged, as it were, the supremacy of Chinese civilization. L. S. Yang's reminder that "Chinese even in remote antiquity seem to have indulged in comparing barbarians with all kinds of animals" (Fairbank, ed., 1968, p. 27) serves as prelude to Chu Hsi's more structured hierarchy of five categories: Chinese man, barbarian, animals, plants, and minerals.

Ming despotism centered around an exalted emperor whose powers owed something to the Mongol predecessors the Ming had displaced, and the Ch'ing conquest of the seventeenth century found even more able and active rulers who shaped the final structure of the institutions of imperial absolutism. While Manchu censorship and attempted thought control sought to eliminate explicit denigration of barbarians (as something that might strike too close to their own carefully preserved ethnicity), the Manchus supported and enforced Chu Hsi orthodoxy as a device to legitimate the imperial and cultural hierarchy presided over by the ruler of China. As a result, the Ch'ing dynasty was—verbally at least—more intransigent about and insistent upon the centrality of the imperial order than its predecessors. The rigidities of this world view, in other words, while very much the product of a millennium of Chinese history, also reflected the particular situation of the ruling dynasty. Ch'ing "illegitimacy" probably operated to increase the Ch'ing compulsion to conform.

Ch'ing rule was also remarkable for an activist military and foreign policy on the continent that established the modern boundaries of the Chinese state. This policy was particularly active in the eighteenth century. Emulating his grandfather, the K'ang-hsi emperor, Ch'ien-lung waged his greatest campaigns in Central Asia, where the western Mongols were defeated in the 1750s and the Tarim Basin was taken over by 1760. Expeditions were sent to Tibet in 1720, in 1727–1728, and in 1750. The Gurkhas of Nepal were subdued in 1790–1792. Military force was also used against Burma (1776–1770) and Vietnam (1788–1790). Imperial China was thus expanding its borders during the same period that Russia was extending its sway to northern Central Asia. As F. W. Mote points out in Chapter 3, "it is impossible to imagine that the territorial enlargement would have happened without the presence of

25

the alien Manchu dynasty and its special commitment to military achievement in Inner Asia. . . . The boundaries of the Chinese state as we know them today do not derive from the glories of Han and T'ang; they stem directly from Ch'ing imperialism.'' Until the Napoleonic wars, Ch'ing military power was superior to that of its possible rivals, and long thereafter the Chinese were still able to marshal astonishingly large forces for successful action in Turkestan and Tibet.

The primacy of Inner Asia for Ming and Ch'ing strategy can also be thought of in terms of a division between maritime and continental China or between littoral and hinterland. It was continental China, Fairbank suggests, that developed the imperial tradition and perfected the institutions of the agrarian and bureaucratic order. Maritime China instead developed to the south. Its traders explored the coastal waters of East and Southeast Asia, developed merchant communities throughout Southeast Asia, developed venture capital, and gave first priority to commerce. For a brief period in the first third of the fifteenth century, when the Ming court authorized the great maritime expeditions under Cheng Ho, it seemed possible that the extension of imperial influence throughout Southeast and South Asia might assume a high priority for the Chinese state, but with a change in political currents, the land frontiers and military security of Inner Asia once again resumed their traditional priority. In these terms the appearance of the West in the nineteenth century can be seen as a reactivation of the potential of maritime China.

It would be misleading, however, to see continental and maritime, hinterland and littoral, as mutually exclusive concerns or typologies. Important integrative elements kept them together. Maritime China always affected the hinterland directly, sometimes in ways that are only now becoming understood. Traditional assumptions about China's economic and cultural autonomy are belied by the facts of early modern economic history. This is nowhere more clearly seen than in the impact of the world economy on China in early modern times. Ping-ti Ho has credited the introduction of food crops from the New World, notably the sweet potato and corn, with a major role in the economic and population growth of early modern China. W. A. Atwell's research shows that China absorbed a very large part of the silver that entered world trade routes as a result of the exploitation of new sources in the New World and in Japan. Thanks to this, silver became the basic medium of land tax payment in late Ming times. The rapid increase in the quantity of silver provided a stimulus for economic growth of many sorts, the number of periodic markets in rural areas increased, traditional industries expanded, new industries developed, and the production and use of cotton goods increased dramatically. There was, Atwell (1977, p. 5) concludes, ''much more money in circulation at the turn of the seventeenth century than even a few years previously. . . . Japanese and Spanish American silver may well have been *the* most significant factor in the vigorous economic expansion which occurred in China.'' Japanese copper, already a major factor in Ashikaga-Ming trade in the fifteenth century, became in the sixteenth century the Chinese mint's principal source for copper cash, which circulated as the basic currency. Steps by Spanish and Japanese authorities to limit silver and copper exports to China produced quick reverses in the Chinese economy and resulted in forced-draft measures for the development and exploitation of new sources in the southwest province of Yunnan early in the Ch'ing period. In the nineteenth century the flow of silver out of China in exchange for opium brought by British ships produced critical conditions quickly recognized by Chinese officials. As Mote has written elsewhere, "by 1644 China [was] a part of world history, deeply affected by the movement of silver in the world's trade, by the dissemination of crops and foodstuffs which would transform its agriculture, and by weapons and warfare, plagues and products which bore in on the daily life of the Chinese people" (1977, p. 195). All this, in other words, long before Ch'ien-lung's haughty dismissal of Lord Macartney with the assurance that "there is nothing we lack, as your principal envoy and others have themselves observed."

The economic facts were slow to become part of the Chinese world view. Central Asian trade routes ended in Peking, at the heart of the dynasty. They traversed semiarid stretches long considered central to the rulers' ethnic and security considerations. World trade routes, however, ended far to the south. They were in the hands of private traders who dealt with principalities dimly seen and poorly understood. Official representatives of Peking frequently assumed that the difficulties and distance of those trips must constitute an index of the importance of the China trade for the countries concerned, and imagined that their ultimate resource lay in the power to stop that trade altogether. Lin Tse-hsu's stern warning to Queen Victoria in 1839 can stand as example: "Of all that China exports to foreign countries, there is not a single thing which is not beneficial to people. . . . Take tea and rhubarb, for example; the foreign countries cannot get along for a single day without them. If China cuts off these benefits with no sympathy for those who are to suffer, then what can the barbarians rely upon to keep themselves alive? . . . On the other hand, articles coming from the outside to China can only be used as toys." In view of such benevolence, he argued, how could the British justify bringing in a poison like opium? (quoted in S. Y. Teng and J. K. Fairbank, 1954, p. 25).

All these elements of the Chinese world view—cultural and normative superiority over less advanced neighbors, a conscious policy not to value or seek outside ideas and goods, and an agrarian bureaucratic polity facing its hinterland rather than its maritime borders—limited the likelihood that China would "seek wisdom throughout the world" in the manner announced by Japan's government in 1868.

CHINA'S WORLD ORDER

The Chinese world order in late imperial times was structured in such a way as to integrate the practical realities of security and power with the theoretical and ideological assumptions of centrality. The emphasis on centrality, the institutional expression of China's cultural ascendancy, has been most re-marked upon, for the tribute system of late imperial China was an elaborately structured expression of ritualized inequality and hierarchy. Under its work-ings China showed itself as middle country, surrounded by culturally de-prived dependencies whose rulers accepted Chinese investiture and thereafter were admitted to a protocol for tribute and trade.

It had not always been so. In preimperial centuries a multistate system had existed. It was sometimes invoked by nineteenth-century leaders as a pos-sible precedent for the multistate international order to which China found it-self having to adapt. Although ancient Chinese history might conceivably have served as a model, in fact the development of the imperial ideal and the pretensions of the imperial autocrat combined to establish a more compelling precedent for policy and theory.

Even during the imperial era, however, there were precedents for devia-tion from the full assumptions of centrality and superiority. Admittedly these were the product of weakness and not of choice. During periods of instability, when "China" was itself divided or only one of several continental powers, Chinese governments sometimes found it necessary to conclude treaties, thus showing the capacity to live in a world of states and to regulate relations through legal rather than normative means. Sung China several times worked out treaties with its neighbors to the north that were negotiated and worded on a basis of relative equality, with careful avoidance of terminology sugges-tive of hierarchy, and with mutual pledges of good faith and oaths of sincer-ity. Yet it is also true, as Herbert Franke points out, that in internal documents Chinese memorialists and officials continued to disparage the states with which they were negotiating. The mere fact that a treaty was con-cluded, he grants, "shows *a priori* a weakening of China's power and the ex-istence of a multistate or dual-state system" (Franke, 1970, p. 57). These treaties also differed from western-style treaties in that they consisted of two unilateral declarations, sworn separately, somewhat like the American and Chinese statements about Taiwan issued at the time of the Nixon visit in 1972. Nevertheless, the fact remains that a multistate system existed for several centuries and that many treaties between states were concluded during this period.

The Sung dynasty's concessions to security and reality were continued by later dynasties who treated Northern and Inner Asia differently from South-east Asia. To the north and west of China were Central Asian peoples whose writing systems, cultural assumptions, and economic patterns were very dif-ferent from those of intramural China. They also presented a more urgent security problem than did other dependencies. Their goods, especially their horses, were critically important to Chinese military force. China, in turn, produced the food surplus and iron and other craft products that were essen-tial to their welfare. Consequently, they received different treatment in pro-tocol and policy.

The Manchus set up a special ministry, the Border Dependencies Control Office (*Li-fan Yuan*). This had its origin in the special ties the Ming had forged with the Mongols and also acknowledged the contribution of Mongol banners to the Ch'ing military and security system. Outer vassals (*wai-fan*) in Central Asia were often brought to heel with military force; the great Ch'ing military expeditions have already been mentioned. Central Asia was of vital importance, but the vast distances and technological problems of control in Central Asia also required realism and practicality. Mark Mancall has shown that Ch'ing rulers were willing to work on a basis of relative equality in their negotiations with Russian representatives in the eighteenth century. This pattern extended to dealings with less formidable principalities. Joseph Fletcher's account of Ch'ing relations with Kokand, in present Russian Turkestan, shows a high ability on the part of Chinese negotiators to stretch theory to fit the facts of Chinese power, even at a time when the tribute system was functioning most fully and satisfactorily. On China's other borders, however, where security was less threatened and trade was more important than diplomacy, relations were most structured.

The Ming dynasty formalized, and the Ch'ing perfected, the tribute system. Advances in navigation and commerce brought Ming maritime expeditions to Southeast Asia, South Asia, and even the coast of Africa in the fifteenth century. The world order was not so much that of a world of states as it was of an "empire without neighbors," and the patterns that resulted were designed less to honor China's superior civilization than civilization itself. Mancall provides a convenient summary of this outlook: the emperor carried out rites required for the continuing harmony of the universe, and failur to perform the proper rituals in his presence was in effect a discordant note in the universal order. The tribute relationship extended the social structure of civilization into realms beyond the immediate power of the emperor. It was always bilateral and never multilateral; and since one partner was ruler of China, it represented also the institutionalization of hierarchy (Fairbank, ed., 1968, pp. 63–72). This, at any rate, is the ideal pattern that dominates the Chinese accounts.

The tribute system was elaborated most fully for states ruled by elites familiar with Chinese writing and precedents and ecologically similar in that they were sustained by the intensive rice economy familiar to China. Located in an arc that extended from Korea through Southeast Asia, these states were graded in order of importance by the frequency with which they were permitted to send official missions to China. Thus even during the crisis years between 1860 and 1894 Korea presented tribute annually, Liu-ch'iu (Ryūkyū) eight times, Annam (Vietnam) five times, Nepal four times, and Burma once. Chinese rulers conferred titles, gave official seals, permitted the use of the Chinese calendar, provided passport tallies for tribute missions, and legitimated rulers through investiture. In Peking the reception of such missions was the responsibility of the Board of Rites. The assumptions of the system were normative; China conferred the benefits, and the tributaries were eager to come and to learn. Classical expressions could be invoked to explain this, as *Mencius,* III, A, 4, 12: "I have heard of men using the doctrines of our great land to change barbarians, but I have never yet heard of any being changed by barbarians." This rhetoric found its way into official correspondence in the nineteenth century, when the "English rebels" failed to conform to the proper pattern of expressing gratitude for favors.

Normative phraseology was also invoked to cover foreign trade. Tribute and trade, as Mancall phrases it, were "paired integrative mechanisms." Tribute was never a mere "cover" for trade, but stood as a requirement for regular trading privileges. It was an absolute condition for audience with the Son of Heaven. Trade was carefully administered, on a contractual basis, between formally authorized Chinese and non-Chinese trading partners. The parties to the agreement were expected to be long-enduring bodies rather than individuals, and the locus of trade was normally at the outer edges of imperial power. The Russian border, Foochow, Macao, and the Canton stations were appropriate selections; so were markets on the Korean and Mongol borders. The early Ch'ing rulers, and especially K'ang-hsi, were willing to increase trade, and until the end of the Canton system a significant share of profits from trade was funneled directly into the palace at Peking. It was also perfectly reasonable to consider trade an example of imperial benevolence to needy foreigners who had come so far to bring their spices to China in exchange for China's silks and tea. At Canton authorized western merchants (notably the British East India Company) interacted with authorized Chinese guilds (the *cohong*) in a pattern that endured into the 1830s.

One may note some parallels among China's East Asian neighbors. In Japan the Tokugawa rulers limited trade sharply, but they found it useful to tolerate a Dutch trading station at Nagasaki, the outermost fringe of Tokugawa direct administration. Similarly, Yi dynasty Korea permitted a Japanese trading station at Pusan, the tip of the peninsula.

In early modern times China's structured world order also constituted the reference point for the international relations of its neighbors. Relations between Korea and Japan were immensely complicated by problems of protocol and forms of address that had their origin in Korea's desire to conform to what was appropriate for a Chinese dependency and Japan's insistence on avoiding any suggestion of formal membership in that world order. In recent writings Ronald Toby has shown that the Tokugawa decision in favor of seclusion derived from the realization that formal membership in the East Asian world order was impossible without ritual subordination to the middle country. It is noteworthy that the system had neither room for countries unwilling to acknowledge China's ritual superiority nor need to force them to do so. Thus *The Chinese World Order,* which takes up China's neighbors one by one, has no need or place for treatment of Japan, a near neighbor, the most "Confucian" after Korea, and one whose institutions and culture owed so much to Chinese example. This despite the fact that there were periods of considerable formal contact between China and Japan, and that informal, private trade with Chinese merchants continued on Japanese terms at Nagasaki throughout the Tokugawa years. The normative official histories and imperial edicts thus do not by any means contain the entire story of China's foreign relations. They do, however, describe the ideal. The Chinese court could not make formal exceptions to that institutionalized ideal without placing its own self-image and legitimacy in question.

Ch'ing concerns about their legitimacy, rendered somewhat suspect by their barbarian origins, probably contributed to an additional rigor and inflexibility. Certainly China's Confucian neighbors were conscious of the paradox. Korean intellectuals regarded the fall of Ming China to barbarian invaders as disastrous to the survival of civilization, and Ch'ing envoys were routinely referred to as "barbarian messengers" (Haboush, ms.). Similarly, the Japanese in Tokugawa times found it convenient to denigrate Ch'ing rule as barbarian and improper. Japanese Confucianists of the eighteenth century vied with their Korean counterparts in affirming themselves as the bearers of the true learning, while Japanese students of western learning found it possible to criticize their country's Confucian conservatives by pointing to the fate of Confucian China under barbarian rule.

It is now possible to address the questions posed earlier in this chapter: were the Chinese world view and world order barriers to a rational and purposeful response to the West and its knowledge, institutions, and technology?

Our response has three parts:

1. China's world view, expressed in the normative assumptions of the official ideology, did indeed make a flexible adjustment difficult. Those assumptions were particularly rigid and absolute in Ch'ing times because of the institutional authoritarianism and cultural defensiveness of the dynastic rulers.

2. China's tribute system and world order were most structured and prescriptive for the maritime dependencies of Southeast Asia. The West was expected to fit into this inappropriate setting at Canton.

3. There were, however, other precedents in China's past, and many examples of theory being moderated in the interest of practicality. Methods for meeting the challenge of the West could surely have been worked out by an able and imaginative leadership. The problems may best be laid at the door of those who espoused the world view, and the considerations that led them to cling to it, rather than credited entirely to the world view itself. The problems were also institutional, in the form of a military state that made little allowance for regional differences, which changed suddenly in the early nineteenth century, and political, in the form of a regime far more concerned with internal than external subversion. But equally important hurdles to adjustment were implicit in the fact that the nineteenth-century outsiders who challenged the system came carrying their own normative expectations and had at their disposal the means to make Ch'ing pretensions seem particularly bizarre and inappropriate.

The Western Advance on China

We have seen that at the boundaries of the empire a large volume of foreign trade could be carried on with a considerable degree of flexibility alongside the ritual of the tribute system, often by the very merchants involved in official trade. Western trade with China began as a side eddy of tribute system relationships with the countries of Southeast Asia. In the early nineteenth century this trade showed a startling change in volume, scope, and economic impact. It came now to center on contraband, reducing the flexibility possible for Chinese officials. Simultaneously its western administrators showed less flexibility and insisted on formalizing arrangements in conformity with (from the Chinese point of view) parochial rules newly designated as international. For the purposes of modernization, which would have required adoption of a program of cultural and technological borrowing from the West, this conjunction of events posed serious problems.

CANTON TRADE TO OPIUM WAR

The Canton system, which developed between 1760 and 1834, shows the possibilities and limitations of informal exchange on the borders of the empire. In volume it became very large; in form the proprieties were observed by delegating it to licensed Chinese monopolists (the *cohong*) who were subordinated to an imperially appointed superintendent of maritime customs. Foreign merchants were expected to deal with the Chinese monopolists, to arrange their schedules and activities according to Chinese direction, and to abide by regulations designed to minimize their participation in and knowledge of Chinese society.

Despite this hierarchic subordination, as Wakeman terms it (*Cambridge History of China,* vol. 10, pt. 1, p. 163), foreign trade and traders became important to many levels of the Chinese establishment. At the apex was the superintendent of maritime customs. A representative of the Imperial Household Agency, he was an agent of the throne and remitted directly to its coffers as much as 855,000 *taels* a year. This official stood outside the provincial hierarchy, and enjoyed a status ranking comparable to, though after that of governors-general. Thus Peking was directly involved in and benefited from a trade it professed to scorn. At a later date the "Consoo fund," based upon a tenth of the Chinese monopolists' profits, became a large sum that went to purposes as varied as the privy purse, Yellow River banks repair, and defense costs. The East India Company, as authorized monopolist on the British side, for decades advanced payments to the monopolists of the *cohong* to enable them to meet their commitments, and thus became very important to this system.

Trade was originally based on an exchange of woven cloth, English wool, and Indian cotton for Chinese tea and textiles. For most of the period it was heavily (two to one) unfavorable to the East India Company, which until the nineteenth century made up the imbalance with American silver, and thereafter with the silver deposited to its account by private merchants who also carried on trade. Small wonder that the Chinese assumed the trade was essential to the foreigners, who came so far to carry it on; they believed it beneficial to their country too, since it increased the flow of silver. In addition it was enormously profitable to all officials through whose hands its revenues passed.

The early decades of the nineteenth century saw a sharp change in the nature of this trade. When the tea supply became more stable as Chinese cultivation increased and transportation routes to Canton improved, the guarantees to the *cohong* merchants were discontinued. The East India Company monopoly in India was ended in 1813, and its monopoly at Canton was slated to end twenty years later. Deadlines for new working arrangements were complicated by the decline in demand for Indian cotton, by social disorder in south China, and above all by the discovery of Indian opium as a crop that could more than balance the English trade deficit at Canton.

Its production in India spurred by the East India Company, and carried by private traders to the China coast, opium became for a time the single most valuable commodity in international trade. Political disorganization, social disorientation, and corruption at many levels combined to accelerate its spread throughout China. Silver, which had long flowed into China through foreign trade, now drained out of the country in exchange for chests of opium. It was in this setting that the East India Company's monopoly came to an end and representatives of the British crown began their campaign to secure formal trading privileges for England on a basis of equality. Chinese officials were frequently complaisant and corrupt and willing to cooperate, but the government of the middle country could not openly countenance a trade so harmful to the country. Chinese officials demanded an end to the import of opium, while English representatives sublimated the issues, portraying them as security of property, freedom of trade, the protection of English law for Englishmen, and diplomatic equality. There is no reason to question Hsin-pao Chang's measured conclusion that "without neglecting other factors, it is justifiable to say that the direct origins of the clash in 1840 lay in the opium traffic and England's insistence on extraterritoriality in China." Since the "opium trade and extraterritorial rights were of vital and immediate concern to the governments and people of both countries," ingenuity and subterfuge could provide no solutions (Hsin-pao Chang, 1964, pp. 214–215).

THE UNEQUAL TREATIES

The Opium War (1839–1842) and the Treaty of Nanking that concluded it began the process that is curiously referred to as the "opening of China." In this process Britain, France, Russia, and to a lesser extent the United States forced China to accept their interpretation of international equality and to abandon its own assertions of ascendancy. It must be remembered that international equality was a doctrine of recent date. Franke reminds us that the Christian states of Europe differentiated between their obligations to each other and their obligations to non-Christian principalities. The Ottoman Empire, he notes, was formally admitted to "full equality" under international law only in 1856. Wang Gung-wu states it more sharply: "The present theory of equality in international relations grew out of interstate rivalries within a closed Christian-European civilization on the eve of European expansion, and . . . this equality was practiced in only a limited context until the twentieth century" (Fairbank, ed., 1968, p. 61). It would thus be more accurate to describe conflict between the western countries and China in the nineteenth century as one between two systems, each of which ascribed inferiority to the other.

The West proved more powerful, and the resulting pattern of treaties imposed upon China is usually referred to as the Unequal Treaty System. The Anglo-Chinese War was the first of an unbroken series of setbacks for the Ch'ing. Internal rebellion alternated with external aggression, which was usually justified on the grounds that the hapless dynasty was not living up to agreements it had made under duress.

Between 1842 and 1895 China lost every one of its five wars and was required to pay the winners' costs. Its principal ocean and riverine ports became open to foreign commerce and residence. Beginning with the 5 treaty ports provided for in the settlement of the Opium War, the open ports and trading sites came in time to number approximately 100, of which all but 22 were forced open by treaty with one power and became accessible to other powers through the most favored nation clause. The arrangements ranged from formal alienation of territory (Hong Kong), to concessions governed by foreign consuls (Tientsin French Concession), to semiautonomous settlements (the Shanghai International Settlement, formed in 1863 by merger of the British and American settlements and governed by a council elected by the foreigner plutocracy), to areas simply set aside for foreign residents but subject to Chinese administration. Extraterritoriality meant that foreign law everywhere followed foreigners, however, and as applied in commercial disputes, protected their employees and protégés as well. Mixed and foreign courts probably had a strong tendency to "keep the flag flying." The most favored nation clause meant that China could negotiate only across-the-board settlements with all the treaty powers, and thus operated as a ratchet for the extraction and extension of privileges. Tariff arrangements, fixed by treaty and held at a flat 5 percent *ad valorem* for much of the period, meant that China was unable to control its trade or protect infant industries. The Shimonoseki Treaty added the right for foreigners to develop manufactures in treaty port areas, thereby making it possible to use cheap Chinese labor and avoid even the modest tariffs that were imposed on outside products.

The Imperial Maritime Customs, an agency that collected the tariffs for China, the new postal service, and even the old salt gabelle gradually (as income was hypothecated for foreign loans) became foreign staffed. Missionary rights, first introduced into the system of treaty rights by France, extended foreign residence and influence beyond the areas of the treaty ports and created in Chinese Christians a group vulnerable to local prejudice and eligible for western compassion and protection. The dynasty tried to give missionary authorities official status in the hope of minimizing conflict, only to create more. At the end of the century the disastrous Boxer antiforeign paroxysm, initially anti-Christian and antimissionary in its focus, brought new and crushing indemnities as well as provision for foreign legation guards that supplied China experience for garrison officers as different as Joseph Stilwell and the Japanese strategist Ishiwara Kanji.

It is small wonder that the western advance has come to dominate most accounts of nineteenth-century Chinese history. Although twentieth-century writers have been quick to identify imperialism as the source of their society's difficulties, and indignation has risen with the tide of nationalism, closer examination shows a considerable range of interpretation and emphasis. Nineteenth-century writers like Wei Yuan, while recognizing that western power posed unprecedented problems for China, were confident that reforms would set the country on the right track. Some modern historians have suggested that China's experience and flexibility in foreign relations enabled it to accommodate much of the treaty system to Chinese tradition. Fletcher argues that early nineteenth-century agreements with a principality in Turkestan, which included provisions for extraterritoriality, trade, most favored nation treatment, and fixed tarriffs were similar to China's treaties with European nations, and Fairbank suggests that "the treaty system supplanted the tribute system as a device for incorporating the foreigner into the universal state presided over by the Confucian monarchy of the Son of Heaven," just as "barbarian invaders of China had often acquired the dominant power in the Confucian state without destroying its political structure" (1953, pp. 464–465).

Both suggestions can help explain the form, but not the thrust, of the treaty system. What was new about the treaty system was that it extended to China proper concessions that were previously known only on the frontier. And what was new about British participation in Chinese government was that the new barbarians were far more powerful than the old, only marginally interested in sharing in the glory of the imperial order, and very intent upon national advantage.

An evaluation of the significance of the nineteenth-century treaty port system for Chinese modernization nevertheless suggests there were some positive effects along with the many negative ones. There were probably some financial gains, although no one questions the fact that the dynasty's income, augmented or not, remained far short of what was needed for an effective modernization program. Since the dynasty's tax income was limited by the nature of its institutions and the precedents of its ruling house, the growth of customs revenue in the nineteenth century produced a significant increase in the government's resources. The English authorities of the Imperial Maritime Customs also constituted an exception to the demoralized and increasingly centrifugally oriented officialdom.

Another new source of income was the *likin,* an internal transit tax first levied in 1853 on grain carried along the Grand Canal and gradually applied by almost all provinces on almost all commodities (despite, it should be noted, the consistent objections of the treaty port powers). The total gain for the central government was substantial, with imperial revenue in the 1880s and 1890s nearly double what it was in mid-century (Feuerwerker, 1969, p. 65). This revenue was not, however, fully at the government's disposal. Local authorities retained most of the *likin* income, of which perhaps 20 percent reached Peking. *Likin,* fully exploited as an emergency tax for Taiping suppression, became a principal source for the support of regional military developments. Not enough reached Peking to finance attempts to cope with the unbroken military and institutional crises of the century. The entire income from the Maritime Customs ostensibly went to the central government, but precisely because it was a secure, separate, and quantifiable resource, it was soonest encumbered by treaty port powers as a guarantee for the indemnities and loans that multiplied during the downward cycle of defeats and antiforeign outrages. Furthermore, the costly navy which was the fruit of much government expenditure helped little, as it was sunk in the Sino-Japanese war.

A comparable ambiguity attends the powers' assaults on Chinese sovereignty. From the Treaty of Nanking in 1842 to that of Shimonoseki in 1895, China found its maritime borders modified but also clarified as English, French, and finally Japanese power demanded the independence or cession of tributary dependencies in Burma (1885), Vietnam (1887), Liu-ch'iu (1874), and Korea (1895). Cessions to Russia in Northern Asia held Chinese borders at the Amur (1860), while Chinese resistance to further Russian claims retained as Chinese what became known as Sinkiang (1881). But as pointed out in Chapter 3, the treaty powers in some way bolstered Chinese sovereignty by this process of border definition. As international law became the norm for interstate relations, the continuous assault on Chinese sovereignty was accompanied by a recognition of Chinese sovereignty over what remained, and the Manchu conquests in Central and Northern Asia became legitimate and recognized as Chinese—except, occasionally, by the Japanese, who developed doubts about the Manchu homeland.

The treaty ports themselves provide material for further reflections on the ambiguity of the western impact. The largest of them provided centers for Chinese capital and development that were safe from bureaucratic expropriation and extortion. They also came to function as examples of a different and more modern society; one marred by shameless racism and discrimination, to be sure, but one also remarkable for lighted streets, public transportation, and impartially administered law and order. The ports were also centers for western missionary activity in education, medicine, social service, and philanthropy that made a significant contribution to the amelioration of conditions of life at a time when whatever safeguards the old society could offer were under assault from social disorder poorly controlled by a distracted officialdom. If the West introduced opium, its emissaries also led in campaigns against the new evil as well as helping to combat more ancient wrongs like footbinding. The ports were centers of modernity in terms of education, publication, business, and thought.

In terms of political stability, on the other hand, the assault on Chinese sovereignty that led to the treaty port era can only be deplored. It is difficult to see what ameliorating factors could have made up for the loss of control over ports, trade, finance, and aliens. Mention should, however, be made of the claim (by Westerners) that the powers tended to prop up the throne and the charge (by Chinese nationalists) that they did so after they had bent it to their will. The issues here relate to the loyal service rendered by the Imperial Maritime Customs, the defense of Shanghai by troops under foreign command during the Taiping insurrection, and the willingness of the powers to tolerate the return of the Manchu court to Peking after Anglo-French forces seized the city in 1860 and again after the Boxer suppression had forced the Dowager Empress to flee in 1900. Each of these steps, however, was motivated by the foreigners' perceived self-interest and their desire to continue a profitable status quo. With the possible exception of the service of the Imperial Maritime Customs, it is probable that the importance of these events for long-range politics in China was much exaggerated by the foreigners and their critics. There were as yet no clear alternatives to Manchu rule in sight. Moreover, each step of this "assistance" to the throne was made necessary and possible by a prior intervention that weakened the throne more than its "rescue" strengthened it. It may nevertheless be that the powers did delay institutional change to some degree after first making it desirable. Having learned to live with the dynasty, they preferred it to any alternatives they could imagine.

Spheres of Interest and the Scramble for Concessions

It was to be expected that the assault on Chinese sovereignty within the borders would be accompanied by a loss of Chinese control over border dependencies and the end of the tribute system. Contiguous territory was ceded—Hong Kong and Kowloon to England and the Maritime Provinces to Russia. Tributary states were forced into new orbits—Liu-ch'iu to Japan, Burma to England, Tongking, Annam, and Cambodia to France, and Korea to Japan. Still the Treaty of Shimonoseki that concluded the Sino-Japanese War in 1895 was the first to transfer a major territorial unit inhabited by Chinese (Taiwan) to a foreign power. H. B. Morse considered it a turning point, grouping the process in his pioneering three-volume work by subtitles as one of combat (1834–1860), submission (1861–1893), and subjection (1894–1911).

To contemporaries the war's stark revelation of the inadequacy of the institutional and military measures of modernization that had been taken up to that point suggested the possibility that the treaty port era might be giving way to a division of China into areas of regional dominance. Russia would compete with Japan for dominance to the north, Germany would set its eyes on Shantung, England would dominate the Yangtze Valley, and France the southern provinces adjacent to its new empire in Indo-China. Chinese patriots began to fear for the survival of their country.

Within two years of Shimonoseki the crisis seemed to be at hand. Russia, Germany, and France, who together had forced Japan to give up its demand for Liaotung at Shimonoseki in the Triple Intervention, were the first to demand their pay, and the British were not far behind with demands for equal treatment. Concessions, loans, and guarantees followed in quick succession. In each of these zones the dream of Chinese resources and the hope of a vast Chinese market attracted bankers and investors. The preferred method of "opening up" a sphere was through railway rights, while the required assurance that no competing line could drain off profits could only be secured through formal definition of a "sphere."

The new sequence of concessions and the alarm it aroused help to account for the reform movement of 1898, which failed, and the Boxer paroxysm of 1900, which threatened to place all of Manchuria in Russian hands. The same set of events prompted the United States and Great Britain, through the Open Door notes, to place the powers on record as defending Chinese sovereignty.

With the suppression of the Boxer movement and the imposition of even more stringent controls on the Chinese government thereafter, an era of formal foreign assaults on Chinese sovereignty came to an end. The temporary absence of the Manchu court from Peking during the Boxer aftermath made clear to all parties that the Manchus had become part of the new pattern of privilege and that open competition for division of the "Chinese melon" would be costly and destructive. Within China itself, the aftermath of the Japanese victory and the Boxer disaster brought realization of the futility of further resistance to change. A decade of vigorous modernization moves incorporated ideas of constitutional representation, modern education, abandonment of the traditional examination system, and construction of a modern military force. Peasant rebellion had raged and had been crushed in virtually all parts of China during a half-century; external crisis had found the powers cooperating, then competing, and now seemingly content to abide by their gains while their mutual jealousies and rivalries were transferred to other theaters of alliance and, shortly, war.

Although nineteenth-century China's relations with the treaty powers were full of disaster and humiliation, it would be easy to exaggerate their impact on the land mass of China and on the masses of Chinese. Paul Cohen has argued persuasively that the westernized world of the major treaty ports with its orientation toward change remained little more than flotsam on the deeper currents of Chinese society and tradition, and that true change came only when inland China began to stir. The Cantonese emerged as a modern banking and business class, served as middlemen between Chinese and western traders, and spread their contacts overseas through trade and emigration, producing the first students, converts, reformers, and revolutionaries. Thus to some degree the West helped to energize part of China and to create divisions instead of a unified response.

More important, however, is Cohen's reminder that nineteenth-century Chinese leaders had to respond to a situation of which the West was only a part. Domestic insurrection figured far more importantly than foreign aggression in the priorities of government leaders and the Confucian-minded gentry. It can be argued that the western presence made the social unrest more destructive by diverting governmental attention from that first priority, however, and that the social unrest made it more difficult to meet the western threat.

Nevertheless it is striking to note in Feuerwerker's analysis of the economic impact of the West that, despite all the special privileges western traders received, their impact on the Chinese economy long remained modest. Inland distribution of goods, he points out, remained dominated by Chinese merchants who operated through traditional channels of trade. Outside the major treaty ports foreign merchant houses were unable to establish ties with rural Chinese distributors. Chinese demand for goods from the West was limited and was handled mostly by the native marketing system. A sharp growth in commerce began only in the first decade of the twentieth century, and until then, "the foreign merchant in late Ch'ing China increasingly served rather than controlled the Chinese commercial system." The actual process of exporting and importing was conducted primarily at Shanghai and Hong Kong and remained almost completely in foreign hands until the 1920s, but "outside of the major treaty ports, the structure of trade and the institutions which facilitated it had not changed greatly by 1911 from what they had been a half-century before" (Feuerwerker, 1969, p. 58–61).

Despite the alarm and the threat, China was not divided into spheres by the powers. John Schrecker has shown that late Ch'ing officials became skillful in their use of international law to limit foreign rights to what was called for by strict construction of treaty provisions. Despite the privileges accorded foreign traders and their products, they were unable to extend their influence and their goods far beyond the major treaty ports. A Hong Kong, Shanghai, and Tientsin "corridor" (to use Cohen's term) reactivated the littoral, but the base of political and economic power continued to lie farther inland. The influence of the international context for modernization efforts was harsh, but later chapters will develop the theme that the key to those problems lay in Peking and not in Shanghai or in western capitals.

International Comparisons

China's world view was indeed of a grandeur unique in its continuity and unchallenged by genuine peers. Not that assumptions of imperial grandeur were necessarily unique: claims of universal kingship have been made by many empires throughout history, including the empire of Byzantium. What was unusual in the Chinese case, Benjamin Schwartz suggests, was that in China these claims were coupled with specifically Confucian criteria of culture. What was unique to the Chinese case was the fact that those proclamations of continuous and solitary splendor had accorded so closely with the facts of East Asian experience and had seemed to be reinforced by the workings of the Chinese world order.

When we consider the response of the Chinese to the events that befell them in the nineteenth century, three possible comparisons present themselves. The first is that of the Ottoman Empire in its period of decline. Fletcher has pointed out that "the European trading powers' demands for extraterritoriality in Asia had been inspired partly by the capitulations they had secured from the Ottoman porte at Constantinople"; as has been pointed out, the Ottoman Empire was the first nonwestern world order to be brought to terms by the newly industrializing West. Yet the differences easily outweigh the similarities. Ottoman power had always grown alongside that of other powers, and was never a world to itself. To a much greater degree than China's, Ottoman rule was over people of different ethnic and religious persuasion, with the result that the first signs of Ottoman faltering brought rebellion on all the fringes of the empire, rebellions that in turn offered opportunities for western imperialists. With the possible exception of one to the north, China's rebellions offered no such opportunities. Ottoman territory—Mediterranean lanes, the Bosphorus, Greece—was also of immense strategic importance to the European powers, and Ottoman crises constituted a much greater invitation for European intervention. This was shown by the sequence of European conferences held to deal with "the sick man of Europe."

A second case is that of Romanov Russia. The defeats of the Crimean War produced a speedy response culminating in the reforms of the 1860s, which brought an end to serfdom and prepared the way for modern institutions in education, government, and the military. Nevertheless the contrasts again outnumber any similarities. Russia had already, under Peter, inaugurated a program of limited European-style administrative reform, and it thereafter consistently functioned as a member of the European international order.

The best comparison is with Japan. Most of the treaty system was fastened on Japan as it had been on China. China and Japan were ''opened'' in the same process of western expansion, often by the same agents. The figures of the China coast reappeared in the ports of Japan. Jardine, Matheson and Company and its rivals dominated Yokohama as they did Shanghai. Harry Parkes, Rutherford Alcock, Ernest Satow, and others who figure large in Japanese history got their basic training in China. Le Gendre, the American who served as Japanese Foreign Office adviser in the invasion of Formosa in 1874, had developed his ''expertise'' as American consul at Amoy immediately before. The unequal treaties that were forced on the Tokugawa government in the 1850s and 1860s were substantially identical to those negotiated with China in the first round of European advance. Extraterritoriality, the most favored nation clause, a 5 percent tariff, and ''new'' treaty ports (especially Yokohama and Kobe) changed coastal Japan as they had changed parts of coastal China.

The dissimilarities may nevertheless be more important. Japan was approached a few decades later than China. Word of what had taken place in China was widely diffused throughout Japan and alarmed Japanese leaders enough to rule out a military resistance that might have brought on a Japanese version of the Opium War. Local experiments in resistance were tried at Shimonoseki and Kagoshima with disastrous results. A shattering Tokugawa defeat in the 1850s might have produced political disorganization before the programs that strengthened the southwestern fiefs had had time to mature.

In Japan the powers, and especially England, had no fear of strengthening the southwestern fiefs that ultimately overthrew the Tokugawa, for their representatives and social systems were no different from the regime that seemed to be obstructing foreign trade. In China the alternative to Ch'ing rule seemed a rabble tinged by madness. When, for a brief moment, junior consular officials thought the Taiping might promise reform as well as trade, they were put off by evidence that the rebel religion was fully as insistent on the middle country as its Confucian opponents. ''Whereas God the Heavenly Father has sent our Sovereign down on earth, as the true Sovereign of all nations in the world,'' the ''Mandate'' handed an English visiting party read, ''all people in the world who wish to appear at his court must yield obedience to the rules of ceremony'' (Thomas Taylor Meadows, 1856, p. 262). The victory of Japan's insurgents in 1868 had results quite different from those that would have followed a Taiping overturn of the Ch'ing.

Japan's treaty system never progressed to formal alienation of territory, western missionaries did not receive rights in the Japanese interior until Meiji times, and there were never discussions of spheres of influence or of dividing Japan. A more effective response helped make such moves impossible or unnecessary, but there were also differences in the intent and intensity of the foreign impact.

Western expectations and intentions in Japan were consistently more limited and instrumental than they were in China. For the European powers Japan was beyond China and secondary; for the United States it was on the way to China. No one expected great financial or trade advantage from the opening of Japan. There were never merchant profits comparable to those produced in China by the exchange of opium for tea or silver. In fact, opium never figured as an item of trade in Japan. Perry thought he was racing British admirals bent on opening Japanese ports, but in actuality Admiral Sterling had orders to hold back and let Perry take the lead. As London saw it, the most favored nation clause would in any case extend all benefits gained by America to Britain, as it had extended England's gains in China to America. After the ports were opened, the China trade also outweighed that of Japan in amount and in importance. Textiles and, later, oil "for the lamps of China" became larger items for western shippers than did comparable items for Japan.

It may have been useful to western powers to have an East Asian accomplice in their advance on China; it was certainly desirable for the Japanese to "join" the West. Japanese diplomats took the lead in securing a western-style audience when the T'ung-chih emperor attained his majority in 1873, and Japanese publicists wrote about the need to dissociate their country from oriental and Chinese stereotypes in western eyes. Japan secured vital rights of manufacture for the western powers in the Shimonoseki treaty in 1895, and emerged as the Asian ally of Great Britain in 1902. Japan was thus consistently more fortunate in its international relations than China, and it was never as fully integrated into a pattern of dependent, "colonial" trade. It was able to avoid almost all foreign loans and foreign investments, to hire and then dismiss foreign technicians, and finally to enter the international alliance system as a major partner in the early years of the twentieth century.

Nevertheless, in comparing the response of Chinese authorities to these events with that of their Japanese counterparts to less serious setbacks, one is struck by the fact that less danger produced more consternation in Japan. Several explanations can be suggested for this.

The first would be that of scale. The initial disruptions in China took place at Canton, far from the capital, while in Japan the center of activity was near Edo, the shogunal capital. Shogunal officials worked hard to keep the foreigners at some distance from the imperial capital at Kyoto, preferring to keep them at the center of Tokugawa power. Chinese officials tried to keep them at the periphery and to protect the administrative center. If China had had two centers of political authority, and two loci of legitimacy that could have been engaged in a struggle about the foreign issue, the comparison (and the story) might have been closer. Second, in Japan the foreign problem was at the forefront of public concern; in China it took second place to the far greater danger posed by domestic insurrection for over a decade.

Third, China's experience and flexibility in foreign relations and Chinese officials' fears of punishment at the hands of the distant court, were sufficient to encourage the depiction of the early stages of the treaty system as the application of traditional measures of barbarian control. Japan's greater seclusion had been so evident to a country united by alternate residence of the service nobility at the shogun's capital (*sankin-kōtai*) that there was no way of minimizing the importance of the concessions that were made to the foreigners.

Official rhetoric put forth by Manchu leaders to explain away the concessions can be interpreted as obscurantist indifference to outside danger or ignorance of what was at stake in an effort to depict a compromise with necessity as conformity with tradition. Given an unenlightened Manchu court, sycophant officials, and insistent foreigners, one could predict a good deal of this. The imperial clansman Kiying (Ch'i-ying), in receipt of Secretary of State Daniel Webster's missive couched in rhetoric developed, as Foster Rhea Dulles has pointed out, for communication with American Indian chiefs ("Now my words are, that the Governments of two such great countries should be at peace. . . . I therefore send to your Court Caleb Cushing, one of the wise and learned men of this country. On his first arrival in China, he will inquire for your health") could assure Cushing that its beauty brought tears to his eyes and then excuse its crudity to the court by explaining that "of all the countries it [the United States] is the most uncivilized and remote. . . . Not only in the forms of edicts and laws are they entirely unversed, but if the meaning be rather deep, they would probably not even be able to comprehend" an imperial reply. Official accounts of the audience the foreign representatives forced upon the T'ung-chih emperor in 1873, Fairbank notes, describe the western ministers as struck with terror, their trembling hands dropping their papers as they struggled to respond to the emperor's kindly questions.

This deliberate distortion of reality had no counterpart on the Japanese side. No one ever suggested that the presence of foreign envoys in Edo constituted an ingenious extension of the *sankin-kōtai* system under which the Tokugawa shogunate compelled feudal lords to reside in Edo. From the first the foreign powers were described as a genuine threat. Although a few shogunal officials proposed using French assistance to control the southwestern domains that seemed to be getting English encouragement, their superiors would have none of it. Nor, it should be added, was the French government in favor of intervention in Japanese politics.

On the other hand, as Wang Erh-min, points out (*Cambridge History of China*, vol. 11, pt. 2), nonofficial comment in China showed a considerably more intense concern than official rhetoric suggests. By the 1860s many writers were warning that China was "facing a change the like of which had not been seen in thousands of years." Translations were becoming increasingly common, as were travelers' descriptions of their experiences in foreign countries. The scale of this activity, while well below that of the same decades in Japan, where accounts like Fukuzawa's *Seiyō jijō* (Condition in the West) and *Gakumon no susume* (The Encouragement of Learning) reached literally millions of people, was nevertheless great enough to invalidate attribution of China's inept handling of foreign affairs to an obscurantism intrinsic to the Chinese world view.

The pattern of collaborative, then competitive, and once again collaborative exploitation the treaty powers developed in China constitutes thus an unusual and rather special category in the history of imperialism. Sharp competition between the powers, the vastness of the land, and its underlying unity made "normal" or full imperialist rule impossible. Sun Yat-sen later tried to convey this difference by describing his country as a "hypo-colony." China was, he said, "the colony of every nation that has made treaties with her, and the treaty-making nations are her masters." Further, he thought, "subjection to one power is a far higher and more advantageous position than subjection to many powers." In China imperialists had power to obstruct without responsibility to manage. A deep sense of humiliation came to mark Sun's generation, which developed a keen awareness of the nature and dimensions of imperialist encroachment.

The treaty port era thus inaugurated a full century of Chinese weakness and humiliation. That century had begun with a few treaty ports. It went on to substantial alienation of territory, and for a time threatened violation of the sovereignty and unity of China. China's central government, hard pressed by domestic disorder throughout the nineteenth century, unstable throughout the first quarter of the twentieth, and fighting for its life against Japanese imperialism the second quarter of the twentieth century, was in no position to counter these moves effectively. Internal weakness thus resonated with external pressure.

At the same time, the western advance contributed much that was important to Chinese modernization. Western enclaves spread the awareness of the modern world and information about it throughout many areas of coastal and riverine China. Missionary schools became gateways to the languages and knowledge of the modern world. Together with their employees and converts, missionaries translated a good deal of the literature of the West, and by the end of the nineteenth century individuals like Timothy Richards were important forces for reformation and change through their personal influence and their publications.

Foreign traders with their goods and processes also forced modifications in many branches of the Chinese economy. Investors and technicians in the race to develop water and land transport undoubtedly speeded effective unification and communication. The foreign presence was particularly important in providing quick access to modern military equipment for a society in constant turmoil. Yet it would clearly have been preferable and more effective to have had this effort under Chinese control and at Chinese initiative. The foreign presence also intensified the cultural bifurcation between periphery and inner core. In the absence of a political leadership deeply committed to the task of institutional reform, extensive exposure to the western world often served to isolate individuals from the political elite rather than increase their value to it. Meiji political and intellectual leaders gained credibility from trips abroad; Ch'ing emissaries and specialists usually had to struggle to reestablish their reputations upon their return. The difference lay not with individuals' world views, aptitudes, or flexibility. Numerous individuals and groups in China reached an intimacy and familiarity with aspects of the modern world that make them seem far more "western" than their more taciturn contemporaries in Meiji Japan, but without comparable ties to the power structure of their society, their influence and role remained marginal.

This discussion leads to the conclusion that the questions with which we began cannot of themselves elicit answers adequate to explain the tortuous course of China's struggle for modernization. The international context of traditional China did indeed create problems for the appropriation of knowledge from abroad, and the circumstances under which the foreign challenge presented itself made appropriation of its examples particularly difficult and unlikely. But though the examination of Chinese views and western aggression will not provide solutions, it will add important dimensions.

The basic conflict was thus between a Chinese order that was fully structured and unchallenged and a western order that was beginning to assume its modern structure, full of vigor, and reinforced by modern knowledge and technology. The western world view and order, without the technology that accompanied it, would have seemed as bizarre to later historians as the Chinese order came to seem to the startled westerners who witnessed the disintegration of Chinese military forces in the face of their own, much smaller, units. That the conflict, until the Sino-Japanese War of 1894, centered along the coast and on the sea, where China's technological handicap was greatest, served to emphasize the hopelessness of the struggle.

In sum, while the Chinese international system and world view were indeed unique in their strength and persistence, they did not within themselves bear the major responsibility for China's response to the challenges of the modern century. There was nothing to hamper Chinese mastery of diplomatic arts and international law, and evidence of Chinese negotiators' superior diplomatic skill is abundant. There does indeed seem to have been in Ming and Manchu times an intensification of Chinese belief in the virtues and sufficiency of the Confucian order, and this may have slowed the response of those in authority. Yet that was clearly no longer a factor by the time the nineteenth century drew to a close.

The new international context of the nineteenth century, on the other hand, while it provided challenge, incentive, and example, also provided handicaps and humiliation; it forced commitment of new sources of revenue to obligations incurred through defeat and frustration; it forced the construction of a modern naval and military force, which was destroyed in the war with Japan. The international order provided means and prevented their use, and provided a challenge only to channel and deflect the response. At the core of the problem was a Chinese context in which political decline, population growth, and social upheaval and economic change forced upon a faltering political system choices for change it was unable to accept. Despite all the foreign assaults, China remained one; but despite all the claims of imperial centrality and unity, internal disorder produced a downward devolution toward regional and familial priority.

CHAPTER THREE

Political Structure

PREMODERN CHINA IS NOTABLE FOR HAVING DEVELOPED over the two millennia of its imperial era political forms similar in their structural features to those of modernized societies. The centralized bureaucratic structure of the imperial Chinese government, for example, prefigured in many significant ways the workings of modern bureaucracies. The change from that base to a modern bureaucracy would seem a smaller and simpler step than a change from an aristocratic oligarchy to a merit-status bureaucracy. Yet clearly no particular set or sequence of conditions is necessary for modernizing change, for some states with aristocratic oligarchies did in fact achieve modernization more quickly and more completely than China. The base from which change occurred in China must contain the explanation of this and other complexities of China's wayward path to political stability as a modernizing nation. We must start by examining that base, seeking an understanding of the capacities for modernizing political change that appear there and of the circumstances under which they were displayed.

Both the earliest modernizers and the most successful of the latecomers to modernization, such as Japan and Russia, exhibited the conditions of a well-defined state, firmly established sovereignty, well-grounded political institutions, and an effective, centralized civil authority. In particular, China's very early possession of some of the most "modern" prefigurings of political modernization, for example, those that Gilbert Rozman in Chapter 5 calls "precocious" features in terms of social integration, calls attention to the compelling enigmas in China's postponed development—or deflected development, or alternatives to the development—of other features of modernization. That anomaly of the precocious and the postponed will be a recurrent theme of this chapter.

For two thousand years or more, certainly longer than any other existing nation, China has been in continuous existence as a well-defined state. Since the consolidation in 221 B.C. of what in English is called the Chinese Empire—misleadingly, since it did not (until the Ch'ing dynasty) resemble the Roman, the British, and other empires in amalgamating several civilizations and states under the imperial sway of a culturally distinct overlord—there has been government of the form peculiar to the unified Chinese state. This government has always been committed to the notion that there can be but one legitimate government for all the Chinese people, even when it was unable to attain that ideal. Its centralized political institutions have frequently been required to compromise with localized internal competition, such as regionally autonomous warlordism, or coexisting claimants to universal hegemony, but such compromise has always been considered a temporary aberration by all the parties concerned. Nor has that concept of a centralized political order conterminous with the extent of Chinese civilization and enfolding all the peoples who shared in it, regardless of racial identity, been challenged even when Chinese or alien rulers struggled among each other. Nor have the political forms of the Chinese state been rejected or seriously challenged, from within or without. On the contrary, China has been the model, the exporter of political ideas and forms. The imperial institution itself, and many of the political forms associated with Chinese government have been adopted or adapted far beyond China, and few if any alien forms gained cognizance or credence there, until the beginnings of modernization in the mid-nineteenth century. All the significant institutional innovations that occasionally stemmed from alien conquest represented adaptations by alien rulers to their problems of ruling in China, and were perceived by the Chinese (not incorrectly) as developments in Chinese government. The essential point is that China's political structures possess unmatched continuity of development without having been threatened or challenged in the eyes of the Chinese themselves. In the intramural world of China's cultural experience, government was a hallmark of civilization, and civilization was unique to, or synonymous with, China. That still was true when the western powers demanded that China conduct foreign affairs more along western lines, leading to the creation in 1861 of an entirely new institution called the Tsung-li Ya-men, which was called the Foreign Office in English; even that was at best a superficial addition to the Chinese machinery of government. Significant replacement of traditional institutional forms by modernized "western" ones (such as legislative bodies) and newly devised Chinese ones (for example, the Examination Yuan) did not occur until the twentieth century.

Imperial China, then, had as stable and as full political institutions as any other premodern nation, institutions founded on the enduring secular, ethical vision of Confucianism, firmly grounded in long historical reality, with elaborately specialized and differentiated subdivisions, and operated according to highly rational, fully recorded "regulations and precedents" (*tse-li*) by professional bureaucrats whose status was achieved by meeting objective criteria. Through those means it conducted an orderly political control over territories whose people regarded themselves as legitimately subject to its uniform, centralized procedures. In short, its modern-sounding government displays to an intense degree of development the kinds of attributes that, one might posit, should be conducive to the early stages of transition to political modernization. We must discount for the shortcomings in actual realization and recognize that the Chinese political ideal was more ambitious than the technical means of its implementation—especially in the field of communications—could sustain. Even so, the late empire's best "protomodern" features would seem to have equipped it superbly for an easy transition. Yet we know this did not happen. Not surprisingly, widespread building of telegraph lines in the late nineteenth century did not greatly improve, or even change, Chinese government. Ray Huang has warned against regarding Chinese political institutions as failed or imperfectly realized prototypes of western, that is modernized political institutions (1976, pp. 6–12). In an important sense, perhaps, the very fullness and perfection of the Chinese political ideal, to whatever imperfect degree it was realized, was itself a stumbling block. Such fundamental changes as enlarging the scope of governmental responsibilities, or of creating regular mechanisms for active popular participation in government, were effectively forestalled by the overwhelming stability and ethical rightness of the old political order. All "old orders" supply controlling factors limiting the society's capacity for change; in China's case, what is special, if not unique, is that the forces of stability (whether we label those reaction, senescence, or native sensibility) were nurtured by so full a panoply of broadly satisfying ideal alternatives to real political change, that is, not just amelioration of evils, that any strong domestic demands for change were very slow to emerge. Who could conceptualize and justify the changes? What social forces could the society generate that would demand profound institutional innovation? It is difficult to imagine a course that history might have taken to produce modernization in China's government that would not have had to include the diffusion of specific elements from the West's evolving political systems and concepts, and compelling demonstrations of their superiority, before Chinese leaders would be ready to transform rather than merely to renovate Chinese politics.

Yet, having stressed stability as a powerful force in Chinese history, we must not subscribe to the foolishness of an "unchanging China," or to institutional traps that had effectively sealed China's society into mere prolongation of its old modes. By the end of the Ch'ien-lung emperor's reign on February 8, 1796, to choose an arbitrary milepost, significant changes in the quality and the operational effectiveness, if not in the form, of Chinese government were beginning to become evident. China's interactions with the world beyond its borders—with areas of no direct political contact—were intensifying but not well recognized or understood. Disruptive influences originating from abroad were therefore beyond China's control. Perhaps the most obvious of these was the change in trade. Trade in commodities had made China since the sixteenth century a major repository of the world's silver, but from the early nineteenth century on, it was beginning to drain China's silver rapidly away. The consequences of this change were vast indeed, and quite unprecedented in China's political experience. Other changes more wholly internal to China, however, were no less important. In particular, the relation between the rulers and the strategic elite in its administrative and nonadministrative roles had undergone profound changes during the Ch'ing dynasty, changes affecting the quality of political performance and the morale of its performers. The resultant administrative deterioration described in detail in the classic study by K. C. Hsiao (1960) portended profound changes in the management of Chinese society. Whether all these changes signaled that a mere dynastic changeover was in the offing, or that more profound dislocations and discontinuities were involved, is a problem much debated by scholars.

Throughout the nineteenth century the larger features of the political structure continued to operate; a few significant structural modifications (discussed in the section ''Local Power,'' in this chapter), took place under conditions of the very greatest social stress. Still, in 1911, the imperial order was quickly and easily overthrown, cast off with no lingering chance of being reinstated. Thus, formally speaking, the largest of all changes, political revolution and the demise of an ancient polity, occurred overnight. Many discrete features of the old political order survived that revolution, but they were no longer parts of an ancient imperial system sheltered from searching scrutiny. The lines of political change became inconsistent, even contradictory, for almost four decades, until the communist revolution of 1949 established a new pattern of political control, not without its own contradictions and inconsistencies. The search for a new political stability after 1911 is discussed in Chapter 9; in this chapter, the gradual loss of stability through the nineteenth century is shown to reveal the infirmities of the old Chinese political order's bases as a modernizing world impinged upon it.

Sovereignty

China's sovereignty in the nineteenth century must be discussed in two contexts; the exercise of rulership within the Chinese state, and the integrity of China's sovereignty vis-à-vis other regional and world powers. Our hypotheses are that the imperial institution, to have been an effective instrument for guiding the processes of early modernization, would have had to have been a secure and stable focus of the Chinese people's (or, at least their elite's) loyalty and political attention; that its powers would have had to have been great enough to will and to legitimize the social changes needed; and that the Chinese sovereignty would have had to have been capable of surviving the

50

stresses induced by the violent interactions with the other sovereignties that encroached on China throughout the century in order for the Chinese ruler to retain effective leadership of state and people. Was Chinese political guidance in fact effective in these ways? We find pluses and minuses on all three scores.

POLITICAL CONSCIOUSNESS

The Chinese have long possessed a well worked out political theory about dynastic legitimacy and how the power to rule over their state can be attained. The Manchu rulers, though alien conquerors, attained legitimacy as sovereigns in China by their successful conquest in 1644–1645, which was reaffirmed by their successful suppression of extensive nativist rebellion in 1673–1681, and by the ideals they invoked in both cases to explain their success. The initial political resistance to them was of two kinds. There was the expected, theoretically based attitude of a generation of the elite formally bound by previous service to the Ming, requiring that they refuse to shift allegiance and service to any successor dynasty. There was also a new element in that seventeenth-century change of dynasty: some Chinese thinkers and statesmen had come to question the right and the rightness, in theory, of any aliens to acquire dynastic legitimacy in China. This new issue lent added meaning to the longstanding formalities of loyalist sentiment at the beginnings of the Ch'ing dynasty. The potentially racist content of anti-Manchu resistance was to smolder on, threatening to reemerge, as it finally did in the nineteenth century. Despite that historically novel element in the early Ch'ing political scene, by the end of the seventeenth century, Manchu legitimacy was securely acknowledged in Chinese political theory and in social fact. The theoretical foundations of legitimacy were expressed in the doctrine of the Heavenly Mandate (*t'ien ming*), an ancient formulation in continuous use for 2,500 years, the only device for claiming the legitimacy enjoyed by all the more than twenty dynasties, native and alien, throughout all of imperial history. The doctrine is unusual, if not unique, in political theory. Because it remained current it is important for understanding the end of the imperial era. Moreover, just as the political circumstances of the late Ch'ing period were conditioned by it, so were certain key modern terms and concepts of political life in some measure derived from it.

Before describing Mandate theory, we must note that the polity it validated displayed a changing character over the two millennia of China's imperial era. While invoking the Mandate doctrine, the bearers of political power progressively intensified the authoritarianism of the Chinese monarchy. By Ming and Ch'ing times they had achieved something approaching a true despotism (insofar as the available communications and capacities for integration and control would allow—in other words, something far short of modern totalitarianism).

This was not accomplished without considerably distorting the pristine

51

doctrine. In Europe since the Renaissance, we see the progressive growth of constitutional checks on monarchic absolutism; the opposite trend in later Chinese imperial history has produced one of the environmental factors conditioning Chinese expectations toward government even among the liberal-minded enemies of such tendencies. Late Ch'ing political reformers did not repudiate the doctrine as a basis of imperial or governmental legitimacy as much as they appealed to the libertarian potential in its early formulations, as found in the *Mencius* and other Confucian texts. Some of China's inability to achieve more thoroughgoing change both during and since the late nineteenth century seems to stem from the general reluctance to part with old terms wholly; instead, the tendency has been to redefine them partially.

In the terms of this remarkable political doctrine, cosmic forces, naturalistically conceived at the level of political philosophy yet compatibly apprehended as "divine" or superrational in many other contexts, somehow grant the responsibilities of governing to a family head and his descendants, in order to discharge the functions of "the father and mother of the people" (*min chih fu-mu*). Each ruling line's (dynasty's) fall was implicit in the manner of its rise; rebellion was a heinous political crime when unsuccessful, but when successful it was the proper means of recruiting the founder of the inevitable successor dynasty in response to the public will, which in effect gave expression to the will of heaven. Every ruler in the succession of a dynasty's tenure had to add to its cumulative merit by ruling well ("for the people") or detract from the store of its validity, leading ultimately to the loss of the sustaining cosmic support. Each new dynastic founder was required to break with the demonstrated weaknesses and errors of the previous dynasty by making some institutional reforms and ritual changes, thus generating a measure of renovation of politics and society. Marion J. Levy, Jr., has observed that "in the past, few societies were characterized by renovating structures of social change as was traditional China" (1966, pp. 487–488). The change of Mandate and the political acts associated with it were among the mechanisms of institutional renewal that characterized China.

At the same time, however, each successor *within* a dynasty was bound to adhere to the institutions decreed by the founder. Although not so intended, we can see that this worked as a mechanism ensuring the end of a dynasty when institutional lag made social problems severe. Long tradition in Chinese didactic historiography had created a myth—and a potent expectation—of a cyclic life through which each dynasty would pass, with a vigorous, renovating founding, then an age of peace and prosperity, then one of decline, followed by a final phase of breakdown, open rebellion, and the struggles of a new founding. Theory and myth also provided that some dynasties, by unusual exertions, might achieve a "mid-point restoration" during the phase of decline, and that an earned reversal of fortunes could bring about a new lease on the dynasty's *te* or *virtus*—its power and moral vigor.

Thus no Chinese dynasty could claim in theory a perpetual right to rule;

the imperial institution was founded on the concept of its periodic replacement. Although loyalty to it became, by the later imperial millennium, the overriding political virtue every dynasty cultivated among its administrative and military elites, a discerning eye for the course of events was also prudent. For the enduring stability of the cosmic order and of human society underlay the somewhat more temporary, yet scarcely flimsy stability of a reigning dynasty. The Ch'ing dynasty even at the end could claim and receive service (even if not a highly committed loyalty) from a majority of its officials, and at least a passive, apathetic support from a majority of its commoner subjects, although it could not claim in theory a perpetual right to rule.

Should we then state that a gradual "impairment of sovereignty" was the expectation, making the nineteenth-century failure of performance less disturbing because people were prepared to understand it? Did it, by the same token, encourage gradual disaffection? Although the weakness of the dynasty's performance was ever more clearly demonstrated, and elite loyalties were tinged with cynicism, this did not automatically cost the dynasty the services of its strategic elite. In part, this was because its most serious enemies—the rude and outlandish Taiping rebels and the rude and outlandish Europeans—were also the natural enemies of the elite, even of the common people. The myth of mid-point restoration provided a real means of combatting both, and of revitalizing commitments to the enduring verities, and to the dynasty. Thus that flexible but demanding basis of power could keep an officialdom aligned with the throne until the last minute, but it also prepared it to accept the inevitability of dynastic collapse once the facts were demonstrated. Thus also the powers of the Chinese throne could be and were diminished by the internal disorders and the external disasters of the nineteenth century, and by Chinese judgments on these events. Likewise, its powers were reinforced, to some extent reconstituted, by the demonstrated success in quelling problems, and in having earned a mid-point restoration in the 1860s and 1870s. Again, the throne was the more seriously damaged by the subsequent relapse from seeming dynastic revitalization during the painful decades of the 1880s and 1890s. The need constantly to fall back on military means of maintaining the proper order of mankind was especially disheartening to those who took dynastic legitimacy theory seriously, and most thoughtful Chinese still did so, regardless of the merits of the reigning dynasty.

The theoretical questions regarding dependence on force were moot when a new conquering dynasty still wielded unchallengeable military force, but once order had been restored in the founding, military force was not theoretically justifiable as more than a secondary sanction, standing behind the primary sanction of civil governing that itself was supposed only to reinforce the suasive power of ethical legitimacy. The foundations of the imperial institution were strongly antimilitaristic. And, for practical as well as for theoretical reasons, no dynasty could retain power for long by primary recourse to its

53

secondary sanction. The Ch'ing had long since passed the founding phase of military action; moreover, it had long since lost that capacity. When the time came it could fall much more easily—with much less wrenching of the social fiber than in the fall of the French or Russian monarchies, or than in the denaturing alterations of the English and the Japanese monarchies. Yet, in 1911, its succession by a radical new polity was by no means implicit in or greatly encouraged by its fall. "Revolution," the Chinese term for which is still "the withdrawal of the Mandate," was at best a transvalued concept in 1911; real revolution then and since has required a great many conceptual components beyond those adequate then to bring down the Ch'ing dynasty only to leave China with unformed alternatives. That the last imperial dynasty should end and a republic should nominally replace it in 1911 was a phenomenon more wondrous than real.

We must conclude here that the Chinese basis of monarchical authority and power contributed some stability to politics by its reassurance that even bizarre events and profound disasters were within an understandable pattern, and by guiding political attitudes along standardized lines. Also, however, it contributed to an acceptance of dynastic changeover, and probably made the events of 1911 both less traumatic and politically less significant than they might otherwise have been. Yet, by 1911 there were also new elements in the Chinese awareness, so that the ancient Mandate theory was not alone—as it always had been previously—in shaping the Chinese responses to the fall of the dynasty as an item of political change. Among the new elements was a new concept of revolution itself, transmitted from the French and the American and other western experiences. The concept was new even if its radical newness was significantly qualified by the derivation of its name (in Chinese) from the ancient and honored Mandate terminology.

LEADERSHIP: DYNASTIC INTERESTS

There was no institutional separation of and no significant distinction between reigning and ruling in the later imperial era. That is, there was no seat of competing powers—a shogunate, patriarchates, a council of barons—apart from the throne. Nor did the political system provide for a symbol of the state apart from the throne; the primary ritual symbols, such as the Altars of the Land and the Grain, were the property of the reigning dynasty, not of the Chinese people. Moreover, the ruler was essentially a political figure. In both Russia and Japan the throne possessed or could quickly assume a much more compelling religious significance, although in Russia the divinely ordained throne shared religious powers with a strongly institutionalized church. In Japan, a reigning imperial house with no popular recognition or ruling powers before the Restoration of 1868, could nonetheless by the end of the century claim a divinity that touched the religious activities of the entire nation very directly through a mass state cult. In short, it could build on latent capacities in Japanese religion and statecraft to produce a divinely enhanced imperial authority. The Chinese imperial institution possessed certain religious attributes and patronized many state cults, but its religion-derived power and authority were rendered relatively weak by the fact that Chinese religions themselves were institutionally weak. Further, the rational, secular foundations of political theory, at least at the higher philosophical levels, severely limited the benefits that the throne could gain from its many kinds of identification with popular religion. In a milieu of nonexclusive truths, the Chinese throne by late imperial times tended to play all the possibilitites for all possible gains, but it achieved little of the numinous aura that surrounded reigning symbols in some other early modernizing states, and that has greatly enhanced the authority of political leaders in many.

As for the ruling monarch, there was no institutional provision for sharing the ultimate powers. K. C. Hsiao has succinctly described the basic political circumstances of the Ch'ing period:

> The government of the Ch'ing dynasty, like preceding regimes, was an autocracy ruling over a society in which . . . the interests of the ruler and the subjects were divergent and to some extent incompatible. The imperial rulers were therefore compelled by practical necessity to maintain as firm as possible a control of the vast realm in order to insure political stability and thus to perpetuate their regime. Because they could not have confidence in their subjects or count on their loyalty, they sought to render the latter submissive and subservient by a variety of devices calculated to immunize them against all thought and action that might prove detrimental to imperial security. The fact that the Ch'ing rulers were conquerors from an alien ethnic group made this necessity all the more obvious and urgent. . . . It is important . . . to identify the precise position of the gentry and literati (or potential gentry) [see the section ''Local Leadership,'' in this chapter] in the imperial system. Owing to their personal qualifications and social status, they exerted considerable influence upon the multitudes of common people in the village and towns. It was from this elite group that the imperial rulers recruited their administrative servants. Leadership in their home communities and services in the administration, however, did not cause their interests to become identical. In fact as well as in theory, scholar-officials remained subjects of the Son of Heaven and, together with commoners were objects of imperial control. Those who in their capacity as government officials functioned as mediums through which imperial authority was brought to bear on the masses, were at the same time part of ''the people'' over whom and ostensibly for whose benefit the emperors ruled. (1960, pp. 501, 505–506.)

Hsiao's is not the most widely encountered analysis of political power in late Ch'ing times, but it is persuasive; above all, it is important in calling attention to the character of China's administrative elite and of its roles in relation to the throne. As a component of the political order, the administrative elite will be discussed more fully in the section ''Local Leadership'' later in this chapter.

Political Structure

The ruling house of the Manchu dynasty together with the chief imperial clansmen and the higher Manchu nobility, linked in a tribal clan structure quite different from China's family- and lineage-based social structure, can be considered to have formed a ruling caste. Participation in the ruling powers enjoyed by the emperor and that small caste was tightly restricted and circumscribed. The emperor alone could make, or approve, final decisions, although under very special conditions, as in a regency, that power could be exercised in his name. There was no alternative or substitute for, or way of bypassing, his decision-making role. Moreover, no decisions were in theory beyond his competence, whether political, judicial, military, ritual and religious, or even philosophical, literary, and artistic. If the basis for that broad imperial involvement had long been developing in theory, by late Ch'ing times it was also true in fact that a succession of hyperactive emperors had ruled for two hundred years, involving themselves in ever-widening spheres, but especially in those having implications for their dynastic security. They continued to accomplish this with the aid of a small circle of advisers in which imperial relatives dominated. The burdens of supervising and implementing policy decisions, and of arriving at strategic decisions with the fullest possible command of the relevant intelligence, were institutionalized during the 1720s in a newly created Grand Council (*Chün-chi-ch'u*) (Silas Wu, 1970, esp. p. 84ff.). This enlarged the flow of and control over open and secret information available to the throne, information of an extent and quality probably not achieved in any other premodern society. The consequences for political performance were primarily inhibitory; the council enlarged the play of suspicion and intimidation and eventually reduced the elite's initiative and responsibility in both its administrative and nonadministrative roles. Yet at the same time the theoretically unlimited powers of the ruler, unlimited that is except for the ultimate limitation on dynastic tenure inherent in the Mandate theory, were raised to higher levels of actual practice. Under the heightened authoritarianism of the Ch'ing dynasty, the rulers' most honored and most responsible administrative associates were constantly reminded that not in theory and still less in practice could they transcend the status of servile subject. There was no possibility that the ruling caste of high Manchus together with an administrative elite drawn principally from the Chinese population might form a ruling class.

In the system of China's imperial institution as it had evolved by late imperial times, the omnicompetent autocrat, even in times of no particular stress, still had to be at least a relatively competent and attentive individual. In that respect, the Ch'ing dynasty's impressive record in the eighteenth century faltered in the nineteenth. The Chia-ch'ing emperor (1796–1819) came to the throne amid the corruption and demoralization of the Ch'ien-lung emperor's declining years. He was able to survive an impending administrative crisis and to restore a measure of effectiveness in government, but his was not an inspiring or dynamic reign. The Tao-kuang emperor (1820–1850) was the last Ch'ing monarch who strove to reign and rule in the model of his more successful predecessors even though made cautious by fiscal crisis and awareness of other dangers. He was the first emperor in all of China's history to be humiliated and forced to acknowledge defeat at the hands of the western powers. His clansman the Manchu nobleman Ch'i-ying negotiated under duress the Treaty of Nanking in 1842 that ended the First Anglo-Chinese War, better known as the first Opium War, and ceded territory and granted extraterritorial rights to the conquering British. His son, the Hsien-feng emperor (1850–1861), was only twenty when he came to the throne, and he remained an immature and confused imperial symbol throughout his distressed reign. He was dependent on Manchu advisers and on Chinese officials in the provinces to conduct the Second Anglo-Chinese War and to attempt the suppression of the Taiping rebellion. That largest of all domestic disorders in Chinese history still raged through the southern half of the country when the emperor died in 1861 from extremes of self-indulgent behavior, a refugee in Inner Mongolia from the French and British occupation of Peking. His vast summer palace on the outskirts of the capital had been looted and burned by the European occupiers, inflicting a further blow to Manchu imperial and Chinese national dignity. Late in 1861 the regency for the five-year-old successor to the throne, established in accordance with Manchu house law, was overthrown in a coup that made the subsequently notorious Dowager Empress Tz'u-hsi the de facto ruler of China, to remain that almost continuously until her death in 1908. In 1875, after the suspicious death of her son who had recently achieved his majority, she again engineered a plot, this time bringing her three-year-old nephew to the throne in violation of the Manchu succession law. By that manipulation she regained her regency. Her rise to power in 1861 had come through a shocking palace plot, and her exercise of power through extended regencies of women (as co-regent with a politically inactive empress), although not unprecedented in Chinese history, violated Manchu house law. Her long retention of power, by means widely looked upon as illegal, corrupt, and immoral, and the generally flagrant pattern of her rule, were quite without analogue in the last thousand years of the imperial institution. Although she was by no means an incompetent person, all the excuses that might be made for her as an achieving woman in a man's world cannot obscure the fact that she was not politically conscientious from the point of view of either dynasty or nation and was not a far-sighted ruler. Above all, the regularized abnormalities in her exercise of surrogate power, with the many attendant evils of factionalism and corruption that her status and her means induced, further weakened a sorely beset dynasty.

This brief review of the succession of nineteenth-century rulers allows us to ask the obvious question: to what extent was sovereignty impaired by the decline of the imperial leadership? That decline occurred at a conjunction of other circumstances: the humiliating assaults from abroad, and the compromises of centralization that emerged as the Manchu ruling caste was compelled to rely to an unprecedented extent on Chinese regional military and political powers, organized amid crisis to save the dynasty from the massive rebellions of mid-century. Internal weaknesses spawning new forms of competitive regional strength, along with intrusive forces and territorial encroachments, together produced a disabling of Chinese sovereignty in contemporary western eyes. In fact, the European powers decided after 1860 to prop up the Chinese monarchy, the better to serve their own interests in having a stable government in Peking to honor the new treaties they were forcing upon it.

To talk of sovereignty in the context of premodern China raises, however, a serious question of applicability. It is a rather recent concept in western political thought, having arisen only in sixteenth-century Europe in intellectual discourse on the duties and rights of kings conducted against a background of highly legalistic conceptions—whether derived from divine, natural, or the emergent conceptions of civil law. The Chinese definitions of the powers of the state and its head stem from quite different conceptions, scarcely, if at all, legalistic. It is very difficult therefore to discuss the subjective Chinese sense of whether the powers of the emperor and his government had been impaired or nullified, in terms fully congruent with western discussions of sovereignty. Nonetheless that sense of the issue is important in the assessment of the Chinese state's role in modernization. The Manchu rulers, despite assaults on their dignity and the decline apparent in their individual qualities after 1820, continued to reign and to rule, to function as the central element in the day-to-day workings of their government. We can safely conclude that the rulers of the nineteenth century were decreasingly able to conceive or to will significant social change, much less to implement it. Insofar as modernization might have gained from more than defensive adaptation to crisis, hesitatingly implemented in straitened circumstances, the political leadership of the late Ch'ing was able to contribute nothing.

TERRITORIAL INTEGRITY

Another aspect of sovereignty remains to be mentioned; that is, sovereignty as it bears on the territorial integrity of the state, and impairment of sovereignty as seen in encroachments on the exercise of full ruling powers within the state's boundaries, or wherever it claims the right to rule. Here again the West's legalistic conceptions of sovereignty were incongruous in the China of 1800. Yet in this case China mastered the concept and its legal methods well enough to apply them skillfully in treaty negotiations as early as the 1870s, whether or not they had fully displaced earlier Chinese concepts by that time, or by the present.

Between the beginning and the end of the nineteenth century China suffered serious losses of sovereignty. By the treaties of Nanking in 1842, Tientsin in 1858, and Peking in 1860, involving principally Great Britain and

France, but also Russia by 1860, and other powers in lesser extent (the United States from 1844, Japan from 1871), China progressively lost the control of its ports, its foreign trade, its finances, and the regulation of aliens in its interior. Under the provisions of the so-called unequal treaties China lost power in several areas of domestic governing. By the end of the century the nationalistic definition of "Chinese-ness" had become prominent; throughout the twentieth it has become perhaps the dominant political force. By the late nineteenth century the humiliations coming to be perceived in the unequal treaties were a liability to the legitimacy of Manchu rule for having allowed those encroachments, despite the Mandate theory's guarantees of Manchu legitimacy. A new nationalism was beginning to fuel conspiratorial movements using slogans that demanded a "withdrawal of the Mandate" from the Manchu dynasty, and that term, as we have already noted, was soon to acquire the meaning of "revolution." Thus, even if the pattern of western encroachment did not immediately appear as an assault on Manchu sovereignty in Chinese eyes, and could be institutionally accommodated, the delayed reaction to it was all the more powerful. Ultimately that reaction destroyed Manchu sovereignty, and led to a potent redefinition of the concept of sovereignty for the Chinese.

Despite a relatively smooth accommodation to the western powers in the treaty ports, the Chinese were quick to realize the threat to their national interests posed by those same nations in other quarters, especially along the Inner Asian frontier which had been secured by Manchu imperialist wars in the eighteenth century, and which for millennia had been the frontier of threatened national defense. The Ch'ing court came close to war with Russia in 1880, then skillfully negotiated a modern-style treaty in the Russian capital and signed the Treaty of St. Petersburg in 1881, which secured Ili and Chinese Dzungaria in exchange for Russian trading privileges in China. Chinese Turkestan was elevated to the status of a new province, called Sinkiang, in 1884, and included the Ili region as its westernmost extension. The drive to accomplish province status for Sinkiang was conducted by Chinese, not Manchu statesmen, and is witness to a growing Han Chinese identification with the empire beyond the Chinese *Kulturgebiet* that Manchu policies had created more than a century earlier. Treaty making under international law was essential to gaining that victory, and was an instrument skillfully used by the Chinese thereafter.

The pattern at work as the Chinese modernized their conduct of foreign relations under the pressures of having western concepts of sovereignty and international law imposed upon them (discussed more fully in Chapter 2) ironically enough can be interpreted as favoring the Chinese in several ways. On the one hand, the successful encroachments of the western powers could be accepted as within a pattern of relations with barbarians, thereby limiting the sense of Chinese loss. Only later did a redefined sense of Chinese interest weaken emperor and dynasty while strengthening the new national basis for

59

Chinese cohesion. On the other hand, the imposed definitions of sovereignty and of international law as the norm for interstate relations drew firm boundaries of political right enclosing the territory of China, where the Chinese themselves had been content with more ambiguous demarcations that were no longer enforceable; moreover, the new boundaries by and large secured an empire for China at a time when the builders of that empire were no longer capable of maintaining it. Finally, the tool of international law, culturally alien at the beginning of the period of western encroachments, was one that the Chinese learned to use to their newly perceived purposes. They did not succeed in abolishing foreign courts on Chinese soil until World War II, but as early as 1880 they skillfully defended Chinese interests against the western powers, through treaty negotiations. Thus the impairment of Chinese sovereignty, in some ways and after some delays and losses, actually led to a strengthening of China's territorial sovereignty by the end of the nineteenth century.

The redefinitions of sovereignty also led to some absurdities. One of those is the West's frequent anachronistic error of looking upon the tribute system, the old international order replaced by international law and diplomacy in the nineteenth century, as if it had been a recent western device of international relations. As recently as the 1970s, the United States Department of State published maps showing a circle of supposed Chinese territorial claims enclosing half of Asia. This is based on the false notion that countries at any time in the past participating in the Chinese tribute system were by that token subject to Chinese suzerainty as defined today, hence under irredentist claims by the Chinas at this time. Most Chinese themselves were not confused by that issue as they emerged from a culturally defined ''Chinese-ness'' into a nationalistically impelled concept of Chinese sovereignty. Yet, seeing the West's willingness to be anachronistic, the Chinese have not been unwilling to strengthen their position in Tibet for example by reference to a relationship that, before the mid-nineteenth century, was not construed as involving Chinese territorial claims.

A long-range view leads to the conclusion that Chinese sovereignty, in terms of the imperial institution, was weakened and eventually rendered useless by western power and the imposition of western concepts; but in terms of bringing the modern Chinese national state into being and arming it with solidarity and cohesive political goals, Chinese sovereign rights and powers were rendered adequate, by those same changes, to the needs imposed by a modern world.

The Exercise of State Power

CENTRAL GOVERNMENT: ADAPTATION TO NEW NEEDS

The larger the geographic and demographic mass of the premodern state, the more its strategies for distributing powers between center and province, or, as in traditional China, within the three-tiered administrative structure of center, province, and local (prefecture and county) levels of government, reveal the character of government. China has always been the largest of societies and one of the vastest of states, and throughout the two thousand years of its imperial era it evolved varying strategies for achieving desired political results in the provinces. From the time of the statist policies governing the unification of the empire in the third century B.C. on, it also demanded, in large measure unrealistically, exceedingly high levels of effective centralization in all its major tasks. China's precociously modern-sounding achievements in some aspects of government, like its nonachievement in others, can help clarify our understanding of the conditions that prevailed in China as modernization began to affect it.

Our general hypotheses in this connection are as follows: (1) strong centralization of a country's administration aids the coordination of efforts and the mobilization of resources to support modernizing trends; (2) highly differentiated and specialized institutional development prepares for the steady enlargement of the political role typical of the course of modernization; (3) articulation of center, province, and local levels in administration makes an important contribution to efficient governing; and, (4) a tradition of experienced, competent administrators familiar with standardized procedures is crucial to the expansion of political means necessary for modernization. In what degree did these conditions obtain in Ch'ing China, especially in nineteenth-century Ch'ing China?

One might with much fairness claim that ancient China invented one important model for all postfeudal-type bureaucracies serving centralized political orders, and that we can see in China continuously evolving parallels and, occasionally, the actual prototypes for all modern bureaucratic procedures. Long before Ch'ing times, rational bureaucratic modes had standardized all administrative operations, replacing local particularisms and thoroughly denying all rights to regional autonomy (except for non-Han peoples in border areas). Lingering traces of village communalism and localized authority at subadministrative levels had been thoroughly undermined; as K. C. Hsiao has noted: "The idea of local self-government was alien to the system of rural control. Any local initiative or community life that was displayed in the villages was tolerated by the government either to facilitate control or because interference was deemed unnecessary" (1960; 1967 ed., p. 7). The idea advanced from the nineteenth century on by some western observers that the village community in China was a "communalistic democracy" or a "free, self-governing community" because the formal structure of local administration did not reach down to the villages, has been thoroughly discredited. (See the discussion of this issue in Hsiao, 1960, pp. 261–264.) Households in all towns and villages, in groupings of tens and hundreds, were *assigned* responsibilities for keeping order and delivering taxes, responsibilities that were met through organized group action. But land taxes and service duties were levied on separate households, not on communities. Village communities as such had no control over property. In law and in custom they had no communal rights, even of negotiation, in settling their relations with the supervisory arm of government at the district level. China thus had long preceded Japan and Russia in making the entire society at the level of household and individual responsive to the central government's directives. Yet it does not follow that China was more effective than premodern or early modernizing Japan and Russia in drawing resources to the central government from the farmers and craftsmen who constituted village society, or in levying recruits for its armed forces, or in communicating new attitudes and values to its masses. In part that is because the late imperial government in China set itself more limited political purposes and goals. More important, probably, the explanation of China's differences at the level of local government lies in the dynamics of China's family-centered society, or as the sociologist phrases it, in the problems of the general structure of control in the explicitly and implicitly kinship-oriented society (Marion J. Levy, Jr., 1966, pp. 430–435), of which traditional China is an extreme example. This will be more fully discussed in connection with the political characteristics of the strategic elite. It was the elite's relationship to village society that determined the character of the central government's control over its common people. Here, however, our focus is on the structure of central, provincial, and local government.

The long-range trends in the distribution of powers between the inside (nei)—court and capital organs—and the outside (wai)— provincial and local government—reveal the priorities of the rulers. Throughout 2,000 years of centralized imperial government, the clear if gradual trend, clearer and less gradual through the 500 years of Ming and Ch'ing, is toward a gain in the powers, prestige, and size of the administrative organs at the center, at the expense of the powers and prestige of those outside the capital. At the same time, in another pair of nei-wai alternatives, the powers of the Inner Court— the emperor and his supporting staff—consistently gained at the expense of the Outer Court—the highest-level central offices and postings in the civil service bureaucracy. Although ranked civil service officials, including some at the highest levels, staffed both Inner and Outer Courts, and some of the highest ranked held concurrent appointments in both, the significance of the structural changes is that the Outer Court, symbolizing the heights of success in the civil service and the pinnacle of gentry prestige, gradually lost its collegial deliberative, policymaking, and policy-vetoing powers, powers that early in the imperial era had made it a bureaucratic and social elite counterbalance to the autocratic emperor. Those powers had been greatly diminished during the Sung dynasty (960–1279) and early in the Ming dynasty, in 1380, the offices of chancellors or "prime ministers" were abolished, removing the supervisory headship of the entire civil service corps, and transferring prime ministerial functions to the throne. As no properly constituted cabinet system was allowed to replace the advisory functions of the chief ministers, emperors came to carry vastly increased routine burdens of paper work with only makeshift secretarial and administrative assistance. Although gradually during the fifteenth and sixteenth centuries a corps of grand secretaries came to fill these assisting roles, this did not restore to the Outer Court the functions previously lodged there. The Ch'ing dynasty rulers left that situation unchanged until the early eighteenth century when the cabinetlike, semisecret Grand Council was established by the power-sensitive Yung-cheng emperor. With symbolic significance, the Grand Council had its offices deep within the Inner Palace, adjacent to the emperor's private quarters, and away from the daily activities of even the Inner Court. The transfer of powers from the Outer to the Inner Court was complete.

Although headless, the Outer Court grew slightly in size and scope of routine functions during the Ming and Ch'ing periods. Of a total of about 12,500 civil offices throughout the country in late Ming times, half were in the capital and half were distributed among 15 (more or less) provincial and 1,500 local locations (figures based on C. O. Hucker, 1958, p. 12). Chang Chung-li has calculated that in the nineteenth century there were approximately 20,000 civil posts of which half were in the capital, the other half distributed among roughly the same number of provincial and local offices as in Ming times (1955, p. 116). Although the population of the country had trebled during this time, the staff of government had grown by about 60 percent. The local civil service officials, averaging five at each county unit, saw the average population of their districts grow from 100,000 to 250,000 during the Ch'ing period. A highly specialized and differentiated structure of administration at the capital contrasted starkly with government at the local level, where bureaucrats of the same training, background, and competence as those in the capital were required to serve as generalists in a very broad range of political tasks.

Clearly the metropolitan offices and their functions were of far greater import to the rulers than was the conduct of local government. Yet, enigmatically, they did not attempt to take advantage of the state's extensive orderly administrative resources to expand government operations, exploit the potential for revenues and resource mobilization, or provide themselves with a larger and more active political instrument for achieving dynastic or national goals. Could they have done so? The question is crucial for analyzing Ch'ing China's capacity for modernizing change.

The strength of the Ch'ing state has provoked nagging debate among China scholars. How meaningful for the exercise of political power was its structured centralization of administrative decision and function? Were Ch'ing failures to respond to early opportunities, later urgent needs, for stronger state management a consequence of policy decisions, or did they stem from power limitations that left little choice? Among the possible answers, two are most important: (1) the Ch'ing state was initially militarily strong, and its civil government grew markedly stronger as a result of early eighteenth-century administrative refinements, but these civil means of achieving greater control eventually were self-defeating, inducing weaknesses which were aggravated by social crises in the nineteenth century; (2) the Ch'ing state was always structurai. y weak, forced to compromise its authority to gain elite support. In the nineteenth century it merely lost its earlier semblance of strength without undergoing serious devolution of its already flawed administrative capacities.

With respect to some of the issues central to modernization, either answer will do. Yet for others it is important to establish a pattern of gradually diminishing political strength in order to explain the changes in society that bore on the pattern of early modernizing in the nineteenth century. In a sense, any government is as strong as it is perceived to be. But the early Ch'ing military and political machine clearly demonstrated its power to coerce as it worked its will on a vast subjugated population. The weight of evidence seems to support the view that the Ch'ing state remained genuinely strong until the mid-eighteenth century; it continued to be overwhelmingly successful in its wars, in the suppression of dissidence, and in enforcing uniform governing. True, it bound itself to very low revenues via its taxes on the population at large, and maintained its fiscal system by means that favored its Chinese elite. Nonetheless, it enjoyed revenue surpluses until late in the eighteenth century. Also, it paid certain costs in the means it found to induce the Chinese elite to serve the dynasty, but it gained the elite's essential services without releasing it from oppressive formal subservience. If the Manchu rulers were sinified in the process, the Chinese granted them in return a powerfully strengthening legitimacy in their hold on the Mandate. The Ch'ing displayed all the essential aspects of real strength that it appears to have wanted until the late eighteenth century. When it could display few or none of these in the nineteenth century, more than its subjects' perceptions of the dynasty's capacities had changed; its political means as well as its command on the power to coerce were weakened, adulterated, and debased. Perceptions in fact lagged decades behind the actual changes in circumstances.

The details of these changing political capacities cannot be set forth here at length, but some aspects of the process by which change occurred must be mentioned. Despite flaws and elements of administrative clumsiness, the centralization of the early Ch'ing state had been carried as far in actual administrative practice as any premodern state. To emphasize its negative aspects, intimidation and control of provincial and local government, and of the society, were particularly well developed. More positively, the government was staffed by able and highly regularized bureaucrats expected to report fully and systematically, in triplicate, on all acts of their governing, who were subject to elaborately developed administrative laws and precedents—in short, who satisfied the requirements of our hypothesized conditions favoring political modernization. We must assume the Ch'ing government chose not to exploit fully its relatively centralized state institutional structure when it still might have done so. Two early and mid-Ch'ing exceptions display the anomaly inherent in that choice, strengthening the argument that failures elsewhere resulted from decisions or from inertia, but not from weakness per se.

The first exception is the often overlooked fact that during the seventeenth and eighteenth centuries the Ch'ing state, by military means, had added to the domain of Ming China a vast empire on the north, northwest, and west, extending far beyond the lands then occupied by the Han Chinese population. By the nineteenth century, it had created a Chinese pattern of civil government for much of that imperial accretion. As an empire-building regime, Manchu China was as successful as Romanov Russia, and like Russia, it laid the foundations for a far more enduring imperial presence in the twentieth century than that of the British, the French, or the Dutch. Despite the West's assault on China's territorial integrity in the nineteenth century, western concepts of sovereignty which then prevailed internationally served to acknowledge and guarantee China's Inner Asian empire as a continuing part of the Chinese state. Ch'ing China had a government and a military force as able in accomplishing territorial aggrandizement as most states of large extent, although it is impossible to imagine that the territorial enlargement would have happened without the presence of the alien Manchu dynasty and its special commitment to military achievement in Inner Asia. In its recent anti-USSR stance, Peking has often defined Inner Asian territorial claims by references to Han and T'ang history; in that it only misuses and muddies the historical record. The boundaries of the Chinese state as we know them today do not derive from the glories of Han and T'ang; they stem directly from Ch'ing imperialism.

The second exception to the passivity of Ch'ing policy is to be seen in the case of Yunnan. During the eighteenth century, the Chinese state was capable of directing and achieving a full-scale, forced-draft development of Yunnan, a border province in the southwest suddenly thrust into strategic importance because of its copper mines. Copper was the basis of the Ch'ing monetary system (silver circulated in ingots, but was not coined). About 1700 the principal source of supply, Japanese export copper, was cut off, creating a crisis, and forcing China to explore and develop the newly discovered mines in Yunnan. The growth capacity of the premodern society, under bureaucratic supervision, was demonstrated to be quite extraordinary, when the central government decided to accomplish overall social growth in a province, within the "traditional" means at its ready disposal. Internal migration was encouraged, new offices of local and provincial government were created, autonomous aboriginal districts were transformed into directly administered districts, schools and cultural facilities were implanted, roads and canals were built, and the mines were made to produce vast amounts of copper within a short time, to solve a national problem. By the nineteenth century, however, the development was over, and the province languished.

Nonetheless, the territorial expansion in Inner Asia, and the one example of province-level planned development appear to demonstrate that the state had the means to enlarge its governing role when it chose to do so. We see, however, no other outstanding demonstrations of the Manchu ruling caste's will to exploit the state's capacities. Even at the height of its powers in the eighteenth century, it had little interest in any statist goals beyond the negative ones of surveillance and intimidation for security reasons. By the nineteenth century its purposes and goals were still more negative and defensive, and its means were severely diminished. The conditions for achieving modernization that resided in the powers of the central government, therefore, were less likely to be used as the need to do so became more urgent.

When we compare the state's capacity to recognize opportunity or urgency, and the pattern of its responses to demands upon it in the nineteenth century, the evidence for decline becomes the clearer. The hypothesis about modernizing capacities of relevance here is that governments prepared by their premodern experience, both structurally and philosophically, to assume new functions and capable of recruiting competent and committed personnel in large enough numbers to perform the tasks, met one of the conditions crucial to effecting modernizing changes. The special functions that the Japanese and the Russian governments had assumed prior to modernization, and which were unusual in countries at that stage, included control over domestic prices, foreign trade, and well-developed networks of communications and transport. Also, to a certain extent, these governments supervised expanding systems of education and had the experience and organizational capacity to manage large-scale public works and land reclamation projects. Furthermore, government guidance in social ethics helped to standardize behavior and attitudes. As for the second part of the hypothesis, both nations had relatively large elites, adequate in training and commitment to perform the new tasks demanded of them.

How does nineteenth-century China compare? Much of the answer has already been stated or implied. As regards unusual extensions of governmental roles, we can suggest some obviously comparable Chinese developments. Long before the nineteenth century, despite, or perhaps because of the vast extent of the empire, the Chinese had developed an elaborate system of communications and transport serving both public and private interests. (Note the comparison of Ch'ing China and Tokugawa Japan in this regard in Rozman, 1973, pp. 92–95.) In existing institutions, public attitudes, and available skilled labor lay the basis for achieving an extensive system of public education. China had the most extensive record in world history for large-scale public works and land reclamation projects. Chinese society would seem to have had as promising a beginning point as any nation in these respects, unusual though they were in premodern societies. But in some of the other respects other tendencies are apparent. For example, Ch'ing China had developed early in the eighteenth century a system of reporting that brought to the emperor on a monthly basis both confidential and public data on market prices of basic commodities from all the districts of China. That information, however, seems to have been exploited primarily to provide a check on the reliability of provincial and local officials, not to control prices or manage the economy. As another example, Ch'ing China had, from its government's point of view, an effective system for controlling foreign trade. That system was so unbending and irrational in the eyes of the principal trading nations that they repeatedly made war on China in order to impose their trading practices and laws; eventually they assumed by force the management of China's customs in order to extract indemnities from that assured source of revenue, indemnities to pay for the wars that had given them the right to interfere. And, another example: China had a well-developed native banking system with a full range of instruments of credit, transfers of funds, and other banking facilities. The system had long supported China's entrepreneurs, some of whom were involved in essential government operations such as salt distribution and logistical support of border garrisons. Yet when the government had to make large loans in the nineteenth century it was forced by its foreign creditors to borrow from western bankers. Its own native bankers, some of whom were attempting to make the transition from old-style money shops to modern banks, did not develop modern banking capacities and methods that would have made them competitive with the western banking establishment in China. The Chinese government's loans were floated abroad; no native banks had the organizational capacity to mobilize Chinese resources on a large scale until after World War I.

Thus the Chinese record is very pointedly one of latent capacities either not recognized and used for the kinds of goals we are considering here, or of capacities stymied by conditions beyond the control of the Chinese. In both circumstances, a supine central government failed to exert the kind of leadership that was particularly significant for modernizing change in the histories of the more successful late modernizers.

ARMED FORCES: THE CHANGING PLACE OF THE MILITARY

The crucial role of soldiers in twentieth-century Chinese politics stems directly from the military history of the nineteenth century. This in turn is comprehensible only in relation to the faltering Ch'ing army of the late eighteenth century. Only such a long-range view can account for the militarism of recent times.

The Manchus, drawing mostly on Mongol models (Farquhar, in Feuerwerker, ed., 1968), created their "machine of conquest" at least two decades before their conquest of the Ming dynasty in 1644. With their banner armies, enlarged to include eight banner units each for Manchu, Mongol, and Han subjects, they conquered China in 1644–1645. This ingenious organizational form combined hereditary military households into self-contained units, wholly oriented to sustaining their professional fighters. It was a triumph of social planning, precisely suited to the Manchu nation's goals of conquest. Yet by 1673 when the Rebellion of the Three Feudatories virtually required the reconquest of China, the banner forces already had grown weak. The new Green Standard Army, made up of Han soldiers and led by Chinese, was needed to put down the rebels who had quickly engulfed half the country. The Manchu conquerors were thus forced to fall back on Han to fight Han for them, despite the old cliché about China's use of non-Chinese for its professional military forces.

Throughout the eighteenth century, the banner forces of about 200,000 troops were complemented by the Green Standard armies, which on paper numbered about 600,000. These two branches of the Ch'ing military together absorbed four-fifths of eighteenth-century state budgets. Each succumbed to its own forms of corruption and degeneration. Despite the Ch'ien-lung emperor's grandiose military adventures, mostly conducted on the borders, both the banners and the Green Standard forces were proven useless at the end of the century by domestic disturbances they could not quell.

The Ch'ing dynasty thus offers a curious anomaly: it began as a conquest state that had organized its tribal society under hereditary military aristocrats with its social organization aimed at total mobilization for war. It then conquered the world's largest society, which also had immense standing armies and a long military tradition. Thereafter, the Ch'ing was unable to sustain the effectiveness either of its own banner forces or of its auxiliary Chinese army. Yet after the success of the "second conquest" in the 1670s, these alien rulers were not seriously challenged for two hundred years (until the 1850s). They were not expelled or replaced until 1911. What, then, was the role of the military in relation to the security and stability of the Chinese state?

The Manchus, like all other Chinese dynasties, long maintained their ruling position by a mystique of legitimacy, and by other carefully cultivated normative means of reinforcing authority. Of course they had to police minor dissidence with local forces, and they maintained the appearance of commanding powerful means of coercion. But for two hundred years, their armies did not have to be in constant readiness to defeat great domestic enemies. Moreover, as a conquest dynasty from beyond the Great Wall, the Manchus moved China's defense frontier from the wall line separating sedentary and steppe societies far back into Inner Asia; they helped to demilitarize China by also dominating portions of the outer steppe. Thus Ch'ing China was not normally an armed society. Traditionally, for centuries before the Manchus, China had possessed no military caste or knighthood. Although both the Ming (through its *wei-so* garrison system) and the Ch'ing (in its Chinese banners) had made an effort to establish hereditary military households, this practice was contrary to the workings of Chinese society. It did not function well enough to maintain a Chinese soldiery; much less did it give rise to a Chinese knighthood, a Han warrior class. When social stresses and political failures led to large-scale banditry, millenarian movements, or uprisings of ethnic minorities, the Ch'ing state was ill-prepared to cope. The Manchus had no choice but to call up the ethnically differentiated armies—the banner garrisons and the Green Standard Army—but these soon inspired more contempt than awe. How could a state that normally did not rely directly on the means of coercion to sustain government find such means quickly and effectively?

The Manchu and Mongol military aristocracies had functioned impressively during the initial decades of the Ch'ing conquest. In particular, the Mongol banners, although smallest of the three, seemed to have retained their fighting qualities. Manchu officers and nobles had been rewarded so lavishly that, as plump parasites on Chinese society receiving far more than the common banner soldier, they had little incentive to remain in fighting trim; the hard life brought no further rewards. In comparison with another displaced military aristocracy, the samurai of Tokugawa Japan, the Manchu military aristocracy lacked discipline. Moreover, they were not drawn to alternative bureaucratic careers, perhaps because these functions more normally were assigned to the Chinese, who had performed them for many centuries. In any event, instead of finding other functions in which performance might have sustained their morale, the professional military leadership in Ch'ing society became ever more useless. The decay of the dynasty's military power by 1800 is not, then, surprising.

The transformation of the Chinese military system in the nineteenth century is nonetheless very surprising. That change was induced by grave threats to domestic order, arising mostly in Central and South China, often among incompletely assimilated non-Han minorities, from the 1790s on. From the 1820s to the 1840s, regional disorders began to generate a new form of local or provincial defensive response. Unlike the longstanding impromptu police—the local militias that always could be called up by county and prefectural magistrates on the basis of the *pao-chia* registrations—the new units were upgraded militia, recruited by local gentry leaders. They used the organizations of lineages, and the prestige and funds of local family notables. Such armies were found to have great development potential. Whenever regional disorder grew to a scale that the ordinary forces could not handle, they replaced both the incompetent national armies and the previous village guards. This new organizational form came to be known as the *t'uan-lien*. Tseng Kuo-fan hastily organized his Hunan army to defend his home province against the Taiping incursion. The essence of Tseng's system was that he recruited highly committed men through their lineage connections. He sought quality instead of quantity, trained the men rigorously, paid them well and rewarded them for success, and paid much attention to their ideological commitment. In particular, Tseng's "Hunan Braves" encouraged natural leadership qualities by quickly advancing soldiers of demonstrated ability, whether or

69

not they were themselves elite types by education or status. That could not have happened in a setting of closed social classes, or under an aristocratic officer corps. It was peculiarly Chinese.

Tseng's model was adopted in other provinces, under his guidance. The court, which trusted Tseng and needed him desperately, allowed him wide authority in fighting the rebellion. One of his junior colleagues, Li Hung-chang, was asked to organize a *t'uan-lien* army in Anhwei, Li's home province, and subsequently, he was assigned by Tseng to lead that army in the defense of Shanghai in the 1860s. A fellow provincial of Tseng's, Tso Tsung-t'ang, with a similarly created army, was assigned to the command in Chekiang. Such leaders in coastal cities and treaty ports, particularly Li at Shanghai, cooperated with western military men, observing their weapons, training methods, and tactics. Such leaders recognized the superiority of western small arms and light artillery, of western naval vessels, and of gunboats that could be used in support of land maneuvers.

Although like most everything Tseng Kuo-fan advocated, the *t'uan-lien* form of local militia had venerable antecedents in name and in reality, both in Ch'ing and in earlier history, as it was developed by Tseng to meet the nineteenth-century rebellion crisis it in fact became a distinctly new element in the realities of late Ch'ing political power. Moreover, its further evolution was linked to another novel element: western advances in organization and technology. It simultaneously became linked to a still further novel component: the new means of financing armies at provincial levels when direct control was assumed over treaty port customs revenues, and a new tax, the *likin,* was levied on commerce. All the elements were in place for the emergence of a powerful military-political instrument without precedent in Ch'ing experience.

The development of new provincial armies under scholar-bureaucrat leadership was in keeping with the age-old Chinese ideal of civilian control of the military. China also had long experience with provincial leaders who acquired military power and used it to defy central authority, thus leading to regional decentralization and warlordism. The Ch'ing dynasty, reassured by its strengthened military position, nonetheless moved dangerously in the direction of decentralization, although the country did not yet fall into warlordism and dissolution. The extent to which it ever recovered from the regionalism accompanying the mid-century crises is much debated by scholars. Some insist that the central government's appointive powers and fiscal oversight prevented the post-Taiping provincial leaders from retaining significant autonomy. Others see a mere facade of imperial formalism, which did not prevent military regionalism from persisting after the end of the crisis or even increasing toward the end of the dynasty. If the latter view is, as seems probable, more accurate, the Ch'ing dynasty nonetheless was exceedingly fortunate in having domestic enemies whose suppression led to new regional military powers. Those enemies were so repulsive that, as alternatives to

Manchu rule, they stood little chance of winning over the population at large, much less its natural leadership in the strategic elite. There was no real danger that the potent new provincial military system, under its scholar-bureaucrat-militarist leadership, would be turned against the dynasty. It would not ally itself with such rebels.

Tseng Kuo-fan, the prototype of the scholar-bureaucrat turned regional commander, disbanded his Hunan Braves as soon as his military tasks were accomplished. But the concept he had established of the private army, regionally organized and personally loyal to its commander, survived in the Anhwei army of Li Hung-chang and in the commands of certain other scholar-official generals. The Ch'ing state never regained fully centralized control over all of its military. Nor were its banner and Green Standard forces ever restored to their pre-nineteenth-century standing. It is thus all the more noteworthy that normative forces kept those regional armies consonant with dynastic interests (without abandoning regional interests) for half a century. No threats to the Ch'ing dynasty came from the new military until, at the very end, Yuan Shih-k'ai used his military power to betray both the dynasty and the revolution. Yuan is the pivotal figure in the transition from regionalism to warlordism; he epitomizes the disintegration of the political hegemony that heretofore had prevailed.

Philip Kuhn refers to "the militarization of the gentry" in the mid-nineteenth century. Eventually, however, the gentry was trapped by that development. It was unable to retain control over this change, to maintain the traditional primacy of civilian authority over armies. Leadership, gentry or other, all became subject to military interests. This was a militarization of Chinese politics, and it affected all participants in politics. Yet even when, at the height of the warlord era, the entire political process was subordinated to military sanctions and force decided all policy issues, the military was unable to accomplish its goal of reunification of the state. At their height, therefore, militarist governments were weak in a crucial sense. They laid credible claim to regional powers, but were only dismembered arms of the Chinese state that for a time ceased to exist as an integral unit. The warlords' enlarged political roles were fated to be confined in polities of diminished significance.

Other modernizing states have consciously and purposively pursued the potential for development that is inherent in armies. The Chinese state was denied this option, because the extraordinary nineteenth-century effort of the legitimate polity to preserve itself put military power into the hands of regional leaders. Military needs, discovered in the mid-century rebellions, became the most urgent and pragmatic tests of western technology. Li Hung-chang and other new commanders played the leading role in recognizing the superiority of certain imports and in responding positively. They not only hired western military advisers and purchased western guns and ships, they also sponsored a considerable array of western schooling, in order to grasp technological innovation more thoroughly and ensure its more rapid assimilation in China. This expanded awareness of the potential for modernization, however, was achieved only within regional military contexts. It was not sponsored throughout China by the central government; it was not a practical matter of national policy. Modernization, as sponsored by regional leaders in the mold of Li Hung-chang, in fact became a tool of rivalries. Development was very uneven. There was a persistent failure to establish and implement national goals, especially in areas of particular interest to the regional leaders.

It is remarkable that neither the military nor the political potential of the new armies was ever fully realized. This can be seen most clearly in cases such as that of Li Hung-chang. Li was eager to be the most powerful Chinese official in the Manchu-Chinese state. His control of regional wealth, his access to opportunities for entrepreneurship, and his factional leadership all derived from command of the Anhwei army. He accepted the ambitious role of chief minister, controlling the metropolitan province, dominating the central government as partner of the Empress Dowager, making domestic policy, and monopolizing foreign policy for more than a quarter-century until his death in 1901. But he also accepted the limitations of that role. Normative controls continued to operate over him; they did not prevent personal aggrandizement of many kinds, but they kept him loyal to dynasty and ruler, even when that could be demeaning, costly, or hazardous.

Li's modernizing impact was nonetheless sharply limited by his own goals. If we look at this case from the point of view of the military as an agency of modernization, we can see that the state's interests were not served. Li's main concern was to keep his regional power base one step ahead of any potential rivals, and to remain strong enough to defy a weak central government—while simultaneously drawing satisfaction from being its most honored servant. He was surely no rebel, but he failed to perceive and serve China's largest interests. For example, little effort was made to use military modernization as a means to make China the equal of other great states. This contrasts with what Li's contemporaries did in Japan. All modernization policy under Li was erratic, its development spotty and slow, because it was never linked to the state as the implementing vehicle. China's only quick modernization at this time was ungoverned, and took place largely in treaty ports under the aegis of businessmen.

The efforts of modern scholars to make of Li Hung-chang a far-sighted statesman of self-strengthening in the Chinese state do not bear scrutiny, fascinating though his long career truly is. He was a skilled political manipulator at the foundering court of the iniquitous and self-serving Empress Dowager. There his immense personal gifts were misused. Because he monopolized the front on which important change was most possible and yet realized so little of it, he serves well as the symbol of China's missed opportunities to achieve better government in the wake of the strong restoration impulse. Therefore, he also must be seen as the godfather of China's twentieth-century militarist malignancy (discussed in Chapter 9).

THE FISCAL BASE

The state revenue system of the Ch'ing dynasty embodied both the strengths and the weaknesses typical of the political structure as a whole; it also displayed changes parallel to those in other aspects of the government and the society. Following the crises of the mid-nineteenth century, structural change in the fiscal system was larger and more important than in other aspects of government, and anticipated further, twentieth-century changes.

Principles underlying the taxation system had prevailed throughout most of the 2,000 years of the imperial era: the state recognized the free tenure of land, and it drew its revenues primarily from the production of the agrarian sector of its population. The revenues from state monopolies on commodity production and distribution were next in importance. Of these the salt gabelle was by far the most important in Ch'ing times, regularly supplying 10 to 15 percent of the annual revenues. Taxes on commerce, including import and domestic customs tariffs, were relatively insignificant until the second half of the nineteenth century. Contributions, primarily those encouraged by the government that took the form of "sale" of ranks, titles, and even offices, could account for as much as one-third of the state's revenues for relatively short periods under special conditions, as during the first half of the nineteenth century when military emergencies forced the state to exploit this time-honored yet readily debased mode of raising money. Other sources of income were of negligible significance.

The land tax included both the *fu,* the tax on agricultural production, nominally levied according to the amount of land held with rates varying according to its productivity, and the *yi,* labor service imposts levied on adult males. Since the value of both was calculated in money and consolidated in one schedule of payments, they can be taken together as the "land and service imposts," or, more simply, "the land tax." In fact, however, neither component of that tax was apportioned on the tax-paying units (landholdings, adult males) according to the principles that underlay and justified them. The *li-chia* machinery for registering land and persons for tax purposes is discussed together with the *pao-chia* policing system later in this chapter in the section "Base-level Organization," as an aspect of local government. Here it is necessary to anticipate some elements of that discussion in order to clarify the weaknesses of the late Ch'ing state's fiscal base.

In Ch'ing times, at the county (*hsien*) level the magistrate was the chief tax collector. He was responsible for registering households and their members, for keeping registries of landholdings, for levying taxes according to the central government's stipulated norms and methods as set forth in various statutes (especially in the *Complete Book of Land and Labor Imposts,* which contained detailed figures for each county, and was supposed to be revised every ten years), for collecting the payments and issuing receipts in triplicate, for punishing defaulters, and for storing and shipping the commodities and money received. Assistance and supervision were supplied by the circuit and provincial levels of government, above the county. Below the magistrate's office was the so-called decimal system of machinery for registration and collection, the *li-chia,* which overlapped with the other decimal system structure of administration the *pao-chia.* The machinery of subcounty administration degenerated, or evolved, throughout the dynasty's reign, but it never failed to provide a mechanism for taking regular revenues from the productive rural sector of the society, a matter on which the Ch'ing state placed high priority. The ideals, however, that defined the system had always lain beyond full realization. Ming compromises dictated by the expense of meeting the nominal management requirements were allowed to persist into early Ch'ing, and eventually were acknowledged in Ch'ing statutes. First, the labor service imposts were fixed in perpetuity at the levels recorded for 1711, making the need for an accurate decennial census of all taxpayers irrelevant to the tax system. In most cases, the census degenerated into a routine repetition of existing figures. Then, reverting to the earlier Ming system, the labor service imposts were absorbed into a single payment with the land taxes in 1723. Finally, in 1772 the long-lapsed cadastral survey procedures for registering changes in landholdings were abandoned, with fixed quotas replacing direct apportionments, thus making the other socially responsible base on which the system rested meaningless. No full survey had ever been carried out under the Ching, and no more were attempted. To be sure, as new lands were opened to cultivation, they were to be recorded and taxed, and ownership of all lands was supposed to be recorded and referred to in apportioning the quotas. But fixing the amounts to be collected from the households registered in the *li-chia's* groupings of tens and hundreds was done by tax clerks on the basis of records that they increasingly tended to look upon as their private property, and, inevitably, according to their awareness of local interests. These changes in the machinery of taxation were, in a sense, highly rational from the state's point of view. They were workable, and at relatively low administrative costs, whereas literal application of the original system would have been impossibly cumbersome and expensive. As long as the supervisory role of the central government was maintained with the efficiency built into it by the system-minded Yung-cheng emperor (reg. 1722–1735) and the strategic elite in the localities was largely responsible to the public good, the worst abuses were avoidable, or correctable.

The Ch'ing emperors gave the taxation system much of their attention, but they complicated their objectives by fixing and rigidly maintaining low norms for the tax rates. The state sought to gain moral credit from this, and emperors often bragged to their subjects that the Ch'ing had outdone all earlier dynasties in realizing classical ideals of frugality and restraint in taking from the people. Simultaneously, the state probably earned some goodwill from the scholar-officialdom by letting most of the wealth of localities remain there instead of sending it off to the national treasury. The ideals were seriously vitiated by realities, however. The low tax levels did not provide sufficient revenue to cover costs of governing, but could not be raised, so surcharges were added to the grain taxes. Some became statutory surcharges; others remained irregular, subject to varying application. Altogether these added perhaps 30 percent to the taxpayers' burden. Labor service imposts also were made subject to analogous increases, usually in the name of special circumstances. Where grain taxes were lower, as in the poorer North China provinces, the labor imposts tended to be higher. Any emergency or irregular problem—from suppressing bandits to rebuilding city walls and public buildings to preparing for an imperial tour of inspection—could be made the excuse for proper or improper calls for extra labor service, whether commuted to cash or paid in labor. Also, while the state made a great show of granting remissions of agricultural taxes in times of disasters, exemptions from labor service were seldom granted.

Thus we find anomalies in the fiscal system, both in the inadequacy of its machinery to meet the ideal requirements, and in the contradictions between the ideal of low taxes and the need for more money. The land tax with surcharges that had become regularized by statute supplied 70 to 80 percent of the state's revenues in the mid-eighteenth century. That percentage is typical of the entire period from the fourteenth century to the nineteenth. It dropped to about 35 percent of the state's revenues by the end of the dynasty, revealing the impact of the structural changes in the post-Taiping fiscal system. Between the mid-eighteenth century and 1911, the absolute amount received from the land tax doubled, from about 50 million *taels* to about 100 million, while the population more than doubled. The various taxes on domestic and treaty port commerce, that is the *likin* and the customs tariffs, were the new and rapidly growing source of revenues from the 1850s on, yet even with these, the Ch'ing state continued to draw very small amounts of the society's wealth for its uses. Yeh-chien Wang, from whose definitive study, *Land Taxation in Imperial China* (1973) most of these figures and interpretations are drawn, believes the total tax burden at the end of the dynasty was about 2.4 percent of the GNP, and surmises that it was lower then than it had been at the middle of the eighteenth century when the state was strongest. He writes:

> In retrospect, the greatest defect of the Ch'ing land tax administration was . . . its inability to capture increased income as the economy grew. Moreover, its decentralized nature deprived the imperial government of a controlling hand over the management of the country's largest source of public revenue. Consequently, the land tax in China played a diminishing part in government financing in the late Ch'ing just as public expenditure was greatly expanding and thereby the need for additional revenue enormously increasing. Should the land tax, like its counterpart in Meiji Japan, have played the crucial role in the fiscal system of late Ch'ing, not only the financial condition then but also the political development of modern China might have been decisively different (p. 131).

Implications for modernization in that analysis of nineteenth-century China's fiscal base are clearly indicated, but one further implication for the deterioration of administration should also be stressed. The fiscal structure shifted from primary reliance on the land tax to large-scale reliance on taxes on commercial goods in transport (the *likin,* instituted in the provinces after 1853) and on the newly established (1858), foreign-managed Imperial Maritime Customs revenues from import tariffs. Both represented not only shifts from labor at the point of production to commerce at its main arteries of distribution, but also shifts to easily controlled bottleneck points, away from the traditional broad reliance on political management at base levels of society. Also, the new commercial taxes were under the supervision of governors and governors-general in the provinces, not under the management of the central government's Board of Revenues. Although the central government appointed the regional officials and could remove them for malfeasance, that did not offset the shift from central to regional initiative, and did not in fact prevent large-scale irregular and improper impositions of *likin* by provincial and local interests. Moreover, even though abuses were limited by fear of arousing popular antitaxation riots, and nonstatutory surcharges and other irregularities were limited by elements of consensus among the local elite working with local magistrates, and by convention about what was excessive, nonetheless the clerks represented the interests of the local strategic elite. As other changes in the society were tipping the balance between central and local interest in favor of the locality, the restructuring of the fiscal base was in important ways consonant with that change, and anticipated the decentralization of the early twentieth century.

Finally, because so little revenue was drawn away from locality and region to the central government's treasury, the potential for regional particularisms to flourish at the expense of national integration was created. Yeh-chien Wang has calculated that even in the most prosperous decades of mid-Ch'ing, the total government revenues amounted to no more than 5 or 6 percent of the annual grain production of the entire nation. The landlord income of Szechwan, the largest province, as calculated by Chang Chung-li, equaled that amount (as quoted in Perkins, 1969, pp. 176–177). Gentry income was derived from services and from entrepreneurship more than from land. If the state was relatively poor in comparison with governments of other premodern societies, it was not because the society was impoverished. Perkins states that by the beginning of the nineteenth century, "central government revenues had risen little if any over the levels of the late fourteenth century, but China's population had risen five or six times" (1969, pp. 176–177).

It has been calculated that the annual revenues of the Ch'ing dynasty, in its still prosperous mid- and late eighteenth century, were about 45 to 50 million *taels* of silver (excluding the tax surcharges retained for local and provincial use). Of that, 10 million supported the central government (three-fourths went for military expenditures) and about 25 million *taels* was allocated for provincial and local government expenses (three-fifths went for the military). The central government normally accumulated a surplus at the rate of 7 or 8 million *taels* per year (Immanuel Hsu, 1970, pp. 79–80). Although the military expenses took a large share of the total, they purchased no active military capacities to support expansionist activities after the mid-eighteenth century, but went largely to subsidize hereditary Manchu garrisons that had little military value, as the troubled nineteenth century was to demonstrate. The Manchus were a steadily impoverished conquering nation, drawing little in material rewards from their Chinese subjects while becoming assimilated by them. The eighteenth-century revenue surpluses masked the fiscal dilemma that was to catch up with the government in the nineteenth century.

The rulers of the state were aware that much of the wealth was retained in the provinces, and that the strategic elite absorbed much of the excess, both through its salary overrides and, more important, through all the private ways for drawing money from status. The rulers may well have looked upon that as an appropriate and an administratively cheap way of rewarding the elite. They may have felt that by stressing the normative restrictions on elite behavior they were in effect programming the use of much of that money to local uses in the state's interest. But, when the normative controls no longer worked so effectively, as during the last century of Ch'ing rule, rulers had no ready administrative means for regaining control. The structural changes in the fiscal base both reflected and contributed to the late Ch'ing political weakness.

NATIONAL COMMUNICATIONS

For millennia the Chinese imperial state had used its public works agencies to build and maintain a national system of post stations with couriers for government communications, roads linking all provinces and their major cities, and canals used by the state and by private commerce. The society also had used printing longer and more pervasively than any other, and by the late imperial era, a private publications industry flourished, as did central and local government printing activities.

The political order relied on the state's communications network for official purposes, but government did not require or seek a public informed about its day-to-day activities. The active participation of the governed was not a feature of government, and the state recognized no interest in having a citizenry informed beyond the realms of ethics and duties. The government of Ch'ing China did, however, have a stake in improving communications, for it used a vastly expanded information network to enhance its surveillance capacities. A secret memorial system was established in the early eighteenth century as a check on the performance of officials, particularly on the accuracy of their enlarged required reporting on local conditions through the open memorial system. The improvement of this communications network was pushed to the limits possible by premodern means. But, in general, the Ch'ing state attempted to perform tasks of direct governing that were beyond the means of its technology and was forced to make compromises, though without abandoning the larger ideal. The supervision of local taxation, already discussed, is an excellent example. Modern communications would have and eventually did provide the enlarged capacity, yet as the new technology of communications was becoming available in the late Ch'ing, the government was slow to modernize facilities so that they might serve the new levels of its needs.

Only in the late nineteenth century did a modern press, modeled on that of western nations, begin to develop, and for several decades it was confined to the treaty ports. The telegraph network began to develop only in the 1880s, when foreign-managed modern postal services also emerged. Railroad building was not significant until the turn of the century. The changes in national communications that eventually were to have so large an impact on government did not assume large proportions before the early twentieth century. Throughout the nineteenth century we can observe what had been, in early Ch'ing times, a remarkable premodern set of instruments of national integration gradually becoming by the late nineteenth century somewhat ridiculous hangovers of a disappearing era.

Local Power

PROVINCIAL GOVERNMENT

In Chinese history, the province means something quite different from what the word conveys in European history. In China, provincial level government had been the most volatile of all the components of the political structure. Prior to the thirteenth century there had been no "provinces" as such. The intermediary organs of administration were the circuits, like the fifteen to twenty *chien-ssu* of Sung times, but called by other names in other periods, which as agencies of the central administration, had primarily supervisory functions over the counties. The eighteen provinces of Ch'ing times go back directly to the twelve to fifteen provinces (*sheng*) of Ming, and beyond that to thirteenth-century developments in Jurchen and Mongol rule over the Chinese, whereby branches of the central government secretariat (*sheng*) were established in the regions, at first to serve primarily as military headquarters during the campaigns of conquest, later to provide supervision over the circuits, prefectures, and counties. During the Ming the province served as the base for three separate administrative functions: (1) surveillance and judicial; (2) fiscal and general civil administration; (3) military. The Ming central government did not allow these to coalesce into an integrated provincial administration. Province-level offices remained functionally distinct, reporting directly to their superior agencies at the capital. The Ch'ing province was somewhat more fully coordinated, and received stronger fiscal powers, but the basic Ming pattern continued. In keeping with the Ch'ing penchant for dual staffing of all offices as a means of control, governors-general (sometimes called viceroys) overlapped in function with governors. There were eight of the former, with jurisdiction over one to three provinces, and fifteen of the latter, three of whom were not under governors-general. Usually where jurisdictions overlapped, the senior figure was a Manchu and the junior a Chinese, although during the military crises of the mid-nineteenth century Chinese appointees came to dominate both levels. Ch'ing governors, where they served alone, or governors-general where they were present, had a general oversight over the province and all its civil and military activities that was greater than in the Ming or earlier, and it may be possible to detect a trend toward province-level resolution of the intermediate supervisory dilemma in Chinese institutional history. In a standard work a leading authority, Ch'ü T'ung-tsu, seems to contradict himself, saying on the one hand that "all administration was under the control" of the governor-general where one was present, otherwise under the governor. On the other hand, in discussing the work of the provincial treasurer, he states: "The central government also had full control over the financial affairs of the local government. In fact, the provincial treasurer and other local authorities were agents of the central government in the collection of taxes." (See the useful chart of provincial government in Ch'ü, 1962; 1969 ed., p. 5; the quotations above are from pages 6 and 7.) As Ch'ü clearly states, provincial government was a link in the centralized administration, important in the articulation of routine procedures between central and base-level organs. Although its fiscal supervisory powers were enlarged in the early eighteenth century, the province was an intentionally weak instrument for integrating regional political action; it was certainly not intended to mobilize regional loyalties. The provinces did not become voices of a unified provincial interest identified with and expressing the subculture and traditions of the region. When provinces began to serve those purposes in the late nineteenth century, the breakdown of centralization was at hand.

Under the crisis conditions created by the Taiping and other mid-nineteenth-century rebellions, the province level of government suddenly acquired what were to be temporary regional powers beyond the central government's direct supervision. One of the most important of the emergency powers was the power to levy the *likin* and to retain its revenues for support of the new regional armies organized by leading Chinese gentry elements to defend the province. Thus commerce for the first time in the history of the dynasty became a major source of revenue, military structures were based on provincial or regional interests, and the centralized control was formally diminished, actually destroyed. Once so compromised, the central government never fully recovered its control. Nonetheless the rebellions were suppressed, peace was restored, and the dynasty prolonged. Emergent regional power interests had discovered the advantages of regional organization and sought justifications for continuing the reliance on *likin* revenues, for maintaining armies for local use, and for influencing if not dictating appointments to all levels of civil and military office in the province. Thus the regionalism of the Taiping period became the father to the warlordism of the postrevolutionary early twentieth century. (See "Armed Forces: The Changing Place of the Military," earlier in this chapter, and "Armed Forces and Warlordism," Chapter 9.) The volatile province level of government became the bane of centralized imperial rule; at its most independent, it could destroy the articulation between the center and county level units, working at cross purposes with the center's mobilization needs, interfering with the rational recruitment and appointment procedures of the bureaucracy. After about 1865 these developments in general undercut all of the hypothesized political conditions conducive to modernization. That did not in itself, of course, preclude modernizing change, but it denied it the integrating and guiding support of the central government.

As the central government's control over the provinces weakened during the late Ch'ing, the opportunity for hastened modernizing change within the more effectively managed provincial unit, when guided by an exceptional provincial governor, increased. The careers of Liu K'un-i and Chang Chih-tung, the two most eminent of late Ch'ing provincial leaders, show that very clearly.

Liu K'un-i (1830–1902) was a mere licentiate from Hunan, on his way to take the higher examinations, when Tseng Kuo-fan's Hunan Army called him to emergency service in 1855. After ten years of outstanding military and administrative achievement, he was rewarded with direct appointment to the governorship of Kiangsi (1865–1874). Thereafter, except for a period of retirement in the 1880s, he served as governor-general of Kiangsu, Kiangsi, and Anhwei, based at Nanking. He was in that important regional post from 1890 until his death in 1902. He thus owed his career to the Hunan Army and to Tseng's dominant place in the post-Taiping political world.

Chang Chih-tung (1837–1909) was a northerner from Chihli province (modern Hopei) whose career was more conventional. An outstanding Confucian scholar and writer, he placed third in the palace examination that ranked the *chin-shih* degree winners of 1863. He served in various court offices until he was appointed governor of Shansi in 1882. Thereafter, he made his entire career in high provincial posts, most importantly as governor-general of Hupei and Hunan, based at Wuchang (combined with Hankow and Hanyang to form the present Wuhan) from 1889 to 1907, with minor interruptions.

Chang was a persistent opponent of Li Hung-chang, the dominant figure in the central government in the last quarter of the nineteenth century, thus exacerbating the tension between center and province. Like Li, however, both Liu and Chang had to stoop to winning the personal favor of the Empress Dowager to make their careers. Chang in particular is an ambiguous figure, sometimes accused of hypocrisy and sycophancy because of his vacillating attitude toward the reformers of 1898 and more especially because of the tone of his relations to the Empress Dowager. Such were the conditions of political life during that half-century; he could not have stood apart and exerted influence. Despite this adaptiveness, Chang was a strong force for the rational promotion of modernizing developments against the reactionary faction in the late Ch'ing government. He sponsored the building of the Peking-Hankow railroad over its objections. He promoted the development of the Han-yeh-p'ing coal and steel complex, which made Hankow a major base of modern industry. Liu and Chang both struggled to improve the fiscal conditions of their provinces and used the increased revenues for projects within the regions they governed. Both stressed the development of modern industries, arsenals, mints, book publishing houses, schools—and especially, modern military training for provincial forces. Their strong joint stand against the Boxer Rebellion in 1900, guaranteeing to the western powers that they would suppress the uprising throughout the Yangtze provinces, not only limited the western intervention to the north but also stabilized the situation, and made it possible for the Empress Dowager to disassociate herself from the failed rebellion in 1900. She could thus return to power as the suppressor of this disruptive movement. Because of her large indebtedness to Liu and Chang in that crisis, she favored them and allowed them to influence the "progressive reforms" that her court sponsored after 1901. Their ideas assumed great significance, not only because they represented provincial demands, but also because the changes they advocated were based on a fervent though adaptive Confucianism. (See "Armed Forces and Warlordism" Chapter 9.)

Even the most energetic and admirable of provincial leaders contributed to the emerging pattern of regional separation and the concomitant loss of centralized integration. That pattern also produced opportunities for negative political performance on the part of less admirable local officials, ultimately aiding the divergent regionalism of militarized politics. As far as the quality of government is concerned, the most damaging aspect of regionalism was that it induced a crucial retrograde step: it transformed the (ideally) depersonalized relations among proud bureaucrats of achieved status into (ideally) personalized relations of loyalty among power grabbers in regional governing hierarchies dependent on military power. That these leaders were often defensively arrogant and ignorant, even when competent, only increased the sense of decline and frustration of those bureaucrats and old elite figures who observed them.

In its impact on the bureaucracy's workings, the militarization of politics was regressive. Since this change did not quickly produce a more rational or a more effective mode of governing, yet did induce a further demoralization of the governors and a growing cynicism among the governed, along with a widening incongruity of ideal and actual patterns that was in various ways dysfunctional, it contributed importantly to the prolonged era of ineffectual governing. Thus, if we hold that effective governing aided the modernizing changes in Japan and Russia and elsewhere, China by contrast was deprived of an analogous aid.

The demoralization of the entire political milieu was so pervasive by the turn of the century that it is difficult to reconstruct in our historical imaginations the tone of the older bureaucratic society that existed into the post-Taiping era. The distorted phase of its late nineteenth-century decline fills our field of vision.

As the provincial level of government lost its articulating function, adding to the imbalance between center and the base level of society, the consequences for modernizing change in late nineteenth-century China were mostly negative. There is one exception, partially realized in the republican era and later. As the precociously achieved rationality of the old bureaucratic order declined, evident in the transition from a rotting eighteenth-century centralization through nineteenth-century regionalism and on into twentieth-century warlordism, China gradually was made susceptible to forceful, direct military action. This was not characteristically benign. Yet in some unusual cases it made possible more efficient alternatives to the bumblings of a disintegrating remnant of a formerly effective though limited central government. That gain was expensive in many ways; the bureaucracy, for example, was permanently debased. Yet ultimately the militarist governments, albeit of widely varying political hues, were decisive for the course of Chinese politics in the twentieth century.

BASE-LEVEL ORGANIZATION

Local government in late imperial China had its base level in the counties, many of which have retained their names and more or less their boundaries for 2,000 years. They are the genuine base of localism, local pride and identity, local history, and local custom. Deeply entrenched local interest was directly confronted by the officials sent to staff the *hsien* government, servants of the central government who were always outsiders.

Above the counties were prefectures (*fu*) and a variety of subprefectural units (*chou, t'ing, chün,* and the like). Prefectures had supervisory powers over the subprefectures and counties except for a small number of subprefectures, which were directly under provincial administration, as were also the prefectures. All of these units—counties, subprefectures, and prefectures—were reorganized as *hsien* under the republic, thus eliminating the complicated hierarchical relations among them, and classifying them all, in theory, as self-governing units. They became, after 1958, the framework within which the new commune organizational form in the communist restructuring of government was imposed; thus the *hsien* has been the truly enduring unit of local political organization.

Under the Ch'ing, as under earlier dynasties, the more than 1,500 counties kept tax, census, judicial, and legal records, and prepared reports on all aspects of their governing; copies of records and of reports were sent to the prefectures, to the appropriate offices at circuit and province level, and on up to the capital, although at each level the county originals might disappear in summary reports and statistics. Reviews were made at each level of each aspect of governing. Reactions to the report and new policy directives initiated from above were duly noted and recorded at each level on the downward course of the centralizing power flow.

Above the prefectural level were administrative subdivisions called in Ch'ing times *tao*, or circuits, headed by circuit intendants. Each province had from three to nine. Their offices included a varied and shifting assignment of censorial and surveillance, judicial, fiscal, educational, military, and other specialized postings. Their functions were both supervisory and expediting; they were the place at which specialists were provided to assist the most important (from the thrones's point of view) local operations in government.

But it was the county magistrate and his staff of three or four civil-service-ranked administrators who constituted the base level of formal government. They were appointed by the Ministry of Personnel at the capital on the basis of its examination and merit rating records; after appearing there in person to receive their appointments, and to be impressed again by their personal relationship to the central powers, they were sent off to their postings, always in some other than their native province. In addition to this small corps of officials serving usually for three-year terms in a district, there was a permanent corps of subofficial clerical personnel, clerks, and runners. They staffed the six operational divisions of the magistracy corresponding to the Six Ministries of the central government, and other clerical offices. They might number only 100 in a small and poor county, and up to 1,000 in a large and rich one. They were on permanent appointment and were local residents; they often knew as much as the magistrate about his job and more about local conditions. All kinds of patterns among the possible combinations of good and bad, clever and obtuse officials and their equally varied clerical aids could be found, and the quality of local government varied accordingly.

In addition, in Ch'ing times the custom arose and became general for magistrates and prefects (also higher-level officials) to maintain their own privately recruited and paid staffs of private secretaries (*mu-fu, mu-yu*). In part, the need for their services reflects a need for more specialized abilities in specific aspects of administration, such as tax collection, document drafting, and fiscal, judicial, and other matters. The need for division of labor and limited specialization was met, thus, not by the civil service where the examinations continued to stress the general literary cultivation of the candidate, but by other means. In fact, people who might otherwise have been in the pool of the highly literate from which the examinations drew their degree winners became private secretaries, and some eminent private secretaries of the nineteenth century in service to high-ranking officials were themselves holders of the higher degrees, although that was not usual. The career of private secretary, a local specialization in some prefectures (many late Ch'ing private secretaries came from Shao-hsing in Chekiang) also can be looked upon as the beginning of one of the alternative career patterns that emerged in the nineteenth century. It was like others in being imitative, in values and life styles, of the "single career" in officialdom, and in its symbiotic relationship to officialdom. It was a potentially important source of diversified human skills for modernization.

Although the use of the private secretary brought specialized skills to the Ch'ing government, it also reflected some less positive features of political life. The need for such assistance was real, but it was heightened by the increasing pressure of surveillance and intimidation under which officials found themselves. They could not afford to make mistakes, and when they made them, they could not afford to have them known. Reliance on private secretaries with specialized skills to solve problems encountered in a county was in large part the shrewd and safe response to higher-level pressures; it was not a vigorous and creative response to local problems. At the same time, magistrates and other officials could not easily afford to prevent mistakes this way. Official salaries were unrealistically low even with their regularized "integrity-nourishing" supplements, and private secretaries' salaries were high. The clerical and other subofficial staff members in the district offices were allowed to collect surcharged fees for services rendered in their offices, and by that dubious and corrupting means were able to support themselves—even to prosper. Magistrates and other officials had no recourse other than to similar practices; the able and success-oriented magistrate in a moderately well off county could become wealthy and was more or less expected to do so, but even those of sterner integrity had somehow to pay their expensive secretarial staff out of their own pockets. When we examine the revenues and disbursements of the late imperial state, the costs of civil government appear remarkably low, and by any criterion, they were. But, the major costs appeared on no fiscal records, and came directly from the population of the county. Being a stranger on a short-term assignment encouraged many a magistrate to indulge in "scraping off the top soil" (*kua ti-p'i'*), exploiting his post and earning the contempt of the natives.

The scope of governmental responsibility and activity at the base levels is an index of a government's capacity to hasten modernization, if it so chooses, since in all known instances modernization has led to a proliferation of governing tasks. Quite apart from that issue, however, the scope of governmental activity at the base level indicated the extent to which the Chinese government acknowledged its own responsibility for performing local social services, but not necessarily the full extent of the services it thought should be performed. It had choices in deciding how certain things should be done.

Tax collection based on well-maintained records, public order and security, encouraging morality, educating for public service, administering justice, maintaining communications—such matters were the inescapable core responsibilities at the base level. Beyond these, a broad range of social services useful to an orderly society was recognized, including public elementary education, medical services, care of orphans and the indigent aged, free burial services, emergency relief, and many others. Furthermore, more capital investment in public works was required than the government could afford: roads, bridges, and canals had to be maintained, public buildings had to be repaired and replaced, city walls had to be built or repaired, and the like. All such local government welfare and public works activities occupied a marginal zone in which the line between official and private obligation could shift one way or the other. The highest level of formal government responsibility in that zone appears to have been reached during the Sung dynasty (960–1279), when a revived Confucianism sought to supersede Buddhism by secularizing many religious activities spawned earlier by the social gospel of Mahayana Buddhism. Throughout the Sung, and with some lingering impact during the Yuan or Mongol dynasty (1279–1368), some of those activities came to be partially institutionalized under the metropolitan prefecture at the capital, and also at the base level in local government. That they were not more fully and enduringly "nationalized," but eventually reverted mostly to the private sector, may have resulted from the private sector's providing so effective—and so much cheaper—an alternative. It was also during the Sung period that a new kind of elite service stratum emerged under the stimulus of the civil service recruitment system, then in the heyday of its development. That system and the kind of elite it recruited persisted until the end of the imperial era, forming the strategic elite that dominated the society of the later dynasties. The members of that elite who were not in office at any time outnumbered those who were; as nonadministrative elite, it evolved roles analogous in many ways to those it performed in office and found its own ways of paying the costs. An unofficial extension of governing ensued, and remained a necessary complement to formal government.

The growth of unofficial governing by the nonadministrative elite seems to have been greatly stimulated again in the sixteenth century when the assertively self-reliant and socially conscious school doctrines of the neo-Confucian idealist philosopher Wang Shou-jen (better known as Wang Yang-ming, 1472–1529) swept through Chinese society. The impact on popular education and welfare was particularly strong. In earliest Ch'ing times something of that broad acceptance of social responsibility and altruism still motivated large numbers of the elite, contributing positively to the morale of local government. That morale, however, was largely dissipated under the severe control mechanisms imposed by the new Ch'ing government, especially from about 1700 on. Wang Yang-ming's teachings on inwardly directed action were decried in partisan reactions against his school. Some of that reaction had set in before the Manchu conquest, but the aspects of reaction important to us here are those encouraged by the new Ch'ing government. In village society, passivity with a streak of cynicism became the norm in daily life, even though some strains of Confucian optimism and altruism survived. The regime's reliance on informal government to keep rural society healthy continued; the performance lagged.

The special problems of local government in the nineteenth century have been exhaustively analyzed by K. C. Hsiao in his *Rural China: Imperial Control in the Nineteenth Century*. It is a comprehensive account of administrative deterioration, largely induced, he believes, by the negatively inspired, overly suspicious control techniques developed by the early Ch'ing rulers. Not only did these bring a declining political performance from the administrative elite, these same individuals experienced the deteriorating conditions in their roles as nonadministrative elite. Resident in their home communities and looked to for the performance of strategic services, they became both more eager to protect their own interests and less willing to serve public causes. Some historians also argue that by and large the intellectual vigor of the educated stratum also declined under the stultifying conditions of Ch'ing controls. The elite's inability to analyze correctly the decline in Chinese society and danger to the Chinese state and, therefore, its slow response in generating renovating pressures, also contributed to decline. The various aspects of decline constituted a problem that vigorous government leadership at the top could have reversed, but as we have seen, the Ch'ing imperial house could not, in the nineteenth century, produce a Peter the Great or a Meiji Restoration. A tighter control on corruption had been achieved in the quarter-century following the Ch'ien-lung emperor's death in 1799. Subsequently, a brief reversal under an aroused Chinese gentry leadership took place along with the mid-point restoration euphoria of the 1860s and 1870s. A strong call for a rehabilitation of Chinese society at any time might have revived this resource for better government, and the implications of that for modernizing change could have been vast. That strong call did not come until after this social resource had already been violently eliminated, in the third-quarter of the twentieth century.

The village in China displayed certain structural features not closely analogous to those of the village in Japan and Russia, nor standard for most premodern societies. Some of those features have already been discussed in this chapter and are more fully analyzed in Chapter 5. Certain hypotheses, some of which will be explored briefly here, have been generated about the relevance for modernization of the political structures at the village level.

The hypotheses about the village level of political administration focus on village-state articulation, the assumption being that "the village is where most public functions were executed," and that the state's effectiveness at this level was a key to its capacity to guide those changes the state perceived as being in its interests. Structural growth, providing for the enlarged functioning of local government was necessary to Japan's and to Russia's modernizing changes and is assumed here to be significant in all modernization. It also could be aided or retarded by features of the local political system. Violence and instability were controlled at the village level; taxes were collected and national service recruits (for the military and for public works) were enlisted at the village level. During the early phases of modernization in Japan and Russia, when the old style village life was still more or less intact, a congruence of authority patterns at the village level was required, if these and the new tasks of an enlarging governmental role were to be carried out.

The Chinese political order in Ch'ing times, in contrast, appears to have bypassed the natural village as the base for governing, no doubt by design. The nineteenth-century Chinese village displayed a wide variation of size and form; it might be a hamlet of four or five households, or a village of several hundred households. It might rely on periodic markets in a larger neighboring village or have daily access to its own street of stores. The configuration of rural nineteenth-century China has been described by many writers, perhaps most succinctly by K. C. Hsiao (1960, pp. 10–24). Some generalizations are possible despite the wide variations in many features.

The Chinese village does not display some of the features implied by the general hypotheses about the village level of government. As noted in the section "Territorial Integrity" (this chapter), the villages and towns had no formal government and lacked community institutions responsible for political life within, or designated by higher levels to govern. Hence, the village was not part of a continuous line of authority leading to the center. Nor were towns and villages communal entities in terms of property ownership or corporate responsibility for taxes, service levies, or keeping the peace. They were concentrations of households, and as such were of course the site of public and semipublic functions. Yet the organizational base for those functions was not expected to be the village or town as such. It was, on the contrary, the family or lineage organization, the marketing or guild organization, the temple or religious organization, and occasionally an educational institution. For those tasks that had to be performed directly at the local level—collecting taxes and policing, virtually the only "public functions" assumed by the government—a subadministrative level of political agencies was maintained. These were superimposed more or less uniformly on the entire rural society without primary reference to the natural settlement boundaries. As set up in the first decade of Ch'ing rule in the mid-seventeenth century (but borrowing old precedents), these were the *pao-chia* and the *li-chia* and, in some parts of China, the *she*.

The *pao-chia* was an organization constructed by grouping households or *hu* into units of 10 called *p'ai* which in turn formed parts of larger groupings of 10 *p'ai* called *chia* (or 100 households), and 10 *chia* (or 1,000 households) called *pao*. This structure was to maintain order and detect lawbreakers through mutual surveillance and group responsibility. It also could be used to develop a militia for use as an adjunct of the national armies.

The *li-chia* was a parallel but originally distinct organization of households for tax-collection purposes. In it, 10 subordinate households, or *hu*, under an eleventh or supervising household formed one *chia*, and 110 households in 10 *chia* formed a *li*.

Their assigned functions were separate, and each network of parallel but distinct organizations was directly responsible to different subdivisions of the county government offices. Since both these organizations were established by the Ch'ing government at the same time to be not only functionally separate from each other but also kept distinct and apart from the natural pattern of town and village, it must be assumed that conscious policy dictated this form. The Ch'ing government, in its obsession with control and surveillance, adopted the pattern of duplicative and mutually intimidating offices and staffing at many points. Nonetheless, in the mid-eighteenth century the tax-collecting *li-chia* functions, including the census registration carried out for tax and service obligations purposes, were made subsidiary to the *pao-chia* policing offices for administrative purposes, although the two networks of organized households still were to be kept separate. In the succeeding century and later, many magistrates found it expedient to adjust the *pao-chia* and *li-chia* boundaries to make them conform to natural settlement boundaries. In some cases, the *chia* units of the one system came to be confused with the *chia* of the other, both in the public mind and in administrative practice. Moreover, in some parts of China an antique organization of households (usually fifty households) formed a *she*, a ritual community that might have both religious and secular functions; this was given official recognition by the Ch'ing government, and might be merged with the *li-chia* or the *pao-chia* structures. In some regions the *she* were conterminous with villages, but in others a large village might contain several *she*. In short, a confusion of systems had developed by late Ch'ing times, and a rationalization of the subadministrative structure of government was long overdue (Kuhn, 1970, esp. pp. 93–99). It was never attempted.

The nineteenth century was one of protracted administrative deterioration at all levels. The effectiveness of the system in articulating the political needs of center and locality, and in integrating rural society with national purposes must be assessed against that background. Several conclusions are apparent:

1. The Ch'ing government had created and tolerated inefficiencies in social management in the interest of enhancing its control through surveillance and intimidation. Unlike the Ming dynasty at the time of its founding, the Ch'ing regime did not display a positive concern for the health of rural society except to forestall or correct conditions producing disorderly, ungovernable people. Nor did it place a high priority on drawing resources from the village level of society. Not surprisingly, the mechanisms for local governing went from an original state of planned clumsiness to one of decrepit clumsiness.

2. The geographic extent of the Chinese state was so vast that before communications could be modernized, effective management was in any event a

tenuous matter. Uniform measures could be decreed, and nationwide systems could be implemented, but uniform performance at desired levels could not be guaranteed. The 1,500 county units of local government still could function relatively well when officials were vigorous and committed, but the Ch'ing prerogatives stressed dynastic security, and bred both cynicism and timidity, not vigorous effort.

3. The subadministrative structure worked as well as it did because the strategic elite of the society, in its public and private roles, accomplished a measure of integration and control. It espoused a value system that, even as social myth, even when cynically misused, maintained a certain congruence between political acts and social attitudes. The elite's pervasive links throughout the social fabric helped to maintain its interest in an orderly society, from which both it and the government gained materially—and which also was the basic desire of the whole society. Its members provided an informal supervision that helped to prevent the breakdown of the system even when they did not maintain its full workings to the maximum interests of the ruling caste.

Nonetheless, from the point of view of the responses that might have hastened China's early modernization, the subadministrative network of governing structures by which government was extended beyond the magistracy into the rural level was a weak and defective system. It was not an adequate base on which to build a larger role for the government. It was always subject to a sharp decrease in central power as it extended over great distances to many end points. By the nineteenth century, when that central power was itself incapacitated, Chinese government in the counties degenerated into a system highly dependent on compromises and on readily corruptible personal factors. It faltered in delivering taxes and policing China. By the mid-nineteenth century the land-tax revenues drawn from the *li-chia* system were so unreliable that the emergency financing necessary to keep peace internally and to suppress rebellions had to rely on ad hoc levies of the *likin* and on the Maritime Customs revenues. In both cases, the government had to draw wealth from society at bottleneck points rather than from the entire social mass. A temporary regression of this kind was not in itself unprecedented, but by the time the Ch'ing dynasty was terminated the conditions under which China had to work her way out of that political failure were new. Governing for new purposes at the local level remained government's most intractable task, from the late Ch'ing on into the republican era.

LOCAL LEADERSHIP

All discussions of the many aspects of local government inevitably lead to an issue repeatedly mentioned: the special character of China's premodern strategic elite. In discussing the imperial institution earlier in this chapter in "Central Government: Adaptation to New Needs," it was argued that Ch'ing China was ruled by a small caste that excluded the Han Chinese scholar-official elite, even though that elite provided the country's administrative bureaucracy, up to the highest levels, and dominated its society. That issue and some of its ramified implications, although treated in Chapter 5, call for further discussion here.

If we use as our criterion Chang Chung-li's definition of "gentry"—that is, persons who had achieved in their own right the lowest official status of *sheng-yuan* by examination, or *chien-sheng* by purchase, hence all of higher official status as well—the elite was a large social group. His figures give 1,100,000 individuals in those categories in pre-Taiping times and 1,400,000 in post-Taiping times (1955, pp. 111–113). The official status accorded to these persons did not extend to their larger family group, nor was it inherited by their children, even though in most cases their families were similar in qualifications and were perceived by society to have "marginal gentry" status. With their immediate household members, that most limited definition of gentry formed an elite group of at least 5.5 million persons in pre-Taiping times and over 7 million thereafter. If our definition of the elite is to include examination aspirants similar in qualifications to the successful examinees, we would have to multiply that figure considerably. Gilbert Rozman rather conservatively (Chapter 5) assesses the size of the elite, defined as degree holders, landlords, and rich farmers, as perhaps 5 percent of the population, or perhaps 25 million persons, more or less, in the mid-nineteenth century. There are problems of definition and of counting the group's membership, but by any reckoning the elite was a large group, a talent pool of native ability and experience, even when lacking directly pertinent education and skills. A significant social resource, with a high potential for assuming some new roles, its impact on the total society was not attenuated by isolation or small numbers. It also overlapped significantly with the entrepreneurial elite of commerce and money. Because officials provided the overwhelming model in matters of life style, values, and social behavior for all persons of elite status, the nature of the Chinese bureaucracy as a subset of the Chinese elite was important to the management of society far beyond its formal roles as administrators and agents of imperial control. Although the importance of the bureaucracy is a broad social issue, our concern at this point is with its implications for politics.

To quote again from K. C. Hsiao:

> That the interests of the scholar-officials did not necessarily coincide with the imperial interests can be readily seen . . . while the innermost wish of the dynastic rulers was to perpetuate their regime, their professed intention was, as the time-honored Confucian formula had it, "to benefit the people." Under ordinary circumstances, the gentry and literati were inclined to accept all this quite readily; they had more than one reason to lend their moral or actual support to the imperial regime. For one thing, the Confucian facade of imperial ideology agreed with the intellectual tradition in which they were brought up. Moreover, the continuation of the dynasty promised continued enjoyment (or continued opportunities to secure

the enjoyment) of the coveted immunities and privileges of their status. The interests of the gentry who entered officialdom were most closely interwoven with the interests of the existing regime; these men therefore had an even stronger motive to uphold it than the rest of the elite group. These two sets of interests, however, remained distinct and might drift apart when the circumstances that held them together drastically changed. (1960; 1967 ed., p. 506.)

The cynicism of the dynasty in proclaiming its altruistic purposes was quite characteristically matched by the cynicism of the elite in serving it. When crisis befell the dynasty, the bureaucracy could look elsewhere. Even in ordinary times, when the dynasty was not under unusual stresses, the bureaucratic elite had other concerns than those of dynastic well-being; its leadership within the elite stratum faced it directly with all its larger interests in society:

> It should be noted that only a small fraction of the gentry served in the government at any given time, and that they did not necessarily remain in office for life. Retired functionaries, expectant officials, and degree-holding scholars far outnumbered officials in active service. These nonadministrative members of the gentry, like commoner literati, were inclined to be more concerned with their personal and family interests than with helping the emperors to control their domain. For besides being gentry, they were heads of households, taxpayers, and perhaps also landowners, with interests that might sometimes be harmed or threatened as a result of imperial policy or local misgovernment. Owing to their status, they were in a better position to protect these interests, but the very necessity for protection revealed their true position in society: they were privileged subjects but not members of the ruling class. One can hardly overlook the fact that not a few members of the gentry acquired their status precisely to secure better protection of their families and property against encroachment—not to satisfy their wish to serve the imperial cause. (Hsiao, 1960; 1967 ed., pp. 506–507)

The gentry and literati elite was the indispensable component of governing; it constituted the instrument for carrying out both the formal and the informal tasks of governing, roles, as we have seen, that were complementary and necessary. China's scholar-bureaucrat elite is designated here a ''strategic elite'' as that term is often used in the social sciences although, in the western experience, strategic elites are thought of as appearing and proliferating only during the West's recent experience with open societies. The old Confucian scholar-officialdom had for long centuries possessed a monopoly on administrative functions, a privilege it gained through merit and achieved status. Its members did not thereby become rulers, and their privileges were highly circumscribed. They could not (with statistically insignificant exceptions) inherit their privileged status. They had neither inherited nor acquired *rights* of political participation. They could not demand or reasonably expect political roles on the basis of having ''constituencies'' in their social group, their region, or other segment of the nation. They lacked therefore some of the most significant politcal characteristics of elites with which we are familiar from other premodern societies. The Chinese gentry and literati elite was granted its status and its formal political roles as achieving individuals; its members filled those roles at imperial pleasure. The higher they rose the more directly they came under the surveillance of the rulers.

They indeed possessed authority (as distinct from power) by the force of social values granting to persons of their ideal qualifications prestige and respect—with opportunity for misuse of that. In many cases they also possessed or could be expected to acquire wealth—that is, economic power—in varying degrees. But wealth, in that society, was at best weakly protected, lacking strong legal guarantees (especially vis-à-vis the state), so wealth gave its possessors little sense of fulfillment nor the security to be independent of the political system, or to pursue paths apart from the family's corporate life. Political service may have drawn many just for the material rewards, but their far more enduring and demanding alignment was with family interests. Some scholars argue that the elite could exercise peripheral but rewarding political powers beyond the perceived concerns of dynasty and state; even if that was so, it could not truly participate in the powers of the rulers. The prominent exceptions to that rule do not come from the Ch'ing period.

Thus, although China's was an open society, its achievers, represented above all by its bureaucratic elite, did not have many open roads before them. They had to submit to severe social limitations on individualistic achievement or be regarded as "fantastics and eccentrics" (to use James Cahill's terms). They perceived the fact that economic power while real, was fragile in their society, not often worth taking as a goal in its own right. They also felt their exclusion from full participation in the highest exercise of political power. For most members of the elite, those bars to alternatives effectively reinforced the society's full approval of family-centered achievement. The family and the lineage could absorb all their achieving capacities, and success in the bureaucracy could easily become no more than a step in that direction. At first the Ch'ing dynasty apparently saw subservience to family goals as a useful curb on behavior, but by the mid-eighteenth century it had perceived dangers to its prerogatives latent in strong family and lineage organization (Hsiao, 1960; 1967 ed., pp. 348–357). Despite certain countermeasures, the state could not prevail against the primacy of family and clan claims. As the dynasty alienated its bureaucratic elite by its political cynicism and gave evidence of its declining political powers in the nineteenth century, the tenuous balance between state and family, between center and locality, was shifting. Yet where it could, the state used responsibility to family well-being as a threat to curb potential dissidence.

By and large, that "dissidence" did not mean political dissidence; it meant politically irrelevant pursuit of family wealth, status, prestige, and privilege in ways that could damage the conduct of government without attacking it. Only as alternative careers developed, as byproducts of the intrusive social changes of the mid-nineteenth century and thereafter, did individuals of elite educational and social qualifications begin to justify and agitate

92

for political change, either as disillusioned loyalists or as political dissidents. Even then, the agitation took place outside the structure of politics, in the new private sectors developing under the wing of extraterritoriality. When radical reform was proposed at last from within the government by members of the administrative elite, as in 1898, it was couched in sincerely held but eccentric Confucian terms. That failed politically, but the experience greatly intensified the modernizing thought currents, and again raised the exciting possibility for political heroism within bureaucratic careers. A brief era when deep social change could be advocated, even if defensively and to some extent camouflaged in old-style loyalist rhetoric, followed, in the first decade of the twentieth century, the last decade of the old imperial system. By that time, other modernizing alternatives had acquired more significance. The opportunity for the Ch'ing state to use an immense potential resource in its bureaucratic elite to effect strengthening changes in politics and in the society was never as large as Japan's successfully realized opportunity to mobilize its elite in the mid-century restoration there, because of differences in the social dynamics of the two countries. But a different political leadership nonetheless might have used that resource, in 1875, or in 1900, or even in 1925. None appeared that could do so.

What is meant by "differences in the social dynamics" between China and Japan—or between China and any other society that comes to mind? This usually ignored subject merits discussion. In Chapter 5, Rozman concludes that social patterns and practices in China "all supported a different kind and, in some respects, a greater degree of family and lineage cohesion than in Japan and Russia." He speaks of various ways "in which Chinese society reduced class consciousness in favor of family solidarity." The primary affinities, those within lineage-connected groups of families, tended to be vertical because no family units comprising a lineage were ever all at the same stratification level; the larger and more successful a lineage, the wider the vertical spread. The small family, and the lineage to which it belonged, functioned as the social context of highest priority in determining individual attitudes and behavior. In times of economic or political stress, or of other need, the small farmer did not look first to other small farmers in neighboring villages with whom to make common cause so as to survive their common distress; he looked up and down (but mostly up) the lines of his lineage. At times an integrating religious doctrine of the kind the state always, and the elite usually, labeled "heterodox teachings" (or worse) might induce a measure of coherence among the common people of a locality without primary reference to kinship lines. But even here family units usually made the decision to join because neither government nor the neighborhood would be apt to see such participation as an individualistic act and would hold the family and lineage responsible. Moreover, spontaneously devised degrees of fictive kinship customarily were instituted to link the members, hierarchically, as if in lineages. The primacy of the kinship claim is clear among the poor of society, and it was even more fully to be observed among the better off. Success in society was attributed to, and further contributed to strong family and lineage spirit of solidarity, to cooperation, and in some degree (with wide regional variations in the forms) to organization.

Because elite status was neither ascriptive nor securely possessed, an individual surely felt more deeply affected by his family's history than by the concerns of the dynasty. An exception might be found in the very small minority of individuals caught in the turbulent events of dynastic changeover, but even here lineages persisted while dynasties fell and were succeeded. The ideology and the laws of the state proclaimed that *hsiao*, or filial submission within the family and lineage, took priority over *chung*, or loyalty to the dynasty, that is, the state. The "divergent interests" to which Hsiao alludes above, to which members of the administrative elite might be devoted instead of being singlemindedly devoted to the state's interests, were quite normally their proper family interests, even when improperly pursued by the misuse of privilege and prestige. Political performance thus was deeply affected—one can say that faulty performance was induced—by private concerns that even the state had to acknowledge as possessing the highest ethical value.

How does the power of the Chinese family differ most markedly from that in Japan, or Russia, or other societies with which comparisons are most pertinent? How did the distinctive features of the Chinese scene come into being? The Chinese lineage is structurally different from that found in Japan or Russia, and the psychology of Chinese familism is much more intensely developed, as well as being different in content. The answers to why those things are so lie at least in part in two elements of the historical background.

1. In China every individual possessed a surname, and by reason of that a lineage identity, at least as far back as the third century B.C. No other society's experience with that feature of social organization is much older than the beginnings of its modernization. Lineage identity meant much more to behavior and values in China than just the identity of "X the son of Y the son of Z," and only the small aristocracy in most other societies had more than that identity. Over the long span of their history as a totally lineage-identified society the Chinese developed powerful social values and organizational forms stemming from the ritual, religious, ethical, and legal significance of lineage identity. To illustrate, surname exogamy, despite its inconvenience in a society having rather limited surname variety, was required by law of all Chinese until the Revolution of 1911, and is still strongly reinforced at all levels of Chinese society by a lingering sense of taboo. The *surname* was seen as the widest extension theoretically conceivable of a common descent group, yet held deep significance for daily life. The *lineage* is a fully documentable and limited common-descent group, and its binding hold upon its members is accordingly the stronger.

2. China has had many times the longest experience of any civilization with the general circumstances of an open society, therefore a society in which

all individuals were aware of and to some extent pursuing upward mobility strategies. The family set the immediate, and the lineage the outer limits of the social group within which cooperative behavior for realization of that goal was to be effected. Diverse and intricate means had been tested and proven, through two or more millennia, for enlarging the effectiveness of family and lineage institutions. All individuals were under great pressure to subordinate impulses that might deviate from the family group's interests, which were envisioned as tasks enduring through generations. Only a few individuals such as Buddhist monks and nuns found a personal escape from the pressures to conform to family interests, and even Buddhism came to explain their lives, not too convincingly, as a kind of alternative service to family and society. Such exceptions to the norm aside, no ordinary individual could achieve the highest goals by himself. Nor did he have to achieve them alone, or achieve them completely, to be counted a worthy successor. The consequences of one's behavior accrued to the honor of one's ancestors and the benefit of one's descendants. Everyone worked for those long-range goals. The privilege of service to the state, with all its precarious rewards, was only one among the means available, although no doubt the one most admired, often the one the most rewarding materially.

The state could not destroy that competing focus of attention and interest, and so it attempted to find effective ways to join in. Many ostentatious ways were instituted for rewarding families and lineages when an individual member's behavior was outstanding. Each case was processed through the bureaucracy, and both ritual and material rewards were issued through the appropriate offices of government. The not wholly identical state and family views of the rewarded individual's contributions to their welfare were masked in vaguely overlapping Confucian phrases. The right to erect a memorial archway in one's lane to a "chaste widow" or other exemplar was granted to both official and commoner households in increasing numbers through the Ch'ing period. After outstanding service to the throne, or a reasonable semblance thereof, officials above a certain grade could petition for titles and honors for their more immediate ancestors. In more truly exceptional cases, an inheritable privilege might be granted to descendants, for a limited number of generations. Among commoner households, model elders, in their roles as household heads, were honored at village wine-drinking rituals. By such means the "good families" were identified with order and security, and with their attendant rewards. The rulers, and no doubt most subjects, genuinely valued order and security. The families so honored gained the rewards, and the state gained, or hoped to gain, an inexpensive extension of its control.

Several conclusions are suggested by the foregoing:

1. Sun Yat-sen found to his dismay that the Chinese were as "a plate of loose sand" instead of possessing the national solidarity he wished to see. Mao Tse-tung struggled to teach the Chinese that they all had primary identities of a class character and a natural affinity for class cohesion; not surpris-

ingly, they were slow to learn that, despite his efforts. Both were wrong in their pronouncements concerning the political implications of Chinese social structure, as they probably were aware. The similarly hortatory pronouncements of the Ch'ing rulers came somewhat closer to recognizing the real nature of Chinese society, but were no more effective in turning the patterns of social dynamics to their dynastic interests. Their error was the hypocrisy with which they mouthed Confucian virtues to mask their more direct interests.

2. The masses of the Chinese population were grouped into small families and forged into lineage chains that dangled vertically more than they sprawled horizontally (because the meaningful gradations of wealth and status were highly differentiated, even among the relatively poor). The elite were members of lineages that displayed even greater vertical differentiation among the family units. Such vertically extended lineages were dominated from the top, wherever that was located. Especially in a period of heightened political controls, cautious conservative behavior at all levels best served the prospects of all. The conservatism of Chinese society was based on an awareness of social realities.

3. The scholar-official elite's ability to penetrate deeply into society and, when of the will to do so, to supervise surveillance over its lower levels while vividly projecting the example of its success, naturally complemented the state's combination of intimidation and enticement as its method of control. As the state weakened, its methods for controlling the elite tended to disintegrate, and the elite's desire and ability to restrain society at lower levels also weakened. The widely observed and documented administrative deterioration of late Ch'ing signifies a weakened administration, with a decline in benign or constructive informal governing by the nonadministrative elite, and hence a less governable population.

4. Despite the effect observed above, the Chinese social system was committed to order, and profound disorder was the exceptional consequence of extraordinary circumstances. Although politically apathetic, the Chinese people well understood the practical benefits of welfare, education, family cooperation, and the acceptance of leadership. Lineage activities provided models for constructive action, and interlineage cooperation could sometimes extend the model. Chinese society was pervaded by downwardly persuasive models and upwardly imitative aspirations. The notion, sometimes encountered in writings on China, of a normally two-tiered society, in which turbulent masses were perpetually at odds with an Apollonian elite, overlooks the nature of the social structure.

5. Under normal conditions the government could manage its limited role relatively cheaply, yet to mobilize the society for goals other than those widely perceived as compatible with family and lineage interests was extremely expensive and difficult. For example, mobilizing soldiers to defend the empire was virtually impossible with any degree of voluntarism. The

revealing exception was Tseng Kuo-fan's success in rousing the population of Hunan early in the Taiping rebellion to defend hearth and home against outlandish (though Chinese) marauders by appealing to genuinely popular values, and by using the authority structure inherent in the region's society. The conditions prevailing in that success were not easily replicated elsewhere in that century, or in the next.

6. In some important ways, the local society in the late nineteenth century, freed from effective surveillance and under degenerating central political guidance, was able to respond resiliently to provide compensating organizational strengths. This, however, often further weakened the cause of good national government because it allowed the currently dominant lineages in a region to achieve uncontrolled degrees of antisocial self-aggrandizement. By breaking up the more normal openness of society and slowing or freezing upward and downward mobility, it could allow an abnormal structure of local control to harden into an enduring set of misused power structures. This complemented and abetted the worst features of regionalism, later of warlordism. The health of Chinese society in many regions was approaching a low ebb by the end of the Ch'ing.

Legal Structure

CONFLICT RESOLUTION

In describing a society's way of handling conflict resolution, we must consider the extent to which the society relies on codified norms, whether in the form of justiciable law or of ethical procedures for mediation and conciliation. The extent to which litigation is used and whether the judiciary is independent and functionally specialized are also important in understanding a society's institutional resources. Collective, rather than individual, responsibility for antisocial acts or antistate behavior is characteristic of many premodern societies. Ch'ing China's means for controlling conflict and resolving disputes can be briefly characterized here; in many senses they are more a matter of social interaction than of the operation of specialized political institutions.

Chinese political thought has debated the merits of controlling society by ethical norms (characteristically to be applied through ritualized social practices), rather than legal instruments, continuously since the fifth century B.C. Nominally the Confucian means favoring social action and moral suasion have been accepted as the standard for the society since the first century B.C. But the empire's institutions have nonetheless relied heavily on legalistic means, on penal codes, on penalties and punishments, and on effectively regularized modes of bureaucratic and private behavior. Despite the extensive government support of depersonalized institutions for maintaining standards of behavior, no independent judiciary ever developed. Nor did the concept of a transcendent law arise. The laws were instruments of the state, and they were applied, along with other instruments, by officials without much specialized legal knowledge. True, magistrates by Ch'ing times felt the need to have a legal specialist among their private secretaries, showing that the government was not tolerant of errors in the application of the laws. But, that is quite another thing from having a specialized, let alone an independent, judiciary. When he was exercising his judicial functions, the multicompetent magistrate who headed the county government was investigator, prosecutor, defense attorney, judge, and jury. At the apex of the authority structure, the omnicompetent emperor was lawgiver and highest judge, at least in theory. The Ch'ing dynasty, like all its predecessors, issued its penal code, and more systematically than most, it compiled voluminous precedents to guide the judicial process. Moreover, the society knew a full panoply of contracts and legal instruments, and litigation was an everyday feature of Chinese life. Nonetheless, litigation was expensive, dangerous, and very uncertain; it was also demeaning and somewhat unworthy of good people in the eyes of many upholders of the society's ideals.

For these reasons it is not surprising that the government itself strongly encouraged mediation and conciliation in disputes that involved less than homicide or one of the ''abominable'' crimes. The pressures to avoid and to resolve conflicts within the family and within the community were very powerful. Magistrates would repeatedly urge such a course on plaintiffs and defendants in most cases that reached the district *yamen*. A wide variety of ingenious means to bring about settlement was well known in all communities. Characteristically, these means involved intervention of a respected senior figure, investigation and discussion of all aspects of the disputed issues, ritualized admissions of error or guilt, payment of token or real fines, and the witnessing of the settlement by members of the group or the community in some social setting, usually a feast paid for by the person judged to be in greater error. The fact of conflict usually was tantamount to the admission of some degree of guilt or error by all parties, and was an expense to all involved, whether the settlement was by conciliation or via the magistrate's court.

When such private means failed, there were, however, regularly established processes for adjudicating lawsuits, keeping case records, making appeals, and reviewing judgments at higher levels. Legal means could be used to settle small-scale conflicts if the parties insisted or the community found no better alternative.

Large-scale conflicts, from riots and spontaneous disorders to banditry, subversive movements, and rebellious armed uprisings, were the great fear of the Ch'ing government. The hope was that mutual surveillance and group responsibility would deter such social disorder, and that harsh punishment would intimidate would-be malefactors. But the amount of force available to a district magistrate was quite limited. Calling up the local police or guard units or the militia to suppress a disorder, would bring to the central government's attention a problem that an able magistrate should have detected early and solved by other means. And, if local forces were unable to restore order and apprehend and punish the wrongdoers, the magistrate would suffer punishment for having allowed the problem to get out of hand. Thus, all the weight of circumstances favored covering up the facts, concealing the scope of problems, and hoping they would disappear. To recognize that a social problem existed and to deal with it frankly and forthrightly, whether by solving a social inequity or suppressing a defiant force, was seldom the best course for a magistrate. Yet when a problem would not disappear, ruthless suppression was encouraged, for intimidation was an important component of the Ch'ing governing system.

The nineteenth century witnessed in China the largest social upheavals in human history, proof that the Ch'ing government lacked the capacity to resolve major social conflicts before they could become large-scale internal disorders. In view of the unprecedented nature of many of the components of nineteenth-century history in China, the government's failure to recognize the full scope of the society's problems is easily understood. Yet many of these problems, as this chapter has repeatedly stressed, were themselves part and parcel of the Ch'ing style, the consequence of the particular ways in which it adapted the Chinese political tradition to its particular sense of its place in history.

After the great mid-nineteenth-century rebellions, a weakened and defensive government was forced to rely on regional military and political forces as the lesser of evils, in order to keep the peace. Local peacekeeping forces proliferated, and in many cases exploited their regions. At the same time, the rising sense of social insecurity encouraged secret associations of semilegal, semibenign character to offer protection to their members and friends, at ever higher cost to the society as a whole. Secret gangs of course also had opportunities to monopolize aspects of organized crime such as smuggling, extortion, and political graft. Their profits could be used, often had to be used, to support certain officials and to defy others. The various forms of the local society's investments in what can be most broadly described as "the costs of social safety" became a heavy drain on resources by late Ch'ing times. The continued increase in these costs and decrease in the quality of government clearly implicit in that spiraling disintegration of central control bore its inevitable fruit in the era of full-scale warlordism that followed the Revolution of 1911.

To summarize, Ch'ing China lacked any precocity in its legal institutions; they were curiously different from many features of the society and its political structures that, prior to the nineteenth-century administrative deterioration, can be seen as embodying an early achievement of conditions favoring modernization. The features of the old society that induced heavy reliance on extralegal solutions to most small-scale conflicts nonetheless served the society well; these social means were inexpensive and effective, and they provided community instruction in the social values even as they operated to maintain them. Yet when the morale and the performance of the government, and of its strategic elite, failed in the nineteenth century, these normative controls were weakened. Large-scale social disorder was the more readily engendered, and the less effectively combatted. This failure of government was consistent with the others discussed here: all display a China that retrogressed politically during the Ch'ing dynasty, and that possessed starkly diminished political resources for facing the challenges brought to its doors in the nineteenth century by a modernizing world.

Interest Groups

SPECIAL POLITICAL INTERESTS

When we talk about the relation of modernization and a nation's special political interests, we are concerned with those somewhat independently established elements in society, such as religions with well-institutionalized churches, business and commercial groups with strong financial powers and operating bases, and military castes or cliques, or military components of elites, having power and political influence. It is difficult to find important examples of these in nineteenth-century China. In Japan and Russia the absence of strong competing interests (and, simultaneously, the presence of effective social organization under strong political leadership) presumably lent force and capacity to the government during the early phases of modernization. Structurally, nineteenth-century Chinese society and politics were in very few ways analogous to Japan's and Russia's, yet Chinese society too was lacking in strong organizational elements between the state at one end and the family at the other end of the organizational spectrum. The Chinese state traditionally had no strong competition from a hereditary aristocracy, from a church, from well-organized merchant capital, or from a politically potent military component. As we have seen, the contest was between the strength of the throne on the one hand, and the claims of family and lineage on the other. A gradually deteriorating political leadership allowed that balance to shift in favor of local interests during the nineteenth century. From the viewpoint of certain social theories, as evident, for example, in Chinese communist historiography, it is plausible to assert that a special political interest in fact developed in the form of a cohesive gentry-elite bloc, but that assertion is not demonstrated, and probably is not demonstrable. The interests of individuals in that status were diffuse at best in the nineteenth century, and by the end of the Ch'ing era, these individuals tended to identify their interests with new and different political concerns.

Thus we must conclude that a discussion of special political interests does not hold much potential for explicating the political factors in China's early modernization. By the beginning of the twentieth century, however, several special political interests had become important and had acquired the capacity to exist in some measure outside the control of the Chinese government and to be the agents of some degree of change. These developments, discussed in the remainder of this section, all stemmed from the western presence in China after 1800.

THE TREATY PORTS

In 1800 limited trading, but trade with a potential for considerable growth, was carried on through Macao and Canton. The age of mercantilism was drawing to a close, marked by the dissolution of the British East India Company in 1834, and international competition in trade was growing. Insoluble conflicts with the Chinese imperial government, represented by its agents in Canton, about the circumstances under which foreign trade should be conducted led to the Opium War of 1839–1842, and to the use of further force to achieve treaty revisions. In the late 1850s and early 1860s, as a result of these unequal treaties, sixteen treaty ports were opened at important coastal or river transshipment locations. Governed under western law, the treaty ports became alien enclaves. The larger and more important international settlements such as those at Canton, Shanghai, and Tientsin, came to dominate trade, banking, and industrial development in China. From the first the treaty ports were important because they were beyond the reach of the Chinese government and thus were demonstrations of other kinds of political behavior. Even their Chinese inhabitants were insulated from Chinese legal and political controls, though they remained less independent of Chinese social norms. Eventually the extraterritorial settlements became bases for direct involvement in Chinese politics. They also spawned social and psychological change.

Much merchant capital was concentrated in the treaty ports by the later decades of the nineteenth century. International banking, to the end of the Ch'ing era, was dominated by the western banking interests (Feuerwerker, 1969, pp. 60–61), but from them the Chinese learned about and increasingly emulated the new banking practices. They provided the model for transforming native banking organizations. New shipping companies and industrial installations representing Chinese bureaucratic capital, such as the China Merchants' Steam Navigation Company and the Han-yeh-p'ing Ironworks, began the attempt to compete with western enterprises by imitating them. For example, Han-yeh-p'ing was built with equipment from England and Germany, and its Chinese technicians were instructed to use the plant as a school for learning western technology (Ayers, 1971, p. 168).

The Chinese Imperial Maritime Customs inspectorate was created by the English and American consuls in Shanghai as an emergency response to the fall of the Chinese old city of Shanghai to the Taiping rebels in 1853; from that act grew the modernized Maritime Customs of the nation, headed thereafter by Englishmen working for the Chinese imperial government. That led to the founding of the modern postal service, also under foreign direction, and to many additional services that were models of efficient modern government. They provided some of the mechanisms through which China and the West interacted. (The diplomatic dimensions of this interaction are discussed in Chapter 2.) The impact of the large foreign trading companies on Chinese business growth was somewhat similar in involving Chinese business, financial, and political leaders in new social contexts. (The economic aspects are discussed in Chapter 4.)

The political consequences of the treaty ports are less clear. The official view in Chinese communist historiography is that China was slipping into a "semicolonial" condition in which imperialist capitalism became not merely a special political interest but the dominant influence over the Chinese nation and its government. Such a characterization has little basis in fact. But, by the second half of the nineteenth century the treaty ports held foreign and Chinese economic interests that could bring certain influences to bear on the Chinese government. At times they stabilized the imperial government by ensuring its fiscal soundness, and at times they could induce the imperial government to invest in modernizing activities, such as transport, communications, arms procurement and arms manufacturing technology, technical schools, translation, and scientific training. These economic interests also possessed economic power, which could be used or misused, diverted to regional interests that weakened the central government, or applied to foster interregional competition. The treaty ports have often been seen as negative factors in China's political development, much resented by the Chinese because they exploited and corrupted; at the same time they engendered nationalistic reactions that in the twentieth century would come to impel strong forces for change. In the nineteenth century, however, the treaty ports and the alien economic activities they harbored were still too far removed from the life of the nation to have constituted a major special political interest. Yet their existence undoubtedly encouraged their western inhabitants, perhaps also some of their Chinese inhabitants, to believe that the treaty ports exerted great influence on Chinese politics, and on domestic matters in general. For decades westerners wrote of the Taiping rebellion as if the limited military activity around Shanghai to which they contributed had in fact been the crucial factor in the rebellion's eventual suppression. Such myopia is characteristic of the western assessment of the western role in Chinese history, in the nineteenth century and since.

There is no doubt that the larger and more important treaty ports developed a cultural life somewhat apart from that of the nation as a whole. They developed extensive publishing businesses served by concentrations of writers, many of dual cultural capacities. A growing flood of newspapers, journals, and books began to have a significant impact on the communication of ideas. Much of the growing nineteenth-century Chinese criticism of the

Chinese government was produced in and disseminated from the treaty ports. In the twentieth century these special interests, developing under the protection of foreign law and encouraged by the exposure to alien cultural forms, also came to be politically significant.

Religion has been a special interest in countries in which a strongly institutionalized church possessed some measure of political importance, but in China the indigenous religions (including also the wholly sinified Buddhism and the regionally important Islam of the late imperial era) cannot be seen as special political interest groups of genuine significance for political life. Christianity as purveyed by the influx of Catholic and Protestant missionaries during the nineteenth century did, however, become a special interest capable of embarrassing the government, of forcing indemnities upon it, of diminishing Chinese sovereignty, and of bringing various other pressures to bear. In spheres of education, medical work, and the management of philanthropy and social service, as well as in fostering a broad knowledge of the non-Chinese world, thereby changing attitudes in ways that favored modernization, the Christian religion was becoming a force that would be significant for change in the twentieth century.

Finally, the treaty ports were the bases from which technological and organizational transformation of the Chinese military was transmitted to China. The modern weapons produced in Chinese shipyards and arsenals, at first under foreign supervision, were essential to the partially successful efforts to modernize China's military capacities during the later decades of the nineteenth century. The impact of the new military is best seen in careers such as that of Yuan Shih-k'ai. He started as a regional military commander under the sponsorship of Li Hung-chang in the early 1880s. He had the foresight to lead the way in modernizing the military forces under his control, and in seeking a firm control over politics by reliance on the power to coerce. Foreign experts aided in the training of his New Army, and after the beginning of the twentieth century he sponsored the Officers' Training Academy at Pao-ting which used German military advisers and was to play an important role in the efforts to modernize China's military forces. This represents but one of many links between the western presence and the growth of regional military, hence political, power. Earlier we noted that the new Maritime Customs revenues were crucial to the suppression of the mid-century rebellion, setting a pattern that was exploited by Li Hung-chang in the 1870s and 1880s. Yuan Shih-k'ai was the direct heir to Li Hung-chang's power and position; it is clear from their careers that the treaty ports were instrumental in providing them opportunities for developing new kinds of power, and that the enhancement of their military means to power underlay all the rest. (This is discussed more fully in the section "National Communications," in Chapter 9.)

New forces like Yuan Shih-k'ai's New Army were convincing evidence that China could achieve certain kinds of modernization by making the political decision to do so. At the same time, however, the comparisons with Russia and Japan, which could not be hidden from the Chinese people after the disasters of the 1890s, when Yuan Shih-k'ai was unsuccessful in dislodging either the Russians or the Japanese from Manchuria and Korea, gave full evidence that a weak government (even with the services of Yuan Shih-k'ai) could not provide effective leadership even for guiding the aspect of modernization most crucial to its own security. China lost all its foreign wars throughout the nineteenth century. Early in the twentieth century, the military phases of the Revolution of 1911 were played out at comic opera levels of military involvement. The end of the imperial era was accomplished without any massive or protracted civil war, and its decisive steps were politically achieved.

The treaty ports held out the potential—the model and the means—for the technological modernization of the Chinese military but did not thoroughly effect that. After the fall of the last dynasty, through the warlord era, China's military system remained only rudimentarily modernized, yet China's politics became fully militarized. From the late Ch'ing on, the world's largest society was held at bay by military machines that possessed (perhaps fortunately) only the capacity to inflict medieval brutalities. By preventing a political reintegration of the nation, and in other ways, they resisted rather than led modernizing change in the sphere of politics. (Warlord politics in the early twentieth century is discussed in Chapter 9.)

One can conclude that the western presence, conveyed through the treaty ports in significant degree, added new elements and offered new kinds of options to China's domestic politics. These elements did not in themselves, however, become a new special political interest in the governing of China.

International Comparisons

We have discussed politics here largely in terms of social factors. Two or three other aspects of the late Ch'ing circumstances of the Chinese strategic elite, especially its active administrative elite, may be mentioned for comparison with the officialdom in other modernizing societies. One aspect has to do with the Chinese elite's links to service. The official career has been described as being on the one hand so attractive as to have induced the existence of a virtually single career society. On the other hand, we have stated here that service was secondary, in the self-interest calculations of Chinese potential and actual bureaucrats, to the more demanding ethical and practical values of family and lineage. These are not necessarily mutually exclusive, for if they represent contradictory attitudes, they could be kept in balance by strong and effective political leadership of the state. Clearly, no other career returned as much public esteem as did official rank and substantive appointment; the material rewards were also perhaps of greater benefit to family and lineage than were those gained from other careers, since office provided a means of securing and enhancing gains, even as it could also expose one to dramatic losses. Despite the importance of these links to service, they seem not to have given the Chinese state as strong a command over the lives or the performances of its bureaucrats as one might imagine. Merle Fainsod in discussing the role of the bureaucracy in the modernization of Russia proposes a category of "ruler-dominated bureaucracies" to which we might well assign the Chinese example, yet in tsarist Russia, probably also in Tokugawa Japan (if not at the shogunal level, within the domains), the ruler's domination of his bureaucratic elite appears to have been more complete.

The use of land as a reward for service, therefore as a control over the servitors, also seems to have worked more effectively in Russia and Japan. Land or its revenues was conferred along with the associated feudal titles and privileges in both Russia and Japan, although the forms varied somewhat. Primogeniture made these rewards both hereditary and safe from inheritance dissipation. In China the acquisition of land was indirectly favored by service but was only indirectly threatened by failure to serve; the link to service was neither clear-cut nor necessary. Second, landholdings, like other property and wealth, were diffused among family members by inheritance. Thus they did not remain integral assets that could assume make-or-break importance to an entire lineage because of the behavior of one individual and his family, as could the estates of an aristocrat-bureaucrat in another society who was threatened with reduction to commoner status. In China, loss of land and status were commonplace happenings in the history of any family, and one that achievement strategies could deal with on a long-range basis. Land, thus, was a relatively weak form of imperial leverage over the Chinese bureaucracy.

Third, the state in China could not, and had not for many centuries attempted to force its service elite to live concentrated at the capital under intimidating surveillance, as in Japan, nor did it develop a metropolitan society to which the elite felt it must belong, thereby becoming susceptible to surveillance, as in tsarist Russia. Instead the members of China's bureaucratic elite retained their attachment to their native places, dispersed throughout the length and breadth of a vast land. Many of them participated also in the life of regional metropolises that might be less "provincial" than the capital, that element of centralization being less complete in China than in most other societies. Most bureaucrats spent by far the larger part of their lives away from the capital, much of it in their native regions. In that way they maintained essential links to lineage and locality.

Finally, like Russia and Japan, the Ch'ing state attempted to maintain uniformity of thought and expression; it did this by controlling to some degree education and preparation for the civil service examinations and, to a larger extent, by maintaining a literary inquisition. A uniform world view was, however, provided by social factors that the state did not need to control; its manipulation of highly contrived control mechanisms in fact failed in its intended purpose of making bureaucrats more reliable because the Ch'ing state gave too high a priority to making them passive. This made them less reliable in terms of initiative and commitment—that is, where the health of politics and society suffered directly. This feature of Ch'ing state controls was counterproductive for governing.

In the light of the special characteristics of the Chinese civil service bureaucracy and of the elite defined by its recruitment system and subservient to its norms, those features of Chinese social structure that made effective political management and control so problematic throughout Ch'ing China cannot but draw our attention. In the deteriorating conditions of the nineteenth century, the failure of that control became fully apparent and was increasingly relevant to China's performance in modernization.

We believe there were structural as well as practical limits on China's capacity to be despotic. Those who stress the total extension of bureaucratic power in China as the defining criterion of a society in which the class structure is entirely based on the relations of the entire population to despotic state power, and to its bureaucratic apparatus, would seem to have overlooked the primacy of familism, its ideal foundation in social ethics, and its structural dynamics.

Bureaucracy and family were the two dominating organizational contexts of traditional society, but they were never equal. Family and lineage organization was prime, bureaucratic organization secondary to it in importance for the social order. With the weakening of the government in late Ch'ing, a degenerated form of the bureaucracy was left to maintain the daily operations of government. When the ruling caste had become decrepit, and the operations of government debased at the top, the bureaucratic performance had also become sadly shrunken in scope and quality. The strategic elite had to make hard choices between increasingly incompatible alternatives of guarding the government's interests and guarding its own, interests truly incompatible even though both were describable in the same rhetoric and still could be harmonized in ideal terms. It is not difficult to see why the cause of effective governing lost out.

CHAPTER FOUR

Economic Structure and Growth

THE CH'ING ECONOMY RESEMBLED THAT OF OTHER PREMODERN SOCIETIES in its low level of per capita production and its primary reliance on muscle power for energy. The economy was, however, also characterized by private contractual behavior in land and labor markets of a sort often associated only with modernizing societies, and the limited role of the public sector set China off from other large-scale empires. These various features coexisted in a huge economy in which small producing and marketing units exchanged resources, goods, and services within large regions that conducted relatively little commodity trade with each other.

As in most premodern societies, agriculture in pre-twentieth-century China contributed as much as, if not more than, 65 percent of the gross domestic product. Commerce exceeded industry (that is, handicrafts) in contributing the balance, and no less than 70 to 80 percent of the work force worked part or full time in agriculture. The Chinese economy also resembled that of other premodern societies in its exclusive reliance on energy supplied by the sun, wind, water, wood, animals, coal, and human muscle power, with the last being most widespread and conspicuous.

While still premodern, however, the Chinese pattern of production and exchange had numerous modern elements: the widespread use of money; long-established and widely accepted legal behavior and institutions that encouraged rational choice by organizers of production and commerce; the widespread use of contracts to minimize risk and uncertainty; highly competi-

107

tive markets characterized by ease of entry and exit, numerous suppliers and buyers, and little product differentiation. Individuals with family support readily contemplated occupational change and social mobility. Few obstacles hindered transactions in land, labor, and commodities. Under these conditions, individual households allocated their resources to the highest paid users in order to satisfy their desired goals.

China's economy also appears distinctive in other respects. First, the very large population, over 400 million in 1850 (see Chapter 5 for more details on the population and its growth), presented a formidable barrier to commercial integration and large-scale division of labor. Despite notable long-distance trade in luxury items and in certain daily commodities like salt, scale and geography severely limited national economic integration. In addition, the state's restricted interest in promoting economic change meant that the private sector operated with little interference or direction. Except for normal market competition, China did not develop any dynamic economic force at or below the central level that would have stimulated more extensive economic integration or reorganization. Problems of scale and leadership very likely made a more centralized economy difficult to achieve; they also meant there was little effort to capitalize on the powerful commercial forces present in numerous local areas.

Finally, the very flexibility of the local economy enabled households to meet their immediate needs and to eliminate acute scarcities of resources that might otherwise have necessitated more thoroughgoing official and community action. For instance, in the absence of high rates of taxation or other obligations to distant authorities or absentee owners, villages and households could develop and maintain resources generally adequate to meet the basic needs of their expanding populations. To a remarkable extent increases in the supply of food, clothing, and shelter kept pace with a population that more than doubled (perhaps even tripled) from the mid-seventeenth to the mid-nineteenth century. In this chapter and the next we indicate some of the roots of local resilience as well as its long-term vulnerability.

We divide our coverage of the history of Ch'ing China into three periods. The first extends for roughly 150 years, encompassing a brief segment at the end of the seventeenth century, the entire eighteenth century, and roughly the first quarter of the nineteenth century. During this period China experienced gradual economic growth with little sign of serious famine or major slumps in production. Population increase seems to have been continuous for much of this period, and economic conditions remained largely favorable. Persistent government surpluses, vigorous merchant organizations, and sustained increases in rural production and employment opportunities all reflect the overall prosperity of the early and mid-Ch'ing economy. Later we consider why these favorable trends may have had an adverse effect on modernization.

The largely descriptive historical evidence suggests that by the second period, which began in the late 1820s, economic growth had begun to slacken.

Was this new economic situation caused by growing population pressure on limited resources, or did other economic factors cause aggregate demand to weaken and thereby adversely affect the employment of resources, especially labor? Was this slower growth, perhaps decline, caused by a scarcity of land or by the shortage of silver associated with changes in foreign exchange? The authors of this volume are inclined to favor different interpretations of this period, but in this chapter we put primary emphasis on external factors to explain the state of the economy. The second period ends with the outbreak of rebellions between 1850 and 1865, which caused production and population to fall and plunged the economy into a sharp decline.

The Chinese economy in the third period was subjected to greater influence from foreign relations than it had been previously. By 1865 the economy again was expanding, as economic relations with other countries gained in importance. Trade with foreigners made possible the emergence of a very small modern sector. Yet prior to 1895, foreign capital, technology, and trade remained minimal and were confined largely to a score of city ports.

The Economic Foundation

THE INSTITUTIONAL CONTEXT

The Chinese state, under the direct leadership of the emperor, had the power to influence the behavior of organizations primarily concerned with production and distribution. It could redistribute property rights, determine the size and regularity of the tax burden, regulate markets and the money supply, maintain and develop the economic infrastructure, such as irrigation systems and canals, offer subsidies for various purposes, such as famine relief and land reclamation, assist in making new technology available, and perform a host of other services. The economic records of many Chinese dynasties provide ample evidence of the state's active concern in these areas.

By the late imperial era the state had reached an accommodation with the populace that ruled out major changes in many of these areas. The legal and institutional arrangements of Ch'ing China were relatively secure. The state did not take an activist role in reshaping the economic environment, but it did work to create a favorable one. It gave incentives to organizations to operate more effectively, and it favored measures that would ensure a stable environment for individual households, perceived as the primary producing organizations.

Stability resulted from various state actions. At first confiscating land and assigning bannermen portions of northern counties as estates, the conquering Ch'ing rulers then reassured landowners with policies that protected property rights, imposed a relatively light (and over most of the dynasty, at least a nominally unchanging) tax burden, and promoted famine relief. The state initiated new laws that chipped away at privileges long enjoyed by local elites of the Ming dynasty, who had derived much of their income from large land-holdings. These laws sought to protect the laboring class that farmed these estates and to repeal the land-tax exemptions of the local elite. The state instructed local officials to subsidize families reclaiming land for farming. Moreover, the state spent considerable amounts to restore irrigation works and water control systems, to rebuild roads, and to revive the system of grain storage for relief when harvests failed. Such reassurances provided strong inducements to encourage the private sector to increase the supply of resources, to use land and labor more intensively, and to make all inputs more productive.

The Chinese state also gathered information of value in regulating the economy, especially in difficult times. The Ch'ing leaders monitored seasonal food-grain and fiber prices from all provinces to observe if any areas began to suffer severe shortages. When price increases were noted and shortages confirmed by provincial memorials to the court, the emperor ordered that commodities be shipped from other areas or tax arrears canceled. Yet information deemed vital in other countries, like Japan and Russia, fell beyond the purview of the state. There were no detailed assessments of merchant property and wealth. More important, land records were long out of date and wildly inaccurate; the state did not survey and raise the land tax when land values rose. The land tax remained fixed for long periods, and only when a serious fiscal crisis emerged did the court order provincial officials to add a surcharge to the existing land tax.

The legal and regulatory environment encouraged household initiative in farming and handicrafts. Few restrictions were placed on opportunities within the private sector to allocate labor, accumulate capital, expand the stock of wealth, and increase the output of goods and services. Households, singly or occasionally in partnerships, produced for highly competitive markets. Within these markets, households—whether producers, brokers, or merchants—resorted to customary law in drawing up contracts to facilitate the exchange of resources. Contracts also mitigated against risk and uncertainty. Some were formal and written, signed by both parties, but most were probably informal and verbal.

The legal system and customary law, the state's role in regulating markets and fostering incentives, the practice of divided inheritance, and the economic autonomy of the household all favored the acquisitiveness of households. The Chinese are justly credited with a strong work ethic, a high motivation to plan, and a willingness to use resources flexibly in response to changing opportunities; they were largely oriented toward the accumulation of wealth, characteristics encouraged by the relatively modern set of institutions affecting household economic behavior.

The contrasts with other premodern societies are striking. In Russia serfdom operated as one of many formidable institutional barriers to the reallocation of resources between households, and in Japan regulations, such as sumptuary laws, handed down from community leaders, domain authorities, and national leaders restricted the economic behavior of households. Awareness of economic problems increased in China around the second quarter of the nineteenth century but did not readily lead to a reassessment of the institutional setting. In Japan and Russia, on the other hand, in the 1850s and 1860s pressures quickly mounted for legal reform, changes in property rights, and revocation of privileges granted to particular groups. The smooth operation of local institutions in Ch'ing China, their flexibility and apparent applicability in the modern era, reduced the Chinese leaders' perception of a need for change. Paradoxically, these factors quickly proved to be a drawback—a barrier to meaningful change.

GROWTH MECHANISMS AND PHASES

The evidence on growth rates in premodern economies rarely permits precise measurement. Nevertheless, there is enough scattered information on the Chinese economy to allow us to hazard some general statements about pre-twentieth-century economic patterns.

During the Ch'ing dynasty, agriculture, handicrafts, and services all grew gradually. When the rate of increase in population was slight, as appears to have been the case early in the dynasty, economic growth rates probably exceeded population growth rates, producing a per capita increase consistent with historical descriptions of recovery followed by rising prosperity up to the early eighteenth century. On the other hand, when economic growth slowed, as in the second quarter of the nineteenth century, and population continued to increase markedly, per capita conditions were likely to have deteriorated. On the whole, it is doubtful that the growth in production and exchange exceeded the rate of population increase as it did over much of the period 1750–1850 in Japan and Russia. Apart from the economic slowdown that began in the 1820s and the severe losses resulting from the devastating rebellions after mid-century, it is not possible to differentiate economic growth rates during most of the Ch'ing period. More could be said about particular local or regional dislocations, but research has yet to show how they fit together in an overall picture.

The mechanisms that made possible gradual growth, averaging perhaps 0.2 to 0.5 percent per annum, are fairly clear. It is certain that cultivated farmland did not increase at anything like the rate of population growth, but the sown area per year may have increased, and the cropping of land become more and more intensive. The principal growth mechanism was the increased use of labor. Average yields per unit of land rose as more labor was applied.

Commercial growth was associated with a more intensive settlement pattern; marketing centers and cities became more densely packed within a locality or region. The most detailed study of this process, focusing on the city

111

of Ningpo (Chekiang province) and its hinterland, is by Shiba Yoshinobu (Skinner, 1977, pp. 391–439). He shows how the Yung River drainage basin, the immediate hinterland of Ningpo city in eastern Chekiang, was first brought under control in the tenth and eleventh centuries by sluices, dams, and floodgates. Over the next seven centuries the region became more populated, developing several medium sized cities, perhaps as many as 600 market towns, and nearly 9,000 villages. By the mid-nineteenth century, the Ningpo region had become densely populated with 70 percent of the farmers growing cotton and many people specializing in fishing and water transportation. Merchants in Ningpo city (with an estimated population of 250,000) operated deposit banks (*ch'ien-chuang*), which financed most of the trade of the region, particularly the long-distance coastal and interior trade. Ningpo's hinterland was heavily dependent upon the commercial activities and urban demand of Ningpo city. In the 1880s Ningpo went into decline as Shanghai assumed greater commercial importance in nearby southeastern Kiangsu, but the growth of Ningpo and its economic hinterland still illustrates the expansion of key economic core areas, an expansion that rested chiefly on flourishing commerce and a prosperous agricultural base.

Local and regional commercial integration remained an important force in the Ch'ing period. Examination of commodity prices offers insight into this process.

In the 1650s local market systems still remained fragmented, and interregional trade had barely revived from the destruction that accompanied the dynastic transition. For these reasons, severe commodity price fluctuations lasting for as long as a decade or more were recorded in such areas as Shanghai. Yet, the long-term price trend for goods and services during this time was still downward as recovery became widespread. At the beginning of the eighteenth century, the key commodity prices for silk and rice slowly began to rise. Violent price fluctuations lasting a decade or so never recurred, and short-term price fluctuations of three to five years' duration became the typical pattern. If other commodity prices also moved similarly, and there is reason to believe they did, the pattern of a gradual demand pull with moderate shifts in commodity supply produced a cluster of prices along a gradual, rising trend line.

Throughout the eighteenth century, when good harvests yielded an adequate food and fiber supply, prices were stabilized, which enabled handicraft producers to reap profits and promote the economic welfare of those living in towns. Poor harvests reduced supply and increased commodity prices, thus reducing the living standard of many city dwellers. Local scarcities were neither long nor severe. The market invariably conveyed signals of these scarcities to other areas, and merchants responded by supplying the necessary goods. If this step did not stabilize prices and eliminate scarcity, the state intervened and sold its grain reserves or hired merchants to import grain.

Unfortunately, the historical evidence does not permit us to determine with any certainty whether relative prices were shifting during this period. The record provides hints that scarcities did develop, but apparently substitutes were found which prevented critical scarcities that might have blocked the growth of production or forced technological changes to emerge. Clearly, the Chinese conserved energy as much as possible. For example, S.A.M. Adshead estimated that by 1800 China perhaps produced only 13 million "energy units for a population of 300 million, or roughly one unit for every 20 people" which was about half the energy produced by western Europe with a population of 200 million (1973, p. 21). When costs of salt production threatened to rise because of the rising expense of firewood, coal, and natural gas (*chien-yen*), producers shifted to solar heat (*shai-yen*).

What was the long-term mechanism by which gradual economic growth and population expansion took place? On the demand side, the money supply of silver and copper increased sufficiently to allow the population to carry out transactions and spend for contingencies and to meet the demand for liquidity. Producers of harvested crops, handicraft products, and services had sufficient funds to advance payments for labor and raw materials and were satisfactorily remunerated in copper cash or silver.

On the supply side, households engaged in complex transactions to exchange resources to correct for resource imbalance and scarcity. Every able household member worked or performed some task to augment household income. Producers used their savings or those of kin and friends to organize production. They kept production costs low by substituting cheaper materials and labor for more expensive ones, and they knew how to take advantage of market opportunities. The highly competitive market structure encouraged intensive use of resources and spurred their allocation to the activities yielding the highest reward.

The state maintained sufficient law and order to minimize market uncertainty and encourage exchange in all markets, both local and distant. When harvests failed and provincial or regional prosperity was threatened, officials rallied to import grain and lower taxes. The degree holders also used part of their wealth to supply such local services as education and harvest relief and to repair transport. Finally, periodic redistribution of wealth took place, so that new households moved up to replace those formerly powerful but in decline. The complex interaction of state supportive policies with the private sector's activities, a highly competitive market system, local elite spending to support the infrastructure, the continual redistribution of wealth, and a growing money supply made it possible for supply to increase and, perhaps, keep pace with rising demand.

Before 1780 the Ch'ing economy experienced a modest demand pull inflation, caused by an increase in the money supply, a gradual rise in the velocity of silver and copper circulation, and the first phase in a sustained growth in population. As a result market demand increased. Between 1780 and 1820, however, prices moved upward more slowly. Although the state had to suppress the White Lotus rebellion (1796–1803) in five provinces, spending about 120 million silver *taels* and greatly depleting its treasury reserve, the economic indicators for prices and foreign trade, and the copper-silver exchange rate showed no distress signs. If the state had been compelled to raise taxes to bid for more resources from the private sector, households would have competed with the state for these resources, and commodity prices would have risen, but no sharp inflationary upswing occurred at this time. Because the state had spent from treasury reserves to mobilize resources to suppress this rebellion, new demand was created. Meanwhile, the money supply and its velocity of circulation rose as treasury surpluses were spent. These expenditures very likely stimulated economic activity and increased employment in some areas, thereby probably offsetting any output decline in regions directly affected by the rebellion.

The economic situation changed after 1826. Between 1801 and 1826 some 74.6 million *yuan* of silver had flowed into China because of a favorable balance of trade at Canton. But between 1827 and 1849 roughly 133.7 million *yuan* of silver flowed out of China. As discussed in Chapter 2, this unprecedented silver outflow, especially from Kwangtung and Fukien, came about because silver was used to pay for smuggled opium. As a result, a sharp rise in the copper-silver exchange rate took place and was recorded even in northern provinces like Chihli. Those parties normally receiving silver hoarded their silver rather than spending it, which reduced the velocity of silver circulation. As silver continued to leave the country, it became scarce, and as a result, spending in both factor and product markets greatly declined. Southeastern provinces suffered severe deflation, thus causing the first great economic crisis since the founding of the Ch'ing.

The court immediately recognized the economic implications of the outflow and hoarding of silver. In 1828, for example, when the shortage of silver in Soochow prefecture enormously depressed trade, the court instructed the prefectural governor to use 200,000 *liang* of silver from state reserves to buy an equivalent amount of copper in the market. If silver prices declined, he was to buy silver and replace the amount borrowed. Similar edicts were issued in other areas at various times. Officials memorialized the throne, citing the disastrous effects of the silver shortage on trade and proposing, without success, that the court mint new coins or certify as legal tender various foreign currencies then circulating.

Why did this silver shortage have such a deflationary impact on the economy? Many urban merchants advanced silver to their brokers to buy raw and semiprocessed materials from market towns. The rural suppliers of silk, tea, sugar cane, the betel nut, and the like greatly depended on these advances to hire laborers and prepare their deliveries. Therefore, when the flow of silver from town to countryside declined, the production surpluses that villages marketed in the towns also declined, so that commodity exchange between villages and cities contracted. Landowners and wealthy farmers hired

114

fewer part-time laborers and rented to fewer tenants. The flow of cash wages thus declined, and households had to restrict their spending, leading to less exchange in local markets and between distant markets. Household spending for luxury goods declined, fewer opulent ceremonies were performed, and fewer people attended temples, shops, or restaurants. As the deflation dragged on through the 1830s, moderating only slightly at times, the number of people out of work increased. Many families even had to leave their communities to seek work elsewhere, so that a floating population of unemployed became more conspicuous.

The silver shortage also increased the burden on landowners of land and grain tribute taxes. Tseng Kuo-fan in 1851 described these new conditions as follows: "[Taxes] are paid mostly in money, rarely in kind. . . . The common people's income from the fields is rice. When they sell the rice for cash, the price is very low . . . they exchange the cash for silver, but the price of silver is very high." Farmers and tenants had to sell more of their grain for cash to exchange for silver to pay their land tax. Even debtors repaying their loans in silver found their debt burden had greatly increased. The increased tax and debt burden forced many households to restrict their spending for goods, further weakening market demand and reducing the profits of many producers.

After the sharp falling off of production and exchange between 1850 and 1865, the economy revived. The basic characteristics of the earlier Ch'ing economy remained, and gradual growth appears to have resumed. A relatively separate treaty port sector injected new mechanisms for growth—new technology, increased foreign trade, and altered institutional arrangements—but these had only a minor impact on the economy as a whole.

In summary, the Chinese premodern economy functioned rather smoothly, growing gradually primarily by means of widely available labor. If growth had resulted more from other kinds of inputs or from policy decisions, it might have become a more meaningful objective. Whereas Russian leaders, with expansionist goals and hostile neighbors, eagerly sought growth, and Japanese domains competed to achieve a comparative advantage in products for long-distance trade, the Chinese leaders lacked a similar stimulus. They did not, at least until well into the nineteenth century, face disconcerting budget deficits, and they did not feel the pressure of a privileged social class, such as Japan's samurai or Russia's serfowners, that demanded action to relieve its deprivation. Chinese leaders lacked the experience of having to search for new sources of economic growth.

COMMODITY MARKETS

The private sector in China produced and marketed an enormous quantity and variety of goods. In this section we consider four major commodities—rice, cotton and cotton cloth, silk, and tea—to see if any factors can be identified that bear on our understanding of China's foundation for modernization.

We can probably assume that in the Ch'ing period, somewhat under a third of the total cropped area was devoted to rice, certainly the most important commodity in the economy. (In the 1930s, roughly 26 percent of the cultivated land was in rice, and the area had declined since the turn of the century.) The adoption of the early maturing Champa rice seed, extensive irrigation, and improved fertilization during the sixteenth to eighteenth centuries had enabled more and more areas to produce two kinds of grain crops per year and had increased the grain yield per sown area. This transformation had started in the lower Yangtze area and spread elsewhere. By the Ch'ing period rice was cultivated throughout central China, with millet, corn, and cotton next in importance.

Interprovincial shipments of rice to grain-deficient areas were handled by private merchants. Hankow, for example, served as a key collecting point for rice shipped to the lower Yangtze provinces (where the average annual deficit in the eighteenth century has been estimated to have been as large as 1.4 million metric tons). Rice moved into Hankow from secondary markets, having been shipped there by rice brokers who purchased it in periodic markets from farmers who needed cash. The flow of rice through the markets was sometimes erratic because many wealthy rural households could afford to store rice and then sell when prices reached their zenith. These actions tended to reduce price swings. Not only were the owners of storage facilities so numerous that no one of them could influence prices, the number of rice merchants and brokers in various markets was also very great. Competitive market conditions existed, in which prices changed each season according to supply and demand, yet a uniform price prevailed in a market at any given time. Since these conditions seem to have existed not only in the region surrounding Hankow but in other grain market systems as well, three main implications for the economy follow.

First, profit margins of brokers and their merchants fluctuated according to market conditions, but the rate of return on this investment did not rise over time. Second, technological and organizational improvements affecting production, transportation, and distribution did occur, albeit slowly, preventing any acute, long-term scarcity of supply. Finally, labor-intensive procedures characterized all stages of production and marketing, and these conditions persisted over time. The Ch'ing rice market and production structure not only proved capable of feeding producers and consumers alike in the many thousands of periodic market systems near the sources of supply and of shipping needed quantities of rice to distant markets to feed millions of urban consumers and rural residents who specialized in cash crops, it generally accommodated population growth as well.

The next commodity, cotton, came increasingly to be preferred over other fabrics because it was easy to wash and dye, durable, comfortable in warm or cold weather, and attractive. It also yielded far more fiber per unit of land than other fiber plants. By the mid-fifteenth century, cotton had spread over much of China, and by the early eighteenth century many regions grew the plant not only for local use, but also for export to areas where spinning and weaving were heavily concentrated. Rural households were able to plant cotton in sandy soil with food crops. This along with the fact that cotton required considerable labor for soil preparation, weeding, and harvesting, meant that families with little land but with some extra hands favored its cultivation over other crops.

Farmers ginned their cotton with homemade ginning machines, and then spun fibers and wove cloth for their own use. Many farmers sold their cotton to brokers who shipped it to markets, such as those on the Soochow plain. In such areas, rural families who did not grow cotton were able to buy it to spin and weave into cloth for sale to cloth merchants. These families had idle hands, especially women, who could spin yarn and weave cloth while the men worked in the fields. These part-time farming families then sold the cloth to brokers and cloth merchants who independently or on a subcontracting basis purchased the cloth to ship to cities for calendering and dyeing. In other areas such as Fukien, farmers planted crops such as sugar cane, and after selling the crop used the proceeds to buy raw cotton which they then spun into yarn and wove into cloth for sale to the market. Instead of merchants advancing funds for spinners and weavers to ply their trades on a putting-out basis, part-time farming households in villages financed yarn and cloth manufacturing themselves.

However, some cloth processing was organized on the putting-out system and flourished in towns, especially in Soochow. Merchants advanced funds to an agent (*paot'ou*) who hired workers, purchased a stone for calendering, and arranged work schedules so that the fulled cloth could be delivered at a prescribed time. Merchants then sent the cloth to dyeing establishments, financed and organized either by themselves or by independent means; once dyed, the cloth was sold to wholesalers who shipped it to other merchants at markets in the interior. Cloth production was made up of several fabricating and finishing stages in which brokers and merchants were responsible for moving the goods and financing and organizing their processing. Each of these stages involved many producers and buyers so that these separate markets were extremely competitive; they were never integrated vertically through large-scale organizations. Highly labor-intensive methods characterized production at each stage. Although technological advances occurred gradually, there was no technical breakthrough, as happened in England, to create machinery that could depend upon water or steam as a source of power. Apparently the numerous markets functioned so effectively as to eliminate scarcities; as a result, inducements for artisans to tinker and devise labor-saving methods were weak.

By the early Ch'ing period, sericulture was well established in the lower

Yangtze region, but silk, our third commodity, was produced in many other regions as well. Long recognized as a luxury good, but with many varieties and a wide price range, silk was still widely used by many social classes. The Chekiang-Kiangsu silk culture relied upon the mulberry tree, and rural households typically grew several of these trees and farmed rice or coarse grains for food. Some of the same households either raised cocoons or sold mulberry leaves to households that produced cocoons, and spun the silk threads for sale to brokers or merchants. The silk thread was then sold to weaving establishments in towns. After the silk cloth was dyed and embroidered, it passed to wholesalers who sold it to foreign merchants or to other markets in the empire. Raw material production and spinning were confined to villages and market towns, financed by part-time farming households, and dependent upon brokers and merchants for transfer of silk thread to the weaving establishments of the towns.

Silk weaving was organized on the putting-out system, financed by silk merchants who contracted with master weavers (*chi-fang*) to hire workmen, assemble weaving implements, and weave the silk cloth under a single roof. The various stages of production and finishing were also organized on a highly competitive basis, and again very labor-intensive methods prevailed. Brokers and merchants also played a crucial role in integrating markets so that vertical integration under large-scale production proved neither profitable nor necessary.

Tea, the fourth major commodity, grew throughout Chekiang, Fukien, and Kwangtung. These areas exported their tea to foreign lands as early as the seventeenth century. Statistics available from the early 1730s show that exports rose considerably thereafter to over 100 million catties (50,000 metric tons) in 1850. Households in the mountainous interior cultivated tea on hillsides. Families hired laborers to help plant and harvest the tea. They received advances of copper cash from brokers and merchants and delivered packets of dried tea. Many of these merchants established small sheds and hired from twenty to thirty men, women, and children to fire the tea and package it for the long haul to such city ports as Canton. These same merchants received advances of money from wholesalers on the coast to whom they delivered boxes of freshly dried and packed tea; the wholesalers in turn delivered this tea to foreign merchants or agents of the East India Company. The foreign merchants had initially advanced silver to the wholesalers to supply tea at a scheduled period. In this way, the tea trade came to be largely financed by silver imported by foreign merchants.

Thousands of households cultivated tea, and countless brokers, small merchants, and large wholesale merchants competed with each other to buy this tea. Therefore, the price of raw and processed tea in the interior as well as in Canton and other port cities was competitively determined by the forces of supply and demand. As foreign demand rose over the eighteenth century tea prices also rose, but at any given time a uniform price prevailed in each tea

118

market. Production methods remained very labor intensive, brokers and merchants linked the different regional markets together, and foreign merchant capital came to play an important role in financing the industry in such provinces as Chekiang, Fukien, and Kwangtung.

For rice, China developed a substantial interprovincial and interregional market, and for cotton and cotton cloth, interregional trade was also important. Silk and tea became valued commodities on the international market as well as products for regional specialization within a national market. Tens of thousands of ships plied the Yangtze River and other major waterways or navigated the southeast coast moving these commodities and others as well. Nevertheless, on a per capita basis or in relation to total amounts of goods produced, long-distance exchange was not so impressive. By comparative standards, exchange was relatively localized. Both the vast scale of the society and the decentralized distribution of demand mitigated against a massive accumulation of goods in particular areas. For reasons discussed in Chapter 5, the concentration of resources in cities was relatively slight. Local marketing flourished, long-distance trade was notable, and yet the overall pattern of exchange was dispersed. National leaders did not strive to produce a more concentrated accumulation of goods as in Japan and Russia and elsewhere.

FACTOR MARKETS

Within the premodern Chinese economy, the labor and skills of household members as well as the land and other capital owned in common were allocated to many different pursuits. Most handicrafts and processed farm products were produced in villages and consumed at home or exchanged in local markets. Some handicrafts were also located in the marketing centers, each the focus of an area comprising roughly fifteen to thirty villages. In both villages and periodic markets, producers often had to hire labor or increase the land at their disposal; they acquired these resources in the factor markets. Let us consider land first.

According to official Ch'ing records, the cultivated area increased about 40 percent between 1661 and 1851. The crop index rose and yields increased. The farming of new lands in once peripheral areas—such as the northeast, northwest, and southwest provinces—greatly increased, so that cultivated land outside the regions settled for over 1,000 years, or what Yeh-chien Wang refers to as "developing regions," came to represent more than one-third of the total cultivated land area of the country, a much larger fraction than at any previous time. Not only had the state encouraged this settlement of new land by supplying draft animals and granting tax relief for the first three to five years of farming, but it had pooled its resources with those of the private sector, to rebuild old irrigation facilities, construct new dikes, and control large rivers. By the mid-eighteenth century the state relaxed its efforts and

119

shifted the responsibility for maintaining river projects and irrigation systems onto private owners.

The clearing and farming of new lands were accomplished by the wealthy, who combined their resources to drain swamps and irrigate dry land, by well-to-do households who obtained official permission to clear land and invited other families to farm the land as tenants, and by poorer families and former soldiers and bond servants, who settled in more inhospitable areas, such as the highlands of the Han River basin. In many areas the new arrivals could only begin to farm or find work by renting land or working as farm laborers. For this reason, the percentage of tenant and laboring households in these new communities was very high. Only after much time had elapsed did these poor families acquire land of their own or achieve a part owner-part tenant status.

Regional land tenure patterns were also influenced by the decline of large estates in the late Ming and early Ch'ing periods. The Ch'ing state in the late seventeenth and early eighteenth centuries eliminated such privileges as not having to supply corvée labor or pay the land tax. Many estate owners soon found they could no longer manage their estates with their bond servants, especially when the bond servants began fleeing to other areas to farm their own land. To counteract this, many estate owners in Anhwei and Kiangsu began giving land to servants on a perpetual leasehold basis, which allowed for transfer to heirs, for sale, and for rent collection.

Differences in climates and yields also produced variations in land-tenure patterns. In the north, the great instability of harvests discouraged long-term leasing and renting of land, and annual rents, geared to the expected harvest, were common. In the more abundant rain-fed areas of the south, the higher, stable yield conditions made farming less uncertain, and farmers and their tenants sometimes opted for land rents as a fixed percentage or even a fixed amount of the harvest. This practice may have encouraged tenants to invest more resources in their plots, thereby stabilizing and elevating yields over time, so that tenant and landlord alike benefited. Rents, whether fixed or fluctuating, were based on only one or two prime crops, so that the tenant's other crops were rent free.

In central and southern China a long-term tenant system became widespread. Tenants frequently sold their rights to others or transferred them to their male heirs. This system gave the hereditary tenant all the rights of proprietorship and therefore an incentive to improve the land, while the absentee owner worked elsewhere, collected his rent, and paid the tax. Finally, the more developed irrigation and water transport systems of these same central and southern provinces produced high yields and supported more commerce and handicraft activities, which provided rural people with more employment opportunity. Families farmed part-time, frequently rented land, and worked at a variety of other occupations to earn a satisfactory livelihood.

Contracts between families to rent and lease land should be regarded as an arrangement to correct resource imbalances within households. Short-term tenure contracts allowed households to put their land and labor to their highest paid use. These contractual arrangements made it possible to use scattered parcels of varying size fairly efficiently and encouraged the labor-intensive farming methods so well known in China.

Many large families owned hundreds of hectares of land in the early Ch'ing period, but few of these estates remained intact for more than a half-century. Even so, land distribution continued to be unequal—in some regions very unequal. More households acquired some document—a permit to clear land, a receipt showing payment of the land tax, a deed showing transfer of land—to attest to their ownership rights. County magistrates occasionally adjudicated disputes over these claims, but households preferred to rely on a third party to mediate disputes. The increase of private rights to land certainly provided a powerful incentive for families to specialize and produce for the market. This development further diminished the role of acquired status in Chinese society and increased the role of contract, whereby families acquired mobility and the opportunity to become wealthy.

For the economy to have grown after 1700, the labor force and its employment also had to expand. Parents recognized that more labor power was indispensable to family wealth. Chinese culture had always dictated that families arrange early marriages, and that the newlyweds produce children. If this proved impossible, families arranged to adopt sons-in-law from within or without their lineages. Working at a very early age in light tasks supervised by their elders, children by their teens performed field work, labored in handicrafts, carted goods, and assumed household duties without supervision.

Villages were rarely self-sufficient, perhaps marketing from one-fifth to one-half of their crops and handicrafts. Most households farmed while allocating some of their labor to a wide range of occupations and services. The occupational diversity within villages reflected the close connection of handicrafts and agriculture.

Large numbers of poor peasants sold labor services. Some laborers worked on a daily or monthly basis and then returned to the family farm, while others worked for a year or longer as agricultural workers or semiskilled laborers in handicraft production. In cities on the Soochow plain or in other prosperous areas, workers congregated where handicraft was located, worked for short periods, and then returned to their villages. Informal labor markets sprang up in these cities; buyers went to negotiate a day's work and wage. Occasionally worker riots erupted in these cities as some semiskilled handicraft workers demanded higher wages or opposed new city taxes. In spite of these disturbances, this free-floating work force never remained organized for any length of time.

On the whole, markets for land and labor were flexible and open, which made possible their intensive use and eased the transfer of rewards, both temporary and permanent, between producing units. Of course, land was inherently scarce, and labor became ever more abundant—a contrast to the pattern of development in Japan. Very high rural population densities increasingly prevailed in central and southeastern China. The ease of exchange on factor markets may bear some responsibility for this and for the continued increases in the labor supply. The declining land-labor ratio reflected the use of surpluses to support an increasing number of social units. Meanwhile, the state failed to tax very much of the surplus produced by these social units. More restrictions on the use of land and labor in Japan and Russia were part of their early efforts to enable households to meet higher tax obligations and to ensure a large flow of resources out of the village.

The Allocation of Resources

INCOME DISTRIBUTION

Information on the distribution of income and wealth is very scanty. Western travelers in the 1830s and 1840s appear to have been singularly impressed by the widespread similarity of living standards of the majority of people whose material conditions were alleged to be more than adequate. Robert Fortune in 1847 offered the following observation: "In no country in the world is there less real misery and want than in China." Pockets of opulence were rarely mentioned because the wealthy managed to conceal their life style behind high walls. Studies of food, drink, clothing, and housing are still in their infancy. Therefore, only an impressionistic account of income level and distribution is possible.

Provisional estimates by Chang Chung-li (1962) give a very rough sense of how the degree holders earned their income. In the 1880s the annual income flowing to this class came to around 645 million *taels*. About 52 percent of this came from property rents and mercantile services. Income from office, including regular and extra income, amounted to only 121 million *taels* or 19 percent of the total income. As noted in Chapter 3, degree-holder households constituted over 7 million persons or roughly 2 percent of the population.

Chang Chung-li's very rough estimate of gross domestic product for this decade comes to 2.7 billion *taels*, but comparisons with Yeh-chien Wang's estimate of 12 billion *taels* for 1908 and Liu and Yeh's (1965) calculation of 20.8 billion *taels* for 1933 suggest that, even accounting for growth and inflation, Chang's figure is too low. If, in effect, the real GDP was much higher, the degree holders' share of the total would be much lower than Chang's 24 percent estimate. Even so, the qualitative evidence for the late nineteenth century certainly attests to the huge disparity of income between degree holders and commoners.

Although the distribution of income and wealth was unequal by modern standards, certain factors prevented it from becoming more unequal over time and creating a rigid social structure. A principal factor was that because of the custom of dividing all household wealth equally among the male heirs, redistribution occurred each generation, which probably made the pattern of income distribution fairly stable over long periods. Larger wealth-accumulating units, like lineage trusts or estates, frequently set aside some wealth to produce an income for educating and caring for various progeny. Well-defined lineage rules prevented the entire dispersal of this wealth, but income flowed to households of different social status and income.

A second factor affecting the redistribution of wealth was the complexity of the household life cycle. Households that achieved stem or extended form eventually broke up to form new households and repeat another life cycle, but during these cycles resources were exchanged between households or even within households as wealth was transferred from parents to sons.

Ceremonial expenditures were a third factor. A wedding or funeral compelled households to spend heavily from savings accumulated over a long period. Sometimes families even sold or mortgaged land and other assets to pay for their expenses.

Because of the economic significance of competitive examinations taken to earn a degree and perhaps to enter the bureaucracy, the absence of legal barriers to transactions, and the equality of inheritance among sons, the redistribution of wealth in China may have been greater than in other premodern societies. Not only did Chinese households aspire to a better future, they often had a reasonable chance of realizing that wish.

CONSUMPTION, SAVINGS, AND INVESTMENT

An economy with a fluctuating per capita income equivalent to perhaps $50 in the United States is very poor by modern standards; yet in some ways Chinese poverty was mitigated by special circumstances and was less acute than in many other premodern countries. The English tea expert Samuel Ball pointed out in 1848 that the Chinese laborer had a living standard considerably above that of the Indian agriculturalist and not very much lower than the European peasant. By 1900, however, this comparative perspective had changed. Europeans described China's poverty and backwardness in vivid brushstrokes.

We know very little about the consumption patterns of the common people for this time. Surveys of urban and rural household budgets made during the 1920s and 1930s may provide a clue as to what these patterns might have been in an earlier period, although using these to make inferences about the past is of course risky.

First, rural households relied upon product and factor markets to obtain perhaps as much as 30 to 35 percent of their total cash income. A survey of rural families in northern Manchuria in 1934 showed that 45 percent of total household income was in cash, but 8 percent of this cash came from loans, sale of assets, and loan repayments. If these are excluded, cash income amounted to 37 percent of total household income. John L. Buck's rural surveys showed that between 1921 and 1925 farm sales exceeded 50 percent of total farm earnings whether the family rented, owned part and rented part, or owned all of the land it cultivated. The late imperial economy presumably was highly monetized. The very wealthy households undoubtedly had a higher annual cash flow.

Second, the average propensity to consume was high because per capita income was so low. Most households spent as much as 60 to 80 percent of their expenditures on food alone, the rest for clothing, shelter, and miscellaneous goods and services. The ordinary Chinese dressed simply; his household contained the barest of essentials—a table and some chairs—and roofs were primarily of thatch, except in the towns and cities. Aside from festival days, the daily diet was plain with coarse grains and sweet potato, instead of wheat and rice, as the mainstay.

Third, as income rose so too did savings, but only the very wealthy could afford to save much. There probably was a very high propensity to save from cash income at the higher income level. The degree holders, merchants, and landlords were the principal savers. The degree holders constantly acquired cash from the many services they rendered; merchants and landlords always received a large cash flow from sale of goods, rents, or loan repayments. Most of this cash flow was eventually hoarded as silver or copper cash, deposited in ch'ien-chuang, or used to buy land or structures as a financial investment. The Chinese possessed a powerful speculative drive, the wealthy always competed to buy land, structures, precious metals, or stocks of grain and industrial crops in the anticipation that their rise in value would net a high rate of return.

We are given a fleeting glimpse of the saving and spending habits of the elite from the household account kept by an official in the Board of Works who lived for more than a quarter of a century in Peking (Chang Te-ch'ang, 1970). Li Ts'u-ming lived in a fashionable section of Peking, employed three or four servants, and eventually acquired three concubines. Li's mother had sold some land in their hometown of Shao-hsing (Chekiang province) for him to purchase a degree. In 1870 he became a chü-jen and later a chin-shih with a fifth grade rank. Between 1871 and 1889, Li's total income came to 16,863 taels, of which 31 percent was in gifts. In only one year, 1887, did his expenditures exceed income. His total expenditures came to 8,462 taels of which he gave 10 percent in gifts and rewards. All the elite exchanged gifts just as it spent hugely for feasts and entertainment. Whether one received more than one gave the higher one advanced in officialdom is unclear, but gifts had to be given if one's career was to be successful.

Contrary to the accepted view that officials never lived on their incomes, constantly overspent, and resorted to corruption to make ends meet, Li carefully watched the spending of every copper *wen* piece and recorded it faithfully. Li certainly lived comfortably, and what he did with the more than 8,000 *taels* he saved is not mentioned in his financial records or daily diary. What seems clear from his case is that officials had diverse sources of income. Li lectured, rendered services, received gifts, and, of course, wrote. If Li's case was fairly typical of the 15,000-odd officials in Peking, the elite lived comfortably on its income, stayed out of debt, saved considerably, and worked hard.

If the masses of people consumed most of what they produced and earned, thereby saving little, the household, rather than the individual, had to be the major saving unit. As individuals pooled their savings, the household collectively bought and sold and even accumulated some wealth. Household members organized their resources as a cooperating unit and allocated their labor and physical resources to the highest bidder. All earnings, including those received for goods or services sold in the market place, were pooled. Household consumption was restricted to the tolerable level, and the remaining income saved. With luck, hard work, and thrift, a household might accumulate enough to produce or buy capital goods or to purchase assets for speculative purposes. The desire to do one or the other was dictated by the risk attached and the expected rate of return. As one would expect in this labor-abundant, land-scarce economy, the rate of return for buying and using capital goods was low, perhaps not higher than 3 or 4 percent per year or what a household generally earned by investing its capital to farm.

We have practically no information on the rate of return for alternative financial investments in late imperial times. For example, we simply do not know whether a household with 100 *taels* of cash savings might have preferred to invest in a handicraft business, to buy grain and sell it later, to purchase some land, to lend at the prevailing interest rate, or to spend for a tutor to instruct a clever son in the hope that he might pass the imperial exams. These were some of the possibilities available for those with savings. The only rate of return possible for most households, namely that from farming, remained low because of the low marginal productivity of farm capital. The small demand for funds to buy and produce capital goods also reflected this low rate of return in farming and handicraft. Technological progress was simply not sufficient to increase the productivity of capital; it merely made land more productive and saved land resources. Had technological change increased capital productivity, the rate of return to capital stock might have increased.

The elite used its savings in two ways. A large share was spent to maintain a comfortable life style. Part of these expenditures represented income transfers to other elite to ensure social and political advance. The remainder was spent on projects that in fact created physical capital and to a lesser extent even improved human capital. For example, the degree holders organized and financed irrigation works, bridges, city walls, roads, and the like; they also founded schools, temples, and institutions devoted to famine relief, and gave to charity—activities that marginally at least enabled the common people to develop their minds and bodies.

Villages financed their economic projects by requesting each household to contribute an assigned quota of money. Business partnerships in handicraft or commerce operated in the same way, each member donating a share of financial capital to the organization. Farming households also saved in order to finance inventory accumulation, produce handicraft tools, and improve land through irrigation.

The demand for credit arose primarily because of urgent consumption requirements that suddenly exceeded current income and came from the poorer and more well-to-do households alike. Funds for loans came from the savings of the wealthy. Small short-term loans were supplied by friends or kin, often without interest. Interest rates in the eighteenth century were roughly the same as in the early twentieth century: 2 to 3 percent per month. For larger loans, a borrower resorted to a go-between who would seek out a kinsman or a moneylender, such as a grain dealer, merchant, landlord, or official. A contract was usually drawn up between the lender and the borrower stating the amount of the loan and the property pledged or mortgaged to repay it. The very poor without any ties to the wealthy had to resort to pawnshops.

For these reasons, then, only a small supply of savings was channeled into the maintenance and augmentation of capital stock. A major redistribution of income would not have increased savings or altered this pattern of investment, for the prevailing ethos of late imperial China would merely have transmitted the same values and beliefs to a new elite to make for similar spending and saving habits.

The successful operation of the highly competitive market economy and the contractual arrangements developed by households to overcome scarcity help explain the society's ability to support such a large and continually growing population. Technological refinements were aimed at preventing a decline in the productivity of land and at making use of the abundant labor supply. But these efforts did not raise the productivity of the existing stock of capital. The economic system kept expanding until it was confronted with the devastating effects of deflation—namely, rising and widespread unemployment. Then the system became increasingly unstable.

TECHNOLOGICAL INNOVATION

The Chinese cleverly and with great skill devised ways to use their more abundant resources. For example, farmers transported topsoil from their fields to nearby piles of waste and then back to the fields to fertilize their land, or moved soil and mud from swamps and rivers to enrich their fields. Wu Chin-yu, governor general of Yunnan and Kweichow in the early nineteenth century, spoke of the "hundreds of strategems" tried to drain the copper mines, and of the "limitless expense" of digging deeper to find more copper. For producing more salt, workmen adopted the slower, more labor-intensive method of evaporating brine through solar energy rather than using fuel to boil the brine in large vats.

Without abundant land but possessing abundant labor, the Chinese might have concentrated on producing capital to offset the scarcity of land. Instead, technological advance concentrated on means of using labor more intensively while trying to save land. For example, progress in farming technology in late imperial times mainly involved increasing the cropping index or obtaining more crops per year from the same unit of land. Although great efforts were made to reclaim land and expand the land area, in the older economic core areas supporting the highest population density, efforts continually focused upon improving practices to raise overall yield by cropping the land more intensively.

Extending irrigation, controlling large, unruly rivers, applying more fertilizer per unit of land, and selecting better seeds after the harvest were the main ways that farmers improved productivity of their land. Most of these activities required more and more labor. For example, the transfer of river mud to fields or the removal of topsoil from fields to make compost to apply on the fields before plowing certainly raised yields over time but required huge amounts of backbreaking labor. As a result labor productivity probably did not rise very much, if at all. The same was true for farm capital. As the quantity of traditional farm capital expanded, its quality or the new technology it embodied, scarcely changed. Therefore, the productivity of farm capital remained very much the same over time. The average and marginal productivity of capital continued to remain low, and for this reason the stock of farm and even handicraft fixed capital obtained a low return. Those with savings to invest were neither encouraged to purchase nor induced to produce capital goods because higher returns could be obtained from holding income-earning assets such as land, inventory, *ch'ien-chuang* deposits, and the like. Capital stock did not increase rapidly, and its productivity remained very low.

The Chinese people merely refined rather than substantively improving their technology. In 1313 China already possessed water-powered machines for twisting hemp and silk; Europe also had these. Five hundred years later, however, China had still not been able to take advantage of its former high technological level. Whereas Europeans had developed new sources of energy and invented machines to increase the productivity of labor and capital, the Chinese had not. Instead, the Chinese had reverted entirely to using labor power to operate multispindle machines for silk and cotton cloth.

Part of the explanation for this paradox must be attributed to the attitudes and behavior of the elite who did most of the saving and could have encouraged technological change and more investment in capital stock if it had so desired. In essence, the elite was obsessed with proper moral behavior and the proper way to rule. As Chapter 6 shows, its energy and time were chiefly spent in debating these issues by reference to complex texts which required many years to master. The cultural ethos necessary to nudge these mental efforts toward mastery of physical phenomenon by either trying to transform the environment or developing principles to understand it did not exist.

The Role of the State

THE PUBLIC SECTOR

The state was not greatly involved in the management and control of the private sector. State organs carried out ceremonial functions, maintained a modest defense force, operated a transport and communication system, and used a judicial system to preserve order. The Imperial Household Agency (*nei-wu-fu*) controlled only a small number of estates and managed certain small luxury-producing organizations. At times its revenues were large and contributed to the state's income when real need arose, but its share of total economic activity remained minuscule. Finally, the state operated salt and copper monopolies, but mostly by co-opting merchants to organize production and exchange.

In the first few decades of Manchu rule the state deeply involved itself in affairs of the economy but thereafter withdrew and allowed the private sector to evolve by its own momentum. First, the Manchus in the 1640s seized nearly 560,000 hectares of land in twenty-nine counties around Peking and gave these to ranking officers and nobles in return for their support. These lands were worked by Manchu and Chinese bond servants and managed by estate managers, many of whom had been brought to the area from Manchuria. The Manchus never recompensed the Chinese for their property. Yet in the next one hundred years much of this land reverted to the Chinese, because Manchus sold or mortgaged it to extricate themselves from debt.

Second, the Manchus attempted to carry out a land survey for the purpose of collecting a new land tax. In districts of Shantung and Honan officials tried to survey the land, but they quickly recognized that the task was too difficult: there was too much unowned or never reclaimed wasteland. They argued that this land could be registered when households began claiming it as private property, and it could then be taxed to encourage the new owners to put it to productive use. In 1663 the state tried for the third time to launch a country-wide land survey, but officials abandoned their efforts when they failed to obtain sufficient land records from landowners, and the task of surveying unreclaimed land simply became too costly and difficult.

Rather than try to regulate or even gather precise information about the entire economy, the state preferred to manage certain organizations it considered important for raising revenue, ensuring economic stability, and maintaining political power and control. The state's interests became largely confined to the production and distribution of salt and copper, the collection of grain price data, the stabilization of the harvest and the control of famine through water conservation works and grain distribution, and the supplying of food to the northern capital of Peking. The state also collected taxes which went first for financing local administration, the remainder being sent to the provincial and central governments. Finally, the state also owned properties and managed certain organizations through the *nei-wu-fu*.

The state had traditionally exercised monopoly control over salt production and distribution because of the large tax revenue to be tapped. The Ch'ing adopted the salt monopoly system developed during the Ming and refined it. In the major salt-producing areas peasants and fishermen worked the salt yard to produce a brine, then boiled or let it evaporate into crystallized salt. Peddlers and agents of merchants purchased salt at the yards and shipped it to depots on the Huai, the Yangtze, and other rivers, from which merchants then moved the salt into the provinces for sale to consumers. Some people produced and sold salt illegally from the salt yards, but in spite of such smuggling, the state managed to increase salt output significantly during the eighteenth century. Thomas A. Metzger's study of the state salt monopoly shows that rather than incorporate nearly a half million salt workers and traders into the bureaucracy, the state "allowed them to retain a private or semi-private status and also become involved in a complex web of cooperation with powerful merchants whose interests sometimes conflicted with its own" (Willmott, 1972, p. 19). To this end, the state established agencies in salt-producing regions which gave merchants permission to ship salt providing they paid a salt tax. During the eighteenth century salt production kept pace with demand and tax revenues increased for the state.

The court tried to control copper production in order to regulate the supply of money, and to this end officials established a virtual monopoly over copper production. Yunnan province supplied about 90 percent of the copper produced in the country, and between 70 to 80 percent of the copper mines were located there. Between 1740 and 1811, Yunnan produced between 10 and 11 million catties (5,000–5,500 metric tons) of copper. About 6.3 million catties (around 3,100 metric tons) were exported to Peking for minting coins; the rest went to provincial mints. The state exerted greater control over copper than salt. Merchants had to purchase a certificate to open a mine and had to sell their copper directly to a state agency responsible for shipping it from Yunnan. Numerous, small-scale merchant partnerships employed between 10 and 20 workers to mine copper, but many large mines also were operated by merchants from Hunan, Hupei, Szechwan, and Kwangtung; they formed partnerships with investments amounting to as much as 200,000 silver *taels* and employing 20,000 to 30,000 workers. Local officials were required to provide support and protection for shipping copper to the mints.

Officials had long contended that the market could not always supply sufficient grain to consumers when poor harvests caused great swings in prices, thereby bringing severe hardship to certain classes of rural people and possibly promoting violent disturbances. Like previous imperial dynasties, the Ch'ing established a grain storage system to make food and seed available on demand or to permit borrowing when private supplies were exhausted. Cities had large storehouses (ch'ang-p'ing-ts'ang), and in large towns officials used tax funds to buy and store grain. In market towns the local elite established granaries (i-ts'ang), and villages established small granaries called she-ts'ang.

The she-ts'ang system spread during the eighteenth century if Kiangsi province is at all representative of the country. In 1742 the grain storage capacity in Kiangsi amounted to 200,000 shih, but by the 1750s this had doubled. In the early nineteenth century this grain storage and distribution system appears to have operated effectively to prevent grain scarcity from causing sustained widespread distress. K. C. Hsiao and others have argued that the granary system in the late nineteenth century declined because the local elite simply found it too difficult and costly to maintain. Perhaps private grain merchants, dealers, and wealthy farmers began storing and speculating in grain, so that the market system gradually corrected for seasonal scarcity, but this is a matter deserving further research.

Currency and Fiscal Issues

In 1687 the Grand Canal resumed operation. This transport system collected the grain tax in Shantung, Honan, Kiangsu, Anhwei, Chekiang, Hupei, Hunan, and Kiangsi and shipped it to Hui-an and T'ung-chou cities for final delivery each year to Peking. About 4.5 million shih of grain or roughly 400,000 metric tons might have moved along the canal each year. This transfer required at least 6,000 boats, which moved in fleets of 30 to 100 ships. Along the canal were sixty-one military stations with an undetermined number of soldiers to supervise the collection and shipment of the grain tax. These troops had received about 6.8 million mow or around 450,000 hectares to support themselves and their families. The resources mobilized by the state to supply grain to Peking were enormous. The state purchased these resources in towns bordering the canal, and these expenditures provided the basis for much of the commercial expansion along the canal, especially in western Shantung. By the early nineteenth century some officials began questioning the usefulness of the canal, arguing that some cost saving could be achieved if grain were shipped by sea instead. In the late nineteenth century the throne ordered that tribute grain be shipped by sea.

During the early Ming period officials used the li-chia control system in villages to mobilize corvée labor to build new irrigation systems and to expand large river embankment schemes to prevent flooding. An unprecedented development of water control projects took place at that time. When the li-chia system began to disintegrate in the sixteenth century, the maintenance of these projects gradually shifted to large landholding families who mobilized their tenants and other villagers. The collapse of the Ming state also meant that the power of many local landholding families weakened, which in turn ruined many water conservation systems. The Ch'ing state at first spent large sums and ordered local elites to take the lead in rebuilding water conservation systems and irrigation networks in their areas. As these began functioning again, their annual upkeep and management again shifted to village landowners, who organized their tenants and hired laborers to make periodic repairs, and to degree holders living in market towns.

The state also managed a fiscal system that had built-in incentives to re-claim and develop land. Previous imperial systems had established local con-trol organizations which collected grain and other commodity taxes and mo-bilized corvée labor. Households had to supply labor at their own expense. The Ch'ing state broke with tradition by doing away with the corvée system. Moreover, when the state abandoned its aim of registering all land, many owners evaded the tax and those that paid did so at rates set during the Ming period. Any increased yields resulting from land improvements accrued to the owners.

The elimination of corvée labor was achieved by combining a poll tax on males (*ting*) eligible for corvée labor with a grain tax for different grades of land. By 1736 this new tax, now paid in silver, had been extended to all prov-inces except Shansi, Taiwan prefecture, and Kweichow. By the mid-eigh-teenth century the land tax had become an assigned quota collected and either paid by households designated by local officials or rotated between households by agreement with officials.

Most landowners still registered their land and paid a tax to the collecting households or to an assigned tax office. But perhaps as many as one out of three or two out of five landowners never paid a tax because they had never registered the land they had developed or purchased. As time passed, when the state required more tax revenue because of some military crisis, officials simply levied a surcharge on an area's existing land tax.

Like the Ming before it, the Ch'ing established a bimetallic system of cop-per and silver throughout the empire. In 1644 the new government created two separate offices in Peking for minting copper coins: one to mint coins for paying banner military units, the other to mint coins for hiring workers for state enterprises that produced commodities for the court. The government prohibited private minting or sale of copper abroad. In the major cities of fourteen provinces the state operated mints to produce copper coins. Con-sumers used these coins to buy goods and services and reckon their accounts. Farmers exchanged copper cash for silver to pay their land tax; handicraft managers used it to pay their workers' wages. The state increased the supply of new copper coins rapidly in the 1650s and then more gradually until 1720; thereafter the annual issue fluctuated between 230 and 437 million *wen*. But during the next fifty years the supply of copper coins failed to keep pace with demand, mainly because many people melted copper coins to make copper products for sale. Recognizing this, the state issued laws prohibiting such activity and tried to increase copper production from its mines in Yunnan.

Silver became a major component of the money supply during the Ming period. China produced little silver, but, as discussed in Chapter 2, merchants, who exchanged silk and other items for silver, brought a great supply of New World and Japanese metal into the country. During the eighteenth century silver poured in at a rate of around 2 to 4 million silver dollars every year.

It became the unit of account by which the state calculated income and expenditures. The state treasury kept its budget surpluses in silver, and the court used silver for all intragovernment money transfers. Local officials used it for their financial transactions, merchants for funding their brokers to buy goods, and rural people for paying the land tax and grain tribute tax.

The state set the official exchange rate between silver and copper, but the free market rate naturally fluctuated according to supply and demand for each currency. From the 1730s to the early 1780s, the silver-copper exchange rate fell and remained below the decreed rate. The supply of silver had increased more rapidly than that of copper, and copper coins continued to be withdrawn from circulation, mainly for commercial purposes and hoarding. From the early 1810s to the 1840s the exchange rate rose considerably above the decreed rate as the supply of silver failed to increase as fast as the supply of copper coins.

This bimetallic currency system worked sufficiently well in all economic regions to allow spending to rise as demand increased. Neither the state or private sector seemed to experience difficulty in conducting business. Shops for exchanging silver and copper flourished, and local officials controlled private counterfeiting. It was not until the 1820s and thereafter, when the money supply shrank, that a protracted deflation forced business activity in many areas to be curtailed, thus creating considerable unemployment and forcing people to seek work elsewhere.

STATE POLICIES

Why did an industrial spurt occur after 1895 but not before? The conventional explanation is that the Confucian ethos and China's social and political institutions prevented officials and the court from perceiving the necessity to modernize and catch up with the West. Assuming the court's perception of the gains from modernization changed rapidly after 1895, could values and attitudes have undergone such rapid change? Perhaps, but other explanations are also possible.

One such explanation is that many officials and members of the court, including the Dowager Empress Tz'u-hsi, did not perceive the advantages of modern technology because they believed that Chinese economic organization and technology performed satisfactorily to provide full employment and maintain adequate living standards. Another explanation is that the same group believed that the adoption of modern technology would produce profound dislocations in the economy and society and cause widespread unemployment. There are many examples of Ch'ing officials opposing the adoption of modern technology on the grounds that it might cause serious unemployment of Chinese workers. For example, the opposition to the Woosung railroad in 1865 was based on such an argument, and the governor of Kwangtung province, Mao Hung-pin, pointed out that animal-driven carts would be no match for foreign railways, so that great hardship for the people would result. Similarly, some officials opposed foreign demands to build railroads in China on the grounds that easy entry of foreigners into the country could weaken the country's defenses, which rested on natural geographic barriers. Still others expressed a concern for graveyards and for the potential disruption to native transportation and commerce. A final explanation is that the most powerful faction at court led by the Empress Dowager greatly feared any new threat to its power which modernization projects in the empire might produce. In other words the ruling elite's obsession with retaining power outweighed any concern to strengthen the empire's defenses against foreign aggression.

Indeed, between 1865 and 1895 the recovery of the economy and its gradual expansion likely lulled the court into a feeling of complacency. The land-labor ratio had increased in the fertile grain-producing areas of the lower and middle Yangtze River. From 1874 to 1893 prices rose gradually. The economy experienced neither prolonged deflation nor serious economic difficulties, with certain local exceptions: for example, economic activity declined in the Canton Delta area during the early 1860s when trade shifted to Shanghai and other ports. Again, economic decline set in along the Grand Canal in Shantung during the 1870s when grain tribute began to be transported by sea. Finally, between 1876 and 1879 Shansi, Honan, Chihli, and Shantung suffered an unprecedented three-year drought claiming 9.5 million famine victims.

Rhoads Murphey (1970) has argued that even the emergence of new city ports involved in foreign trade, like Tientsin and Hankow, did not have much effect upon the economic activity of local markets in North and Central China. The court still denied foreigners the right to build manufacturing enterprises in China, and any Chinese who wished to import foreign machinery had to obtain permission from the court which meant going through official channels. Although China had signed a series of treaties with foreign countries giving them virtual free trade rights in certain city ports, western manufactured articles barely penetrated the interior because of their high prices and marketing difficulties caused by local transit duties. The main disruptive effects of imperialism would only arise after 1895.

As late as 1900, westerners like Jeremiah W. Jenks and Robert Hart urged the Chinese to reform their monetary system by adopting the gold standard. Chinese officials rejected such advice because they recognized that the declining price of silver in the late nineteenth century had lowered the official exchange rate for foreign currencies, thus stimulating exports, curbing imports, and helping to create a favorable trade balance. The automatic devaluation of the exchange rate had definitely given China substantive foreign trade benefits for several decades. Foreign businessmen found China's monetary system complex and baffling, but Chinese merchants were accustomed to it and used it effectively.

A majority of officials also argued against suggestions that the court replace the traditional official communication system between Peking and the provinces by a modern post office. They pointed out that the old system handled the volume of despatches quickly and effectively, and that a new postal system would simply increase unemployment.

When the Ch'ing government did endorse an official's request to establish a modern industrial enterprise, the state-managed enterprise usually turned out to be an expensive failure that hardly whetted the court's appetite for more. For example, Chang Chih-tung proposed building an iron and steel works which was supposed to promote related industries, such as a domestic railroad system. The Han-yeh-p'ing Iron, Coal Mining, and Smelting Company at the very outset of operations incurred high unit production costs and made a poor showing. Chang had erred in locating the iron works too far from iron ore and coal reserves and had purchased the wrong machinery to process ore with a high phosphorous content. High unit costs meant a low profit margin, so the firm had to use its working capital to pay investors their dividends. As a result, the company never had sufficient funds to improve operating efficiency, reduce its unit costs, and increase production. The court remained unimpressed by the so-called advantages of modern manufacturing.

Had the court in the late 1860s committed itself to promoting modernization, a different pattern of economic development might of course have resulted. For example, had the court between 1867 and 1875 given more support to the Kiangnan Arsenal by providing raw materials, intermediate goods, and transport facilities, the arsenal would not have had to rely on costly imports that raised production costs prohibitively. Even without such support, the arsenal by 1875 had assembled fourteen vessels of western design, thirteen of them powered by steam. In 1875 Li Hung-chang, believing the arsenal's production costs were far too high and that western ships could be purchased more cheaply, ordered the arsenal to change its production mix and concentrate on military ordnance. As a result, China failed to modernize its maritime transportation system and had to continue to rely on foreign ships to move its goods. The Japanese imported ships too, but were able to substitute their own ships more quickly.

The Tsung-li Yamen and the Imperial Maritime Customs Services had been established by the Ch'ing court to deal with foreigners and obtain more tax revenue. But these offices possessed limited power. Furthermore, the court felt uneasy with them and used them only out of necessity. The court and officialdom alike regarded these agencies as outside the permanent structure of government. They had been created out of unusual conditions and were expected to disappear when the need for them disappeared. Such an attitude perhaps explains why no office like the Ministry of Agriculture, Industry, and Commerce was established to promote the use of modern technology until after the turn of the century. The court simply did not recognize the need to develop China. As provincial officials lacked the authority to initiate modern enterprises without permission from Peking and could not freely import western machinery, nothing could be done without leadership from Peking. Not until after the Treaty of Shimonoseki in 1895 was the legal barrier to importing machinery removed. And only after 1898 did the court reverse itself and finally pledge to promote modern business development.

Between 1879 and 1891 total tax revenues in cash and silver scarcely changed, and from 1891 to 1895 they rose only 11 percent. The state could see no compelling reason to introduce sweeping fiscal reforms. Only after 1895 did it begin to extract more revenue from the private sector: between 1895 and 1909 total taxes doubled, because the state at last committed itself to promoting industrialization. The state could only raise taxes by drastically increasing surcharges on land or imposing the *t'an k'uan* or extraordinary levies. The court permitted coins to be debased, and local officials limited the amount of such coins they would accept for tax payments, in effect raising the grain tax. As Yeh-chien Wang has pointed out (1973), levels of taxation remained remarkably low throughout the entire Ch'ing period. Had the state wanted to mobilize more revenue for modernization projects, it would have had to carry out a massive land tax reform. It is truly questionable if the Ch'ing state had such a capability.

FOREIGN TRADE

Because the state did not build new conduits to carry information and technology to merchants, artisans, and farmers, nor provide support for new industries, the response of the private sector to foreign trade after the 1860s was bound to be hesitant and slow. Yet the private sector still demonstrated considerable adaptiveness and at times even responded vigorously. New organizations of production and exchange developed in many districts. Cotton textile production underwent gradual restructuring in response to changes in the price and quality of imported yarn. The sericulture industry shifted to steam-filature-reeled yarn production in the 1890s when this new technology first became available in China. Such changes occurred primarily in the city ports where wealthy people began to congregate because the ports offered greater security for property and life with less interference from the state.

In the hinterland, however, painful readjustment and rising unemployment sometimes resulted. Machine-made yarn completely displaced hand-

135

spun yarn in Shensi and Kweichow, and in many other provinces the displacement was widespread. The shipping of grain by sea on steam-powered ships instead of along the Grand Canal on traditional junks and the displacement of water traffic by railroads stretching across Hopei and Shantung created much unemployment and social unrest in many regions.

The major development in the handicraft cotton textile industry after 1870 was the rapid increase of yarn imports, which rose some fortyfold by 1900. Domestic prices had risen gradually, while foreign yarn prices declined below those of native yarn; in addition foreign yarn was of far higher quality than the domestic. As a result spinners could not compete, and entrepreneurs found it more profitable to buy foreign yarn for the warp and combine it with handspun weft to produce a more durable and higher quality cloth. Meanwhile, hand spinning began to disappear. In 1875 virtually all yarn was handspun, but by 1905 probably only about half still was. After 1900 foreign and local machine-spun yarn mills began appearing in Shanghai and Tientsin. Their main buyers were weaving establishments in rural areas. Over this same period cloth imports rose only twofold, fluctuating greatly every few years. Cloth imports circulated mainly in the city ports, only entering the countryside where local weaving was sparse.

The trade expansion of the 1870s and 1880s stimulated silk exports, especially from Kwangtung. In 1881 there were only 10 or 11 silk-weaving factories, but by 1891 there were 50 or 60. By 1906 most of these were concentrated in Shun-te county (24) and Nan-hai county (45), with others in Hsin-hui, San-shui, and Hsiang-shan counties. A total of 176 establishments employed 60,500 village women. Although China's exports of silk products steadily rose over this period and silk producers' sales in the world market were profitable, by 1900 China's share of reeled silk in the world market was being reduced by Japan and Italy whose machine filatures produced more silk yarn of even higher quality. Japan had adopted modern technology in silk reeling and sericulture in the early 1870s, but China did not shift to the machine filature process until the mid-1890s. In 1894 there were only 10 firms in Shanghai reeling silk by this new method, and 7 of these were foreign, but by 1910 there were 58 reeling establishments.

The usual explanation for this delay is that: (1) the government did not encourage new silk reeling and sericulture methods; (2) domestic producers remained content with traditional methods; (3) the costs of establishing silk reeling mills were too high; (4) state taxes bore too heavily upon merchants; and (5) quality control of silk products declined as adulteration occurred. The first factor is probably most crucial. Had information about changing world silk market conditions in the 1870s been gathered, evaluated, and taken seriously by any authoritative group, the sericulture industry might have modernized much sooner. Chinese silk producers could have benefited even more than they did from world trade growth if they had shifted sooner to the modern filature process. But ignorance of these market conditions remained widespread. When businessmen began to see that market conditions had changed, they shifted quickly to modern filatures. Their ability to do so suggests that the scarcity of capital and the tax burden were not crippling. And most likely any firms that actually practiced adulteration lost their customers.

The emergence of new establishments using steam filatures greatly increased the demand for cocoons and raised the price of raw silk, producing a sharp change in the household handicraft industry. Many households formerly reeling silk now found it more profitable to supply only cocoons and raw silk, whereas those households that remained in reeling experienced a decline in demand for their output.

The tea industry neither experienced an organizational change nor acquired modern technology. Yet tea exports increased after the 1860s, then declined after 1900, apparently because of competition from Japan, Ceylon, and India, whose tea was both superior in quality and cheaper than Chinese tea.

During the 1870s and 1880s the Chinese tea industry demonstrated its ability to increase supply to meet rising demand. In Hunan, for example, tenants specializing in tea production shifted more land into tea shrubs, and tea growers hired more workers. More merchants entered the market and established tea firing and drying establishments in which the processed tea was packaged before being shipped to the coast. These processing firms operated in a highly competitive, localized industry that lacked controls over the quality and price of raw tea. They made no effort to investigate world developments in the tea trade so as to prepare for change, and they failed to learn of the scientifically planned tea plantations of South Asia until much too late. For reasons already mentioned, the state also failed to take the lead in providing information and improving the quality of tea.

Agriculture responded to new foreign trade stimuli by supplying more industrial crops such as beans, cotton, hides, oil seeds, tung oil, sugar, tobacco, hemp, and animal products. Between 1876 and 1895 the export value of industrial crops rose from 3.8 to nearly 18 million Haikwan *taels*, but silk and tea exports only rose from 62 to 72 million Haikwan *taels*. Exports of industrial crops continued to rise rapidly, and between 1911 and 1915 their value exceeded that of silk and tea exports.

Was the expansion of agricultural exports achieved at the expense of grain production for the home market, in particular for cities? Grain imports to supply the cities did rise steadily over this period, but agricultural import and export trends alone cannot tell us whether production on a per capita basis for the home market rose, remained constant, or declined.

The following agricultural trends are only conjectural because production data are not available. Between 1870 and 1910 the average crop area per farm in the North China region, Szechwan, the upper Yangtze region, Kweichow, and Fukien gradually declined. In the lower Yangtze region, it rose until the early 1890s and then fell, but not to the level of 1850. Therefore, as the rural population gradually recovered during this period, the crop land-labor ratio fell. Second, for at least nine provinces—the agriculturally rich, largest, most populated areas—after 1865 nearly half the districts frequently reported below normal harvests. Part of the cause for this seems to have been the constant flooding of the Yellow River. Third, after 1900 certain districts in North China increased their crop specialization in response to the new trade opportunities opened up by expanding urbanization, foreign trade, and railway development. Under these circumstances, households could have obtained increased returns to labor by supplying more specialized products for local trade and export and still maintained constant grain production per capita.

The comments of travelers and residents give us some sense of the state of agriculture during this period. The laconic remarks in the reports submitted by the European officials of the Imperial Maritime Customs merely describe the annual fluctuation of the harvest and unchanging rural conditions. The comments of Japanese travelers invariably stress the poverty and backwardness of rural areas as compared to those in Japan, but conclude that a great potential for developing agriculture existed. Finally, the Chinese themselves did not profess any great alarm at the state of affairs in agriculture. By the 1910s, however, some writers nostalgically looked back on earlier decades as a period of missed opportunities when new policies might have increased production.

Qualitative evidence suggests that agriculture perhaps did manage to expand after 1865 so that production per capita rose slightly or at worst remained constant. The scope for increasing yield within this agrarian system was certainly still very great. The introduction of new seeds and fertilizers, the prevention of crop loss through improved water control and weather reporting, and the restoration of land that had suffered ecological destruction were only a few of the measures that could have been initiated by the state and the local elite.

Two existing economic problems probably became more serious after the 1860s. Both required state policies to correct, but the remedies would not have been expensive, and local markets would have functioned more efficiently thereafter. The difficulty of deploying factors of production from organizations already in decline (as seen, for example, in the history of the Grand Canal) became more serious in the late nineteenth century. The other problem was ecological: many examples of deforestation, ruined farmland, and ineffective water control can be cited to show its growing severity. The new course set by the Yellow River through Hopei and Shantung caused salination and drainage problems in many areas after periods of prolonged flooding. Numerous lakes along the Grand Canal had been used as a source of water to elevate the canal's water level when junk fleets moved northward. After many communities along the canal diverted canal water to irrigate fields, there arose drainage and salination difficulties along the canal, and severe damage to the canal itself.

International Comparisons

By premodern standards, the Chinese economy over most of the Ch'ing period—especially before the 1820s—was largely successful. On an intensively cultivated agrarian base, it supported a growing population, permitted a proliferation of market systems, and, with few exceptions, avoided prolonged or widespread famine. The people's livelihoods were protected, and long-range household planning for increased prosperity was facilitated. At the same time, state revenues were regarded as sufficient to meet perceived needs. In support of these objectives, the money supply expanded at a fairly stable rate, factor and product markets functioned rather efficiently, and grain reserves and distribution practices alleviated occasional severe food shortages. Under conditions of general poverty typical of premodern societies, the Chinese may well have achieved as much success in meeting perceived household and state needs as any other people prior to the modern era.

China was unusual in its key organizational underpinnings, which permitted the private sector to operate relatively unfettered. Among them were the practices of customary law and the flexible policies of state organizations themselves. Households continually entered into exchanges with each other or shared resources, and customary law agreements, especially when formalized in written contracts, made promises fairly binding and minimized uncertainty. Households also combined to form economic organizations like merchant partnerships, guilds, and irrigation associations. The ability of households to work together for certain common goals and still produce benefits and rewards for each household in the collectivity greatly depended upon their compliance to customary law. The state, on the other hand, left many decisions and transactions to the private sector and did not itself engage in costly intervention and regulation. Yet state organizations helped to offset occasional, critical scarcities within the private sector by maintaining flood control projects, distributing grain when necessary, and expanding the money supply to meet demand. Low taxes gave local areas more flexibility in using their own surplus resources.

In the mid-Ch'ing period, China's economy combined a high degree of decentralization with the extensive use of money, credit, and contracts, the organization of production and exchange within highly competitive markets, and unfettered household choice. In Japan and Russia, to the extent that similar modern features evolved during the seventeenth, eighteenth, and early nineteenth centuries, they were accompanied by growing centralization and a greater urban concentration of resources. Clearly neither central nor local governments in China exerted the leadership seen in these other two countries for overcoming patterns of decentralization.

As late as the mid-1890s imperial China had not made much headway in reforming its fiscal system, revamping its laws, and encouraging private enterprise to adopt foreign technology. The military defeats China suffered at the hands of the English in 1842 and again in 1856–1857 and at the hands of the French in 1881–1884 never unleashed the shock waves produced in Russia between 1853 and 1856 by the Crimean War or in Japan in 1853 by the arrival in Uraga Bay of Perry's "Black" ships. Russian and Japanese leaders recognized more quickly than China's rulers the need to launch reforms to strengthen their economic foundations and upgrade their military power. They turned to their privileged classes, the nobility and samurai, for help.

The existence of a large, privileged class, with broad claims to resources and income, can be of enormous assistance to the state. The Russian nobility and the Japanese samurai possessed qualities of leadership that could be channeled into the successful establishment of modern enterprises. Moreover, these privileged classes had access not only to their own great, though varying, personal wealth, but, through their elaborate social networks, to the wealth of others. The tsarist and Meiji rulers initiated fiscal reforms that encouraged them to develop new sources of income, in part by cutting off the old. For example, the Meiji government eliminated the traditional stipends to daimyo and samurai, but still provided them with bonds that yielded some income. The emancipation of the serfs in Russia reduced noble landholdings and eliminated corvée labor, but the nobility in turn received compensation from the former serfs or the state. In both countries, there was a widespread attitude that the old elite status and privileges were decrepit and had to be changed. State leadership in reform coupled with a sudden change in economic circumstances for the old elite proved a stimulus to modernization without any parallel in China.

CHAPTER FIVE

Social Integration

V IEWED THROUGH OUR HISTORICAL TELESCOPE, CH'ING CHINA stands out as a prosperous-looking giant among the multitude of premodern societies. With its record of sustained population growth, its increasingly dense distributions of periodic markets, its unparalleled numbers of very large cities, its widely dispersed and nationally coordinated civilian and military bureaucracies, its fluid social mobility patterns, its reliance on literacy, and its limited but still important reliance on achieved status and formal contracts for an unusual array of personal relationships, China cuts a robust figure. These long-nurtured features bear witness to an extraordinary premodern society nearing its peak by the eighteenth century.

Exceptional as China may have been over a long stretch of history, were its social conditions in the Ch'ing dynasty conducive to rapid modernization in response to contacts with already modernizing countries? If we measure China's preparedness not against the immense variety of societies scattered across the entire sweep of premodern history, but against that of Japan and Russia—who were to become rapidly modernizing latecomers—as they entered the nineteenth century, the Chinese record can be assessed in a new and more meaningful light. In terms of the growth, distribution, and mobilization of human resources, how did social integration (the interdependence of the units within a society) in Ch'ing China compare with that in Japan and Russia? By making comparisons with Japan and Russia, can we clarify the elements of social structure that stalled China's mobilization effort during the late nineteenth and early twentieth centuries? Can we also uncover potential assets that lingered on awaiting the catalyst of a new environment? If these efforts prove to be reasonably successful, then we should also be able to pinpoint in Part Two steps essential for accelerating the pace of modernization.

China in the sixteenth century abounds with evidence of population growth, of large-scale upward mobility through the well-lubricated channels of the examination system, of urban expansion and organizational innovation. The seventeenth century bears the imprint of civil war and of further disorder following the Manchu takeover: decline in the middle third of the century followed by recovery may well have left the population and the urban sector no larger at the end of the century than they were at the beginning. By the onset of the eighteenth century, Chinese society had resumed its dynamic thrust, entering a period of unprecedented long-run premodern population explosion, of apparent organizational vitality, and at least on a local level, of smoothly functioning traditional patterns seemingly able to persist in perpetuity with occasional slight renovation. As indicated in Chapter 3 and later in this chapter as well, there were already factors at work in the eighteenth century detrimental to future modernization. The record of the nineteenth century belies the basis for optimism in the previous century; signs of possible overpopulation (or at least of increasing pressure on existing resources) came as a prelude to abrupt depopulation followed by gradual recovery, and inherited forms of social organization failed to meet challenges of both internal and external origin. These special problems of the nineteenth century, which were accompanied by several major rebellions, may have exhausted China's ability to respond decisively to the onslaught of modernizing states, but apart from the war-torn years of the 1850s and 1860s, they probably did not undermine the further gradual maturation of premodern structures.

However imprecisely this chronology may characterize and lump together aspects of societal development that require exact definition and measurement, it conveys an image (which will be supported below) of sporadic or gradual evolution in the Ming and Ch'ing periods rather than one of sustained and rapid premodern development. When compared with the more spectacular changes in Japan and Russia during the same centuries, the indicators of social change reveal China to be already well endowed in some ways, but markedly less dynamic in others. China in the mid-nineteenth century appears to have been less favorably prepared for modernization than Japan or Russia.

Between 1550 and 1850, China exhibited a mixed record of resource growth and mobilization. The population increased greatly and kept increasing at a pace that at least matched and may well have exceeded the growth in food supplies and other resources. Thus per capita social indices reveal no striking changes. The percentage of Chinese in cities and the pattern of social stratification remained roughly as before. No marked organizational restructuring can be detected. Indeed, as has been shown in the preceding chapters, the leadership took little interest in reorganizing communities or extracting increased quantities of resources. China boasted many of the world's largest cities and a dense network of marketing places, but these conditions did not reflect any rush of new migrants to cities or any widespread emulation of new styles of urban consumption. Beginning as perhaps the world's most developed society in 1550, China did not experience any sharp break with past patterns. Even so, China's impressive legacy from earlier periods left it fairly well endowed along many of the dimensions to be considered below, particularly with regard to local conditions.

During the half-century after 1850, China's initial modernization under the impact of treaty ports, foreign trade, and military inferiority proceeded exceedingly slowly. Timid government initiatives sank in a sea of inertia. No sign could be found of such measures of substantial early modernization as a demographic transition with falling mortality and fertility, a marked upsurge in social mobility, a sharp rise in literacy, an urban takeoff, an appreciable decline in periodic markets, a breakdown in the extended family ideal, or a shift to a modern large-scale governmental bureaucracy. In fact, starting with a high base level on many of these measures, China may even have been changing in a direction contrary to what is expected as modernization takes root. For each of these indicators of transformation and for others as well, we should seek to find out how the lack of dynamism after 1850 reflects or was a consequence of the earlier conditions of China's society. In Chapter 11 we treat the period after 1900 when social change gathered steam amid a complex interplay of assets and liabilities for modernization inherited from the past.

Human Resources

POPULATION

In a premodern setting characterized by high fertility, high mortality, and low rates of immigration and emigration (conditions China shared with a large number of societies), population growth can result from modest increases of already high birth rates or, more typically, from reductions in death rates. It can best be understood through age-specific birth and death rates, which unfortunately are lacking for premodern China. In their absence it is necessary to work with highly aggregate statistics of the temporal and spatial components of the natural increase in population. For the analysis of population growth, regional data offer a better starting point than national data. They also take us one step closer to the important task of distinguishing the differential impact of population growth at the level of the household and village, in cities and counties, and in a variety of organizational settings.

Table 5.1 summarizes the broad currents of population change by region. The data for 1850 and 1950 are based on relatively complete enumerations at roughly these dates, the 1750 statistics blend somewhat later provincial break-

Table 5.1   Population of China, by region (in millions).

	REGION	1550	1750	1850	1900	1950
NE	(Manchuria)	1	1	2	5	41
N	(Hopei, Shantung, Shansi, Honan)	40	60	97	105	142
NW	(Shensi, Kansu)	10	17	29	29	41
E–C	(Kiangsu, Anhwei, Chekiang)	41	55	112	96	96
C	(Kiangsi, Hunan, Hupei)	30	37	79	74	74
SE	(Fukien, Kwangtung, Kwangsi)	16	25	52	56	63
SW	(Szechwan, Kweichow, Yunnan)	12	20	58	65	93
		150	215	430	430	550

Sources of Data: These data rely heavily on statistics presented by Ping-ti Ho, *Studies on the Population of China, 1368-1953,* pp. 281-83. The 1750 figures total 215 million rather than the 180 million noted in Ho's appendix (p. 281), which corresponds to Ho's conclusion that the actual population at this time "was at least 20 percent more than the officially registered population" (p. 46). The estimates for 1550 are loosely based on provincial population data of 1393, on scattered gazetteer figures for the late Ming and early Ch'ing dynasties, and on impressions of which areas were growing faster than others. Totals may not add up because of rounding.

downs with an estimated 1750 national total, while the figures for 1550 and, to a lesser extent 1900, represent educated guesses. Even if the 1550 figures were found to be in error by as much as 20 or 30 million persons, it would still be clear that between 1550 and 1750 China's total population rose fairly slowly; these estimates indicate an average annual rate of growth of roughly 2 persons per 1,000.

1. For the years before 1750 regional variations are not pronounced, but the least densely settled extremities of the empire—the northwest, the southwest and the southeast—all exceeded the national growth rate, as most likely did the north to a lesser extent.

2. Grain production as well as other economic indicators could easily have kept pace with or even somewhat exceeded population growth.

3. Consequently, for this period, including the first century of the Ch'ing dynasty, there is no reason to regard the level of natural increase of population as a barrier to improved living conditions.

During the period 1750 to 1850, and perhaps beginning somewhat before, China's population growth accelerated and assumed a different regional distribution. The average annual rate of growth for the country as a whole approached 8 per 1,000, although the rate climbed to an even higher peak in the eighteenth century and then gradually declined. The fastest growth prevailed in the southwest, where immigration from other regions proved important. Elsewhere annual provincial growth mostly ranged between 5 and 9 persons per 1,000 residents.

Sustained population growth at a remarkably high rate for a premodern society occurred in China for roughly one century. About that the records are unambiguous. The impact of that growth has proven more troublesome to assess. Despite the introduction of New World crops and some expansion of acreage and improvements in yields, agricultural production at best kept pace with the rising population. Even if Dwight H. Perkins (1969) is correct in his assessment of long-term stability in the critical relationship between people and food, it is unlikely that the same generalization would hold for the period 1750–1850—the century of peak population growth. There is every likelihood that in this decisive period on the eve of the new challenge from abroad, the natural increase in population exceeded the rate of agricultural development; neither a noteworthy internal migration to sparsely settled areas nor a marked increase in agricultural productivity in already settled areas accompanied the national population spurt. Even if the most optimistic conclusion is drawn that a constant per capita output resulted, China can still be distinguished from Japan and Russia, which were adding to their per capita agricultural surplus during the same years.

Circumstantial evidence points to the conclusion that the population growth undermined China's foundation for responding to exogenous forces of modernization. The highest rates occurred in the regions most capable of generating a surplus in rice. The amount of rice produced did increase substantially, but it was largely consumed locally in the central, east-central, and southeast regions. Within local marketing communities the circulation of resources reached a high volume; however, only a relatively small amount trickled into the cities. Had population growth been curtailed, a larger part of this potential surplus could have been channeled into long-distance commerce and urban consumption. In turn, had the surplus been extracted through taxation, rents, or commerce, pressures would have mounted—as they did in Japan—for households to make decisions that would have led to a reduction in the population increase.

By 1850, following the gradual slowdown in population growth during the first half of the nineteenth century, the Chinese population was approaching a new equilibrium at approximately twice its 1750 size. At best, this equilibrium rested on about the same balance as before between population and material resources. At worst, it signified a meaningful reduction in the margin above subsistence. The devastation of wartime conditions during the 1850s and the 1860s, accompanied or followed by severe famines in northern provinces during the 1870s, even caused population decline in certain regions. After a period of recovery, an improved land-person ratio may have contributed to better material conditions. And increased rents and taxes may have absorbed some of this surplus, accounting for the absence of full recovery in the size of the population within certain provinces. Yet, for the crucial period of 1750–1850, our main finding is one of population growth limiting the potential for present and future resource mobilization, especially in the regions where that potential could have best been realized.

This century (1750–1850) of rapid population growth by premodern standards may have sealed China's fate in the subsequent period of initial responses to the forces of modernization. During the same century in Japan, where highly intensive agriculture also resulted in high population densities, the population had remained virtually stable while per capita income rose. In Russia population growth for at least part of the period benefited from vastly expanded grain production in previously sparsely settled areas. In China, on the other hand, the premodern social structure somehow favored the survival of expanding numbers even at the expense of existing welfare and comforts (several of the following sections will return to this point). The pivotal period when the old equilibrium was upset must have been the three generations before 1820 when growth reached a peak. It is, therefore, necessary to trace back to the height of Ch'ing prosperity the conditions supportive of continued population growth that only gradually, and perhaps belatedly, succumbed to harsher economic circumstances.

China may have been an early case of a nation strangled, for purposes of later modernization, by its own fertility. It is easy to lose sight of this because China's population explosion occurred precociously, prior to substantial contacts with modernizing countries. The earlier surplus that might have been converted to new purposes in the transformation after 1850 was partially dissipated through the century of growth between 1750 and 1850.

In comparison with other premodern countries, the sustained Chinese growth after 1750 seems to indicate a low variance around a fairly high annual population growth rate. Not only did China in this period apparently suffer from relatively few of the subsistence crises so widely recorded elsewhere, it must have achieved both a high degree of local prosperity and a relatively equitable system of distribution supplemented by adequate grain flows between areas. The small fraction of the world's arable land located in China managed to support up to one-third of the world's population with what seems to have been for most a satisfactory diet. The mid-Ch'ing period clearly stands out for premodern conditions conducive to population growth—along with the seventeenth century in Japan and the eighteenth and early nineteenth centuries in Russia—but in China growth continued unchecked even as resources, potentially available as surpluses, were depleted.

In contrast, China's population did not grow as rapidly as that of other countries between 1850 and 1950. It dropped sharply from roughly one-third to barely one-quarter of the world's population during that time. The minor redistributions of population that occurred within the country probably enhanced its capacity, after a period of recuperation, to generate a surplus for economic development. The rice-growing provinces in the east-central and central regions did not fully recover from the population losses suffered during the Taiping rebellion, while regions less devastated by war managed slight population gains. The southeast continued to be the source of emigrants leaving China. The new equilibrium between birth and death rates—a return to

146

low rates of growth—that prevailed nearly everywhere remained premodern in nature; mortality was not yet showing the effects of new techniques for extending the average age of life, and fertility continued at a high rate. In contrast, some other areas of the world, including Japan and Russia, experienced declines in mortality that resulted in increased numbers reaching the years of childbirth and an accelerated pace of population growth.

Two further aspects of population growth should be mentioned. First, changes in the average age of females at marriage and, of indirect interest, in the percentage of men who never married could provide some clues about population growth rates. A lowering of these figures could have contributed to the doubling of population in a century, and these figures may have risen again, reducing total fertility. Indeed, as population growth proceeded, it may have taken longer to accumulate the money needed for a bride price, thus raising the age at marriage. In any case, the age of marriage in China remained much lower than in western Europe, and a higher percentage of women married. (According to the Buck survey data for 1929–1931, the mean age at first marriage was remarkably constant from region to region at 21 for men and 17 to 18 for women. See George Barclay et al., 1976, p. 609.)

Second, changes in the sex ratio may reveal a fluctuating incidence of female infanticide, which apparently remained far higher in China throughout this period than in Japan or other countries for which data exist. According to statistics for North China, the ratio of men to women may have dipped below 115:100 in times of considerable population growth and climbed as high as 120:100 at other times. For instance, Ch'ing hsien (Chihli province) reveals an adult sex ratio of 119:100 around 1875, while more rapidly growing Chinan fu (Shantung province) had an overall adult sex ratio of 109:100 in 1837. Wide variations between localities may be studied for new insight into this ratio. The possibility must be considered that increased female infanticide rates operated as a brake on population expansion during the nineteenth century. Underenumeration of the female population may also be a factor (Rozman, 1982).

Later marriage and increased female infanticide may not have been the preferred means for curtailing the growth in population, but they were available. Explanations for the slowness to perceive this need and the relative insensitivity of the fertility schedule to pressure upon agricultural resources must be sought in later sections of this chapter, including those concerned with family structure and inheritance practices.

What were the consequences of sustained population growth in eighteenth- and nineteenth-century China? A land squeeze occurred at the level of the household and the village. The practice of equal inheritance among all surviving sons, which incidentally may have been a major barrier to population control, led to an increasing fragmentation of holdings. New households appeared in large numbers, each with a reduced acreage within the same village boundaries. The number of villages expanded much more slowly. Despite the prolonged period of increasing population density, and shrinking arable land per capita, neither households nor villages made any discernable structural reforms. No mechanisms existed for adjusting to this changed situation. As a consequence, households had less to pass on to their surviving sons and villages had more claimants for their limited land. Perhaps the rising unemployment during the second quarter of the nineteenth century referred to by Ramon H. Myers in Chapter 4 can also be attributed to these conditions.

Population growth over a wider area evoked two contrasting responses. Where the response did not require government initiative as in the expansion of cities and the proliferation of marketing centers, per capita rates did not fall. Chinese urbanization remained about 6 percent, and the number of local markets rose in proportion to the population. Where the emperor and state bureaucracy would have had to take vigorous action to increase the number of counties or to add new officials, however, little or nothing was done. The average population per county doubled between 1750 and 1850 without remotely corresponding additions to the official bureaucracy. The high degree of decentralization customary in premodern times became exacerbated, diluting the potential for later official efforts to increase control and coordination. Complexities of administering large numbers may have contributed to the signs of declining administrative efficiency. As at the village level, awareness of population growth did not elicit any meaningful governmental action to deal with its consequences.

STRATIFICATION AND OCCUPATIONAL DISTRIBUTION

Major changes in stratification are difficult to document for the period 1550 to 1850. Of course, after their arrival in Peking the Manchus displaced the old Ming imperial family on the top rungs of the ladder in favor of their bannermen comprised of Manchus, Mongols, and early supporters among Han Chinese. This strengthened the position of a military elite, some of whom now assumed high civilian posts, but it did not lead to an upgrading of the military profession in general. Otherwise the four idealized occupational categories—the literati, the peasants, the artisans, and the merchants—all persisted roughly as before. Scholar-officials and degree holders aspiring to prestige and official position constituted the highest calling, peasants were a diverse classification bridging all income and status distinctions, and artisans and merchants, despite being at the bottom of the idealized rankings, also exhibited great diversity, from the lowly hawker to the powerful salt merchant.

To describe the distinctive characteristics of Chinese stratification the following labels are appropriate: (1) open-class society, (2) single-career society, (3) area-wide occupational specialization in the export of talent, (4) petty landlordism based on an overwhelming prevalence of small land concentrations, and (5) tenancy rather than wage labor among the agricultural poor. In each of these respects China contrasts with many premodern societies, including Japan and Russia. We will elaborate on these terms and then take up the urban population separately.

1. The open-class nature of Chinese society refers to the absence of legal barriers blocking upward or downward mobility into any of the major social strata. What made China distinctive was the continuous flux in its elite population, broadly defined to consist of the literate degree holders (some of whom received recognition in the form of official posts), landlords, rich peasants, and (actually, if not ideally) wealthy merchants.

Two avenues provided access to this select 5 percent or so of the total population: literacy and advanced education, as demonstrated in government-organized examinations, and wealth, normally invested in land, but easily transferred to commerce or money lending. While many degree holders came from well-to-do landlord families and others converted their degrees into wealth, the overlap was far from complete, and these two criteria were clearly differentiated. Holders of lower degrees did not necessarily enjoy much wealth, and until the nineteenth century big landowners had difficulty ensuring that at least one family member secured a degree. Aspirants to both degrees and landholdings were numerous, and examinations open to nearly all as well as inheritance practices contributed to a steady turnover. For a time during the early Ming dynasty, movement between social strata had been more restricted, but from at least the sixteenth century, legal barriers scarcely interfered with a fluid society.

2. Aspirations for official appointments and examination degrees so dominated as an ideal among the educated and wealthy that China can be labeled a single-career society. Yet, as F. W. Mote points out in Chapter 3, from the middle of the Ming dynasty acceptance of alternative careers became increasingly evident. Mostly these careers were linked in some way to the careers of officials and not only made possible but encouraged the acceptance of officials' values and the imitation of their life styles. The ideal continued to dominate through imitation as other careers emerged. For instance, estate managers, pharmacologists, and irrigation technicians acquired specialized skills, which they often put at the service of the degree holders. China's open-class pattern, however, continued to focus attention on the most desired career, in contrast to Japan and Russia, where closed classes made elite positions inaccessible to most and channeled interests into a multiplicity of careers.

Other careers existed as consolation prizes, or, with the family's future in mind, as a means to gain resources necessary for pursuing the road to officialdom. Indeed, the brevity of official appointment, even for the most successful, meant that different careers might easily be considered. These careers did not involve specialized professional training and did not become attractive alternatives to government service. Rather there seems to have been a readiness to shift among various long-established positions compatible with literati status, such as teaching by the classical methods. For some, investments in land, trade, or pawnshops provided income that made it unnecessary to pursue a career or enabled them to engage in voluntary community work, such as contributing to public works projects.

3. A striking element of Chinese stratification is the degree to which the prospects of people engaged in specialized jobs away from home depended on support from others from their place of origin. Some counties developed a reputation for exporting individuals with particular skills, such as talented bankers or private secretaries, and contacts were established that ensured continued opportunities for native sons. Organizations of merchants from the same home areas occupied an important place in the life of major cities. Native place ties operated in other premodern societies too; yet the lack of corporate organizations, professional groupings, and self-perpetuating urban elites in China increased their potential importance.

4. Perhaps because of the open-class nature of the society, substantial population growth, and equal inheritance practices, land ownership did not become concentrated. Many small landlords rented out scattered plots, but with rare exceptions individuals did not accumulate large concentrations or consolidate their holdings. Regional and local variations were considerable. Only in a few areas did the corporate holdings of lineages represent a major share of the land. In general, the total holdings of small owners dwarfed those of large owners; no estate mentality emerged in Ch'ing China. Indeed, well over 90 percent of landholdings belonged to private owners, motivated by the objective of maximizing household income. A clear contrast emerges between Chinese fragmented holdings and the aristocratic or serfowner estates of Europe.

5. Given the prevalence of scattered plots continually divided through inheritance or sale, in most regions hiring labor semed less advantageous than self-cultivation or renting to tenants. Tenancy, which carried with it various legal rights, predominated as the mode of working holdings beyond what the landowner's family could farm. This combined with the small-scale landlordism created a village environment without sharp gradations. The large numbers of part-owners and part-tenants blurred the line often found elsewhere between landowners and hired or serf labor. More will be made of this point in Part Two.

Data from the *Chin-men pao'chia t'u-shuo* (a valuable collection of local maps and population records) for T'ien-chin county (Chihli province) in 1842 add some specificity to our comments on social stratification. This unusually urban county dominated by the Grand Canal and the Hai River linking Tientsin to the sea cannot be taken as representative of China, but it can illustrate some conclusions that we believe have wider applicability. For instance, in the sixteen rural subareas into which we divided the county, the percentage of households recorded as hired labor ranged between 6.3 and 43.2, with all but three subareas between the minimum figure and 16.6 percent (Rozman, 1982). For the county as a whole, the number of registered ordinary households (*yan-hu*) equaled almost six times the number of hired labor households. In rural subareas peddlers were as numerous as or outnumbered shopkeepers; however, in Tientsin shopkeepers were twice as numerous

The listing of households by social strata may well indicate the perceived status order of the period. At the top of the hierarchy were degree holders followed by salt merchants. Shopkeepers preceded ordinary households, who preceded service personnel such as government clerks and runners. Omitting minor categories, next on the list were hired laborers and peddlers. Finally at the bottom were boatmen, fishermen, and then beggars, priests, and monks. This hierarchy reinforces widespread impressions that religious personnel lacked the clout in China that they had in many other countries and that degree holders enjoyed top billing.

Separate county surveys of social strata completed at the beginning of the twentieth century in northern China permit us to obtain a general impression of the division of the population into the four officially designated classes. These surveys reveal that in eighteen counties with close to 4.5 million total population, 90 percent of the 1,880,000 occupational designations referred to peasants, 4 percent to merchants, 3 percent to literati, and roughly 2.5 percent to artisans. Another listing for roughly one-fifth of a prefectural city in Shantung during the 1870s (in which close to 4,000 persons were enumerated) indicates that 55 percent of the households engaged in commerce, 11 percent in crafts, and 11 percent in government (Yamane Yukio, 1963). Of the remainder of the households, 9 percent derived a primary income from agriculture, 6 percent were degree holders or engaged in educational pursuits, 3 percent were soldiers, and the remaining 5 percent comprised religious personnel as well as miscellaneous categories. The high percentage in commerce, particularly the large numbers dealing with foodstuffs and the marketing of other rural products, highlights the city's dependence on the countryside, while the figure of 90 percent peasants probably masks the nonagricultural pursuits peasants engaged in on a part-time basis.

Within urban areas, the pattern of social stratification displayed some striking characteristics. Cities fell far short of a monopoly in the concentration of wealthy customers since much of the luxury consumption in Chinese society occurred in rural areas. As a result, the distribution of merchants and artisans was unusually rural oriented. Perhaps somewhat exceptionally, only one of sixteen rural subareas in T'ien-chin county recorded fewer than 5 percent of households as shopkeepers and peddlers. Craft production in particular developed on an extremely small scale, and artisans constituted a smaller portion of the urban population than is usually true in other countries. Moreover, government personnel were not numerous in China. On the other hand, merchants and peddlers, many of whom engaged in rural-urban exchange, represented a large percentage of the urban total.

From the above, it seems reasonable to visualize Chinese cities—even more than other premodern cities—as occasional switches along the numerous tracks linking villages, primarily shuttling the flow of resources between destinations. Even the composition of a city's population better reflects its role as a modest integrative force than as a model for emulation or as an engine capable of generating substantial change. Cities did not stand out as places of residence for persons who ranked high in the social hierarchy. Apart from a small number of officials in administrative centers, government personnel were either soldiers or clerks and runners—the much demeaned subordinates and hangers-on of the magistrate. Absentee landlords—at least until late in the Ch'ing dynasty—remained a rather weak force. Lower degree holders had little incentive to migrate into a setting where what modest chance they had for influence, prestige, and special service occupations such as teaching would be squandered. Administrative capitals without dense commercial concentrations did register a disproportionate number of degree holders and, of course, large cities supported powerful merchants, but the overall pattern blunted the image of elitist urban living. A move to the city often meant dividing the lineage and simultaneously maintaining entrepreneurial activities in the city and at the original, often rural, location.

The most evident changes during the initial thrust of modernization occurred in the cities. Probably somewhat more wealth began to be channeled into cities with an increase in absentee landowners and with growing commercial specialization for export and long-distance markets. The prestige of examination degrees declined, leaving it unclear which occupations warranted respect. Perhaps the most changes can be observed in another dimension of stratification, that is, power. The relative position of the magistrate within the city declined, the privileged bannermen concentrated in several large cities became a less potent force, and the magistrate's subordinates lost some of their inadequately checked power to collect taxes and preserve order. Urban wealth by the beginning of the twentieth century could be more readily converted into influence and power.

In the treaty ports, a new commercial elite, rather removed from the traditional status hierarchy as a result of its foreign connections, developed. Moreover, throughout the country the unity of the elements that made up the elite seems to have been gradually shaken by the wartime devastations, foreign intrusions, and policy responses of the mid- and late nineteenth century. The opening of additional channels of elite mobility created a problem of accommodating new forces in old coalitions. Elite frustration, especially on the part of lower degree holders losing out to villagers with more localized sources of authority, may have mounted. By the end of the century, the longstanding unity of the elite coalition that had cemented the integration of Chinese society was showing cracks.

In brief, the overall pattern of social stratification in Ch'ing China appears to have been highly stable; it erected few legal barriers to social mobility and operated with little government involvement. China's dispersed elite largely fended for itself; it had few official employment opportunities and few

demands placed upon it. The Chinese elite straddled city and village, remaining largely rural and only temporarily living outside of local systems.
While members of the Japanese and Russian service nobilities grasped at
higher levels of urban consumption and new sources of revenue to support
them, the Chinese elite continued to strive for achievement that might lead to
recruitment into the small bureaucracy or to invest in land to support local
consumption. Then in the 1860s and later, when the dispossessed samurai
and serfowners struggled for sources of income and employment that could
compensate for lost privileges, the Chinese elite still had no reason to feel
dispossessed or to alter its behavior. Having long blended more easily into the
rest of society, the Chinese degree holders and large landholders could not
easily be separated or induced to take new roles. They did not develop new
patterns of consumption, lead the way in the commercialization of agriculture, or shift quickly to new occupations and investments in the opening
phases of modernization. Having long had available opportunities to shift resources into land ownership or education for elite status, Chinese merchants
did not easily perceive themselves as a distinct group whose achievement depended on foreign or state-sponsored reorganization.

Further evidence of the different patterns of premodern social change in
Ch'ing China and these other two countries is the lack of growing occupational differentiation in China. Within a standard marketing area of twenty
or thirty villages a variety of part-time and full-time activities met local needs,
but submerged as they were in an overwhelmingly peasant environment, few
actually severed their ties with the routine demands of the agricultural cycle.
The local division of labor took almost complete ascendance over more broad-
based specialization. This contrasts especially with Japan, both with its larger
urban-based elite and merchant and artisan populations and with its growing
differentiation of occupations in rural areas.

We close this section with one note of caution. The emphasis on factors
missing in China ought not to obscure the presence in China of numerous elements of social stratification generally absent elsewhere but present and expanding in Japan and Russia. China had a sizable, educated elite, many
skilled merchants and artisans, and experienced peasants able to produce
large yields per acre and to use innovative techniques. Probably few populations anywhere in the world before 1800 could match the Chinese as scholar-
officials, merchants, craftsmen, or peasants. When other conditions were
met, these skills could be energetically channeled into the tasks of
modernization.

STRATIFICATION AND SKILLS

As population grew, the percentage of degree holders, like the percentages in
other strata, did not change noticeably. Government employment of degree
holders failed to keep pace with population growth, and even rising quotas for

the number of degrees granted at examinations and by special purchase lagged behind the expanding number of eligible male candidates. To some extent, officials allowed for more access to government posts by reducing the service of county magistrates, but the number who benefited remained negligible.

Not only did the size of the official bureaucracy remain roughly as in the preceding dynasty, its distribution and internal regulations did not change substantially. The presence of several officials in a county with hundreds of thousands of people could scarcely affect local customs, particularly when in most cases these appointees were not well acquainted with urban life or with local conditions in general. Nor did the meager circulation of officials and degree holders between cities create a vanguard with new tastes in education and consumption to emulate. China's literate elite contrasted with those of Russia and Japan in being less urban, less mobile, less dependent on government sources of income, and less conscious of the alternatives to traditional village life. Buoyed by varied sources of income, this dispersed and unorganized elite proved difficult to mobilize for new objectives. United by ideology and national allegiance, degree holders remained separated by location and local organization.

China's literacy rate may have long remained at the forefront of the premodern world, yet during the Ch'ing dynasty it apparently did not rise. Urban and rural literacy continued at a high level; perhaps one-quarter to one-third of adult males had learned simple reading (and the recent estimates of Evelyn Sakakida Rawski in 1979 reported by Sally Borthwick in Chapter 6 range even higher). The gap betwen male and female literacy, however, remained enormous; no more than a few percent of women received similar preparation for reading. While this gap between the sexes resembles what has been observed in Japan and Russia and the overall literacy figures are between the high figures reached in mid-nineteenth century Japan and the much lower ones in Russia, the rate of change trailed far behind Japan and, at higher levels of education, behind Russia too. If dynamism on the eve of initial modernization is a criterion for comparison, as it should be, then clearly Chinese literacy contrasts with that in the other two countries.

Two distinct levels of education characterized the male population. The majority of men had two or three years of instruction in tiny village schools and achieved a minimal functional literacy, helpful in occasional commercial or land transactions and in keeping family rituals and other records. Widely exposed to calligraphy on doorways and shrines and to written public communications, they acquired a smattering of knowledge about the outside world and about orderly ways of interacting with it that were less accessible to illiterate persons. A minority, which can be calculated on the basis of scattered estimates (as in the information presented by Chang Chung-li, 1955 and 1962) as roughly 4 to 8 percent of the male population, reached a far superior degree of learning; they competed in the examination system in local county capitals. The ability to write complex essays on learned subjects obviously signifies a high general level of education that could be applied to other goals.

One of the striking but understandable features of this unusual record of literacy in Ch'ing China is how little it appeared to contribute to the adoption of new techniques for dealing with problems of production and administration. New skills applicable to agricultural or industrial production or to more efficient taxation developed slowly. There is little evidence that large numbers of Chinese in 1800 possessed skills or knowledge of the world beyond nearby areas superior to those of their ancestors 200 years earlier.

After 1850 the rise of treaty ports and the growing specialization of production in their vicinity somewhat altered the occupational structure, and, as a consequence, entry into the most prized positions of a nonagricultural nature increasingly required knowledge of imported commercial procedures, modern technologies, and recent advances in military organization. For merchants, artisans, soldiers, and officials, this knowledge could best be acquired in urban areas. Foreign consumption standards and new-style schools attracted more landowners and their children to the cities, and a modern education became identified with urban residence. Nevertheless, in their early stages these changes occurred so slowly as to be barely perceptible against the background of continuity with the past.

In summary, the human resources of China increased substantially in quantity, but showed little dynamism in various measures of occupational diversity, literacy, and technical skills. Between 1550 and 1850 the population nearly tripled, but little change occurred in the distribution of skills and jobs. Of course, in these respects, China continued at what was undoubtedly a high premodern plateau. After 1850, primarily as a result of civil war and intense foreign penetration in some port cities, a different pattern emerged. Population abruptly declined and only slowly recovered its previous size, while in some parts of the country new sources of wealth and training gained somewhat in appeal. China shows no evidence of major indigenous change toward bettering the quality of human resources during conditions of peace and growing prosperity. Yet Chinese resources reached a level of achievement in the nineteenth century that could have been an asset for modernization; in several areas China had long possessed the very conditions that Japan, and to a lesser extent Russia, had so recently realized.

In terms of its population, China lacked certain features that facilitated the rapid modernization of Japan and Russia. While total population was growing rapidly, evidence on the relation between population growth and material resources indicates that Chinese families were not making decisions that would maximize the resources available to each person. While there were impressive concentrations of merchants and artisans in big cities, evidence on the overall growth in nonagricultural occupations indicates that Chinese communities did not reveal much division of labor indicative of wider integration between areas. While national literacy rates were high, evidence on increasing literacy and specialized skills associated with the expansion of a large elite many of whom were engaged in administration within urban centers indicates that Ch'ing China did not show the effects of recent premodern transformations evident in Japan and Russia.

Patterns of Settlement

RURAL

During the Ch'ing dynasty the number of villages in China rose to upward of 700,000, and perhaps even close to one million, while the number of marketing centers increased even more rapidly to a total well in excess of 35,000 and perhaps even above 40,000. These enormous totals indicative of the vast area and the unprecedented size of China's population dwarf figures for any other country at any time prior to the twentieth century. One consequence of this vast scale was a low degree of integration between regions, corresponding to the relative isolation of the largest cities from other cities of a like size normally many hundreds of miles distant. Another consequence was the continued dominance of Chinese cities on a list of the largest urban centers in the world; in the early nineteenth century six of the ten cities in the world with 500,000 or more residents could be found in China. The scale of the society helps to account for the anomaly of so many great cities without a high level of urbanization or a pronounced urban presence.

Of course, among such a large number of villages, great diversity existed. While some remote areas had scarcely emerged from self-sufficient farming, other villages near prosperous cities depended upon relatively commercialized agriculture. Furthermore, land productivity, tenancy rates, and population differed considerably among villages. Yet, certain generalizations do seem to be firmly grounded in the records of many areas.

In a variety of ways, cooperation at the level of the village did not reach the heights of community solidarity evident in Japan or Russia. The Chinese village lacked precise boundaries, its leaders could exercise little control over degree holders and rich landlords, and land transactions occurred as individual matters rarely subject to village-wide intervention. Separate temples, lineages, families, and landlord-tenant relations grouped some villagers together in activities that did not often extend to the village as a whole. Of course, some cooperation did occur, notably on matters of water control and on occasions of civil disorder. The contrast is between these limited forms of solidarity and the more pervasive village organizational efforts in other societies.

A related conclusion is that in China lines of interaction with the outside world generally did not reinforce village solidarity. Household representatives journeyed individually to a nearby periodic market. Degree holders cultivated personal ties with others of equal status, and if they achieved sufficient rank, these ties extended to the county magistrate.

For the majority, contacts with government functionaries often acquired a private character rather than devolving on the holders of public positions. Indeed, the widely noted weakness in the subadministrative *li-chia* and *pao-chia* systems of joint household responsibility attests to the circumventing of public village-wide responsibilities through less official and less formalized channels.

Furthermore, the village lacked controls over what were broadly defined as the inherent rights of families. The individual family possessed rights, inviolable except by higher state authority, to dispose of and to acquire land as self-cultivators, landlords, or tenants, or any combination thereof. No obstacles prevented ownership of land in other villages. Families could subdivide holdings, send sons to sojourn elsewhere, or split the inheritance in ways that threw into flux any efforts to give continuity to intergenerational hierarchies of households. In various respects, family-centered rights took precedence over village authority. Understandably, single-lineage villages could achieve greater solidarity because residential propinquity was reinforced by kinship bonds.

Perhaps because of the weakness of village-wide functions as well as the remoteness of county administration, the Chinese marketing area acquired various features of a community (Skinner, 1964–1965). Precise boundaries delimited areas containing on the average fifteen to thirty villages in which individuals periodically came together not only to buy and sell basic goods, but also to be part of a community for such activities as entertainment, arranging marriages, and exchanging information about the outside. The circulation of goods and services reached a rather high volume within the marketing area of 2,000 to 3,000 households, but contact with areas beyond was more limited.

It is striking that few people were moving away from rural areas in Ch'ing China as compared with Japan and Russia during the period in question. In Japan and Russia rural areas regularly sent large numbers of migrants to cities. Moreover, in Japan by the early nineteenth century a large-scale exchange of young servants and apprentices occurred between households in different villages. In China the predominance of degree holders and wealthy landowners who not only maintained a residence in their native villages but also lived there the year round extended to all elements in the population and all family members except daughters who were obliged to marry out; with few exceptions, people remained at home whenever possible although they hiked periodically to local markets in neighboring settlements.

Wedged between the closely joined household and the standard marketing area, which acquired so many of the features of a community, the Chinese village did not, as a rule, achieve a high degree of integration. Nor should the rather irregular control emanating from the overburdened magistrate and his little-respected underlings and supplemented by the somewhat independent powers of local degree holders and large landlords be construed as firm outside administrative control. Finally, although commercialized agriculture prevailed, circulation patterns generally favored exchange concentrated within small clusters of villages rather than strengthening ties with large cities.

URBAN

The percentage of the Chinese population that resided in cities rivals or exceeds figures in most parts of the premodern world, but trails the high figures reached in Russia and especially in Japan. It appears possible that for close to 1,000 years (and perhaps for as long as 2,000 years) the Chinese urban population fluctuated around 5 to 7 percent, and although a long-term upward rise seems likely, some scholars argue that the Sung dynasty achieved at least as high a figure as the Ch'ing some 700 to 800 years later. Neither the Ming nor the Ch'ing periods nurtured the spectacular acceleration in urban growth witnessed in early Tokugawa Japan or, to a lesser extent, in eighteenth-century Russia.

Why did city populations only increase at approximately the rate of national population growth? Did a meager agricultural surplus—so often assumed to be the limiting factor in premodern urbanization—bar any hopes of generating further urban expansion? Did excessive state intervention stifle commercial initiative, as much of the comparative urban literature presupposes? For both these last two questions arguments can be cited to support affirmative answers. If overall population growth between 1750 and 1850 exceeded agricultural growth, then had not the cities lost possible resources from the countryside? Furthermore, if merchants and artisans were perceived as the lowest of the four idealized occupational categories and could only with difficulty resist arbitrary taxation or confiscation in judicial proceedings, then did not state actions encourage channeling resources away from urban pursuits?

On the basis of a more comprehensive perspective, the most telling comparative evidence compels us to reject or at least to revise substantially the conclusion that inadequate production and state coercion blocked urban growth. Both the amenities available to rural Chinese and the abundance of local exchange suggest that notions of a shortage of resources must be amended by awareness that much more could have been extracted from standard marketing areas and funneled into cities. Presumably for some extended time this potential surplus persisted at a rather high level before it was partially dissipated by the requirements of feeding more mouths. Finally, customary statements of the negative impact caused by an absence of urban governmental autonomy ignore the fact that in Japan and Russia, where governmental activities also extended out over the surrounding countryside, urban growth was exceptionally high.

The Chinese city did not act as a magnet for either the poor or the wealthy. Without the means to purchase land, the poor gravitated toward tenancy and wage labor at those times during the year when pressing farming needs drove rural wages well above urban levels. The well-to-do remained within a short distance of their landholdings, finding both earning potential and consumption opportunities almost on a par with more distant cities. Indeed, as Mote (1970) has observed, in few respects did cities differ from the countryside. In its architecture, its consumption styles, and the flowering of its learning and arts, the city offered remarkably little special appeal for even the leisured, landholding elite. Many of the most attractive conditions could, to a notable extent, be duplicated in rural areas.

Of course, some characteristics of cities were distinctive: a greater density of population supported specialized shops and functions, and the inhabitants predominantly engaged in nonagricultural activities (which did not exclude cultivating small plots). Most important, from the walls of the administrative city radiated the symbolic presence of imperial government. Of the approximately 1,400 cities with 3,000 or more residents in the early nineteenth century, at least 80 percent functioned as seats of county government, and close to half of all cities in excess of 10,000 population added functions of prefectural and, in some cases, provincial administration. Their imposing city walls, which in most instances no longer wholly contained their markets, shops, and residences, represented the majesty of governmental authority. Reinforcing this impression, the large compound for the magistrate's office and for other state activities and the special temples standing as monuments to the city's role within a vast empire alerted the populace to a set of associations that emphasized order and harmonious interaction with the world beyond.

Whereas Japanese and Russian administrative centers attracted a larger percentage of the population and exerted more control over the rural populace, Chinese cities substituted symbol for reality. Their massive walls, measuring in most cities from one to four miles in perimeter, encompassed all manner of urban functions. Symbolically, the wall, which had once served an important defensive function, separated the city as a whole from its hinterland and preserved continuity with the past. In Japan only the castle at the city's administrative center, with its stone wall and surrounding moat, received such symbolic attention. In Russia, except in certain older cities, only some public buildings along a main street imbued the administrative city with a special presence. In Chinese cities change perforce occurred within the walls of tradition or by accretions along the boundaries they defined.

From the perspective of harmonious premodern rural-urban interchange, China presents a model of stability. The problem of a sharp gap between the city and the countryside did not become pronounced. Neither the state nor the established elite nor a rising middle class prodded the urban milieu into a new relationship with its hinterland. Undoubtedly the imposition of treaty ports and the burgeoning among them of Shanghai, Tientsin, and other coastal centers somewhat altered this pattern in favor of a distinctive urban existence capable of luring new residents and conferring on them a separate identity, but the effects only became substantial as the Ch'ing dynasty neared its end.

The conclusion to be drawn is that the urban sector did not stimulate change as it had in the other two countries. While the total urban population roughly kept pace with overall population growth, Chinese cities did not serve as magnets or models for rural dwellers. Unlike cities in Japan and Russia, the urban sector lacked impressive new signs of vitality except in the externally generated treaty ports.

Correspondingly a second stage of rural-centered diffusion of handicraft industries, stores, and ways of life did not develop. Rural-centered and market-town craft industries and stores were widespread at an early date in China; yet, lacking a new urban impetus, no basis existed for imparting new vitality to these establishments on the basis of a wider circulation of goods. They supplemented and operated within the context of the periodic market rather than replacing it or prospering independently.

The Urban Hierarchy

A relatively efficient (that is, geared to the movement of goods to higher level cities) network of central places emerged in Japan and Russia during their periods of rising urbanization; yet at the most local level China offered more abundant opportunities for marketing. The Chinese achievement rested on a high degree of local circulation—on a marketing system functioning, to a great extent, so as to eliminate scarcity and not so much to provision cities. These conditions fostered rural population growth and reduced the desirability of settling in the city.

Detailed calculation of the ratios between the numbers of settlements at each level reveals major blockages in the flow of resources from the countryside, if we are correct in assuming that urban population figures are indicative of the amount of goods arriving in the city. Although the number of marketing settlements per capita in China remained below the figures for eighteenth-century England and France, it exceeded the numbers in Japan and Russia. With about 12,000–13,000 persons per market in the early nineteenth century and a successively decreasing population necessary to support a market thereafter, China boasted at least one-fourth as many more such settlements per capita as Japan and Russia. On this basis, it would seem probable that the Chinese peasants flocked to market in greater numbers.

Community exchange designates the circulation of goods within the confines of the standard market. China's noteworthy achievement in this scale of exchange probably oriented the individual household more than in Japan and Russia to the market mechanism and to independent judgments about production and consumption. This finding corresponds to our earlier conclusions about a relatively skilled, literate, and growing population in rural China.

What accounts for the considerable scale of community exchange in China? Three essential factors deserve mention. First, by the Ch'ing period China possessed vast productive capacities and skills. Lack of production capabilities did not act as a decisive barrier to exchange, as it did in some pre-modern societies. Second, rural organization generally isolated the individual household as a unit of economic decision making. Landowners and tenants alike operated to maximize commercial sales without serflike obligations or patronage expectations in time of need. An exception that lends credibility to this generalization is that in a few northern areas where lands in support of the bannermen in Peking reduced large numbers to tenancy, periodic markets were more sparsely distributed. Third, the outside world placed relatively few demands on the community; tax rates were low and most rent recipients resided within the area. These characteristics of Chinese society contributed to a high degree of interaction at the community level.

At other levels of the urban network, the situation was decidedly different. Five-country comparisons indicate that the Chinese ratio of four small, standard periodic markets for each intermediate market far exceeded the ratios elsewhere; only in Russia was this high ratio approached. The high value of this ratio signifies that in China goods did not move out of the standard marketing areas in as large amounts as elsewhere. Merchants did not adequately compensate for the low rates of taxation by transporting large amounts to higher-level markets. The purchasing power within the basic marketing area absorbed more of the available goods relative to the demand from outside.

Also counted as local exchange was the turnover at local markets in cities of 3,000 to 10,000 population. The fact that there were five or six times as many intermediate markets as local cities even more sharply sets China apart; in Japan and Russia the comparable ratios were close to 3:2. These figures indicate most decisively that goods failed to move up the local urban hierarchy in large quantities. (Again our reasoning presumes that fewer cities signifies a smaller flow of goods. Reinforcing that conclusion is the evidence that Chinese city dwellers did not control as large a share of their society's wealth as did a corresponding number of Japanese or Russian urban residents.) Cities of 3,000 to 10,000 population numbered somewhat over 1,000 in China; however, if circulation had reached the volume seen elsewhere they ought to have been in excess of 2,500 or 3,000. These figures demonstrate that the main inefficiency (from the viewpoint of future needs) in the Chinese movement of goods occurred within the county or between adjacent, local administrative units. Of course, what was inefficient for the mobilization of resources into cities can be appreciated as supportive of superior rural incomes and opportunities.

What accounts for the weak circulation of goods between intermediate markets and those in local cities? Administrative inaction certainly must be emphasized here; for as population multiplied, no new administrative centers were established. Taxation did not increase and, unlike what happened in

Japan and Russia, the relatively small numbers of elite residents in cities did not win a greater share of the revenues from village landholdings. Rural areas captured a large part of the goods placed in circulation.

Middle-distance exchange carried goods that had already been gathered at local cities to prefectural and other large urban centers. At the level of medium sized (10,000–29,999) and large cities (30,000 or more residents), which benefited from such exchange, China's urban network does not appear inefficient. Although China did not have quite as many cities of 10,000 to 30,000 proportionately as did Japan, it far surpassed Russia. And in the ratio of cities of 10,000–30,000 to those of 30,000–70,000, China actually stands out with about 50 to 60 percent more cities than would be anticipated from the Japanese figures and many times more than the Russian ratio would yield.

Finally, for the largest cities supported by long-distance exchange, China does not appear at either extreme on the scale. The roughly 6 million residents in its ten largest cities are close to the proportional data from the other countries (Rozman, 1973 and 1976).

Overall, the Chinese urban network emerges as strikingly effective in serving rural dwellers and, at the same time, in light of the needs for concentrating resources in the period ahead, as inefficient in channeling resources upward to larger settlements. The major points of inefficiency operated not at the extremes in the settlement hierarchy but in local exchange beyond the standard marketing area. The high degree of administrative centralization typical of Japan and Russia, especially as evidenced by the abundance of small cities of 3,000–10,000 population, was absent in China.

Even before modernization started in Japan and Russia, the dimensions of the urban pyramid began to change. At least in some regions, the number of periodic markets at the already narrow base of the pyramid declined; during the second half of the nineteenth century these markets would largely disappear. Meanwhile some resettling occurred, in Japan favoring the largest and smallest settlements at the expense of cities with 10,000 to 500,000 persons. After the 1860s while urbanization proceeded slowly for a time, intensive competition pitted city against city in a struggle for survival under new conditions. China's more wide-based pyramid missed any such unsettling experience. On the one hand, the base grew even wider; except perhaps near a few flourishing treaty ports at the end of the century, periodic markets did not decline. On the other hand, adjustments occurred in lower Yangtze cities and along routes plied by steamships or newly bypassed, like the recently silt-blocked Grand Canal. The treaty port impact was blunted; new cities failed to alter substantially the patterns of domestic trade or to create a multiplier effect for more inland and smaller cities. Symbolic of their fringe status, the rapidly growing cities of Tientsin, Tsingtao, Hong Kong (under British rule), and Shanghai, among others, dotted the Chinese coastline. Despite the realignment of commercial and transportation ties for certain transactions toward a small number of ports under foreign domination, the same basic urban conditions as before prevailed over nearly all of China.

Throughout the Ch'ing dynasty, China had held on—despite minor adjustments—to its earlier legacy of administrative divisions and settlement patterns. While Japanese and Russian leaders vigorously imposed far-reaching regulations on the distribution of administrative cities and territorial units, including spurts of urban relocation and construction of new cities, the Chinese clung to tradition. They did not take an active hand in extracting the surplus and directing resources to elite groups or to the support of cities. In addition, sharp regional imbalances in these other countries contributed to an integrated national market impossible to duplicate over the immense scale of China. No leading regions pulled others along, no urban sector impelled rural transformation, no small administrative centers pressed new claims on their hinterlands, and no major cities operated as engines of change.

Patterns of settlement did not exhibit the features identified as useful for the modernization of Japan and Russia. If attention centers not on the relative order or prosperity in villages but on their solidarity and direct responsiveness to outside controls, not on the number of large Chinese cities but on the percentage of the population in cities and its record of expansion, and not on the number of periodic markets but on the efficiency of settlement distribution at various levels in the central place hierarchy, then Japan and Russia provide a vivid contrast with China. What was at stake is more than failure to match the Japanese and Russian record. It was, we believe, a matter of China not possessing an urban network capable of serving the needs of a program of modernization. In Part Two, this theme reemerges in a twentieth-century context.

Organizational Contexts

FAMILY STRUCTURE

By all rights, family and kinship ties should constitute the first theme for a study of the social structure of premodern China. Our not beginning with this subject does not reflect a reduced sense of its importance, but rather a desire to establish first a context in which family and kinship conditions can be considered. Demographic, stratification, and settlement patterns all set limits on and, by the nature of their main contours, focus attention on particular aspects of family structure.

A combination of pervasive indoctrination about family matters and diverse practices that reinforced family controls distinguishes China even from other premodern family-centered societies. Ideally the Chinese family approached self-sufficiency and never had cause to give preference to any considerations but those of family and, to a lesser extent, lineage. It was to remain stationary on ancestral lands, preserving the link with previous generations and ensuring the worthiness of successive ones. Rather than dividing its property, the family was to pass it along intact to all male progeny who would remain together in a single joint and extended household. The family might share in lineage-centered ownership of ritual as well as development property and even in lineage-organized investment away from home. Although in various respects the ideal could not be realized, it operated without as many constraints as has often been assumed. Marriage and inheritance practices, ceremonial activities, land tenure, mobility strategies, village organizations, religious associations, and forms of production and distribution all supported a different kind and, in some respects, a greater degree of family and lineage cohesion than in Japan and Russia.

Household size in China conformed to figures from other premodern settings. The national average fluctuated around 5.3 persons per household with noteworthy, and still little studied, disparities between areas. (A large majority of prefectural data for the mean household size ranges between 4 and 7 persons.) As elsewhere, roughly 80 percent of family members consisted of the married couple, or a survivor of an earlier marital bond, and their children, that is, the nuclear family. At some point in the household cycle, a stem family involving three generations (or an extended family consisting of two or more married couples) often appeared, but high mortality rates reduced its duration.

The introduction of a new member into the family provided an important occasion for reaffirming familial bonds. The Chinese lavished considerable resources—perhaps more than did Japanese or Russians—on the ceremonies, bride price, and dowry associated with marriage or birth. They also obeyed more stringent and extensive rules forbidding endogamy even among persons with a common surname. Somewhat successful efforts to preserve the "virtue" of widows by keeping them from remarrying, strict provisions against sexual experience outside of marriage for the vast majority of women, and encouragement of blind marriages in which the couple met only at the ceremony all emphasized the hold of the family, represented by its male head, over the individual. Of course, this marriage model proved more monolithic for the elite than for the poor peasant. Other premodern societies also practiced arranged marriage, but without the full range of supporting customs found in China. In Japan, for instance, many areas accepted premarital sexual experimentation and a form of trial marriage in which the actual registration occurred only with the birth and survival of a child. Earlier marriage in China coupled in some parts of the country with greater seclusion of women (usually those of higher economic status) reduced individual choice further. Marriage was nearly universal for women; except for widows and some unusually poor men, single-person households were practically nonexistent.

Inheritance practices differentiate China more from Japan than from Russia. In China two valued objects were inherited: property and lineage rank and seniority. Primogeniture did not exist in the former, but it was present in the latter. Sons shared equally in the property, but ordinarily the eldest son received the ancestral tablets and could anticipate a larger voice in the management of lineage property—slightly offsetting the lack of primogeniture in property. To diversify its old-age insurance, the couple sought to rear as many sons as possible. Whereas infanticide in some villages of Japan eliminated babies of both sexes, in China it was overwhelmingly sex selective, resulting in a high sex ratio favoring a surplus of males. In Russia equal division of village communal lands to all able-bodied males (with preference for married couples) would also have encouraged a preference for male offspring, but there population growth occurred without the same degree of female infanticide.

In Japan the family's property was passed on to only one son, and in Russia the village assumed a major role in property redistribution; only in China did family inheritance involve everyone, including women whose marriages were arranged with awareness of the holdings coming to their husbands once property was divided. Ideally, married sons would continue to reside together in a single household, but, in fact, when two or more sons survived to maturity, the pressures for creating separate households almost always prevailed not long after their marriages or immediately following the death of their father. Because each son received an equal share, more people were caught in the far-reaching nets of family controls.

The prevalence of the family farm, whether owned or rented, likewise reinforced the autonomy of the household. Land tenure relied on respect for legal contracts and an active real estate market. A constant flux existed in property assets. Family labor reserves determined the amount of land to be farmed, which led to frequent decisions to rent additional parcels out or in. Such transactions blurred an individual's predominant status as landlord or tenant, yet preserved the vitality of the independent family unit. This is just one of the ways in which Chinese society reduced class consciousness in favor of family solidarity. The impermanence of village social hierarchies, the multifaceted character of tenant-landlord relations, and the presence of degree holders and other elite persons within lineages embracing the poor reduced social class identification. Primary loyalties cut across stratification lines.

As far as farming was concerned, families customarily gave each son roughly the same opportunity—however limited it might be. For other pursuits the household head had to decide on how best to use available resources. The most important decision normally concerned education; most pupils spent only two or three years in school and did not cause a major drain on funds, but for others the costly preparation for state examinations had to begin early and required difficult choices. By hiring a tutor or securing enrollment in a private class nearby, by forgoing some of a son's labor time and meeting study expenses, and eventually by providing travel expenses to exams, the family—many with lineage support since schools often were operated by a lineage group—was gambling on a strategy for upward mobility. In Japan and Russia schools were organized for a particular social class or represented a community decision; education was less exclusively bound up with the individual family or kinship group.

Paradoxically, to the extent a family proved successful in its endeavors, the likelihood of increased outside loyalties rose. A Chinese family's decision to invest in education for a particular bright son tended to launch him on a course of involvement with nonfamilial connections. The sociology of "*t'ung*" ties discussed in the next section began at that point to compete with the family's allegiances in ways often new for that particular family.

Either the community or the family can assume responsibility for some of the important decisions in a premodern society. In comparison to Japan and Russia, the balance in China rested decidedly on the family's side. Of course, village cooperation helped meet pressing needs for irrigation and water control and for crop watching and, in emergencies, collective defense, but as in education the family predominated in almost all spheres of activity. In China a less stable ordering of households prevailed. Correspondingly, Chinese identified more closely with lineages, which provided a measure of security for relatives within the village. The awareness of degrees of relatedness reached a height unrivaled elsewhere; Chinese terminology, for example, distinguishes far more degrees of kinship than Japanese or Russian. Although except in areas in the southeast, the Chinese lineage rarely acquired substantial resources or major controls over the household, it offered a framework for mutual support and united action that partially compensated for and represented an alternative to community organizations.

Religion remained somewhat more household oriented than in Japan or Russia. Although in Japan the household also was the locus of most religious activities, the Shintoist stress on community provided more balance. Temples and shrines abounded in China; so the household cum lineage while functioning as a wholly self-contained unit of ancestor reverence certainly did not operate as the exclusive base for anticipated supernatural contact. Indeed, a certain tension existed between the independent religious authority of the family head and the cooperative religious ventures centered in merchant guild halls and village temples. Religious activities permeated all collectivities. Numerous village-oriented cults can be identified. More numerous, however, were the ancestral halls founded by lineages and grouping together a fraction of the village's households. Also in evidence were intervillage temple activities and secret societies that did not take the village as the religious community.

Nonagricultural production and distribution also substantiate the impression of an unusually family-centered society. The putting-out system of domestic industry was highly developed, and most commercial operations were conducted on a small scale by separate household units.

Ideally speaking, the family and secondarily the lineage took precedence in every one of life's decisions. Perhaps, the appropriate slogan would have been "serve the family," as the slogan in the PRC has been "serve the masses." Outside the kinship setting there were few guidelines as to where authority might be found apart from the distant, imperial bureaucracy. The legal system gave clear precedence to loyalty to family over loyalty to state, and officials were expected to go home on leave from their jobs to perform lengthy mourning rites. Only assignments to posts distant from their homes gave some assurance that officials would be insulated from family and localist priorities.

These characteristics of the Chinese family and lineage had many positive implications for the stability and vitality of the premodern social structure, but they also had some negative implications for the creation of conditions conducive to modernization. The dearth of external restrictions freed the family to maximize its population growth and its resource intake. The inclusivity of lineage ties and the high rates of social mobility attributable to inheritance practices blurred social boundaries and reduced the potential for change. Because the family was accepted as the unchallenged unit of control the state was unable to assert its authority more vigorously. It did not place its personnel in rural areas. It did not tax heavily or impose major, new claims for goods and services. And it did not seek to withdraw local elites on whom it had conferred degrees from the family or lineage context in which they were employed as private teachers and local spokesmen.

This description of the Chinese family structure suggests that control mechanisms would be highly vulnerable in a period of rising individualism brought on by modernizing forces. Outside of the family and kinship context, alternative bases of control and coordination remained fragile. When family restraints broke down or were irrelevant, individualism by default was common. In this respect as well as in the various buffers supporting family autonomy cited above, China differed from Japan and Russia.

INTERMEDIATE ORGANIZATIONS

How were people organized within the cities and villages of China? Did the existing organizational base offer a good foundation for the reorganization essential to modernization? To begin, let us simply list the types of organizations in which individuals operated. In addition to the household, lineage, and village-wide associations at the grass roots and the imperial civilian and military bureaucracies at the summit, mention should be made of: (1) subadministrative bodies involved in police control, tax collection, and population registration; (2) educational associations, primarily comprised of degree holders, perhaps formally associated with an advanced school or informally joining individuals such as officials who had passed an exam in the same year; (3) business organizations in which merchants, artisans, and hired laborers or households working on a commission basis interacted with others in similar professions; (4) religious associations, often weak and temporary, but claiming some allegiance and responsible for some kinds of devotional as well as social activity; (5) public works associations, often created on a temporary basis to raise funds or to meet pressing needs for water control; and (6) illegitimate societies (characteristically including a religious or doctrinal element) operating clandestinely to smuggle salt or opium, to engage in some

167

other illegal traffic, or on occasion to plot violence, the most extreme form of which appeared as attempted rebellion. Despite the scarcity relative to Japan and Russia of approved organizational contexts between the centralized state apparatus and the family and lineage, several groupings existed in which we can look for distinctive Chinese features.

In rural areas, these groupings mainly operated informally and centered on marketing places. Often they were organized in imitation of lineage structure and created fictive kinship relationships. Wealth, examination degree status, and kinship ties guided these contacts between the leisured, the commercially minded, and the occasional supplicant for a favorable governmental ruling, or for some intricate personal financing or, perhaps, for a delicate arrangement of marriage through a matchmaker. From a comparative perspective, China may have displayed a dearth of formal arrangements for such local intervillage contacts (related to the weakness of the village as a unit of organization and to the scarcity of administrative bodies in rural areas) and relied more extensively on the prestigious degree holders rather than on the wealthy landowners. The very flexibility of these Chinese arrangements in comparison to the fixed nature of the corporate village may have diminished perception of the need to create new organizational structures in response to changing circumstances.

In urban settings, more permanent associations evolved. Smaller cities operated without finely differentiated organizations, corresponding to the absence of specialized stores; many trades might be clustered together in a single guild. Larger cities developed more complex arrangements. Middlemen under wealthy merchants hired transport workers or unskilled industrial employees and assumed responsibility for them. Separate guilds existed for each of the main trades, and, at least in the great regional cities, care might even be taken to specify their separate neighborhood spheres of activity. These associations operated with government permission; they received privileges, paid rather paltry taxes, and from time to time made sizable contributions to special public works projects. The existence of guilds and related associations gave members some security against competition and assured authorities of active cooperation in the arbitration of conflicts that might disrupt order in the cities.

In the absence of close governmental regulations and closed social classes, guilds operated in a highly fluid and competitive environment. Yet, given the low formal status of merchants and the constant turnover in officials, some options were lacking for legitimizing and solidifying their role in society. They could neither challenge the preeminence of officials nor gain assured protection. They therefore developed organizations with unusually secure bonds between members and tried to carve out controlled sectors for themselves. Relying on kinship and native place ties, these organizations succeeded in isolating outsiders within an alien environment. Conscious of their separation from the urban community as a whole, and of their dependence on guild associates, individual members closely identified with these organizations.

The concept of *t'ung-hsiang* refers to the common local origins of persons who associated together. Second only to family and kinship ties, and accommodating nepotistic hiring practices, it established the main criterion for recruitment to organizations and association through business relationships. Although *t'ung-hsiang* was by no means peculiar to China, it pervaded the Chinese setting to an extent perhaps unmatched elsewhere. Developing during the Ming dynasty and proliferating under Ch'ing rule, *hui-kuan* and other commercial organizations joining men from a common province, prefecture or, less frequently, county became dominant at the apex of urban business life. Merchants from a few areas, who replenished their members with local talent, dominated banking activities and large-scale trade in various commodities over much of China. The potency of *t'ung-hsiang* ties extended from regional cliques in the civilian and military bureaucracies to farm migrants who, despite centuries of life in a new province, maintained identification with their area of origin.

Why did outsiders so decisively gain the upper hand over the more numerous local urban population? The answer must lie in superior organization, which by virtue of isolation could somewhat diminish kinship obligations. Operating on a larger scale, the outsiders could more readily channel needed personnel and capital into the most profitable pursuits. Through their *t'ung-hsiang* associations, they united to settle disputes and bring order in a potentially competitive environment. Thus they reaped benefits that were shared with the home area and rested assured that relatives back home would be cared for and would have available similar employment opportunities, and that in case of illness, death, or other personal hardship the proper action would be taken in the city on their behalf. The success of such organizations provides a meaningful commentary on the nature of the organizational vacuum between family and state that they partially managed to fill.

Other *"t'ung"* contexts likewise bridged the formidable gap between individuals without kinship ties. Passing an examination in the same year or sharing a patron or teacher could reinforce common territory of origin as a principle of association for urban sojourners. These perceived connections offered a measure of security that persons with the same *"t'ung"* identity would not permit other parties to take unfair advantage of one. Even in rural areas, this concept existed; for instance, investment or credit clubs usually worked in some kind of *"t'ung"* context with each member benefiting in turn through an arrangement determined by lot. As an organizational principle, *"t'ungism"* indicates a fluidity and impermanence to associations that generally favored family-centered and nepotistic practices over professional or interest group identification. Notable as an exception, special arrangements sheltered the prestigious careers in bureaucratic service in which, since an official appointment was far from one's family residence, professional loyalties were accorded precedence by default.

To an unusual extent the Chinese pattern of commercial organization appears to have siphoned resources away from the big cities. Of course, new investments were centered in appropriate urban locations. But funds also went to merchants' home areas, just as they ended up in the locales of successful officials. They were expended in land purchases, in educating sons to become officials, in opulent consumption, and in extending the area's business enterprises in other locations. In contrast, Japanese and Russian merchants had little choice but to funnel resources into their local enterprises. To a much greater extent, they were not outsiders and did not have available alternative uses for their profits.

Before 1900, this organizational pattern over most of China scarcely changed. While the operations emanating from the treaty ports expanded, domestic trade remained under the control of such traditional forces as the Shansi bankers or similar territorially based alliances of merchants. Some regional realignments occurred as witnessed in the proliferation of Kwang-tung and Fukien *hui-kuan*, but the old patterns persisted.

Within the largest cities some interesting developments did occur in commercial organizations. The foreign settlements described in Chapter 2, which operated independently of Chinese law, especially exerted an impact in this area; yet even apart from their direct influence, the urgent government demands for revenue beginning with the Taiping rebellion induced more reliance on guilds. Perhaps this continued an earlier trend of relaxing restrictions on such groups. If so, it now produced the added result of gradually broadening the criteria for membership; new more broadly based commercial organizations appeared, and *t'ung-hsiang* criteria operated more flexibly, extending perhaps to a larger geographical unit or to businessmen engaged in unrelated trades. More powerful guilds strengthened the representation of merchants in city governance. Nonetheless, even with the vulnerability of certain groups of transport workers and merchant associations to the reorientation of trade routes and with the emergence of the comprador as a new type of businessman, the basic organizational forms persisted.

STATE ORGANIZATIONS

Comparisons between China, Japan, and Russia yield a paradox in the distribution of official government personnel. The vast countries of China and Russia produced highly center-oriented distributions; for instance roughly half of China's civilian bureaucracy was stationed in Peking. Even sizable cities or large administrative units elsewhere were often assigned only a few officials with a small professional staff. In contrast, in compact Japan most cities of even 5,000–10,000 inhabitants boasted large bureaucracies. In China, the bureaucracy did not expand markedly, and its objectives remained roughly constant—a legacy of the Ming dynasty. Little effort was made to extend its control over resources; it did not become growth oriented. Thus it should be characterized as center oriented but not committed to centralizing control over resources, as a source of continuity and not a force for change.

Japanese and Russian authorities repeatedly devised new challenges for their growing administrative staffs. In Russia, foreign models and military challenges jolted leaders into action aimed at increasing revenues and improving administrative direction. In Japan, the high costs of life in Edo as well as intense competition between *han* sparked even more far-reaching measures. Only in China were governmental objectives deemed compatible with what was long assumed to be a permanent freeze on taxes announced in the early eighteenth century. No pressing external objectives were recognized, and even the more serious threats of internal rebellion scarcely dislodged this attitude. A continued belief that the ideals underlying the existing system best met the welfare of the people remained the underlying rationale for preserving the status quo. Indeed, limited resources and long experience had produced impressive results in terms of peace and prosperity.

In various ways, the Chinese government acted to create and preserve a society held together by ideology far more than by formal organization, by grass roots stability far more than by local, regional, or national integration. In conformity with the doctrines of a Confucian state, the leadership became reconciled to a sparse bureaucracy necessitating a low level of local penetration. Aware of the difficulties in controlling a larger or more dispersed national bureaucracy, the Chinese officials accepted a skeleton of government outside of the major capitals. While forgoing expansion of local outposts, the state also forestalled the development of an indigenous administrative elite on the subcounty level and acted to disperse large-scale or potentially powerful organizations. Even the continued presence of groupings of ten households through the *pao-chia* or *li-chia* systems of collective responsibility had such limited and often unrealized scope that it could not be taken as a sign of a tightly organized society. Dispersal prevailed over mobilization as an organizing principle.

While the pillars of the bureaucracy—consisting of the examination system, the spatial and hierarchical distribution of offices, the organizational objectives and the means assigned to achieve them, and the Confucian ideology identified with the imperial system—remained firm, some changes occurred in the selection and advancement of personnel and the internal rules designed to increase organizational efficiency. These changes, by reducing the professionalism of officials in local outposts, even further circumscribed the capacity of officials to mobilize resources. The average years of service for a *hsien* magistrate fell, and the potential for reappointment in another post or for advancement declined. Long years of study with little direct relevance to the tasks of governance scarcely prepared the magistrate for a short tenure in a difficult and complex office.

Lack of experience had no consequences for policy making, since the magistrate was bound to follow directives from above; however, in implementing policy he could actually function with more impunity vis-à-vis superior officials than in Russia where the governor closely supervised local officials or in Japan where *daimyo* inherited the entire staffs and ingrained precedents of their ancestors. The magistrate's initiatives centered on the selection of his staff and on the collection of taxes; yet even in these matters the import of his decisions could be tightly circumscribed. Being an outsider in the county, often without knowledge of the local dialect, the magistrate could not easily avoid reliance on the staff inherited from his predecessor and on the influential local degree holders. The magistrate in Ch'ing China, a novice with little time to get to know the area and limited to supervising a narrow range of functions in which poor performance could lead to strict penalties, was in no position to innovate on major matters despite the lack of direct guidance in most areas. Peking's distrust of local administrative power obliged the magistrates to act in a conservative fashion.

A comparison of the magistrate with the local authorities in Japan (the *daimyo, daikan,* or *bugyo*) or in Russia (the *voevod*) indicates that the Chinese government took a much less active role in transferring resources to cities. Low taxes and small salaried staffs gave the magistrate less wherewithal for pumping resources out of the village. Moreover, the magistrate's power was more sharply curtailed by the rural elite (degree holders) than was the power of urban-based officials in the other countries. Any irregular collections that were added to the tax payments could be sent by the magistrate, aware of his brief tenure, to his own local area or siphoned off by underlings from scattered bases around the district. While the Japanese and Russian officials acted under pressure to increase deliveries of resources to the central cities, the magistrate was only expected to meet relatively low tax quotas which might remain unmet or be reduced in times of calamities.

Through its administrative arrangements, the Chinese government sought to curtail the development of autonomous organizations yet at the same time, it did not move to extend its own organizations. During the nineteenth century, pressing local needs made this status quo outlook a less tenable position. For purposes of local security and fiscal strength, the state partially approved the formation of new organizations led by degree holders. Rather than being under the state's control, these new local alliances represented a further source of fragmentation—often for the self-protection of particular locales or elite groups. The first steps may thus have been taken toward a vertical organizational structure reaching down to the family, but in the short run these responses to deteriorating social control probably only contributed to further local fragmentation and the inability to draw upon a stable set of authority relationships to mobilize resources.

In Japan and Russia, the state took the initiative in expanding the organizational capacity of the society. Administrative needs led simultaneously to the enlargement of govermental activities and organizations and to the promotion of intermediate organizations that could readily be held responsible as adjuncts to state agencies. In China the state did not take similar initiatives; its inaction in the face of population increases, commercial growth, some territorial expansion, and eventually civil disorder may well have lowered the organizational capacity of Chinese society to respond to markedly new conditions from the middle of the nineteenth century.

In summary, Chinese organizational contexts appear quite different from those in Japan and Russia. Fewer constraints operated on family autonomy. Indeed, such a panoply of supporting structures propped up the priority of family concerns that no simple conversion to other sources of authority could prove successful. Commercial organizations, to an unusual extent, represented outsiders committed to channeling resources away from rather than into the cities in which they operated. Moreover, our appreciation of the vaunted imperial bureaucracy ought to derive mainly from how much was accomplished with so little, not from any evidence of deep penetration into the workings of local areas. At times, the Chinese had successfully mobilized for large-scale efforts. But the state had not moved to establish an organizational framework for sustained accumulation of resources. Organizational continuities befitted a slowly evolving—even a locally prosperous and unfettered—premodern society, not a mobilized society responsive to stepped-up efforts aimed at rapid social change and even less a society challenged by the forces of modernization.

Redistributive Processes

MOBILITY

In any society major changes in wealth, prestige, and occupation occur between generations within a single household and less frequently for individuals during the course of their adult lives; however, the rate of change in these measures of stratification varies among societies as do the avenues available for mobility. In China, the legal barriers to such changes were minimal, and the main avenues of examination success, transactions in land, and commercial entrepreneurship stretched into every community.

Chinese society recognized and encouraged social mobility to an extent that few other premodern societies did. Government employment could be aspired to by males from nearly any background whose persistence paid off in meritorious achievement on fairly administered examinations. Moreover, the government managed to manipulate prestige evaluations to the extent that degree holding brought enormous recognition in all local areas. Given the inevitable overlap between different aspects of stratification, at least a modicum of wealth and occupational change often resulted. The reverse side of this conveyor belt of opportunity was that downward mobility resulted either from a genuine lack of ability or merely from inertia. Each generation had to repeat the accomplishments of its predecessors to ensure that family prestige did not slip away.

The examination system, in which millions from each generation participated, set the tone for the entire society. For the vast majority, skill at farming and a mixture of good fortune and proper guidance in family matters contributed to differentials in wealth. With the accumulation of some surplus, families often turned to higher yielding but riskier investments, such as pawnshops or commerce. Change appeared gradually, as visible improvements in production and accumulation depended on the amount and quality of land that was cultivated and on the level of commercial transactions. Good fortune depended on the age and sex distribution of family members, roughly stated as the ratio of producers to consumers (although in fact everyone but the smallest children and most infirm was both). The choice of a hard-working daughter-in-law and the couple's success in producing male offspring affected the family's capacity to save. In some regions of China, the reluctance to allow women to work in the fields increased the influence of the sex ratio on household prosperity. Through slow increments a peasant family could increase its landholdings. The reverse could also occur, particularly because of equal inheritance among sons and the existence of concubines in some well-to-do households which increased the likelihood of more than one surviving son. Within a few generations even large fortunes would ordinarily be largely dissipated. Comparable flux should be assumed in smaller holdings as family wealth rose and fell from generation to generation. Relatively few impediments stood in the way of this fluidity.

Some factors that limited mobility require no explanation. Large numbers of poor households could not provide education for their children and faced a severe burden in overcoming chronic debts and in saving after paying out high rents on the land they farmed. Indeed, in some communities hereditary tenancy and chattel slavery signified an ascriptive inferiority contrary to the society's ideals. Part of the elite enjoyed hereditary status as members of the banners that had originally conquered China in 1644. Learning for practically everyone centered on the family and thus normally involved preparation for the same occupation as the parent of one's own sex practiced.

Other barriers to mobility may have escaped much notice. They inhere in the organizational contexts described above. Associations of persons from a common area of origin mainly served the migrant with means, who, after achieving success or training at home, followed a well-defined path. What happened to the poor fellow without connections? If the impersonal urban job market was indeed much more constricted in China than in Japan or Russia, then the conversion from peasant to urban hired laborer or merchant would have proven more difficult to make. Nevertheless, even for many poor migrants to cities the *t'ung-hsiang* identity probably could serve in a general way to provide the needed connection. Others might fall in with socially deprived groups such as beggars, bandits, and prostitutes.

Overall, the evidence suggests that intraclass mobility for peasants and for the elite was greater in China than in Russia or Japan. For merchants and artisans a similar conclusion would also seem appropriate given the relative dearth of privileges and fixed obligations for specific Chinese groups. Clearly interclass mobility into and out of the elite occurred much more frequently in China. Moreover the rich peasant in China could easily convert funds into merchant status and vice versa—a stark contrast to both Japan and Russia. Probably in only one avenue of mobility did Chinese traffic lag—most conspicuously in comparison with the ideal—even where the absence of legal barriers would seem to have speeded the flow; the Chinese poor found it extremely difficult to achieve upward mobility through the urban sector. A proportionately smaller urban sector not experiencing rapid growth and dominated by native sons and strong organizations of outsiders from particular areas could not welcome many migrants driven by desperation into the cities. As James L. Watson (1977) indicates, even the most unsatisfactory rural conditions, as long as they provided security, were deemed superior to urban migration. Only in famine conditions did poor people sometimes flock to the cities, and their march could usually be headed off by foresight in distributing relief to affected areas.

Fixed statuses in other societies restricted opportunities for interclass mobility and often cushioned the impact of changes in life's fortunes. Many households had relatively fixed places within such associations as state organizations of the elite, merchant groups, and village hierarchies. In Chinese society, the dearth of intermediate organizations may have increased the fluidity of movement; there was little to restrict one's rise or fall. Mobility in China was centered more in the family and less in intermediate organizations. Perhaps as a consequence, there were few new channels of mobility in Ch'ing China.

Migration

This subject remains little explored in the literature on premodern China. In the absence of analyzed and interpreted statistics on migration, it is necessary to draw tentative conclusions on the basis of fragmentary data and information bearing indirectly on migration.

From the level of urbanization in China, it is possible to conclude that the flow of rural-urban migrants remained rather slow. Because inheritance practices granted each son a stake in village property and in ancestral shrines and tablets, it seems likely that community bonds restricted permanent movement to the city. The widespread presence of elite households and of lavish consumption in rural settings suggests the lack of a strong pull to the cities on those with means. If one considers elite migration, China can be clearly distinguished from Japan and Russia where alternate systems of residence produced a regular circulation of local leaders between local areas and the largest cities. If one examines migration of young adults without means, China can again be distinguished from Japan, where it was common to send family members away to serve in other households. In both these situations migration represented a rather unusual act in response to special circumstances.

Despite the absence of legal barriers, the Chinese did not flock to cities. The urban percentage remained fixed at a level well below the rising levels in Japan and Russia where, paradoxically, some legal restrictions did operate. Even during the period of peak population growth—and presumably greatest pressure on land resources—Chinese cities at best maintained roughly a constant percentage of the total population. Large, unruly urban crowds rarely created a menace—further indication that the destitute and unemployed did not gravitate to the cities.

Of course, different types of cities and sections within or outside the city walls exerted different appeals to migrants. Cities and urban wards varied sharply in their occupational structure, mean household size, and attractiveness for the wealthy, as indicated by degree holders, and for the poor, as indicated by beggars. Yet, in general, neither push nor pull factors operated with much force; in contrast to the situation in Japan and Russia, in China large numbers were not motivated by family structure or local landowning practices to escape the village, nor by attractive job opportunities created by expanding urban functions and state mobilization efforts to enter the city.

In various ways, the Chinese pattern of migration might be traced to two circumstances: the adequacy of rural services and the absence of a powerful urban elite or state leadership core able to make the city into a markedly different environment. The Chinese rural dweller was served not only by an extensive marketing network for goods, but also by traveling recreation such as temple fairs, storytellers, theaters, and preaching monks. Since its wealth was not being drained off into the city, the rural family could enjoy a standard of living that could not be readily bettered. In turn, the urban sector did not emerge as a magnet for migrants because the state did not take aggressive action to transform the cities and endow them with a self-perpetuating elite and a privileged core of merchants.

With the establishment of treaty ports, the efforts by local and regional associations to establish *hui-kuan* and *t'ung-hsiang* organizations in the growing cities intensified. The level of rural-urban migration probably rose marginally. Apart from these indicators, migration patterns prior to 1900 do not appear to register any notable responses to the new forces of social change. Migration to rural areas occurred primarily in the southwest and, beginning in the nineteenth century, in Manchuria. Although it was an important factor in the rapid growth of these regions, on a national level, migration was on a small scale.

MARKETING

The primacy of local circulation over the channeling of goods into large cities has already been discussed under "Patterns of Settlement" earlier in this chapter. The commerce, voluminous for a premodern society, circulated primarily in rural intracommunity exchange.

China's ratio of population to marketing settlements (roughly 12,000–13,000 persons per market) may have lacked the advantages of either extreme found in other countries. The lower ratios in England and France (6,000–10,000 persons per market) produced a vibrant exchange conducive to the relatively uncontrolled mobilization of resources in a society initiating modernization. Unfettered popular participation in commerce conceivably led to a gradual buildup of resources in the community, vast amounts of which found their way into cities. In contrast, the higher ratios of overall population to markets in Japan and Russia (about 17,000 per market) when combined with other evidence support the conclusion that more resources were removed from rural transactions and placed directly under outside authorities. Added outside control in mobilizing resources, leaving less to be taken directly to market, probably improved the capacity to respond to external stimuli in early modernization. Even if China had reached the point of vibrant community exchange, the circulation of resources, as we have seen in the section on the urban hierarchy, was impaired for wider areas of exchange. Nor did high levels of taxation or rents draw large quantities of goods directly into higher-level central places (Rozman, 1976).

The continued appearance of periodic markets in China (to the extent that the ratio of population to markets fell instead of rising as in Japan and Russia after 1860) further indicates a move in the direction of the first-comers to modernization in 1700 rather than that of the rapidly modernizing latecomers in 1800. In the late nineteenth and early twentieth centuries, markets formed faster than the population grew in almost all areas of China. Even if we cannot take this indicator as adequate evidence that rural community consumption outpaced urban accumulation, it suggests that at a time when resources streamed in ever larger quantities into cities in Japan and Russia, Chinese marketing remained rural oriented (Rozman, 1982).

There is ample evidence to show that redistribution beyond standard marketing areas was unusually low in China. Rents and taxation also contributed to this situation. Provinces with large grain exports did produce high levels of tenancy, presumably a factor in the accumulation through rents of resources that might otherwise have gone for consumption. Yet, in many provinces tenancy rates remained low, tenancy generally did not signify absentee or large-scale ownership, and even absentee owners with sizable holdings normally resided nearby and did not create a powerful force for the removal of resources from the community. A clear contrast exists with Russia's large-scale rent payments (actually serf obligations) and marketing by the local elite to support its urban and urban-induced consumption standards.

An even more striking contrast characterizes redistribution through taxation. With the exception of Peking, which received tribute, urban centers benefited only slightly from rural taxes. Most important, this condition resulted from the low and falling real levels of taxation, discussed in Chapter 4; the falling levels were particularly evident in the land tax which brought in the bulk of revenue. Although for a time in the mid-nineteenth century the rising value of silver and the falling value of rice caused the rural tax burden to rise, over the final half of the Ch'ing dynasty taxes mostly declined. Furthermore, some of the local fees that added to the tax rate did not lead to outside accumulation but rather to redistribution to governmental underlings within the local area. By a factor of at least three or four, the land tax brought in a smaller percentage of the land produce than in Japan.

In summary, redistributive processes all reveal communities that although not isolated from the surrounding society, were comfortably self-contained as measured by modest rates of exchange with the outside. If interest focuses not on the legal acceptance of freedom for migration, social mobility, and marketing, but on the actual volume of these movements of human and material resources, then China lacked several of the features identified as important for Japan and Russia. Conditions favored upward mobility within the local community unless a strong organization already promoted the interests of persons from this area within a particular city. Shopping trips to the local market involved large numbers, while few migrated outside the marketing area. Goods to a large extent circulated locally. Land could easily be owned in nearby villages. Labor could readily be hired in or out, independent of village boundaries. Together with the remarkably low level of government involvement in redistribution through taxation, these conditions fostered local autonomy and, most likely, help account for persistent population growth.

Personal Relationships

CONTRACTUAL ORIENTATIONS

Nepotism and contractualism both reached unusual proportions in China. The former so predominated in local areas that the only powerful organizational foci in the society not based on kinship emerged among individuals away from home; laws of avoidance isolated officials from the demands of relatives, and the principle of *t'ung-hsiang* to some extent contained kinship claims for merchants away from home. Neither the government bureaucracy nor guilds directly challenged the priority of family concerns; they worked around them or built on them in a separate environment, which only a small minority in the society experienced.

Legal contracts provided an orderly method of interaction between households. Transactions in land, labor, and credit long exhibited an impersonal, contractual pattern. (Examples of such contracts can be found in the work of Fu-mei Chang Chen and Ramon H. Myers, 1976.) The relation between landlord and tenant generally maintained this pattern. Specific obligations and responsibilities would normally be waived only when a community consensus was reached that harvest conditions did not warrant full payment of rent.

Perhaps more than in other premodern societies, interfamilial relations operated through proper introductions and go-betweens. Arranged marriages did not simply give respectability to an informal decision by the couple; they confirmed a highly impersonal process of selection based on clear-cut criteria and the experienced skills of a matchmaker. Merchant-customer and employer-hired laborer relations also often depended on formal introductions.

Despite conspicuous elements of choosing people based on who they were rather than on what they could do (evident, for example, in the magistrate's preference for contracts with degree holders and in *t'ung-hsiang* relationships in general), Chinese social practices rested on a pervasive framework of customary law often upheld by state regulations. These arrangements assumed equality before the law of all parties to the agreement and a high degree of literacy among the parties and their witnesses. This framework made possible household strategies for upward mobility and undoubtedly contributed to the vitality of redistributive processes within the local community.

China may have given unusual weight to contractual arrangements; yet they operated within a pervasive and enduring family-centered context. Indeed, this puzzling combination may help account for the weakness of intermediate organization. In other words, impersonal mechanisms, including contracts and markets, enabled the household to operate successfully as an independent entity.

During the nineteenth century, with the deterioration of local government (described in Chapter 3), the state became a less reliable source of support for orderly, contractual relationships. The personalized, often nepotistic, forces in the society became more pronounced. Yet, these trends are but a faint glimmering of the forces that were to be unleashed in the early twentieth century.

LINES OF AUTHORITY

Individualism as a determinant of behavior was weak in China. Strong family solidarity took precedence, and important decisions were made by the family head. These are not unusual features in premodern societies. Although in certain western countries an individualist ideal (often associated with the ideal of romantic love) was emerging, elsewhere the group's hold over the individual remained virtually unchallenged. What was distinctive in China was the context in which controls over the individual operated.

In Japan and Russia, family loyalty also was highly valued; communities stressed mutual responsibility within the household, and, at the same time, leaders favored collective obligations among groups of neighboring households. Several differences with China can be noted. First, these societies managed to provide more reinforcement for family controls. In China, various systems of mutual responsibility among households, such as the *pao-chia* system, appear not to have worked as well or in as many contexts. Village-wide collectivist activities were relatively weak; other types of formally constituted neighborhood bonds also proved tenuous. Second, outside of the family setting, the Chinese was freer to act independently of any reference groups; individualism by default resulted from a dearth of alternative organizational forms. The individual functioned in terms of relatively few intermediate organizations not directly connected with or patterned on the family. Once outside of the demanding family context, there were few controls. Secret societies, rebel bands, or religious sects arose despite government vigilance. Of course, the individual rarely operated outside of the family context in the absence of extraordinary circumstances.

In all three societies young married women and children were subjected to the most stringent demands for obedience and conformity. The future of the household depended on their proper behavior. Prior to the initial penetration of new influences in China during the late nineteenth century, these lines of authority within the household remained unambiguous. In contrast, there is more evidence of new trends in the cities of Japan and Russia, especially among the self-perpetuating urban elites including commercial elements. The notion of a separate city culture or personality type and distinctive expectations for individuals in particular social classes had wide popularity in Japan and Russia.

Apart from the family, and in some localities, the lineage, clear lines of authority were missing in China. Mutual responsibility could not be aggregated easily at the village level and through larger units beyond the village. These conditions made joint action and mobilization on a large scale difficult except under charismatic leadership associated with secret societies.

The very qualities found in Japan and Russia of village collectivism, direct hierarchies of power, and potentially unconditional loyalty to a national authority figure were less evident in China. As discussed earlier, villages had few joint responsibilities and powers while their ostensible headmen were often upstaged by degree holders. Given the large scale of counties and the virtual absence of a subadministrative elite, no basis existed for a direct hierarchy of power reaching from community to national leaders. In short, one might surmise that family solidarity in China did not allow for strong alternative orientations or for nested loyalties culminating outside of the local community.

For personal relations in general, this comparative approach to China identifies a pattern of discrete family-centered and lineage-centered local solidarities bolstered by a loose array of potential *t'ung* organizations and by the impersonal workings of highly contractual customary law for exchanges and purchases of land, labor, and credit. This pattern leads to fragmentation and localism. Its full development probably requires widespread literacy, commercial exchange, and acceptance of the main tenets of the national social structure and ideology. Once ingrained, it seems to be an enormously difficult pattern to dislodge. Even in the early stages of modernization, the sinews of this family-based loyalty structure remain strong while the task of reaching into each community to nurture a new and well-organized hierarchy of loyalties proves formidable indeed.

International Comparisons

In terms of the vitality of local conditions, Chinese society achieved an early and substantial development; in terms of the integration of local communities into wider areas, China reveals a lack of development that continued into the nineteenth century. Locally China sustained remarkable population growth, occupational diversity, literacy, social mobility, contractual interaction, and exchange through marketing. These conditions generally fostered the attitude that superior performance would be rewarded and that the rural community provided adequate services compared to what might be available by leaving it.

One might have expected a society with such local vitality and so rationalized a social system to have modernized more quickly than did Japan or Russia. After all, the major achievements of Chinese civilization appear remarkably modern in character: market forces prevailed, and low or moderate taxation did not seriously limit the options of communities or households, the achievement ethic flourished, and a fluid social class system made possible an orderly and relatively predictable environment for the pursuit of mobility strategies. Yet, the record of these three countries suggests that other conditions are more conducive to modernization as a latecomer.

Among the many factors mentioned in connection with China's limited capacity for broad-based accumulation of resources, we would reiterate three especially significant contrasts with Japan and Russia. First, sustained population growth in already densely settled China meant that the basis for using traditional resources for broadening the surplus was declining, whereas in Japan with tight community controls on the number of households, and in Russia with rapidly expanding grain production in previously sparsely settled areas, the potential surplus was growing. Second, the increasingly urban orientation of Japan and Russia contrasts with China's decidedly rural orientation. Both administrative measures requiring increased movements of resources into cities and pressures from elites residing in urban areas contributed in Japan and, to a lesser extent, in Russia to waves of urbanization, to rural transformations under the influence of new urban forces, and to relative centralization of wealth and population in very large cities and in local administrative centers. The Chinese state did not adopt new policies in pursuit of urban concentrations, and the Chinese elite remained dispersed; consequently the network of cities was markedly decentralized. Third, the overwhelmingly family-centered organization of Chinese society was associated with a dearth of intermediate organizations that could operate as counterweights and with a dispersed distribution of resources. Outside of the family and kinship context, alternative bases of control and coordination remained fragile. Intercommunity linkages and community organizations as well lacked the strength of those in Japan and Russia. Furthermore, the demographic and organizational constraints we have noted likely worsened during the course of the Ch'ing dynasty, and, although it is uncertain whether the urban constraints worsened, they do not seem to have showed any improvement either. Thus not only the basic features of social structure, but also their pattern of change contrast strikingly with the vast gains in conditions conducive to modernization made in Japan and Russia over the seventeenth to nineteenth centuries.

China lacked particular elements of social integration, especially at the local or county level, where the assets of separate communities might have been merged. It was lightly taxed. Its elite remained scattered and rural in orientation. Villages lacked solidarity. No spurt upward occurred in the urban percentage of the population. The family and lineage were rarely constrained by outside organizations. Communities were unusually self-contained in their redistributive processes and in patterns of personal loyalties. Resources remained available for family use, cementing styles of consumption and ceremonial expenses that would prove difficult to dislodge and contributing to population growth that would complicate accumulation of surplus resources.

This complex of social conditions could not simply be overturned by new state initiatives. In Japan and Russia centuries had been required to build an infrastructure capable of mobilizing the resources of scattered communities. Elites had been concentrated and reequipped; settlement patterns had been reshaped with the effect of funneling resources up the urban hierarchy; organizations intermediate between the state and the kinship group had taken root. Family decisions and local autonomy had been circumscribed by countless decisions affecting redistributive practices and personal relations. Without this social infrastructure, the Chinese state's initial modernization efforts inevitably proved narrowly limited and unsuccessful. Compounding the task ahead were the enormity of Chinese society and the embedded state of community-centered resources.

CHAPTER SIX

Knowledge and Education

T HE ROBUST DEVELOPMENT OF PREMODERN CHINA commented on by Gilbert
Rozman in Chapter 5 is as evident in education as in other fields. Skills and
common values were widely distributed across the population to a degree
perhaps unequaled among other premodern societies with the exception of
Japan. Public and private record keeping and communications rested on
command of the written word. Education was universally prized, and both in
structure and content had an orientation toward achievement, universality,
and rationality. Secular schooling had been the norm for centuries. Yet
China's progress toward modernization has been halting. Is the apparent
similarity of values illusory? Did Chinese education fail to attain its proclaimed goals, or is it possible that in their very realization lay subtle traps,
crosscurrents that militated against change? What assets and what debits did
the intellectual and educational life of the Ch'ing bequeath to twentieth-
century modernizers?

Chinese educational institutions shared certain characteristics with other
premodern societies in which education has left the home but not yet taken up
residence in an institutionalized school system. Many functions today thought
appropriate for formal education—such as technical and professional training
and much research—were carried on informally, and formal education was
itself largely private, voluntary, and local, lacking any administrative structure and often without permanent buildings or funds. Other features—secularization, rationality, a high literacy rate, and state support of a limited
number of higher educational institutions for the elite—China held in common with advanced premodern states like Tokugawa Japan and (except for its
low level of popular literacy) eighteenth-century Russia; still others, chiefly
the examination system, were unique to China. In assessing the contribution

of each aspect of education to China's modernization, one should beware of considering merely the convertibility of indigenous educational forms into their modern counterparts—institutions of primary, secondary, or tertiary education. One must also take into account the context of education: the social, economic, and political interrelations that may make the traditional an aid to modernization or the apparently modern a diversion.

Government and education have been linked in China since Confucius trained his followers in the principles of virtuous rule in the fifth century B.C. The relationship, still fluid in the Chou dynasty, was formalized under later dynasties. The state had a twofold interest in the results of education: the selection of talent for use in administration, and the transformation of the people through familiarity with the precepts that guided the lives of their betters.

The enlistment of talent through local recommendation and its more deliberate cultivation through salaried students attached to the court had begun 2,000 years earlier, in the Han dynasty. By the later Han, each group's fitness for office was tested by examinations in the Confucian classics. Students and their lecturers were supported not only at the court but in provincial-level schools, and educational officials were appointed to the provinces; that is, the foundation of later dynasties' examinations and state schools had been laid. Under the Sui the examination system or *k'e-chü* was established as the dominant route to office in an attempt by the imperial house to counter the power of aristocratic families, a policy continued under the T'ang. Government schools were set up and examinations held at the county level, but since the opportunity to take the examinations was not confined to students at the schools their functions gradually atrophied despite later attempts by Sung reformers to restore their status. Under the Ming and Ch'ing the examinations became entrenched as the only method of recruiting talent for high government office. The academies or *shu-yuan*, which had arisen in the Sung as centers of free discussion challenging the dominance of the examinations, were also drawn into their orbit; scholars used their regular essay competitions to brush up their examination technique.

"The transformation of the people" was in Confucian theory to be achieved primarily by the example of the ruler. Mencius had mentioned with approval the schools of the three dynasties, but apart from Ming attempts to set up a network of community schools and Ch'ing endeavors to sinicize border tribes through free schools, the state usually left formal education at the elementary level in private hands. The moral welfare—or ideological control—of the mass of their subjects was nonetheless a matter of some concern to emperors of the last two dynasties. Both Ming T'ai-tsu and the Ch'ing K'ang-hsi emperor framed a set of moral maxims for popular consumption; the sayings of the latter were elaborated by his son, the Yung-cheng emperor, into what Miyazaki (1976, p. 23) calls an Imperial Rescript on Education (on the analogy of that issued by the Meiji emperor). The rescript, or Amplified

Instructions, was to be expounded regularly in public places for the edification of both the literate and the illiterate, in lectures known as the *hsiang-yueh* or rural compact. An edict enjoining faithful performance of the lectures—to be carried out by local officials—expresssed confidence that they would "open the minds of their hearers. Not only will the careful and compliant delight in them; even the wild and unruly will feel some constraint."

Although the historian Ch'en Tung-yuan has characterized the two millennia of imperial rule as a period of "scholar-nurturing education" (1937, preface, p. 3), the majority of those who attended school had no higher goals than learning to read and write, with a view to personal advantage rather than Confucian self-cultivation. To these basic skills technical or commercial training might be added, under the guidance of parent or master— the latter usually involving indentureship as an apprentice. Yet the schools developed no separate track for nonacademic needs; despite the pragmatic goals of its patrons, even elementary school education was dominated by the classical curriculum tested by the examination system. Texts at the private schools or *ssü-shu* were cast in Confucian mold as early as the first century A.D., and tutors continued to teach the classics for another nineteen hundred years. Popular familiarity with the main themes of Confucian texts can be attributed in part to the humble village schoolmaster.

The dominance of Confucianism within the schoolroom did not mean it held unquestioned sway outside it. Indeed, it is worth remembering that there is in Chinese no word for "Confucianism," which is, in a sense, a construct of western scholars. A commonly used equivalent is *ju-chiao,* or the teachings (set of beliefs, school of thought, doctrines) of scholars. This usage points up the distance between scholarly studies and the beliefs of the masses, who were more likely to profess adherence to Buddhism (*Fo-chiao*) and Taoism (*Tao-chiao*). These faiths performed an integrating function from below, being followed by scholars in their idle hours. Cultural integration was also achieved through popular ballads and drama, almanacs, and handbooks of general knowledge. Non-Confucian elements were not, however, important in formal elite learning.

Another phrase often used to comprehend the essence of Confucian teachings was *"san kang wu ch'ang"*—the three bonds and five relationships that regulated family and state through the subordination of subject to ruler, son to father, and wife to husband. These represented the established social order, to be defended against attacks from outside—the barbarous values of the West—and within—erosion by ill-disciplined rowdies and heretical rebels. That they were not always taken completely seriously by the masses is reflected in the frequent portrayal in popular literature of the Confucian scholar as a namby-pamby prig, cast into the shade by dashing heroes or warriors or strategists. These teachings did, however, leave a legacy of shared norms in family behavior—the propriety of wifely submission and filial duty—and a sense that moralizing was an appropriate government function.

185

Whether they led in practice to greater docility on the part of the masses seems doubtful in view of the frequency of rebellions in Chinese history.

Confucianism did not rule the marketplace or even the magistrate's *yamen:* economic exchange—from family transactions to interregional exchange—rested on sophisticated legal arrangements and accounting procedures, and government administration, as Thomas A. Metzger (1973) has shown, involved far more than adherence to Confucian pieties. What was taught in schools was, however, congruent with customs and values outside them. Education dovetailed with practical needs, providing their basic tool—literacy—and at the same time acted as a gauge of social status as determined by the elite.

Popular Education

The widening of functional literacy beyond the ranks of a tiny minority is required for the extension of the new knowledge, techniques, and modes of social organization involved in modernization. This appears to have happened in premodern Japan and northern Europe. It has been estimated that late Tokugawa Japan had a male literacy rate of more than 40 percent, providing the groundwork for the rapid achievement of universal education and for the regulation and mobilization of the populace in response to new government demands.

The literacy rate for Ch'ing China appears to have approached that of Tokugawa Japan. The exact rate is difficult to ascertain: no statistics are available prior to the twentieth century, necessitating a disproportionate reliance on surveys of the 1920s and 1930s. A sample age cohort measured in the 1930s gave a male literacy rate of 40 percent for males over fifty. Estimates made in the Ch'ing by contemporary Chinese scholars range from less than 30 percent to a hyperbolically low 5 percent. Difficulties are compounded by lack of clarity in the definition of literacy: "knowing one's letters" could refer to anything from rote memorization of elementary primers to the basic literacy required for keeping accounts and writing letters, to the high literacy—familiarity with the classics, ability to compose essays and poetry—possessed by the scholar-gentry. The latter probably included between 5 and 10 percent of the male population. There must have been an equal number of the professionally literate, subofficials, clerks, merchants and traders, military men, and clergy. Overall, as Evelyn Sakakida Rawski's recent study (1979, p. 23) has shown, functional literacy in the eighteenth and nineteenth centuries was probably "greater than has previously been supposed. Basic literacy was unevenly distributed between males and females, with perhaps 30 to 45 percent of males and only 2 to 10 percent of females possessing some ability to read and write.'' A more precise estimate seems impossible on present data; nor is it possible to determine from available figures whether the rate of literacy was rising or falling, though it has been surmised that increasing commercialization during the late Ch'ing would have involved increased literacy, especially in the cities.

At the elementary level, the difference between urban and rural access to education was not great. Many sources bear testimony to the ubiquity of the village school. Shu Hsin-ch'eng recalls that in his childhood in Hunan at the end of the nineteenth century, the passer-by could hear the chanting of lessons in every hamlet of ten households. Only poverty prevented a village from hiring a teacher and setting up a school (with private schools or *ssŭ-shu* the two were synonymous; unless a school possessed its own property, it did not exist independently of its current teacher). The fact that schooling was not simply an urban phenomenon, but flourished in all but the most sparsely populated and poverty-stricken rural areas meant that Ch'ing China had a relatively even base on which to build the structure of a modern school system. By the time such a system came to be established, however, the modernizers of the late Ch'ing had resolved to make a new start rather than build on old foundations. It was in spite of, rather than because of, the attentions of educationalists that indigenous forms of schooling persisted for some half-century after schooling on the western model was introduced.

In social terms, schooling had a restricted but not exclusive distribution. ''Mass education'' in the modern sense—the compulsory attendance of every school-age child—did not of course exist. Tuition fees were required at most schools, limiting attendance to the sons of those families with some disposable income and no pressing demand for labor power. Fees were flexible, since it was in the schoolmaster's interest to take as many pupils as he could control; the sum paid was negotiable depending on family circumstances, and could be paid in installments or in kind. The cost of schooling rose with the amount of attention given the pupil. The dearest was that of the family school where a tutor was hired for the children of one family and its associates. In such cases, daughters as well as sons might receive an education; there was no objection to female schooling as such, but only to the impropriety of a girl's mixing with the opposite sex outside the home. The south had some schools for girls taught by women, but these appear to have been unknown in North China. For those who could not afford fees, there were community schools which hired a teacher out of an endowment of property for the education of the poor but talented. These included the charity and lineage schools of Central and South China, which subsidized the education of poorer members of the clan. Such schools were intended for the succor of the deserving and not as vehicles of universal education: recorded charity schools, according to Evelyn Sakakida Rawski, ''provided negligible opportunities for education'' (1979, p. 184). Even if one assumes considerable underrecording it seems unlikely that free schooling reached as many as one in twenty of the school-age population.

An attempt to bring a different kind of enlightenment to the poor was made by missionary educators in the last half of the nineteenth century. Their clientele was initially restricted to those without hope of rising in society through the examinations; foreign-run schools were an object of contempt among the gentry until the state espoused the value of foreign qualifications at the beginning of the twentieth century.

Schooling was undoubtedly widespread in Ch'ing China, but quantity of education cannot be identified with quality. To the difficulty of the Chinese script must be added the difficulty of the texts with which the young reader struggled. Even beginning primers were written in classical Chinese rather than in the vernacular; the simplest of them, the *Three Hundred Character Classic,* dated from the Sung, while another popular text, the *Thousand Character Classic,* was a literary tour de force written in the sixth century A.D. With the *Hundred Family Names,* these formed the staple of childhood education. Their rhymed couplets served basically as character mnemonics, though a good deal of simple moral, historical, bibliographical, and general knowledge was conveyed to those who penetrated their meaning. The core of the curriculum, the Confucian Four Books, was written in even more archaic language; and the final stage of the reading course, the Five Classics, required specialized scholarship. None of these books had been written for children, and it was assumed that only adults could comprehend their teachings; their meaning, therefore, was usually not explained to the pupil until he had memorized them in toto, a stage usually reached by the age of twelve or thirteen. For those whose education broke off before this stage, even the literal meaning of the words in these texts was often a mystery. But as recent research has shown (Evelyn Sakakida Rawski, 1979), the classics were not the only route to literacy for young Chinese, though they were the standard one. Many from nongentry families had recourse to *tsa-tzu* or glossaries whose contents—names of tools, clothing, animals, plants, buildings, and so on—were more readily apprehended than the abstractions of even the most elementary primer. In addition, professional and amateur storytelling and balladry constituted an informal preparation for reading; once the plot and the words of a story were thoroughly familiar, deciphering the printed text required a relatively low level of skill.

The everyday uses of literacy for the bulk of the population in Ch'ing China can be divided into three main categories: convivial, technical, and business or adversary. Under the first head comes the celebration of events in the seasonal or individual cycle—the composition of couplets for the New Year or for a birth, marriage, or funeral. The local schoolmaster was often called in for such occasions. One may also include the reading of romances, ballads, and ghost stories, which were commonly retold to a wider audience. Under the second come technical manuals for a craftsman or farmer and the technical knowledge purveyed through more general works such as cheaply produced encyclopedias for everyday use. Almanacs provided every household with the details of the rural calendar. Business or adversary uses of literacy, the third category, covers the contracts required for commercial and domestic dealings—buying and selling, record keeping, mortgaging, tenancy agreements, marriage, and adoption—official documents—public notices, household registration, taxation requirements—and the disputes and litigation arising out of these. There is some evidence that the drawing up of contracts, a complex and specialized task, was carried on within particular families. To a greater extent than in premodern Europe or Japan, literacy in China functioned not simply as a tool of communication but as a talisman, a weapon. In Chu The's words, "Since tax collectors, officials and soldiers respected or were afraid of educated men, my family decided to send one or more sons to school." There are many other examples of relatively humble families who resolved to redress the balance by educating the next generation. Where lawsuits in rural areas were concerned, the village schoolmaster could again be called in to write plaints and pleas; since either side could hire him, however, it was obviously best to have an educated man in the family. Among those affected by this way of thinking was Mao Tse-tung, who recalled: "My father . . . wanted me to master the Classics, especially after he was defeated in a lawsuit because of an apt classical quotation used by his adversary in the Chinese court."

The accumulated skills of the bulk of the population provided a desirable foundation for modernization. Whether and when these were called into play depended in part on the rate of economic growth—slowed by a population some ten times the size of Japan's, and a land area twenty times as great—in part on the attitudes and policies of China's elite, the scholar-gentry.

Knowledge and Education among the Elite

No sharp cutoff point existed between popular and elite education. Certainly, the son of a "household filled with the fragrance of books," whose parents could afford a private tutor, acquired a better education than a boy attending classes with "ten odd students in a small room, all squawking nonstop," memorizing "a lot of nonsense syllables," in the words of Ma Hsu-lun. But both could learn to read from the same text, and a change in family fortunes or variations in individual ability could mean that the latter would succeed while the former failed. The possibility of such a rise, however remote, assured the population of the justice of the social order in much the same way as the log-cabin-to-presidency myth sustains belief in democracy in the United States.

Education was desirable because the ruling class reproduced itself largely by means of a highly competitive examination system; anyone who passed the first (county) level had legal privileges (immunity from corporal punishment), social status, and the opportunity to become an official through passing examinations at the second (provincial) and third (metropolitan) level. What this meant can be seen in a poem by one of the Sung emperors:

> In books there are houses of gold;
> In books there are a thousand bushels of grain;
> In books horses and carriages abound;
> In books can be found women with faces of jade.

In popular form, the message was repeated in proverbs—''Become an official and make money''—and inspirational verse:

> The emperor values heroes bold, and writing would have you learn.
> Other occupations are lowly in rank; study alone is high. . . .
> The court's full of nobles in purple and gems; scholars, every one.

Although only a small percentage of those who embarked on the study of the Four Books sat the examinations based on them, and only a fraction of examination candidates passed even the lowest examination, the goal of success dangled before every boy who learned to read, while its benefits were borne in—through stories, plays, and displays of official pomp—even on the illiterate. Schooling gained a large part of its prestige from association with elite culture and a large part of its utility from association with elite power. The identification of educational achievement with entry to the elite has to a large extent persisted to the present day.

Modern reformers have inveighed against classical education as being impractical, not related to the needs of daily living. In fact, a classical orientation was probably inevitable given the social structure of Ch'ing China. Not only membership in but dealings with the elite required a knowledge of its language; to have confined one's course of study to simple, everyday language and locally observable phenomena, the goal of later educationalists, would have been to receive a second-class education. Reading ''dead books,'' on the other hand, could have immediate utility. The social status accorded knowledge was linked with mastery of a philosophy of governance rather than with increased productivity or efficiency, so that a literary education was valued not only by scholars but by peasants, craftsmen, and merchants.

Popular and state interest in education coincided in the examination system. The examination system selected men for offices on an impersonal, equitable basis; quotas were allotted by region, and the identity of candidates was carefully concealed from examiners. The system was highly centralized; the emperor himself conducted the last stage in the final examination, emissaries direct from Peking supervised the provincial examinations, and even the lowest or county level was supervised by the court-appointed provincial director of studies. The system thus possessed many of the characteristics of a "modern" institution: it was centralized, operated on a national scale, and fulfilled a rational bureaucratic function implemented through a series of impersonal, universalistic regulations. There were, however, certain differences: as Max Weber observed, "the examinations of China tested whether or not the candidate's mind was thoroughly steeped in literature and whether or not he possessed the ways of thought suitable to a cultured man and resulting from cultivation in literature . . . this education was on the one hand purely secular in nature, but on the other, was bound to the fixed norm of the orthodox interpretation of the classic authors. It was a highly exclusive and bookish literary education" (1951, p. 121).

The literary nature of Chinese criteria for office has often been contrasted, implicitly or explicitly, with western specialization. The comparison is somewhat overdrawn, since few sections of western bureaucracies recruit specialists into administrative positions and many indeed discourage a specialist orientation. The outstanding example of the generalist is perhaps that of the classically educated civil servants who administered the British empire, whose own selection process was influenced by the example of the Chinese examination system, but the tendency is still evident today.

Similarly, the socialization aspect of the selection process has its counterpart in western bureaucracies; new recruits are tested for compatibility with established members of the hierarchy. In China, where the emperor topped the hierarchy, loyalty to the ruling house was mandatory, if often passive and perfunctory. In addition, recruits had to be worthy representatives of the wider community of scholars, for it was as patron of Confucian learning that the state appointed talented men to office. Since this was "*the* body of learning, artistic as well as moral, which . . . lent itself more easily, for examination purposes, to aesthetic exposition than to practical implementation" (Levenson, 1968, p. 41), it is not surprising that examinations measured literary style and calligraphy as well as intellect and scholarship. Literary artifice was taxed in particular by the "eight-legged essay," an elaborate form which was peculiar to the examination system. Essay topics consisted of quotations from the Four Books, which the candidate enlarged upon from the standpoint of the speakers in the chosen passage—a convention that enabled him to get by with being totally ignorant of events after the third century B.C., since their introduction would have constituted an anachronism.

The examination sessions themselves were a test of nerve, stamina, and meticulous care. At the provincial level, candidates were locked into the examination compound for nearly three days, eating and sleeping in tiny examination cells. C. T. Hu, quoting the *Ch'ing-ch'ao ye-shih ta-kuan*, writes that the ordeal required "the sprightliness of a stallion, physical strength of a donkey, fortitude of a beetle and perseverance of a camel." Natural selection must have ensured that many officials possessed these qualities in addition to more bookish abilities.

The examinations functioned both to maintain internal bureaucratic norms and to legitimize the position of office holders among the gentry from whom they were selected. If the selection process emphasized tractability rather than independent judgment, this was probably not contrary to the intentions of those who devised and ran it. As an institution, the examination system was by no means devoid of potential for change; simple imperial fiat abolishing the eight-legged essay (a Ming introduction) in favor of the topical essay (used in the T'ang and Sung) would have immediately broadened the studies and outlook of candidates without doing violence to Confucian propriety. Yet such an order was never issued, because the institution was inseparable from the men who operated and participated in it. The former group owed its legitimacy to the mastery of existing forms, the latter had spent years—often decades—attempting to acquire the same mastery. Together they formed a powerful vested interest. Their conservatism need not be attributed to the eight-legged essay per se, but rather to their investment in the status quo. (The medical profession in the United States in some ways forms a similar pressure group today.) These men succeeded in preserving the examination system unchanged into the twentieth century—by which time it was too late for change, and more radical modernizers had their way.

The number of candidates sitting the examinations always outnumbered the quota for degree holders; the ratio could be as high as forty to one. Unsuccessful scholars did not find their talents totally wasted, however. The compliant took positions as teachers or private secretaries; the disaffected few fomented unrest. The Taiping rebellion was led by a failed scholar.

In addition to the examinations, the Ch'ing government, like its predecessors, maintained a hierarchy of schools crowned by the Kuo-tzu-chien in the capital, with prefectural and county-level schools, some seventeen hundred in all, forming the base. These were staffed by the prefecture or county's educational officials. All those who passed the lowest level of the examinations—approximately 270,000 in the last half of the nineteenth century—were automatically enrolled as "students" in these schools, and the best among them were chosen for enrollment in the Kuo-tzu-chien. Their enrollment, however, was purely nominal, requiring no attendance and laying down no course of study. Listening to the occasional lectures given by the more conscientious educational officials or being present at the performance of Confucian ceremonies gained students no advantage in the examination system, the raison d'être of their studies. By the nineteenth century the educational function of these schools had dwindled into nonexistence. If the reality had withered, however, the form remained, and figured prominently in late nineteenth-century discussions of the desirability of establishing a modern school system.

From the eighteenth century on, the Ch'ing court also patronized academies or *shu-yuan*. Attempts at official regulation—of the course of study, the promotion of academy heads, and so on—combined with scholarly aspirations for an official career to lessen such intellectual autonomy as the academies had preserved from previous dynasties. Fiscally and administratively, they retained a degree of independence—being funded locally by donations from official, gentry, or merchant sources—but this was not often reflected in departures from the examination curriculum, which was as dear to local worthies as to the emperor.

The greatest contribution to Ch'ing intellectual life was made by those academies that were centers of Han learning (a school of classical interpretation sometimes referred to as the school of empirical research), and by others that gave equal place to Han and Sung learning (the neo-Confucian school whose interpretations were followed in the examination curriculum). Such institutions were well placed to profit from the disestablishment of Sung Confucianism for which they had prepared the way. Hunan's Lu-liang Academy, in 1907, encouraged its students to read widely and critically in Chinese classics and history; their studies were illumined by the lectures and example of the head. In 1907 however, this academy was already an anachronism within the new school system; the following year it was made into a lower primary school. Proponents of the new system could not afford, either intellectually or financially, to give quarter to the old.

Despite their cessation as institutions, the great academies—the Hsueh-hai T'ang in Kwangtung, Nan-ching and Cheng-yi in Kiangsu, Lien-ch'ih in Chihli—may be considered to have made an indirect contribution to early twentieth-century intellectual and political life through the men who received part of their training in them: Liang Ch'i-ch'ao, Chang Ping-lin, Huang Hsing, Wu Chih-hui . . . a roll call, in short, of some of the most influential figures in the reform and republican movements. All of them traveled a considerable distance beyond the most radical reinterpretations of their scholarly masters, but one must at least consider the possibility that their youthful training in open-minded inquiry and high purpose fostered their later capacity to conceive and act on a synthesis of Chinese and western thought.

Two other settings served as meeting places for scholars: the imperially sponsored bibliographical projects of the eighteenth century and the private staff of top provincial officials of the nineteenth. The former created a climate in which the school of empirical research flourished. Its special field was classical philology, undertaken as an instrument to test the authenticity of the Confucian canon. Building on the researches of Yen Jo-chu and Ku Yen-wu in the seventeenth century, this school sought to regain the true meaning of the classics. By the end of the Ch'ien-lung reign its work had degenerated into a rigid and sterile methodology. Studies in more practical fields had been inhibited by the Ch'ien-lung emperor's literary inquisition, the other side of his patronage of the arts. The emperor had not only ordered the destruction of works on the Manchu conquest, frontier regions, and defense, but also prescribed heavy penalties for their possession. Although actual executions were few, the threat must have reminded many of the need for circumspection.

A return to some previously forbidden topics was made in the first half of the nineteenth century, when, as Susan Mann Jones writes, "provincial officials . . . began to recruit scholars to write about the administrative crises confronting them—border defense, military strategy, and the breakdown of major bureaucratic institutions like the grain transport system and the Yellow River conservancy" (1974, p. 42). The men who wrote on these topics were not themselves in the pay of the government but were hired by a particular official as members of his private staff. They were friends as well as employees. In addition to this group, coteries of scholars at odds with current policies turned to questions of northern and maritime defense. Renewed concern with practical problems appears to have arisen from a sense of dynastic weakness; this perception, however, had to be conveyed cautiously. Even Wei Yuan's classic of statecraft, the *Huang-ch'ao ching-shih wen-pien*, seasons analyses of late Ch'ing problems with a liberal measure of flattery of the dynasty.

Twentieth-century revolutionaries explained lethargy in Ch'ing intellectual life as a result of Manchu repression of the natural genius of the Han Chinese. Their picture of intellectual decline was much overdrawn and their explanation biased; the Chinese emperor Ming T'ai-tsu had been the first to issue a blanket prohibition of private scholarly intervention in politics, a prohibition simply repeated by the Ch'ing rulers. Recent scholarship has given a different picture of competing schools, shifting factions, and pragmatic problem solving. Yet one must remember that most scholars operated, albeit adroitly, in a politically restricted world, where lese majesty threatened death. Everybody had heard the story of the scholar beheaded for having included in his examination paper two characters which, capriciously interpreted, could be seen as forming a decapitated version of "Yung-cheng," the title of the reigning emperor. The fact that such a once-in-a-century occurrence was unlikely to affect oneself or one's son or brother did not really matter; the warning was internalized and set unconscious limits on thought and action. The petition calling for basic reform presented to the throne by metropolitan examination candidates in 1895 was shocking not simply because of its content but because it breached the prohibition on scholars meddling in political matters.

A related theory, popular among nineteenth-century westerners and a later generation of Chinese, was that Confucianism was to blame for China's slowness to respond to the West. Confucianism may have bred a sense of public responsibility, but it was one that ran in well-defined channels. Brilliant and outspoken eccentrics like Kung Tzu-chen were unrewarded by the system, and W.A.P. Martin believed he was characterizing the typical Hanlin (member of the highest academic body) when he wrote:

> It is doing our Hanlin a species of injustice to compare him with the Academicians or even with the commonalty of the West, in a scientific point of view; for science is just the thing which he does not profess, and that general information which is regarded as indispensable by the average intelligence of Christendom is to the Hanlin a foreign currency, which has no recognized value in the market of his country. (1880, pp. 33–34)

A more balanced but equally critical verdict is given by Chang Chung-li, who sees Confucian conformity as state determined:

> The constant drilling in traditional Confucian moral principles and the writing of formalized essays kept the minds of the gentry so occupied that they had little time for independent thought and study. [Two thousand years earlier] Ch'in Shih-huang-ti had tried to control the scholars by forbidding them to read the classics, but the Ch'ing government tried to control them by making them read the classics. Their thought was channeled into the lines of official ideology in which the aspects of authority and discipline in the Confucian tradition were emphasized. (1955, p.198)

Confucianism as a philosophy was not inimical to trade, technology, or foreign dealings. But in imperial China Confucianism was never just a philosophy: it was a ticket to office, a weapon in faction fighting, a tool of control, a badge of status. Western learning, which performed none of these functions, interested only the exceptionally curious and far-sighted.

Science and Technology

The nexus between classical learning and access to prestige and power meant that nonliterary skills were neglected in both the private and the public manifestations of formal education. Although the study of mathematics, law, and medicine had been officially sponsored under the T'ang and Sung dynasties, by the Ch'ing specialist subjects had given way to classical studies. Skill in these fields thus became the province of professionals—doctors, private secretaries with training in law or accounting—or of amateur enthusiasts. The former were often failed or aspiring examination candidates who needed an income while they studied, not specialists in the modern sense of the word. Doctoring and teaching often went in tandem; both were respectable if not inspiring vocations for a literary man. For medical training, one took for master a practising doctor; for administrative, someone with years of experience as the private secretary of a high official. Military skills were likewise learned from a master, who imparted training in feats of individual prowess rather than group drill. An examination system for military degrees parallel to that for civil degrees existed, but it had far less prestige.

Channels of transmission for the researches of scholar-amateurs in such fields as geography, waterworks, astronomy, or mathematics were equally informal. Such interests were regarded as personal hobbies rather than disciplines with a defined body of knowledge and methodology; the all-embracing nature of the Confucian canon meant that it included all the social sciences and humanities, while subjects such as medicine imitated the Confucian style of learning with "classics" of their own. It was not until the advent of western education that the related concepts of independent disciplines and modern discovery, as distinct from the elucidation of meaning inherent in the classics, made headway in China.

Chinese experience differed from that of Europe in that secularization of thought was not a problem for Chinese thinkers schooled in a this-worldly Confucianism. The foundations of what Hu Shih calls scientific method had been laid by the school of empirical research, a school Susan Mann Jones (1974) has characterized as marked by a sense of skepticism, of relativity, and of professional competence. Unlike their European counterparts, however, eighteenth-century Chinese thinkers lavished these qualities on a narrow section of the social sciences—history and philology—neglecting not merely the natural sciences but political, economic, and military studies, an omission only partly redressed in the nineteenth century.

No rigid orthodoxy prevented Chinese philosophers from studying the natural sciences: no dogmas informed them that the earth was flat, man guilty of original sin, or creation completed at four in the morning in the year 4004 B.C. Individual philosophers did indeed achieve remarkable scientific insights. The Sung philosopher Chu Hsi, for example, explained the fossil shells found in mountain rocks as remnants of an age when the mountains were under water and the rocks, mud. But they did not elaborate such insights into a system. The major scientific work that was achieved, as by the late Ming botanist who preceded Linnaeus in the taxonomy of plants, was often carried out in isolation and met with official indifference.

The very secular, rational, and nondogmatic attitude of Confucianism in the sphere of the natural sciences may have contributed to their lack of development. Chinese thinkers did not have the stimulus of competing systems with absolute claims; any amount of experimental observation could be absorbed into the capacious framework of Chinese general knowledge, and there was little compulsion to explain away contradictions or reconcile opposed theories about the natural world.

Lack of intellectual systematization was paralleled by informal social organization, so that the indigenous tradition of scientific investigation was ill-equipped to hold its own against its nineteenth-century western variant. What remained to be carried over into the twentieth century was less a body of knowledge or a methodology than an attitude, "seeking the truth from the facts," a slogan that the school of Han learning had made its own in opposition to what it considered the empty metaphysics of Sung neo-Confucianism. That is, scientific values grew from the clash of ideas in the human rather than the natural sciences; the former was the main arena in Chinese thought. It is interesting to note that this slogan has so far maintained its influence that it has become the battle cry of a new school of practical learning in the People's Republic today.

Knowledge and skills associated with service to the state or the community had a respectability not accorded those solely concerned with making a living. The skills required of a craftsman, peasant, or trader were not considered part of general knowledge and were not included in even the most liberal curriculums. Even basic numeracy was seldom taught in schools. Preparation for occupations belonged to the world of work, not of schooling, and the requisite skills were usually obtained on the job—either at home, for simple accounting, agricultural techniques, and handicrafts, or, in a more commercial, less intimate arrangement, through apprenticeship to a firm. Most apprentices would learn the rudiments of reading and writing at a *ssǔ-shu* before embarking on account keeping and the use of the abacus under their employer. More specialized training in a particular technology was also acquired through a master-pupil relation.

One should not exaggerate the extent to which technical knowledge was removed from the public domain. Some cheap and widely circulated encyclopedias purveyed information on agricultural techniques through cartoons, making it readily accessible to the semiliterate. Many technical manuals existed. But in many cases, as Needham points out, "social factors prevented the publication of the records which the higher artisans certainly kept" (1969, p. 23). In these circumstances even simple mathematical knowledge could be tinged with a sense of initiation, as witnessed by the title of a work on the abacus quoted in Rawski: *New edition of the secretly transmitted orthodox methods of abacus calculation, for the convenience of scholars and commoners.*

More practical knowledge than that involved in the composition of the eight-legged essay might well have come to the fore had the latter not been compulsory for the examinations. A glimpse of the possible direction of an examination-free schooling may be gained from looking at some old-style schools operating in rural Szechwan in the 1940s. Organizationally they preserved the structure of their forebears, but the sociologist Liao T'ai-ch'u found that "subjects such as the use of the abacus, essentials of funerals, weddings and contracts and the attending of cows have been accepted into the szu shu curriculum" (1949, p. 56).

Although a wide body of technical and scientific knowledge existed in Ch'ing China (C.P. Ridley has pointed out the diversity of texts that could be found on subjects as specific as marine biology), it was not highly systematized or standardized and was often not transmissible outside a personal relationship—unlike classical learning, whose practitioners and texts were so numerous as to reduce the importance of any one master to any one pupil, and whose knowledge was standardized by examination procedure. The discovery that in the West, in Liang Ch'i-ch'ao's words, "farmers have scholars in farming, craftsmen have scholars in craft, merchants have scholars in commerce, and soldiers have scholars in soldiery" (1896) was a revelation not because China lacked a high level of achievement in many of these fields, but because their association with scholarship was unprecedented.

Western specialization struck the Chinese not on its own merits but because it seemed to account for western victories. In the aftermath of the Second Opium War, three schools were opened to train interpreters and specialists in foreign affairs in Peking, Shanghai, and Canton. Over the next thirty years, a number of naval and military schools, a mining school, and a school of telegraphy were set up by a handful of central and provincial leaders alarmed by the western threat. Like indigenous technical training, that given in these schools was not highly regarded. Their foreign associations were an added disadvantage: the first students at Peking's language school were ostracized for having surrendered to the foreigner. As Knight Biggerstaff observes, the schools "were generally regarded by the Chinese as completely outside the regular concept and system of education" (1961, p. 31). The majority of gentry members despised them, while the mass of people were ignorant even of their existence. Nonetheless, they did play a role in accustoming high officials to state intervention on behalf of western learning. Chang Chih-tung, for example, moved from patronage of reformed academies to the foundation of specialist schools to advocacy of a national school system in which western learning would occupy a place equal to Confucian.

Reformist leaders were less successful in the promotion of study abroad. A project to send boys to study in America was called off when it became evident that the first group, sent in 1870, was losing touch with its homeland. Thereafter, no government students (apart from a handful sent to Europe) went abroad until the late 1890s, a situation in striking contrast to that of early Meiji Japan, where the government recruited specialist foreign teachers and sent abroad students who were given high positions on their return.

Because there was no strong government direction, missionaries have often claimed credit for the spread of western learning in China in the late nineteenth century. By 1896 thirty-six Protestant missionary bodies were operating in China, and almost all of them ran schools. If Roman Catholic missions are added to their number, it is apparent that many thousands of children were receiving religious education. Pupils were not necessarily, however, given much "western learning" beyond biblical studies, so that mission schools appeared even less attractive than government schools to most members of the gentry. Exceptions began to emerge toward the end of the century: by 1896, the Methodist Anglo-Chinese College in Shanghai could claim 2,000 alumni "scattered throughout China in the telegraph offices, the Custom Houses, Yamens, etc." The same mission ran a school for girls "from the higher class families, who have hitherto refused to send their daughters to an ordinary mission school" (*China Mission Handbook*, 1896). By the turn of the century, six Protestant missions had collegiate departments offering a general education in western subjects.

Those directly exposed to western education were few. A wider audience was reached by translations conducted under government and missionary auspices—with missionaries achieving a double prominence, for ex-missionaries such as W.A.P. Martin and John Fryer did much of the early government-sponsored translation. The translating effort, begun in the 1860s, had produced by 1900 a harvest of books dealing with modern science, mathematics, history, military science, and education. In addition, free renderings of works on political economy and even versions of European novels were beginning to capture a popular market.

Even more effective than translation in preparing the way for the acceptance of western learning were the works of popularization and propaganda written by Chinese who stood between two worlds, the "marginal men" of the treaty ports. From their vantage point, both China's weakness and the West's strength were alarmingly clear. Cheng Kuan-ying's clarion call, *Warning to a Prosperous Age* (written on the eve of the Sino-Japanese War), called on the Chinese to undertake radical change for the sake of their country's survival. His readers included the Kuang-hsu emperor, Sun Yat-sen, and the young Mao Tse-tung, each of whom attempted, in different ways, to put his words into effect.

Education and Values

Education has always imparted other skills than those set out in the curriculum. In societies with a modern school system, children often receive in the classroom their first introduction to fixed hours, set tasks, group action, and external authority. Schooling in Ch'ing China performed some of the same functions. The schooled certainly acquired the habit of application, even if they did not carry it as far as the models in their first reader (one of whom tied his hair to a roofbeam, while another jabbed his thigh with an awl to prevent sleep from overtaking him while he studied). Rote learning, the basic pedagogic technique, trained the memory, while writing developed steadiness of hand and meticulous care. Many of these values have been carried over into present-day society; even at university Chinese students commit many of their lessons to memory, and at a lower level the ideal school may be one that sets its young pupils to writing characters before breakfast and has them back after dinner to pursue the same task. In Ch'ing China, however, these accomplishments were characterized by the fact that they were solitary. Even rote learning was sung out individually and not in unison, each pupil proceeding through the classical texts at a different pace. Harsh discipline kept young students' attention fixed on their task (at least while the teacher was present), but this was seen simply as a transition stage to the internalization of diligent sobriety, not as a foretaste of permanent external regulation. No external hierarchies or fixed routine strengthened the teacher's hand or the pupil's resolve, no senior or junior classes sandwiched the schoolboy into place; the process of learning cultivated self-regulation, self-discipline, rather than mass organization. Once past infancy, conformity rather than simple obedience was fostered.

The work life of an official was as unconstricted in organizational terms as the schooling that prepared him for it. Liang Ch'i-ch'ao writes that even metropolitan officials "had very simple office work and very few deadlines to meet, facts that enabled them to take up studies day and night behind closed doors, and when time allowed, to meet with friends of similar interests to compare notes and ask each other questions" (Liang trans. Hsu, 1959,

p. 73). Gentry members living off rental income or the interest from loans naturally had even more discretion over the use of their time, but even those of the educated who worked for others—schoolteachers, private secretaries, doctors—had roles that were not sharply defined and hours and conditions of work that were even less so.

Modern Chinese enterprises early experienced problems of industrial discipline; in the late nineteenth century the Kaiping Mining Bureau found great difficulty in keeping workers through the summer months, when their labor was presumably needed on the farms. Ellsworth Carlson quotes a foreign engineer writing of the same mines in 1912 as estimating that "the output per man was from one fourth to one seventh of that of an American worker, depending upon whether a low or a high degree of skill was required" (1949). Rawski has suggested that the Chinese were well prepared for industrial life by the cooperative work involved in tasks such as rice planting and by habits of industry and thrift enjoined both by social norms and the need to make a living. These attributes may indeed be valuable in small-scale owner-producer enterprises, but they are not identical with those required of the work force in modern industrial production. Factory work requires time rather than task orientation; the latter may indeed be a hindrance when only a single repetitive task, isolated from the end product, is required of the worker. Punctuality, obedience, precision, and uniformity become the new virtues outweighing even thrift and hard work. Judging from reports on lapses in industrial discipline in the 1966–1976 decade in China, the problem has not yet been resolved.

To see education in terms of the imparting of skills or even knowledge—whether related to the needs of modernization or to the functioning of premodern society—is an anachronistic perspective. Education in Ch'ing China was for its participants and promoters acknowledged to be primarily a matter of the inculcation of values, moral standards, norms of conduct. When Ito Hirobumi attempted to impress on the Confucian scholar Wu Ju-lun the importance of giving equal attention to moral, intellectual, and physical education, Wu's reply revealed his conviction that the two former, at least, were inseparable: the practice of virtue, he said, required intellectual comprehension of its teachings. Confucianism was the mainstay of state ideology, and according to Confucian teachings the correct ordering of an individual life was reflected in family harmony and the stability of the state. An examination essay of the late Ch'ing on a passage from the *Great Learning* gives the orthodox neo-Confucian interpretation of these tenets:

> When of old teachers taught, there was the lesser learning to lay a foundation and the greater to perfect their talent. Their achievement lay in perfecting themselves, their range extended to perfecting objects outside themselves. Steeped in the Way, they were not limited to superficiality; only then could they call themselves learned men . . . themselves possessed of unspotted virtue, they wished constantly to ex-

pand it . . . so that the family, the state, the world could all reach it through this learning . . . the people's minds are not open, so one must make them over anew by promoting education and raising talent. The people's customs are not of solid worth, so one must make them over anew by making a point of good faith and carrying out right acts. The people's will is not set right, so one must make them over anew by turning aside from the deviant and combatting the heterodox. (Shang, 1958, p. 226)

This passage illustrates the way in which Confucius's teaching on human relationships was used for the ends of the state. Through it, the scholar would have his ambition curbed, his intellect channeled, and would become a suitable instrument of government service; through it, the common people would be roused from the brutishness of their native customs to become truly men.

The bulk of the population saw more immediate and personal benefits in education than the abstract goals of maintaining the social order under the ruling dynasty. Yet for them, too, Confucian tenets were a fundamental part of education. Writing of the 1930s, Liao T'ai-ch'u comments that villagers were reluctant to use new textbooks rather than the classics, even doubting whether the former actually contained the characters "invented" by Confucius or whether they had created a different set! Informal as well as formal teaching ensured that such precepts as filial piety and female subordination were as familiar to the illiterate as they were to the literate.

The official ideology permeated the community to an extent that modern states—including the current leadership of the People's Republic—might well envy; yet this ideology was not the conscious creation of current rulers but the confirmation and reinforcement of deep-rooted social norms owing their sanction to texts written before the fourth century B.C. It was thus effective in maintaining stability but not easily manipulated in the interests of change, and indeed could become a barrier to change when that was presented as an alien threat to time-honored values.

International Comparisons

The Charter Oath of the Meiji emperor pledges Japan to "seek for knowledge throughout the world in order to strengthen the foundations of imperial rule." At the same period in China, the T'ung-chih Restoration was under way. What made the one country seek solutions outside its borders, and the other turn first to its own tradition for answers? How far can the different reactions of China and Japan be related to differences in education and intellectual life?

One is struck by the unity of the intellectual world inhabited by the Chinese elite. After neo-Confucianism's unacknowledged incorporation of Buddhist tenets, the debate was between different schools of Confucianism rather than between Confucianism and any outside force. Daring spirits might turn to a reexamination of the competing schools of the Warring States period, but no non-Chinese creed was considered. In Tokugawa Japan, on the other hand, Confucianism was itself a borrowing from outside. Buddhism still had a certain intellectual vitality, and Shinto occupied an unshakable position in national ritual. In addition, a small school of foreign learning was growing up around the Dutch at Nagasaki. A composite picture of the world was no new thing to the Japanese, who had behind them more than a thousand years of choosing and assimilating at their own pace. To a lesser extent, the same can be said of the Russians from the time of Peter the Great. The Chinese, however, had been subjected to repeated waves of "barbarian" conquest, to which they reacted by a reexamination and reaffirmation of what it meant to be Chinese.

Greater alertness to the problems western contact was bringing China might have been stimulated by including in the examinations current affairs topics and questions on western learning. Such a change was not easily made, for every scholar had invested decades in the study of the current topics and every official owed his position to them. It was not, moreover, in the court's interest to solicit the opinion of men outside the government on how state affairs should be managed. Pure science could have been incorporated into the examinations with less difficulty—indeed, the earliest reform was the inclusion of an optional mathematics paper—but it is doubtful whether abstract study of the sciences was much use in the absence of industries or research bodies in which scientists could be employed. The specialist government schools and missionary schools started up in the last half of the nineteenth century had difficulty attracting students of high caliber for the same reason. The most prestigious occupation, that of officialdom, was closed to their graduates but there were few other outlets for their skills. This situation contrasts with that of Meiji Japan, where the government moved swiftly to tie office to modern educational qualifications.

Levels of popular skills and education in both Tokugawa Japan and Ch'ing China were considerably higher than those found in Russia over the same period. Like Japan, China possessed a high rate of male literacy, affording it a basis for sophisticated commercial, legal, and administrative systems. Elementary schooling was accessible to those with a small surplus income in both urban and rural areas; in addition, free schools or subsidized places catered to the poor but talented. Universal education in the modern sense was not a goal, but the government made sporadic attempts to ensure that all were familiar with Confucian principles and civic duties. It proved difficult, however, in the absence of strong government leadership or a rapidly expanding economy, to convert Confucian loyalties to modern patriotism and business acumen to modern entrepreneurship.

CHAPTER SEVEN

Summary: Eighteenth and Nineteenth Centuries

To assume that any failure to deal effectively with modernization must result from some special defect would be a mistake. On the contrary, the process of modernization is in general so difficult that what requires explanation is why any group of people is successful with these patterns. In what follows here we try to draw together those elements of difficulty that arose in China, but it must be remembered that what is special about China is not the difficulty itself but the particular set of factors that produced it.

International Context

In the nineteenth century the Chinese world view was based on convictions of centrality. To a large extent this view was accepted by neighboring societies with satellite status in political respects (Inner Asia), ritual respects (much of Southeast Asia), literary and cultural respects (Japan), or all respects (Korea). Chinese assumptions that the middle country, which had developed out of regional ascendancy, was central made few provisions for equality or competition, and they were conditioned by limited consciousness of cultural borrowing in the past. In terms of security, Inner Asia held higher priority than maritime areas, and most Chinese were unaware of the economic importance of the outside world in the transmission of crops and currency.

This world view made a flexible adjustment to modern knowledge, institutions, and technology difficult. Moreover, the assumptions in the view became more rigid and absolute in Ch'ing times because of the authoritarianism and cultural defensiveness of the Manchu rulers. Though precedents existed for acting flexibly, including interacting as equals with other countries, they were regarded as signs of weakness and ignored. A further barrier resulted from the fact that the setting into which the West was expected to fit at Canton before 1840 was the most prescriptive and the least appropriate for mutual accommodation. In short, China's world view impeded realization of the urgency of reform; throughout the nineteenth century it delayed the introduction of basic changes necessary for modernization.

Although the predisposition to look abroad for wisdom was not high, it would be an oversimplification to attribute this slowness in borrowing to a preoccupation with a simpler and grander past. Rather, the slowness resulted from inherited limitations in Ch'ing institutions as well as from inherited ethnocentrism. Other precedents existed that imaginative and able leaders could have used in the mid- or late nineteenth century to work out methods for meeting the challenge of the West, but the highly placed governors-general who led in the efforts at institutional change usually ran afoul of factional and political barriers. China's problems of adjustment were affected by its world view, but that was only one of a complex of institutional and intellectual limitations.

The West won in the conflict between two systems, each of which ascribed inferiority to the other. The Opium War and unequal treaties that followed introduced serious violations of Chinese sovereignty through the enforced provision of facilities for foreign trade in port cities, which first numbered five and grew to more than ten times that number. A fixed tariff, extraterritoriality, the most favored nation clause, and, ultimately, on-shore rights of manufacture limited the Chinese capacity to control and channel foreign trade. Chinese leaders could no longer impede the penetration of foreign influences, ideas, or goods. The results of these defeats were not entirely negative. The impact on taxes and state revenues was mixed; they increased, but much was locally appropriated. Sovereignty was impinged upon, but paradoxically the definition of national rights and borders also resulted in a de facto confirmation of Chinese sovereignty and borders at other points. The impact was unambiguously harmful in its political consequences for a faltering dynasty hesitant to undertake major changes. It was, however, also helpful in exposing Chinese to the example of more modern conditions, providing a long-term impetus to strive for modernization. Eventually (at the beginning of the twentieth century) the foreign impact led to a decade of vigorous reforms, incorporating much that had been learned from the outside.

Thus the international environment is not the principal cause of China's tortuous start in modernization. The western impact remained a limited one. It did not reach far into inland China and did not strongly affect the economy, particularly the structure of internal trade. For all the importance of international pressures, therefore, internal affairs were more important in the weakening of the government during this period.

Political Structure

Prior to the onset of the social changes associated with modernization, the Chinese state had long existed as a political structure characterized by centralized direction of highly bureaucratized institutions. Beginning in the mid-seventeenth century, it had come also to include a vastly expanded empire in Inner Asia that extended Manchu (Chinese) rule over many non-Chinese peoples. It was a firmly established state system, deriving its authority from deeply entrenched ideological foundations and long-accumulated historical precedents, and having the unchallenged endurance record for all governmental systems. China's political institutions had elaborately specialized and differentiated subdivisions and were run by professional bureaucrats according to highly rational, fully recorded regulations and precedents. In many respects, China was well equipped for the modern transformation.

The political order and the entire society had been vigorous and expansive at many points in history but had been particularly so from 1500 to 1800. To the chagrin of twentieth-century Chinese who, unlike their forebears, have been intensely nationalistic, China in the nineteenth century proved to be the world's prime exemplar of political failure and humiliation. For the first time in 2,000 years the Chinese found themselves confronted by peoples who did not take Chinese greatness for granted—who, indeed, were not even aware of it. China could neither keep peace within, nor repel aggression from without. Explanations for this failure have ranged from domestic economic crisis to deteriorating social relations to intellectual sterility to the West's exploitation.

China's failures in the nineteenth century can in large part be explained by the vulnerability and consequent erosion of its political structure. The political system was not simply, by its nature, increasingly out of step with the changes going on elsewhere in the world and the needs imposed on China by the concurrent impact of intrusive new political challenges. Rather, its disastrous nineteenth- and early twentieth-century record displays an internal and internally generated decay of the old political order.

The ''success'' of the Chinese state prior to the late eighteenth century can be explained as a phenomenon of balance between potentially countervailing forces, a balance that was gradually upset. Governing consists of an elaborately differentiated set of political tasks carried out by formally institutionalized means as well as by related, informally conducted, but highly regularized means. In China, these means included the role played by the strategic elite and its social group both in and out of office. The elite's performance of governing tasks in the interest of the state and, in large measure, in the perceived interests of the whole society, was balanced against the competing interests of all members of society expressed by their family and lineage organizations. Between the lineage-based context at one end of the spectrum and that of national government at the other, we can discern no organizational contexts of great import for politics.

China was vulnerable because its basic political stability rested on special forms of family and lineage stability, which were themselves highly vulnerable to the impact of modernization. More specifically, its quite remarkable political system was overburdened by excessive administrative centralization, the result of patterns inherited from the Ming dynasty and the increase of population in the eighteenth and nineteenth centuries. Special tensions in the political structure introduced during the Ch'ing dynasty also contributed to the decline.

Legitimate political power in Ch'ing China was held exclusively by the imperial nobility of the Manchu society, who were perceived by the Chinese generally as a foreign and lesser people, and whose leaders had to struggle throughout the dynasty to be regarded as the equals of the Chinese. Always before political power had, ideally, been held by a dynasty that shared power on the basis of merit in an open class system. As the strategic elite, the Chinese scholar-officialdom and its associates, although limited in its access to the highest positions, nonetheless exercised authority, held prestige, and provided models of upward mobility for the entire Chinese (even the Manchu) population.

The Manchu-led government monopolized the organization of society and both defined and directed all centralized political action. The Manchu ruling caste, despite its thorough assimilation into Chinese cultural patterns by the eighteenth century, did not acquire a significant base in Chinese society outside of politics. Its power base was sustained by the banner system of military organization and, increasingly after the conquest phase, by manipulating or at least by benefiting from the normative patterns of Chinese thought and practice, both public and private, both familial and political.

Chinese familial and lineage organizations and interests, like their ideological supports, were all-pervasive; their strength and ubiquity can scarcely be appreciated by analogy to any other society. For the individual they took legitimate primacy over other considerations. A principal task of political leadership was to maintain a consonance if not an identity of those interests and the state's needs, to keep the formal and the informal tasks of governing at the highest levels possible.

Building on the cumulative experience of 2,000 years of imperial practice, and further adjusting the operation of its coordination and control devices to satisfy its own insecurity as alien conquerors, the Ch'ing dynasty ruled vigorously but unwisely; its rulers upset the balance of state and family interest. First of all, the Ch'ing rulers enhanced the effectiveness of controls (of both inducement and intimidation) to the point of stultifying activism and initiative in performance within the bureaucracy. Second their patently hollow maintenance of the grand norms induced a growing cynicism among Chinese associates in government. Their overcontrol spawned underperformance. The public cause—engaged, committed governing, especially at the local level where the informal extension of governing was carried out to greatest social effect—lost ground before family and lineage-centered aggrandizement.

Above all, strains between the Manchu overlords and the Chinese bureaucrats created an alliance between the Chinese bureaucrats and informal Chinese groups with interests inimical to the bureaucracy. Those who previously had been held at bay became allies to an unprecedented degree. A bureaucratic order characterized by a strong element of rationality was undermined by this new alliance and by compromises of central power, Confucian altruism, and regularized procedures.

From the point of view of China's traditional political standards, administrative deterioration had set in even before the disasters of the early and mid-nineteenth century introduced intrusive elements. As those disasters compounded the compromises, the deterioration went further, but the dynasty lingered on under conditions of increasing de facto decentralization and regionalism. By the end of the nineteenth century, the working of the political structure was being altered in a way that can be described as "debureaucratization." The compromises of the nineteenth century rendered meaningless the rationality of the Chinese bureaucracy. The old standards of merit and relevance were debased by the personalized relationships evident in new power structures. Formal and informal tasks of governing were altered, and the latter in particular came to be linked ever more extensively to lineage and family interests at a time when the traditional route of upward mobility was becoming less accessible. Elite status tended to become ever more secure, as it became linked to the new power relations in society and government. Nepotism, the universal corrupter of mobility, increased.

Social abuses of regional and local government intensified as a changing strategic elite shifted toward unchecked aggrandizement. Local government, especially government at the village level, had never been strong, having no general legitimized institutional base in politically integrated units below the county level. The field was open for local mismanagement. The previously strategic elite was no longer strategic to the functioning of a well-balanced national system, susceptible to forceful national leadership and checked by the demands of a vigorous normative component in social relations. That elite, of changed recruitment and composition, gradually became strategic to the exercise of illicit power in regional and local successor systems. An elite whose attention had been focused for 2,000 years on imperial government at a national level had its attention decentralized—shifted—to a local basis which had previously been the domain of the out-of-office elite and hence highly dependent on those in office.

A secondary explanation for the slowness of concerted responses to the new challenges in the nineteenth century is that the very fullness and perfection of the Chinese political ideal was itself a stumbling block to modernizing changes; the overwhelming stability and ethical rightness of the old political order forestalled fundamental changes. The forces of inflexible stability, little if at all adaptive, were nurtured by a full panoply of broadly satisfying ideal alternatives to real political change. Confucian thought was resilient enough to respond to a changing world. Because at the initial phase of foreign impact it clothed China's response in native garb and provided Confucian justifications for much of it, small steps were taken that forestalled explosive, profound change. It is difficult to imagine a path toward modernization that would not have had to include compelling demonstrations of the superior adaptability of the West's evolving political systems before Chinese leaders would have been ready for transformation rather than mere renovation of Chinese politics.

The framework and the character of China's politics changed deeply and irrevocably at a time when China was increasingly being integrated into worldwide changes and becoming involved with agents of such change. Modernization was neither entirely forestalled by political weakness nor constructively channeled by political agency in nineteenth-century China. Some of the changes described under the rubric of administrative deterioration possessed the potential to evolve into more effective political forms in postimperial times, especially those changes linked to the increasing role of regional military power in the conduct of government. More frequently, we observe only the protracted decline of old forms, and the frustration of the nation-state's political goals.

Various aspects of governmental decline might have been reversed by vigorous government leadership at the top. But the Ch'ing rulers did not attempt to make much use of the state's resources to provide themselves with a larger and more active political instrument for achieving dynastic or national goals, and increasingly, they lost that capacity. The late Ch'ing state's defensive, hesitant, ad hoc adaptations to crises contributed little, if anything, to modernization. Chinese rulers of the nineteenth century were decreasingly able to conceive or to will significant social change, much less to implement it. The political structure was largely irrelevant to purposeful action toward modernization. Its failure is a primary explanation for China's slow start in modernization.

Economic Structure and Growth

The economic strengths of Ch'ing China largely reflect a commercialized, agrarian system in which nearly all households could strive to accumulate land and other forms of wealth. The widespread use of money and contracts and highly competitive markets helped make mass participation a reality. There were few legal barriers to the flexible use of land, labor, and commodities to maximize household income. Under these favorable conditions for the redistribution of wealth, a not inconsiderable number of families made the transition from rags to riches, or, no less likely, from riches to rags within a few generations; on a smaller scale, there was constant flux in the economic standing of large numbers of landowners, tenants, and merchants. With few exceptions, social categories record a temporary status, not a permanent condition. The open class system had an economic as well as a legal base.

In this system the state played a limited role. Primarily it maintained the legal and institutional arrangements that gave the population a stake in weighing opportunities for production and commerce. It was content to regulate the conditions for trade to some degree without becoming deeply involved in management and control of the private sector. The Chinese state did not, as some have suggested, restrict and suppress merchant initiative to the point that an environment hostile to commerce prevailed. Although Confucian ideology assigned merchants the lowest rung on a four-class social ladder, and there is ample evidence to show that merchants found it advisable to secure through family connections the protection of officials and prominent degree holders, commerce normally operated with few obstacles from above. At all periods Chinese merchants could, and some did, become powerful and prestigious even though they were not supposed to convert their wealth to these ends. Nor is it correct to conclude that the Ch'ing state relied heavily on monopolies, relegating the private sector to a peripheral role. The state's few monopolies were strictly limited; only the salt monopoly brought in much revenue. After the early decades of the Ch'ing dynasty the state adopted a low profile, favoring the private economy but controlling abuses by powerful households. Incentives favoring commercialization over long-term investment were strong; the tendency was to take both capital and talent out of merchant activities and invest them in land and office seeking. Commerce was even a ladder of social mobility for some without sufficient resources to farm, and successful artisans often became merchants by their very success. Finally, graft and corruption were built into a system that ostensibly allowed its experts in economic allocation no legitimate access to political power nor its experts in political allocation any fully legitimate access to great economic accumulation.

Officials did not perceive a need for a more active state involvement in the economy. This is demonstrated throughout Ch'ing history until late in the nineteenth century, especially in the longstanding freeze on taxation first proclaimed under Emperor K'ang-hsi. State intervention mainly meant regulation to keep the system functioning smoothly. As for foreign trade, it was not perceived as an important source of benefits. Instead Chinese leaders were preoccupied with controlling and limiting it as well as with the possible advantages native merchants could gain from becoming involved in it.

What accounts for the continuation of a system that gave such clear precedence to the interests of the private sector over the public sector? How can we reconcile this "imbalance" with the contrasting "imbalance" within the political system, which favored the central forces of autocracy? It seems likely that concentration at the very center and dispersal within scattered localities combined to defuse pressures for state action. National leaders, drawing on the wealth of a vast country, could obtain adequate taxes for their own and their key supporters' needs. Occasional military campaigns or suppression of rebellions could be financed from accumulated surpluses. The nature of the political system precluded pressure from local and regional governmental interests to mobilize resources at their level of operation. At the same time, limited state intervention and low taxation satisfied most household interests; as a means to forestall rebellion and to satisfy local elite goals, the system was consonant with long-supported Confucian objectives.

The Chinese were acutely aware of prices as a reflection of the equilibrium of market forces. State oversight and readiness to intervene when conditions went awry helped produce a remarkable stability in markets during the mid-Ch'ing period. Yet what distinguishes China is the state's acceptance of a role primarily limited to maintaining certain economic balances. China was startlingly laissez-faire for centuries before Adam Smith, but with a difference—it was laissez-faire not by ideal, but by default.

Other features of Ch'ing history reduced the likelihood that the state's involvement would be perceived as too limited: (1) The economy managed to grow with few signs of serious slumps or unmet needs until the second quarter of the nineteenth century. (2) Government surpluses persisted until the rebellions of the nineteenth century. (3) The very scale of the economy under conditions of premodern transportation and communications inhibited commercial integration and state control. In a smaller society aggressive state involvement in the economy might have brought substantial rewards to the center. In a political system with more tolerance for regional concentrations of power, an activist state might have stimulated regional resource accumulation. The scale of Chinese society, however, was enormous, and its leaders did not countenance regionally oriented economic policies. But a time bomb was ticking away in the combination of the extraordinary population increase of the eighteenth and nineteenth centuries and the bureaucratic developments already mentioned.

Waves of problems disrupted the stability of the Ch'ing economy: (1) currency-related problems beginning in the 1820s; (2) difficulties caused by the devastating rebellions of the 1850s and 1860s; and finally (3) the mounting international pressures entering through the treaty ports. New pressures arose for the state to take action: to limit the importation and distribution of opium in order to reduce the outflow of silver; to increase revenues in order to crush rebellions or to counter foreign military incursions; and to promote economic recovery after natural disasters, wartime depopulation, and some unemployment resulting from imported goods and foreign competition. But the state did not take far-reaching measures; it procrastinated. Without the backing of the state to provide new information and technology, the response of the private sector to foreign trade was hesitant and slow, even though the private sector still demonstrated considerable adaptiveness.

The economy's recovery and gradual expansion during the final third of the century likely lulled the court into complacency. As before, the flexibility of local economies enabled them to meet immediate needs and to contain problems that might otherwise have necessitated more thoroughgoing official and community action. In these circumstances the court and many officials were slow to perceive how serious were China's problems. They also feared that the adoption of modern technology would produce dislocation and that certain innovations like railroads would make China more vulnerable to foreign aggression, while other changes might strengthen a potentially rival elite. Above all, it was the history of restricted state economic involvement, and the resultant use and distribution of resources within local communities, especially given the high levels of local self-sufficiency, that complicated the state's responses to new challenges in the nineteenth century.

Social Integration

China stands as perhaps the closest premodern approximation to a society possessed of the modern achievement ethic. It created an orderly, predictable, and surprisingly unfettered environment for the pursuit of upward mobility by individual households. For a nonmodern society, China was remarkably open and achievement oriented. Over an extended period, the Chinese created enduring monuments in (1) a fluid social class system with opportunities for vast numbers to aspire to achievement and reward, rather than a largely frozen hierarchy of serfdom or self-perpetuating aristocracies; (2) a market mechanism with relatively easy reallocation of contractual rights and investments, rather than burdensome levies by the state and inescapable financial dependence on serfowners or others; and (3) a mutuality of interests between a professionalized state service and locally vital family and lineage solidarities, rather than an intense local suspicion of outside authority. Nevertheless, these did not survive the change in context produced by the introduction of modernized patterns from outside. Exceptional local literacy and learning, flexible household decisions to purchase land or to engage in commerce, and elite humanistic ideals and feelings of responsibility to community-wide interests, do not suffice to bring together resources.

We reject the argument that in earlier centuries China's vaunted stability of social forms and extraordinary record of structural continuities reflect a stagnant society or an absence of sustained social development. But we do find that through most of the Ch'ing period, new methods of mobilizing resources were not developed while the old ones became less adequate as a basis for governance and development. Neither at the level of local administrative areas nor at the regional or national levels can we observe a broad-based accumulation and concentration of human or material resources. Small administrative centers did not press new claims on the production of surrounding areas, nor did large cities operate as engines of change, pulling the cities and villages around them in their wake. Local vitality—with households actively

211

marketing their goods, educating their sons, and accumulating land—was insufficient to establish a base for centrally directed change. Over the long term the unplanned consequences of community vitality—population growth and a high tolerance for localized consumption—made mobilization of resources all the more difficult. Beneath the centralized, imperial bureaucracy, which normally functioned well in preserving order and a stable economy within a premodern setting, China was a weakly integrated society. To draw together the goods and talents of local areas, as might have been done through deliberate and concerted efforts over centuries, required a massive reordering of social arrangements. The prevailing arrangements drew support from a deeply embedded foundation in local communities; to dislodge them required more than well-meaning leaders and short-term policies. New arrangements would have to overcome ancient inertia, especially given the eighteenth- and early nineteenth-century population boom, the special patterns of decay, and the new forces.

During the late Ming and the Ch'ing dynasties, intercommunity interdependencies and forces of integration did not develop significantly. Existing administrative mechanisms became more center dominated, but there was little sign of local control becoming more centralized. Indeed, the difficulties of administering large numbers of people, especially given the growth of population from 200 to 300 million over the second half of the eighteenth century and to more than 400 million by 1850, probably contributed to the decline in administrative efficiency. Had population not grown so quickly, a larger part of the potential rural surplus might have been channeled into long-distance commerce and urban consumption or extracted through taxation, rents, or commerce. Had population remained quite stable, as it apparently did in the late eighteenth and early nineteenth centuries in Japan, local surpluses might have triggered more of an export orientation for local settlements and marketing communities. Previous population growth may have destroyed the key to ''what might have been.''

Increases in local production (offset by population growth) did not become a basis for restructuring social relations, nor did marketing mechanisms show much per capita change. Instead, Chinese society made do with a pattern of settlements conducive to local exchange, aimed primarily at local self-sufficiency. China became relatively inefficient in funneling resources outward to larger settlements. In short, the Chinese did not develop more effective methods of tapping the productive base of the countryside. The elite as well as the masses lacked a strong commitment to the goals of resource centralization; local leaders did not develop new patterns of consumption, lead the way in the commercialization of agriculture, or shift quickly to new occupations and investments in the opening phases of modernization. Except in the family and kinship contexts, control mechanisms began to break down as the balance between local interests, represented by degree holders, and the centralized state was disrupted, and even the family and kinship contexts were themselves vulnerable under modernizing conditions. Alternative bases of coordination and control remained fragile. New ones were not developed save on paper. Only a skeletal network of organizations existed between households or lineage and the state bureaucracy. In view of China's highly visible central institutions with their internally concentrated authority, it is easy to overlook the genuinely decentralized nature of the society that had always underlain the centralized elements. Under the new population pressures and the new needs for universal coordination and control, these elements of decentralization, which had worked so well for so long, proved an impediment to national purposes.

Various social indicators, such as urbanization, market proliferation, administrative bureaucratization, and education, place China among a select group of premodern societies with substantial development. China had built an impressive record of early achievements, but during its late imperial era—particularly under the Ch'ing dynasty—it was not among the societies possessing a degree of dynamism that signified accelerated change within a premodern context. Large numbers of Chinese families climbed the social ladder; there is, however, little evidence of the intense merchant competition and displacement, the improved status and increased migration of wage labor, and the reorientation of household achievement strategies associated with Tokugawa society. Around 1800 China boasted roughly half of the world's ten great cities that topped 500,000 in population and, in all, supported a respectable 5–6 percent of its population in cities; yet its urbanization hovered around a plateau long since reached, without the spurt of growth that brought countries such as Japan, England, and France to levels three or four times that found in China. The Chinese state did not create new administrative centers, launch new commercial ventures, or make new demands on social groups. In other respects as well, the dearth of reorganization left the earlier foundation for change ill-suited to support a sudden push for concerted action.

Knowledge and Education

Levels of knowledge and education in Ch'ing China were indeed remarkable. Literacy was widespread among the male population (of whom an estimated 30 to 45 percent possessed basic literacy), traditional technology was highly developed, and commerce and law rested on written documents even at the village level. Seekers after national unity could have invoked the values of a common written culture including at one pole the Confucian classics and at the other popular romances, or the mechanics of a nationwide system for the transmission of government orders. Similar features in Japan were conducive to rapid modernization; what differed in China's case?

Critics of traditional education have tended to take for granted those advantages China shared with other premodern advanced societies and to focus their criticisms on distinctively Chinese institutions—the examination system, the academy, and the private schools or *ssŭ-shu*—and on the frame of mind said to be engendered by their exclusively classical curriculum. Such critics appear to underestimate the potential of indigenous institutions for constructive change. That little in the organizational structure of the examination, academies, or *ssŭ-shu* militated against breadth of learning or practicality was evident in tentative nineteenth-century reforms. Nor should the narrowness and conservatism with which Chinese education has been charged be ascribed to the study of classical literature per se. Rather, difficulties in adaptation appear to have arisen from the unusually strong link between level of education, status, and power, a link whose wide acceptance was at the same time a source of stability and legitimacy for the existing order and a barrier to its replacement. An elite relatively satisfied with its position saw no compelling reason for change, and the upwardly mobile were for the most part content to submit their claims to the adjudication of the examination system. This pressure for achievement sanctioned by the government and one's peers may have lessened the drive toward technological specialization, but it ensured high motivation in the pursuit of academic excellence.

The majority of the Chinese elite saw little relevance for its status in the sources of knowledge outside its own heritage: there was little equivalent to the Japanese readiness to recognize native and borrowed systems of thought as equally valid. At the same time, a variety of historical precedents, philosophic schools, and differing interpretations of Confucianism gave considerable scope for alternative stances within Chinese tradition, and a thorough classical education may have prepared those who received it for a later synthesis of Chinese and western thought. Western science and technology were slow to take hold for social rather than intellectual reasons. Confucianism was not intrinsically inimical to the development of science, and indeed its secular, rational approach and conscientious search for the truth have been valuable legacies to later inquiry.

Among the mass of people, knowledge and education were acquired through the formal and informal channels of the school, the work place, and the home. Education in the first of these concentrated on the reading of classical texts, with more workaday skills, such as mastery of the abacus or a trade, relegated to the other two. The training thus acquired was functional given the demands of Ch'ing society and economy, but its private, decentralized nature meant that it could not be readily deflected toward the provision of standardized up-to-date knowledge and techniques and politically desirable attitudes; would-be modernizers therefore attempted to replace rather than revise it. That training of this kind was not an absolute barrier to commercial and industrial development can be seen from the rise of overseas Chinese entrepreneurs in the later nineteenth and early twentieth centuries.

Ch'ing China's educational arrangements were relatively well adapted to the maintenance of the existing political structure, social values, and productive capacities. Had a strong government been able to act on them directly, or a rapidly changing market indirectly, it might have been possible to use the groundwork they had laid for China's modernization while gradually eliminating redundancies and anomalies; problems of scale and control, however, meant that the process of transformation was slowed for several decades. Furthermore, the lack of dynamism in Ch'ing education as a force for new and diverse forms of social mobility and as a source of nationalism left a heritage of inertia that took time to overcome.

The Basis of Change

The underlying pattern reflected by these five aspects of Chinese society in the century or two before 1900 suggests the conclusion that some elements of its heritage that might have served as a point of departure for its modern transformation were declining; other elements that represented the strongest bulwarks against conversion to modernity retained and were even strengthening their vitality; and, perhaps of greatest importance, many elements that had early roots in China and bore the potential to facilitate rapid change remained dispersed and without the organization necessary if they were to be centrally controlled and directed.

The decline was most evident in the institutions of the central government, which were losing their ability to rally the Chinese elite to perform civic duties vital to the public good and to administrative vitality. Not only did the center become more isolated, but the effectiveness of the provincial level of administration, which depended on the center for its authority, also weakened. This development resulted in part from the Chinese elite's reaction to the inflexible restrictions of the dynasty and was facilitated by the continuing vitality of the family and lineage associations, through which the gentry asserted its local influence. The end result of this process was an increasing preoccupation with short-term personal and lineage gains, often at the expense of broader considerations.

Many examples of the preservation of forces that stood in the way of a modern transformation can be found in Chapters 2–6. Inclined to seek models in their own past rather than in other societies, Chinese were slow to show curiosity about the revolution in science and technology that was transforming the West. Other barriers were the low level of taxation and state economic leadership, the slight development of local cities which might have integrated commerce and social interaction on a broad scale, and the unflagging adherence to classical modes and content of education. Over centuries little reorganization was attempted—virtually nothing occurred to displace the powerful forces that would make difficult the realization of the considerable potential represented by Chinese skills and resources.

215

Summary: Eighteenth and Nineteenth Centuries

China had been the virtuoso among societies in her ability to cope effectively with problems of organizing a large territory and a very numerous population. Nor was this "coping" a minimal matter. If a line is drawn in history at the seventeenth century or at practically any time during the previous millennium, the case could be argued, some believe convincingly, that no peoples can lay claim to higher incomes per capita or to a more equal distribution of opportunities to win a large share of such income, to higher levels of literacy, to more sophisticated arts and crafts, to more highly developed commerce, or to markedly more elaborate adornment of such marks of "civilization" as the fine arts of sculpture, painting, calligraphy, and music, the intellectual arts of philosophy and knowledge in its varied forms (save that we know today as "science"), and the minor arts of cooking, gracious living in general, and humor, or the arts of governance and even war. Those traits deemed relevant for national strength and prosperity and for household enterprise and initiative were present to an unusual degree; and yet there remained unrealized potential for creating a powerful state or a dynamic society capable of mobilizing resources or taking concerted action. The nineteenth-century basis from which change toward modernization took place, however subject to incremental change, seems by the criteria invoked here little advanced from what it would have been centuries earlier. With hindsight, it is not difficult to find examples of missed opportunities long before the era of confrontation and humiliation: opportunities for becoming alert to new international forces; for extending the reach and the competence of government; for reallocating economic resources away from scattered and localized consumption; for increasing urbanization and reshaping the impact of the urban sector on the countryside; and for improving education and knowledge with direct application in diverse careers. Inertia on these fronts still visible during the late nineteenth century was the legacy of centuries of little or no social reorganization.

Maps

Maps 1 and 4, which are reproduced from other sources, differ in their spellings of some city names. Each set of spellings is widely encountered in writings on China. Examples of alternate spellings for the same city are Yang-chou and Yangchow, Su-chou and Soochow, Ning-po and Ningpo, Ch'ang-sha and Changsha, and K'ai-feng and Kaifeng. Throughout the text we have attempted to conform to standard usage, which agrees in some cases with one of these maps and in some cases with the other.

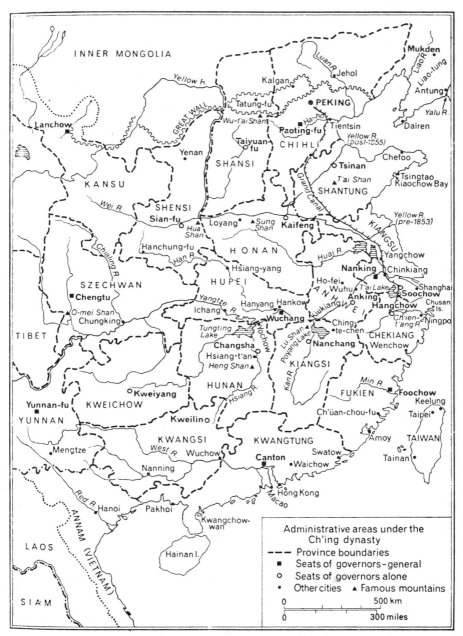

China proper in the nineteenth century

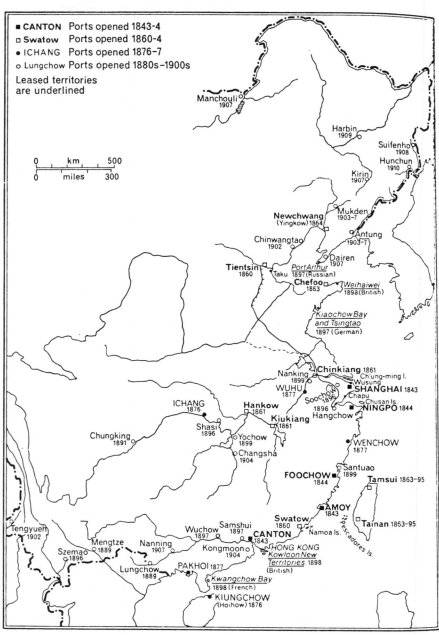

0   km   500
0   miles   300

Manchouli
1907

Harbin
1909

Suifenho
1908

Hunchun
1910

Kirin
1907

Newchwang
(Yingkow) 1864

Mukden
1903-7

Antung
1903-7

Chinwangtao
1902

Dairen
1907

Tientsin
1860

Port Arthur
Taku 1897 (Russian)

Chefoo
1863

Weihaiwei
1898 (British)

*Kiaochow Bay
and Tsingtao*
1897 (German)

Nanking
1899

Chinkiang 1861

Ch'ung-ming I.

Wusung

WUHU
1877

Soochow
1896

SHANGHAI 1843

Chapu

Chusan Is.

ICHANG
1876

Hankow
1861

Kiukiang
1861

1896

NINGPO 1844

Hangchow

Shasi
1896

Chungking
1891

Yochow
1899

Changsha
1904

WENCHOW
1877

Santuao
1899

FOOCHOW ■
1844

Tamsui 1863-95

Tengyueh
1902

■AMOY
1843

Mengtze
1889

Nanning
1907

Samshui
1897

Swatow
1860

Tainan 1863-95

Szemao
1896

Wuchow
1897

Kongmoon
1904

CANTON ■
1843

Namoa Is.

Pescadores Is.

Lungchow
1889

PAKHOI 1877

*HONG KONG
Kowloon New
Territories* 1898
(British)

Kwangchow Bay
1898 (French)

●KIUNGCHOW
(Hoihow) 1876

Growth of the treaty port system

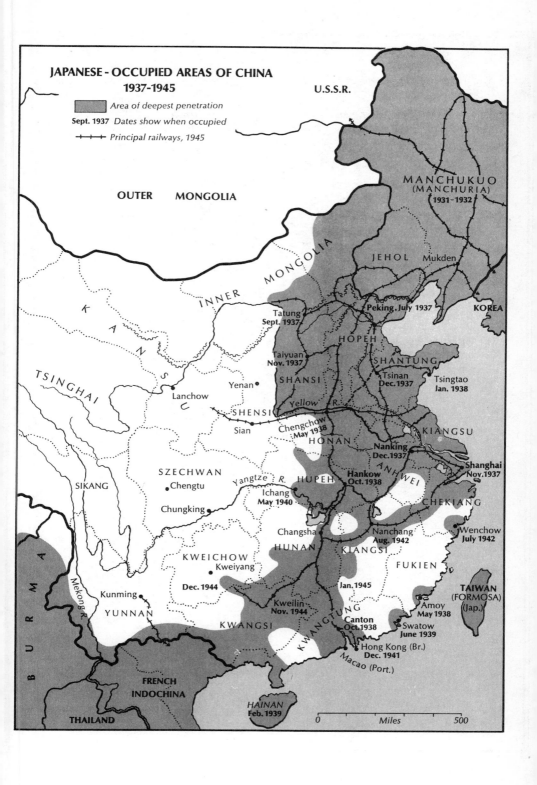

JAPANESE - OCCUPIED AREAS OF CHINA
1937-1945

Area of deepest penetration

Sept. 1937 Dates show when occupied

+++++ Principal railways, 1945

U.S.S.R.

OUTER MONGOLIA

MANCHUKUO
(MANCHURIA)
1931-1932

JEHOL   Mukden

INNER MONGOLIA

Tatung
Sept. 1937

Peking, **July 1937**

KOREA

HOPEH

SHANTUNG

KANSU

Taiyuan
Nov. 1937

Tsinan
Dec.1937

Tsingtao
Jan. 1938

TSINGHAI

Lanchow

Yenan

SHANSI

Yellow R.

SHENSI

Chengchow
May 1938

Sian

HONAN

KIANGSU

Nanking
Dec.1937

Shanghai
Nov.1937

SZECHWAN

Chengtu

Yangtze R.

HUPEH

Hankow
Oct.1938

ANHWEI

CHEKIANG

Chungking

Ichang
May 1940

SIKANG

Changsha

HUNAN

Nanchang
Aug. 1942

KIANGSI

Wenchow
July 1942

KWEICHOW

Kweiyang

Dec. 1944

FUKIEN

Kunming

B U R M A

Mekong R.

YUNNAN

KWANGSI

Kweilin
Nov. 1944

Jan. 1945

KWANGTUNG

Canton
Oct.1938

Amoy
May 1938

TAIWAN
(FORMOSA)
(Jap.)

Swatow
June 1939

Hong Kong (Br.)
Dec. 1941

Macao (Port.)

FRENCH
INDOCHINA

THAILAND

HAINAN
Feb. 1939

0   Miles   500

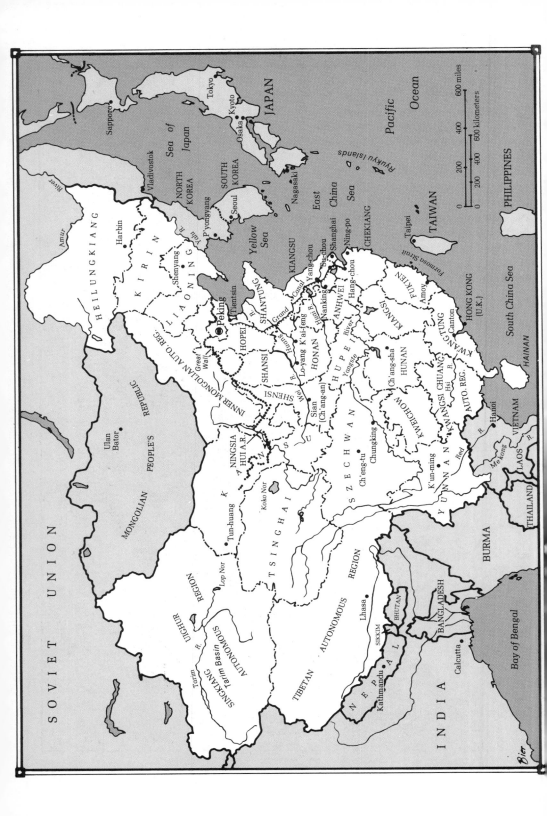

PART TWO

The Transformation

The Twentieth Century

CHAPTER EIGHT

The International Context

O<small>UR CONTENTION IN</small> C<small>HAPTER</small> 2 <small>WAS THAT THE INTERNATIONAL ENVIRONMENT</small> in which China met the West in the nineteenth century, while highly un-favorable, was not the principal cause of China's tortuous road to moderniza-tion. Military and diplomatic setbacks were certainly serious, and the conse-quences in foreign debt and humiliation unquestionably diverted energies and resources that might otherwise have been directed toward programs of in-ternal change. Yet they might also have acted as a spur to intensive programs of defensive modernization like those adopted by Russian and Japanese gov-ernments in the nineteenth century. They did not, and there is no basis for supposing that fewer setbacks or less humiliation would have produced more or a different response.

China after the Boxers

The Boxer Rebellion of 1900 marked (with the possible exception of the Cultural Revolution of the 1960s) the last effort to meet China's problems through a radical rejection of modern ideas and technology. It was shown to have failed when an international rescue mission forced its way into Peking in August 1900, resulting in the rescue of the foreign legations and the flight of the court. The Boxer Protocol that China signed with twelve powers a year later marked a watershed in China's relations with the outside world. It rep-resented the high point of foreign controls on Chinese sovereignty and reve-nue, but it also put an end to talk of division of Chinese territory between the treaty powers. It convinced even the most xenophobic of old-style conservatives that thoroughgoing programs of institutional change were desperately needed, and thus marked the beginning of a series of governmental reforms.

The Boxer Protocol provided for Chinese expressions of regret, the punishment (including death for four) of ninety-six officials, payment over a period of forty years of 450 million *taels* with interest, a lower and uniform tariff set at 5 percent, an enlarged and fortified legation quarter, and the razing of Chinese forts and the establishment of foreign garrisons from Peking to the coast and to Shanhaikuan. The indemnity was guaranteed by native customs, the salt monopoly, and the Imperial Maritime Customs, which was given control of customs within fifty *li* of all China's treaty ports. China was not to be permitted to import foreign weapons for two years. Forty-five cities in which foreigners had been killed or mistreated were to be punished by a five-year suspension of civil service examinations. Chinese ambassadors were sent abroad, and within China expiatory monuments were erected to apologize and atone for the Boxer excesses. The foreign powers were convinced that the Chinese elite had to lose "face" and status in order to see and show the error of its ways; the Boxer Protocol was an expression of that belief.

In another sense, however, the protocol showed the powers' helplessness and frustration in their efforts to force China to change according to their will. There was no longer talk of the division of China between the powers, something that had been feared by many Chinese patriots. The powers had discovered that a central Chinese government was essential, and since they had no alternative to propose, the court was permitted to reoccupy the looted and ravished capital after it had shown its contrition.

It now became common for the powers to express their concern for fair play in China. The most celebrated instance of this was the Open Door notes that United States Secretary of State John Hay prepared in response to British suggestions in 1899 and 1900. These proposed that England, Germany, and Russia not interfere with treaty ports and that within their spheres of influence they not levy higher harbor or railroad charges against foreign goods than they did on their own. Although motivated by wishes to set up standards of foreign competition in the Chinese market, and not particularly effective, the "Open Door" phrase came to have additional overtones of concern for Chinese sovereignty and self-limitation on the part of imperialist powers.

The focus of competition for advantage in China between the powers now shifted from division to development, and the advance was led by bankers instead of gunboats. Railway development, increasingly welcomed by a Chinese officialdom that saw the need of better communications, seemed to hold the promise of "opening" inland China for foreign manufactured goods. Rail lines also brought with them the promise of access to mineral rights and rural markets. The capital required was so large that foreign cooperation was the rule. Franco-Russian (1895), Anglo-French (1896), Anglo-German (1896), Belgian (1898), Anglo-German (1898), and a succession of later consortium loans combined to fasten a burden of foreign indebtedness on China that was very heavy when measured against an annual budget receipt calculated at only 100 million *taels* by foreign ministers in 1900. Much of this was predicated on the invaluable Imperial Maritime Customs, removing it as a source for other possible modernization needs. In post-Boxer years China's annual remittances on foreign debts stood at 42 or 43 million *taels* annually, a sum almost half the central government's slender receipts and larger than the entire imperial revenue had been a century before. Subsequent decades saw multiple defaults lighten this burden, and many of the concessions promised were never taken up because of the political turbulence of China in subsequent decades, but this "financial imperialism" with its inexhaustible opportunities for corruption gave twentieth-century Chinese a sharp distaste for foreign imperialism as rapacious and exploitative.

Yet this same economic exploitation placed new emphasis on the maintenance of Chinese unity. North of the Great Wall, Chinese territory was in greater danger. As Manchu power declined, the relatively lightly populated Manchu homeland, because it was close to vital security and economic interests of Russia and Japan, neither of whom were enthusiastic about open door competition close to their borders, was jeopardized.

Russia provided the first threat. After the siege of the legations at Peking had been lifted, the Russians showed little readiness to give up the Manchurian centers they had occupied in the course of "Boxer suppression." Since Russian "assistance" to a discountenanced Manchu court in 1860 had been rewarded by cession of the Maritime Provinces, there was good reason to expect Russian requests for additional privileges in Manchuria. Proposals Moscow made for a special position were so onerous that the Chinese government appealed to other powers for help in resisting them. Russian recalcitrance on Manchuria was combined with a hard line on special privileges in Korea. When the Russians refused Japanese proposals to work out spheres of influence, the Japanese turned to Great Britain for help, and in 1902 secured the protection of the Anglo-Japanese Alliance. A year later, with the departure of Count Witte, Russian policy was surrendered into the hands of the hard-liners and brought on the Russo-Japanese War of 1904–1905, in which the Japanese posed as champions of the territorial integrity of China.

After the Japanese victory was sealed at the Treaty of Portsmouth, however, Japan took over Russian attitudes as well as Russian holdings in South Manchuria. Japanese leaders felt that their gains, which had been won at heavy cost, were essential to their new security needs in Korea, and they showed no readiness to open them to international competition in which their country might fare poorly because of its shortage of capital. Instead they worked out a new series of guarantees with Russia on Mongolian and Manchurian rights in 1910 and 1912 whereby each agreed to respect the other's zone. Within China, meanwhile, an awareness of the danger to the north led to administrative changes in 1907 whereby Manchuria was reorganized as three eastern provinces, and thrown open to unrestricted Chinese settlement.

Thus China's response to having a foreign war fought on its territory was a move toward centralization and administrative rationalization in Manchuria.

Within China south of the wall the Boxer disaster had led to steps of institutional modernization, which were accelerated after Japan's demonstration of its ability to hold its own with the great imperialist powers showed the advantages of modern institutions for national strength. The initial steps toward institutional reform were taken by the repentant Dowager Empress at the urging of the dynasty's principal Chinese servants.

The most conspicuous political effort was a movement for constitutional government. Legal and administrative reforms were related to this, and the German and especially the Japanese examples were important. The court sent learning missions abroad and hired foreign consultants. Chinese statesmen credited the Japanese victory to Japan's modernized institutions. As those had been conferred from above, so should a Chinese constitution. In 1908 the court announced a nine-year preparatory program (modeled on that of Japan between 1881 and 1890) under which provincial assemblies would meet in 1909, a national assembly in 1910, and a parliament in 1917. Lower assemblies would incorporate local elite, while at the higher levels half the representatives would be metropolitan bureaucrats appointed by the court and the other half would be selected by provincial assemblies. Thus the constitutional apparatus was to give voice to lower officials and gentry, who would then support the central elite. Wherever possible, the new order was related to the old. Gentry registrants provided the base for apportioning elected representatives, and a property qualification was adopted to secure a responsible electorate, as had been done in Meiji Japan. In the first election, which was held in 1909, 90 percent of those elected were degree holders. Despite their conservative design, the representative institutions produced unexpected results. The local gentry quickly saw them as a device for protecting itself against the demands of central bureaucrats whose motives and venality it distrusted. The court's growing awareness of the need for change impressed observers, but the dynasty fell before its schedule of administrative reform was carried out.

In education the same years brought shattering changes. In 1905, the year of Japan's victory, the examination system was declared ended. The structure of degrees and titles was to continue as before, but the path to their acquisition was now to be through new schools and new learning. This meant a permanent change in the institutionalization of rewards and sanctions for ability in China.

The educational shifts had been proposed for several years. Critics had long deplored the impracticality of the examination essays. K'ang Yu-wei's plans for reform in 1898 had incorporated new standards for educational achievement and reward, and in 1904 the court had decreed a system of national schooling. The 1905 decision against the examination system was nevertheless revolutionary: it represented an uncritical shift from classical to foreign standards. The highest rewards were reserved for those with the most extended educational experience abroad, ranging from three years in Japan or the West to a one-year stay in Japan. Chinese education continued to be predominantly foreign oriented from this point until the establishment of the People's Republic. Regulations in 1904 specified that all teachers in colleges and universities were to be foreign educated or products of foreign-style research institutes.

The consequence of this was a rush of students abroad. Japan, the nearest, cheapest, and apparently the most appropriate model for emulation, was the initial target of thousands. By the time of the Russo-Japanese War there were at least 8,000 Chinese students in Japan. Most of them worked out makeshift educational arrangements, for the Meiji education system was not prepared for this sudden challenge. Chinese students congregated in Tokyo, where they organized along provincial lines. Many were there on scholarships given by their provincial government. They came from all parts of China, but the more conveniently located and politically active provinces of Kwangtung, Hunan, Kiangsu, and Chekiang sponsored the largest numbers.

In 1908 the United States remitted half of its share of the Boxer Protocol for Chinese education, making possible the establishment of Tsing Hua University as a preparatory school for study in America. Between 1911 and 1917 over 1,100 Tsing Hua graduates continued to the United States for higher education. Generous numbers of Chinese students also pursued higher education in Europe, especially in France. Western education had particular prestige, and the hundreds who traveled to the United States and Europe were proportionally more successful than the thousands who participated in the ebb and flow of the early student movement in Japan. In time Japanese institutions were prepared to educate better prepared Chinese students too, and numbers of Chinese graduates increased despite a decline in the total number of Chinese. Japanese influence was particularly strong among Chinese army officers, many of whom studied in Japan.

A student movement of these dimensions was pivotal in the experience of a generation, and it was also traumatic for the regime that sent them. Because of the political turbulence of China in the decades that followed, the students neither came from nor returned to a structured setting. Japan's experience in the Meiji period, when a large-scale migration abroad and widespread employment of foreign teachers gradually gave way before a growing system of domestic education in which the foreign experts were eased out at the earliest possible moment, provided striking contrasts. Meiji Japan was developing a structured system of examinations for education and bureaucratic service just as China was giving its system up.

Despite the court's attempts to integrate modern education and politics with traditional standards of degree holding, gentry rank assigned on the basis of foreign study could not easily be assimilated into a new structure. For thousands of the students the old learning was no longer true or useful. During the years around the Russo-Japanese War, a growing tide of translation into Chinese included a growing literature in science, technology, and the social sciences. These categories included over 60 percent of the total. New terms, new vocabulary (much of it Japanese in origin) came into Chinese. A traditional degree of *sheng-yuan*, granted on the basis of exposure to the new learning and often for foreign study, did not work toward the convergence of morality, learning, and public service as in earlier days.

The single most important effect of the new travel and learning was probably its impact on the development of Chinese nationalism. Chinese students in Japan were immediately and powerfully struck by the pervasive impact of Japanese nationalism. Students in Tokyo were often the objects of condescension and derision because of their dress, their queues, and their country's weakness, and they developed a reactive solidarity in which nation loomed larger than province or lineage. In Japan they were free, indeed encouraged, to organize against Russian refusal to evacuate Manchuria, obliged to watch Russian and Japanese armies march across Chinese territory, and affronted by special measures the Japanese government took to restrain their political activities and undisciplined behavior. Student strikes were mounted in protest, and student anger directed against the apparent complacency of Ch'ing diplomats in the face of national insults.

Student unrest abroad resonated with similar movements along the Chinese littoral from which the majority of the students had come. Movement between Japan and the China coast was constant, and publications and translations circulated easily between them, especially in the treaty ports with their foreign control. It was an era of intense emotionalism, stirred by the romantic imagination of a generation beginning to encounter the sorrows of Werther. This was true also in Japan, where authorities after 1906 began to be alarmed by the suicides among a generation of "anguished youth" no longer stirred by the passion of nation building; Chinese youths had better reasons to be anguished because of their personal and national problems. Occasional spectacular patriotic suicides—in China against foreign railway loans, and in Tokyo against newspaper derogation of Chinese student character—showed the strident tone of a new nationalism. Mass meetings and sensational pamphlets warned against the dangers China faced. Emotions were stirred by foreign railway loans that threatened to open the Chinese hinterland to the influence of a foreign imperialism for the profit of a central government that was perceived as rapacious and corrupt. The foreign issue presented an irreproachable device for attack. When a Japanese shipment of contraband arms was shown to be a violation of Chinese sovereignty in 1908, large-scale meetings of women resulted in the formation of a National Humiliation Society whose emotionally charged meetings were announced as preparation for suicide. As a result of the student movement the stirrings of change, strongest along the paths of modern commerce and influence, also reached beyond them to affect areas and groups that "awakened" to a consciousness of danger and disaster. The old elite was beginning to crumble, and a new elite was not yet structured to take its place.

Naturally this was also a setting that encouraged revolution. Sun Yat-sen's revolutionary organization (*T'ung-meng-hui*) was formed in Tokyo, and his cooperation with other groups from Central China was worked out there. The events that toppled the dynasty in 1911 represented a convergence of all these trends: gentry opposition to railway loans and central government intervention in Szechwan; refusal of "new" army groups, many led by officers trained in Japan, to provide support; and quick recruitment of youthful students, revolutionaries, and secret societies by *T'ung-meng-hui* members who had the makings of an ideology of revolutionary nationalism and republicanism.

The impact of the events of this decade on China's programs of modernization was very great. Throughout China, and particularly along the coast and river points of communication with international contact, there was a rising consciousness and awareness of national weakness and danger. Most direct were the additional symbols of national humiliation imposed by the Boxer Protocol. There were new and larger foreign loans that seemed likely to affect the vast Chinese hinterland through programs of communications and raw materials development. And there was the power of the Japanese example with its impact on the large and unstructured student movement.

Indirectly, the late Ch'ing program of administrative and educational reform removed powerful restraints of the old structure without providing new values in their place. Instead it substituted rather clumsy rewards and incentives for the newly disorienting diversification of educational experience. Innovations of representative institutions provided outlets for the expression of distrust that provincial elite had long held toward the central government. As a consequence, institutions designed to increase support and provide stronger consensus for the national government worked instead to articulate suspicion of its moves for centralization. Throughout all this, the increasing scale of participation and greater perception of a hostile international environment raised the consciousness of crisis. Student strikes, commercial boycotts, and petition campaigns began to give voice to larger numbers of Chinese. While still a minuscule portion of the millions in the hinterland, these protestors were becoming a minority that mattered. In sum, at a time of growing need for symbols and structures of national unity and leadership, China's existing structures were losing their ability to inspire respect and exercise control.

Republic to Washington Conference

China's international environment in the first decade of the republic was one of rapid change. Shortly after the fall of the Ch'ing dynasty World War I brought the collapse of empire in Turkey, Russia, and Germany. While the major treaty powers fixed their attention on the struggle in Europe, Japan emerged as the principal contender for influence on the continent. The United States responded as the principal defender of Chinese sovereignty. The Washington Conference at the end of the decade represented an attempt to restructure comprehensively international guarantees and rivalries in East Asia. China's governmental instability made it particularly difficult for it to respond to this international instability, and opinion within China fluctuated between optimism and despair with perceptions of a promising and a hostile international setting.

At the time of the Chinese Revolution of 1911 the reaction of the treaty powers ranged from jubilation in the United States because of the apparent victory of parliamentary institutions and republicanism to alarm in Japan because of the success of revolutionary ideology so close at hand. Japan's conservative military leaders considered intervention on the side of the Ch'ing government. Sun Yat-sen, who was in the United States at the time of the outbreak of revolution, journeyed first to England to seek help in restraining Japan before he returned to a triumphant welcome at Shanghai. His priorities in this illustrate the perception leading Chinese held of the overwhelming importance of foreign roles in Chinese politics.

In fact, however, foreign influence took a different path. The other treaty powers were no less desirous than Japan of finding a successor government that would be able to maintain order and carry out China's treaty obligations. After Yuan Shih-k'ai, who was delegated by the Ch'ing court to negotiate with the revolutionary leaders, secured the Manchu abdication in return for his own nomination as president, the powers saw in him the necessary "strong man" that the situation required. The Reorganization Loan that he secured helped him to take a strong line with his republican rivals, flouting their parliamentary expectations and assassinating one of their chief leaders.

The "Second Revolution" that Sun Yat-sen tried to launch in the summer of 1913 failed completely, and Sun and his associates once again found themselves in exile. Yuan would have been a powerful opponent even without the Reorganization Loan, for he had a dependable military following and access to regional taxes as well as the experience of high office to help him. Nevertheless the revolutionaries perceived his victory as made possible by foreign intervention, and their new dependence upon outside support led to some years of desperate maneuver in which Sun Yat-sen went farther with promises of possible rewards for outside assistance than Yuan Shih-k'ai ever had. It was a climate in which the desperate need for foreign help seemed to corrode the idealism and naiveté that had characterized the romantic image of the last decade of the empire.

While the western powers engaged in a desperate struggle for survival in Europe, Japan dominated East Asia. Japan seized the German holdings in Shantung as its war contribution under the Anglo-Japanese alliance, and then consolidated its gains by securing agreements from its military allies.

232

The Twenty-One Demands of 1915 represented a clumsy effort to secure Chinese agreement to Japanese primacy in parts of China important to Japan against the uncertainties of the postwar world. They called for Chinese recognition of transfer of Shantung holdings from Germany to Japan, extensions of leases in Manchuria and Inner Mongolia that Japan had taken from Russia after the Russo-Japanese War, joint Sino-Japanese administration of an iron complex in Central China, promises that, "in the interest of preserving China's territorial integrity," China would make no assignments along its coast to any other power, and, in Group V, a set of "desires" that would give Japan primacy in Chinese development plans. Although the Japanese government saw the demands as a way to forestall future misunderstandings, Chinese negotiators saw them as alarming portents of Japanese aggression. Japanese clumsiness in negotiating made it possible for the Peking government to appeal to western, and especially American, opinion for help. Japan finally eliminated the items in Group V, but resorted to an ultimatum to secure Chinese agreement in May 1915.

It is difficult to exaggerate the psychological impact of this incident. The gains for Japan proved insubstantial. Manchuria could have been negotiated separately, Shantung was restored to China by provisions worked out in 1922, the iron works became debt ridden and unprofitable, the age of seeking bases and ports along the coast was at an end, and Group V was eliminated from consideration. Yet for much of the outside world, and certainly for United States Minister Paul Reinsch (who wrote that "it fell to me to counsel with Chinese leaders as if I had been one of their number") a protective partiality for China against Japan was now established in a tradition that would influence Reinsch's disciple Stanley Hornbeck three decades later. For Chinese opinion, the Demands constituted a central outrage; the day of Peking's capitulation became commemorated as "National Humiliation Day."

After 1915 Japan continued to be the most powerful outside force in Chinese politics. In 1916 Yuan Shih-k'ai erroneously banked on Japanese approval for an attempt to establish a new dynasty. A transitional figure, Yuan harbored monarchical hopes from the first. As "president" he had issued an Audience Act and carried out regular ceremonies at the Altars of Heaven; he began these in an armored car, changed to a vermillion coach, and ended in a sedan chair. He began the ceremony dressed in a field marshal's uniform and then changed into sacrificial headgear and robe. But his monarchical attempt failed completely. Everywhere in China opinion was opposed to this combination of usurpation and betrayal. Powerful regional army commanders in the southwest opposed it, and, not least important, Japan made clear its disapproval and seemed likely to assist Yuan's military rivals. Yuan died that year.

Shortly afterward General Terauchi, who headed a new Japanese government in 1916, tried to use the opportunity to build order out of the warlord confusion that followed the failure of Yuan Shih-k'ai. His government encouraged a decision by the Peking government to join the allied side in World

War I, meanwhile channeling military and economic aid to China through a War Participation Bureau. The Russian Revolution of 1917 made it seem urgent to build an anticommunist defense on China's northern border, and some 150 million yen (about $80 million) was poured out as loans to Chinese government agencies for development projects. The "Nishihara loans," as they were known, helped Japan's cause very little. Most of the money was wasted, and its repayment became only one more item of disagreement between Japan and Chinese governments. The few modern divisions the loans financed were soon destroyed in China's civil wars. Japan's warlord allies too often proved little more than elaborately decorated and plumed birds of passage, and as they left the scene Japan inherited chiefly dislike and resentment for its efforts to collect interest on the loans.

During these same years China's halting political development was outsped by developments in Chinese popular awareness of the nation's predicament. The large labor force that was sent to the western front as China's contribution to the war effort became the object of a campaign for mass literacy that served as a model for future campaigns at home and as a focus for many intellectuals' greater involvement with the plight of ordinary Chinese. Japan's well-advertised foreign policy miscalculations produced large-scale indignation among groups of Chinese theretofore scarcely conscious of national affairs. China's civilian elite had looked forward to a postwar settlement that, it was hoped, would provide the opportunity for China to restore its dignity in international affairs. The rhetoric of Wilsonian democracy struck responsive notes among East Asian intellectuals, and Wilson's refusal to permit American participation in the Reorganization Loan for Yuan Shih-k'ai, like his announced refusal to recognize Japan's gains from the Twenty-One Demands, encouraged young Chinese to expect a future international order with more justice.

The Nishihara loans brought demonstrations by Peking University students, who marched to government buildings to demand an end to their government's collaboration with Japan. When, in 1919, the fourth anniversary of the Twenty-One Demands humiliation approached, and when word came from the Versailles Conference that Japanese negotiators had succeeded in holding their allies to honor secret agreements relating to Shantung, which had been worked out prior to Japanese entry into the war, gigantic demonstrations broke out directed against the officials who had collaborated with the Japanese; the May Fourth movement, as it became called, ushered in the age of modern Chinese nationalism. The May Fourth movement has become a milestone in modern Chinese history and nationalism. The demonstrations for which it became known were directly inspired by popular, and especially student, perceptions of a hostile international environment. In a broader sense the movement went well beyond antigovernment demonstrations. Campaigns for substitution of the spoken vernacular for classical Chinese in formal writing, for popular education, and for new and more strident values of struggle to replace "effete" Confucianism stirred a new generation.

The decades that followed the Chinese Revolution of 1911 thus saw the emergence of a popular perception of Japan as a principal barrier to Chinese aspirations of national equality and sovereignty. They also saw the emergence of the United States as the principal opponent of Japanese domination of Northeast Asia. The end of empire in China, in Russia, and in Germany, and the relative weakening of England and France because of the losses and costs of World War I, thus inaugurated a new Pacific competition between the emerging expansionisms of Japan and America. Wilsonian rhetoric and the institutionalization of the Wilsonian dream of an international league, signaled the beginning of a new era of cooperative effort to help the reconstruction of China.

It is clear that in this period the consciousness on the part of large numbers of Chinese that the international environment was somehow obstructing their national development grew steadily. The results of this consciousness were positive in that the rising tide of indignation contributed to a national consensus and psychological participation that brought more Chinese to share alarm for their country's plight and problems than ever before. Throughout the modern world and especially the underdeveloped world the willingness of people to be mobilized to action for national purposes has had an important effect on programs of modernization. No one doubts that the manner in which the Meiji government was able to recruit support in the name of the nation was a significant factor in Japanese modernization. On the other hand, China still lacked an effective government that could combine continuity with purpose. Without such leadership, the events of the decade tended to activate, and indeed to radicalize, without mobilizing China's intellectuals. The results of this were negative in that the resulting sense of frustration and disillusion tended to deepen distrust in authority and contributed to extreme division and to extremist solutions of radicalism and militarism in the years ahead.

Nevertheless, the international environment also offered new patterns of hope and example, which came from Moscow, Tokyo, and Washington. Moscow sent the thrill of social revolution in a backward land and messages calling for an end to "imperialism." Washington, in the person of Wilson, contributed hopes of international order and friendly assistance. Tokyo continued to train thousands of Chinese in modern learning and established particularly close ties with the military cadets who were beginning to command Chinese armies. Japan's modernized institutions were also beginning to show a "second generation" relaxation of the military rigidity that characterized the now elderly Japanese elite. "Japan" meant student radicalism and parliamentary government as well as the Twenty-One Demands of 1915. The setting in China was thus far from funereal, for it vibrated with energy, growth, and movement. Furthermore, despite Chinese perceptions of handicap, the international environment, problematic as it was, still did not constitute the decisive element in China's political difficulties. No outside power saw its aims achieved, for China's complexities defeated each in turn. This would continue to be so in the Washington Conference era.

The Washington Conference Era

The decade that falls between the Washington Conference and the Japanese seizure of Manchuria constituted a new division in China's international environment. At Washington in 1922 a network of international agreements replaced the piecemeal arrangements, of which the Anglo-Japanese Alliance was the most important, that had existed earlier. The Nine Power Treaty committed its signatories to respect China's territorial integrity and political independence and renounce further efforts to achieve spheres of special influence. Equal commercial opportunity for all was pledged, thus legislating the Open Door principles.

China thus seemed to be in less danger than before. Of the empires that had threatened it, two had collapsed; Germany had lost its holdings in Shantung, and Russia, consumed with internal problems, was no longer a danger in the north. Britain and France, weakened by their losses in World War I, were no longer expansive, and Japan was to agree to return Shantung shortly after the Washington Conference.

Despite this, few actual gains were scored. Existing privileges for foreigners remained as they were. Foreign settlements and concessions remained in place, and large numbers of Chinese continued to live under foreign governance without representation. Worst of all, China lacked a government capable of dealing with these problems. Imperialism, capitalist exploitation centered in foreign enclaves in the port cities, and warlordism now became firmly associated in the minds of Chinese nationalists. Although Chinese unity was less threatened by imperialistic action, Chinese opinion was more vehemently antiimperialist than ever before. The real roots of that vehemence were to be found in frustrations growing out of the chaos of internal politics, where the kaleidoscopic shifts of power in warlord coalitions and the ebb and flow of strong men across the political stage were the despair of a generation.

The spokesmen of that generation coupled imperialism with political disunity. Chiang Kai-shek wrote that "the secret activities of the imperialists were actually the chief cause of the civil wars," Mao Tse-tung agreed that "revolutions in China failed one after another because imperialism strangled them," and Teng Hsiao-p'ing (Deng Xiaoping) told American reporters in February 1979 that he himself had become involved in politics in his youth because of foreign interference in China.

The grounds for impatience and irritation with foreign intervention were at least threefold. The first was the foreign position in China's greatest cities, especially Shanghai, the center of modern publishing, industry, and political organization. The May 30 Incident of 1925 was in response to the shooting down of protesting Chinese workers by British-officered police in Shanghai. Nicholas Clifford's recent (1979) study shows the tortuous course that strike, boycott, and demonstration had to take to secure even minimal adjustments there. In June of that same year Anglo-French troops killed fifty-two Chinese by shooting into a demonstration at Canton, prompting a related strike and boycott there. A second irritant was the continued presence of foreign officials in high positions in the Maritime Customs, an organization whose income-producing potential made it the great prize in the intermittent civil wars. Even under the Nationalist regime that took power in 1927, customs income averaged fully one-half the national government's budget; other sources of revenue were largely controlled by local authorities. Thus this foreign-officered organization, controlling sums partly hypothecated to foreign obligations, served as a magnet for competing warlords. The third irritant was the clear possibility that outside influence could count for more on actors in a fragmented China than it could on a central government. Such foreign influence was most constant in the north, where the Japanese reached an agreement with Chang Tso-lin and tended to protect him from overthrow in order to maintain the stability of the area most important to them. Other powers, too, frequently maintained contacts with the headquarters of several warlords for similar reasons, and, in view of the Japanese military training of the men who officered China's armies, Japanese military meddlers probably outnumbered others.

Nevertheless the influence of such representatives was very limited, and for the most part the governments they represented did their best to restrain their nationals. As the American diplomat MacMurray phrased it in 1924, "We have no favorites in the present dog fight in China; they all look alike to us"; the hope was rather that "somebody, whoever it may be, licks his rivals . . . in other words, that they fight it out to a conclusion" (Iriye, 1965, p. 28). Yet clearly the tone of that comment would raise more irritation than its content would allay. The powers' fastidious attitude toward Chinese disunity brought them no more popularity than direct intervention would have done.

In fact the most purposeful foreign intervention in China was devoted to unsuccessful efforts to build unity and strength there. Iriye divides the events of the decade into three sequential initiatives; the Washington powers' attempt to build a new order, the Soviet effort to sponsor and support the Northern Expedition, and the Japanese initiative in Shantung. Only this last was designed to slow that unification. All three failed.

The principal Washington Conference powers were agreed on the need for cooperative moves to help China achieve unity, but they found that the political disorder in China prevented common action. They discussed holding conferences to arrange tariff reform, but when one convened in Peking in 1925 it was forced to disband hurriedly because of the overthrow of the host government. There were more cooperative programs of aid than ever before; movements for flood and famine relief, literacy campaigns, and campaigns against opium found public and private agencies working together. But little of this contributed to Chinese political stability, and at times, as when insistence upon the free export of rice as stipulated by treaty contributed to famine emergencies, treaty "rights" could contribute to new wrongs.

The most important foreign intervention in Chinese politics in the 1920s was that of the Soviet Union, which was not a signatory to the Washington agreements. Russian help for Sun Yat-sen's Kuomintang came in the form of money, arms, the establishment of the Whampoa Military Academy, instructions to the fledgling Chinese Communist Party to join in a united front, and high level counsel coordinated by Michael Borodin. This organizational assistance proved highly successful, and helped guarantee that the forces that moved north from Canton would be very different from the lackluster units of the warlords they faced.

Yet in the end Soviet efforts to use the units they had helped form failed totally. After the death of Dr. Sun, Chiang K'ai-shek, as head of Whampoa and then as general of the armies that moved north, was full of doubt about his Soviet advisers and totally without doubt where his Chinese communist collaborators were concerned. By advancing the timing of the Northern Expedition he escaped Soviet control at Canton, and by using the support of anticommunist forces in Shanghai he anticipated a communist takeover attempt by a massacre of real and suspected communists in Shanghai in 1927. Next the "left wing" Kuomintang, no less than Chiang, became disillusioned about Soviet purposes and expelled its Soviet advisers. Chinese communists, responsive to Stalin's desperate efforts to convert failure into success, staged a series of risings, the last of which were at Canton and Changsha in 1928, that cost them most of their followers. Chinese realities had defeated Soviet plans, as they had the capitalist imperialists earlier. The Nationalist government was established at Nanking in 1927.

The significance of the decade of the 1920s for Chinese modernization was very great. Despite the turbulence and political disunity of the period it saw the emergence of a surprisingly clear consensus on national goals, one that was shared by millions of Chinese. National unity took first place. The recovery of national rights from foreign powers was expected to be a result of such unity, and social justice, however vaguely defined, would follow.

That these were universal demands could be seen even during the disunity of the warlord era. The more successful and important contenders for national power among the warlords usually campaigned with slogans against imperialism and "bad" landlords. The Northern Expedition showed that antiimperialist sentiment was widespread, for as the armies moved north a surge of antiforeign and especially anti-British sentiment produced protests, strikes, and boycotts throughout China that brought violence at Shanghai, Canton, Nanking, Chungking, and other treaty ports. Immediately afterward the treaty powers began to agree to return privileges; at Hankow and Kiukiang (February 1927), Chinkiang (1929), Weihaiwei (1930), and Amoy, (1930), and the Belgian concession at Tientsin (1931). The exasperation of the Chinese people was thus beginning to make it possible for the new national government to do things that previous Chinese governments had not been able to do. China announced its intention of setting new tariff schedules in 1928, and within ten months the powers, including Japan, had agreed to those schedules.

The establishment of the Nationalist government thus met the first and most strategic of the needs for programs of modernization. The government was staffed at many points by modern-educated men drawn from coastal, "modern" China, which was also the area under its control. It was prepared to make extensive use of outside advisers in programs of modernization. Its writ expanded slowly as warlords who began with formal subordination gradually found it necessary to affiliate more fully. To the south the Chinese Communist Party had remained defiant in its mountain redoubt, but its future seemed extremely uncertain. China seemed within sight of unification and effective central government for the first time in the twentieth century. New developments in international affairs blighted that hope.

The War with Japan

Within a few years of its establishment the Nanking Nationalist government found its international environment dominated by an attack from Japan on its territory, its sovereignty, and finally its life. The Japanese destroyed the Nationalist government as a viable regime by forcing it into expensive military measures that took precedence over internal reform, by driving it into the hinterland away from its supporters and its revenues, and by forcing it into dependence on the least modernized sectors of the Chinese society and the Chinese economy.

During the Northern Expedition, Japan's policy toward China had reflected the importance of internationalism, parliamentarianism, and commerce in the years after World War I and the Washington Conference. Japanese exporters had been influenced by the growing tide of Chinese nationalism and the boycotts of the decade. China had become steadily more important to Japanese business and during this same period the support of Japanese business was becoming more important to Japanese political parties also. Consequently Japanese policymakers were sensitive to Chinese public opinion in the populous areas of Central and South China, and Foreign Minister Shidehara resisted suggestions for stronger measures that were urged upon the government during the disorders in the Yangtze Valley in 1926 and 1927.

As Chiang Kai-shek's armies moved from Central to North China in 1927 and 1928, however, a new Japanese government, headed by Baron General

Tanaka, faced new questions about priorities. Tanaka's intervention in 1927 and again in 1928 against the Nationalist armies in Shantung denied them transportation routes for a time, but did not represent a political decision. Japan's chief concern lay with Manchuria, which was of immense strategic importance and seemed vital to future industrial expansion as well. Its principal political figure, the warlord Chang Tso-lin, had long been the beneficiary of quiet Japanese support, but after he developed larger political ambitions and occupied Peking, Manchurian politics became hopelessly entangled with those of China. In 1927 Tanaka convened a conference to discuss Japan's course; it was later credited with the formulation of the "Tanaka Memorial," a spurious document that mapped out full aggression in China; but its formal recommendations did in fact propose continued support of Chang Tso-lin in Manchuria. Chang, however, was not in Manchuria but in Peking, and was forced to retreat from Peking by the advance of the unification drive in 1928. Staff officers of Japan's Kwantung Army who wanted a stronger policy saw to the murder of the warlord in June 1928 as his train was bringing him back to Mukden. He was succeeded by his son, who soon formally recognized Kuomintang rule in Manchuria. In 1929, shortly before his fall from power, Tanaka's government too recognized the new Nationalist government.

That same year a political party government took office in Tokyo, just in time to inherit the blame for the world depression and financial crisis and to worsen its effects by returning Japan to the gold standard. New staff officers of the Kwantung Army now worked closely with confederates in the Tokyo General Staff to lay plans for direct action in Manchuria, while the London Naval Conference, designed as a continuation of Washington Conference agreements, sparked controversy over issues of civilian-military primacy. The Manchuria Incident of 1931, in which the Kwantung Army inaugurated an era of violence in Japanese politics, transformed the politics and policies of the interwar years. Military adventurism on the continent resonated with military and ultranationalist extremism within Japan. Conservative leaders in Japan reluctantly reached accommodation with the more conservative wing within the military establishment, preferring expansion on the continent to an ideological crusade against the Soviet Union, and choosing military participation in bureaucratic rule over a radical restructuring of Japanese society in the name of a potentially revolutionary "Shōwa Restoration."

The chronology of Japanese advance is familiar. On September 18, 1931, Japan's Kwantung Army staged an explosion on the tracks of the South Manchurian railway as a pretext for military action that led to the swift occupation of all of Manchuria by February. That same month an independent Manchukuo, "ruled" by the last Ch'ing emperor, as regent, and (1934) as Emperor K'ang-te, was established. From January 28 to March 4, 1932, Japanese naval and military troops also intervened at Shanghai against the Chinese 19th Route Army, an incident that created a demilitarized zone around the settlement, and, indirectly, led to the assassination of a Japanese prime minister. In 1933 Japanese forces occupied the province of Jehol, and, a year later, the Ho-Umezu Agreement secured the withdrawal of Chinese troops from Hopei. In 1935 an autonomous East Hopei, and then a Hopei-Chahar Council (December) was established as a sign of Japanese determination to deny the Nanking government control over North China.

In the summer of 1937 clashes between Japanese and Chinese troops near Peking led to the China Incident, which escalated swiftly into full-scale war between Japan and the Nanking government. By the fall of that year the nationalist capital had been removed to Chungking, and the Japanese found themselves victorious in hard-fought campaigns to take Soochow (November 20), Nanking (December 13), and Hangchow (December 24). Tsingtao, Hankow, and Canton fell during 1938 as the Japanese extended their control along the coast and along major communication routes.

This aggression came as the Nationalist government was beginning to achieve some of its major goals for the recovery of Chinese sovereignty. By 1930 China had recovered tariff autonomy. Nine countries had surrendered extraterritorial privileges in China, and only France, Great Britain, the United States, and Japan retained those privileges. Increasingly effective boycotts were giving the Nationalist government leverage in its campaigns for the recovery of rights.

The Nationalist government was also making headway in its campaign of political unification. Chang Hsueh-liang, the "young marshall," had brought Manchuria into the Kuomintang fold. A provisional constitution was adopted in 1931. Kwangtung was brought into the union in 1936, and Szechwan in 1937. Steps toward a modern currency, forced by American purchases of silver under New Deal legislation, laid the groundwork for economic unification. Modern finance and budgeting methods were introduced. Communications made rapid progress; the Hankow-Canton Railway was completed in 1937; telegraph, telephone, and radio communications improved, and many thousands of miles of new motor roads were built.

In addition to all this, Chiang Kai-shek's armies were making headway in a series of "extermination" campaigns to crush or at least contain the communist movement. After the disasters of 1927 Mao Tse-tung and Chu Teh had joined forces in the Chingkang mountains, on the border of Kiangsi and Hunan, and from there moved to south Kiangsi, which they made the base of a Chinese Soviet Republic. Communist strength grew slowly but steadily in the years that followed, several times through the defection of large bodies of Nationalist and warlord troops. In 1930 Chiang launched the first of his campaigns. The fifth, which got underway in October 1933, caused enough hardship in the communist area to produce the Long March of 1934 which ended with the Chinese communists in their new and remote base in Yenan. Chiang's determination to crush them there led to the Sian Incident of December 1936, in which he was kidnapped by the forces of Chang Hsueh-liang, who had been driven out of Manchuria by the Japanese. He was released at communist insistence, and agreed to a united front against the Japanese.

Chiang's campaigns against the communists had been hampered several times by demands that he turn against the Japanese instead; this pressure now gave the communists safety in their area of Northwest China. Thus the war with Japan, which forced Chiang to abandon his military campaign against the Chinese communists, probably saved the communists from military destruction and provided them with the setting in which they could compete on equal terms with the Nationalists.

The importance of the war with Japan for Chinese nationalism and politics cannot be overestimated. Japanese atrocities (notably at Nanking) and brutality (notably in the campaigns against the communists of North China) contributed to the rise of nationalism among people of every sort. The forced evacuation of "modern China"—students, civilians, and urban elite—from the cities of the coast to inland China produced powerful pressures of "psychological unification" and identification between sectors of Chinese society theretofore only marginally interrelated. The enforced separation of the Nationalist government from its social and economic support—urban bourgeoisie and customs duties—made it dependent on a much less modernized military and landholding elite in the interior of China, and that part of the eastern China elite that stayed in place was discredited in the years after 1945 and highly vulnerable to communist criticism. Finally, the long years of impotence in which the Nationalists could do little more than wait for deliverance from the Japanese produced lethargy, corruption, cynicism, and a war weariness that equipped that government poorly for the renewed competition with the communists that followed the Japanese surrender in 1945.

The war against the Japanese, in short, destroyed the Nationalist government as an effective agent for the modernization of China. It also contributed to the tide of nationalism and made impossible any postwar extension of foreign privileges in China.

The Civil War

In 1945 Chiang Kai-shek seemed to have achieved total victory, and Nationalist armies returned to occupy the coastal areas from which the Japanese had driven them. Four years later Chiang was in Taiwan, his military strength and his government defeated by his communist opponents. An upset so startling inevitably contains material for sharp controversy in interpretation, and the argument is far from over. The focus here, however, is limited to the question of intervention by outside powers, and the consequences of such intervention, or lack of it, for China's progress toward modernization.

The Nationalist-communist struggle did not have its origins in the struggle between the United States and the Soviet Union, but helped to create and worsen that competition. The Nationalist-communist united front had fared badly during the war years, especially following the 4th Route Army clash of 1941 in which Nationalist troops ambushed communist units. Chiang Kai-shek used a large part of his strength after that to isolate the communist areas, and by 1943 American observers estimated that as many as 400,000 Nationalist troops were involved in a blockade of communist areas. The fact that the communists controlled large areas of North China by then, and maintained an armed force of at least one-half million men, showed that Nationalist fears of competition were well grounded. On several occasions communist forces mounted offensives against the Japanese, who responded with total destruction in "free fire" zones, but for the most part they chose to conserve scarce material and to incite, rather than attack, the Japanese. Similarly, Nationalist armies, which bore the main brunt of Japanese pressure, waited for outside help to defeat the Japanese.

After Japan surrendered, the Nationalist-communist rivalry came to the forefront. United States representatives had feared this, and saw in it a danger to postwar cooperation with the Soviet Union. At the Yalta Conference in 1945 efforts were made to secure Soviet cooperation by offering to return the "former rights violated by the treacherous attack of Japan in 1904," although those "rights" had of course been extorted from China by the tsarist government in 1898. In addition, during the waning months of the war, efforts were made to build a modern force under the leadership of General Joseph Stilwell that would serve as the support of a coalition government to include communist as well as other non-Kuomintang elements. The policy of peaceful unification, unfortunately, had little basis in Chinese politics, for the principal contenders for power had been at war with each other intermittently for nearly two decades. Their distrust was deep and well founded.

After the Japanese surrender the United States transported half a million Nationalist soldiers to North and Central China, while American marines landed to accept the Japanese surrender in the Tientsin-Peking area. The Soviet Union had already occupied Manchuria, and promised, in line with a recent agreement with the KMT, in which the nationalist government accepted the decisions that had been reached at Yalta, to time its departure with the Nationalist arrival. In December 1945 President Truman sent General George Marshall to China to work out the path toward a coalition government. In talks that followed both sides agreed to hold the areas they had occupied, while truce teams would supervise the truce. Marshall returned to Washington in March 1946, his task apparently going well; by the time he returned in April it had failed.

The truce agreements failed first of all in Manchuria, an area that the Nationalists were determined to reclaim despite American warnings about priorities. Although Soviet forces gave communist troops the arms and equipment they had taken from the Japanese, the Nationalists won a major victory in May and June of 1946, which served to convince Chiang Kai-shek of his military superiority. At this point the United States, which was anxious to limit and if possible end the civil war, embargoed further military support for China. Chiang Kai-shek now decided to occupy the Manchurian cities, where his best divisions were surrounded and forced to surrender in October 1948. Critics of American policy argued that a shortage of supplies produced a garrison mentality in Nationalist military circles, while defenders of United States policy retorted that the basic contrast was between communist morale and discipline and Nationalist war weariness and incompetence.

While Soviet assistance in the form of Japanese equipment was clearly important (and in violation of the Soviet-Chinese treaty), total American assistance to Nationalist military strength was far larger in amount. All Chinese leaders realized the importance of the Soviet and American roles. In January 1945 Mao Tse-tung and Chou En-lai proposed a visit to Washington to discuss matters with President Roosevelt, probably in hopes of bypassing what they saw as an unfriendly American embassy in China, but received no invitation. After the Communist defeat in Manchuria in 1946, Stalin invited Chiang Kai-shek to Moscow to work things out there, but that invitation also was declined.

It is unlikely that either visit would have made much difference in the final outcome. Stalin's invitation was presumably based upon a healthy respect for Nationalist military strength, a respect that would not have outlived that strength. Mao's visit would not have increased Nationalist trust in the United States, and it would certainly have contributed to the intensity of American political warfare after the civil war resumed.

China was much more than a cockpit of international rivalry. The United States was unable to guide the course of events despite a very large effort to do so. Because of its efforts the United States became an object of widespread criticism in China; Nationalists wanted more assistance, and others blamed the civil war on American aid. In 1948 Chinese cities were swept by anti-American demonstrations. By then the breakdown of governmental efficiency and spiraling inflation made continuation of that civil war highly unpopular. All evidence points to the fact that the Soviet Union was surprised by the speed and decisiveness of the communist victory and poorly prepared for it. Soviet occupation forces had hurriedly dismantled Manchurian industrial plants after their entry in 1945. The politics of the civil war were made in China, and rooted in recent Chinese history.

The significance of the civil war for programs of modernization needs little comment. Although the cities were turned over with little violence and minimal physical destruction, communist sabotage of communication lines during the struggle created serious problems. Postwar inflation went far to destroy the middle class as an economic force, and probably made it easier for the new regime to destroy it as a political force. The political ineptitude of the Nationalist government, combined with the war weariness of the Chinese people, also eased acceptance of the new regime in its early months.

The People's Republic: The Soviet Tie

The establishment of the People's Republic in October of 1949 marked a clear turning point in China's response to its international environment. The new government found itself able to act with full restoration of national sovereignty. China had not been in full charge of its foreign relations since the treaties that ended the Opium War in 1842. The western allies had renounced their treaty rights in 1943, but the new communist regime was able to renounce all loans incurred by previous governments as well. The Soviet Union, claiming the privileges it had been promised at Yalta, was able to reassert former Russian influence in Manchuria for a time, but within a decade those privileges too had been surrendered. All that remained of the nineteenth-century humiliations was the border to the north, where the Soviet Union retained the Maritime Provinces that had been surrendered to it in 1860, and Hong Kong and Kowloon to the south.

The Peking government also saw the survival of Taiwan under Nationalist rule as a remnant of outside interference in Chinese politics. American support for the Republic of China, first uncertain and then strengthened as a consequence of the Korean War, conditioned China's perception of its international environment strongly and ruled out the "final" unification of that province with the mainland during the 1950s. By the 1960s it was probable that the Taiwan regime had recovered enough self-confidence and military power to deter invasion from the mainland with or without American support. But its existence in no way weakened the fact that China now had, for the first time in a century, a government with armed forces capable of protecting its borders. It fought the United States to a standstill in Korea in 1952, improved its borders with India a decade later, defied Russian threats in the 1960s, and launched a punitive expedition into Vietnam in 1978. The PRC established an international presence in the communist and nonaligned world and managed to claim its UN seat and reverse United States policy in the 1970s. Under the leadership of Chou En-lai it fielded a team of expert diplomats who gained respect as the representatives of an increasingly major power. This was an accomplishment no other modern Chinese government had been able to perform. China had unusually accomplished diplomats in the twentieth century, but they invariably spoke from weakness.

China's major problem has been centered around the question of what its involvement in the world economy was to be. After an initial decade of close relations with the Soviet Union, a period of experimentation with other courses ranged from nearly total isolation to the internationalization of the late 1970s.

The People's Republic made an initial commitment to the Soviet bloc. It may not have been an entirely free choice, for the resumption of American aid to the Nationalist regime in the closing months of the civil war was read correctly as a hostile act. The United States nevertheless experimented by leaving some of its diplomats and nationals in place in China at the time of the political change, but the harsh treatment they received at communist hands confirmed the initial hostility.

Immediately after the establishment of the People's Republic, Mao Tse-tung traveled to Moscow. The length of his stay there—nine weeks—so soon after the establishment of the regime indicates the importance of the visit for him and the difficulty of securing guarantees of help from Stalin. What Mao secured was a thirty-year alliance against aggressive action by Japan or any Japanese ally (the USA) in addition to Russian promises of credits and technological assistance. The Russians received confirmation of the South Manchurian economic and political footholds they had been granted earlier by the Nationalists as a result of the Yalta agreements. This treaty, together with the peace treaty between the United States and Japan and the Japanese-American Security Treaty that followed in 1951, laid out the terrain for East Asian international relations for the next quarter-century.

Hostility between the United States and the PRC deepened with the outbreak of the Korean War, and became conflict with Chinese participation in that war in 1951. The Soviet Union had encouraged Chinese entry, but the Chinese hesitated until the American drive to the Yalu in December of 1951 threatened to destabilize their northern border. Chinese participation in the war was expensive in manpower, but it was rewarded by extensive Russian military assistance that made the modernization of the People's Liberation Army possible. The performance of Chinese armies also stirred national pride, and the war provided the external crisis under which massive national drives against alleged class enemies could be carried on within China.

China's First Five Year Plan (1953–1957) seemed to meet many of its goals in economic development. China was emerging as an attractive model for third world countries. Chou En-lai represented his country at the Geneva conference on Southeast Asia in 1954 and at the Bandung conference of non-allied countries the following year. In 1957 Mao Tse-tung, having crushed the "Hundred Flowers" movement and established stronger control over intellectuals and universities, traveled to Moscow a second time, this time for the Conference of Communist Parties. Now he called for a hard line at all points, and interpreted the Soviet Sputnik as a sure sign of an early communist victory in the world struggle. Mao was apparently disgruntled by the reception of his proposals, but upon his return to China he showed his own determination by precipitating the Quemoy crisis, crushing resistance in Tibet, and, especially, launching the Great Leap Forward.

Soviet assistance in the first decade was large scale and important to China's modernization programs. National planning, ambitious goals, an emphasis on heavy industry, and large-scale imports of entire plants marked a new stage in industrial development. In the first eleven years of communist rule the Chinese imported over 5 billion dollars' worth of machinery and equipment, over half of that in complete plant projects, the largest from the

246

USSR. The vast majority of this aid came from socialist countries. Dern-berger (1977) shows that even Poland and Hungary, China's fourth- and fifth-largest suppliers, together provided more than did all the countries in the noncommunist world. The Soviet Union provided 56 percent of China's imports of machinery and equipment, and the communist countries together provided thirteen times China's imports from the noncommunist countries. This, again, was not an entirely free choice for the Chinese, for China's Korean War participation subjected it to a boycott of materials of potential military importance (the CHINCOM list) that was even more restrictive than the list (COCOM) applied to the Soviet Union. China's debt was large. Some 12,000 Soviet technicians came to China. Over 25,000 Chinese technicians, and thousands of Chinese students, were sent to the Soviet Union, and Russian became the primary foreign language taught in China.

China ended this dependence on the Soviet Union for reasons that were political, strategic, and ideological. The death of Stalin and the rise of Khrushchev, followed by the de-Stalinization program, affected the Chinese party negatively and Mao Tse-tung's position adversely. The Stalin cult never flagged in China. In 1957 Sputnik seemed to bring visions of technological superiority and communist victory, but Khrushchev's willingness to talk to American leaders seemed an alarming indication of Soviet untrustworthiness. Russian promises, and failure, to share atomic technology with the Chinese heightened this distrust.

Mao's Great Leap Forward of 1958, an attempt to forge ahead of Soviet example and defy Soviet doubts, thus represented a direct challenge to Soviet leadership. It was also an economic failure, one so great that it produced challenges to Mao's leadership in the Chinese Communist Party. Chinese agriculture, which had been slated to carry the cost of industrialization, failed badly under the pressures of radical communization. Agricultural crisis and serious shortages led to a revamping of priorities.

The 1960s and "Self-Reliance"

In the early 1960s the abrupt departure of Soviet technicians left the Chinese unable to complete many projects, unable to provide spare parts for equipment on hand, and forced to modify Soviet procedures to meet Chinese needs. Failures in the agricultural sector inevitably produced greater caution in imports of foreign technology, and the revelation of the shortcomings of foreign dependence strengthened such caution.

There were ideological reasons for the Chinese stance that coincided with economic and international realities of Soviet disfavor. A vigorous emphasis on the wisdom of Mao Tse-tung made a virtue of self-reliance and peasant wisdom. An emphasis on equality coincided with the priorities that were assigned for agricultural development. Technology was deprecated as less important than correct social and political policies, and seemed to relate to the foreign origin of the processes to which it was appropriate.

Internationally, the American effort in Southeast Asia maintained the Cold War in full vigor, and constrained the Chinese to cooperate with the Soviet Union in assistance to North Vietnam despite the growing ideological differences with the Russians. Elsewhere in the underdeveloped world, however, the Chinese maintained a rival presence and competing aid program. Emphasis on "countryside" at home was combined with a vision of the world struggle in which China stood as the natural leader of rural societies over against the industrialized countries, and especially against the two superpowers. "Development" in any ordinary sense was spurned, and a separate Maoist path was the goal.

Despite the vehemence of the political rhetoric, however, Chinese imports of plants and equipment fell off more slowly than might have been expected, and in key areas of national security the Chinese leadership made no pretense of applying ideological rigidity. Key groups of nuclear physicists were kept at work and not permitted the luxury of ideological reconstruction in agricultural work, and China staged its first nuclear test in 1964. Imports of plants and technology too, after a low point in 1962–1963, rose for several years, and purchases began to be sought in Japan and Western Europe.

The Great Proletarian Cultural Revolution of 1966 brought most of this to a halt. Dernberger correctly describes the Cultural Revolution as "the Maoists' last stand against the technological imperatives that had been generated in China's socialist revolution over the previous two decades" (1977, p. 245). Others suggest that the egalitarian measures of that decade were possible only within a setting of withdrawal from the exigencies of the international economy (Ch'uan and Kraus, 1975, p. 238).

Whatever one's interpretation, there can be little argument that the policies of the Cultural Revolution represented a self-imposed isolation. Formal education was drastically modified and higher education suspended completely between 1966 and 1970. Students were sent from school to the countryside, and the folk wisdom of the country substituted for the modern learning that had been sought from abroad. In this setting egalitarianism could flourish, but at a very low level as specialized training was renounced and derogated. Foreign trade, including imports of technology, plummeted.

Some students have seen in this a "modern" reversion to nineteenth-century conservatism, when modernizers used the slogan, "Chinese learning for fundamental principles; western learning for practical application" (a variant of the formulation used three decades earlier in Japan by Sakuma Zōzan, "western science, eastern morality"). In a sense, Mao's call for ideology over expertise was designed to prevent infection from abroad. Yet the contrasts seem to outweigh the similarities. Nineteenth-century Confucians were trying to justify and legitimate necessary technology, but the slogans of the 1960s tried to deny technology an independent or value-free role, and insisted that it had to be subservient to politics. There is merit in Richard Baum's counter-suggestion that the 1960s, with their insistence on nationalizing even technology, reversed tradition to read "western learning as foundation, Chinese learning for application" (1975, p. 325).

During the last half of the 1960s China was probably more inward looking than it had been since imperial times. Its foreign trade in 1970 was only slightly larger than it had been ten years earlier, and even in 1976, after several years of vigorous reversal of the foreign policies of the decade, China accounted for only 0.7 percent of total world exports.

The 1970s and "Four Modernizations"

Beginning in 1972 the PRC changed course again to embark on a massive program of importing foreign technology and expertise. Every year since then has brought additional commitment to a stronger role in international society. The schools have been revitalized, examinations have been reinstated, students have traveled abroad, and foreign students have been invited to China. Technical imports include complete plants again, and in larger numbers than in the 1950s.

Changes in the international environment made this possible, as did the overthrow of the so-called Gang of Four following Mao's death. The United States abandoned its attempt to prevent the overthrow of noncommunist governments in South Vietnam, Laos, and Cambodia and withdrew its forces from Southeast Asia. China's concern with the stronger Russian military and naval presence in East Asia, one that now extended to an alliance with Vietnam, made it view the American-Japanese tie as a constructive restraint on possible Soviet adventurism. Japan's defense forces, which had been decried as harbingers of a new imperialism and militarism in the 1960s, were now described in China as necessary attributes of national independence. Chinese pragmatists took over leadership in Peking after the death of Mao Tse-tung and purged the radical Gang of Four, announcing instead the "Four Modernizations" in military, economic, educational, and agricultural development. Foreign ties and contacts were essential for each. As the regime scuttled its radicals at home, it sacrificed its radical allies abroad, especially in Japan.

The shift began before the death of Mao. In the summer of 1971 President Richard Nixon announced his intention of visiting China. When he did so in February 1972 the United States and China agreed, in the Shanghai Communiqué, to normalize and improve their relations. Separate positions were announced on the issue of Taiwan, but the United States agreed to abrogate its defense agreement with the Republic of China and to withdraw its forces. Japanese Prime Minister Tanaka in his turn traveled to Peking that same year. Japan abandoned its recognition of the Republic of China and restored its embassy in Peking, maintaining ostensibly nongovernmental offices on

Taiwan for commercial and diplomatic needs. The United States followed this example in December 1978 when it extended formal recognition to the People's Republic, and Japan and the People's Republic signed a Treaty of Amity and Friendship that same year. Vice Premier Teng Hsiao-ping's visit to the United States in January 1979 brought a formal end to three decades of hostility and invective.

The Chinese turn to the noncommunist countries for technical and economic ties brought vigorous campaigns by Japanese and western traders to extend loans and export goods to China. Japan had emerged as China's principal trading partner early in the decade, and negotiations in 1978 included ambitious plans for the exchange of Japanese plants and goods for Chinese coal and oil. The dimensions of China's capacity for payment remained uncertain despite the heroic expectations western traders once again formed of the China trade, but no one doubted that the new turn in the international setting would be advantageous to rapid economic development in China. For the first time a strong and effective government, able to marshal resources and allocate priorities, faced developed nations eager to extend their industrial goods and technology in return for markets and materials.

World View, International Context, and Modernization in China

In Chapter 2 consideration was given to the Chinese world view. Writers have suggested that the sinocentric, middle country approach made it particularly difficult for China to respond to foreign example. The question has received little attention in this discussion of twentieth-century Chinese responses for the reason that it does not seem very relevant.

China's perception of the world order in the years after the Boxer Rebellion was based not on perceptions of its own superiority but on perceptions of danger, and the examples of modern institutions in Japan, the United States, and the Soviet Union were in turn attractive to reform-minded leaders in late Ch'ing, Nationalist, and communist periods. Nothing in the Chinese tradition prevented efforts for massive transplants in the early 1900s, the 1930s, the 1950s, and the 1970s.

It is also noteworthy that the tradition of a Chinese world order did not stand in the way of twentieth-century China's development of a corps of professional diplomats of unusual ability. During all the trauma of China's warlord and republic disunity these professionals, whose job security was far higher than that of their counterparts in other branches of government, compiled a distinguished record in international conferences and world organizations. Their adroitness, fluency, and sophistication made them world citizens.

The distance between the diplomat and the agriculturalist, and between the internationally oriented port city and the inland village, is great in many countries, and perhaps nowhere greater than in the vastness of China. Problems of scope and of scale have created enormous difficulties for regimes trying to guide change in China, and the twentieth century has seen these magnified by changes in the international environment.

Not all of these changes were completely disadvantageous. The end of empire, European-style, left China with an annoying foreign presence and influence in its treaty ports, but spared it further assaults on its sovereignty and territory. In the 1930s treaty enclaves even operated to slow the Japanese penetration. The appearance of empire, Japanese-style, removed the western privileges and substituted for them a short-lived military occupation whose crudity contributed to the rise of Chinese nationalism and the resolve of the masses for national independence. This determination came late; later than in Japan and Russia, though perhaps earlier than in India and Iran. Lateness is important, for the technological gap between China and more modernized countries in the twentieth century was considerably greater than that between Japan and the West in the mid-nineteenth century. Japan's early missions to the West in the Meiji period returned home invigorated by the consciousness that the West's modernization was of recent date, and that Japan was probably not more than forty or fifty years behind.

One way of showing how the international environment harmed Chinese modernization is to ask how it might have been more favorable. The answer seems clear. Chinese control of Chinese tariffs, Chinese ability to focus and apply foreign investment, and Chinese ability to restrict the flow of foreign arms into China would have improved the scene, to say nothing of Chinese freedom from Japanese encroachment in the Nationalist era. All of this would have come sooner had China had an effective national government. The lack of that control made it more difficult to develop an effective national government, but did not prevent its development. Effective government had to wait for the substitution of political for familial priorities and the replacement of private by public concerns. What mattered was less that the Chinese public revenues were committed to foreign indemnities than that those revenues were too low and that they represented too small a percentage of the national income; what counted was not that treaty port privileges undermined the authority of Chinese government but that that authority itself was not sufficiently intense to do the task set for it. China's need was for effective central government able to command and allocate resources. The Nationalist regime in the late 1920s seemed to be building toward this when it was deflected by foreign invasion. The communist regime in 1950 completed its work. Its reforms have, as Okita Saburo writes, "provided an egalitarian base for the work ahead. In a sense China has succeeded in distributing poverty equally— not wealth. . . . If," he continues, "China succeeds in carrying out modernization without jeopardizing this egalitarian society, it will be a unique accomplishment in human history" (1979, p. 1105).

251

International Comparisons

Although many comparisons might be suggested for twentieth-century China's course, the twentieth-century efforts at nation building that have come out of a background of colonialism seem inappropriate. Sun Yat-sen correctly contrasted China's subservience to many countries to a colony's dependence upon one; clearly the latter produces a very different form of cultural and political influence.

Two comparisons, however, may be suggested as instructive. The first is with Meiji Japan, and the second with the Soviet Union. The Meiji comparison has been explored by Ezra Vogel (1979) and is drawn on here in part.

Meiji Japan, like the PRC, was extremely conscious of a foreign threat, and used that threat to build popular consciousness. The Meiji state was able to build upon the past, but also to strengthen that past, by press and propaganda emphasis on the young emperor; the PRC similarly emphasized the infallibility of its Chairman Mao. Meiji Japan based its early administrative structure on the service and loyalty of a core of samurai from southwestern domains. The inner group had worked together for ten or more years in pre-Restoration days, and most of them had had administrative experience in domain affairs. The experience that tied the PRC leadership together was the shared danger of the Long March of 1934–1936.

The Japanese leaders came to power in their thirties, when their ability to learn was high. They competed eagerly for inspection tours and diplomatic missions abroad to familiarize themselves with the world that had opened before them. The communist leaders in China, in contrast, were in their fifties, the survivors of two to three decades of civil war and strife. China's leadership was clearly less ready for travel, for new experience, and less open to foreign influence and example. Like the Meiji group, however, it had also profited from administrative experience gained during the period of the PRC's incubation in Kiangsi, Yenan, and wartime communist-ruled areas. The Japanese regime took power relatively little scarred by civil violence. The Restoration wars, though sharp, were of short duration, and the violence of Restoration days had for the most part been carried on by other samurai than those who became the Meiji leaders. In China, however, the conflict that had begun in the mid-1920s continued to the establishment of the PRC with very few breaks. The consequence of this for bitterness, distrust, and coercion was very great. It was a good deal more divisive (and dangerous) to be categorized as pro-American in the 1950s or pro-Soviet (Russian) in the 1960s in China than it ever was in Meiji times. One setting made for accommodation, the other for extremism.

An additional contrast is to be seen in the accommodation of the new regimes to the larger international environment. The Meiji leaders matured in an international climate that seems, in retrospect, full of rather obvious choices. State enterprise was considered characteristic of despotic and

"Asiatic" regimes, while capitalism and international trade were the special features of progressive states with powerful economies and armies. By mid-twentieth century, however, this consensus was long gone; the Russian revolution had from the first exercised a powerful attraction for Chinese intellectuals as an example of rapid development in a backward country. Again, the Meiji leaders concluded that growing countries acquired empires. They came to this conclusion in an age of empire, and their own security interests seemed to emphasize the importance of empire to their ability to control their environment. This decision seemed natural and even desirable to members of the imperialist order, and brought them alliance with England and the protection of the British fleet. The Chinese communists, in contrast, developed in the atmosphere of twentieth-century nationalism and antiimperialism, to which they added a distinctive anti–great-power emphasis of their own in a profession of affiliation with the weak, underdeveloped, and small, the "country" against the "city."

The other comparison is with the early Bolshevik regime, a generation closer in time. The Soviet leadership, like the Chinese, came to power in the aftermath of a destructive war, one that dissolved a government and society. Its early reception was conditioned, like that of the PRC, by the war weariness of its people.

It also came out of a struggle for leadership, though one that had been waged more with books, slogans, and charges than with the bullets the Chinese had experienced. It was no less divisive. Without the experience of administrative work and problems that the Chinese communists had acquired in areas under their control, the Bolsheviks found themselves hard pressed to make things run. They had numerous individuals of popular appeal and intellectual brilliance among their number, but lacked the disciplined corps and army that followed Mao Tse-tung. It would require the discipline of the Russian civil war, followed by the brutal authoritarian police rule that Stalin fashioned, to produce the discipline of the modern Soviet state.

The international environment in which the Bolsheviks appeared was far less favorable than that experienced by the Chinese. There was no friendly communist state to which they could turn for arms and aid. Instead, the western powers and Japan intervened in 1918 in hopes of throttling the revolution at its birth. Even after the intervention failed, the Soviet state was a pariah in international circles and organizations, left out of the League of Nations and unrepresented at Washington and other conferences.

Russian isolation, and "socialism in one country," were thus to a large extent a predictable response to a hostile environment. As with China, however, the fear of infection from abroad did not keep Russia from importing and purchasing strength where it could be found. Plant and military imports, and military exchange arrangements with the newly developing German army, were actively sought.

The Nazi danger brought relaxation of the bans against the Soviets, and lend lease aid was essential to Russian survival in World War II and probably pivotal in Russia's strides in technological modernization thereafter. Similarly China's break with and alternative to Soviet control were major elements in American willingness to explore a new and friendlier relationship in the 1970s.

In one sense the Soviet leaders, like their Chinese counterparts, worked to "create" a new element in the international context. The propaganda of anti-imperialism in the years after the Bolshevik revolution, while designed to forward Russian security interests, was also a powerful leaven among colonial intellectuals and students around the globe. Maoist espousal of the underdeveloped and "country" of the world against the industrial urban giants seemed, in the 1960s, to capture some of this same appeal.

CHAPTER NINE

Political Structure

CHINA WAS A "LAGGING LATECOMER" TO MODERNIZATION: the rapid transformation that occurred in Japan and Russia between the 1860s and 1940s did not begin in China until the first half of the present century. China's traditional integrative system, embodied especially in preparation for, recruitment to, and service in official careers, was destroyed in the first decade of the present century. This was equivalent to abolishing the old social order, but by means that entailed decades of degeneration and dissolution. The political order underwent rapid formal, if superficial, alterations in the decade after 1900. Political power was radically decentralized after 1912. Political behavior, particularly in relation to local governance, was largely freed from the old regularizing influences. The opportunity for rapid change would seem to have been at hand, but the leadership to guide it was supplied only falteringly until after 1949.

The course of political change has been vitally affected by the increasing demands of the Chinese people for policies generally consonant with economic and technological modernization, whether these have brought warships to the armed forces or kerosene to the lamps of ordinary people. The problems that required governmental action in this century have been many and pressing. China's poverty and weakness were highlighted by the largely fruitless exhortation to "enrich the country and strengthen the military." The key to economic and social improvements was widely seen to lie in better government. But, by about 1915, it was already scarcely possible to speak of a "Chinese government" except as a collection of uncoordinated, regional systems. As the consequences of government inaction aroused widespread dissatisfaction, the demand for Chinese unity and national strength took priority over other social goals.

The transformation since 1949 has been rapid, but has been concentrated in the reestablishment of strong authority; many of the new political ideals projected by the revolutionary government have remained unfulfilled. The issue of how firmly the new government has been centralized is debated by specialists. The scant extent to which participation has become general in politically meaningful ways and modern political values have been nurtured became the subject of common outcry in China in 1978 and 1979, as the communist regime led in the denunciation of China's recent political failings. A final assessment of many such issues is not yet possible. It is clear, however, that the political structure of China has been fundamentally and, without much doubt, irrevocably altered in the third quarter of the twentieth century, in some ways continuing processes of change underway since the middle of the nineteenth, if latent for much of that time.

Sovereignty

POLITICAL CONSCIOUSNESS

For all its imperial millennia, if not longer, China was a unified cultural area, even though its governing apparatus could not always maintain political unity. Its ideology was centralist, ethical, and universal, in other words, specifically nonnational. The changing conditions of national life in modern times challenged these ideals much more fundamentally than ever before. The formal legitimacy of the state changed in the period of modern transformation.

Traditionally, the legitimate state was the throne. The emperor was responsible for the people, indirectly and symbolically, and in a cumulative sense—the dynasty's legitimacy depended on its ability to bring social order to the people. The need for a center that could maintain order by regularizing attitudes and behavior was seen, by bureaucrats and dynasts alike, as the rational basis of sovereignty.

Legitimate rule was not traditionally tied to the interests of any particular national or social group. For centuries, no such group became politically self-aware on a sufficiently large scale to challenge in terms of its distinct goals the basic ideas underlying this long-lasting polity. At least by the middle of the nineteenth century, however, the conditions of empire-wide political life in China were slowly changing under strong new influences, some imported and some indigenous. New and old political forms, and political consciousness, in varying combinations, rose to compete with the old universalistic legitimacy of the state. There emerged a new emphasis on the urgent need of modernization for the large national group.

Scholars disagree whether modernization, by 1911, had given gentry families (since 1905 no longer even theoretically recruited to that status by competitive examination) a chance to maintain their influence without changing their basic interests (Ichiko in Wright, ed., 1968) or instead had already altered the nature of their main political concerns (Wakeman, 1975). When we compare the political consciousness prevailing among China's strategic elite at mid-nineteenth century with the interests of its counterparts at the turn of the century, we can see very large changes in its political concerns. Nevertheless, it is striking that the fall of the dynasty, the somewhat increased emphasis on ethnicity within the state, the increased urbanism and cosmopolitanism of many leading families, and the open reliance on guns rather than virtue to muster support for rulers did not basically undermine general acceptance of the concept that sovereign power in China must be central and should at least claim to be moral. A changing political consciousness provided new definitions of means and goals, reforming rather than wholly rejecting the Chinese past, even in the radical decade of the 1920s; it was one factor in the course of political change in this century.

The Manchu dynasty is usually said to have been saved in the 1860s in the course of defending a civilization, by an aroused elite who put its group interests ahead of racist or nationalist appeals. This cliché of modern interpretation is not wholly acceptable; yet it seems clear that in the mid-nineteenth-century rebellions, the dynasty gained support by representing the status quo. The alternatives to traditional values were not yet powerfully attractive to any sector of the society.

The successful anti-Taiping leaders were committed to renewing the dynasty through reform. They planned to accomplish this through a fundamentalist revival, recruiting for positions of political leadership better men, who through moral influence would improve the conditions of life at the basic level. Even though these social reforms were not broadly implemented (and the dynasty was only superficially renewed), the leaders of the 1860s and 1870s were convinced reformers. Their guiding concepts were drawn largely from the ancient arsenal of Confucian political ideas, which were archaistic in content. Their models lay in the Chinese past, and they located the crux of the problem in deficiencies of the material and ethical well-being of the people. Altruistic, paternalistic reform zeal, coupled with faith in Chinese values, has remained central to the changing political consciousness in the twentieth century, even though specific details of its content have shifted. The relative values assigned to reform and revolution are discussed below, as an aspect of another change in political consciousness; but Confucianism remained important as a source, sometimes unacknowledged, of reform methods and goals in succeeding decades.

The capacity of the essentially nondogmatic Confucian thought system to generate corrective influences from within was paralleled and reinforced by renovating mechanisms of the social order. Old Text and New Text schools of Confucian thought developed out of the recurring controversies over the correctness of the dominant orthodoxy. In the late nineteenth century, the Old Text conservatives, although unwilling to abandon the Confucian ideal of government by virtue, nevertheless gave great weight to the traditional (but strictly speaking, anti-Confucian) search for wealth and strength, the statist goals of earlier imperial regimes. The New Text search for institutional reform and the Old Text struggle to justify a more pragmatic statecraft interacted with each other to produce both the abortive reforms of 1898 and the dynasty-sponsored reforms of the decade after 1901.

Despite the resilience of Confucian political thought, which allowed some change and thus forestalled explosive, profound change, the ground of political thought nonetheless, through successive accommodations, shifted. The new political consciousness retained Chinese emotional content but represented a real, albeit partial, alteration of values. In the shifting conceptualization of the proper object of Chinese loyalties, the Chinese past has remained central to the validation of China's future greatness, but most of the rest has changed. The focus of Chinese loyalties once was upon ethically bound, ethnically neutral, state-free, politically unencumbered, universalistic cultural ideals. Now it is on the Chinese people, variously defined, and on their state as a distinct political entity in the pluralistic modern world. The Chinese national consciousness is no longer ethnically neutral; it is now bound to a particular state; and politically, that force encumbers all the population of China, and even many Chinese living abroad. In short, it is political in specific new senses. This transvaluation was well under way by 1900 and was virtually complete by 1940. That there was rightness in Han service to the non-Han Manchu dynasty was scarcely arguable in the nineteenth century; that there was evil in Chinese service to the Japanese conquerors was scarcely arguable in 1940. The driving force of Chinese nationalism has been by far the most potent component of the modernized Chinese political consciousness.

Both the myths and the realities of race and of nationalism have been important in the changing Chinese political consciousness. It has become customary to say that during the last two or three decades of the nineteenth century, a universalistic culturalism was displaced by a new kind of patriotism, in which the Chinese nation-state itself became the prime focus of loyalty. "Culturalism" and "nationalism" are particularly imprecise as mutually exclusive terms. It is questionable, at least, that we see a diminution of pride in Chinese civilization among the strongest nationalists in the present century—whether they be conservatives like Liang Ch'i-ch'ao in the post-1898 reform era, or iconoclasts in the May Fourth Movement, or even leaders of the present day.

Nonetheless, the idea of a transvaluation of Chinese loyalties is useful. A changing perception of China's place in the world, which gradually eroded the ancient Confucian universalism, was, despite some native roots, largely the product of Chinese absorption of western ideas in the past century and of interactions, whether friendly or hostile, with the western presence in China. It is thus an index of Chinese adaptability and of Confucian change.

Anti-Manchu racist sentiment in late Ch'ing China fueled nationalism in the conspiratorial revolutionary movements before 1911; but once the dynasty fell, the racial issue disappeared, because Manchus are about one-quarter of one percent of China's population. Sun Yat-sen, who conceived the Revolution and devised its political program, announced immediately on the founding of the republic that the Manchus were one of the five great races comprising the Chinese nation, welcoming them to full and equal status in the republic. That paralleled the gesture that the Ming founder had made to the Mongols in 1368, after expelling them from China and founding a new dynasty under an ethnically Han imperial house. More recently, a similarly expansive policy encouraging the absorption of non-Han peoples into a multiracial China is evident in the changing usage regarding the designations for "Chinese peoples" and "Chinese languages." Divisions among the Han languages, such as Mandarin, Min, Wu, and Cantonese, are now by political fiat declared to be mere dialects (ignoring the more usual linguistic criterion of mutual intelligibility for dialects). At the same time (and again ignoring linguistic criteria), Manchu, Mongolian, Tibetan, T'ai, and other minority languages are put on a par with the Han tongues, and as a group are called the "Chinese languages." The political fact that their speakers are all subject to one government has made them one linked group of languages. A parallel change now also applies to the ethnic groups; all are "Chinese" peoples by political fiat. The relation of race to nation thus has undergone a politically determined redefinition in the twentieth century. This process echoes Confucian universalism, which is otherwise largely disappearing; but it is now made to serve modern concepts of nation building. How fully this has created a genuine political solidarity, and has actually changed the thinking of either the Han majority or the non-Han 5 percent, cannot be ascertained. There is some reason to believe that it has failed to solve all regional political problems, especially in Tibet. Racial integration goes forward at the expense of meaningful minority separation and distinctiveness.

Looking beyond the domestic issues, one can perceive a shifting focus of racial hostility in the international relations of China since 1900. Anti-European, anti-American, and anti-Japanese sentiments—quite apart from anti-Manchu feeling—had a significant base in the coastal provinces and near the foreign trade ports in the early nineteenth century. The phrase "China's traditional xenophobia" is often used by writers, especially by those whose acquaintance with traditional China is limited to the nineteenth century. There is no basis for xenophobia in any of the defining canons of Chinese civilization, nor much evidence of it in the Chinese historical record until the last hundred years or so.

Resentment against Westerners in China was sometimes expressed in violence, and this tendency increased from the 1840s on. In 1900 the Empress Dowager, along with some leading statesmen, saw in that resentment an instrument for aligning her alien dynasty with the Chinese people. She hoped to deflect a measure of the growing anti-Manchu (more basically, antidynasty) political agitation. She also had more personal reasons for resenting the Europeans in China: they had clearly sided with K'ang Yu-wei and the recently suppressed reform group, and they clearly preferred the imprisoned Kuanghsu emperor to herself as the actual head of the Chinese state. Thus when, in the summer of 1900, the Boxers in North China began killing foreigners for reasons of their own, the Empress Dowager played a wily game of outwardly deploring their excesses while secretly encouraging them. The twentieth century thus begins with the siege of Peking, the invasion of the capital by the army of the Eight Powers, and the ignominious flight of the Empress Dowager and her court to the Northwest Provinces. Subsequently, she denounced the Boxers and made amends to the foreigners; but her foolish maneuver cost her dearly and increased popular antiwestern feelings as well.

The Revolution of 1911 erased the anti-Manchu issue; but as nationalism grew, so did antiwestern sentiments. Chinese attitudes display in varying degrees ambivalence, arrogance, and latent xenophobia. In the 1920s, the British as the dominant western power, bore the brunt of the antiwestern action. The new Soviet government, because of its Karakhan Declaration in 1919 and other moves, ostensibly to renounce its imperialist privileges in China, became for a time the most admired foreign government (even though an influx of unfortunate and often unsavory White Russian refugees into Manchuria, Tientsin, and Shanghai lowered the Chinese esteem for Russians more generally). To some degree from 1919 on, but especially after 1931, the Japanese conclusively outpaced all western powers as the most hated alien power. Anti-Japanese feeling was widespread, in fact almost general. It was officially sponsored by two of the three wartime governments in China. It was the mainstay of KMT cohesion, and the War of Resistance for a time made a genuine national hero of its prime symbol, Chiang Kai-shek. The anti-Japanese cause was simultaneously the basis of the communist appeal to the people of some regions in which it strove to achieve control. Whether ultimately that spur to intensified nationalism better served one side or the other in the KMT-CCP struggle is still vigorously debated among scholars, but neither of those nationalistic regimes could have been strong without it. After 1949, in a quick turnabout, the United States was projected as the number one enemy in communist China. In another manipulated turnabout, the Russians were made to bear the onus of animosity after 1960.

Racist sentiment and nationalism in the Chinese political consciousness are evidence of politicization and increasing subjugation to the state's perceived interests. Such forces have a powerful potential for political mobilization; under the communists, the government has tried to guide their rise and fall. As foreign policies have changed (and this is most obvious in Chinese policies toward the USSR and the USA), public scorn of foreigners has alternated with public friendship for them. The Soviet Union was involved in important policy and leadership disputes of the People's Republic during

1953–1954 and 1959 especially, and during the decade of the 1960s, the PRC government had unfriendly relations with both superpowers. After the Cultural Revolution, the dangers of Soviet expansionism were highlighted by border incidents and emphasis in Chinese media. Antiforeign feeling was based partly in Chinese international interests, but it also could help to increase domestic Chinese unity. Official communist statements emphasized the idea that the foreign enemies (Japanese, American, or Russian by turns) were governments, not the innocent common people of the countries in question.

LEADERSHIP

The year 1905 marks the watershed between old China and new; it symbolizes the end of one era and the beginning of another. It must be counted a more important turning point than the Revolution of 1911, because it unlocked changes in what must be the main institutional base of any government; the means of awarding status to the society's elite and of staffing the administration. The republican revolution was a product of Chinese who worked mostly abroad, in conspiratorial groups; it displaced the throne, but it had few other revolutionary objectives as classically defined by the French, nineteenth-century, or Russian revolutions. It did not have an aristocracy or a church to disestablish; it had no closed social classes to open. The principal large-scale integrating institution of the old society was abolished in 1905, with the imperial proclamation terminating the Chinese civil service examination system, although revolutionary social consciousness played no role in this change. The examinations had functioned as the nexus of traditional China's social and political dynamic. They were the operational device for sustaining the Confucian state orthodoxy. They were the means of granting privilege and channeling upward mobility. They formed the Chinese pattern of social ideals. With their abolition, the entire society lost its characterizing institutions. This change was arguably as important for political structure as the victory of the communists in 1949.

The examinations were not abolished by a conspiracy from without, but by leading Confucian statesmen who sought a rational plan to renovate their nation's politics and institutions in modern times. This was a profound change, intended to be implemented in successive steps of political development. The plan was gradualist, not explosively revolutionary. The movement for renovation, generated within the Chinese system, echoed many steps that Confucian thinkers had advocated in the past on the basis of preimperial political thought; it followed the pattern of the examinations' establishment, for instance, and of the governmental institutions for recruitment that evolved through the Han, the T'ang, and the Sung dynasties. The act of terminating the examinations sapped the roots of the social integration that had been reinforced in many steps over a period of two millennia. That act's unintended, gradually realized consequences were far more important than all those apparently foreseen by its scholar-official promoters in 1905. It threw away the old compass before providing a new one, and it contributed to a subsequent era of unguided social drifting.

The abolition of the examination system occurred in the course of a thoroughgoing plan for educational reform. The need for changes in schooling had been seen by the unsuccessful reformers of 1898, so this issue became a focus of concerned official thinking and an element central to the court-sponsored reforms of 1901–1911. Here we will only touch on the political implications of this crucial alteration in culture.

The statesmen who formulated the education reform proposals for the court in 1901 and immediately thereafter were Chang Chih-tung and Liu K'un-i, governors-general respectively of Hunan-Hupei and Kiangsu-Kiangsi-Anhwei. Both had been named "participants from the provinces" in a new Office for the Management of State Affairs, created by the Empress Dowager in April 1901. When Chang and Liu were appointed, they immediately advocated "revision" of the examination system, more or less following proposals initiated by K'ang Yu-wei in 1898. In his justification for the change, Chang prominently used the slogan that he had made famous in his stirring "Exhortation to Study," which was first published in 1898: "Chinese learning for fundamental principles [*t'i*, essence]; western learning for practical application [*yung*, utility]." The *t'i-yung* formula, which was and is quite superficial, nonetheless was useful in that it justified western learning as a proper concern of Chinese statesmen.

Chang's ideas on the examinations were a Confucian's response to western civilization, which he perceived as an indispensable technology if nothing more. Chang presented his plan for revising the examinations with elaborate justifications from the Chinese classics and from imperial statements by earlier Ch'ing rulers. His plan was only a part of a general scheme for reorganizing the entire Chinese political system (Wolfgang Franke, 1960; Ayers, 1971). In the original reform proposals of 1901 and 1902, the civil service examinations were to be continued but western learning would occupy a place equal to that of the Chinese classics. After Liu K'un-i died in 1902, Chang saw the matter through alone. The reform proposals were adopted by the court, but they failed to win the general response that would have given them practical significance. Chang therefore shifted his views, first urging gradual abolition of the examinations within ten years, then (after recruiting Yuan Shih-k'ai and other provincial leaders to his cause) proposing the immediate abolition of the system. This last proposal was hastily adopted by the Empress Dowager and the court in 1905, and it took effect in 1906.

Chang's hope was that a new national school system, capped by the newly founded Peking University, would soon provide graduates with the best of both Chinese and western learning. The old system of state examinations died quietly. But no new system quickly emerged for educating heirs to China's old strategic elite or for screening new graduates to find worthy officials. The coherent guidance of society and government once provided by the examinations was not to be regained for half a century.

The resulting changes in education were disappointing to Chang. He spent his last years, until his death in 1909, attempting to institutionalize the place of Confucius as the sage of a new Chinese society to come. Chang now saw clearly that the abolition of the examination system had undermined classical education and gravely weakened the influence of traditional values. Within a decade of his death, a virulently anti-Confucian movement had begun to possess the new schools and to stir the hearts and minds of China's educated youth. Of more importance for political change, education, except for the new military training, became peripheral to the conduct of government, for military government replaced almost all civil authority. A new elite recruited through military advancement took over many of the functional roles of the old scholar-official elite, in a general transformation of the management of Chinese society in which the civilian components of local and regional elites also were transformed.

By the 1920s warlords large and small, dominating areas ranging in size from half a county to a whole province or more, provided a spectrum of types of the new local leaders of Chinese society. Their social backgrounds varied immensely. Some, such as Yuan Shih-k'ai or Wu P'ei-fu, had attained relatively high educational levels or gentry status. Others came from less auspicious backgrounds: Chang Tsung-ch'ang, the notorious "dog-meat general" of Shantung, had a father who was a head-shaver and a mother who was a shamaness. The real problem was not, however, that transitional modernization brought some shady personages to power. The essence of China's difficulty was that this process destroyed a time-tested procedure for selecting good leaders and replaced it with nothing except the ability to muster coercion.

Even after the warlord period, from 1927 to 1937, provincial leaders were still overwhelmingly soldiers. Sixty-three percent of the governors in this decade had military educations, and fully 84 percent had military careers. Only 13 percent had civilian university educations, and 18 percent had mainly civilian careers (computed from Tien, 1972, p. 140). As in traditional times, most of China's leaders followed one career, but now that vocation was military.

This aspect of the change in local leadership could have worked constructive consequences for China's modernization had a unified system of militarized government for the entire nation emerged, and a rationalized, disciplined administration been installed. Instead the nation was fractured into units, most of which had only short-range survival goals. They benefited from the degenerated character of local power. A society that depended on much informal governing, provided by its local elite, now found the character of that elite changing, largely for the worse.

Political Structure

When the Manchu dynasty collapsed, the territorial divisions that warlordism introduced threatened the end of national political unity and political style; of even deeper significance, they dissociated ethics from politics and fostered a radically new view of China's place in the world. After 1911, China lacked a central leader who could perform the symbolic and integrative roles of the emperor. In this respect, China contrasts with Japan, where the *tennō* had become a common focus of loyalty for conflicting leaders from many regions and callings. The tsar in prerevolutionary Russia attempted to play this role, despite widespread disaffection among the intelligentsia. But in China, until the late 1920s, the nation had no widely obeyed leader. Warlord aspirants lacked overwhelming power in war, and had no other major claims to suzerainty. When Yuan Shih-k'ai tried to fill this role, first as dictator of the republic and then as emperor in the "Great Constitution" (*Hung-hsien*) reign, he failed to restore dynastic authority. By the end of 1915, he could not control the military governors he had appointed, especially in the south. Yuan had worshipped at the Temple of Heaven, as only the emperor was properly allowed to do; but he had firm support neither from any large popular base (as imported democratic ideals would prescribe) nor from his military subordinates in important provinces such as Kiangsu. Later twentieth-century leaders, especially Chiang Kai-shek and Mao Tse-tung (to some extent, even current communist leaders), also encouraged the recovery of the ritual and emotional supports to their leadership, drawing on both traditional and new models.

Formal centralism pervaded the framework of the 1912 republic, the KMT's official structure established in 1927, and also the People's Republic of 1949. Federalist ideals had occasional support: from provincial assemblies during the last four years of the Ch'ing, from warlords wishing to preserve their local suzerainty during the second decade of the century, and from a variety of liberals in the early 1920s (Chesneaux in Gray, ed., pp. 96 ff.). All were somewhat influenced by western models, but all proved to be temporary, unimportant in the long term. In a modernizing world environment, China's lack of modern communications meant that the country had de facto federalism. But this was never widely acknowledged, certainly not as an ideal. The "central country" by definition had a center.

For the communists, centralism resonated well not only with inherited Chinese ideas about sovereignty, but also with the notion that sages (Marx and Lenin) had found new principles of politics. The communists were consistently antifederalist during the 1920s. After their dispersal to guerrilla bases for the next decade and more, however, different leaders in different bases were often out of communication with each other and with comrades in the urban areas. The communists were in practice a loose federation. Until the capture of Japanese radios during the late 1930s, many of their leaders, in isolated groups, had to make decisions independently. The wartime diffusion of radio techniques would have been less important, if the will to find and follow a political center had not already been set, in both Chinese and imported traditions.

The centralist ideal of Chinese legitimacy survived the modern process better than its ethical ideals did. This was so in both the KMT and CCP, and it was so despite China's practical decentralism, which until mid-century resembled the clichés of an end-of-dynasty situation more than a new founding. Military control was the basis of order in the early modern period, and the civilian primacy of traditional government was an early casualty of transformation. As guns spread more widely, regional administrations became dominant. Civilians acquired firearms on an unprecedented scale during the early years of the republic, and governments became increasingly militarized as the number of soldiers in China increased sharply (Kapp, 1973, pp. 10 ff.). Railroads allowed increased control within many of China's provinces and regions that are natural topographical and trading units. But modernized means of transport did little to unify the nation during the first quarter of the century. Prowess in writing based on the classics was replaced by prowess in commanding armies as the central preoccupation of rulers. Victory was the only test of rulership. No gateway to legitimacy replaced the imperial examinations.

The communists, both in Kiangsi and at Yenan were not different from other regional Chinese regimes in this respect. The CCP's internal organization, like the KMT's, was more modernized than that of most warlords, because of Soviet models and because of leaders who had much experience in relatively modern cities. But the communists' relations with other local and national political organizations were based largely on the military power they could muster.

Especially in the 1930s and 1940s, Mao's new style of political leadership took form. The long-term survival of the party's urban-experienced leadership depended on a return to the cities, the modern centers of national life—and thus on the mobilization of forces to effect that return. By 1936, the CCP had retreated to northern Shensi, one of the most deeply impoverished, hard-scrabble, least modernized regions in all China. Although three major historical dynasties had emerged from Shensi, the center of Chinese civilization had long since left this cradle. During modern times, especially in the north of the province, brigands were more notable than mandarins. The road back to cities such as Peking, Shanghai, and Changsha, where top communist leaders such as Mao, Chou, and Liu had spent much time in their youths, was a hard path that required social change if they wished to remain leaders. Indeed this path required "modernization"; but to the extent they defined that idea at all, they did so in a political way. It was a slogan, not a social index. The commitment of this leadership was not abstract but pragmatic; it aimed to establish central leadership with new techniques of mobilizing social forces, just as various warlords hoped to achieve the same goal by using new kinds of weapons.

The communists justified their early-modern political tactics more elaborately than most other groups of the period. Mao apologized by mocking a possible accusation against the CCP: "'You are dictatorial.' My dear sirs, you are right, that is just what we are. . . . We deprive the reactionaries of the right to speak and let the people alone have that right" (Mao, IV, 1965, p. 1480). The concept "people" is not burdened by any definition that might hamper political maneuvering. At different times, it might include anyone who was patriotic or anti-Japanese, or anyone who was antilandlord, or only lower-middle and poor peasants and proletarians who had been organized by communists, or a presumed silent majority whose interests were represented by some (but not most) party members. Those outside this group could be opposed by any means.

Mao's notion of struggle was as flexible as his notion of society's main groups. Not until his 1957 speech "On Contradiction" did Mao attempt to distinguish an "antagonistic" tension, whose resolution would be identical to one of its original elements, from a "nonantagonistic" one, whose "synthesis" would share characteristics from both the original "theses." Even then, the procedures for applying this distinction were vague and open to much interpretation—by Mao himself, while he lived. This ideology preserved the old centralism while draining it of any potential restraints.

The center for communists was also geographical. Yenan after 1936, and then Peking after 1949, were extolled as major sources of inspiration, because they were capitals. In recent times the imperial palace, especially its Chungnanhai compound (where the CCP leadership lives) and its T'ienanmen Square (where a monument inscribed by Chou En-lai stands), have been scenes of political marches and demonstrations. Lesser shrines have included the old guerrilla base of Chingkangshan, the model commune at Ta-chai, and Mao's birthplace at Shaoshan.

Personal centralism and the hero worship of Mao were condoned by the object of the cult himself—and sometimes even by his political rivals. Mao, referring to Khrushchev's 1956 criticism of Stalinism, once remarked that Khrushchev might have remained in power longer if he had sponsored a broader cult of himself. The persistence in China of purely symbolic political centralism is dramatized by Mao's status after the failure of his Great Leap Forward policies, when he retrea ed to the "second line" of practical leadership. Mao's party opponents praised the central leader in public, even while they ignored his policy suggestions, apparently because they felt that such action would help to legitimize their whole organization in the eyes of the Chinese people.

TERRITORIAL INTEGRITY

The territorial integrity of China in the present century was genuinely threatened by internal political disintegration during the warlord era, especially when some warlords became pawns of foreign powers. It was still more seriously threatened by Japanese attempts to build a continental empire; the Japanese Twenty-One Demands, which would have given Japan a foothold, were rebuffed in 1919, but Japanese armies were temporarily more successful after 1931. Other threats have been less real or less urgent. There have been a few signs of ethnic separatism in some border areas throughout this century, and state policies have not been automatically applied in minority areas such as Sinkiang and Tibet by local authorities of KMT or CCP governments. Such tendencies have generally lessened over time, however; and the conditions necessitating them appear to have been slowly altered.

With hindsight, even the genuine threats to China's territorial integrity can be seen as having generated spontaneous resistance; and they allowed regimes to reinforce nationalist cohesion. China has drawn, and to some extent still draws, some political unity from a readily aroused awareness of state territorial interests. The era of warlordism is discussed elsewhere in this chapter, as is the issue of national cohesion under the communist government since 1949. Only the problem of China's ethnic solidarity demands further comment here.

The geographical extent of China's sovereignty in this century was inherited from the Manchus. Within this area the population is 95 percent Han Chinese, so identification with the Han-dominated state has raised problems of conflicting loyalties for only 5 percent of the people. If culturally sinified members of the Chuang, Hui, Yi, Manchu, and Korean nationalities are subtracted, this percentage is even lower. However, the non-Han groups were local majorities in one-third of China's territory as late as the middle of this century. In some of those regions, China's boundaries with other countries divide the non-Han minorities: Mongols, Uighurs, and Kazakhs live on both sides of China's borders with Outer Mongolia and the USSR, for example; T'ai, Shan, and many other groups straddle the boundaries with Burma, Laos, and Vietnam.

Natural barriers reinforce parts of China's borders. Elsewhere there are buffer peoples between the Han people and the politically dominant groups of adjacent large countries. Partly for these reasons, China's formal borders have remained largely unchanged during the present century. For example, neither Russians nor Chinese have for many decades officially extended their full sovereignty to large territories occupied by Turkic peoples within the opposite empire (even though some protectorate and condominium arrangements were established under the CCP, KMT, and before, they projected foreign influence without foreign sovereignty).

Several of the large frontier areas within China—the northeast, Tibet, and Sinkiang—have had particular modern histories that are worthy of special mention. After 1949, up to 1960, the policy of "leaning to one side" preempted Chinese assertions of interests vis-à-vis the Soviet Union. Since then, irredentist claims against the USSR have been a large item of political education and a sometime source of domestic solidarity. PRC claims to three coastal areas that are populated by the Han people (Taiwan, Hong Kong, and Macao) have at least temporarily been pressed less insistently because of concern with the Soviet threat, and because the government of the largest of these areas is already Chinese and the governments of the other two are amenable to some PRC influence.

The northeast included the homeland of the disappearing Manchus. After their dynasty's fall, this large area's Han majority, and its Chinese warlord Chang Tso-lin, made it one of China's independent regions. Despite occasional and partial cessions to Russia or Japan, and despite the massive occupation of Manchuria by the Japanese as a heavy industrial base in the 1930s and early 1940s, this important area has had an increasing Han population over many decades and is now one of the most developed regions of China.

By contrast, Tibet was assimilated to suzerainty and then sovereignty by China, largely because the British and Indians were unwilling to prevent that development, and also because the Tibetans have been too weak to do so. Sinkiang, like Tibet, probably still has a Han minority, but foresight and organizational work by the late Ch'ing bureaucrat-general Tso Tsung-t'ang prevented the loss of this large province from the empire. After some transitional condominiums with Russia during the first half of this century, Sinkiang is now tied to the main parts of China by a railway and other modern communications.

Since 1950, the Chinese have systematically fostered the migration of Han Chinese into such border areas, while declaring that Stalin's policy on the handling of minorities should guide their political solutions to ethnic problems. This policy, in effect, continues the Chinese imperial tradition (as Stalin continued the tsarist one). Large minorities such as the Chuang become increasingly sinified. Smaller groups, especially those living in mountainous areas or near sensitive borders such as the Kazakhs, are exempted from many political campaigns of the Han areas. Nominally, the folk cultures of all minority groups are honored, in compensation for the loss of political autonomy. Because non-Han are one-twentieth of China's population, whereas non-Russians are one-half of the USSR's, the Chinese government has not faced minority problems on the scale of those in the Soviet Union, or in India and many other modernizing countries. In this respect, China's ethnic solidarity comes close to equaling Japan's. This should be an advantage for China in the modernization process.

The Exercise of State Power

CENTRAL GOVERNMENT

In the last decade of Ch'ing rule, China replaced many institutions of the old imperial government with new and experimental organizations, modeled on western forms. The complex steps of this reform reveal both some rational development and some fortuitous circumstance. At first, new institutions were more names than realities. Gradually, never fully, they acquired substance; but the importance of these first steps lies more in their break with the past than in their realization of anything permanent.

The Empress Dowager outmaneuvered K'ang Yu-wei in the abortive Hundred Days' Reform of the summer of 1898. That story did not end, however, in the success of her antireform show of power. The reformers' radically conceived political program was intended to be implemented in a spirit of moderate gradualism, but in fact they were too eager, and their haste contributed to their downfall. Their program for sweeping change brought to a climax the growing confrontation between those who had accepted the principle of institutional change, after Japan's defeat of China in 1894–1895, and those who could not. That confrontation pervaded the entire strategic elite. It was echoed in the new press that had been born in the treaty ports since the 1860s. It was debated in the schools, especially those that had been reinvigorated as centers of Confucian inquiry during the Restoration decade. This confrontation might have remained at an impasse much longer, had not the Boxer crisis of 1900 created new conditions at court and throughout the government. Returning to Peking early in 1901 from her exile in the Northwest Provinces, the Empress Dowager in January issued a proclamation reproving herself for political blunders (a time-honored gesture of Confucian rulership), and calling for reforms. This held more meaning than she intended. The context and the precedents were traditional; the substance, though flimsy, was to emerge as something quite new.

In 1900 the Eight Powers—the United States, Japan, and the principal European states—had sent military forces to occupy the Empress Dowager's capital, repeating in some ways the experience of 1860–1861 (the crisis that had first brought her to power). Forty years later, she recognized that a different set of conditions had come into existence, particularly in relation to the foreign presence as a continuing factor in Chinese government. The January 1901 proclamation was directed as much toward foreign powers as toward her own government and people.

At the turn of the century, China experienced its deepest political crisis in four decades. In meeting that crisis, the government revealed the unprecedented extent to which awareness of the foreign presence and familiarity with alien ideas had grown during those forty years. The political history of the next eighty years centers on China's attempts to adapt imported forms that had largely superficial impacts on a society responding to many profound challenges.

K'ang Yu-wei had sought to achieve a constitutional monarchy on the Japanese and western models in 1898, seeing in that culturally incongruous institution a means of saving Chinese civilization. He had accomplished a first step toward a synthesis of western and Chinese political values. In the process he not only threatened the power structure of the court, but also enraged much of the Chinese scholar-official elite. Subsequently, in an unrelated development, a popular antiforeignism had appeared in North China, the Boxer movement of 1899. Covertly, it was taken up by the court, though it possessed no qualities compatible with the dynasty's professed values (nor, as the sequel showed, with its real interests). In the wake of a political and military debacle induced by that blundering policy, the weakness of extreme conservatism was fully exposed. The Empress Dowager, in her hasty flight and uncomfortable exile, then adopted institutional reforms of the K'ang Yu-wei type (while continuing to denounce K'ang), the inevitable choice among her policy alternatives. Her intentions were, no doubt, cynical. No doubt they included intentions to mollify foreign diplomats, display the resilience of her regime in crisis, and focus attention on the new tasks ahead. Whatever the tactical advantages she perceived in that choice, it was a turning point in China's political development—not so much for what it achieved, as for what it acknowledged. Political concepts not derived from Chinese tradition (even when, as in K'ang's thought, they were made compatible with Chinese values) were now to be made a central feature of the Chinese political system. An era of new political forms was inaugurated.

Chief among the new institutions were provincial and national deliberative assemblies, a preparatory stage to provincial and national parliaments. According to plan, these assemblies would have ratified a constitution, installed a premier and cabinet responsible to the parliament, and promoted democratic participation through elections. (See the brief account of the steps outlined and taken, in Ch'ien Tuan-sheng, 1950, ch. IV.) Such reform measures had been widely publicized throughout China by K'ang Yu-wei, Liang Ch'i-ch'ao, and their followers; after 1898, they continued their efforts from their base in Japan. These measures were discussed, understood, and accepted by a widening sector of the Chinese public, although still not by a broadly representative one.

After 1902, Yuan Shih-k'ai, governor-general of the metropolitan province including Peking, became the most important Chinese official at court. He was thus a rival to leading Manchu nobles, and the resultant last-hour resurgence of Manchu power interests contributed greatly to Han-Manchu friction. Yuan's overweening political ambitions led him to become the principal proponent of the reform ideas submitted by other senior Chinese officials in the provinces. The eminent regional innovators, governors-general Chang Chih-tung and Liu K'un-i, proposed numerous changes, the most important of which led to the abolition of the civil service examinations in 1905 and the reconstruction of the education system. Chang and like-minded reformers also argued that Japan's astounding defeat of Russia in 1905 came about because Japan had adopted a constitution and Russia still had not done so. The call from the provinces for a constitutional monarchy was becoming insistent.

Shortly before the deaths of the Kuang-hsu emperor and the Empress Dowager in 1908, an Outline of Constitutional Principles (*Hsien-fa ta-kang*) was promulgated. Study missions had gone abroad to investigate the workings of constitutionalism in other countries, as they had gone from Japan a generation earlier. Also as in the Japanese case, the Chinese delegations were most favorably impressed by the authoritarian system of Wilhelmine Germany. They admired the Meiji imitation of the kaiser's constitution. Whereas the Japanese had sent their ablest men for serious study of western governments, however, the Chinese missions that had most credibility at home were composed of relatively incompetent Manchu nobles accompanied by incompetent interpreters. The proposals they brought to the Empress Dowager that earned her approval were garbled notions that reassured her unduly about the safety to the dynasty of undertaking a constitutional monarchy. In 1906, the government was reorganized along the lines suggested by a study commission. The regency, set up in 1908, expected to implement the constitutional reforms.

As the Manchu-Chinese rivalry for position and power at the court intensified Yuan Shih-k'ai became the voice of the high Chinese officials, while the Manchu nobles used the ill-understood constitutional reforms as a device for redesigning the central government in ways favorable to themselves. Late in 1908, Yuan Shih-k'ai was dismissed. At the center, the Manchu regent became the first incumbent of the new office of premier. In the provinces, as provisional assemblies began to function they became forums for Chinese reform interests, contesting with the court.

Improvement of government, or even essential changes in the power structure, were in practice not promoted by such debate. Nonetheless, in the space of a few years, power struggles at high levels had shifted from a setting of traditional institutions to one of premiers, cabinets, ministries with new functions, and provisional assemblies—all of which justified their political acts with reference to a new outline of constitutional principles.

The Revolution of 1911 took a further step, which was deeply shocking to many ardent reformers of the previous dozen years: it abolished the emperor as head of state and replaced him with a president. This represented a shift of models, from the constitutional monarchies like Germany and Japan to the constitutional republics like France and the United States. One may speculate that such an important change reoriented (or ''reoccidented'') China's political structure from realizable goals at that time to more difficult objectives, but the country really had no choice, because its monarchy had become a debased and unusable national symbol. Despite the overthrow of the imperial institution, it can be said that the new republic's institutional forms were nonetheless directly in the line of development started by the reform proclamation of January 1901.

Struggles to launch the republic were complicated by Yuan Shih-k'ai's interference. He was the strongest military leader in the nation, and his control

of that semimodernized instrument of power made him the key man in negotiations between the collapsing imperial regime in Peking and the revolutionary government in Nanking, under the provisional presidency of Sun Yat-
sen. The revolutionaries were compelled by the force of circumstances to
hand the presidency over to Yuan, whose inauguration took place in Peking
on March 10, 1912, after two months of devious plotting. No political goals of
reform or revolution meant anything to him; the presidency was merely his
vehicle of supreme power. Even after his death in 1916, the presidency long
remained the plaything of Yuan's warlord successors. There was, quite literally, no central government thereafter, until the Kuomintang in 1927 succeeded in establishing the second republic of China, based in Nanking, and
began to reverse the dissolution of the Chinese state.

When the KMT came to power in 1927, however, it did so under a new
political program devised by Sun Yat-sen shortly before his death in 1925.
This espoused ''democratic centralism,'' under a single-party system on the
model of the USSR. The KMT republic thus represents a third shift of
models, this time from the constitutional republic model of western democ-
racies to an ideally far more unified state, only nominally democratic, but
looking to the future establishment of full constitutional democracy after a
period of ''political tutelage.'' The failures of western civilization, which
seemed evident to many Chinese in World War I and in the liberal West's
unfair treatment of China at Versailles, contributed to the shift away from
Sun Yat-sen's earlier, more liberal ideals. That shift occurred within a politically disintegrating China, one still resisting the military unification that was
only half-completed by the KMT's Northern Expedition. The practical problems of making a more direct transition to fully democratic processes were apparent to many Chinese. These difficulties made the abandonment of liberal
ideals more acceptable, at least in the short run. The KMT governmental
model was virtually identical with that of the CCP. The two parties, although
they became rivals for mastery of China and had sharply contrasting ideologies, did not represent a clear-cut rivalry of competing political forms. Constitutional democracy was never realized at the level of popular elections,
multiparty politics, or representative legislatures.

Nonetheless, Chinese communist experience with political forms took a
somewhat different route from that followed by the KMT. Chinese communist organizations, for two decades after 1927, prospered only in rural environments. Although the party's leadership had much urban experience and
consisted largely of ex-students, farmers replaced workers as its main political
support. Some communists, even before their expulsion from China's cities in
the late 1920s, had sought to restructure village politics and mobilize large-
scale popular support. The first CCP effort to achieve such mass backing was
a local experiment with what are called peasants' associations, under the Hai-
lu-feng experimental governments, along an especially impoverished stretch
of the Kwangtung coast. This presaged the radical land reform of the Kiangsi

Soviet, where most CCP members who were willing to leave cities had congregated by 1930. They established a "Soviet" state, based on the ability of urban-educated cadres to organize rural farmers, and on earlier attempts of the Kwangtung and Hunan organizers to do so. This effort failed; the Kiangsi Soviet was destroyed not only by strong military forces launched against it, but also because it lost support from some local leaders who were disadvantaged by its policies (some of which, incidentally, Mao also opposed within the CCP at this time). The communists had to find another, less extreme kind of land reform, before they could realize their modern aim of wider direct support for the government they wished to establish. Their failure to accomplish this in Kiangsi was one cause of their need to move northward on the Long March, and of a sharp drop in party membership.

In Yenan, as in large areas of the North China plain which the communists occupied intermittently, land reform was a tool of CCP organizers who mustered support for the party. In these areas, and from 1946 to 1952 throughout the country, land reforms of various kinds were conducted. But Chalmers A. Johnson (1962) has shown that the basis of their later expansion across wide areas of North China was inadvertent Japanese arousal of Chinese nationalism in the harshly occupied areas of North China. The Chinese Communist Party, now ruralized, had a leadership with much experience in modern, urban organizations (Lewis, 1966). This government was often the only effective nonpuppet leadership available, in areas where the Japanese military presence made Chinese farmers aware, as many had not been before of nationality. It was able to function there because the top communists could work in both modern organizations and rural areas. They could survive in rustic peripheries, under attack by modern forces.

Farmers organized by ex-urbanites proved to be politically powerful. Although the rise of communist power is sometimes explained as mainly a rural phenomenon—resulting from peasant nationalism and agrarian inequalities—the modern talents garnered by the CCP from its founding were also crucial to its fortunes. A comprehensive study of the ecology of Chinese communist success in rural areas (Hofheinz, 1969, p. 77), shows that no single factor, either modern or traditional, correlates geographically with early communist expansion as well as the mere presence of CCP organizers in rural areas. This suggestion is not tautological; in fact, it points to the crucial importance of efficient political organization, in a society that had lost so many of its traditional bases for large-scale integration.

In Kiangsi and Yenan, a communist elite was formed that had extraordinary continuity into the post-1949 period. The top communist leaders of the PRC were not drawn mainly from poor backgrounds. They were less low class in origin than several of the most prosperous and notorious warlords. Some of the top CCP leaders were similar in background to many of the central-government elite of the Nanking decade. On the whole, the communist leaders were from small capitalist or rich farmer backgrounds: Mao Tse-tung,

273

Chu Teh, Liu Shao-ch'i, Lin Piao, and Teng Hsiao-p'ing all basically fit this mode. Some, such as Chou En-lai, came from gentry or landlord backgrounds. (The only notable proletarian-born CCP leader during this period was the less important Ch'en Yun. See Scalapino, 1972, pp. 71–72.)

The ratio of party members to population has been far less than the 5 percent norm for communist parties in many countries. At least before 1979, it probably never exceeded that portion, even of the people in areas under CCP control, except during the Long March from Kiangsi in 1934–1935 (see Table 9.1). During the PRC years, the party has increased greatly in size, from somewhat over 1 percent of China's population to somewhat under 4 percent. The CCP has grown irregularly but quickly since mid-century, at an annual rate of over 7 percent.

Both the party and the army appear to have been disproportionately urbanized, although full statistical data are not available. The broader geographical distribution of CCP members has also been somewhat uneven; in 1956, for example, Shantung had about three times as many party members per capita as Chekiang. Distribution by job is also not uniform, and some functional fields (the military is the extreme example) are far better represented in the CCP than others. The distribution of all party members by types of occupation in 1956 was perhaps as follows: agriculture, 58 percent; military and related categories, 21 percent; industry, 10 percent; finance and commerce, 5 percent; education, 4 percent; transport and communications, 4 percent (calculated from *Chung-hua nien-pao*, 1957, p. 136).

Restriction of entry into the national leadership is pointed up by the fact that China, like the USSR, has increasingly become a gerontocracy. The average age of leaders on the top CCP committees has risen almost constantly. This process began to reach some natural ceilings only in the 1970s. The Kiangsi Central Executive Council in 1931, for instance, had an average age of 31 (Waller in Scalapino, ed., 1972, p. 51), whereas the CCP Politburo in 1956 had an average age of 59. The full members of the Politburo in 1976 averaged only seven years older than in 1958; so the mean age of the top leadership had advanced only a bit less than half as fast as the calendar—despite an intervening Cultural Revolution, and despite the passing of many old leaders.

To some extent, this elite stasis affected lower political and administrative levels also. Lack of access to posts held by aging leaders was naturally frustrating to younger talents. For middle-aged cadres who were already somewhat high in the party, there was no longer any equivalent of the higher imperial exams, which could have provided a generally agreed criterion for promoting some and not promoting most of them. Without a common standard of this kind, acquiring political positions was largely a matter of factional connections with the few leaders at the top.

In such a situation, some mid-level leaders might favor change in policies as the main content of policy, because change might create new posts and

Table 9.1: Growth of communist organizations (by thousands of members).

YEARS[a]	PARTY MEMBERS	REGULAR SOLDIERS (CCP UNITS)	YOUTH LEAGUE MEMBERS	POPULATION IN AREA UNDER COMMUNIST CONTROL	POPULATION IN CHINA (MAINLAND)	5 ÷ 6	2 ÷ 5	2 ÷ 3 (× 100)	PARTY SIZE (1950 = 100)
1921	.057	0	—	0	522,000*	0	—	—	0
1927	58	c. 0	50	c. 0	537,000*	0	—	—	1
1930	122	—	75 +	—	544,000*	0	—	—	2
1934	300	350	—	c. 9,000*	552,000*	2	3.3	86	5
1936	30*	50	—	600*	553,000*	0	5.0	60	1
1937	40	92	20	c. 2,000*	553,000*	0	2.0	43	1
1943	790	465	1,193	81,000*	555,000*	15	1.0	170	14
1945	1,211	880	1,500*	91,000*	555,000*	16	1.3	138	21
1950	5,822	5,000	3,000	547,000*	556,000*	98	1.1	116	100
1953	6,612	3,500	9,000	583,000	583,000	100	1.1	189	114
1957	12,720	2,500	23,000	640,000	640,000	100	2.0	509	218
1959	13,960	2,600*	25,000	669,000	669,000	100	2.1	537	240
1961	17,000	—	—	694,000	694,000	100	2.4	—	292
1964	19,000*	2,800*	22,000 +	734,000	734,000	100	2.6	679	326
1973	28,000	3,200*	30,000	899,000	899,000	100	3.1	875	481
1977	35,000	3,500 +	—	966,000	966,000	100	3.6	—	601

a Usually c. mid-year, depending on availability of data.

* These are less reliable estimates; figures in different sources were, however, similar.

Sources of Data: Estimated or computed from *Chung-kung yen-chiu yueh-k'an* (Research Monthly on Chinese Communism) 1972, no. 7, pp. 20, 27–28; Central Intelligence Agency, 1977, p. 8; Gittings, 1967, p. 305; Harrison, 1972, pp. 294, 314; Johnson, 1962, pp. 73, 192–193, 210–213; Nelson, 1977, p. 2; Pringsheim, 1962, pp. 75 ff.; Schran, 1976, p. 2; Schran, 1978, p. 642 (uncertain interpolations also using the Central Intelligence Agency source); Schurmann, 1966, p. 129.

radicalism might expel the occupants of old ones. Mao Tse-tung often spoke of the need to purge lethargic bureaucrats and party members who had lost their revolutionary enthusiasm. Against his rivals, in the Cultural Revolution particularly, he was able to use many upwardly mobile deputy heads and second secretaries who wished to see higher posts vacant. Neither radicalism in policy nor the expulsion of old cadres became permanent, but the pressures implicit in the CCP's elite recruitment structure affected its political style.

Armed Forces and Warlordism

The military reforms sponsored under Li Hung-chang's aegis (see "Armed Forces: The Changing Place of the Military," Chapter 3) led directly to Yuan Shih-k'ai's dominance of the early twentieth-century court. This led in turn to the era of warlordism in the 1920s. Consideration of militarized politics in the present century can, therefore, best begin with some observations on Yuan's career.

Yuan did not spring directly from the Li Hung-chang apparatus of the 1890s, although he succeeded to its failing control. Nor had most of the warlords of the 1920s and thereafter been Yuan's underlings. At each phase of a centrifugal process, local holders of military power gained further freedom from civil restraints, and survived by competing against other militarists. Yuan initiated the final phase of that process. Unlike Li, who used regional military power to become the dominant figure in court politics, Yuan and others of his kind devoted themselves in the last two decades of the century to provincial or regional tasks, as governors-general of two or more adjoining provinces. Their local success occasionally enabled them to exert some influence on national policy and politics. Yuan's career was thus fostered by a different aspect of the regionalism of late Ch'ing political development. In this period, some provincial statesmen exerted strong, often "progressive" influences in their own areas. After 1900, such provincial leaders could, in some significant instances, speak as the strong voice from below, demanding that political interests beyond the court be heeded in institutional reforms. Two of those statesmen have been already mentioned. Chang Chih-tung and Liu K'un-i were truly outstanding figures, able to think deeply and even radically about the failures of the 1898 reforms. They sought other solutions to the problems defined by Confucian statecraft, and ironically from their Confucian ground, they proposed reforms that would terminate the Confucian era. They were vigorous proponents of the military modernization that was realized experimentally within their regions. They thus incidentally sponsored Yuan Shih-k'ai's rise to controlling power in North China and at court, after the death of their longstanding political rival and opponent, Li Hung-chang.

Both Liu and Chang, emphasizing the need for military modernization, had been advocates of strong resistance, to the Russians in the Ili crisis of the 1870s and in the war with France in 1884. Chang created a model "Self-strengthening Army'' as early as 1895, after the Japanese defeat of China, while he was serving at Nanking. The court saw the excellent results achieved by the German training of his small force, and it adopted his proposal that such methods be imitated in the metropolitan province near Peking. A "Newly Established Army" was thus begun, on Chang's model; it was placed under the supervision of Yuan Shih-k'ai, then a young scholar-official by purchase, who had distinguished himself over the past decade as staff officer to the Chinese forces in Korea. Yuan created a new military training academy, first near Tientsin (1895) and later (1903) at the provincial capital of Pao-ting, again using German and other foreign advisers. From a core force of 7,000 officers and men, Yuan gradually expanded his army, taking some units to Shantung as his provincial army when he became governor there in 1899. In 1901, after Li Hung-chang's death, he returned to the court as his successor. Yuan assumed Li's concurrent positions as governor-general of the metropolitan province and Pei-yang commissioner. In the latter post, he had responsibilities for defense, customs, and foreign affairs in North China; this office had been created in the 1860s to manage special problems arising because of the treaty ports and the foreign presence. Yuan's Newly Established Army came to be called the Pei-yang Army. The dozen years following Yuan's death were subsequently called the era of the Pei-yang warlords, and this name accurately reflects the consequences of Yuan's leadership in military modernization after 1895—consequences that Chang Chih-tung and Liu K'un-i could not have anticipated. Chang and Liu hoped that the Newly Established Army might become the core of a truly national force; but in fact, it remained the private possession of another regional leader. From the first years of the twentieth century, it was in rivalry with the so-called Nan-yang armies, the successors of provincial armies established by Liu and others in the Yangtze provinces.

Yuan's new army in Chihli province became his private instrument for gaining extraordinary political power. Its officer corps, from the start, was full of his personal underlings who owed him primary loyalty. The structure of Yuan's officer corps was profoundly different from that of Tseng Kuo-fan and other provincial leaders at mid-century; the old Hunan Army and its copies were led by gentry and stressed strong lineage and local loyalties. Tseng's armies, by promoting men of low rank who demonstrated ability in the field, generated new leaders, and thus may have raised some persons who had little gentry learning or cultivation and could be sometimes criticized for unnecessary violence—nonetheless, the Hunan Braves and their like were subject to the restraining influences of the local social milieu. They could pursue alternative, nonmilitary careers in their home social settings, and some of them later did. They had strong identifications with their provinces. In contrast, Yuan's new officer corps was recruited from many provinces. The primary loyalties of these men were to the training academy itself, to their class of fellow graduates, to the military profession, and above all to Yuan as their "overlord" through a metamorphosed conception of the academy director as "teacher." This was an intensely personal relationship unrelated to the values of family, lineage, and local feeling that are important to many basic contexts of Chinese life. Hence this loyalty also lacked the mutuality and the subordination to larger and longer-range goals that guided relationships derived from families and localities. The new militarists were not wholly freed from those features of Chinese life, but they had a monopoly on coercion within personal networks of a new kind. It is not surprising that their dominance should produce a period of dismaying social confusion and retrogression, earning the hatred of both the old strategic elite and the new intellectuals. The warlords shared the ideals of neither, and their behavior was acceptable to neither.

After Yuan came to power as president of the republic of China in 1912, he was supported only (but adequately) by the militarist base he had created in the previous fifteen years. Upon his death in 1916, the central solidifying feature of the warlord power bloc, the personal obligations that other generals owed to him, was removed. Lingering authority in Yuan's old organization gave temporary advantage to Tuan Ch'i-jui, who as premier was the leading Pei-yang figure in the succession under President Li Yuan-hung. Soon a number of rivals for control of the would-be central government appeared on the scene. Each held a region by means of a personal army, and each vied for occupancy of the national capital, Peking. The Kuomintang clung to tenuous bases in the far south, wherever it could align itself with sympathetic militarists. The Pei-yang successors, in full hierarchical array, held private meetings to decide the fate of government; but soon they took to fighting over the spoils and rapidly formed competing factions and alliances, with shifting real military power. Their political arm, the An-fu Club, was heavily subsidized by the Japanese. The political process was totally usurped by generals who controlled the means of violence.

Warlord governments varied greatly in stability and effectiveness. The quality of regional regimes had in fact varied considerably since the 1860s, but now they lacked any formal unity. The partial hegemony that continued through the end of the empire was now completely smashed. Until 1927, the western powers continued to view Peking as the capital of China, and they recognized whatever government possessed that city. At the same time, they also dealt with regional authorities on a de facto basis as necessary. Ordinary Chinese could also cross the lines from one warlord area to another with no difficulty, as could most trade. A growing national system of public and private universities continued to serve the entire nation, and so did the publishing industry, modernized communications, the press, and the cinema. China's cultural unity was not threatened by the political fragmentation; in fact it was strengthened by various movements in thought and culture. In many politically important ways, however, China could not act as a nation. Under the warlords, this became obvious to all, and the sentiment of nationalism was spurred by recurrent and humiliating demonstrations of China's political weakness.

The devolution of the Chinese state was pivotally caused by Yuan Shih-k'ai, who had let his new conceptions of politics (and his personal ambitions) free him from the normative limitations under which his predecessors such as Li Hung-chang had functioned. Yuan's blatant amorality fed the festering cynicism and operational irregularity of the late Ch'ing, leading it into the last phase of the debureaucratization of traditional China. No transcendent claims to altruistic service, to public propriety, to commitment for political ideals (old or new), or to probity in private life, could any longer be effectively imposed by government. Usurpation of the political process by armies deprived politics of its identification with what had long been, in ideal and in varying degrees of practice, an honored achievement in China, a stately career in public service. This particular refinement of Chinese civilization's evocative model of the good man was long the main guarantee of governmental performance. It was now rendered, at best, a hollow shell of its former extensive reality, and at worst a caricature of that. Individuals might still respond to the old ideal; but the previously civilian, now strangely and partially modernized conditions of a militarized political life would not allow many to do so.

The warlord transformation of Chinese politics had deep implications, both destructive and constructive, for the on-going process of modernization in Chinese society at large. The end of old models led many to seek and believe in alternatives. During the heyday of warlordism, the intellectual world witnessed its most radical and iconoclastic era; the Chinese communists were more radical then than more recently; in fact China's entire intellectual community was subject to extremes of skepticism, rejection, and innovation. Much of the intellectual searching was nationalistic; values for modern times were sought in the Chinese heritage. Political theories claimed wide attention. The Chinese elite was broadened to include large numbers of graduates from new, westernized schools. Many of these went abroad to find the practical, specific utility that Chinese training seemed to lack. Most returned, expecting careers in government. To a previously unknown degree, leaders of the nation focused its attention on the search for China's international dignity and political stability. If the masses of villagers were largely untouched by these changes, they at least saw more children attending schools, studying textbooks that used Chinese written in a modern semicolloquial style, full of information about other nations and their political systems. China took a giant step toward participating in a shared world culture during the 1920s.

Yet the costs of the era in terms of modernization also were great. Most obvious was the disabling effect of warlordism on government. From the fragmentation of the early 1920s, military interests and regional separatism developed—and they became too powerful for the resurgent KMT to overcome, even during the decade when it held power in Nanking before the Japanese invasion of 1937. The legacy of militarism was political debilitation. If many encouraging phenomena in education, in economic growth, in political experimentation, and in social change of all kinds occurred between 1927 and 1937, they occurred despite domestic and external challenges to effective governing. They did not result from strong political support, and they occurred under conditions that continued to give precedence to military priorities. The "Nanking decade" was at once disastrous and hopeful in different ways.

The attempted reunification of 1927 had great importance for China's political modernization; it was the first serious effort to recreate the traditional geography of state politics on a modern basis. Internationally, it provided China with a vehicle for resisting aggression, for the country's participation in World War II, for its enhanced place in world politics, and specifically for the United Nations' later acceptance of China as an emergent great power. Domestically, the Nanking decade also saw the emergence of powerful new national symbols, and the awareness of new national causes and goals. These symbols prepared the way for wartime mobilization of the people. The post–warlord-era KMT government, despite its internal and external compromises with warlordism, might in a less bellicose international environment have made the successful transition to a new politics of national unification. Because of Japan's invasion, it did not. Yet it made significant contributions to the continuing political development of the nation, particularly at the level of the central government. The hopeful beginning of a national reintegration, after decades of disgrace, is an achievement that more recent propagandists have sought to erase.

The Nationalist and communist governments that came into being in the decade following the warlord era were deeply influenced by warlord politics, but they belong to a new and different era of political history. Warlordism, the dominant system in the immediate postimperial period, ended in 1928. KMT victories over most important regional warlord factions assured an accommodation with the remaining ones. Militarism, as an adjunct to politics, was now in transition to a new stage. Increasingly modernized armies came to serve the one-party state and its proclaimed revolutionary purposes. This stage was partially reached under the KMT after 1923, and more fully under the CCP after Mao Tse-tung's rise to power and especially after 1952. A military stage to achieve national unification was described by Sun Yat-sen in the early 1920s. Sun accepted Soviet advisers for the reorganization of his army, as also of his party and government. The young Chiang Kai-shek, who attended the preparatory school of Pao-ting Military Academy in 1907–1908 and then studied with government support at the Shikan Gakko, the Japanese military academy, was sent by Sun Yat-sen to the USSR for six months in 1923. In the next year he became the founding director of the Whampoa Military Academy at Canton. Chiang thus embodied both the older and newer aspects of modernized military training in China. He was representative of a significant group of Chinese officers who experienced the transition between the period of Yuan Shih-k'ai and the time when hundreds of Soviet advisers came to play a key role. The Japanese role in Chinese military development was also very large, both because of training in Japan and because of instructors at Whampoa and other new military academies.

Pao-ting Military Academy was formally established as the new republic's central military school in 1912, and the National Central Military Academy at Nanking assumed this role when it replaced Whampoa about 1930. These schools, and a number of provincial and other new-style military academies, produced an elite officer corps that contributed greatly to the professionalization of military careers. The military academies were a major avenue of upward mobility for poor but able young men. Some continuity is observable from the Pao-ting Academy of Yuan Shih-k'ai's time: excessive personal loyalty to the director, strong group cohesion, and a tradition of hierarchy based on membership in a particular graduating class, with seniority reckoned by graduation dates. At Whampoa, new elements were added. The students were selected according to more rigid standards, they received intense political training, and they also were given far more modern technical education. Graduates were ideally committed to the purposes of revolution, and they were supposed to be loyal to the school director who now commanded fealty both as teacher and as revolutionary leader. That Chou En-lai and other future communist leaders were Chiang's junior associates in running the academy is significant for the similarity of army-party relations in the KMT and the CCP. Whampoa graduates who made their careers in the communist armies included many of later importance, such as Lin Piao. Whampoa contributed as much to modernizing the Chinese communist military as it did to the Nationalist army.

In military units, success and efficiency often depend on the certainty that subalterns will carry out commands, without pausing to consider the legitimacy of their orders. Bonds of obedience, personal loyalty, and a soldier's obligation to his commander become more important than any policy per se. The history of twentieth-century Chinese politics is largely a tale of what armies, having this kind of integration, can and cannot do well. Soldiers are better at creating a framework for relative authority, by destroying the capabilities of their oppositions, than at making positive policies to increase their own constituencies. The main problem for a militarist is to compensate or sanction his officers sufficiently, so that they will maintain their loyalty to him, and will not set themselves up as concurrent, autonomous, rival warlords.

This problem was epitomized by Yuan himself, who played a central role in persuading the last Ch'ing emperor to abdicate and then had the country's most prominent parliamentary democrat assassinated. He could not, however, muster popular credence for either the old or new claims on loyalty, despite his attempts to use new media for this purpose. China under him saw no emergence of a stronger, more centralist modernizing government, such as spurred progress in Japan and Russia at similar, early stages of development.

Leading officers could, and did, segment China when they were dissatisfied with the rewards from their erstwhile superiors. They were relatively good at fighting each other, but they were unable to unify China. Especially during the century's second and third decades, it was generally true that politicians who had large armies lacked long-term governmental programs, and those who had the ideas lacked the troops.

The main exception to this generalization was Chiang Kai-shek, who after Sun's death led the Northern Expedition to take the most populous parts of the country from warlord control. This expedition was successful especially in East and Central China, although ''residual warlordism'' (Sheridan's term, used by Tien, 1972) crippled the Nationalists' efforts to achieve unification long after 1928. Nonetheless, the KMT and subsequently the CCP developed a politics in which military problems could have the highest immediate priority without policy becoming entirely the captive of those who possessed military means. The army as a tool of the one-party state is a considerable development over the kind of militarism that had been central to Chinese politics since the 1850s. It marks a return to civilian political control over armed forces. This had always been the ideal in China; in a context of modernization it had new implications. The delays of this development, which lasted from the 1850s to the 1950s, cost China dearly in terms of political effectiveness. No early or successful late modernizers had to pay such a high price at a similar phase in the process of modern change. As we shall see below, the communists after their victory at mid-century were able to change the inherited pattern of regional militarism somewhat.

From 1910 to mid-century, the portion of military spending in central government budgets changed very erratically, but on average, very little. The Nanking decade (1928–1937) saw the ratio of military allocations to the whole state budget decrease at an average rate of 6 percent a year. In the two decades after mid-century, this ratio decreased at approximately 10 percent per year.

The number of full-time soldiers in China generally increased over the republican period. In 1918, according to one report, China had about 1.3 million soldiers, of whom only 42 percent had any connection with warlords involved in the national government. (Chang Nai-wen, 1936, p. 10, also gives figures from which it can be calculated that only a bit over half of total military spending in 1918 was associated with the central government.) The number of soldiers expanded greatly during the following fifteen years, and by the mid-1930s China contained more than 2 million soldiers (ibid., p. 307). During the anti-Japanese and civil wars, the quality of statistics on this subject was especially low for political reasons. According to one source, the Nanking government's 1947 claim of over 4.5 million soldiers was inflated over reality by a factor of nearly two. If so, then an estimate for the number of communist troops in 1947 may be added to the revised estimate, so that a possible all-time high ratio of about 1 percent of the mainland's population was engaged in full-time soldiering during the civil war. By 1953, this portion had decreased to about six-tenths of a percent. A trend line for the PRC era (using data from the last note) suggests that the portion of soldiers in mainland China's population decreased by about 3.4 percent annually in the third quarter of this century, or by over 4 percent annually since 1945.

Central influence over the careers of government and military officers in provincial capitals increased after the mid-1950s. Before then, a practical kind of military regionalism was based in large natural administrative units, necessitated by China's slowly transforming communications net. In February 1949, just before victory on the mainland, groups of communist military units that had long been associated with each other were organized into five "field armies," each of which acquired a sphere of influence in the section of China its units occupied for some years thereafter. Each army was dominant in one or two large military regions. To simplify: P'eng Teh-huai's First Field Army was in the northwest; Liu Po-ch'eng's Second Field Army in the central and southwestern provinces; Ch'en I's Third Field Army in East China; Lin Piao's Fourth Field Army was split between Manchuria and the Hunan-Kwangsi-Kwangtung area; and Nieh Jung-chen's Fifth Field Army was on the northern plain around Peking (Whitson, 1973, pp. 498 ff.).

Although political career patterns in the PRC cannot in all periods be adequately explained in terms of these military "loyalty groups" (Parish, 1973), each of the field armies nonetheless established a government under its own cadres in its own region during the early 1950s. Scholars debate the extent to which these large, political-military cliques competed with each other in China's central politics; but there is general agreement that they were important within their own areas, even when their local institutions took new forms because of central decrees. There is more evidence of their significance for national politics in times of turmoil (such as the Cultural Revolution) than at times of relative calm (such as the mid-1950s or the period after Lin Piao's demise). Some years into the era of the PRC, the politics of China's army thus remained transitional, neither fully modern nor fully old. When it was necessary to interact with other military areas or the central government on politically sensitive matters, the local marshals often proved to be national-minded patriots. When central policies were unclear or in chaos, they made their own without difficulty. This was not a warlord situation; for many purposes it meant unified command. However, it was also not totally different from numerous republican situations, especially during the Nanking decade, when essentially autonomous militarists might all fly the same flag, give formal obeisance to the same national leader, avoid giving evidence that China could be divided—and yet create their own local policies at some times.

The military clearly was a most important constituency of the state for much of the modern period of Chinese politics. The decrease of civilian authority had been so long term and severe at earlier times, however, that the situation was not praetorian in the usual sense. Even for times when the military hierarchy became the only effective surviving one in the country, as during the Cultural Revolution, it cannot be accurately said that the army staged a coup d'état, however much its leadership (then Lin Piao) may have wished to do so. The reasons for military intervention into government during the Cultural Revolution reveal more about the nature of China's political structure in the transformation period than any coup could have done. The Chinese remained conscious that their country is a huge ex-empire, and undoubtedly a future world power; it is not a banana republic. The old civilian ethic of imperial times was surely dead, but the top "civilian" CCP leaders all had years of experience as political commissars, working within military units. The top generals were still half-imbued with the notion that civilian logistic support, and thus much civilian supervision of military strategy, were vital keys to the sole purely professional goal any soldier could possibly have: victory in war. By the late 1960s, the guerrilla tradition was not the only important one in China's army but it still had much force. The military did not intervene in politics to depose civilians; it had civilian interests too, and intervened on behalf of civilian ex-soldiers whose radical policies could not be administered easily.

This kind of situation, which became endemic and was based in both communist and warlord precedents, made formal juntas unnecessary. The government's need for the army's domestic role resulted from the politics of hasty social mobilization with political institutions too weak to channel that mobilization. This predicament could exist only in the transitional period, when change easily outran the restoration of structure. The strong traditional bases for state integration had been destroyed, and reliable replacements still had not been found. Radical hopes led to military intervention. There were no means for institution building, until more order balanced the strife.

In 1971, Defense Minister Lin Piao pressed his claim to replace the deposed Liu Shao-ch'i as head of state. Marshal Lin was confronted by a civilian coalition, including Mao, Chou, and a group of "radical" politicians from Shanghai. This diverse (and temporary) alliance separated the defense minister from commanders near the capital; he was involved in an abortive coup and died while trying to flee the country. The military constituency of the state remained extremely important, but the generals allowed a sharp reduction in the army's procurement budget after 1971. In a stunning demonstration of self-conscious civilian dominance, Premier Chou announced in January 1974 that eight of the eleven commanders of China's great military regions would be reassigned to head other regions—although, formally, none of them was demoted. Many of these generals were thus removed from areas where they had served and built friendship networks for more than twenty years. This order is the main evidence that regional militarism in China was receding. The wholesale nature of the shift suggests that everyone involved was aware of the strength of the tradition that had been interrupted.

In very rough terms, it may be possible to estimate the changing openness and directness of army involvement in PRC politics by the portion of CCP central committee members who are soldiers. This index was highest in the Ninth Central Committee of 1969, when about one-half of the members had their current main work in the army. At an earlier period (the Eighth Committee, elected in 1956), the military held about one-quarter of the seats; after their victory in the revolution and their professionalizing experience in Korea, leading marshals may not have desired a larger open representation. In the Tenth Committee of 1973, the military portion was the average of these amounts (three-eighths); and in the Eleventh Committee, it was basically unchanged, at 35 percent. These figures can be interpreted to suggest that China's top soldiers are still assigned to nonspecialized political posts in considerable numbers, that their direct participation has fluctuated widely, and that the degree of this fluctuation is decreasing at a slow rate.

If so, then soldiers will participate less regularly in the details of decisions for functional fields that do not relate to their military specialty. This does not, however, mean that they are becoming much less crucial in the support base of the regime (or in choosing the top civilian politicians).

THE FISCAL BASE

Taxes and talent are needed by any administrative structure, and much of the changing environment for modern government can be traced in changes in the groups that supply these political resources. Economic and social changes—the slow increase of industrialization and of urbanized leadership, entirely atypical of old China—gave rise to new sources of political revenue and recruitment. These changes combined with the demise of the imperial examinations, the traditional entryway for legitimate rule, to create entirely new bases for government.

Even before the end of the Ch'ing dynasty, land taxes had become less important as a source of revenue (see "The Fiscal Base," Chapter 3). Thereafter, the significance of land taxes diminished even further, especially for the central government. New industrial technologies were introduced by the same military and political leaders who had suppressed the major nineteenth-century rebellions. Important gentry families living in these areas thus diversified their interests into manufacturing. Their new economic strength was not mainly established to serve the national polity. Leaders in provinces such as Kwangtung and Kiangsu administered and financed their own local political structures. Many of their policies (for example, not to mobilize popular feeling against foreigners during the Boxer movement in the north) simply differed from policies of the central government. Especially in areas near the treaty ports, these leaders sometimes financed experiments in local administration that were deeply influenced by western models (Elvin in Gray, ed., 1969).

The extent of such efforts, however, was trivial in comparison with China's size. Relative to both Japan and Russia at analogous points in their development, China's investment in technology during the first half of the present century was low. The government did not invest much directly, nor did it build up its tax base by greatly encouraging private investment.

Official and semiofficial enterprises, sometimes in heavy and military industries, were of some importance; but wealth was accumulated most quickly in light industries, especially textiles, most of which were not nationalized or commandeered by the government until much later. Some of the most prosperous industries were long protected from Chinese taxes by being located in treaty ports. Legally, none of the treaties had exempted Chinese enterprises from such taxes; but despite this fact, the revenues were not generally made available to the national government. Modern industry was throughout the century a growing tax base, and in time it became the dominant one, as we shall see below.

By the end of World War I, China already had a network of modernized domestic banks and important light industrial bases concentrated in seaboard cities. A growing rail system helped to integrate some regional markets. But managerial systems of the kinds required to operate large industries, postal systems, or national communications did not display such impressive growth in China as they had in modernizing Japan or Russia. Both of those nations accomplished ''unusual feats of social engineering'' in the changes needed for management of both private organizations and government (Black et al., 1975, p. 146). In Meiji Japan, officials guided the nation's use of resources and skills from the center. In both nations, the governmental role was especially broad and effective.

The Chinese record is one of far more limited government concern for such problems. (Only after 1949 did the CCP launch large new training programs and then mainly for its loyalists.) A few bureaus before mid-century developed good management records, especially in customs and the postal service, both of which built on the work of foreign experts. The railroads, using mostly Chinese engineers and managers, and served by their own National University of Transportation (Chiao-t'ung Ta-hsueh), gave evidence that the Chinese were fully able to accomplish such growth on their own. Some major cities, particularly the national capitals, had model governments in the 1920s and 1930s, in part borrowing from machinery established in the treaty port cities such as Shanghai, whose International Settlement Municipal Council was mostly European. By and large, however, provincial and local governments were little affected.

Development of managerial skills in the private sector proceeded more quickly. Modern light industry, selling goods to markets mostly in the countryside, became China's main means for accumulating both savings and taxes. State-owned enterprises were a notable source of funds for the Manchu court even before its fall. For example, in 1911, state enterprise income (*kuan-yeh shou-ju*) was already alongside the land tax (*t'ien-fu*) as the largest source of the central government's revenue (Juan, 1924, p. 416; K'ung, 1935, p. 4). The fall of the dynasty led to the localization of practically all public enterprises that had previously been in the central government's domain.

Provincial and subprovincial expenditures in the second and third decades of the century were largely military, and they may have approached the high four-fifths of total government spending that was common in the eighteenth century. Revenues came from many sources, and it is at least clear that "the financial resources at the disposal of the local militarist regimes far exceeded those of the central government at Peking" (Ch'i, 1976, pp. 166–167).

Deficit financing soared almost immediately upon the dynasty's fall; it rose from a small amount to four-tenths of the total budget. At a slightly later stage, various commercial taxes (the "miscellaneous taxes" on liquor, tobacco, and much else) reduced the deficit by about half. Chinese governments have readily imposed taxes on commerce, but they have been more loath to levy from industry, which lays more obvious golden eggs. There has been a continuing official incapacity to administer a major agricultural tax equitably without hurting production. The farmers have been taxed indirectly— through the prices they pay for consumer goods made in factories that are either state owned or concentrated and relatively easy for the government to monitor for turnover taxes.

At various times from the 1920s to the 1950s, Chinese governments have announced land reforms that were ostensibly intended to increase rural production and improve the bases for collection. None of these reforms, despite their great variety, was notably successful over the long term, for either of these purposes. Central government revenues came from agriculture largely through the light industrial sector, even when that was small. When land reforms achieved any notable governmental purpose in China during the century's first half—and under the communists they did so both before and after 1949—their significance lay in constituency building, not in tax collection improvement. Light industry, not agricultural change, modernized the way the Chinese farmers paid for government.

After 1952, when the land reform was "basically completed," the countryside lost several million local notables who had been killed, and it acquired many new activists who supported the regime. Fiscal extraction was somewhat increased in absolute terms by the land reform, and then again by the subsequent establishment of agricultural cooperatives and communes (see Vogel, 1969, ch. 3; and Lippit, 1974, p. 146), but agricultural production did not rise much on a national basis. To encourage output, the CCP found it necessary to allocate considerable authority to local units that were too small to monitor effectively.

Modern industry and commerce were by far the fastest-growing sources of direct government income throughout the middle decades of this century. First the anti-Japanese war, and then the civil war, temporarily depressed the ability of officials to use this base, and unsecured deficit financing was the result. In 1936 central government expenditures were already 33 percent greater than income; but by 1940, with further Japanese incursions, the expenditures not covered by receipts rose to 87 percent. In only one of the next five years did this red-ink portion of the central budget fall below 70 percent. In the year of Japan's surrender (1945), it stood at 81 percent. Because of civil war, the government deficit remained over six-tenths of the budget for the next two years, only declining thereafter when the political effects of inflation became more obvious (Weng Chih-yung, 1952, pp. 76–77).

Deficit finance did not completely end with the establishment of the PRC. In 1950, Peking's state deficit was 14.5 percent of government expenditures (Cheng Chu-yuan, 1953, *shang-ts'e*, p. 29). Considerable inflation of the new currency ensued. Of course the KMT regime had done this on a much larger scale, and strong direct price controls by the CCP eventually prevented the inflationary effects from becoming severe. Nonetheless, this early PRC similarity to the previous government's finance methods suggests that the two regimes were not so totally and immediately different as they liked to depict themselves.

One means by which the PRC covered its deficit in the following few years was equally direct: confiscation of the property of politically disadvantaged groups. This method, also, had precedents in early regimes. In 1951, confiscation yielded nearly 10 percent of the value of total government expenditures. Much of this was from the agricultural sector. By 1952, lucrative urban sources of such income were tapped more heavily, with greater results. The Three-Anti and Five-Anti movements, which were directed against the state bureaucracy and the business community, were responsible for financing 23 percent of Peking's budget (ibid., *shang-ts'e*, 35–40). Although the accuracy of published figures on this politically sensitive subject may be suspect, it is clear that confiscation was not negligible in state finance at this time.

The CCP gradually expanded the financial bases of government. As long as the private sector was allowed to continue large-scale production during the 1950s, the communists imposed major turnover taxes on it. The direct importance of agriculture to the fiscal base rapidly declined. In 1936, about 16 percent of the gross value of agricultural and sideline output had been taxed away by various levels of formal government, but this portion fell to 8 percent by 1952, and to 6 percent by 1956.

As early as 1952, fully 57 percent of all state revenues, including provincial budgets, were generated by state-owned firms. Fully 80 percent of all official monies came from public, private, and "joint" enterprises together (Nairuenn Ch'en, 1967, pp. 441–443). Customs and the salt tax were providing only 5 percent of revenues in 1952, although in the 1928–1937 decade they had provided over 70 percent.

Changes during the first few years of communist rule vividly show the opportunities for fiscal modernization that had been lost in the previous fifteen years of war. In 1953, the CCP was already receiving 705 percent more revenue from its state-owned industries than in 1950, but the direct agricultural tax (despite land reform) now brought only 34 percent more. By 1953 also, private and state modern enterprises together contributed 82 percent of the state budget, counting both taxes and direct remittances. (Computations are made from data in Chi-jung Hsiao, 1954, pp. 8 and 10.)

The state budget, by the same token, assumed a vastly greater role in the national economy than previously. After 1954, more than 30 percent of China's total income each year passed through official budgets—more than five times pre-1949 averages. (This experience recapitulated on a much larger scale a similar proportional rise during the Nanking decade in the four years 1931–1934; data in Tien, 1972, p. 83; Nai-ruenn Ch'en, 1967, pp. 141 and 446; Chi-jung Hsiao, 1954, p. 89.) For the remainder of the first decade of CCP rule at least, a ceiling on this percentage seems to have kept it from rising much above the one-third level (despite institutional changes in 1956 and 1958). It may well have risen higher in later decades, for which comprehensive budget data are not yet available.

In 1956, the "transition to socialism" that is, the quasi-nationalization of all remaining large private enterprises, took place. By this time, 65 percent of the state's net income from its enterprises came in the form of direct profit remittances (Donnithorne, 1967, p. 376). By the end of the 1950s, the great bulk of the state's total revenue came from these profits on nationally owned enterprises. The portion is now well above nine-tenths. These transfers to the public treasure are line items in economic plans; they are deducted automatically from enterprise bank accounts. The ultimate burden of financing the state, in other words, falls on the purchasers of modern industrial goods.

Industrial taxes and appropriations both rose to become very high portions of the government's budgets (well over half, in each case, since the Great Leap Forward). But agricultural revenues and appropriations became very small portions of the government's receipts and outlays. A dual economy perforce meant a dual base for direct taxes—even though a major net flow of resources from agriculture to the modern sector continued, because prices were set well above costs for industrial consumer goods. Light industry was the key to modernization financed by government in this period.

The central budget grew at an average annual rate of over 17 percent from 1952 to 1959. Its rise decelerated somewhat in the post-Leap depression and probably averaged below 6 percent per annum from 1961 to 1975; but this is still some growth.

China's modern transformation thus provided a tax base that was more prosperous than any the state had known before. Some aspects of this growth showed its transitional nature: it was uneven, and not until the end of the wars at mid-century did it begin to accelerate notably. Despite major transfers of funds between provinces, regional budgets and fiscal management systems remained important. Finally, the direct revenues and expenditures of the government became almost totally linked to the activities of those few Chinese citizens whose work is industrial. The activities and fortunes of the agricultural majority were affected, but only indirectly.

Local Power

NATIONAL COMMUNICATIONS AND PROVINCIAL GOVERNMENT

During the first quarter of the century, the growth of modern communications in China did not correlate with an increase in central government power. The contrast with Japan served by coastal shipping and even with Russia (despite its immensity) could not be more stark. In China, the first effect of modern communications was not to increase the capital's power over outlying areas; instead, it increased provincial leaders' ambitions for national influence.

By the end of World War I, telegraph services were available in many Chinese cities, and a modern post office offered services that were extensive, even if they were often slow. These gradual developments provided infrastructure not only for provincial cohesion and control, but also for political agitation and resistance. Technology changed the pace and scope of political action by bringing centers of regional power into instantaneous communication with each other. Certain parts of the nation, which had been inert in politics, became concerned and informed. Slowly new kinds of leaders assumed some importance on the national scene.

A revealing example is seen in Yuan Shih-k'ai's last months as the head of China's government. Through the latter half of 1915, he cleverly maneuvered his so-called selection as emperor by manipulating media throughout the provinces, and by leaking a stream of telegrams, ostensibly to test "public opinion" as reflected in the provincial provisional assemblies, but actually to build a semblance of popular support. Yuan in his earlier career had displayed skill in covertly manipulating the court; he now used new communications methods, especially private telegrams made public in newspapers, as he attempted to turn the republic into a constitutional monarchy. The downfall of his imperial aspirations was accomplished by political leaders in the remote provinces of Kweichow and Yunnan, who made similar use of the new instruments of communications. Largely because of the impact of a sequence of daily telegrams, published in the national press, these leaders mobilized antimonarchical sentiment widely in the first months of 1916. Telegraphed declarations of independence by province after province, made in the names of new "representative" political institutions, built an appearance of impending civil war. Attention throughout China became focused on these developments, adding the weight of potential mass involvement to the inherent volatility of the politics of national leadership. Yuan was overcome by political forces that he misjudged. In May 1916, he had been humiliated; by June, his frustrations induced his physical collapse and death.

The head of the Chinese state had become a public figure, in a manner unprecedented for any emperor of the past. The population of China had become his audience in a modern sense. Since the Sung dynasty, for a thousand years, the emperors of China had increasingly become private figures. They were gossiped about within the strategic elite, but were not socially involved with this elite—and they were faceless, unknown figures to the masses. By Yuan Shih-k'ai's time, their personalities and daily acts had become public property.

This technologically induced shift in the means of political action intensified in later years. During the 1920s, the urban proletariat was small, but in response to the theoretically derived demand that it serve as the vanguard of revolution, it became the object of intense organizing efforts. It was propelled by the media into strikes and boycotts and became the focal point in nationally publicized confrontations with the imperialist presence. The KMT-CCP struggle after 1927 included a media war, the KMT controlling most of the radio and news press, and the CCP strong in the literary press and in informal underground communications. In the Sian Incident of 1936, after Chiang Kai-shek was captured and returned to Nanking to shift China's war policy, national attention was concentrated on the person of the leader. A tense population, at war with Japan, was kept up-to-date by frequent news releases on the radio and in the press.

The Nanking government tried but was unable to reverse the dissolution of central government by reinstating strong central control over its provinces. Yet in the 1927–1936 decade it achieved some success in modernizing and integrating the governments of some central China provinces closest to the national capital at Nanking. From the long-range view, the new communist regime after 1949 can be seen as faced with the same problems of reconstructing a centralized authority that had waned for over a century, and then had been nonexistent for almost half a century.

Regionalism, linked to militarism, remained more important than the communists publicized, even after the foundation of the PRC, although the state bureaucracy increasingly contervailed these traditions in periods when national policy debates were relatively muted. The incumbency of Chinese leaders at many administrative and political levels has tended to be quite long. This was no less true in the communist period than it had been in the republican one, or is now in Taiwan. Leaders in related posts built close, personal working relationships with each other, which inevitably became political because of trust developed over many years. Not only in the field armies' large regions, but also in other large and small institutional settings, political groups were partly generated by the low mobility between posts. This inertia encouraged relatively impermeable, cellular organizations (which are often physically encapsulated in walled compounds). Within these units, low mobility between posts encouraged local authoritarianism on the model of a traditional family.

In the country as a whole, new communications infrastructure, the increase of official planning, and the use of campaigns all tended to break down these conditions somewhat. In 1952, the field armies' regional governments ceased to "represent the Central People's Government." After the inception of the First Five-Year Plan in 1953 and of a new state constitution in 1954, the formal authority of central leaders was increased in many fields. Their most powerful means of controlling regional and provincial leaders lay in norms of party discipline. Below the province level, similar rights existed formally for provincial heads.

Because of China's size and lack of economic development, relatively central monitoring of just a few levels of vertical jurisdiction does not necessarily imply effective control of mass action. The administrative span-of-control problem for any high level in China is immense. It is often unknown and not fully surveyed even by the cadres who have to work with it. There are formal similarities between authority patterns in large and small organizations in China, but these do not always imply that the large ones effectively control the small ones, which are so numerous. The trend has been toward centralization but it has been uneven; and in such an immense country, it follows the slow development of communications and the larger groups fostered thereby.

Regionalization to the large multiprovince level was the most important and effective kind of centralization during the first years of the PRC. One of the administrative regions of this period, the truly "independent kingdom" (*tu-li wang-kuo*) that Kao Kang established in Manchuria, became the official bad example of excessive autonomy, criticized especially by central bureaucrats Liu Shao-ch'i and Chou En-lai. Kao was brought to a high central post, purged in 1954, and then committed suicide. The first PRC constitution, in the same year, was designed to create a less regionalized state structure than had prevailed during the early period.

The decline of the large multiprovince units led to greater autonomy at the province level. This was especially true during the quick agricultural collectivization, industrial nationalization, and quasi-liberalization movements that dominated 1956 and 1957. By the anti-rightist movement and the early Great Leap, many important cadres had been physically dispersed from offices in provincial capitals to headquarters in lesser market towns. This meant a decrease of the influence of provincial governments, a further decentralization from that viewpoint. It paved the way for communes, at first outsized ones that attempted to administer too much with too few resources, and then smaller ones, with many important powers over daily affairs increasingly delegated to production brigades and teams.

Any description of this change in authority during the 1950s is necessarily overschematized, because the kinds of power that can be wielded by various levels are in some ways inherently different. Fluctuations of influence in levels

have resulted from many local and infrastructural causes, not just from decisions in Peking or editorials of the *People's Daily*. Reference to that national
newspaper, and a few other party sources like it, has tended to obscure the
continuing, considerable diversity of political life in different parts of
China—although these media have also somewhat reduced that diversity over
time.

The official press, in particular the organs of CCP committees, is printed
for subscription mainly by bureaucratic offices, not by individuals. Between
1950 and 1956, the number of newspapers published at the national, regional,
and provincial levels increased scarcely at all, but their combined circulation
quadrupled (Liu, 1971, p. 134). Throughout the 1950s, the circulation of
these papers septupled. Subprovincial newspapers appeared in great numbers
during the Cultural Revolution, but were eliminated again after it. By Leninist principles, modern newspapers are supposed to play a major role in unifying a socialist country and in assuring compliance with central directives at
low levels. They no doubt help in achieving these aims, largely because party
activists pay some attention to them. But to fulfill their tasks among "the
masses," they must be more than centralist; they must also be widely read.
Local sources of information are often less boring to more readers than the
party's own press. At least in the PRC's first two decades, the circulation of
local newspapers was much larger. Even purist cadres knew that such media
could convey official messages to a greater (if less enthusiastic) audience than
could the more staid, official CCP organs. Also, delays at the post office,
which delivers newspapers in China, mean that local newspapers are usually
more up-to-date than papers distributed from more central places. Through
the late 1960s, this kind of decentralization was general in Chinese journalism. In no place (except Peking city at some times) has the *People's Daily*
exceeded the circulation of other, less completely central sources, especially
limited circulation and nonparty newspapers.

The content of the media became increasingly, though unevenly, centralized and homogenized during the 1970s, but word of mouth, local sources,
and foreign radio remained important. The characteristic virtue of modern
communications technologies (their ability to spread messages to many people
over a large space) has been somewhat separated by centralist ideals from the
characteristic virtues of traditional media (the credibility and interest of their
messages).

Degrees of regionalism or centralism can be indicated by resource flows,
as well as by information flows. For example, government budgets changed
importantly in this respect after mid-century (Lardy, 1975a; Donnithorne,
1967). At first, budget collection was easier for local officials than for central
functionaries, in part because communications and economic-monitoring facilities were only semimodern. As late as 1953, when the basic elements of the
PRC tax system had been established, 80 percent of all government revenues
were still collected by localities (Chi-jung Hsiao, 1954, p. 90). Public com-

pliance patterns and official career patterns were such that subprovincial jurisdictions did this job better than provinces, and provinces did it better than Peking could. In 1959, for example, Chungking remitted 45 percent of its total revenues to Szechwan, and Szechwan remitted 33 percent of its total revenues to the center (see Lardy, 1975a, p. 92). The rate of such remittances has generally been greater for coastal than for inland provinces.

The best indication of nonregionalism in China is the fact that leaders from many scattered provinces have contested for central power throughout the twentieth century. They have done this even when they partly used local bases to bid for national status, and even when localities remained administratively independent of each other to a large extent. Sun was born in Kwangtung, Chiang in Chekiang, Mao in Hunan, Hua in Shansi, Teng in Szechwan—and most of these leaders did not launch their efforts for central leadership from their native areas. Chinese from other places followed them. The country has been a single political stage at most times, despite the long-continued importance of provincialism.

Regionalism became even less frequently tolerated in the 1970s than it had been during the previous two decades. Apparently, the freedom available to leaders at the provincial level has been decreasing (for one kind of statistical confirmation, see Teiwes, 1974, p. 142). This gradual trend toward centralization is evident in the PRC, but it has been unsteady and far less clear-cut than in either Japan or Russia during their transitional periods.

BASE-LEVEL ORGANIZATION

When we turn our attention from the twentieth-century changes at the provincial and regional level to the character of base-level governing, we are usually given a picture of venerable ways becoming increasingly outmoded. In fact, the degenerated conditions of local government have been too uncritically assumed to represent a norm of traditional China. That the workings of local government and society at its base level were being deeply altered by deterioration of the old norms has been stressed throughout this study. The features of late Ch'ing governing, long in the making, were compounded by the extraordinary events of the Manchu dynasty's last century. But our emphasis must be on the extraordinary, not on the hypothetical regularities of "dynastic decline."

The Chinese dynastic cycle concept possesses very little explanatory value for any dynastic era, and it conceals useful explanatory factors in the Ch'ing. The cynicism and disaffection of the strategic elite stem from the opening decades of Manchu rule, and exerted gradually more impact on the operations of government through the 270 years of that regime. Two other factors intensified the loss of balance between center and locality. First, unprecedented population growth in the eighteenth century radically increased the scale of the government's task, while the means remained essentially unchanged. Second, unprecedented destruction and dislocation were caused by the nineteenth-century rebellions. It has been customary to see the former as the product of a dynastic cycle's second phase ("prosperity") and the latter as characteristic of the third phase ("decline"). Contrary to such formulaic interpretations, neither of these Ch'ing phenomena is typical of Chinese experience in other dynasties; both must be understood apart from familiar domestic problems. A third factor, the reversal of the silver flow at the beginning of the nineteenth century and the resulting deflation and fiscal and economic disorder, added to the woes of government. Elite cynicism, population growth, and huge rebellions, in combination by the nineteenth century, substantially altered the tasks and modes of government.

As the members of the elite changed in their private roles as local notables, informal government below the county magistracy changed. The elite became less responsive to a weakened central government's leadership, to altruistic impulses from its Confucian education, and to the need to celebrate its hard-won elite status through public acts of noblesse oblige. Higher status was used mainly to guarantee elite families' economic and political advantages, to prevent downward mobility. Elites became more stable, less legitimate in their own and the society's eyes, more exploitative. Wealthy leaders first abandoned the ideal of the public career in favor of other careers: a profound change in the character of rural society took place when local notables were freed both from responsibility to a supervising government and from restraints imposed by local social settings. Both of these obligations had previously been sustained by the elite recruitment system, which was deteriorating and finally became defunct. The extent to which leaders actually abandoned rural society to become absentee landlords, leaving the management of their properties in the hands of lineage members or hired bailiffs is a matter of regional variation, as well as one of scholarly dispute. To whatever extent it happened, further dislocation occurred.

The old elite had been one whose members achieved their status individually, with much effort; but in the early twentieth century it became, for most members, status with secure local dominance. It was unthreatened by the fluidity and the demands that had existed in the old society. Critical writings and satirical fiction used the term "*lieh shen*" to describe the gentry members who were most susceptible to evil trends in society. Communist writings extend it to the whole elite, and in translation make it come out "degenerate gentry," with perhaps unintended aptness. The rural elite of the twentieth century, whether or not its members were all "degenerates" as individuals, represented a devolution from the imperial society's gentry; it had indeed degenerated in many ways.

After 1911, along with these qualitative changes in the elite, there was a marked tendency to appoint local officials from within provinces, even from within localities, and thus to abandon the old "law of avoidance." Local bosses became more directly and openly the representatives of local notables.

A concomitant change was that new upward mobility patterns, via commerce, the military, the new education system, and especially new careers in the treaty port cities, greatly diversified options for the ambitious and the able. New opportunities freed the upwardly and outwardly mobile from the old patterns of expected behavior and success, just as the perpetuation of elite status freed the rural elite from responsible and regularizing community obligations. Finally, the government had lost its monopoly on the punishments and rewards to which the elite had been subject, so that elite behavior became more varied, "less principled" in Chinese eyes. These developments of course held germs of greater individuality and enlarged personal freedom; in important ways, they were consonant with modernizing change. In the short term, however, they were not remarkably productive of better government.

Writings from the early decades of this century indicate declining morale in many local administrations. The outward forms of social relationships remained much the same, adding to the misleading impression that the old social order was unaffected, that the norms of traditional society were really being perpetuated. The actual changes can best be demonstrated by drawing illustrations from descriptive literature: after the mid-nineteenth century, future rights to government offices, often very substantial and important ones, were put on sale. Examination degrees had long been available for purchase, but now some titles to policy-making posts came onto a new kind of futures market. A title such as "expectant first-class subprefect" could be used to gain the actual office. In most cases, such titles were purchased by well-to-do families for their younger male members, either as a form of future job insurance or just for conspicuous consumption. In the "Introduction" to *Landlord and Labor in Late Imperial China* by Jing Su and Luo Lun (1978, p. 30), Endymion Wilkinson describes a family in Shantung that had purchased four such degrees and offices, but had used none of them. This family was only interested in commerce, and in making money. The family's leader "summed up his attitude toward education by saying, 'There's no point in us studying; the poor kids have already done it for us.' He was presumably referring to the children of the poorer families of his clan, for, even if the landlords were scornful of education, they still recognized its utility, and many provided the funds for clan or family schools. If these landlords did not, on the whole, attempt to climb into the ranks of the Confucian gentry through the regular channels of the examination system, they certainly attempted to raise their status by purchasing official titles. Many of them, too, were active in district and village affairs, sometimes joining the local informal sub-bureaucracy and always using their influence in the local networks of entrenched wealth and power through which the gentry and the officials of the central government acted."

Those comments summarize a full century of a family's history, from the early nineteenth century to the early twentieth, by which time the head of a wealthy family could reflect utter cynicism about education in relation to the practical goals of retaining wealth and achieving status. The high literacy of the old elite now held little relevance. For the lineage, however, education was still of peripheral value; it no longer represented the "main chance," but it offered a kind of supplemental job insurance for lineage members. The single career ideal still existed, but only as the model of some superficial features in an elite life style devoid of cultivation and public obligation. In fact, private or military careers were now pursued with the greatest vigor, even by many leaders in government.

Education was thus separated from the functions it had served in the old society, and this was a profound historical change. The cynicism of this early twentieth-century landlord would have been culturally incongruous a century or even half a century earlier. As wealth and careers were gained in new ways, the political integration of center and locality was diminished. As more routes to high success could be found entirely within regions, there was no need for a successful leader to go through the regularizing influences of examinations at the national level, or to interact with a homogenizing political milieu along the way. Such changes could only lower the prestige and effectiveness of county government. The county magistracy, which had been important for centuries, was no longer the nexus of the national elite's interaction with village society. Localities no longer had any prominent, on-the-spot example of civilian career prestige or success in public service.

These hypotheses agree with more general findings on local government in the Nanking decade. Hung-mao Tien (1972, p. 130) states:

> During the imperial reign magistrates acquired their position through competitive examinations. The destruction of the examination system in 1905 and of the imperial order itself in 1911 shook the foundations of the magistrates' formal careers and removed the source of their authority and power. Although magistrates continued to hold office in many provinces, they now had to live under a different set of rules, which, in the final analysis, were the personal requirements of regional warlords. There were no longer definite procedures or behavioral norms.

The same study finds the educational level of magistrates lower in the 1930s than at the turn of the century, finds that natives of the provinces in which they served far outnumbered outsiders, and finds that duties borne by county governments had declined in importance. Specifically, as county magistrates became subject to warlord politics, taxes were not forwarded to the central government, reports were not made, and the representation of central interests in the county magistracy disappeared. Tax collection was one of the two basic tasks of local government and was traditionally subject to elaborate regularization and control, but by the 1930s, effective bureaucratic oversight of tax collection was nil. Local bosses came to control the fiscal management of local society, because the integrating functions of education and bureaucratic centralization were lost, and no one responsible to China's government was on the scene to do the job. Hung-mao Tien (1972, p. 164) writes thus about counties in the provinces where the Nationalist government made its most intense efforts in the 1930s:

> Some counties had established granaries (*liang-kuei*) staffed by several clerks who were to prepare and maintain grain tax records. . . . Many counties never even had a *liang-kuei*. Instead the magistrates often assigned the grain clerk's job to the headman of an administrative village [Tien's term for *ch'ü, hsiang, pao*, and the like, administrative units, not natural villages], the *hsiang-chang*, who could hardly perform it without relying on families that had traditionally collected land taxes in the area. There are at least two reasons why local administrators had to rely on these people. First, local governments had no proper records of land ownership on which to base tax assessments and were making little progress in compiling them. Thus the relatively comprehensive records kept by the numerous families who had been living for decades on the collection of taxes, and who had become a semi-bur-eaucratic group, were indispensable. Second, many counties were so large that it was impossible to maintain an administrative network down to the village level, forcing the county governments to seek the cooperation of the rural gentry.

By the 1930s, "rural gentry" had become a vague term for families of relatively high social status and wealth; for this period it already lacks the precise definition that it had in the nineteenth century and earlier. What Tien's statement implies is that the remnants of the old *li-chia* tax collection administrative network (which was often combined into the *pao-chia* defense network by late Ch'ing times) persisted under the management of families who had become semibureaucratic local tax managers. This occurred because the county magistrate's office had lost its functions. It represents a shift of control from bureaucratic and semibureaucratic structures under central constraints to local bosses under no such constraints.

In a few places that had central government sponsorship, local government remained active. Sidney D. Gamble offers our most complete description of a county in early republican China in his *Ting Hsien: A North China Rural Community* (1954), based on data collected between 1926 and 1933. County administrative structures and their social services expanded impressively (Gamble, 1954, esp. pp. 125–145). Ting Hsien, however, was a "model county" receiving national and international attention. Hung-mao Tien's data provide a better basis for generalization. Tien found that when the KMT in the 1930s tried to recentralize local administration in the hands of the magistrates, "county government had not been functioning as a center of political authority for decades, and as a result many problems simply went unsolved, especially in the many counties with over a million people" (Tien, 1972, p. 103). A. Doak Barnett, describing a "reformed county" in the immediate shadow of the Chungking government during the war years in Szechwan, concludes by relating inversely the degree of local democracy achieved to the existence of an elected county council:

> The "democratic" *Hsien* Council tends to be an obstacle to, rather than an instrument of, change. The reasons for this should be obvious in view of what has

already been said about social organization in the region. As one high-ranking member of the *Hsien* government expressed it to me: "There isn't a single tenant in the whole Council. Many of the Council members are able men, but they are all men of wealth, education and leisure. They are conservative and aren't interested in changing the *status quo!*" (Barnett, 1963, p. 154)

Where the central government could bring pressure to bear on a county by appointing a vigorous county magistrate, the balance of central and local interests could be regained. But even in Barnett's Pa Hsien in 1947, local society was run by a club of notables who were a "degenerated gentry" compared with the norm for late imperial society. Functionally, they did little, regardless of the institutional innovations in county government. Striking evidence of the failure to make new county institutions work can be seen in the decision of the KMT in the 1930s to reinstitute the *pao-chia* local security administration (see "Central Government: Adaptation to New Needs," in Chapter 3). The alternative road, not taken, would have been to develop elected village governments. "By reviving the *pao-chia* system the Kuomintang allied itself with rural elites oriented toward the status quo. As one writer remarked in the 1930s, 'Heads of Chia and Pao must be local rich peasants or landlords, no outsiders being eligible'" (Tien, 1972, p. 112). By the 1930s, the heads of *pao* and *chia* were the established local bosses in their localities, although a century earlier the *pao-chia* heads had been responsible to central authority through magistrates. Even Gamble (1954, pp. 142–143), in describing his "model county" with its array of new political reforms, writes tellingly that "the usual village government was a headman and a vice-head selected by and assisted by recognized influential men of the village community or representatives of the influential families. . . . The youth of so many of the village heads and vice-heads would seem to indicate that in many cases they were selected because of the prestige of their families rather than for their own leadership."

The device of using village headmen, "nominated by the inhabitants . . . to be approved by the magistrate," had been proposed as early as 1865–1866 by Tseng Kuo-fan for resisting the Nien rebels in Honan, although it was not implemented then (Liu, "The Ch'ing Restoration," *Cambridge History of China,* vol. 10, pt. 1. p. 471). The institutional innovation of elected village headmen could not emerge even in model counties of the 1920s and 1930s, because Chinese rural society was becoming a closed society. Central government had previously been exercised through regular bureaucratic procedures, and a community of interests had been shared by the bureaucracy and the open elite of the old society. In the twentieth century, those controlling and regularizing influences were gone. Local elites became fixed in place, altered their objectives, and assumed ever more fully autonomous roles in local management. The relevance of these changes for modernization is manifold, particularly because they lessened both the central government's capacity to mobilize society and the society's susceptibility to central management.

It has been noted by many writers that the era from the 1870s to the 1940s witnessed a great expansion of secret societies, in the numbers of their members, the scope of their regional influence, and the range of their activities. Some writers see this change as a byproduct of modernization in society (Chesneaux in Chesneaux, ed., 1972, p. 8), but it is not difficult to suggest other explanations. Secret society doctrines had been important in social dissidence since 1790, and the suppression of the Taiping rebellion had incidentally contributed to the spread of clandestine organizations. As local government declined throughout the second half of the nineteenth century, many unusual means to preserve safety were resorted to. Secret societies found an intermediary role in organizing illegal activities, even as they sometimes organized guarantees of safety from other illegal activities and rebellion. As the controls in society loosened, both opportunities and needs increased for mid-level organizations, intermediate between family lineages and the state. By the 1920s, it was clear that most so-called secret societies were closely in league with the new bosses of local society. Nonetheless, the most important of them had their own principles, and retained some independence of action. They were not merely tools of the exploiting elite. Their existence reveals some kinds of social change, but we do not know enough about them to make definitive statements about their causes and wider social roles.

Even though the disintegration of Chinese local politics is insufficiently understood, there is ample indirect evidence for its effects in recent times. Repeated central-government efforts to "penetrate the villages" were undertaken, and social energies were mobilized temporarily when national politics met important interests at low levels.

The CCP land reform campaigns exemplify these developments. As Chapter 3 makes clear, traditional Chinese villages were scarcely political units; they were mainly concentrations of houses. Artificially imposed administrative units, not hamlets, were held responsible for certain tax and police functions by separate offices of the state, and lineages were the bases of most social action. Village leadership meant little, even when it formally existed. The communist land reforms tended to change this situation. The jurisdictions of the meetings that communists called to distribute land, and usually to criticize the landlords, were hamlets. The categories in which these meetings placed households and individuals were wealth groups, not lineages. The rich did not fare badly at these meetings, initially, if they were anti-Japanese.

Subsequently, during the civil war, they often fared very badly. The war was fought not only at battle fronts. Labeling now changed the format and content of local politics. Only a small percentage of local households (in some places, about 10 percent; in many, half that) were branded as landlords or rich peasants; and often three-quarters of the households emerged from this process with the labels of poor or hired landless peasants. But the new labels of this sort prevented free social and physical mobility in subsequent years, in a way that was contrary to either Chinese traditional or imported universalistic standards. The loosening of local political structures, in some other developing countries such as Japan, did not involve such quick imposition of new kinds of criteria, with government sanction, to prejudge individuals after old systems had been cast aside.

In cities, other campaigns in the early 1950s similarly labeled households. Urban individuals therefore acquired new kinds of interests in government decisions. First, police of the newly installed regional governments rounded up comprador capitalists, secret society leaders, and other leaders of noncommunist organizations. The Five-Anti Campaign in businesses then brought "national capitalists" to a greater appreciation of communist power. Proletarian activists could distinguish themselves in these urban campaigns, just as poor peasants could in the land reforms. In each case, a major outcome of these movements was a rise of household members' desires to use their new official titles, if they were good, for future personal benefit in education, work, and other public fields. If the titles were not good, the first item of personal business with government was to see whether the labels might be altered. In a modernizing society, changing quickly and developing many new kinds of activities, relatively permanent labels of this sort had deep influence on individuals' lives, particularly as more resources and jobs fell under government control.

In cities, each person was assigned a changeable, personal "class status" (*chieh-chi ch'eng-fen*) on the basis of the kind of job he or she held, as well as a more permanent "family background" (*chia-t'ing ch'u-shen*) on the basis of the source of income of the household in which he or she grew up. The family label, indicating a social class, followed an individual throughout life and was difficult to alter.

In the countryside, the family-origin labels were usually the sole ones. Since farming was the general occupation, categories based on current work could not mollify persons who had been assigned bad labels in the other system, as sometimes happened in cities. Until "bad class elements" underwent reform, they were not allowed to vote, to express themselves in public, or to hold office without special permission. They could sometimes be assigned undesirable jobs or be put under pressure to move their residence registrations to unpopular places. They were the first objects of criticism in any movement to revive class struggle (such as occurred in 1951–1952, late 1957, 1963–1964, 1967–1968, and locally at other times; see also "Mobility," Chapter 11).

In campaigns, the revolutionary government produced many unintended consequences. Household solidarity was sometimes strengthened in campaigns or by the institutions that mass movements created. Often the communists had to rely on large collectivities inherited from republican and imperial times. For example in the 1950s, the CCP used traditional guilds (*hang-yeh*) as a basis for its efforts to control small urban shops and factories. Where these institutions had not previously existed, or where they were found to be politically unreliable, they were established or reformed. Many of the guilds were later metamorphized into state corporations, which confederated and socialized (nominally or really) most of the country's private nonfarm business enterprises. It would have been impossible for the founders of New China to rebuild the country from scratch, even presuming they wanted to do so. They had to adapt many inherited institutions, because China remained poor and their own resources were far from infinite. When they reused older institutions at local levels, they usually attempted to reform the authority patterns that came with those old units, but their success in doing so was mixed.

The formats of most Chinese politics remain local. This is the prime fact of China's constitution-in-practice, or of any generalization about the influences that shape most citizens' behavior. After the turn of the century at least, politics was no longer integrated with the national theater by the old lineage and career system, nor yet integrated with it by modern means. This is probably one reason militarism played such a prominent role in the country's politics during the next fifty years. China's twentieth-century economic and communications infrastructure could support no other kind of practical constitution than a decentralized one—any modern or traditional ideals of centralism notwithstanding. It is difficult to say much about political transformation in China that is not affected by the vastness of the government's managerial task.

Some sense of the size of the administrative problem that all modernizing governments in China have faced during this century can be given by listing the current administrative levels of this polity. We will describe their general pattern since the Great Leap Forward, ignoring, for the sake of convenience, the occasional changes in the levels' names or official statuses. The typical Chinese citizen, a peasant, has been separated from the nation's central authorities by at least seven major layers of organization (not counting the multiprovince regions, which have sometimes been important also). China has twenty-nine province-level units, each of which has seven or eight special districts, each of which has roughly ten counties, each of which has about twenty-five communes, which average sixteen production brigades, each of which contains seven or eight production teams (either natural villages or large parts of them), and these in turn average about thirty-three households, which contain a mean of 4.4 persons on a national basis.

Although observers of the PRC during Mao's rule, when local information was sparse, often stated otherwise, and despite the fact that communications in China have improved greatly since the 1920s and 1930s, there is no certainty that any political intention from Peking will descend this ladder of levels without being deeply affected by interests at the intervening layers.

The mass campaigns, a major institution used by the CCP to try to penetrate local units, are organized centrally, usually after a national conference attended by representatives of all regions. Such conferences are characterized by long speeches and work reports explaining the current tasks of government, as defined by the center. Representatives break into small groups for discussion, to provide some broader participation and to make sure that the top leadership's line is widely understood. Reports and telephone conferences are subsequently used to monitor performance. "Work teams" (*kung-tso tui*) of ranking cadres from higher offices may then be dispatched to visit lower levels and supervise campaigns directly, in a style inherited from old imperial inspections. Low officials' careers may be judged by their achievements in such campaigns, but the local functionaries must guess whether or not the line that they are given to implement will change by the time any such judgment comes. Campaigns, thus orchestrated at conferences, may strengthen more central control of low-level behavior, if the subordinate cadres believe that the leadership and line will not change soon. On the other hand, campaigns may also weaken such control, if local officials believe that problems or criticisms will follow implementation.

These transformations of political patterns have generally been typified by temporary or permanent expansion of relatively central government control. For example, work places in city and country alike underwent symbolic changes of titles—for many of them, more than once—during the 1950s. New signs were posted outside doors, even if enough CCP experts had not yet been trained to monitor what lay behind them. Demobilized servicemen from the civil and Korean wars often received such training and became important civilian cadres, but the posts to be filled were numerous. Campaigns cowed many old personnel into compliance with new regulations. In the 1956–1958 period "politics took command" either because new personnel were brought in or because old ones were now trusted. The economic depression after the Leap, however, forced the party to relax controls in many firms. Somewhat more stable local structures, in which titles bore greater relation to leadership, were created in the years of party resurgence after 1962. Authoritarianism in these local contexts produced sharp resentment against many cadres, which exploded in cities during the Cultural Revolution. On a recurrent basis, the CCP attempted to control more than it had the resources to control. Indiscipline in its own ranks, and its democratic ideal that the masses must be persuaded of decisions before anything was done, recurrently destabilized local authority. Many mid-level party functionaries were in theory responsible to their lower constituents, but in fact their careers were mainly determined by their superiors. To counteract this common flow in the party's government, certain expedients were attempted.

One such measure was purely bureaucratic: the multiplication and standardization of local offices. In villages, for example, traditional heads had been far less important than informal leaders. Now most production teams had not only heads, but deputy heads and accountants. This kind of standardization at first helped higher levels control lower ones, although the Leap and post-Leap reorganizations of the countryside were very radical. Only 24,000 communes were established throughout China in 1958, but by 1962 there were three times as many. Thereafter, the number was again reduced to about 50,000. Similarly, there were about 500,000 production brigades in 1958, but almost one-third of these were soon absorbed into the rest, so that production brigades became generally coincident with the "higher-level" agricultural producers' co-ops that had been fairly successful in 1956–1957. Local situations, not just national decisions, help determine much national policy in the PRC, despite governmental hopes and presumptions about planning.

Probably most heads of production teams in China are now party members. (Parish and Whyte, 1978, suggest that 70 percent of them in the coastal province of Kwangtung now have membership.) Production teams usually have populations in excess of 100 persons, but a large minority of them still contains no party member. Admission to the CCP in many cases may be a compensation for taking responsibility for team operations, including the sensitive tasks of tax collection and the allocation of produce. This is an important but somewhat risky local job, subject to criticism from constituencies both below and above. Membership in China's foremost organization, the CCP, is apparently used as an incentive to leadership in low-level units, especially the teams. That honor no doubt helps team heads in their work, but the party may need such men as much as they need it.

Technological modernization has thus far been less important for peasants than organizational changes. Decisions on when to plant crops, what small investments to undertake, and how to use labor time were traditionally made in households. In some contemporary villages, a notice board, assigning daily tasks to individuals, is posted publicly so that farmers know what to do. The form of organization is surely modern—in fact, almost industrial—even though farm technology has changed very little in most places and the bureaucratization of agriculture in this kind of setting can damp initiative.

Production brigade headships are apparently the most authoritative local jobs for many purposes in China's countryside. Brigade leaders are to some extent autonomous of higher and lower constituencies so that representation and leadership can often take place. Brigades on average contain about 1,000 persons; their leaders are the "colonels" of the Chinese rural system. The great majority of them are party members, but they retain some independence of higher levels because of a generally great span-of-control problem just above them (the next highest level, the commune, on average contains more than fifteen brigades). Brigade headquarters are ordinarily at some physical distance from the commune seats. In many political and financial situations of local import, they may make decisions. They are far too numerous for provincial, special district, or county cadres to monitor effectively (counties on average contain about 400 brigades each); so if a brigade head can establish rapport with his commune liaisons, he may be reasonably free to lead. Even though commune and brigade officers are recurrently threatened by visits from work teams sent by county and higher levels, the party would have to replace any of them whom it demoted or expelled. The CCP could not afford to do this often.

In urban situations also, campaigns may either restrict or enhance the autonomy of low-level leaders. For example, the downward mobility of managers from capitalist families affected their capacity to lead their socialized enterprises. China is not the first nation in which modernization has destabilized the careers of local potentates. However, sometimes campaigns unintentionally strengthened local leaders. For example, in the field of education, during much of the 1960s before the Cultural Revolution, new directives concerning admissions, curricula, examinations, and many other topics were shot out from the central government so quickly that their frequent changes could be used by low-level officials to justify practically any policy in local schools.

The 1970s saw a resuscitation of the CCP at its lower levels. This development depended on rebuilding the confidence and authority of the city-based leaders who had been criticized during the Cultural Revolution and had withdrawn their services from government. The pattern was not new: just as foreign-associated leaders had been put to flight in 1949, or patriotic noncommunists had been eased from local economic power in the 1950s, the party and its associated organizations had been decimated by the Cultural Revolution. For example, not until 1973 did the Young Communist League, from which the party traditionally recruited its new members, hold new province-level congresses. Even at the central level, contests for power continued with little abatement but were hidden, allegorical, connotative, drawn out, and inconclusive. Premier Chou could run the ministries in a business-as-usual manner; but the future bases of government policy were uncertain, as Mao Tse-tung faded into honored senescence, and then died.

The later decline of government-by-campaign boded diverse and contrary effects on the autonomy of local leaders. But the growth of the communications infrastructure, and the expansion of the number of educated cadres available to the state will probably integrate local and regional leadership to a greater extent in the future.

Special Interests and Legal Structure

INTERESTS, CONFLICT, AND PARTICIPATION

The modernization process in its middle stages tends to create new specialized groups and to increase differences between rural and urban areas. This latter change is a reversal of the norm in traditional China, where town and country were culturally better integrated than in premodern Europe (Mote, 1970, p. 48).

Traditional government administration, whether urban or rural, had concentrated on two functions: the collection of taxes and the maintenance of order. Large projects, especially canals, were sometimes undertaken by government, but the fiscal and police functions predominated. In the late nineteenth century, the quick growth of certain cities such as Shanghai, caused by refugees from rebellions and by early industrialization, led to more public services being provided. The scope of official policy increased, as communications, health, customs, and other functions were expanded. In the late nineteenth and early twentieth centuries, this process often occurred under the auspices of regional governments, and it progressed very unevenly, starting in the prosperous coastal areas. At the same time, new resources were available to finance expanded realms of public policy, at least for some city folk. Slightly larger portions of the population were brought under government purview. But in China, more than in Japan or Russia during their transitional periods, the relevant governments were often local, and many rural areas of the nation were not affected by these changes at all.

The importance of urban support for modernizing government was vividly illustrated in the Nanking decade and the war years. The KMT was vastly better represented in cities than in the countryside. Mid-1930s data suggest that in Shanghai, where practically all the households were urban, the KMT had roughly one member per 200 population; but in Shantung, where 89 percent of the households were rural, there was about one KMT member for each 5,000 people. Even in rural Szechwan, which had greater KMT strength, the density of members was only double that very low rate (estimated from Tien, 1972, p. 30 and Weng Chih-yung, 1952, *"fu-piao,"* p. 17). The KMT lost strength during the 1940s, partly because the Japanese evicted it from China's largest cities during the war. Major differences between the KMT and CCP are not just to be sought in their goals for China (and surely not in their formal or informal decision-making structures) but also in their varying abilities to maintain their organizations during the war, when the elites of both were expelled from China's coastal cities.

Land reform and the Korean War were crucial in structuring the CCP's rural and urban support groups, respectively, in the early 1950s. The party's appeals in country and city were very different. In farming areas, traditional groups were partially replaced by new groups, based on carefully labeled social classes and often led by people who were new to local leadership. In cities, however, the communists' first major political appeal was nationalistic, broadly based, and essentially modern. For a few years after 1949 it could remain so, because the Korean War gave the CCP many opportunities to make demands on noncommunist but patriotic urban groups that, without the war, would have been far less inclined to accept the reforms implicit in these claims. Previously foreign-influenced institutions, including many universities and large enterprises, could be easily reorganized on grounds of the war, as they could not have been without it. Intraparty tension between previous leaders in the "white" (mainly urban) and "red" (mainly rural) areas was recurrent throughout this period; the "reds" sporadically purged "white" communists who espoused less radical policies in productive urban areas. This tension might well have been more severe, if the Korean War had not provided urban cadres with unexpected political resources to compel changes quickly. Internal CCP conflicts of this sort were nonetheless as closely connected to China's partial modernization as were the combined urban-rural bases of CCP success.

New occupational groups, especially in cities, provided expanding sources of government revenue and talent. The CCP organized functional "circles" (*chieh*) in scientific, commercial, and professional fields, through which to monitor such groups. They were not generally attracted to communism, but they were patriotic; so "third force" political parties were set up for them. Their role in politics was subordinated to that of the dominant party, but specialized journals were published for modern specialized readerships: *Jen-min jih-pao* (*People's Daily*) for cadres, *Chung-kuo ch'ing-nien pao* for youths, *Kung-jen jih-pao* for workers, *Kuang-ming jih-pao* for liberals in higher education and science, *Ta-kung pao* mostly for small businessmen, *Wen-hui pao* mostly for teachers, and many others (see Liu Mu and Ch'en Shou-ch'u, 1956, p. 203).

Government patronage of these specialized groups, under either the CCP or KMT, showed their lack of political autonomy. Labor unions, nonruling political parties, commercial and industrial guilds, women's and sports federations, youth clubs, and many other associations were all labeled "mass organizations (*ch'ün-chung tsu-chih*). Interest groups, as such, were not legitimate. Especially in the PRC under Mao, even in movements when such groups were not fully controlled, the presumption was that all mass organizations must serve goals approved by the central elite.

To recruit patriotic talent even after the "transition to socialism," for example, Mao in May 1956 delivered the first version of the "Hundred Flowers" speech, calling for free criticism of officials, including CCP members. This speech was widely quoted and played by tape recorder at meetings for invited noncommunist leaders for several months thereafter. Criticisms of party administration were invited, and they came in a diverse barrage that climaxed in May 1957. Some critics pointed out that the party, in its escalation of campaigns to reorganize economic units, had broken explicit promises of autonomy to noncommunist businessmen and patriots. Others made a contrary complaint: that the party had promised official leadership and resources to many units in exchange for their cooperation and assimilation into new, larger institutions—and after the units were relabeled and consolidated, these supports had not been supplied. Specific charges were aired against cadres who had been arrogant or unfaithful to their constituents. General complaints were aired against rule by campaigns, and against the party's habit of establishing new institutions and then forgetting about them.

The CCP later converted the criticism forums into struggle meetings against "rightists." In the antirightist movement, the party's opponents were sent in large numbers to rural camps. The criticism also gave high leaders a justification for sending many mid-level party members, some of whom had been criticized, from cities to smaller market towns, especially to county seats. Their presence in those places provided the administrative base for the partial decentralization of administrative power that was ordered in early 1958 and was soon called the Great Leap Forward.

The Leap was partly an effort by the top communist leadership, already growing old (on average, approaching the traditional retirement age of 60), to force younger CCP leaders, largely recruited from cities, to recapture in the 1950s their own experience of earlier decades by organizing peasants in rural areas. But this experiment did not work the second time around, because the problems of modernization had changed. In the earlier period, the overwhelming problems had been order and organization; in the later era, all the big political issues were at least partly economic.

The Leap, in immediate terms, was an economic failure. The regime's popular constituency was reduced by the quick depression that followed Leap efforts to collectivize rural incentives and to reorganize rural distribution on a scale larger than the old marketing structure had sustained (Skinner, 1964–1965). The party dealt with damage to its base in cities, and let urban critics dissipate their energies harmlessly by calling for a formalistic "Second Hundred Flowers" movement. After the 1957 experience, this elicited few blooms, because it seemed clear what the sequel would be. Workers were also placated by an expansion of part-time education to employ their time in these slow years. Urban residents were appeased with a partial relaxation of party controls over employment, schooling, and the immigration of their family members to cities. In the countryside, middle peasants were placated by the party's restoration of private plots, and by devolution of the main rural accounting unit to the low production-team level.

As soon as the economy revived after 1962, the party once again moved to narrow and purify its particular constituency. New affirmative action school policies, mandated in 1963, made more education available to the offspring of "workers," "poor peasants," and "lower-middle peasants" (all officially labeled in police dossiers on households). This program was continued for several years. Unionized proletarians benefited disproportionately from the economic recovery, and many of their brethren doing temporary and contract labor became part-time agricultural workers, under programs legitimized by the national government. Rural "work teams" were dispatched in 1964–1965 to revive class struggle. "Political departments," such as had previously existed only in the army, were established in many urban offices to increase political activity there. After the post-Leap depression, work teams and political departments were used extensively to define and mobilize the regime's main bases of support at low levels. Their emphasis on class struggle naturally tended to polarize local politics—but this effect was far greater in cities than in rural areas, where the post-Leap order was stabilized in small units, as

Chapter 11 shows. Especially in urban schools, students from ''good'' social class origins formed clubs that were nascent conflict groups. The division of political formats between modern cities and the rest of China had never before (not even in the civil war) been so obvious. Partial modernization, and investment and wage and household-registration policies that separated urban from rural life, had created two surprisingly separate theaters of Chinese politics. The Cultural Revolution was acted in the urban one.

Divisions in the national leadership became obvious by late 1965, and political splits among urban conflict groups accelerated through the end of 1967. These divisions began in cultural institutions such as publishing houses and universities, then spread to schools, and then to factories, newspapers, and government offices. Not only did this process fracture the social bases of the CCP and of government bureaucracies in cities, it allowed the formation of free-lance political cliques that had only loose connections with any high communist leaders. Their new platforms were almost always couched in socialist language, but the basic frustrations behind the Cultural Revolution—especially the frustrations involved in seeking or protecting good urban jobs— were social in a general sense. They grew directly from previous local CCP efforts to administer, sometimes with more favoritism than fairness, extensive controls over personal careers and life styles. The Cultural Revolution did not become a civil war; nor properly speaking was it even a revolution, because relative peace still reigned in rural areas, and because most army commanders enforced regionally unified political lines. In cities, political constituencies fragmented along quasi-class lines, determined by the benefits or injuries their members had received under CCP rule in the mid–1960s. In China as a whole, however, the main lines of cleavage were regional, just as they had been during most of the republican period. The merely semimodern format of Chinese politics, in the transformation period, never emerged more starkly than in the contrast between urban turmoil and rural nonchalance in most areas during the Cultural Revolution.

Mao distinguished himself from other major twentieth-century Chinese leaders, in the People's Republic as well as the National Republic, because of anarchist strains in his politics that opposed bureaucracy. Maoist policies during the Great Leap and the Cultural Revolution evinced a sometime desire to criticize official institutions. This view did not legitimize spontaneous, autonomous interest groups. It merely authorized their temporary emergence for the purpose of attacking established offices, when Mao as the supreme leader thought the attack was justified on substantive grounds. It was not a democratic doctrine, because approvals for ''spontaneous'' democratic organization were supposed to come on a case-by-case basis from central levels.

''Tendencies of articulation,'' to use Franklin Griffiths's term for weak interest coteries, have nonetheless emerged among business cadres, academics, urban residents, peasant leaders, and other categories of potential political actors. The government has not allowed their open organization as pressure groups. Since the 1920s the only fully political major Chinese organizations have been the two major parties: the KMT and the CCP. Neither tolerated the growth of major dissident groups of full citizen participation. Other Chinese groups (other political parties in particular) remained in existence. Usually composed of like-minded persons, these groups are without major political power. Both before and after 1949, mass organizations have had little meaning for decisions in politics.

Labor unions have remained unimportant, despite the supposed proletarian nature of the PRC dictatorship. Some unions in earlier decades were used by the CCP or were infiltrated or suppressed by the KMT. Both then and now, they are pawns in politics, not kings. Nor have peasant associations transformed the political life of rural China, by developing as autonomous centers of power that might operate effectively above their own small jurisdictions. Eighty percent of the population has remained apart from the initiatives of national politics; their activities in larger formats have been dominated by the CCP.

In other words, the sometime liberalism of a part of China's elite at the century's beginning has proved to be almost entirely ephemeral. Nonliberal models in politics have had far greater influence than liberal ones. Both the CCP and KMT were affected by Comintern advice in structuring their internal affairs, especially during the 1920s. In the 1930s and 1940s, the examples of Stalin and Hitler were important to KMT and CCP leaders; and in the 1950s, the PRC adopted the outward trappings of Stalinist institutions in a wholesale fashion.

Indigenous Chinese forms of organization, derived especially from the recent centuries of disintegration under the Manchus, played a major antiliberal role along with these imported models. As no less an authority than the communist General Chu Teh once pointed out, the division of the CCP into disciplined party cells derives not mainly from the Soviet pattern, but from the structure of the Chinese secret societies as they developed during the late Ch'ing. The same remark could equally well have been made about the early KMT, which under Sun Yat-sen was a lineal descendant of such organizations (especially among Cantonese and Hakkas). Brotherhoods do not owe their internal integration to formal rules; instead, they owe it to familylike, generally hierarchal loyalty bonds that develop between leaders and followers. The self-conscious search by many prominent Chinese for a stable constitution during the twentieth century arises, above all, from the loss of a center of loyalty for administrators and for social groups, which accompanied the slow fall of a whole civilization during recent centuries.

As Tawney once noted, "Political forces in China resemble Chinese rivers. The pressure on the dykes is enormous, but unseen; it is only when they burst that the strain is realized" (1932, p. 161). This applies to the communist era at least as well as to its forebear, the republican period about which it was written. The CCP enforced relatively intense controls, especially in modernized urban areas, to channel people's energies in ways that the government thought would lead to further modernization. The habits of campaigns, dossiers, inspection teams, and work teams meant partial control over the lives of millions. After the Five-Anti Movement of 1951–1952, entrepreneurs could not safely take initiatives in business; it took several years to train new socialist managers to replace them. Intellectuals were repressed by school reorganizations during the Korean War; and then successively again in the Hu Feng Campaign, the antirightist movement, the Second Hundred Flowers, and the Cultural Revolution. Some students of "bad" class backgrounds were prevented by official policies from continuing their educations, especially after 1962. Many faced a choice of becoming peasants or taking nonunionized, irregular urban jobs. These controls were efficient only under some economic conditions, and they fostered frustration in many groups. All together, they encouraged neither stable political institutions nor the development of autonomous political participation.

CONSTITUTIONS AND LEGAL STRUCTURES

Chinese constitutionalism in this century is a quixotic topic, because the nation's leaders have searched ceaselessly for formal institutions to give structure to politics, but without much permanent success. China has really had two kinds of constitutions in these eight decades. Public attention has been focused on formal state charters, such as President Ts'ao K'un's "permanent constitution" of 1923 (which was used, for a brief time, in the immediate vicinity of the capital). A second, unwritten, informal kind of constitution has been more important; its main provisions can be generalized from evident patterns such as the responsibilities regularly assumed in government by military men, and from the political roles that naturally devolved to the regional and local units of so huge a country.

Even before the rise of the republic, in the decade of 1901–1911, new political forms emerged at the national level, changing old patterns of public management and raising expectations that the government would gradually be democratized. Constitutions promulgated by fiat were eventually to be replaced by a constitution drafted in a representative congress and approved by a national referendum. Provincial assemblies were soon to be directly elected, allowing representative participation in the legislative process. The executive branch was to enlarge its political duties toward the citizens in a responsible, multiparty system, providing the panoply of new services that progressive governments then performed. Such expectations were frustrated by the failure of the national government in the warlord era to become more than a claimant to power, by its inability to devote more than superficial attention to improved government. In a few provinces, such as Shansi under the "model warlord" Yen Hsi-shan, political experimentation with new structures was allowed or even encouraged; but participatory democracy did not emerge in any wide area. Eventually, the concept of "political tutelage" under a one-party state superseded all efforts to create a strong central government under an open political system.

Many conscious links with the past were cut in Chinese politics after 1911. The past was no longer the source of approved political institutions, although it remained a source of social ethics and values. New forms in the state, new content in education, and new goals of wealth and strength were accepted rapidly, if superficially. Throughout this century, the Chinese have sought a systematic replacement for the Confucian state that was explicitly rejected by some elite members. Revolution (*ko-ming*) no longer meant mere withdrawal of the dynastic mandate; it meant withdrawal from the comprehensive task of the old politics, which was to make sure that the political system served people in a moral manner. What revolutionaries did, in effect, was to specialize the modern aspects of this task over time, so that its comprehensiveness was no longer important. They felt that the many needed improvements could only be made serially. Good government in one field might imply backsliding in another—yet it should be attempted, for the sake of some quick progress even of a limited sort. Needed rights could justify present wrongs. To promote revolution in some fields, such leaders have regularly been willing to give temporary short shrift to other fields.

This viewpoint permeates many tutelage theories of the road to political progress and is not unique to China. Echoes of it can be heard in developing societies as different as Victorian England and present-day Mexico. J. S. Mill during his later years, in this respect like Lenin or Itō Hirobumi, preceded Sun and Mao in insisting on the importance of a modernizing elite that can see what society needs first, and what other values it may postpone, for its long-term benefit. These thinkers differed in many ways, especially as regards political means. They were together on the notion that a requisite of progress is firm leadership by a group that knows how to direct the energies of the masses into channels that will prove fruitful for modern goals.

In China politics took command, and government was seen by its members as the main source of initiatives that might modernize other sectors of society—economic, educational, and so on. Political development, despite propaganda about it by Chinese regimes, was at the bottom of most government lists of priorities. This has also been a convenient doctrine for incumbents.

After the provisional constitution of 1912 and the "permanent constitution" of 1923, the Nanking government promulgated another provisional constitution in 1931 and then a regular constitution for the Republic of China in 1946. This last document (which is still the supreme law on Taiwan) provides in Article 7 that there should be no legal distinction between persons on the basis of social classes or political parties (see Fu Ping-ch'ang, 1954, p. 1). The first full constitution of the PRC, promulgated in 1954, nonetheless indicated in its preamble that the "broad people's democratic united front led by

the Communist Party of China . . . will continue to play its part in mobilizing and rallying the whole people in the struggle to fulfill the general tasks of
the state during the transition period and to oppose enemies within and without." The 1970 draft constitution contained direct references to CCP dominance over the the government, and Article 2 of both the 1975 and 1978 state
constitutions provided in identical wording that "the Communist Party of
China is the core of leadership of the whole Chinese people." (Article 15 in
1975 and Article 19 in 1978 also contain the unprecedented provision that the
national army is not commanded by any state official, but by the chairman of
the CCP.)

In other words, recent state constitutions instruct China's government to
follow a specific party. In earlier twentieth-century Chinese charters, where
this was not explicit (as in Ts'ao K'un's 1923 effort to garner international
respect for Chinese law so that extraterritoriality might end, or in the 1946
KMT appeal to domestic and foreign liberals while a civil war loomed), the
reality was nonetheless always a government by parties and factions.
Throughout the century, the internal structure of the regime at its top decision-making levels has taken the form of one or more familylike groups. This
has been China's real constitution, and it was the natural outcome of the disintegration, in the late-imperial and transitional periods, of a common basis
for more fully representative rule. Political wills splintered at this time, officialdom represented only some of them, and there was little unity or common
understanding on how to attain good rule. If this situation differed from what
many political actors on the scene have perceived in China's past and hoped
for its future, they have not yet found a way to change it.

An analytically better approach to constitutionalism in China would be to
examine party charters, not state documents. Especially in the communist
period, these charters are short, unspecific, enthusiastic, and constantly revised. They are really manifestoes, not supreme laws. Their main aim has
been to describe the flame of revolution at the times when they were written;
but this has flickered. CCP constitutions do not last long after they are
adopted. No national party congress can meet without writing a new one.
This habit implies deep doubts that the political process can feasibly be stable
in China's modernization, and the expectation realizes itself. The classic
statement of the problem is in the Tenth Party Congress constitution of 1973,
which provides: "The future is bright; the road is tortuous."

These constitutions represent the leadership's perception of the amount of
constancy that is realistically possible in government, so it will come as no
surprise that laws are often ignored or modified in practice. China is not the
first country in which governmental decisions have been highly personalized
and situational. Proceduralism is weak. There is a public sense, expressed by
the leaders in some campaigns, that no useful means to strengthen it exist
without impeding the performance of governmental tasks that are deemed
vital. Many cases of nonproceduralism could be cited here; the most obvious

ones deal with the succession to national leadership. The party constitution of 1969 and the state draft constitution of 1970 were not so dilatory and indirect as most charters concerning the procedures for transfer of power after Mao's expected death. Instead, they straightforwardly named the new incumbent (Lin Piao) rather than wasting words on how he might be chosen. When Chairman Mao died some years later, in 1976, Hua Kuo-feng assumed the premiership (not on an acting basis) without the approval of a national people's congress, even though Article 17 of the state constitution written just the previous year unequivocally required such approval. Not to care about such niceties (even when they surely could have been arranged) can be conceived as a revolutionary position. Attention to formalities has been considered, at least until recently, a less than fully constructive preoccupation in politics.

Even this position is not constant. At the end of 1978, legalism came into vogue. This change had precedents in recent decades; the reasons for the recurrence did not differ from those prevailing in years such as 1923, 1946, 1954, or 1956–1957: the official desire to recruit more talent for state purposes, after an era when the most important state policies had alienated people who could provide needed expertise and initiative. It is unlikely that the 1978–1979 trend will blossom into any basic official commitment to liberal guarantees in politics, even if a succession of future "thaws" over several decades may gradually create an uneven trend toward minor political freedoms in urban areas.

Movements for procedural politics in contemporary China harbor a great ambiguity. Government officials may well espouse the more regular application of laws for the sake of better planning and control. Nonofficial spokesmen, however, can advocate legalism for precisely the opposite purpose, that is, for guaranteeing the autonomous rights of individuals and nongovernment groups. Both of these conflicting rationales for proceduralism are "modernizing," but their content differs crucially. In fact, they indicate an allowance for wide variation in the concept of political modernization. Stalin, for example, was the most widely proclaimed proceduralist in Russian history; his constitution of 1936 was the supreme law of the USSR into the mid-1970s, and the bureaucratic regulations he laid down in many functional areas (including the security services) made state performance more uniform, thorough, extensive, and in fact more predictable than at any previous time in his country's experience. Proceduralism is indispensable to serious dictators in large countries. Stalin's lawyers criticized the less statist thinking of their predecessors of the Leninist period in the 1920s. PRC constitutions owe much to their work, especially to the "Stalin Constitution" of 1936. A liberal view of modernization, however, would distinguish the development of political institutions that repress autonomous participation from those that channel many constituencies into the formation of official policies. This view is bolstered by a few individualist traditions of the Confucian school, but such traditions are usually overwhelmed by the contrary inheritance of centralism.

Traditional justifications for state structures that disallow open political participation are complemented by truly modernizing, developmental justifications for the same thing. The legalist school of old Chinese thought, which has been much praised in the PRC and is anti-Confucian, prescribes severe laws, promulgated dictatorially and applied bureaucratically to assure the dominance of a central arbiter for disputes. Imported liberal theories also prescribe stable procedures; but their aim is completely different, because the legalists had no liberal interest in maintaining autonomous centers of power that could countervail the state or conflict within it. However, legalism and liberalism have some interesting concurrences, too. They both imply doubts that mere moral norms can ever provide a sufficiently stable basis for politics. The collapse of the old system and the rise of modern tasks have given old statist traditions a new lease on life while creating no fertile ground for liberal trends. Strict centralist ideals have been on the Chinese scene for a long time, and they will not soon disappear, even if "democracy walls" recommend that they should.

Neolegalist ideals have been generally victorious in political life ever since the climactic first decade of this century. No *tria politica* has separated executive functions from legislative or judicial ones. The word of the leader who is deemed to preserve order, the moral interpretation of the national teacher, has been as readily enforced as any law. Directives from Nanking or Peking have often been vague. Complex regulations have ordinarily applied only within the bureaucracy, and local variations in implementation have often been explicitly allowed. Coordination and norm specificity have been sacrificed for the sake of mobilization, and for the fulfillment of norms that do not specify details of the actions they mandate. Moralistic movements under the KMT, such as the New Life Movement of the 1930s, are examples of this tendency. The history of the PRC is studded with moral-coercive campaigns, which together made China's formal constitutions almost completely irrelevant to what happened in Chinese politics.

International Comparisons

Comparisons of China's political performance in the twentieth century with that of other latecomers to modernization must focus on China's loss of political unity—its lack of a national government—after 1916, and the struggle to regain it in the following decades through a succession of ever more radical experiments with imported, unevenly naturalized political forms. Full political unity was not reachieved until 1949 or 1950, and political reconstruction according to revolutionary concepts has kept the nation in rapid, uneven, occasionally contradictory, political change for thirty years, despite the continuity of the communist government's control.

Political leadership benefited neither from continuity of the symbolic head

315

of state, as in Japan, nor from the quick replacement of the old, powerfully centralized leadership by the new, forceful, national revolutionary leadership, as in the transfer of power from tsarist to Soviet Russia. China's thirty-five-year interregnum denied it the guiding force of state power during the years in which other modernizing nations most purposively were applying that power to effect modernizing change. Since 1950 China has possessed the features of a strong one-party state apparatus engaged in central planning, but the distinctive characteristics of the base from which planned (and concomitant unplanned) change has occurred have continued to qualify all similarities with Soviet and other ostensibly shared socialist experience.

China undergoing modernizing change has been strengthened by the deeply shared sense of community within "Chinese-ness." It is closer to Japan in its ethnic solidarity, although much of its heritage of Manchu imperial territory has been dominated by local majorities of non-Han racial groups. As with the USSR's 50 percent non-Russian population, China's strategically placed 5 percent non-Han peoples have been politically neutralized by Stalinist policies toward "national minorities."

A feature of political life that China most obviously shares with many other modernizing nations is the transvaluation of cultural pride in the emergence of a powerful nationalism, a process the more remarkable because of the explicit denial of its bases in the premodern Chinese high culture. This process of political change has steadily intensified from the first years of the present century, and has been a hallmark of both the Nationalist and the communist governments, despite the theoretical anomalies in the latter case. The effort to replace Tibetan, Mongolian, and other minority nationalisms with Chinese national identity can be compared with the difficulties of instituting overriding national consciousness in post-1948 India, perhaps also in the USSR and in some other modernizing nations, but the sheer bulk of Han Chinese preponderance has limited the significance of this problem in China.

The ideal of democracy has become a twentieth-century political universal; no government can fail to grant it lip service and to claim to foster its emergence. China compares unfavorably with all other large modernizing societies in the extent of its experience with the mechanics of democratic politics. In contrast with both Japan and Russia, it has no historic experience with elections, elected representative assemblies, democratic constitutions, or other instruments of democratic participation, although it more closely resembles the Soviet Union, which has been retrograde compared with tsarist Russia's record in at least beginning to implement the politics of free choice. The fact that precommunist China had never held a national election (probably not even an open local election until 1980), even within a limited electorate, makes its distance from democracy even greater than that of most other communist countries.

China has shared with many late modernizers the feature of militarized politics. It reached its peak in the warlord era of 1916 to 1927, but a gradual usurpation of the political process by the military had been underway for some decades before that, and only gradually receded thereafter. Compared with the USSR's, communist China's army-party-state has at several points had to rely somewhat more obviously on its armed forces to maintain or recover political stability. It is not clear to what extent the army's vast potential for furthering guided social change has been exploited by the government of communist China.

The international comparisons leave us with a gauge for measuring the remarkable political changes witnessed in twentieth-century China, and strengthen our understanding of the immensity of China's unfinished tasks. They may also suggest that the political component is the crucial, in some senses the independent variable in China's modernization.

CHAPTER TEN

Economic Structure and Growth

Dᴀᴛᴀ ᴏɴ Cʜɪɴᴀ's ᴇᴄᴏɴᴏᴍɪᴄ ᴅᴇᴠᴇʟᴏᴘᴍᴇɴᴛ ᴀʀᴇ ɪɴᴄᴏᴍᴘʟᴇᴛᴇ, but enough are available to paint the following broad picture: (1) Initial growth was largely confined to coastal treaty ports, and agriculture showed long-term stagnation (as well as sharp seasonal variations) in the 1920s to 1940s, while urban industrial growth produced only modest change in the economy's structure. (2) The rates of product growth generally accelerated under the influence of modern changes, with great fluctuations. (3) Sustained growth, especially of industry, began at a very rapid rate in the 1950s, although its rate slowed in the following two decades. Table 10.1, like the chapter as a whole, is based on data that are not definitive. They do, however, indicate that gross domestic product slightly accelerated between World War I and the 1930s. Snaillike though this growth was, it is remarkable for having occurred at all. Frequent harvest failures, disruptions of transport, and widespread lawlessness and political disunity during most of the republican period did not prevent development in some areas and in some periods. The destruction that characterized the late 1930s and the 1940s, however, brought the economy to its nadir at the time of the communist victory, and recovery had to take place in the early 1950s before growth could resume and accelerate.

Between 1916 and 1933, when industrial production increased, most factories still used coal, wood, and crop byproducts, but electrical output nonetheless expanded eighteenfold. The volume of railway freight rose 62 percent, from 2.94 billion ton-kilometers to 4.77. (This increase was more rapid than that of value added in transportation as a whole, indicating the substitution of modern for conventional means of transport; Yeh, 1965,

318

Table 10.1 Estimates of Chinese economic growth

Economic Indicators	1914-18	1931-36	1952-57	1972-77
GDP (billion 1933 *yuan*)	24.26*	29.13*	37.97	102.52
Population (millions)	440*	500*	602	897
GDP per capita (*yuan*/person)	55.1 *	58.3 *	63.1	114.2

GDP per capita (*yuan*/person) *Average Annual Rate of Growth (%)*	1914/18– 1931/36	1931/36– 1952/57	1952/57– 1972/77	
GDP	1.08*	1.27*	5.00	
Population	0.75*	0.89*	2.00	
GDP per capita	0.33*	0.38*	3.00	

Sectoral Share of GDP (%)	1914-18	1931-36	1958	1977
Agriculture	65.9*	62.9*	53.6	33.0*
Manufacturing	16.2*	18.9*	18.5	39.0*
Services	17.9*	18.2*	27.9	28.0*

Gross Domestic Investment (%)	1914-18	1931-36	1952-57	1972-77
1933 Prices	—	5*	16*	20-23*

* These statistics are particularly subject to error; for example, the 1977 sectoral share percentages are based on 1958–1977 growth rates in agriculture and industry, with services treated as the residual to make up total estimated 1977 GDP, so that price weight changes would introduce error into these data even though they indicate general trends accurately. For estimates in this calculation, see Central Intelligence Agency, 1978.

Sources of Data: For 1914–1918, 1931–1936, and 1952–1957 see K. C. Yeh in *Conference on Modern Chinese Economic History,* 1978, pp. 125–158; these data include the northeast. Data for 1972–1977 are estimates based on extrapolations of 1952–1958 data according to various rates of growth. These rates for the expansion of GDP and GDP per capita for the first half of the twentieth century are nearly the same as those estimated by Subramanian Swamy (1979, pp. 25–46).

p. 14) Despite strikes and disruption in the transport of raw materials during the mid-1920s, the production of manufactures such as cotton cloth soared, because of new capacity in the textile industry. The modern sector had to rely largely on foreign trade to obtain the grains and fibers that the agricultural sector failed to provide in this period.

Farm production, as reflected in the output of China's three major crops of wheat, rice, and cotton may have risen very slightly, but farm output mainly fluctuated during the century's first three decades (before declining in the 1940s). Some regions, such as the northeast, exported raw materials such as soy beans, but these exports declined after 1931. Manchuria was unusual—an area with an expanding, marketable farm surplus. The surplus resulted from reclamation of new land and from agricultural diversification, aided by railroad expansion, by a growth of commercial processing, and by vigorous foreign demand in Japan and Europe. As a recently settled frontier amenable to extensive cultivation, Manchuria was atypical. Other areas had more difficulty finding the means to increase per capita production.

After 1949, gross domestic product expanded rapidly, except during recessions caused by the Great Leap Forward, the Cultural Revolution, and political crises surrounding the succession issue around 1976. The gross domestic product rose quickly in the 1950s, but then it fell just as rapidly for three years after 1958. Output stagnated or declined in 1959–1962, 1967–1968, and 1974–1977, with spurts of recovery between these periods. The annual average rate of real economic growth, over the entire three decades after mid-century, was about 6 percent (5 percent if the first years of speedy recovery are omitted in Table 10.1). The annual population increase was about 2 percent. The share of the manufacturing sector's contribution to gross domestic product rose from less than two-tenths in 1952 to about four-tenths in 1978. Agriculture's share of this output value, during the same years, declined from almost six-tenths to about three-tenths. Although the prices used to compare sectors favor manufacturing, there is no doubt about manufacturing's overtaking agriculture as the leading contributor to GDP.

This was quick structural change—more rapid than sectoral changes that occurred in France, Germany, or Sweden during the comparable periods of the nineteenth century, or more recently in Japan. The alteration was not accompanied by a large proportional shift of labor from agriculture to manufacturing, as had been the case for western countries in the nineteenth century and for latecomers to industrialization in the twentieth. Furthermore, this change occurred as land reform was equalizing income distribution within most localities—a situation that contrasts with the earlier modernizing countries mentioned above.

Productivity per capita increased less rapidly (about 3 percent per year after the early 1950s) and was particularly slow to change in agriculture. Irrespective of this poor productivity performance after 1949, the rate of capital accumulation has been impressive. The country has developed a particular kind of socialist system that has great ability to garner savings. By 1978, the share of capital formation in gross domestic product was roughly one-quarter, up from one-twentieth in 1933. Industry (especially socialist light industry, whose product prices can be set high relative to input prices so that government profits are large) has been the main means of gathering savings from both urban and rural consumers. China's means of accumulation have been somewhat different from those of the Soviet planned economy of the 1930s, which placed an even greater emphasis on heavy industry. The PRC has not received large-scale capital aid from other countries (except the USSR for specific projects in the 1950s), and its post-1949 loans have all been repaid.

In summary, Chinese economic growth began slowly before World War I, generally accelerated in the more modern sectors until the 1930s, and then stagnated or declined until 1949. In the decade after 1949, it resumed at a much faster speed, but eventually growth slowed and on several occasions was interrupted—by a brief depression in 1959–1962 and by temporary stagnation in the political unrest associated with the Gang of Four.

The Economic Foundation

THE INSTITUTIONAL CONTEXT

The economic activism of the late Ch'ing court was limited both by foreign influences and by a failure to perceive the full importance of modern prosperity to imperial stability. By 1900, a major fiscal burden faced the government from several sources: first, the court had negotiated a series of military loans from foreign powers beginning as early as 1851; and even by the end of the century, these had still not been repaid. Second, China had borrowed 47.8 million pounds sterling in 1899–1900, to pay Japan after military defeat. The Boxer uprising in 1900 also created indemnities to various foreign powers of roughly 67.5 million pounds. These costs to the government imposed a high burden just as some officials in China first became committed to modernization. The transfer of large sums abroad required the Ch'ing state to relinquish claims to domestic resources that might perhaps have been used for modern projects. In some years during the early 1900s, these transfers, if fully met, would have amounted to roughly 10 percent of the government's total revenue. As pointed out in Chapter 8, however, some of these funds soon came to be used within China, and borrowing also brought in foreign funds for productive purposes such as railway construction.

By 1917, warlord armies influenced the availability of productive factors for agriculture as well as the distribution of goods between treaty ports and the countryside. These armies tended to plunder village economies and levy new taxes on farmers. They absconded with animals, carts, and the sons and hired hands of rural households. They hindered sowing and harvesting and prevented rapid recovery from the effects of natural disasters. Local administrations could no longer be effectively coordinated to mobilize resources either to alleviate scarcity in calamitous years or to promote growth in better times. In 1921, six provinces suffered large floods; and in 1923, twelve had droughts or floods. Crop pests sporadically ravaged the land. Of course, these problems had existed from ancient times, but some Chinese now perceived that the government was not effectively developing the available modern means to solve them. Grain and industrial crops from the interior failed to reach cities as reliably as in the past. The treaty ports turned to foreign sources, and during the early 1920s, China became for the first time in its history a major importer of food. Some foreigners called China the land of famine.

In 1931, a survey that covered 28 million people in fourteen provinces reported that the grain supply fell short of minimum needs by at least 5 percent (Chang Hsin-i, 1932, p. 33). Natural disasters were slightly less destructive during the 1930s, and in the region of Kiangsu and Chekiang, conditions greatly improved as the new Nanking government began to build a new economic infrastructure. The beneficial effects of modern transport, education, and agricultural research nonetheless still spread only a little way inland from the coast or the Yangtze.

The Chinese economy became dualistic, with factory development mainly in scattered treaty ports and improved agriculture mainly in their suburbs. Throughout the vast hinterland, farming, handicrafts, and commerce remained backward, operated by muscle power and still frequently disturbed by the shocks of weather and war. The commercial separation of city from countryside was exacerbated after 1937, when Japan extended its invasion of China; inflation spiraled during the 1940s. Although rural markets did not revert to barter during that decade as is often the case in hyperinflations, the flow of rural products to urban markets slowed to a trickle.

Within a context of increasing military separatism, economic dualism, and fluctuations of economic activity, modern growth nevertheless continued slowly. Within the treaty ports, foreign and Chinese entrepreneurs combined and competed to create a small but solid industrial foundation.

GROWTH MECHANISMS AND PHASES

Impressive economic development from low starting points occurred even between 1895 and 1911. In 1911, the country had 9,618 km of railroad (more than half located in North China); in 1895, there had been only 1,000 km. Up to 1894, only 101 western and Sino-foreign firms had been founded, whose total capital was probably not above 20 million Chinese dollars (Yen, 1955, pp. 116–122, 190). By 1911, there were still only 96 western firms and 40 Sino-foreign firms, but their capital investment had increased to 103 million Chinese dollars. In the same period, 549 Chinese firms began using modern machinery propelled by inanimate power, with an investment coming to roughly 120 million Chinese dollars (Feuerwerker, 1969, pp. 35–38). The number of modern factories continued to increase, particularly during the vigorous industrial booms in the treaty ports during 1918–1920 and 1928–1932. By 1933, their number stood at 3,167 and they employed more than half a million industrial workers.

These new factories supplied large quantities of inexpensive, standard-quality goods, and they had to compete with a well-developed Chinese handicraft sector as well as with foreign imports. Of the total number of modern factories in 1937 (3,935), 22 percent produced cotton yarn and cloth, 23 percent processed food, and 14 percent manufactured chemical products. These plants, which accounted for roughly three-fifths of all factories, absorbed 61 percent of the capital investment and employed 75 percent of the work force.

Furthermore, 62 percent of all modern factories were in the provinces of Kiangsu and Chekiang, with most of these located in Shanghai, Nanking, and Hangchow (Ch'en Chen, 1961, vol. 4, pp. 92, 97).

Although the new factories mainly manufactured consumer goods, perhaps a fifth or even a quarter of them supplied the handicraft sector with intermediary products such as yarn, dyes, and machine-reeled silk. Some traditional cloth centers (as in Shantung's Wei county) and silk-weaving centers (such as Hangchow and Shun-te) came to depend on modern factories for their supplies. Before World War I, their prosperity increased with that of the manufacturing sector, but by the 1920s and early 1930s old handicraft centers felt more severe competition from modern mills producing the same articles (Fong, 1936, pp. 55–56).

Many factories after 1895 began to adopt advanced technology, and vertical integration of manufacturing processes was thus spurred. Textile plants and equipment before 1911 had been based on designs from England and could not use Chinese cotton; they manufactured a yarn of only 10–14 counts. But after World War I, more of them used textile equipment from the United States. Textile engineering improved, and more mills began producing yarn of 20–40 and 60–80 counts. The shift from low- to high-count yarn coincided with the gradual installation of machine weaving. In the period 1928–1932, when this shift became more prevalent, mill design greatly improved, and labor productivity rose. But between 1933 and 1935, the industry suffered a slump, so that idle capacity rose, and many firms incurred such big liabilities that banks acquired ownership. Only after 1936 did the textile industry revive (Chu Hsien-fang, 1936, pp. 2–3). By then, private ownership had given way to considerable state control.

Another measure of the industrial spurt has been provided by John K. Chang's study (1969) of production between 1912 and 1949. There are difficulties in any estimate of 1912 product, but his bold work indicates a remarkable industrial spurt during the republican period. Chang constructed an industrial index based on 1935 prices, taking a dozen manufactured products that represent about 60 percent of the gross output value in the modern sector. He found that the annual rate of growth of industrial output for the 1912–1936 period was 9.2 percent. Production grew at 13.8 percent between 1912 and 1920, and by 8.3 percent between 1923 and 1936. To be sure, the combined product of all modern factories, handicrafts, mining, and utilities still only amounted to 10.5 percent of net domestic production in 1933. If handicraft products are excluded, the "modern" industrial share only amounted to 3.4 percent. But an industrial spurt had nonetheless taken place within an economy of huge size, dominated by labor-intensive methods of production and premodern technology.

The capital-goods-producing part of this modern sector was extremely small, but it provided an important base for expanding the supply of such equipment after 1949. For example, the Wahson Electrical Manufacturing

Co. was formed in 1917 to produce current limiters, feeder panels, and power switches. In 1922, the Chinese National Electrical and Pottery Co. was founded, and three technicians trained at Westinghouse Electric in the United States became the driving force for this firm's growth. It manufactured equipment that could handle as many as 33,000 volts. Similar firms sprang up in the 1920s and 1930s to produce wires, cables, batteries, and a variety of insulating materials. Industry was concentrated in only a few cities, especially Shanghai, but by 1935, more than 400 of the 2,000 principal towns in the country had electric power plants (Moser, 1935, p. 13). Equipment of reasonably good quality was produced at low cost.

Chinese factories expanded in the modern sector, despite competition from foreign-owned firms, imports of manufactured goods, and frequent disruptions of hinterland raw-material and product markets. Under such conditions, how did enterprises grow? The state gave them little assistance; municipal governments in most treaty ports lacked the plenary authority and fiscal control to encourage their growth directly—in fact, these firms sponsored local port governments more than the governments sponsored them. Within the enclaves, there were no controls over prices or incomes, which fluctuated according to supply and demand. Foreign capital moved freely in and out of the treaty ports. Municipal governments provided neither protection nor subsidy to industry, although taxation was also low. These governments supplied only the basic services such as law and order, water, power, and waste disposal.

For example, in Shanghai between 1905 and 1914, the city council established by Chinese civic leaders provided enlightened management to ensure public health, safety, and the movement of human traffic and goods. The council's policies were implemented by an executive committee; beneath the committee was a small bureaucracy, which collected taxes, managed the police force, and provided a variety of other services such as cleaning and lighting the streets (Elvin and Skinner, eds., 1974, p. 260). Chinese entrepreneurs perceived the city ports as oases providing business security and a better life style, havens where they could not only preserve their wealth by investing in manufacturing, but enjoy more freedom to use it.

What were the overall effects of such investment? When the prices of raw materials lagged behind those of finished goods, an investment boom occurred. Entrepreneurs financed this investment partly from business savings and partly from bank credit, especially western bank loans. Their new machines had to be purchased from abroad. Typically, a factory could begin to manufacture products a year or so after it ordered its machinery. But increased competition for raw materials by foreign and Chinese manufacturers gradually bid up prices, and sometimes disruptions in the hinterland also sent domestic raw material costs soaring. Some items, such as wheat, could be imported cheaply, and raw material and food imports rose. Eventually, input prices would converge on the prices of finished goods. Profit margins were thus squeezed, and firms had to cut back their production, creating idle capacity and causing bankruptcies. Foreign exchange-rate fluctuations exacerbated these import and export booms. Whenever the silver price fell relative to the US dollar or English pound, imports appeared to be cheaper than when the price of silver rose.

This treaty port business cycle shows up in the slump period 1923–1926 and the boom period 1927–1931, when foreign trade decreased and commodity prices changed accordingly. In 1924–1925, the prices of yarn and cotton converged, but they diverged in 1927 and 1929. Imports of textile machinery and aniline dyes fell sharply from 1923 to 1925, when the industry slumped; but these imports began to rise in late 1927, and then they soared until 1931 as textile firms ordered new equipment and constructed new factories. During the "golden period" of Chinese industrialization, 1914–1921, the decline of consumer imports and the divergence of manufactures and materials prices encouraged a surge of Chinese investment. Large-scale construction occurred between 1919 and 1922, when imports of construction goods also greatly increased.

The demand for manufactured consumer goods came from relatively prosperous families in cities, whose income elasticity of demand for food and other basic commodities was very low. A study of 1,270 students in Yenching University, Peking, in the early 1920s showed that only 28 percent of average family expenditures went for food (Milam, 1927, p. 430). But for workers' families, three-fifths or even three-quarters of expenditures went for food. Upper-income groups also purchased most of China's imports; the lower-income majority of households bought local handicrafts. If a manufacturing firm wished to expand its market share greatly, it had to sell at a price that lower-income families could afford; this meant competing with the huge traditional sector. Modern firms, therefore, tended to confine their sales to Chinese cities and to markets abroad.

As long as China exported agricultural and mineral goods, whose production did not extensively rely on other sectors, foreign demand did not stimulate new manufacturing. China mainly imported consumer goods, which only satisfied final demand and as Robert Dernberger notes, "served neither as inputs to China's production nor as capital goods to increase China's productive capacity" (in Perkins, ed., 1975, pp. 34–35). These weak domestic-linkage features of China's foreign trade only partially explain why the manufacturing sector remained small, but they reflect the broad characteristics of the Chinese economy at this time.

Tens of thousands of local enterprises still used technologies that relied primarily on labor rather than capital. They exchanged products through networks of brokers and merchants, within a hierarchy of towns and villages that served as periodic marketing centers. Handicraft production was still meshed with the crop cycle. Chinese entrepreneurs had to wait for favorable conditions to organize manufacturing on a factory basis: suitable technologies, profits as attractive as in other investments (real estate, money lending, commerce), and sufficient low-cost loans to purchase machinery. These conditions emerged only in treaty ports, where Westerners also had the freedom to establish banks and other enterprises. Without the markets of these unregulated centers and the presence of large-scale modern foreign firms, Chinese businesses would not have had the incentive or example to organize as they did.

Much has been written about the repressive effects of foreign investments on the Chinese business community, but in fact, these credits had many diverse results. The exact size of direct foreign investment in China is not known, but Remer and Wu Cheng-ming separately calculate that in 1902 it totaled slightly over 500 million US dollars. Their estimates for 1914 were 1,067 and 1,090 million, respectively; for 1930, 2,483 and 2,347 million, respectively. Another estimate, for 1936, places direct foreign investment at a lower figure, 1,149 million US dollars. (Fujiwara, 1976, p. 51). Foreign capital in manufacturing for 1936 was 149 million US dollars, or 13 percent of total investment, according to this estimate. The bulk of external transfers into China in 1936 went to finance foreign trade (30 percent) and to support banking and insurance (25 percent). The largest share of foreign credits thus underwrote Chinese imports and benefited Chinese business firms through bank loans. These external stimulants to the Chinese economy were important.

China's lack of tariff protection is also alleged to have put the economy at a disadvantage. Infant industries could not be fostered; Chinese firms claimed to be at the mercy of foreign importers and manufacturers. It is true that the government before 1928 lacked the financial capability to establish and promote many new manufacturing firms; Chinese businessmen were left to their own devices. But the treaty ports also enabled Chinese entrepreneurs to learn new techniques, borrow funds, and copy foreign business procedures. In these competitive port economies, any businessman could make a profit if he manufactured and distributed his product efficiently. Foreign businessmen had some advantages over Chinese in modern technology and credit, and in knowing about foreign markets. But Chinese businessmen also had advantages over foreigners in hiring labor, obtaining information about local production factors, and selling products domestically. Depending on the state of the market, the net advantage could tip either way. No ethnic group was internally unified enough to set prices or determine market shares for any commodity over the long term. When war came in the 1930s and 1940s, its effects overwhelmed all earlier developments in China's economy.

THE TRANSFORMATION AFTER 1949

The Communist Party that gained power in 1949 was dedicated to making the nation wealthy. As is often the case when a country becomes more unified after years of war, China's new leaders were strong—and factious. Fundamental differences over what kind of society China should become produced violent debates within the communist leadership, which put the nation on a zigzag course of economic modernization.

In 1949, the party confronted a series of severe problems and resource scarcities, which threatened to stymie efforts to launch industrialization or increase farm production: inflation was rampant. A large urban labor force was unemployed. Factories had run down during the war years. Foreign trade was only a trickle and was partially blockaded. Yet China also possessed some assets that could be used to revive the economy quickly. Slack use of capacity was widespread in some industries. There was, moreover, some potential for rapid increases in agricultural production, because with the end of the civil war, labor could return to farms and put more land into production. Factories were rebuilt, and the railway transport system was restored. New organizations were created under official auspices with the aim of shaping most behavior, including economic behavior. In terms of management patterns, an economic revolution occurred in China by stages, during the whole decade of the 1950s.

In this period, the Chinese economy had rapid but unsteady growth. Population increased more quickly than before, at about the same rate as grain. The supply of other foods rose faster. Above all, the state devoted an increasing portion of the gross domestic product to capital goods, which enhanced the capabilities of many sectors. This rapid capital accumulation in the 1950s allowed the acquisition of some modern technology. Increased savings and capital, along with more modern technology, led to an expansion of goods and services.

A paucity of statistics for some years makes it difficult to measure Chinese economic performance exactly, but recent research attests especially to increases of industrial production. Before 1949, the portion of GDP devoted to capital formation amounted to only 5 or 7 percent, depending upon the price measure used. Pre-1949 economic growth was characterized by the slow growth of savings, except in treaty ports. Savings rose to about one-fifth of GDP in 1957. By 1970, they stood at about one-third. The annual growth rate of savings from 1952 to 1970 was almost 9 percent. Rapid economic growth has originated, to a great extent, from the rising savings-GDP ratio. The fast increase of capital stock is most obvious in the industries producing machinery, metals, fuels, and electrical equipment.

China now leads the world in number of machine tools manufactured. Its petroleum and chemical industries have also expanded rapidly in recent years. Prior to 1949, various producer goods industries had been established in Tientsin, Hankow, Shanghai, and Canton. The state gave great encouragement to this sector, particularly during the 1950s, building new plants from scratch at inland sites. Sometimes the Soviet Union provided loans, and often Soviet investment patterns were followed. In 1949, the value of the producer goods sector was only 28 percent of gross industrial output value, but by 1957, its share had risen to 53 percent, and by 1973 probably to 65 percent. The most rapid spurt for this sector took place between 1952 and 1957, when it grew at 26 percent per year. From 1960 until 1971, its expansion averaged around 15 percent per year (T. Rawski in Perkins, ed., 1975, p. 222). Although this growth slowed temporarily in the mid-1970s the producer goods sector nevertheless turned out six times as much in 1975 as in 1957.

Greater savings made possible the creation of more industries, which in turn produced more capital. Certain kinds of capital grew very rapidly, for example in the energy industries. New reserves of energy, especially natural gas and petroleum, have been discovered in recent years, which suggests that China's energy reserves may be broadly similar to those of the USSR or the USA. Yet accessibility is especially difficult in China, and the consumption of energy is much lower than in these modernized countries. Most of the population is dependent on what is normally discarded as agricultural waste elsewhere. During the early 1970s, solid fuels accounted for more than three-quarters of total primary energy consumption (in the USA they accounted for only 19 percent; in the USSR, 39 percent). In 1974, China generated 108 billion kw of electricity, compared to only 7 billion in 1952. In 1974, it produced 35 billion cubic meters of natural gas, compared to none in 1952. And it produced 63 million metric tons of petroleum, but only 0.4 million tons in 1952 (Smil, 1976b, pp. 58 and 62).

With sufficient power thus available, Chinese industry could expand quickly, and it began to develop in areas other than the treaty ports. Heavy industrial plants now extend inland to Paotow and Urumchi in the northwest, and to Chengtu and Chungking in Szechwan. Coastal cities, especially the old ports, have been taxed to finance this expansion, even though they were by no means the sole source of savings. In return, some of them, such as Shanghai, have been authorized to establish high-technology factories of kinds that did not previously exist in China.

Between 1952 and 1957, the gross value of output in the iron and steel industry expanded at an average annual rate of 16 percent, a pace that is fairly representative for most producer goods. For the longer period 1952 to 1976, the annual rate of growth in all industry leveled at around 10 percent. It was considerably higher for producer goods than for consumers' industrial goods (although pricing problems make an accurate assessment of this difference difficult). Even allowing for the three brief periods of decline (1959–1962, 1967–1968, and 1974–1977), this is an impressive industrial growth record since the middle of the century. There is no sure way to calculate what the overall increase would have been if political factors had not caused it to fluctuate widely within fairly short periods.

Farm production quickly revived between 1949 and 1957, but not without some fluctuations in the harvest. Grain production increased at an annual rate of over 6 percent. Cotton output rose at almost 19 percent, a rapid rate attributable mainly to putting idle factors of production to work. However, as discussed in Chapter 11, population also began to expand at a more rapid rate than ever before, 1.8 percent annually for the same period. Living standards for the majority improved slightly, and the supply of agricultural materials for industrialization increased substantially. The state controlled consumption levels, and much of the increased crop production was used to finance the strong industrialization drive it also had launched.

The favorable agricultural trend was reversed between 1958 and 1961, when production declined sharply. This was caused mainly by the radical communization of the Great Leap Forward, which reduced incentives to labor in farming and disrupted market patterns. Farm output regained 1957 levels only in 1965. During the next eleven years, grain production increased at an annual rate of 2.7 percent, and cotton output grew at 3.2 percent. The usual estimate for population growth in this period is about 1.9 percent. Per capita availability of both food and fibers thus very gradually rose. For the twenty-six years between 1952 and 1978, the annual growth rate of farm production appears to have been around 2.3 percent, which is not high compared to other modernizing countries.

Thus, while China experienced a rapid industrial spurt, its agricultural production grew just slightly faster than population. Providing employment and consumer goods commensurate with population growth has imposed a huge burden on the economy. The country remains poor. The people may be, by some standards, adequately fed and clothed, but they do not live with abundance, and many items are stringently rationed. At the same time, China has enjoyed remarkable price stability, with consumer prices constant or even declining before the mid-1970s.

Modern manufacturing has grown rapidly, while per capita income has remained low. In 1977, China's per capita income was probably about 350 US dollars. This compares well (in a country with very little inflation) with a per capita income in the early 1950s of around $150, although by no means did all of the increase go to consumption. The rise of per capita income was led by modern manufacturing, and it has been uneven not just between sectors but also over different periods.

Between 1960 and 1980, China's agricultural growth, like most of its industrial growth, was achieved by an increase in factor inputs, not by a rise in their productivity. Apparently China has lavishly used its natural resources to achieve rapid increases of production. But no country can afford to squander scarce resources for very long. In the past few years, the leadership has sought to improve management, invite foreign investment, increase incentives, and obtain modern technology for the sake of raising factor productivity. If this program succeeds, growth rates for agriculture and light industry may increase.

The Allocation of Resources

Decisions on the use of resources determine how much can be invested, over time, and thus how an economy's structure will evolve. Before 1900, the slow rate of technological change and the minimal interaction of the state with the economy caused a very small share of output to be invested in reproducible capital. Enough savings were generated to divert only a small share of resources into capital.

The emergence of the treaty port economy in the late nineteenth century introduced a new element. These nodal ports, linked to foreign markets, began to use imported techniques, especially in plants established by foreign entrepreneurs who had great financial leverage and access to international markets. This process stimulated a gradual growth of national income and concurrent changes in the structure of the increasingly dualistic economy. The state during this period proved weak and ineffectual, and the treaty ports deserve virtually all of the credit for the modern growth China achieved at this time.

INCOME DISTRIBUTION

Although land was unequally distributed in China, by the early twentieth century a large portion of tenants had quasi-rights to land which were inalienable according to customary law. After 1920, a growing share of households lost some of their land. But land alone did not determine the distribution of income. As households switched their resources back and forth between farming, handicraft, and commerce, they influenced their incomes. Charles Roll found that Fukien province "had a low level of inequality, primarily because of the ability of its households to engage in nonagricultural occupations. Kwangtung, on the other hand, exhibited a low level of inequality because the distribution of farm land was relatively equal" (1980, p. 140). When Roll measured rural income distribution during the 1930s from a sample of 1.7 million households made in 1934, he found an income concentration ratio of 0.44, which coincides exactly with the arithmetic average of concentration coefficients for a large sample of developing countries in the early 1950s computed by Kuznets. In rural China during the 1930s, the top 20 percent of households received 50 percent of rural income, and the bottom 20 percent only claimed 5 percent (Roll, 1980, p. 46).

Income distribution in China after World War I probably became somewhat more unequal, as some cities became prosperous on the basis of slightly more diversified labor. By the same token, as urban income rose, the business community was able to save more and increase its investment.

CONSUMPTION, SAVINGS, AND INVESTMENT

Political decay and militarism after 1911 created havoc in the countryside. Taxes increased, some farmers lost their capital, great migrations of people to the northeast occurred, and famine periodically stalked the land in many provinces. Meanwhile the rural population continued growing, and only a modest portion of this increment could find satisfactory jobs in cities, although a larger number went there.

Rising per capita income and rising consumption standards enabled some city dwellers to enjoy a much better life. In parts of the countryside favored by peace and propinquity to treaty ports, consumption standards also improved slightly. Nevertheless, only the middle and upper classes were high savers and consumers. Low per capita incomes continued in the enclaves, in part because large numbers of migrants from villages came seeking employment. In the large cities of the 1920s, urban census reports showed 65 to 70 percent of the dwellers to be males, particularly those of employable age.

The business community, meanwhile, could expand investment by relying on foreign and domestic credit. Banks multiplied in number after 1900. Chinese *ch'ien-chuang* or native banks served as important suppliers of funds for small firms, and after 1927, the new Nanking government also became important in financial markets. The Nanking government's revenues increased from 334 million Chinese dollars in 1929 to 870 million in 1937. New borrowing rose threefold over this same period, to more than one-fifth of government expenditures (Young, 1971, p. 38). The Nanking government increased its revenue, mainly in the small area it ruled, by taxing landowners and businessmen and by floating bonds. These certificates were purchased by new banks, some of which the government had created to finance industry and communication. The attractive yields encouraged many investors to buy bonds rather than invest in manufacturing. During 1934–1935, in the world-wide depression, ownership of some factories in treaty ports such as Shanghai reverted to banks.

The Nanking government lacked the means to survey land values and systematize the rural tax system. By 1936, however, the government's financial situation had improved, and the economy was emerging from depression. Government bonds could be floated at rates of only 8 percent, compared to 15 or 20 percent five years earlier. In the absence of war, the government might have been able to balance its budget and launch fiscal reforms.

In 1936, however, 84 percent of the government budget went to support the army and refinance internal debt. As revenues increased each year, somewhat larger amounts could be spent for economic projects and services. New agencies for promoting economic development were established within the executive branch of the national government, which carried out surveys and made recommendations for reform and regulation. More new banks and credit associations were created to channel loans to businessmen and farmers. New agricultural colleges and research institutes were formed to develop seeds and improve farm techniques. Academic studies of the deleterious impact of silver exports on farm purchasing power apparently played a role in the formulation in 1935 of an official decree pegging Chinese currency to the

English pound and taking China off the silver standard (John L. Buck in Sih, ed., 1970, p. 190). The construction during this period of railways, roads, schools, and water conservation projects in the provinces under Nanking was very impressive.

Despite these successes, the Kuomintang never succeeded in making even Chekiang and Kiangsu into fully "model provinces." These areas might in time have developed a modern fiscal system that could have mobilized larger resources, but the Japanese army arrived before such an evolution took place. Had the KMT carried out a far-reaching land tax reform, altered East China's dual ownership land tenure system, and encouraged more farmers to use modern technology, it might have been able to garner more revenues for building the economic infrastructure. Chiang Kai-shek, however, was devoted to unifying his nation, and this project consumed resources. Even more important, Japan seized the most lucrative urban tax bases. Modernization was thwarted in the 1930s more for political than for economic reasons.

Had China been able to move more fully into an economic boom during 1937, the upsurge in farmers' purchasing power likely would have enabled more peasants to participate in cooperatives, such as were then being established throughout the Shanghai-Nanking-Hangchow region. More farmers could have purchased high-yield and disease-resistant seeds. This conjecture is not without evidence. On the small Liaotung Peninsula, controlled by Japan after 1906, a transformation of agriculture actually took place. From 1910–1912 to 1920–1921, farm output increased 2.74 percent annually; between 1920–1921 and 1935–1937, the increase was 5.71 percent (Myers and Ulie, 1972, p. 340). This progress resulted from greater efficiency, not the use of more resources. An aggregate input index, weighting factor shares for land, capital, and labor, shows a growth rate of only 0.74 and 3.7 percent for the two periods. Increased output was obtained with relatively little new input, indicating a sharp increase in total factor productivity. The Japanese colonial administration achieved this by maintaining law and order, encouraging local commerce and industry, and sponsoring farmer associations and research stations to improve seeds and farm techniques. These efforts were successful in Chinese farming communities that are fully comparable to villages in parts of North China, and similar programs would probably have brought comparable results in the south, too. Had more time elapsed for the lower Yangtze region to enjoy political stability, more agricultural improvement would have taken place there. Instead, foreign invasion and then civil war cut off this evolution.

THE TRANSFORMATION AFTER 1949

A rising savings-GDP ratio, more modern technology, a rapidly expanding population, and, of course, the restoration of order account for part of the post-1949 economic transformation. It is difficult to impute the exact contribution of each of these factors, but the increase in savings and investment is the simplest, most obvious factor to emphasize first.

After seizing power, the Communist Party soon took steps to divert more income from the private sector to the state, so that new industrial institutions could be created. Especially in the 1952–1957 period, unprecedented amounts of resources were devoted to producing equipment, machines, stocks of raw materials, and intermediate products—in other words, capital. Receipts in the state budget rose from 6,519 million *yuan* in 1950 to 17,560 million in 1952, and then to 29,703 in 1957. This was a fourfold increase in only seven years. This increase in revenue was much greater than any fiscal achievement in the late Ch'ing or republican periods, although revenue trends in the Nanking decade were also upward. The new receipts resulted partly from the communists' agricultural tax, which accounted for 30 percent of internal budget receipts in 1950, but dropped to 14 percent by 1954, and eventually fell to less than 10 percent. During the 1960s, agricultural taxes remained low. Despite mandatory grain sales at state-fixed prices, the peasants did not directly supply most of the capital for China's industrial expansion in the third quarter of the century. These funds were mostly provided by—or at least collected through—modern industries that sold products to consumers at official prices. Profits from socialized industry, taxes on industry and trade, and factory depreciation reserves were the biggest sources of budget receipts. These three categories rose from 67 percent of the state budget in 1950 to 81 percent in 1956 (Choh-ming Li, 1959, pp. 148–149), and they became even more important in later years. Industry, especially light industry, provided the link between most of China's population and the government with its old enclaves and new inland economic centers. Consumer industry was the modern ''tax'' collector in China, the main means to increase savings and fuel growth.

The state spent only one-fourth of its budget for economic projects in 1950, but by 1956, this figure had risen to 53 percent. To supplement its income, and to divert more resources from the private sector, notes were issued through the People's Bank of China, the central bank. These issues were of course inflationary. They covered the state's budget deficits, and they also helped the government claim more resources through inflation. Legal controls on some important commodity prices made this policy politically viable. Note issues probably financed 8 or 9 percent of the public sector's investment income. Thus, this pre-1949 tradition in Chinese government finance continued into the communist era, although its effects were changed in the new institutional framework.

Underlying the capacity of the state to increase taxes and garner more revenue was the party's policy of income redistribution in both villages and cities. The land reform, initiated by the party in most of North China by 1947, was extended to the south in 1949. It was finally completed in 1952, when the land of wealthy households was redistributed to those with little or none. According to Roll's estimate, when land reform ended in 1952 the Gini coefficient (a standard measure for analyzing income distribution) for the distribution of total per capita rural income was 0.22 (1980, p. 139), a reduction of 50 percent from his estimate of 0.44 for the 1930s. The top 10 percent of rural households received only 21.6 percent of the (posttax) income, and the bottom 10 percent received 5.1 percent. Then, between 1952 and 1954, the party confiscated or semisocialized the assets of urban entrepreneurs. These steps may have slightly reduced the income disparity between cities and villages; but most important, they made income distribution in the countryside more equal than ever before.

Land reform eliminated individual holdings in excess of roughly one-half acre. It did not eliminate the classes of farming households officially labeled by the party as "rich" and "middle" peasants. In Kiangsu even in 1952, middle-peasant households still held farms averaging 40 percent larger than those of poor peasants (Ash, 1976, p. 529). After 1956, all households were compelled to pool their implements and farm animals in village cooperatives, to forgo income from their former lands, and to work in production teams for wages. Still, not every household received the same income. Families fortunate enough to have more adults, especially males who did heavier work and received higher wages, earned more income than households with few or no male adults able to work.

The new team farming system disbursed income more equally than had the traditional system. Measures of village land distribution can serve as rough proxies to show rural income distribution in traditional China, and they render Gini coefficients expressing inequality as high as 0.7 and 0.8. The restructuring of property rights between 1947 and 1957 produced a somewhat more equal pattern of income and a collective pattern of rural ownership. A study of income data from four rural communities in different parts of the country during the 1950s showed Gini coefficients as low as 0.17 or 0.25 (Blecher, 1976, pp. 800–805). These extreme coefficients are probably atypical of China as a whole, but they suggest that much leveling had taken place by the mid-1950s. The leveling occurred within communities; wide disparities from village to village largely persisted.

In the cities, where a redistribution of industrial and commercial property also occurred, fragmentary income data reported in the 1970s indicated some wage variation in modern plants. Wages ranged, for example, from about 40 to 125 *yuan* per month in the Shanghai Machine Tool Factory. High compensation has generally been received by very few technicians and cadres, and the average urban industrial worker with full union membership (not including apprentices or contract or temporary workers) probably earned about 50 *yuan* per month in the early 1970s.

Promotions and raises have been based almost entirely on seniority, not on productivity. In this situation, it has been difficult or impossible for managers to dismiss employees who do not work hard. Although material incentives have been mandated periodically in policies from Peking (a wage reform in 1956, bonuses in the mid-1960s, raises in 1977), and although material incentives and piece-rate wages have at other times been criticized on radical egalitarian grounds, managers' lack of power over their subordinates' jobs has remained fairly constant and general. For this reason, material incentives for labor have not ordinarily been strong. Normative incentives, insofar as they have been guided by temporary policy lines from the state, have also been fairly ephemeral. Normative incentives implicit in continuing, small work communities (which are also accounting units) may have been stronger.

If urban-rural comparisons on income distribution are attempted, it is first necessary to distinguish rich from poor rural areas. In the most prosperous production teams, peasant households may receive monthly wages and in-kind payments worth 40 *yuan*, although this is exceptional. Such advanced teams probably include less than 5 percent of the rural population, and many families within them receive less. A worker's money wage in a poor team is about 12 *yuan* per month, plus some income in kind. It is impossible to determine what portion of all production teams in China are this poor, but the average monthly income in the countryside (where average household size is larger than in cities) may be about one-third that of urban families.

China's per capita real income, expressed in 1976 US dollars rose from about $153 in 1952, to $275 in 1970, to $340 in 1976—although not all of this income was received by individuals. This increase represents a 3.3 percent annual growth for the twenty-four-year period (Central Intelligence Agency, 1977, p. 1). If these figures are correct, the performance was fairly impressive for such a populous country beginning with so little capital. If growth continues at about the same rate, per capita income might double by the year 2000 and be roughly US $700. What does this mean in welfare terms for the common man in China? Most of the increased per person production has gone into savings, producer goods for later growth, and increased national strength. The portion that went to individual consumption is small.

Rationing has been the rule for grain, cotton cloth, sugar, cooking oil, soap, and many other consumer goods. Whenever possible, the bulk of resources have been channeled to the producer goods sector, not to consumers. Workers in urban households receive wages, but to purchase most goods, they have to present not only money but ration coupons. These tickets have been issued monthly or semiannually by organizations, usually the corporations producing the rationed products, against the presentation of household registration books certified by the police. Coupons are sometimes exchanged between individuals, despite regulations designed to discourage this practice. Only when the rationing of food became particularly rigid, as was the case during the near famine years between 1959 and 1962, did nutritional difficulties develop. In some areas many people did in fact die.

The list of rationed commodities has changed sharply from year to year, and also varies between cities. In the south, urban adults and teenagers during the mid-1970s received a monthly rice ration ranging from about twenty-eight pounds to sixty-six pounds (dry, uncooked weight), depending upon their work. Individuals in cities received ration coupons for as much as six yards of basic, good cotton each year, but in many areas, the amount was less. Fresh meat was available only in limited quantities, except on holidays. The ration of cooking oil in Peking was half a kilogram per month, but in many other cities, the ration was only half the Peking quota. The soap ration was apparently two bars per person per year; laundry powder was virtually unobtainable. Toothpaste was a luxury item, and those who could afford it had to submit a used tube upon purchase of a new one.

Fragmentary reports about household income and food prices suggest a spartan society, accustomed to scarcity, poor quality goods, and few modern services. This is of course nothing new in China, or in most of the world. A comparison of household income, prices, and food consumption on a per capita basis for cities in 1975 showed that a family of five could expect to spend 60 percent of its income for food alone (Klatt, 1977, p. 408). If this pattern is typical, it is similar to the average household food expenditure during the republican period.

Certain regions have fared better than the country as a whole in increasing food supplies. The three northern provinces of Hopei, Shantung, and Honan became self-sufficient in food by the 1970s, an achievement considering that since the turn of the century the North China plain had been dependent on imported grain from other areas. By 1972, these three provinces were net exporters of grain. In general, consumption patterns in China stabilized and became more egalitarian during the third quarter of the century, but the supply per consumer began from a poor base and grew only a little. The abundance of population and the state's ability to control consumption levels by equalization, and thus to increase savings, have mainly accounted for the high ratio of capital formation to GDP, for low factor productivity, and for usually high rates of growth in industrial output.

Foreign capital goods have represented a small share of the country's total since mid-century, but they have usually embodied modern technology. These imports have improved the quality of China's capital stock, so their small quantity does not fully indicate their importance. By 1955, probably half of imports consisted of machinery, equipment, metals, fuel, chemical products, textile fibers—in other words, capital goods or materials necessary for the expansion of the industrial sector. During the 1950s, virtually half of China's trade was with the USSR. Modern capital acquired from the Soviet Union became a vital component of China's emerging industry. Some factories were of the turnkey variety, built by Soviet engineers and turned over in finished form to Chinese managers. The capital share of imports increased through the 1960s and beyond. By the early 1970s, especially after 1974, China's trade shifted toward noncommunist states, and similar turnkey projects, such as fertilizer plants, were built by American, European, and Japanese contractors. The technology in this new equipment had spin-off advantages for several Chinese industries.

By 1976, about nine-tenths of China's imports were capital goods and industrial supplies, such as steel. Only one-tenth consisted of consumer goods, almost entirely foodstuffs. On the other hand, in 1976 only one-third of China's exports came from agriculture and only one-eighth from extractive industries, including oil. More than half of China's 1976 exports were manufactures, but they were almost all from light industries such as textiles and footwear; few production goods were exported. Although China's coastal economy was far better integrated with inland areas than before 1949, the threefold increase of China's trade from 1970 to 1975 still largely involved the old treaty ports.

The forced growth of capital stock in some industries, especially machine building, contributed to a rise of labor productivity in those sectors. Modern technology, incorporated in the expanding capital of this industry in the 1950s, permitted the productivity of other inputs to rise. In assessing the achievements of any Chinese industry, one must look not just at increases in production, but at the efficiency with which inputs are converted into outputs as well. If gross product rises fast, but the factors used to make it rise even faster, then the performance may well represent a misallocation of resources. When total factor productivity is rising, on the other hand, resource allocation is improving. At least for the 1952–1957 period, total factor productivity in the officially favored machine-building industry rose 7.3 percent and accounted for 25 percent of the growth of total output.

It is likely that total factor productivity remained important as a source of industrial growth in the first eight years after 1949, but by the late 1960s or at least by the 1970s, presuming the capital stock continued to grow at the same rate, total factor productivity in industry had apparently declined. This has been indirectly confirmed by many statements of the post-Mao leadership in Peking. Virtually all factories operate with two or three eight-hour shifts each day, seven days a week. Sometimes factories still operate at less than full capacity, but the general pattern of relatively steady use of machinery may produce an increasing long-run pattern of high capital productivity and low labor productivity—a situation common to many modernizing countries (and also to agriculture, as shown below).

Partly because of declining returns in growth from this mounting reliance on capital, partly because egalitarian ideals have led the communists to place many investments in areas where short-term payoffs are slow, and partly because certain management and labor-incentive policies become less productive as firms expand, industrial growth in the People's Republic has been rapid but decelerating, at least until recently. Although average annual industrial growth from 1952 to 1957 was 16 percent, after 1957 it fell to about 9 percent (using 1957 as a base) for any long period from the mid-1960s to the mid-1970s.

Just as the generally high level of Chinese industrial growth can be partly explained in terms of socialist institutions that forced savings, so also its deceleration before 1978 can be partly explained by equity-oriented political decisions to disperse capital all over the country. As economists such as Nicholas Lardy, K. C. Yeh, and Charles Roll show, geographical scattering of investments was a major distinguishing feature of Chinese economic strategy (*China and the Chinese*, 1976), at least until the year of Mao's death. Allocations of many resources, but especially of capital, have gone to inland places where the external economies for investments were not yet great. In contrast with the usual pattern in other developing countries, Chinese capital was often invested in places where it would not regenerate itself quickly, where it did not enjoy inexpensive access to productive inputs and to markets. Specifically, more money went to inland cities, and less to the old coastal treaty ports, than immediate criteria of collective profitability would have dictated. The future development of inland places may possibly be aided by this investment strategy, but the environments of many new projects did not prove conducive to quick capital turnover. This same, egalitarian, leveling trend is evident if the economy is divided into sectors not along geographical lines, but according to other dimensions such as the average compensation that labor receives, or the administrative levels at which enterprises are managed, or various categories of factory size. The short-term costs of this general economic strategy were probably great (just as the political constituency-building benefits may also have been great). The medium- and long-term costs may also be considerable, if past investment decisions were too rarely based on attention to external economies. It is likely that such decisions in the 1950s and 1960s were one reason, for example, that industrial growth in 1972–1977 was half the 1952–1957 rate.

China's leaders believed that by redistributing private property and then collectivizing it, new productive forces would be released. Their strategy between 1949 and 1957 established the foundations of planning in all major industries. They also succeeded remarkably well in bringing land, except for small private plots, under the control of cooperatives. Production teams used draft animals in common, and households in each team no longer received income from property; they received collective payments instead. Most families continued to gain a small share of their income from poultry, fish, or vegetables that were produced on the small plots, but the new team farming system consolidated most arable land into large elongated fields. Farm machinery gradually made its appearance, at least in prosperous rural areas near the old treaty ports, to prepare the soil or to transplant and harvest crops. Manual collective labor continued to perform four-fifths or more of the work in agriculture. Some of China's traditional crops, especially paddy rice, require field procedures which, if mechanized, would free vast amounts of labor whose alternative uses are not obvious.

The new rural system, so effective in extracting a large share of output for the state through payments for consumer goods, succeeded partly because of the enormous recuperative powers of agriculture after nearly fifteen years of decline during the wars. It also succeeded because of the gradual distribution in the 1950s of new disease-resistant and high-yield wheat and rice seeds. These seeds had been developed by the agricultural research institutes and farm extension units founded by the Nanking government. The cooperative farming system released very little new productive power, despite official hopes that it would do so. All studies of the 1950s show a huge decline in total factor productivity in agriculture. When Fei Hsiao-t'ung in the mid-1950s returned to Kaihsienkung, the village in Kiangsu that he had surveyed in the 1930s, he could only report that the peasants had still not recovered their pre-war living standards.

In 1958, the Maoist faction gained the upper hand, and its Great Leap Forward launched the new commune-brigade-production team system. Large labor teams were organized not only to farm but also to build rural capital projects. This new policy was not, however, combined with an increase in state investment in agriculture. In fact, these new organizations were supposed to finance themselves. The policy proved to be disastrous for the allocation of agricultural resources. Labor was lavishly squandered on projects with little payoff, while field preparation and sowing were neglected. Three years of very bad harvests resulted, which cannot be attributed primarily to poor weather, despite official claims at the time.

It took nearly five years to repair the damage. The government in 1962–1963 began to invest more heavily in agriculture and to introduce price incentives to farmers. Meanwhile, new technology was gradually introduced in the form of chemical fertilizers and especially new seeds. Throughout the 1960s, more irrigation projects were constructed. For these purposes, the team farming system was effective for mobilizing and increasing the supply of agricultural inputs. For example in 1949, the total sown area for all food grains and cotton came to roughly 104 million hectares (ha), but in 1976, the sown area for these crops had reached 142 million ha—a 1.2 percent annual growth. This increase in sown area did not result from reclaiming land, but from increased multiple cropping of the available fields. Cultivated area scarcely increased, because roads and structures took valuable land out of cultivation almost as fast as new land could be found or created. The multiple cropping index was 131 in 1952 and rose to 145 in 1958. Perhaps it was as high as 160 in the mid-1970s.

After the mid-1960s, a major change in China's cropping system began to take place. Previously, throughout the northern provinces, most farmers had obtained three harvests every two years, whereas in the central and southern regions they obtained two harvests every year. Now many farming teams are obtaining three harvests every year in the southern and central provinces, and two harvests every year in the north. In some of the more prosperous parts of the North China plain, one of these harvests is of paddy rice, which yields more calories per acre than do other grains. This new cropping pattern has not taken root in every district, but it has spread rapidly where irrigation is well developed, where early ripening seeds are used, and where large quantities of organic fertilizers can be applied. Inorganic fertilizers are likely to become important during the fourth quarter of the century. Large investments were made in domestic and imported chemical works during the 1970s, although organic fertilizers remained overwhelmingly important through the third quarter of the century.

In irrigation, China's traditional problems have largely stemmed from the periodic occurrence of droughts (especially from March to May on the North China plain) and from the unruliness of some of the largest rivers at other times. During the 1950s, the government initiated many canal-building projects, especially in the north, to combat these problems. As a result, productivity on some previously dry lands was increased. But before the end of the decade, it also became evident that in many areas the water table was being raised because of this new irrigation. Some previously high-producing plots were becoming waterlogged. For this reason, a compensatory campaign to drill tube wells, which can bring water from underground sources to the surface without greatly affecting local water tables, was launched. This development, along with the canals and efforts to build more level land in the north, has allowed an important northward expansion of the one-crop rice area. In the south, drainage canals have helped reduce problems caused by waterlogging in monsoon rains. Although China's traditional technology in agriculture makes dramatic new production spurts generally unfeasible, some improvement of the irrigation network, of the fertilizer supply, and of seeds has at least ensured that grain output will not be outpaced by population.

Water, fertilizers, and new seeds have been the keys to the moderate progress thus far, but Chinese farmers continue to apply great amounts of compost to their land. Frank H. King observed farmers placing six metric tons on every hectare of land in Shantung, when he toured the north in 1910. In 1976, members of the US Wheat Studies Delegation reported that 150 metric tons of organic matter were applied to each hectare of land in the better-farmed communes. For areas around Peking, Shihchiachuang, and Nanking, the amounts ranged from 70 to 112 metric tons.

In 1952, China used only 79,000 metric tons of chemical fertilizer measured in terms of nutrient content—and of this amount, roughly half was imported (Central Intelligence Agency, 1977, p. 12). After 1960, the state began to import still more chemical fertilizer. By 1965, the total supply of inorganic fertilizer reached 2.1 million metric tons, with approximately 640,000 metric tons (slightly under a quarter of the total) being imported. In 1973–1974, China negotiated with foreign manufacturers to construct many high-grade urea and nitrogen fertilizer plants. By 1975, China made 5.6 million metric tons and only imported 1.1 million metric tons (roughly one-sixth of its total supply). By 1980 China was able to provide nearly 18 million metric tons of mostly high-quality chemical fertilizer to its agriculture. If we assume a total sown area of roughly 145 million ha, this means an average of 7.7 metric tons of good manufactured fertilizer could be applied to every sown hectare of land. This could have positive effects on Chinese agriculture, if the irrigation projects and successes with seed research also proceed apace. Farm output might accelerate, although it is not likely that the portion of the labor force in agriculture will decrease very quickly.

China has yet to experience the chemical fertilizer revolution that occurred in Japan during the 1920s and 1930s, and in Taiwan during the 1950s and 1960s. The effects of some seed improvements have been apparent for crops such as wheat and rice, and to a lesser extent for vegetables and cotton. In 1952, only 5.2 million ha (roughly 5 percent of the total grain area) were sown with improved grain seeds. In 1958, about 94 million ha, or 77 percent of the total area in grain, used improved seeds. After 1965, further plant research led to a flow of even more high-yielding, disease-resistant and—most important—early ripening strains. Research institutes and agricultural colleges experimented with different genetic lines, and each year new seeds were distributed to county agricultural research stations and communes. After a year or two of trial use on the experimental plots, the successful strains were distributed to production brigades and teams, which meant that new seeds were being put into commercial production roughly three years after being developed. New varieties have been partly responsible for changes in the cropping system, because with early ripening seeds, plots can be used more times per year.

In exceptionally advanced farming communes around large metropolitan areas, grain yields by 1975 had risen to eight to ten times the 1949 levels. In some of these communes, the wheat yield stood at 1,800 kg/ha in 1965, but it increased to 3,000 kg/ha by 1975. In other cases, the yield was 3,500 kg/ha, compared to 2,500 in 1965. Land productivity in some areas markedly increased between 1955 and 1980, and this effect could become more general as the technology that allows it spreads to more of the Chinese countryside.

On the other hand, labor productivity in agriculture has not risen much, if at all. A survey of 101 cooperatives in Shansi reported trends in output per manhour for five separate crops between 1949 and 1957. An aggregate labor productivity index for these crops declined 5 percent over the eight-year period. Meanwhile, the farm labor expended in these villages, which were located in an arid region of the north where new irrigation projects helped raise yields, nearly doubled. Team farming was established as early as 1954, so that the mobilization of labor to construct more farm capital and apply more organic fertilizer raised crop yields. But the gigantic increase of labor time to achieve these results was not accompanied by any increase in labor productivity. If this case is representative of areas elsewhere in the country, then labor productivity in agriculture did not rise during the 1950s. In addition this productivity almost surely did not rise during the 1960s, when an even greater mobilization of labor took place.

Nor does it appear that there has been an increase in total factor productivity in agriculture. Studies of the input-output relationship in grain agriculture for the 1950s and 1960s conclude that inputs to farming rose more rapidly than production. Total factor productivity declined by 6 percent between 1952 and 1957 and by 8 percent between 1957 and 1965 (Tang, 1971, p. 285; Williams, 1974, Table 13). While such studies can be criticized for the procedures they use to measure and combine farming inputs, changes in the factor shares or weights would not alter the main conclusion. This is a poor input-output performance for Chinese agriculture.

Countries such as France and the United States during the nineteenth century, or Japan and Taiwan in the twentieth century, experienced a rise of total factor productivity in agriculture. In all four cases, this was a most important source of quick growth in agricultural production. In each case, it lasted a quarter-century or more. (In the Soviet Union, total factor productivity in agriculture declined first during the 1930s, and then again in the 1950s and early 1960s, but by the 1970s it was rising slowly.)

In conclusion, it must be said that the communist government has successfully allocated more resources to increasing agricultural and industrial production. But it has done this at great human cost and at times with an extravagant waste of resources. This section has scarcely mentioned the great loss of output that resulted from the Cultural Revolution, or the systematic destruction of universities and research institutes that continued into the 1970s. China's leaders now stress improved administration, more incentives to workers and managers alike, and most important, the need to adopt modern technologies quickly. The state has played a strategic role in the type of economic development described above.

Agents of Modern Economic Growth

Chapter 4 emphasizes that in the late nineteenth century China's top leaders did not perceive the gains to be had from modernization. Differences in ideas about modernization led to serious tensions in the bureaucracy. The court leadership tried to mollify its critics by adopting some of their suggestions; so the strategy of *kuan-tu shang-pan* (official oversight, merchant management) was initiated. This became the basis for many modern enterprises, but these failed to have much effect on the rest of the economy. The system certainly encouraged the activities of bureaucratic capitalists, and of officials who used their power to extend their personal wealth while supervising merchants' enterprises. Some bureaucratic capitalists proved to be innovative, but the majority were not. They did not create industries that stimulated the economy.

China needed entrepreneurial bureaucrats willing to use their official power to encourage new production and markets. Late imperial China had few such men. Republican China had more, but the country in most of that era was politically disintegrated or invaded from abroad. Post-1949 China also possessed some officials of great technocratic abilities, but during most of the three decades following 1949, the top leaders—especially Mao—preferred not to make full use of their bureaucrats with such skills.

THE ROLE OF THE STATE BEFORE 1949

Only after 1895 did the Ch'ing government make a vigorous effort to launch industrial development and modernize the economy. In 1903 Tsai-chen, a member of the imperial household, returned from touring the world and petitioned the throne to establish a department of commerce, the *Shang-pu*. In September, this department was set up and was mandated to promote the activities of new enterprises. The department proposed new laws for single-proprietor and corporate business ventures. It initiated studies of the economy and founded some enterprises directly. In 1906, a new Department of Transport and Communications was created. By 1907, post office mail deliveries had trebled over their volume a decade earlier. Between 1907 and 1918, telephone subscribers increased fivefold and telegraph offices increased threefold (Wang in *Conference on Modern Chinese Economic History*, 1977, pp. 1–17). For the first time, the state had an apparatus to foster a variety of modern enterprises.

The Ch'ing government also tried to consolidate its finances. It ordered that salt taxes be combined into a single national account, to be used for railway building, school expenses, and support of military and industrial development. By 1909–1910, the state spent more of its budget for modernization than at any previous time, although it had not been able to increase its revenues very much. Taxes between 1880 and 1895 had increased slightly. Between 1895 and 1909, the state managed to double all taxes. This was accomplished mainly by increasing temporary surcharges, rather than by revamping the entire tax system (as Meiji Japan had done when it established a new land tax based on the real value of a field's production). These increased surcharges garnered more revenue, but the government was still hard pressed to pay for all the new expenditures it was making, including indemnity payments to foreigners.

Projections for the new republic's budget between 1913 and 1916 show how difficult government finance had become. Revenue forecasts and expenditures declined sharply, basically because China was in an anarchic state, which had dried up its sources of revenue. By 1926, Finance Minister Wellington Koo could report less than 2 million Chinese dollars of nonborrowed revenue. Before the republican government was established at Nanking, the central government had been too weak to have any significant influence on economic affairs except for the mail and telegraph. Provinces were ruled by military elites. While some provincial assemblies tried to achieve greater fiscal independence, warlord control of budgets was the main pattern. Increasingly, surcharges were imposed on landowners and merchants, and a growing share of revenue was spent for military affairs.

During the Nanking decade after 1927, the Kuomintang apparatus had direct control only in portions of Shantung, Honan, Anhwei, Chekiang, and Kiangsi, and in all of Kiangsu. This party had inherited a poor economy and a demoralized, ill-staffed administration. World trade in manufacturing and primary products fell by as much as 30 percent in this decade; the Kuomintang thus had to deal with economic depression, as well as with Japan's seizure of Manchuria. Under these circumstances, it was impossible for the state to initiate major reforms, particularly in agriculture. In this era, conditions for modernization were strengthened mainly by private initiatives, rather than by government spending to develop the economic infrastructure.

THE STATE AFTER 1949

Under the Communist Party, the state created new organizations to affect how society used its resources, how it saved, and how it spent its income. The sections above show that the state increased savings and accelerated capital accumulation, especially for machinery. Policy mistakes and political turmoil produced periodic setbacks, but for a country at such a low level of per capita income, the rate of industrial growth has been high. Through what institutions was this particular kind of growth achieved? It has been argued that in Japan capital accumulation was the major force behind modern economic development, and it seems clear that agencies established in the Meiji period were crucial to this evolution. Is the key to China's industrial development similar?

The state budget and central bank became twin instruments to mobilize revenues and allocate them to the producer goods sector. The communist state obtains its income mostly from the profits of socialist enterprise (although in the very early years, significant amounts were also obtained from commodity and turnover taxes, agricultural levies, sales of government bonds, and some minor taxes). Payments flow to the state from three sectors, industry and commerce, agriculture, and households; and from this budget, allocations are made for capital goods, military defense, welfare, education, and other services. The central bank helps collect the revenues and transfers all legal payments that relate to plans. Communes and enterprises may have deposits in the central bank, and households may deposit savings there. The People's Bank and its branches make authorized credit available to firms for working capital. Enterprises are not legally permitted to hold shares in other firms, or to lend to each other. Public enterprises, collectives, and government bureaus remit their profits and taxes to the state, and they receive funds from the state to acquire capital goods.

The central government has maintained particular control over provincial tax receipts. The developed coastal provinces of Kiangsu, Chekiang, Hopei,

Fukien, and Kwangtung have not generally been able to increase their investment shares from tax and other revenues (Lardy, 1975a, p. 39). The official published budgets do not include all capital, but they do represent an important central control. While decentralization of decision making has been tolerated in communes and many other enterprises, strong control is exercised over the allocation of provincial tax revenues.

Households have been induced by rationing (and sometimes by political campaigns) to save a high portion of the income they receive, and the aggregate spending for some important consumables is planned to match the supply of available goods. Price inflation has thus been low. But to maintain such a high savings-GDP ratio, and to limit spending for the restricted supply of consumer goods and services, a fixed-price system has had to be maintained. Leakages and black markets in this system have often been important, particularly during the "bad years" after the Great Leap. Extensive state controls nonetheless allowed the establishment of a high rate of capital accumulation in industry, and some of the new capital embodied new technology.

A mix of planned pricing, free markets, and informal markets has enabled the economy to extract a considerable flow of resources for capital accumulation, to operate efficiently for some commodities that require particular care in handling (such as vegetables), and to distribute a relatively small supply of consumer goods among a population that has been given the purchasing power, but not the ration tickets, to buy more. In the late 1970s the mix changed in favor of free markets, largely in an effort to meet pent-up demands for consumer goods. An immediate improvement in the standard of living resulted.

CONCLUSION: PAST DEVELOPMENTS AND FUTURE POLICIES

The party's strong impulse to raise the rate of economic growth has sometimes caused planning mistakes, with results that were opposite from those intended. If the state had continued to develop railroad and road transport during the 1960s, even at the cost of slowing the short-term industrial growth rate slightly, China today might not be confronted with serious bottlenecks in delivery and storage, such as have been frequently reported. Also, intensive campaigns have, in some periods at least, caused huge production losses. Disruptions in higher education and in the development of technical manpower during the late 1960s resulted in roughly a decade passing with very few people being trained. Chinese leaders are now hastening to overcome the shortage of scientific manpower. These difficulties have arisen because of the planners' obsession about maintaining an extremely high rate of capital accumulation and because of political activities that have a dynamic of their own, separate from economic needs.

Since Mao's death, the Chinese government has readily acknowledged the existence, if not the cause, of these problems. Hua Kuo-feng, in a major economic speech to the National People's Congress in 1978, was understandably ready to blame all such difficulties on malfeasance by his former rivals, the Gang of Four. He also stated future goals, including a proposal that China produce 60 million tons of steel in 1985. Because 1977 output was about 23 million tons, this plan would have required an average annual increase of approximately 18 percent—a rate comparable only to that of the Soviet Union in its heyday of "steel-eating" growth during the 1930s. Such a proposal implies continued high savings, specifically by means of low urban wages or high rural extraction and taxes, or both (such as Stalin used to finance his similar endeavor).

The problem with the plan was that both of these means were specifically ruled out, for good reasons. Instead, the principle of "from each according to his ability, to each according to his work," has been greatly emphasized. Material incentives, if serious, are expensive, and their cost is potential capital. Their effect on productivity, in China's labor system, is largely unknown. Similarly, the need to keep agricultural taxes low has been stressed, and Mao's 1966 "Letter on Farm Mechanization" has been reprinted to warn against "draining the pond to catch all the fish" and "alienating the masses" by too much extraction from rural areas.

Hua said that agriculture would receive priority over light industries, which in turn would receive priority over heavy industries. But the order of practice may reverse the order of policy quite exactly, in the end. The direct cost of Hua's proposal to "mechanize 85 percent of agricultural processes" by 1985, and the high indirect costs of finding new employment for all that labor, may combine to encourage much investment, instead, in light industries in which capital regenerates itself far more quickly and larger profits can contribute to savings. Military interests, and the well-established Chinese institutions for centralized use of savings, may similarly lead to an emphasis in practice on heavy industry. Development efficiencies and politics will interact to determine the future directions of China's economy. By 1980 Hua's plan had been scrapped, the military budget had been cut, and the priority for agriculture and light industry was being implemented under Teng Hsiao-p'ing's pragmatic direction.

Hopeful plans, political conflicts over them, and progress below expectations have long recurred as threads in the history of China's modernization. After a quarter-century of debate, factions within the imperial court were galvanized into action by Japan's ignominious defeat of China. For the next decade, part of the Ch'ing government tried to mobilize tax revenues and modernize the country. The 1911 political revolution removed the Ch'ing but failed to replace it with a new authority able to modernize China. Even in 1928, when the Kuomintang declared Nanking to be the new capital of the republic of China, state power never fully extended beyond four or five provinces, and it only weakly reached the villages in those provinces. Between

1895 and 1945, modernization took place but with little backing from the state.

The treaty ports along the coast, and a few cities linked to them by rail or water, became new free markets. Singly and cooperatively, foreigners and Chinese businessmen began establishing banks, warehouses, insurance companies, utility companies, and manufacturing enterprises, based on the most up-to-date accounting procedures and technology. Modern practices blended with Chinese business traditions. The new energy channeled and released in these few enclaves launched industrialization. Until Japan invaded the country in the summer of 1937, modern industry developed rapidly in these centers. Tightly integrated with foreign markets through capital transactions and trade, these cities obtained most of their technical advice, finance, materials, machines, and even markets outside of China.

These centers were linked more closely with each other and their foreign markets than with Chinese towns of the interior. The new manufacturing firms frequently found themselves in keen competition with rural handicrafts, although some firms supplied intermediate products to handicraft producers. Modern factories managed to find enough buyers in the treaty port enclaves to justify expansion. New firms multiplied in fits and starts, and a modern industrial complex emerged. A work force of over half a million semiskilled workers and technicians developed, as well as a small class of managers knowledgeable in modern engineering and business practices. This new group, however, made its livelihood under conditions of uncertainty. It greatly influenced enclave politics, but it could not ultimately control the foreign and Chinese governments that deeply affected the environment in which it did business.

In the countryside, farmers and entrepreneurs also struggled under conditions of insecurity. Some districts benefited from new commercialization radiating from the treaty ports. Other districts, whose handicraft production was in direct competition with the modern sector, gradually declined. Still other districts found their traditional markets taken over by different suppliers. This complex process of growth, decline, and readjustment was affected sporadically by political disturbances, military activities, and natural calamities. The result, after World War I, was that farm production fluctuated widely for over a decade, without any marked trend of growth or decline. The fluctuations moderated, but production still only kept pace with population change through most of the 1930s. It declined after the outbreak of world war and later civil war.

In the main coastal provinces, especially those of East China, the Nanking government expanded a modest infrastructure of modern transportation, education, and agricultural research. The beneficial effects of this development did not spread very far inland from the coast or the Yangtze. The Chinese economy became increasingly dualistic, as urban and rural market structures separated from each other. This commercial separation of country from city was exacerbated after 1937, especially during the ravages of inflation in the late 1940s.

The socialist government, after 1949, built up unprecedented control over China's economy and people, in both rural and urban areas. The Communist Party systematically eliminated private property and redistributed both capital and income. Not all the directives from Peking were applied quickly or uniformly everywhere, and redistribution could not radically augment the assets of the poorest households. Nonetheless, these tumultuous reforms greatly reduced the economic power of the business and well-to-do farming classes. The party slowly educated sufficient loyal manpower to replace power groups in many units with loyal cadres and sympathizers. The party also created many new organizations to carry out its policies. The commune, in particular, represented perhaps the most important organizational reform of China's tax system since the *li-chia* and *pao-chia* systems of the Ming and Ch'ing periods. Communes generally facilitate state control of the countryside, yet they still have some independence in organizing resources according to the interests of factions governing those units.

Traditionally, households that had accumulated wealth and then achieved social status and political power had behaved frugally. Such households had always maintained a high rate of savings and had even drawn on the savings of relatives or friends to obtain capital such as land, by which to earn more income. Like rich households of the past, the new socialist state established a high rate of saving and capital accumulation. All enterprises and organizations are ordered to maintain a high accumulation-to-income ratio, either directly through local collective savings or indirectly through remittances to the government. The main means of modern industrial development in China are based on longstanding habits of capital accumulation—now on an unprecedented scale.

This rate of savings enabled China's economy to achieve a high, slightly declining growth rate in industry, averaging around 10 percent per annum since 1952. At the same time, the state has managed to increase farm production at a rate of about 2 or 3 percent per year. If a population explosion had not occurred, this agricultural growth rate might have sufficed to permit a still higher savings-GDP ratio and a still more rapid industrial spurt. Population pressure on limited arable land has meant that practically all of the increments to farm production from new capital and technology have been used to supply new people, not to raise per capita consumption.

Tight rationing of consumer goods remains a major policy in the PRC's modernization. The Chinese people have long been accustomed to spartan living conditions. Food and services are strictly limited and are likely to be so for a long time. Yet from the stock of increasing communal wealth, the state has been able to expand public health and schooling. These consumer services have increased in supply, even though luxuries of the simplest kinds (such as fountain pens, watches, and bicycles) are scarce and expensive. Rationing applies not only to commodity consumption; through the urban household registration system, it extends to security in jobs that support city life styles.

Chinese planners have used complex price policies to guide resource allocation. Their economic organizations rely in theory on centralized planning. In fact, and in some periods, many enterprises have been permitted wide latitude in determining how to obtain the inputs of production and how to dispose of the output. This flexibility, within a formally centralized administration, is a salient feature of the Chinese economic heritage; it is a source of both efficiency and irregularity in the system.

Mao's successors now stress that modernization of the economy is their primary concern. The new leadership has reaffirmed past PRC commitments to a high rate of savings for industrial development, but it has also advocated a new willingness to borrow from the West by sending thousands of students and researchers abroad and buying new capital that embodies the most advanced technology of the day. China's leaders are deeply concerned about the absence of productivity growth in their socialist economy. They have set high industrial and agricultural targets to be reached by the mid-1980s and appear committed to making China a modern economic power by the year 2000.

International Comparisons

Because Japan and the Soviet Union began their industrial marches well before the end of the nineteenth century, they had time to take advantage of technical transfers, which were relatively easy then, to increase exports for growing world markets under the stable protection of a dominant (British) navy, and eventually to borrow from willing international moneylenders. China missed out on these favorable opportunities for modernization, and when World War I came, its industrial foundations remained weak.

China's economic transformation was more like that of certain Eastern European countries before World War II. Early growth in these cases was characterized by an industrial spurt, greater urbanization, and little or no change in the agrarian sector. For example, Gerschenkron notes that in Bulgaria industry expanded at the rate of about 8 percent annually for about twenty-five years and then stopped (1962, p. 202). Meanwhile, agriculture, which had paid the costs of this spurt, received few benefits and was denied capital for investment or reform; agrarian stagnation resulted. China experienced much the same pattern between the two world wars.

Before its leaders could give priority to modern economic growth, China had to put its political affairs in order. This happened at mid-century, a watershed comparable to the calamitous early years of the century when domestic decay and international tensions forced crucial decisions to be de-

TABLE 10.2 Rates of growth of total product, population, product per capita, and estimated product per capita at initial date of period of modern growth for China, developed (modernized) countries, and less developed (nonmodernized) countries.

COUNTRY	PERIOD	DURATION OF PERIOD (years)	DECADAL RATES OF GROWTH			ESTIMATED GNP PER CAPITA AT BASE DATE OF PERIOD (1965 US $)
			Total Product	Total Population	Product per Capita	
China	1952–72	20.0	64.5	24.1%	34.0%	85
United Kingdom	1801/11–1831/41	30.0	32.1%	15.4%	14.5%	227 (1765–85)
France	1831/40–1861/70	30.0	26.3%	3.9%	21.6%	242 (1831–40)
Belgium	1900/04–1925/29	25.0	19.6%	6.0%	12.8%	326 (1865)
Netherlands	1860/70–1890/99	30.0	20.3%	11.7%	7.6%	492 (1865)
Germany	1880/89–1905/13	24.5	32.9%	13.5%	17.0%	302 (1850–59)
Norway	1885/94–1905/14	20.0	24.9%	9.2%	14.3%	287 (1865–69)
Sweden	1885/94–1925/29	20.0	38.8%	7.1%	29.6%	215 (1861–69)
Italy	1885/99–1925/29	30.0	24.6%	6.5%	16.9%	271 (1895–99)
Japan	1885/94–1905/14	20.0	39.8%	11.4%	25.5%	74 (1874–79)
	1904/14–1925/29	17.5	50.7%	13.5%	32.8%	
United States	1869/78–1889/98	20.0	50.0%	24.7%	20.3%	474 (1836–43)
Canada	1870/74–1890/99	22.5	41.8%	13.2%	25.2%	508 (1870–74)
Australia	1861/69–1890/99	29.5	45.1%	36.9%	6.0%	760 (1861–69)
Argentina	1900/04–1925/29	25.0	57.0%	40.2%	12.0%	443 (1900–04)
Mexico	1925/29–1963/67	38.0	59.0%	30.0%	22.3%	215 (1925–29)
Jamaica	1950/52–1963/66	13.5	110.5%	18.5%	77.7%	232 (1950–52)
Ghana	1950/54–1963/67	13.0	49.1%	30.6%	14.2%	263 (1950–54)
Philippines	1950/54–1963/67	13.0	77.8%	36.7%	30.0%	181 (1950–54)
Egypt	1945/46–1963/66	17.5	65.4%	27.4%	29.8%	117 (1945–49)
India	1952/58–1963/67	10.0	41.4%	26.1%	12.2%	77 (1952–58)
European Russia	1860–1914	53.0	30.2%	13.8%	14.4%	—
	1913–58	45.0	35.7%	6.4%	27.4%	—
USSR	1928–58	30.0	53.8%	6.9%	43.9%	—

SOURCE: Ramon H. Myers, *The Chinese Economy Past and Present* (Belmont, Calif.: Wadsworth, 1980). Reprinted by permission. Figures on China are revised.

layed. When these decisions finally could be taken, after 1949, the economic results were as follows:

First, urbanization increased slowly, while the contribution of manufacturing to the GDP increased rapidly and that of agriculture declined. Russia, Japan, and other modernized countries experienced much greater urbanization when their sectoral contributions to GDP altered in the same way.

Second, income distribution in China became more equal both between cities and countryside and within (if not between) agricultural units. In later years, this distribution remained constant or perhaps widened slightly—whereas in Russia, Japan, and other developed countries, income distribution between urban and rural areas became more unequal over a long period, before reaching a plateau and then reversing.

Third, China began to achieve rapid growth rates for manufacturing from a very low per capita income level. Table 10.2 compares total production, population, per capita income, and estimated early levels of per capita income for China and other modernizing countries. While some of the nations in Table 10.2 achieved rapid growth rates over a fifteen-year period, they have not been able to sustain such a performance. China managed at great cost in resources and people, to maintain generally high, if uneven, growth rates until the mid-1970s, and there is every prospect that it will continue to maintain at least moderate rates under the current leadership.

CHAPTER ELEVEN

Social Integration

CHINA CAME INTO SUSTAINED AND INTENSE CONTACT with modernizing societies in the 1840s, which was relatively late; only in the 1860s did its leaders gradually begin to introduce the primary institutions for drawing extensively on foreign interactions; they further delayed until the late 1890s and the 1900s the initiation of basic reforms. With these reforms, Chinese society finally became deeply caught up in the process of modernization—some four decades after a similar turning point had been reached in Japan and Russia. Furthermore, apart from selected industries and some coastal cities, the general social transformation in China remained fitful and slow until mid-twentieth century. In 1949 this society was less modernized and had met fewer of the conditions for accelerating modernization over the long run than had Japan or Russia on the eve of World War I, also a half-century after their major reforms had been launched. Under communist leadership, China at last joined the small circle of countries to experience rapid modernization as latecomers. Once having reached this target (although still nonmodernized), the Chinese struggled to maintain the momentum of change. In the areas treated under the theme of social integration we find a confusing array of policy initiatives and reversals, but we can also discern an underlying strategy to meet pressing problems of modernization and an emergent, distinctively Chinese approach. This chapter considers how measures to create a social foundation for this modernizing society have been dependent on specific conditions rooted in China's past, but have addressed problems observed also in the transformation of Japan and Russia.

Over its first three decades, the history of the PRC bears testimony to two propositions about rapid modernization in latecomers: (1) the means that prove useful in accelerating modernization depend on the specific legacy of social conditions—the historical examples most pertinent to this chapter are listed in Chapter 5; and (2) the continuation of a rapid rate of modernization and the eventual shifting of orientation as a higher plateau of modernization is reached require major changes in approach that vary in their timing but occur with some predictability. This second proposition especially refers to the transition away from the totalitarian means that may help to propel a country rapidly ahead in the early phases of modernization. In the case of the PRC, examples of these early methods that were later criticized are: overconcentration of authority, neglect of law, intolerance of sharp criticism originating from below, rejection of a factual approach in the search for truth, low priority to increases in living standards, a minor role for material incentives for the majority, and puritanical social policies. After an overview, we take up individual areas of social integration and suggest specific propositions for understanding the Chinese experience.

Overview

China's struggle to modernize blends in an uneasy and, from time to time, unstable alliance deeply rooted forces of tradition and vigorously imposed forces of radical transformation. Despite some glaring policy errors and periods of slowed development, the leaders of the PRC have since 1949 largely harnessed these two forces in combination to meet the immediate needs of rapid modernization. Yet, each of these two apparently contradictory forces 'seems somehow more pronounced in the Chinese setting than elsewhere.

There is ample evidence to indicate that through the 1970s considerable continuity with the past remained. Where else has modern growth proceeded so far with so little urbanization, or with so little movement of individuals away from their longstanding genealogical roots, or with so great a state-enforced hold over the individual allotted to the still powerful family unit? Persistent traditional factors of this sort give a distinctive cast to China's course of modernization and enhance the significance of the past.

At the same time, the jolts of radical breaks with the past remain fresh in Chinese memories. Where else has the label "revolution" been applied to so many programs intended to sweep away the old ways? The intensity of the battle between tradition and transformation appears magnified in the PRC; the battle has been raging for several generations, but communist policies have most vividly demonstrated the extreme alternatives that are present.

Decade by decade through the twentieth century, Chinese society has experienced a persistent interplay between the forces of transformation and the

forces of tradition, and between the alternatives of immediate wholesale oblit-
eration of certain traditions on the one hand and gradual shifts without challenging traditions on the other. Of course, much social change found some
middle ground, in part building on traditions and in part undermining them,
but contending forces remained ready to redirect changes toward one extreme
or the other. Without doubt, of the many watersheds from the reforms during
the first decade of the century to the reversal of the Cultural Revolution in the
mid-1970s, the major turning point in this conflict occurred in 1949. The battle between conflicting forces reached a new intensity after the communist victory in that year; the leaders of the PRC enlarged the field of struggle to encompass more diverse groups and more spheres of activity. Nonetheless, the
basic problems of accelerating modernization persisted, and the developments
after mid-century, which addressed and in some cases solved these problems,
can be interpreted within the context of a much longer time span.

Under the stimulus of military defeat, foreign incursions and demands,
railroad building, study abroad, foreign trade, and many other factors, China
around 1900 began to experience much more rapid social change. Only at the
beginning of the twentieth century had the forces in favor of massive change
finally been galvanized into aggressive pressure groups within urban society.
At last, some six decades after the first decisive exposure to the military and
technological superiority of modernizing states and to their ability to compromise China's territorial integrity, and some four to five decades after the
disintegrative impact of the destruction caused by the Taiping rebellion, and
the compromises needed to ward off its powerful challenge, diverse groups
had taken up the cause of finding a new basis for integrating Chinese society.
In particular, individuals representing four distinct backgrounds—each in
direct contact with modern education and with internationally defined role
models—groped for new organizational forms to help realize their goals of
transformation. Civilian political leaders, provoked by the inadequacies of
Ch'ing rule and later of warlordism, sought constitutional checks on autocratic rule as well as bureaucratic reorganization and broadened popular
participation in one form or another. Military officers quickly emerged as the
most decisive pressure group; they found in their improved armaments and
new organizations the necessary vehicle for seizing and consolidating power.
Business leaders gained an opportunity in the waning years of the Ch'ing dynasty to form chambers of commerce and other associations capable for the
first time of fully securing their position within the power structure of each
city. Finally, the emerging modern intelligentsia began to organize to trans-
late abstract principles into national slogans and to propagate social reforms
heavily influenced by practices abroad. Although in the short run, the
negative effect these groups had in destroying the foundation of the old social
order was greater than any good they could possibly have achieved by advo-
cating a new foundation, their efforts gradually gained ground in the struggle

to integrate China anew, a task in which these groups would be deeply involved by the 1920s.

As the reforms of the first decade culminated in the Revolution of 1911, which, in turn, gave way to warlordism and to urban activism on behalf of nationalist causes, new organizations continued to take shape but not necessarily in the idealized fashion some envisioned. Inadvertently, initial political successes opened the way for leadership that was more personalized and faction ridden, more localized and fragmented, and more brutalized and manipulative. Increasingly possessing specialized technical training, officials within the newly created ministries of successive governments were circumscribed by the authority of military leaders. The career military officers proved to be the best organized, best financed, and inevitably, under the harsh circumstances, the most indispensable of the contending groups. To a great extent, their armies filled the organizational void, but in a manner that clashed with the Chinese tradition of regularized, civilian rule. Also in conflict with tradition was the unrestricted rise of certain business organizations and activities. Through political contributions and other organized expressions of their economic clout, business leaders (including merchants and moneylenders in the traditional sector) converted the improved economic situation in the modern sector into an unprecedented lever for influencing state policies and, not infrequently, availed themselves of the greater opportunity for graft and corruption throughout the society as a source of profit and as protection for pursuits of questionable legitimacy. In the climate of the times, they had few alternatives. Meanwhile, freed from the demands and responsibilities of the examination system, the modern intelligentsia split into diverse groups writing for different journals and associated with different foreign-inspired approaches to learning and social reform. Under the banners of nationalism and social justice, they could reach a large urban audience. By deposing imperial rule and eventually much of Confucianism as well, the potential elites that were once so carefully prevented from rivaling the favored degree holders now became less fettered in their basic organizational undertakings, although they remained subject to the arbitrary demands of powerful officials and soldiers. Officials could become professional administrators, soldiers could gain supremacy over civilians in governing the populace, businessmen could actively enter the political arena, and intellectuals could form factions and political parties. Modern elites were appearing in a society weakly integrated at levels above the family and the lineage.

The impact of new forms of social integration during the first two decades of this century is observed primarily in the role of elites and of organizations controlled by them, linking various levels of the society. Cumulative changes from the abolition of the examination system in 1905, to the overthrow of the imperial system of governance in 1911 and the May Fourth Movement against classical learning and associated modes of thought that gathered steam from 1915, eliminated the position of degree holders as the meritorious protectors of local interests and the overseers of the public will. As we discussed in Part One, national, regional, and local disintegrative forces had already in the nineteenth century greatly undermined the effectiveness of this group, which had performed so many functions vital to social order, stable intercommunity relations, and a general atmosphere of justice throughout the society. Its final collapse (obscured by those who would apply the ambiguous label of gentry both to the degree holders and to twentieth-century rural elites) hastened the overall process of social disintegration.

In rural areas, the dearth of organizations above the family and lineage led to stopgap alliances and associations rather unpromising as a basis for a long-term integrated order. Imperial decline and warlordism along with the profits of the opium trade and the need for armed associations to protect local interests contributed to the growth of secret societies, based on fraternal bonds and readiness for militant action. With taxes rising—now more arbitrary and at times even expropriative—with social mobility often channeled into the army and the personal entourages of warlords and their subordinates, with speculation and lending less amenable to customary restrictions and more readily converted into power and influence, and with landlords increasingly living at a distance from their holdings or in some other manner seen as illegitimate and less responsive to the needs of tenants, the tenor of rural life probably worsened even if most living conditions and day-to-day activities remained much as before. The village was clearly not immune to outside influences; penetration could be seen in the fairly rapid abandonment of the practice of binding girls' feet and in the temporary successes eventually realized in crackdowns on the use of opium. But many of the changes in an era of civil disorder, including the reorientation of career patterns without generally improved opportunities, must have reinforced the very local solidarities that inhibited outside control and influence.

Social change penetrated more deeply in the urban environment, especially in the large cities and treaty ports where foreign influences and new opportunities abounded. As described in Chapter 9, public opinion emerged as a force that could be aroused by mass circulation publications. Students and workers, spending much of their time outside of the family context, could be enlisted in efforts to challenge traditional authority. Increasing instances of individual acts of defiance could be observed among women struggling against forms of male supremacy and among youths of both sexes rebelling against the virtually unlimited power of older generations. Programs to organize these urban residents acquired the trappings of major social movements by the 1920s and 1930s. Even in the cities, however, large numbers remained embedded in family, localistic, or paternalistic relationships—often not fully separated from their rural roots—that precluded active involvement in these causes.

While in the 1900s, transformation centered on the replacement of the most visible organizational impediments to modern change, that is, those associated with dynastic rule, and in the 1910s it centered on removing the chief intellectual barriers to modern knowledge, only in the 1920s did transformation come to mean primarily building new types of organizations rather than destroying old ones. In this regard, the revolution of 1927 when the Kuomintang forged a new, if still fragile and in most areas superficial, unity signified a major turning point. Relying on similar elements to consolidate local and regional control as the warlords before them, the Kuomintang in the short run accommodated its policies to the exigencies of internecine warfare and the realities of local social conditions. There was no long run for the Kuomintang in mainland China. Thus the partial integration it did achieve, based primarily on urban organizations, did not represent to the same degree an application of conscious policy and ideology as the long-lasting integration under the preceding dynastic order had or the subsequent much more intensive social integration of the communist order would. It meant accepting the forces that had already filled the vacuum resulting from the decline of the Confucian order. And it meant confirming existing leaders, regardless of the origins of their power or the merits of their leadership.

During the protracted strife of the 1920s and the intermittent civil war between the Kuomintang and the communists of the 1930s and 1940s, state power expanded in two areas where the imperial tradition had long granted it precedence. The first area was surveillance. Through the revived *pao-chia* system and through the discipline internal to an elitist party, social control of political opponents became a preoccupation of local and national leaders alike. The brief respite of relative freedom of association earlier in the century, the duration and significance of which varied from area to area, became an early casualty of increased centralization. The second area of expanded state power was taxation and control over production. In theory, there had been virtually no limit to state intervention in the economy during imperial times, but the immense scale and largely agrarian nature of the society as well as the Ch'ing leaders' eschewal of an active state role apart from surveillance restricted that involvement greatly. The situation changed markedly under warlordism, KMT, and communist rule. Of course, despite a common propensity to nationalize industry, the KMT and the communists differed sharply in the visible targets of their revenue-raising policies and in the means available to them to tap the scattered resources of the society. Most important, where the KMT penetrated the village, it depended on recipients of rent rather than reducing or abolishing rents in the process of securing tax revenues.

Drawing largely on modern elite elements from the military, professional administration (including some of the intelligentsia), and the business community, the KMT reasserted the state's command over much of society (especially the urban sector) and did so with modern means of communications and control. Under its leadership, substantial advances were recorded in the development of modern elites and in their use by the state for purposes of national integration. Within the big, eastern cities a critical social infrastructure now existed for rapid modernization. It included qualities that Chinese society had long nurtured: a diligent labor force responsive to education and skills, a wealth of entrepreneurship and managerial talents, and a capacity to reshape organizations to improve results. But even had there been no shortage of time, some difficult problems would have remained throughout KMT rule.

Most important, Chinese leaders faced an enormous task in coping with the social structure of the village and in more fully involving the village in the urban-led intensification of economic development. Some changes since the nineteenth century may have created a better basis for penetrating rural areas and mobilizing their resources, but major obstacles remained. Transportation and communications were improved, yet the standard marketing community with its orientation toward internal exchange within clusters of villages had scarcely been restructured. Although traditional social obligations honored by the landed, leisured, and literate became more precarious, lineages remained essential in a period of insecurity, and family solidarity in the village remained unassailable. In addition, state efforts to take active control must have been stymied by the absence of obvious targets. There were so few large landowners or powerful individuals among the many men of modest means who had some say in the village. Social boundaries were fluid. Most of those who had amassed power or wealth did not differ greatly in their life styles from their fellow villagers; they remained in residence in the village, were embedded in collectivities involving persons with diverse means, and enjoyed mixed sources of income. The village was characterized by small producing units; it was a society of modest producers who largely consumed for survival and for ceremonially unproductive, but much honored, ways. Most landlords, traders, moneylenders, and others with above average wealth could not be readily singled out to reassign their assets to the state, and removing the most abusive of them would not prevent others from taking their places. On the eve of the communist takeover of an area, as before, strong bonds of kinship and local homogeneity on the one hand and weak bonds of alternative organizations and class solidarity on the other made the villages difficult for either the KMT or the CCP to genuinely transform. At the same time, villages lacked the strong leadership or cohesion to resist land reform and other forms of redistribution; such reforms did not necessarily appear incompatible with dynastic traditions of equalizing holdings and supporting the family farm.

The modern urban sector, despite the city's masses of unemployed and barely surviving residents, and the nonmodern rural sector had diverged sharply during the first half of the twentieth century. To the extent the CCP realized success in recruiting rural supporters, it did so partly by drawing on the city's human resources as outside leaders "squatting" for a time in the village. This could produce immediate gains via land reform and disciplined intervention; however, it would not be an adequate long-range solution to problems of modernization. In the cities, modern employment and educational opportunities did more to transform social conditions. Here the lineage declined more quickly, women and youths sought and took advantage of new legal rights, and life quite alien to rural customs was taking root. Still, vast numbers in the cities had not been assimilated to or received the benefits of the modern sector; traditional attitudes operated as a much more potent factor in the city than did modern attitudes in the village. The struggle for modernization continued in urban areas, but it was only beginning in the countryside.

During the 1950s, the communists succeeded in reestablishing a strong central government, a country with full sovereignty in international relations, and a stable and unified system for economic recovery and growth. The most visible prerequisites for modern development identified in each of the previous chapters had been restored after a lapse of up to a century. Other requirements associated with modern elites had emerged in the urban sector over the previous half-century. In the area of social integration, the establishment of a large and dedicated corps of activists under the leadership of the CCP, capable of reaching into nearly all communities, should likewise be considered a major milestone that made possible many further developments. Through base areas at a time of civil war and Japanese invasion and through the village-by-village mobilization of land reform, communist leaders recruited a network of party members and supporters at their disposal for carrying out all sorts of policies and campaigns. Not since the abolition of the examination system had there existed in local areas across China a corps of individuals inculcated in an ideology that persuaded them of their leadership responsibilities, organized in a hierarchy that led from the village to the local administrative center and on to Peking, and committed to service through their recruitment experiences and their hopes of career advancement. The party card replaced the examination degree as the means of entry into this web of obligations and rewards. Of course, membership in the Communist Party imposed a degree of disciplined obedience and a commitment to transform rather than respect local traditions unknown in dynastic times. Although, unlike degree holders, the party activists could not buttress their claim to superior knowledge of the lessons of history and of the proper social relationships with a monopoly on educational achievement, they represented a potent mobilizing force on behalf of the central leadership.

In the 1950s and 1960s the CCP seized control of the levers of society, that is, the distribution of such factors as land, labor, income, and education. Each major campaign tightened the leadership's grasp over societal resources. Marriage-reform and land-reform campaigns at the beginning of CCP rule somewhat liberated the individual from family control (although not much by international standards), hastened the decline of the lineage as a force that guided family initiatives, and severely curtailed dependency relationships based on wealth. In the process, the most impoverished households gained a more secure basis for subsistence, certain gross injustices and abuses were eliminated, and the state increased its income considerably as it gained a foothold within each village. The first steps were relatively easy because they simultaneously removed obstacles to CCP control and transferred resources from a minority to a majority and from nonessential local consumption to productive state capital formation. (In the absence of serious obstacles after the long-awaited reunification, the CCP intentionally unleashed the forces of struggle and bloodshed in an attempt to shake up rural society during land reform; the process was more divisive than many of its major goals required.) Urban campaigns in the early 1950s served much the same purpose, with the special circumstances that many of the class targets who owned the means of production and many of the occupants of official positions were deemed essential for their modern knowledge and technical expertise. In the short run, they became targets of campaigns against abusing their positions, but many retained responsible jobs.

The second wave of major campaigns differed from the first in its priority for solidifying new organizations rather than undermining old ones. Since the old relationships and privileges most directly attacked in the earlier campaigns were fragile to begin with, they succumbed rather easily. In the mid-1950s there were even fewer obstacles to redistributing resources and to building new organizations; the state apparatus had grown to the point that it could largely accomplish these ends, and, what is more, without disastrous consequences it could take some charge over the vast numbers of organizations that were established. Collectivization and nationalization were completed by 1956 over virtually all of China except some areas inhabited by minority nationalities. While there were few serious barriers to completing these campaigns, there is reason to believe that the organizations that resulted from them fell short of CCP goals for resource control, mobilization, and growth. Collective farms were too numerous, inadequately controlled by outsiders, and subject to too many conflicting pressures to meet quickly their many objectives. The proliferation of state factories and offices encouraged aspirations for privileges in the form of wage increases and job-related benefits, superior schooling for children, and even some sharing of power through reliance on experts. By speeding up the widely anticipated reorganization of society through the second wave of campaigns, the CCP under Mao Tse-tung found itself divided and unprepared for the difficult aftermath of these campaigns.

After two years of uncertain policies, the CCP responded to the difficulties in simultaneously achieving all of its objectives with a third wave of massive social reorganization. It followed a sweeping "anitrightist" purge of educated persons who had been persuaded to voice criticisms during the Hundred Flowers campaign of 1957. Again the CCP transferred local controls upward: many household belongings and private sector activities were transferred to the collective sector, and collective farms were absorbed into much larger communes. Less than a decade after the communist victory, the CCP had carried its policies of social control to an extreme, especially in the rural areas. The accounting unit for management of land had shifted from the household to the large commune with tens of thousands of individuals. Allocation of labor began to take the form of the mobilization of vast armies of workers for seasonal projects. At the height of the Great Leap Forward, a large share of personal income was distributed in kind, depending less on household labor than on available communal resources. A temporarily highly mobilized population obscured a fragile organizational base in which coercion and exhortation replaced opportunity and actual incentives. Winning approval for the social reforms of the Great Leap Forward proved no more successful than hitting the economic targets. The CCP had attempted to carry control and mobilization too far; its leadership implemented hasty decisions without adequate awareness of their possible disruptive consequences and organizational shortcomings. The most radical measures, such as communal mess halls and backyard furnaces, quickly disappeared, but it took two decades before leaders forthrightly recognized other negative consequences, such as inadequate gathering and reporting of accurate information.

Despite the setbacks sustained in the Great Leap Forward—the third wave of reforms—and in subsequent policy reversals, the results of the first two waves remained largely intact. The social context had changed, however, to provide guarantees to the household and the production team (the old village or intravillage neighborhood). On this new foundation of limited material incentives, elements of the new order and the old interests were gradually reaching an accommodation in rural society. This accommodation rested on an understanding that remained in force despite some tampering from above during moments of the Socialist Education Movement, the Cultural Revolution, the Learn from Ta-chai campaign, and the anti-Lin Piao anti-Confucius campaign. In other words, the accommodation based on limited material incentives for households and production teams weathered repeated attack; it was a stable feature that met minimal needs before the post-Mao leadership proposed more substantial incentives in the late 1970s.

What are the basic features of this arrangement, which—despite repeated threats—prevailed across rural China in the 1960s and 1970s and remained largely intact in 1980? At least five dimensions deserve mention:

1. Reward for land, labor, domestic animals, and other factors of production as well as their allocation involves several levels of control from the commune to the individual, with tolerance for a restricted private sector operated by the household and preference given to the production team, the smallest of the collectives.

2. Exchange and redistribution of resources are based on the objective of self-sufficiency made possible by modest state taxation frozen at an earlier level, some degree of material rewards in the form of gradually increasing purchase prices (although these are often matched by rising costs for indus-

trial and consumer goods) and the availability of private markets, diverse services such as education and health care made accessible at the village level, and contracts to village and market town small-scale industries.

3. Selection and control over local leadership permit active community involvement. At the most basic production team level, according to studies based on South China, this is mainly in the hands of local representatives, under guarantees of autonomy in many areas and under the normally limited supervision of brigade outsiders and party members.

4. Tolerance exists for disapproved activities in many areas, including the absence of high administrative pressure for change in family customs and practices that continue to be the predominant mode of interaction in rural areas (Parish and Whyte, 1978).

5. Local strategies for development, making use of available community resources with access to some inputs from outside, are encouraged. This degree of acceptance of local controls, local rewards and benefits, local leaders, local customs, and local strategies all distinguish China's rural policies from Stalinist measures. Nonetheless, in China, as in the USSR, the rural sector was squeezed for two decades without improvements in the standard of living. At the same time, opportunities for individuals to be politically uninvolved or to escape to the city were much greater in the USSR once collectivization was complete.

Local initiative within the context of a decentralized model of modernization is part of an overall approach in which the center keeps basic control and the capacity to intervene based on the information it amasses. The center's inherent powers are revealed in the successive campaigns which from time to time have threatened essential elements in this accommodation with local interests. Even when it functions well, this approach relies heavily on the center's tight controls on political deviance and budgets and on its other latent powers to restrain localism.

Of course, there are many levels between the leaders in Peking and the localities. As Chapter 9 shows, Peking has not had the means to impose tight controls on day-to-day activities. Most administration has occurred at lower levels by officials often quite loosely controlled themselves. The continued growth of small inland cities relative to large, coastal ones enhances the integrative means available in local areas.

Rather than reconciling itself to the collapse of the third wave of reforms in the urban sector, the leadership under Mao Tse-tung decided in the Cultural Revolution to make the cities the major battleground for exerting further administrative pressure. A fourth wave of reforms followed, which revived objectives of the Great Leap Forward and, in narrowing the range of targets, intensified the controls on selected urban behavior. In particular, the most powerful party faction during the fateful decade from 1966 to 1976 sought control over all facets of education and mass information. It curtailed advanced educational opportunities in the city, drastically altered the criteria for access, decimated the ranks of teachers, scientists, and artists, and substantially adulterated the contents and methods of instruction. Only during the late 1970s were these policies reversed, repeating the experience of the late Ch'ing period when educational narrowness was found to inhibit modernization. In the late 1970s Chinese were still groping for a long-term approach to the cities and to the elite who lived there—this time one that would encourage initiative and reward performance and expertise without relaxing the controls that keep the leadership firmly in charge.

The general urban situation continued to reflect tight controls on the distribution of labor. Increased migration out of the city resulted from large-scale programs for sending youths into rural areas. Migration into the city was curtailed and controlled by registration, rationing, and the allocation of jobs to temporary workers by arrangement with their home communes. Previously underused labor of women and the elderly could be mobilized in labor-intensive street factories. Family planning, late marriage, and forced migration policies aimed at reducing the number of couples in fertile ages, rapidly diminished population growth. Although in several periods of intense political struggle factory conditions had deteriorated, the record of industrial growth presented in the preceding chapter testifies to a largely successful short-term strategy for organizing labor and other inputs and for minimizing nonproductive forms of consumption. In the late 1970s, managerial authority expanded, scientific and technical expertise began to be valued again, and inequalities widened as a means of stimulating improved performance.

Whatever the zigzags in policies over the first three decades of communist rule, they reveal a consistent concern with social control, resource accumulation, and growth and national integration through identifying a proper balance among geographical levels. The problems interfering with China's modernization prior to 1949 were faced and largely resolved although with enormous costs and delays in many areas. New problems created under Mao Tse-tung's leadership elicited a stream of reforms starting in the late 1970s. The following sections focus on many of the long-term problems and their resolution in the PRC.

Human Resources

Whether at home or abroad, Chinese have demonstrated unusual aptitude for diligent labor and educational achievement. Stories are legion of Chinese fortitude at work and eagerness to learn, whatever the setting. But the task of converting these talents, so long preoccupied with examination success and official appointment or with the acquisition of an additional parcel of land, to the modern deployment of specialized skills has by no means been simple within China itself. Efficient manpower training and use require more than concerted family support and extraordinary individual capacity for hard work and study; they presuppose a satisfactory blend of opportunities and incentives and an array of social changes that over the long run include a full demographic transition, a decisive transformation in the occupational structure, and a corresponding shift in educational content and purpose. Development of personal abilities demands an organized set of alternatives to past behavior capable of motivating new aspirations. Curiously, leaders of the PRC have, over extended periods, vehemently repudiated the very features that appear now to embody their promising formula for rapid modernization of human resources. During much of the 1950s the demographic component seemed most in doubt; at the end of the 1950s and through most of the 1960s the occupational component may have least complied with long-term demands; and then in the "ten lost years" to as recently as 1976 educational programs strikingly deviated from the talent search to which China eventually returned. In fits and starts, a strategy evolved for balancing the growth, training, and allocation of human resources with societal and individual needs and, in the process, for capitalizing on the impressive potential of China's premodern legacy in these respects.

POPULATION

When China entered the ranks of latecomers to modernization, it manifested a record of sustained population growth and an already staggering density of population that left only modest leeway for further increases in agricultural productivity by means that might realistically become available. Could Chinese leaders somehow accelerate the pace of modernization without the customary interval of rapid population expansion? Could they locate unused capacities and introduce new methods sufficient to keep agricultural gains in excess of population growth? Could they swiftly implement a strategy to curtail fertility sharply? Over the past century, despite moments of failure and long periods of very slow progress, the Chinese largely succeeded in preventing these problems from overwhelming their pursuit of modernization. The problems remain serious, but the successes in the 1960s and 1970s have considerably improved the prognosis for rapid development.

The population of China approximately doubled over the first two-thirds of the twentieth century before birth control became widely practiced. The age of marriage rose appreciably. Then population continued to increase at a rate that would add hundreds of millions of people to the one billion estimated for 1980 even if, as expected, family planning along current lines becomes virtually universal across the country. Should so large a growth somehow be considered a mark of relatively rapid demographic transition? Yes, by world standards for latecomers, it should be. The three phases in the demographic transition distinguished below indicate the gradualness of growth over a long span when other countries were growing more rapidly, the brevity of the period when a sharp drop in mortality preceded a drop in fertility, and the rapidity with which fertility eventually did decline. These phases in China were: (1) pre-1950 when annual rates of natural increase averaged only about 5 per 1,000 with higher rates of perhaps 8 to 10 per 1,000 at times of greatest public security and order; (2) post-1950 and ending anywhere from the mid-1960s to the mid-1970s depending on the area, as annual rates of natural increase climbed to well in excess of 20 per 1,000 and remained there until fertility decline began to match an earlier drop in mortality; and (3) from the late 1960s in most provinces as sustained decline in fertility more than counterbalanced an increase in the number of women of childbearing age, leading to a drop in the annual rate of natural increase to about 15 per 1,000, or even lower according to a 1979 PRC report. Few countries could match China's initial slow drift upward in population lasting as late as 1950, the rapid inception of its fertility decline, or the swiftness with which fertility then dropped; adding the fluctuations prior to 1900, China had "merely" doubled its total population between 1850 and 1970.

The explanation for the population's relatively slow growth in the first phase rests, above all, on the continued high level of mortality, with peaks in the Taiping rebellion, in periods of intensive warlord conflict, in recurrent famine years, and in the anti-Japanese struggle and civil war to 1949. Even in times of relative order and prosperity, death rates remained quite high. Modern hygiene and medicine were not rapidly transmitted to the countryside where, despite a decline in female infanticide, rates of infant mortality remained high and life expectancy at birth did not even approach thirty years (Barclay, et al., 1976). It is also necessary to note that fertility among Chinese women fell far short of what would normally occur among a population marrying so early. Whatever the reasons may have been for greater durations between births, they did not reflect family planning in which the spacing of children significantly widens as new births occur. A similar pattern of early marriage and low fertility within marriage characterized Central Asian peoples of the USSR, where it gave rise to a tremendous population boom (with unusual increases in birth rates) once mortality started to fall. Overall, prior to 1950 prolonged disorder and postponed prosperity preserved premodern demographic patterns and thus restrained population growth until a time when it could be vigorously counteracted. Much of the growth that did occur was absorbed by opening up the northeast for settlement and by migration to other relatively sparsely settled areas.

The brevity of the second phase may result in part from attributes shared with Chinese populations elsewhere and with others long within the orbit of Chinese-based civilization, who likewise experienced a swift demographic transition. Households in East Asia have shown a remarkable quickness in adopting family planning measures, just as they have been notably firm in rejecting divorce as a solution to marital problems. The swiftness of the transition may also reflect distinctive conditions in the PRC. Rather than widespread urbanization inducing change, collectivization and, on this basis, community incentives to restrict households created an environment favorable to birth control. Along with the expected effects of increased educational availability and of new occupational outlets for married women, a concerted effort at spreading knowledge of contraceptive methods and attitudes conducive to family planning reached into the work place, the neighborhood, and the small group. In lieu of massive geographical mobility or genuine opportunities for single or divorced women, changes within the rural community and the intact household reduced the desirability of large families. After a couple of interludes in which the leadership's attitude toward population might best be summarized as "the more the better," sober assessments of the relation between population growth and modernization took over. To secure more supplies from the villages, to enable villagers to improve their lot through both investment and consumption, and to curtail traditional demands on mothers and modern demands for community services, the leadership had to combat large families.

The speed with which fertility decreased (within the limitation of a rising percentage of women in the fertile ages) attests both to the unusual responsiveness of the Chinese population to new situations and to the extraordinary measures available to the communist leadership. The government commanded increasing control over the organized aspects of the nonfamily environment; it fully activated its means of persuasion and the groups capable of applying pressure on family members. With the assistance of production team collectives with self-sufficient strategies and barefoot doctors with essential knowledge and means, the state achieved some success in realigning the costs and benefits of children and the peer pressures in support of family planning. The principal features of this generally successful campaign can be summarized as follows: (1) the unlimited activization of normative pressures ranging from the mass media to the small group; (2) the rearrangement of organizations to draw the individual into groups beyond the household that can press for objectives of their own; (3) dissemination of the means to change behavior; and (4) the creation of a matrix of costs and benefits such that behavioral change will be seen as advantageous by many at both the collective and the household level. Since these features are by no means distinctive to China's approach to family planning, successes in this area may be presumed to result from a combination of a high coincidence of advantages between the state, the collective, and the household and of a more sustained commitment to this campaign by leaders at all levels. There have also been coercive elements in China's family planning measures. In the late 1970s, access to jobs, schooling, housing, rations, and private plots were all restricted for households with excess children. The state began to favor the one-child family. The new policies enhance the material incentives for households to restrict births.

To be sure, Chinese population continues to grow by more than 8 million annually (recent campaigns have dropped the figure sharply). There still exist well entrenched motivations for having many children, such as reliance on them for old-age assistance. Nevertheless the persistence of a serious problem of population growth should not detract from one's appreciation of how much worse that problem might have been.

In the short run, even without population growth under control, Chinese could pursue a strategy of rapid urban-centered industrial growth. But in the long run, given the modest surplus available from the rural sector and the minimal living standards of the rural majority, rapid modernization depends on the real growth of rural production, including the nonagricultural sectors, and on the capacity to keep population increases down.

What additional, overall lessons should be drawn from the Chinese experience with population control? In the Ch'ing period, the Chinese people did not find ways to restrain considerable population increases that at the very least matched production gains. But the regional experience in the mid-twentieth century indicates a different pattern—a propensity for Chinese populations to accept family planning with little delay. It would, therefore, seem likely that among the unusual elements of rationality and calculation in the Chinese peasant heritage discussed in Part One were some that could be speedily activated on behalf of population controls, given circumstances absent in an earlier era.

During the late 1970s the general decline in the use of coercive measures was less evident in population policies. In addition, new policies relied to an unprecedented degree on material incentives and penalties designed to restrict fertility. Late marriage, long intervals between births, and other desired family practices have an increasing financial impact in the form of penalties for those who fail to comply.

STRATIFICATION AND OCCUPATIONAL DISTRIBUTIONS

China's Confucian tradition was premised on the short life expectancy of the individual counterposed to the long-term predictability of social systems, and on the ample opportunities for ups and downs in the fortunes of the household in a setting of only minor fluctuations in the overall per capita indices of the society. Unusually secure conditions for long-range planning in a legally open society intensified the competition for degree holder status and for ownership of land. One would think that these same features of long-range planning and an open society could likewise encourage individual decisions conducive to modernization, but before 1949 instability bred insecurity and rural areas lacked the urban inputs that might have elicited new career options. For a time after 1949 these traditional features actually came under strong attack. Only after the repudiation of the Gang of Four did such notions as "continuous revolution," which minimized long-term stability, and "never forget the class struggle," which, in effect, imposed a closed class system by making recruitment and advancement conditional on class labels, begin to disappear.

Meanwhile, other social conditions were changing; life expectancy at least doubled, many per capita indices climbed, old avenues of social mobility were closed, and collectivities were given the resources to promote new avenues. At last in the late 1970s, a new stability of conditions for generating change and for pursuing household, individual, and community strategies seemed to be emerging in a context of reduced importance for class labels. The positive benefits of some CCP policies must be weighed against the considerable damage of others.

Many of the most interesting and elusive problems of China's modern development bear on issues of social stratification. Among these problems are the articulation of the elite and the masses, the interplay of vertical and horizontal bonds of community integration, and the diversification and accessibility of occupations. In various ways, these problems relate to the size and identity of, and relations between, groups of individuals in different occupational categories.

In the contemporary period, as in the past, a centrally selected elite occupies a critical role between family-centered interests and the objectives of the national bureaucracy. The similarity in function of the degree holder and the party member represents a fundamental continuity of Chinese history. Each ideally feels a direct bond to the national leader and to the guiding doctrines in terms of which all policies are rationalized. Each owes dual local allegiance, to officials representing higher authority and to the communities they serve. The balance tilted to the former for the party member and to the latter for the degree holder; the danger of malfunctioning resulted largely from excessive localism by the degree holder and excessive centralism, at the beckoning of party leaders from the commune level up, by the local party member. In brief, the recruitment and organization of a vast party membership with its deep involvement in virtually all decision making beyond the household unit and the smallest community gatherings continued the traditions of the degree-holding elite. Today there are many leaders both at the village level and in the intellectual community who are not party members; in the past one could also often identify a separate village elite as well as the business elite.

In the interim between the collapse of the degree-holding elite and the establishment of the party elite, rural China drifted along virtually beyond the reach of urban forces apart from coercion and commerce. This cutting adrift of masses of households posed a fundamental problem for China's modernization. In this respect, the contrast with Japan and Russia warrants attention. There the old elites of samurai and serfowners faded quickly into oblivion in the late nineteenth century following a single, sweeping reform. Their decline produced rapid, positive consequences for modernization. Since alternative restraints on behavior and bases for integration had become incorporated into local communities, the displacement of old elites did not disrupt social control and cooperation. Moreover, the separate life styles of these elites made them ready targets: funds previously diverted to ceremonial expenses and various types of luxuries could be greatly diminished and transferred to more productive uses. In contrast, the decline of China's elite removed an important basis for coordination but freed practically nothing for the state's coffers or productive investment; the decline proved disintegrative for long-term community and intercommunity cooperation, nonproductive for altering the balance between consumption and production, and inimical to breaking the pattern of landlordism and tenantry. To be sure, there was some concentration of authority in the hands of warlords, but their representatives never acquired legitimacy as a new elite.

The new framework for social stratification in the PRC rested on the results of land reform, collectivization, and a strategy for rural self-sufficiency. Land reform released much of the large surplus diverted into rents and transferred funds from land purchases and certain forms of debt repayment into consumption by the poor and investment by the state. Collectivization, in the form of production teams and rural strategies for meeting their own developmental needs, created a new organization for channeling and mobilizing manpower. Local party members in cooperation with team leaders could use this new framework for mediating between the general welfare and growth needs favored by the masses and by the national leaders. This arrangement proved adequate to keep resources flowing from rural areas, but it did not provide sufficient protection against recurrent excesses in central policies. Basic modification is required if the rural sector is indeed to take the lead in achieving the "four modernizations" in the 1980s.

Societies vary in the extent to which groups linked mainly by horizontal bonds represent their own occupational or other interests and the extent to which those integrated primarily by vertical bonds allow kinship, area of origin, or some other principle to predominate in interactions beyond the household level. In the transformation of premodern societies, it is common to find a heightened awareness of horizontal bonds, and eventually trade unions and a multitude of interest groups are formed. As described in Chapter 5, the Chinese heritage of strong lineages, *t'ung-hsiang* localism, paternalistic relationships of employment, and open social classes accentuated vertical bonding in which income and occupation were submerged as secondary distinctions. Legal equality accompanied wide inequalities of income and status within cohesive organizations of relatives or business associates. A multitude of small groupings prevailed; even with degree holders present, only a flimsy basis existed for coupling one grouping to another. The very conditions cited in Chapters 4 and 10 as encouraging free negotiation and responsiveness to changing conditions reflect a dearth of strong group structures that could promote organization for modern growth.

The communists sought to replace the old bonds with, on the one hand, a pervasive awareness of a new set of horizontal distinctions and, on the other, a centrally controlled hierarchy that would preempt virtually all vertical relationships. They frontally assaulted the perceptions of status and the criteria for association among the Chinese population. Their conceptions of social class acquired concrete meaning by the labels assigned to households and individuals during land reform, which for over a quarter-century were to be worn, in the minds of the community, like identification numerals stamped onto the skin. The attacks on earlier bases of organization probably further reduced the potential for organized resistance to state directives including those conducive to modernization. The establishment of new organizations such as the poor and lower middle peasant associations to represent a distinct point of view by virtue of common social origins or life circumstances has been sporadic and perhaps harmful to the initiative and diversity best suited to speedy modernization. Instead of developing further as interest groups, mass organizations representing workers, women, and youth were undermined by hastily conceived campaigns under Communist Party control and then destroyed in the Cultural Revolution, only to be revived later. In 1980 steps were being taken to invigorate mass organizations as representative bodies.

Since vertical groupings beyond the household operated on such a small scale to begin with and were so dependent on forms of property holding and labor use that quickly disappeared in the 1950s, it is not difficult to understand their decline. Probably the main beneficiary has been the community bond fostered by the production team, which may not altogether ignore traditional organizational principles. We might conclude that the contradictions between Chinese reality prior to communist control and the subsequent interpretation of that reality solely in terms of class conflict, and between the actual conditions of contemporary collective ownership and the invectives of class struggle supposedly applicable to these conditions do not create fertile soil for the desired organizational development. As enforced in the spirit of the early 1970s, attempts to "democratize" management through revolutionary committees (when they were actually implemented) were one factor leading to a breakdown in factory discipline; efforts to give work groups a strong say in community schools and in student admissions helped to paralyze quality education; and the group's frequent reassessments of work points based partly on attitudes are examples of peer decision making carried to excess. Decisions justified as the will of the masses were often manipulated for personal reasons. Nonetheless, the general cultivation of community power backed by collective ownership, labor use, and public services may have struck some positive chords in the villages and, in some ways, inserted a missing element of village solidarity common to early modernization in Japan and Russia.

Historically, the inhabitants of China, in theory, had diverse potential outlets for their ambitions, although the single career path of degree holder to official mesmerized households of the most ambitious and able, and full or part-time farming claimed the vast majority of households. The problem in the twentieth century was to widen the realistic career options, ensure that they met the real manpower needs of the society, and motivate the best prospects to seek the most crucial jobs. Prior to 1950 the options did widen and even though, because of the dearth of modern schooling opportunities for the majority, many could not exercise them, there was an overabundance of educated persons in many fields and corresponding unemployment. After 1950 options narrowed for the previously educated or well-to-do households; household economic activities were curtailed, geographical movement was restricted, and job turnover was often prohibited. China lost its open labor market. Yet, in the 1950s China gained a blossoming higher and middle school educational system, a burgeoning state bureaucracy, and a booming industrial labor market. In the cities, jobs existed for the educated and the skilled. But the regimentation without proper concern for diversity or management in the Great Leap Forward and, even more, the retrenchment that followed without much opportunity for the younger generation, largely closed the gateway to lucrative and career-oriented employment. Sending urban youths "down" to the countryside and recent arrivals of the Great Leap Forward back to the countryside, and finally decimating the ranks of mental labor in the Cultural Revolution narrowed job choices even further. The diversification of the rural economy starting in the late 1960s created new opportunities, but in a restrictive environment marked by duplication and few quality controls. The greater accessibility to early years of schooling and the scattered distribution of small-scale industries and services of the early 1970s did not realize their potential because of the low quality of training. Tight restrictions on job turnover, promotion, migration, and access to higher education also impaired the development of skills needed for modernization. Only the resuscitation of the intelligentsia in the late 1970s established a new range of possibilities for prospective labor with increased incentives to attract qualified persons.

In general, the modern transformation begins with inequalities determined largely by ownership, with labor and education secondary, and ends with labor and education primary, and ownership secondary. In earlier Chinese history ownership had been so fluid that labor and education acquired greater than usual significance. This led to relative equality, but at a marginal existence, and to common consumption aspirations so that no amount of redistribution altered the propensity to invest in land and to spend for household ceremonies. Further equalization in land reform and collectivization brought with them increased obligations to the state and to collectives; these avenues for investment did not depend on the uncertain prospects of voluntarily deferred consumption by households. But modernization also required increased output and motivated performance of tasks. Excessive equality has often reduced motivation, especially for educated mental labor, for workers without wage increases, and for industrious peasants. In various campaigns when the banner of equality waved most conspicuously, incentives have been least in evidence.

We observed in Chapter 5 that some conditions of stratification were favorable to modernization but others were not. What happened during the twentieth century? First the difficult problem of substituting a modern elite for the degree holders was largely resolved, although in the 1960s the Communist Party became the target of charges that its members were more expert than red. It is ironic that the organization dedicated to the supremacy of Marxist ideology should be attacked for insufficient purity. At the very time when expertise should have acquired added importance, it was assailed. Elite leadership was plagued by excessive and faction-ridden central control and by the paralyzing practices of peer review and decision making dominated by safeguards against innovative and individualistic activities. Second, new horizontal groupings served useful purposes such as building village solidarity, yet they stifled existing and emergent interest groups and set artificial barriers against the old vertical bonds. Finally local job opportunities expanded, but diversification, turnover, and specialization were hampered by, among other things, the absence of an open labor market. In the 1950s Chinese society achieved rapid modernization by creating substitutes for missing conditions in these three areas and then failed to sustain some of the newly established conditions. The task of rebuilding in the 1980s became all the more urgent and difficult.

STRATIFICATION AND SKILLS

The usual path of increased educational opportunity and social mobility into worker, service employee, and intelligentsia professions posed special difficulties for China. Basically, the problem was one of coordination: aspirations had to be kept from deluging the limited positions that would become available in the modern sector. The means were unavailable to accelerate urban growth and city employment as fast as in Japan and Russia, and a situation in which the desire for education in the cities alone would easily satisfy the modern sector's modest requirements could quickly have developed. The temptation would be great to expand one element or another so that educational achievement and urban or rural manpower needs would be out of kilter.

Prior to 1949, apart from some unemployment among those with advanced education in nontechnical areas, the problem of coordination did not become acute because the educational system expanded slowly, especially in rural areas. After 1949, both employment in the modern sector and educational opportunities leading to these jobs expanded too rapidly without adequate concern for the impending oversupply. Then retrenchment in employment preceded educational cutbacks at higher levels; in the next stage educational and employment cutbacks were so severe that the modern sector lost much of its vitality; and by 1980 Chinese leaders faced the difficult task of both meeting the modern sector's manpower needs and coping with massive unemployment among the vast numbers of school graduates.

One of the striking things about Chinese society is the differing opportunities that have been available to successive generations of youths. The bulge created by so many young people taking jobs in the 1950s and the dearth of older workers and employees retiring over the following decades resulted in an absence of new openings and of opportunities for promotion. Job security without job mobility or advancement stifled initiative. Then the enforced rustication and neglect of specialized training for the sizable generation of youths born after the revolution of 1949 created an enormous personnel shortage that became obvious once employment needs in the modern sector were reassessed. Finally, under the stiff new standards for competition, opportunities expanded for select individuals who excelled in education and on examinations even if others would have difficulty finding employment. The curious result of three decades of inconsistent policies, inefficiencies, and disincentives is that large numbers of positions are filled by inadequately trained people, numerous people are unemployed or underemployed and never allowed to apply their talents, and, in general, the work force's performance on the job is well below its potential.

In the villages the improvement in manpower skills largely awaited the communists' takeover. Following vast gains in mass literacy in the 1950s, the late 1960s and the 1970s yielded some gains in middle-level education attuned to local needs for health services, agronomy, teaching, and other applied interests. In the late 1970s both goals were being upgraded at once: middle and higher education primarily in the cities for access to the capital-intensive sector and to the application of international science, and lower and middle education in the villages for meeting local needs in labor-intensive activities and services. The communist leaders, especially during "the ten lost years" had squandered tremendous intellectual resources, but no one doubted the capacity of Chinese society, once limitations on study and career were largely removed, to produce another generation of competent experts.

In summary, China had, despite temporary setbacks, achieved much in the areas of human resources favorable to accelerated modernization. Although population growth still posed a problem, a population in 1900 of 400–450 million with premodern demographic characteristics has been succeeded by a population in 1980 of 1 billion with low death rates and moderate and sharply falling birth rates. A new dispersed elite of party members filled much of the void left when degree holders declined. The commune system as reorganized in the early 1960s, the late 1960s, and the late 1970s gave some encouragement to local strategies to achieve occupational diversity and productive investment in place of the old system of landlordism and rents. Universal literacy was virtually achieved (see Chapter 12) along with a return to a hierarchical, exam-based educational system for access to the modern sector and applied middle-level schooling for meeting diverse rural community needs. Given the basic characteristics of premodern China, the outstanding educational results on Taiwan, and the general rapidity of the demographic transition among Chinese populations, it is difficult to resist the conclusion that successes in the area of human resources were greatly facilitated by the heritage of the population.

Nevertheless, the heritage was far from sufficient—probably requiring more comprehensive transformative measures than had been necessary in Japan and Russia. And the communist leaders vacillated greatly on policies toward human resources, failing in the short run to take advantage of various assets—even decimating earlier gains. Their achievements did not come easily and remained incomplete. At the end of the 1970s they still faced the difficulties of converting from coercive measures, in, for example, controlling births, educational aspirations, job choices, party members, and potential occupational interest groups. In the development of modern scientific expertise, the task ahead seemed uncomplicated, but the wasted opportunities reveal a serious failure of policy that will take considerable time to remedy.

Patterns of Settlement

Just as increases in the availability of education are best timed to coincide with changing manpower needs, settlement changes may be analyzed as more or less in phase with other social transformations. Neither process should be expected to proceed so rapidly that its results are out of step with other conditions. The reflexive response that modernization requires urbanization, the decline of periodic markets, and the integration of villages into ever larger urban hinterlands may be at odds with the short-run needs for speeding modern growth in a particular setting. It is worth noting that Ch'ing China bears a striking resemblance to the common experience of modernization under communist leadership; it compares to societies at comparable levels of development by being "overeducated" and "underurbanized." From the Chinese experience of recent decades, it seems likely that in the modern era similar features could produce positive consequences for modernization. Because they curtail consumption, relatively low levels of urbanization best suit the overall strategy for speeding modernization. Thus, this discussion under patterns of settlement must take into account not only needs for rapid change, it must also consider needs for controlled and limited change.

It took China approximately a century of initial modernization to establish settlement conditions similar to those already evident in premodern Japan. Village cohesion in China mainly followed collectivization in the 1950s. Replacement of longstanding periodic marketing systems began in earnest only in the 1950s. Subadministrative units that could exert a firm grip on village resources may have emerged under the KMT, but they did not become fully operational until the commune system was established and overhauled. Only in the 1950s did the percentage of China's population residing in cities approach the level sustained in Japan during the second half of the Tokugawa period. Whereas cities generated powerful forces of change in Tokugawa society, they barely began to have similar potential as treaty ports developed in China; the full impact of urban forces awaited the improved rural linkages after the CCP took charge. In light of these circumstances and those discussed in Chapter 5, there seems to be little doubt that China experienced much more difficulty than had Japan and Russia in converting and building on its earlier urban network.

Once modern growth had accelerated in the PRC, however, unrestrained settlement changes in the directions anticipated with long-run modernization proved premature. Especially during the years of the Great Leap Forward when tens of millions flocked into cities, when the imprint of periodic markets was hastily obliterated, and when the village unit became little more than a subdivision of large communes, the need for a distinctive, slow transformation along these dimensions became apparent to many. Abrupt change disrupted important social routines and proved costly in resources and incentives. Over the following two decades, rapid modernization proved compatible with, indeed in some measure dependent on, slight urbanization, widespread availability of periodic markets, and buttressing of village and intravillage solidarity at the expense of larger territorial entities.

RURAL

Villages keep growing in China with no relief in sight until at least the end of the twentieth century. That is a fundamental reality of past and present; at no point has urban growth approached the level necessary even to absorb the increase in rural population. Even in the peak decade of urban increases, the 1950s, rural population increased at several times the rate of rural-urban migration. Undoubtedly the fastest rural growth followed in the 1960s when, in addition to high rates of natural increase, cities were made to disgorge recent arrivals and youths and send them to the countryside. All told, what began as a population of 75 million rural households in the mid-nineteenth century had probably reached in excess of 160 million households by the late 1970s.

Population growth is not the only force increasing rural consumption. The pervasive consumption orientation accompanied by a propensity to save for large ceremonial expenses inherited from Ch'ing China has no doubt been fanned by the contraction in opportunities for investment or migration and by the dispersal of resources to persons whose existence had previously been marginal. Increased income meant, among other things, a chance to realize long-accepted aspirations for expenditures on family ceremonies associated with birth, marriage, and death. Furthermore, a deep reservoir of optimism about improving one's family's lot, which had long encouraged the education of promising sons and the hard work needed for accumulating land or undertaking commercial ventures, meant that the desire for objects of consumption, now including diverse products of the modern age, could not be simply dismissed as the fancy of a minority. Given previous Chinese proclivities, it would not prove easy to hold these aspirations in check except as part of a well-constructed framework whereby modest rewards would be associated with concerted family strategies and diligent individual effort.

The Chinese had a choice among three basic methods for keeping yearnings for consumption and advancement in check while fostering modernization. First, there was the possibility of tolerating wide inequalities while depending on the main beneficiaries of the system to become investment-oriented landlords who sponsor improvements, like those evident in prewar Japan and present in areas of China before 1949 and in Taiwan thereafter. A great deal of tinkering with Chinese social structure would likely have been needed before this pattern of growth through wide inequalities could have materialized on a broad scale. After all, prior to 1949 productive rural investments remained meager. Second, there was Soviet-style collectivization with its forced equalization at a poverty level and its large requisitions for the state's investment purposes. This strategy had to be ruled out, sooner or later, as incompatible with the more immediate need in China for expanding rural production and with the traditional alliance between state and peasant in which both found advantage. Although the Chinese pattern over three decades in many ways approached the harsh Soviet treatment of rural life, there are grounds also for concluding that Chinese leaders opted for the third approach of equalizing and, to some extent, motivating; they redistributed the surplus away from the landlords, rich peasants, and merchants and at the same time, although not without some indecision as to how best to go about it, granted peasants limited means to better their lot at both the household and the collective level. This choice required powerful collectives with ample room for initiative and flexibility, in other words, strong village or intravillage organizations as opposed to Soviet intervillage collectives tightly controlled from above. It also required genuine incentives for household activities on a small scale, a convincing justification for the persistence of periodic markets within access of scattered villages still remote from modern transport. Finally, to serve rural needs as well as to meet the enormous appetite of modern industry for resources, it proved necessary to curtail large increases in consumption and services that accompany the growth of large cities and to stimulate on a limited basis growth in small cities that link the countryside to the advances centered in the urban sector. Although in the late 1970s it became clear that since collectivization there have been many Chinese similarities to Stalinist forced requisitions based on little increase in rural income, it is also evident that the Chinese have gone to greater lengths to motivate the rural population.

The contemporary production team, heir to over half a century of administrative realignments, provides the control and coordination of household activities and community resources that were previously absent in China. Its appearance follows such changes from the top down as the dispersal of power to the provincial level, the abolition and then partial reestablishment of the prefectural unit as an intermediary between province and county, the buildup in administrative activities at the county level, the establishment of subcounty districts, the division of districts into townships, and the repeated adjustment in township boundaries in an attempt to make controls effective at the local level. Under the communists, this realignment from above was joined by vigorous efforts to reorganize from below. Land reform dealt a strong blow to lineage and paternalistic bonds, partially releasing the household from old community ties and beginning the process that would lead through mutual aid teams and elementary producers' cooperatives to the establishment of new ties. Collectivization bore the thrust of reorganization from below, taking various forms before becoming firmly settled in production teams under the restrained, but potentially unlimited, control of larger territorial entities. Based on a corporate interest in land and on multiple functions associated with its operation as the dominant accounting unit for using and rewarding labor, the production team integrates rural communities comprised of roughly thirty to forty households. It mobilizes the population on a collective basis, makes crucial decisions with centrally determined guidelines for balancing various types of consumption and investment needs, and maintains an environment in which households can pursue independent, subsidiary economic activities and general strategies for improved conditions and benefits.

On occasion, communist leaders have negated the potential benefits of this rural organizational form by denying the household its main incentives in the form of private plots, pigs, periodic markets, and payment largely commensurate with work performed. They have also submerged the production team under strengthened production brigades or communes centered too far from the household's environs to maintain the symbiosis between family effort or interest and collective response. At other times—and these predominated during the 1960s and 1970s—the selected rural social policies produced unintended consequences visible in the tenacity of household customs, preserved under the influence of the private household economy, and in the increasingly closed character of the community centered on the production team.

On the whole, the communists have transformed the village, controlled it from without, integrated it into a wider territorial system, and, to some extent, penetrated it on a lasting basis. Traditionally, local areas pursued income and power maximization strategies by sending out officials and merchants and holding back taxes and other forms of surplus; now the localities again are pursuing strategies to maximize their gains, but the center succeeds in pumping far more resources from them. The rapid agricultural gains in Szechwan during the late 1970s suggest that increased attention to motivation—allowing households to have more pigs, permitting more private markets, forming small work groups out of production teams, increasing procurement prices, and the like—can shake the rural sector out of its doldrums. Even more serious tampering may be needed if the rural areas are to begin to narrow the gap with the cities.

By the late 1970s the new leadership of China had found rural policies to be seriously deficient. They sought to restore balance by upgrading the household vis-à-vis the production team and the latter vis-à-vis higher level units. They also favored greater incentives and more opportunities for personal initiative and expertise. As in the field of education, the Maoist leadership had gone to the opposite extreme in responding to a one-sided historical legacy. Leaders rejected an elitist educational system geared to achievement of top positions in favor of a modest mass education often hostile to superior performance, and they sought to eclipse the pervasive household orientation by granting almost all power and incentives to the community. These policies did not prevail in many areas, but they still contributed to the agricultural stagnation of the mid-1970s. The call for shifting the balance toward the household and its private subsidiary economic activities accompanied the rejection of coercive measures in 1978. One of the justifications for this shift was the difficulty the state had in securing more resources from the rural sector.

URBAN

It is always necessary to distinguish urban population from urban percentage, but this distinction is especially meaningful in China. In absolute urban population, China once led the world; it continues to rank with the frontrunners. When one considers how much investment in services is necessary to meet the natural increase of the urban population or how many jobs must be generated to achieve full urban employment, it is the absolute size of cities that counts. When, however, one turns to questions pertaining to the cities' share of entrants into higher education or to their share of convicted criminals assigned to labor reeducation, what is at stake is the relative size of cities in the overall population. According to this criterion, China has fallen steadily and is now one of the least urbanized states in the world.

During the Ch'ing period, China's cities failed to establish, as was done in Japan and Russia, various conditions conducive to modernization. As discussed in Chapter 5, cities did not display much dynamism in per capita terms. Over the century of initial modernization to 1953, although urban change did not proceed rapidly, its cumulative effect compensated for earlier inadequacies. While in the 1840s, some 15 million of 400 million Chinese resided in cities with a minimum of 10,000 inhabitants, by 1953 the figure for residents of cities of this size had quadrupled while total population had risen by less than 50 percent. Regional cities, which had previously flourished as entrepôts for diverse goods, were converted into treaty ports deeply involved in foreign trade and serving as incubators for modern elites. Warlords, the

KMT, and the CCP alike bolstered urban controls over resources scattered across their hinterlands. Meanwhile, modern transport extended those hinterlands, and eventually modern industry concentrated in the large coastal cities generated a surplus that transformed both investment and consumption for those with access to this sector. By the mid-1930s, cities had developed a momentum of their own for propelling social change, and by the mid-1950s the modern sector was on roughly equal footing with the traditional sector. What China had lacked in premodern urban dynamism, it realized through the introduction of modern elements.

If conditions for rapid modernization are absent and substitution of modern elements is necessary to produce their equivalents (China was no doubt unusual in possessing conditions that made substitution possible), then it is important to determine the fit between the modern substituted elements and the premodern social setting. The greater the role of substitutions, the more we might expect to find difficulties in the integration of old and new. Modern urban elements remained located in China's large, coastal cities; extraterritoriality, spheres of influence, and Japanese invasion increased the isolation of new types of industry and organization. Throughout most of the 1950s, the Soviet-style allocation of resources probably somewhat redistributed modern features to large inland cities, but it did not fundamentally alter the wide gulf that separated sectors of the society. Thus, in spite of good intentions and some important organizational changes in the 1950s, until the 1960s the difficulties of building on modern outposts in a premodern setting had barely been addressed. Only after the abortive attempt in the Great Leap Forward to make the entire society flower instantaneously did new policies systematically seek to link the new and the old, resulting in semimodern light and small-scale industry, and to reduce gaps between coastal and inland areas, big and small cities, and urban and rural environments in general.

It might be useful to consider Chinese policies as countermeasures to the negative consequences of substitutes for missing conditions. Since the 1960s, policies have not sought just to pile modern elements one on the other, but also consciously to redress the imbalances between sectors. In cities, these policies have focused on two main objectives, curtailing the usual spinover effects of a growing modern sector on rising consumption and services and using nonmodern elements in complementary ways. They circumscribe movement and mobility through a panoply of controls: sending down of excess labor and persons close to the age of marriage and to their chief reproductive years, tight restrictions on registration in cities with preference for temporary migration of persons without their families, and allocations of jobs virtually for life without even the semblance of a labor market. Control policies are premised on nationalization of major producing organizations and collectivization of subsidiary units like the neighborhood factories, which employ women and the elderly who cannot be profitably used by the modern sector and recently youths who would otherwise remain unemployed.

Urban control rests on two organizing principles overlaying the traditional household solidarities now reoriented to the smaller nuclear family. First, extensive controls are vested in the place of major daily activity outside the home—the factory, the office, the school, and the like. As we discuss in the section on organizational contexts, these organizations claim to embrace much of their members' lives beyond the specific functions for which they are formally gathered. Second, the city divides into a hierarchy of territorially based organizations, whose chosen committees become involved in diverse decisions ranging from who is to be sent out to the countryside and who is to have a baby as part of the birth control plan to how community services should be organized to make female labor more efficient. In suburban areas the two organizing principles often overlap since the place of work forms the nucleus of a company town.

Overall, Chinese leaders have taken extraordinary measures of control which may be regarded as successful for keeping the urban percentage from even doubling since 1949, but may seem less successful for allowing an absolute urban increase of at least 100 million and possibly close to 125 million persons—a figure that exceeds any other increase elsewhere in the world over a period of just three decades. Limiting urban growth is both an essential and a remarkable feature of modern China; it is consonant with a program of maximizing labor use where it is most productive and minimizing consumption where it proves most costly.

Because premodern China lacked the urban percentages of Japan and Russia, and because its cities were not as active in generating change or mobilizing resources, the urban sector had to be built up and reorganized in advance of most other modern changes. Treaty ports, the industrial investments of the pre-1949 period, and the long-term emergence of modern urban elites partially met this need. After 1949 burgeoning cities quickly added new functions. In the PRC controls on labor through the place of work and neighborhood committees and controls on movement through household registration, rationing, and other devices helped in the subsequent important tasks of restraining population growth and consumption needs. Yet, wage increases stopped, housing conditions deteriorated, and reduced freedom of movement curtailed the flexibility vital for urban life. Excessive controls created a mood of disenchantment and operated against improvements in labor productivity. In the cities, too, efforts were made to correct the imbalances acknowledged in the late 1970s, but little money has been made available to remedy severe shortages in housing, public transportation, and other services.

THE URBAN HIERARCHY

Comparisons of urban networks in the eighteenth and nineteenth centuries reveal inefficiencies for subsequent modernization in China's settlement pattern, particularly because of the dearth of cities of less than 10,000. During the initial century of slow modernization, this pattern did not alter substantially. The number of standard marketing centers increased faster than population rather than declining with modernization as in Japan, Russia, and Western Europe. The establishment of new county seats also did not keep pace with population growth. Modern developments were concentrated in large cities.

In China in 1953 the distribution of population in sizable cities almost duplicated that of Japan in 1878. In each country, some 11 percent of the population resided in cities with at least 10,000 inhabitants; 9 percent resided in cities of 20,000 or more; and 6 to 7 percent lived in cities of 100,000 or more. Over the following quarter-century, Japan undoubtedly urbanized more quickly; interestingly, in both cases the main thrust came from cities of moderate modern size, that is, well below the 100,000 level. Despite a high concentration of modern industry in a small number of cities, modern organizations and overall growth were widely dispersed. Tantalizing but skimpy evidence suggests that during this interval China was overcoming Japan's initial advantage in cities below 10,000. It seems that rather than urbanizing in an overall sense during the 1960s and 1970s, China primarily developed small cities—many are administrative seats of communes or, in a somewhat larger category, county seats—where it had been notably deficient.

By the late 1970s, China may not have been more than 20 percent urbanized (no more than 15 percent in cities of 20,000 or more), but it had an urban network newly balanced on the side of small cities. It may not have neared the demise of periodic markets, but it had built alternative channels for funneling the bulk of village production into cities. It may at last have created an urban network without major gaps, appropriate for mobilizing scattered rural resources and for stimulating the downward flow of industrial goods. It was also a network capable of fostering rural vitality and of slowing the pace of urbanization.

Three shortcomings in the reorganization of the settlement hierarchy were brought to light in the crescendo of self-criticisms of 1978. First, Chinese planners had long skimped on transportation; the network of roads and railroads connecting cities remained a serious bottleneck for development. Second, periodic markets and other outlets for private production had been excessively stifled in various areas; following collectivization the intermittent attacks on these outlets must have interfered with both the upward and the downward flow of goods. Third, centralized decisions without adequate expertise on urban problems did not result in optimal allocations of investments and personnel. Nonetheless, the overall picture was one of improving the potential for urban-rural and interurban linkages.

In brief, settlement patterns—apart from the frenzied widening of the urban-rural gap in the 1950s and the abortive dislocations associated with the Great Leap Forward and later revivals of some of its elements—became restructured in a way that appears to be conducive to the fastest possible modernization. City growth has been kept reasonably in check and reoriented to smaller cities, village units have been greatly strengthened and placed under the direction of broader territorial entities, and periodic markets persist as one device to give rural households and communities the flexibility to build on traditional and semimodern elements at the same time as the modern urban sector continues to expand.

Organizational Contexts

How have the Chinese solved problems of leadership, coordination, and control? How have they mobilized individuals and households into groups and guided these groups in the pursuit of modernization? Human resources and patterns of settlements may be vital elements in a society's modern development, but they do not directly address problems of collective action nor do they go to the heart of the communist ideology for reorganizing the forms in which people interact—for nationalizing, collectivizing, communizing, and, in other ways, regrouping the population. Representatives of diverse social systems adhere to the common objectives of birth control, expansion of the intelligentsia and of industrial workers, educational achievement, and integration of rural and urban networks through more local growth centers; Chinese communists have no monopoly on these objectives nor do the zigs and zags in their pursuit of them instill confidence that there, indeed, exists an enduring Marxist-Leninist blueprint to be followed in these areas. What distinguishes communists is, to some extent, their long-term goals for society, although these do not clash sharply with more vaguely expressed goals widely held by others, and, to a greater extent, their organizational means and redistributive methods. In this section we consider how the Chinese have balanced the concerns of families, intermediate organizations, and the state.

Prior to 1949, Chinese society continued to show a dearth of organizational development conducive to modern growth, especially in the villages. Two sets of organizations, which, in premodern times, had evolved precociously and in an unusually comprehensive way, jealously guarded their prerogatives against the possibility that other organizations would try to diminish them. The state bureaucracy, supported by its weaker local offshoots, suspiciously clamped down on large-scale organizations not subject to its close control, and the patriarchal household, bolstered by its involvement in a larger lineage organization, ordinarily tolerated other organizations only if they accepted the primacy of kinship principles. Small-scale state offshoots, such as the *pao-chia* or *li-chia* groupings for the purposes of control and taxation, and large-scale kinship-based units found survival difficult on either side of the imprecise demarcation zone between the two main organizational jurisdictions. Developments of the Ch'ing dynasty may have increased polarization into these two extremes; however, when this combination was found wanting as a basis for both social stability and modernization, new organizations were established. They responded to the exigencies of war and disorder better than they met the requirements of modern growth. Under warlordism and KMT rule, the functions of the state government expanded. In rural areas, however, kinship units remained strong, especially lineages which expanded their activities to meet increased needs for security. The victory of the CCP resulted from its ability to organize the peasant population in a time of prolonged disorder and foreign occupation. Peasant mobilization under such circumstances was nothing new in Chinese history, but what was new was the application of military and other disciplined means for mass mobilization to the long-term tasks of governing society. Such slogans as "the mass line" and "democratic centralism" entered the litany of organizational principles for Chinese modernization. The CCP reorganized Chinese society.

Risking the charge of oversimplification, we can distinguish three types of organizational response to modernization. The first modernizing societies relied heavily on intermediate organizations such as factories, local bureaucracies, and stores interacting with families and other primary groups without much state direction. Although Japan asserted greater state direction, its organizational forms largely conform to this first type. The Soviet Union represents the second type. The state commanded the modernizing heights, creating and centrally controlling organizations that were exclusively responsible to the leaders, not the people. The PRC presents a third type of organizational arrangement, balancing intermediate organizations between the pull of the family and the push of the state. As in the Soviet Union, organizations exist at the will of the state; those that preceded the communist movement are not tolerated. But once created, many organizations must operate in a decentralized environment. The discussion that follows suggests that Chinese leaders have created an organizational balance generally conducive to modernization, but have also impaired leadership and expertise in large-scale organizations in ways detrimental to a more efficient performance.

FAMILY STRUCTURE

The guideline for building a communist society, as it has been widely perceived, favors liberation of the individual from the family. This society of the future is to give preference to individual choice of a mate or partner on the assumption that the relationship will persist only so long as love endures, to state-sponsored forms of upbringing and education to the point that parents will play only a secondary role in socialization, and to contraction of the size of the household and its scope of activity until it becomes a secondary social institution. One might expect traditional family goals in a society following this guideline to yield to individual fulfillment, service to society, and acknowledgment of the priority of the interests of wider collectivities. Yet, the Chinese have developed somewhat different perceptions of building socialism and communism. Family practices in many ways do not fit the anticipated mold.

Prior to 1949 the traditional family structure operated as an obstacle to modernization in China, creating conditions of nepotism or blocking the formation of strong intermediate organizations. But in the urban environment less family-centered forms of employment, education, and property ownership were eliciting changes in family life. Indeed, the changes, for which there was little or no administrative pressure or mostly normative pressure, which William L. Parish and Martin King Whyte (1978), upon whose research we draw extensively, find occurring in villages of the PRC, largely duplicate those observed earlier in cities. One finds earlier family division, less solidarity among brothers, reduced cooperation among distant kin, more women working, the decline of dowry, better treatment of the new bride, and a decline in the power of the aged. The urban sector, already in the throes of industrial growth, anticipated the rural transformation to a more conjugal emphasis in the family.

Despite the communist blueprint for the family, some three decades after the establishment of the PRC rural transformation has produced surprisingly few results beyond the changes already visible in the cities before 1949. An accommodation has been reached in which the leadership eschews the use of heavy administrative pressure to produce structural change in the family. Apart from brief attempts in the early 1950s to enforce actively the newly granted rights of free mate choice, divorce, and remarriage, radically disruptive measures of the Great Leap Forward to transfer functions from the family, and the sporadic assault during the urban Cultural Revolution and its rural aftermath on ritual objects and old ways of behaving, the CCP has granted family structure a large measure of immunity. It continues normative pressures against elements of the extended family with some success, while tolerating behavior within the conjugal family clearly at odds with the CCP's professed goals. To the extent persuasive means are employed to diminish such behavior, they are largely ineffective. Bride prices, divorce rates, child-rearing customs, residence, property and inheritance patterns, and other indicators point to the high priority still assigned in the village to obligations owed to the corporate family.

Does this accommodation with the rural corporate family suit China's requirements for rapid modernization? There is evidence that it is costly in allowing large household ceremonial expenses. Moreover, it must be viewed as a limiting factor acting at cross-purposes with goals of rural social transformation that appear from time to time, such as efforts to build up large collectivities and armies of laborers. Nevertheless, in the context of a decentralized strategy dependent on motivated and flexible village participation, acceptance of the corporate family has many positive consequences. The Chinese have found that this accommodation does not prevent women from entering the collective work force in large numbers. By granting the family a meaningful private-sector production role and by making this interdependent with involvement in the collective sector, the CCP has kept alive substantial incentives for hard work and has increased the incentives for cooperative activity. Maintenance of the family's traditional responsibilities, such as old-age payments or aid to broken families, reduces welfare needs, minimizes individual acts of disorder, and supports the main source for motivating achievement-oriented behavior. The alternative of a more suppressed and restless rural populace cut asunder from many of its traditional family ties would not be compatible with the development strategy of the 1960s and 1970s. Likewise the alternative of a rapidly migrating and occupationally mobile populace would be incompatible with this strategy and with the means available in the society. The corporate family complements the program to encourage rural areas to lift themselves up through their own efforts. This approach to a surprising extent accepts the traditional organizational principles of familism and localism.

In recent decades, Chinese have created mechanisms equivalent to the family characteristics important in Tokugawa Japan for reducing population growth and promoting early economic advances. In both societies, the family operated as a basic legal and producing unit; its patrilineal, patrilocal, and patriarchal elements placed extensive controls over individual members and emphasized the welfare and status of the family as a whole. In addition to these traditional elements in China, new features altered the role of the family in ways reminiscent of Tokugawa society. First, the number of households in a village had been effectively regulated through community and household action in Japan, albeit without state intervention. The collective farm economy in the PRC also created conditions that complicated the formation of new households by tightly regulating the amount of land and other means of production available to each household and perhaps by limiting construction of new houses. Second, the size of each Japanese household tended to be constant, while the timing of increases in family size took into account current economic conditions. In the PRC pressures have mounted for a similar outcome; benefits for each household are highly dependent on the hand-mouth ratio, and efforts to maximize that ratio have increased rapidly. Third, opportunity to marry and age of marriage were adjusted in Japan to match available resources with actual household size. Policies in the PRC to increase marriage age in order to save community resources by reducing births and more fully using female labor offer a modern equivalent. The combination of village and household controls produced the Tokugawa mechanisms for reducing births and productively using resources; since the 1960s the combination of the production team and the corporate family with its private plot and household production seems capable of duplicating and, because of modern circumstances, amplifying the economically favorable rural results of the Tokugawa pattern. The Chinese state, unlike the Japanese, is deeply involved in bringing about these changes, especially in its program to reduce the birth rate sharply. The use of penalties to prevent undesired behavior shows that persuasive methods alone have been insufficient.

In other areas, there have been fewer incentives to meet state goals. While the Chinese have stepped back from some ambitious attempts to collectivize family functions and reduce material incentives even further, they have, nonetheless, denied the family adequate incentives to help the rural sector prosper. In some villages, egalitarian measures in general and outright discrimination against so-called bad class elements made a mockery of the principle "to each according to his work." Reforms proposed in the late 1970s seemed designed to reduce such restrictions on family initiative in production.

INTERMEDIATE ORGANIZATIONS

Modern China inherited a dearth of organizations—especially ones that could override kinship and local area ties—between family and state. During the century of treaty ports and increased ascendancy of regional power, new organizations partially filled the vacuum but did not systematically address the lack of intermediate organizations. Underorganization seriously impaired political stability as well as modernization efforts. In a sense, the major political parties of the 1920s to 1940s were competing to demonstrate their organizational superiority—to prove that they could create an apparatus to control and coordinate disparate elements. Finally the victory of the communists in 1949 attested to their success through the CCP in establishing local military units and base-area supporting organizations. They produced political stability largely through their organizational skills.

Could the organizational accomplishments of the wartime CCP and People's Liberation Army (PLA) be transferred to peacetime, developmental purposes? The communists lost no time in reorganizing the society: weakening lineages in favor of village-level groupings and mass organizations, restricting and then nationalizing family businesses, assigning activists and party members to leadership posts in all kinds of organizations. There was no doubt that the CCP could establish intermediate organizations crucial to linking greatly expanded state power and local family-centered authority. But were these organizations appropriate to the needs of modernization?

There are many reasons for thinking that Chinese leaders have erred repeatedly in their attempted reorganizations. Apart perhaps from the production team, which has had to survive various efforts to strip it of functions or to revamp its rules, the organizational record seems pretty dismal. Above all, there has been a pattern of hasty reorganization and, over the long run, inconsistent policies. Despite the willingness of some observers to credit the CCP with the achievements it claimed for itself, a campaign approach to social change has produced unplanned, fitful, and intense transformation rather than carefully thought out, planned, and orderly programs. Leadership changes and struggles have made policies inconsistent. At various times—not just in the abortive Great Leap Forward—inadequate attention has been given to the organizational forms appropriate to the conditions at hand. In their preoccupation with the possibilities of changing individual attitudes through charismatic appeal and the sporadic incitement of class struggle, Chinese leaders have not systematically studied the implications of the organizations they create. Short-lived organizations, such as the Red Guards, have redirected frustrations and disrupted ongoing activities, but long-lasting organizations have found it difficult to regularize relationships for sustained programs.

At the heart of these organizational problems was the central leadership's long expressed ambivalence toward managers and experts. Some carryovers can be discerned from the role of intermediate organizations in the Ch'ing dynasty. Consider the following similarities: (1) Uncontrolled organizations are suspect; permission to form an organization, regardless of its objective, is a privilege granted infrequently and only under stringent limitations. (2) Organizations are not in any way to develop independent political leanings; loyalty and full-fledged support to the ideology of the state and, except in extraordinary circumstances, to the national leader represent a high calling. (3) Members accept the priority of principles that accentuate the organization's service to the outside—in the past, nepotism in the service of the family and in the present, the mass line in the service of society and its national leaders. (4) Within the organization, impersonal rules and formal, contractual relations operate in limited ways; membership demands intense involvement and loyalty. Thus career orientation is downgraded for service, organizational objectives become secondary to outside loyalty, and specialization defers to commitment.

Even more important is the suspicion of the intelligentsia evident in the years of guerrilla warfare and continuously since the establishment of the PRC. In the first half of the 1950s, great opportunity and responsibility were granted to relatively educated persons, but the leaders regarded them as tainted and in need of having their thoughts rectified. Specialists could only relieve their special burden by "dismounting to look at the flowers," being in contact with the masses, and engaging in physical labor. But their situation worsened: hasty decisions from above meant dissatisfaction; antirightist campaigns meant demoralization; simplification of management meant demotions; the *hsia-fang* program for sending people to the localities and the countryside meant dispersals, slogans in place of plans meant disregard; and, after a respite in the early 1960s, the Cultural Revolution and its aftermath meant denigration. As went the intelligentsia employed as experts and managers, so went their organizations. Not even administrative agencies nor the Communist Party were spared from the onslaughts of the Cultural Revolution. Only intermittently in the early 1970s and decisively in the late 1970s did urban China recover from a decade of organizational collapse and deterioration; mass organizations were reformed, educational institutions were reinvigorated, and factories were relieved of the disruptive management of revolutionary committees. Under stronger professional management, able to make fuller use of the talents of experts, and permitted greater flexibility to pursue their own objectives, organizations emerged from a long spell of serious problems. Yet, differences within the leadership remained disruptive.

The administrative buildup of the 1950s greatly alleviated the problem of underadministration even though subsequent campaigns weakened many administrative organs. Questions of how big the government would grow and how minutely it would intervene in local activities remained unresolved. For a time it seemed that diverse interests could be aired through national party congresses and other forums and that the rule of law would become an ever larger obstacle to arbitrary uses of authority. Yet, for most of the two decades from the antirightist campaign of 1957 to the downfall of the Gang of Four and, to some extent, from 1949 to 1957 as well, another style prevailed. Law was played down in favor of individual attitude, mass mood, extenuating circumstances, and class background. From the top leadership on down, factions and personal loyalties took precedence over substantive issues and representation of organizational interests. These circumstances fostered a dossier society, especially in the cities, in which extensive files—records sprinkled with criticisms and self-criticisms from repeated small group sessions and mass meetings—could at any time be used against individuals in positions of responsibility. Oversurveillance lingered on in China, accompanied in the mid-1960s by license to Red Guard youths to assail authorities and specialists and in the following years by mass demotions to physical labor or more serious punishments.

To the extent that state organizations were successful in fostering modernization, their procedures were far removed from the political hysteria of the Cultural Revolution. Rather they offered long-term guarantees in place of disruptive measures that brought insecurity and confined themselves to persuasive pronouncements in lieu of coercive penalties. Direct administration of large, capital-intensive enterprises, where central or provincial control proved most feasible, was matched by decentralized guidance of other firms and of the agricultural sector in general. Oversurveillance posed a serious problem, but much administration was in fact decentralized.

In the area of organizations, it is possible to discern an overall approach that compensates for the earlier absence of conditions conducive to modernization and complements the other new aspects of China's developmental strategy. In 1980 this approach was not firmly implemented. It had passed over many hurdles, but had not yet become securely settled in the fabric of society. Intermediate organizations were still being revamped following the disruptive waning years of Mao's life. Leaders were beginning to promise managers and intellectuals the autonomy and security necessary for able leadership. Oversurveillance may still be stifling personal initiative, and even the planned

388

addition of a firm legal underpinning may not be adequate assurance that surveillance will not take a more regularized form. Despite these shortcomings of the recent past, the organizational framework has largely proven adequate in key areas of production and, once revitalized, can be expected to blend, with less friction and malfunctioning, cohesive family groups, powerful but locally flexible and professionally administered intermediate organizations, and substantial state planning and direction. There still remain decisions in this area that could be critical to the success of the general strategy of rapid modernization.

Intermediate organizations play a crucial role in China's modernization strategy. In rejecting the Soviet, centralized strategy, the Chinese increased the need for flexibly evolving separate strategies in various local organizations. In acquiescing to the continued grip of the family on the individual, they enhanced the need for achieving balance by constraining and guiding individual behavior in organizations apart from the family. And in restricting migration and labor turnover, they placed a heavier burden on each organization to meet individual needs internally. Small study groups are one device for reaching individuals within each organization. Reduced status differentials among members and broad participation in many kinds (but often not the most meaningful ones) of decision making are other characteristics of contemporary China. These devices cannot substitute for the genuine articulation of group interests. Revitalized and new organizations are critical to the "democratization" of Chinese society deemed essential in the late 1970s.

Despite the many reservations one can raise about the appropriateness of China's intermediate-level organizations for continued modernization, it should be noted that production teams have met many longstanding needs of local control and coordination, and modern factories as well as other large-scale urban employers have managed to organize labor for sustained economic growth. Although these organizations may not have been well geared to increases in productivity or consumer satisfaction, they have made important contributions to the modernization achieved over three decades.

State Organizations

As described in Part One, the Ch'ing pattern of underadministration and oversurveillance relinquished access to local resources at the same time as it stifled the initiative of officials and other potential advocates of reform and modernizing change. State organizations were bolstered, of course, over the first half of the twentieth century, and after 1949 the new leadership en route to socialism secured far greater powers for central ministries and other agencies at all levels of government. By 1957 leaders recognized the ineffectuality of a highly centralized planning apparatus in a largely dispersed, agrarian society; they groped for the right mix of central, regional, and local powers and of state and collective authority. On the one hand, signs of regional militarism (prior to the transfer of generals in 1973–1974) and local self-reliance imply a dearth of centralized controls. On the other hand, the profound impact of intermittent national campaigns and the import of sharp criticisms of overcentralization expressed in the late 1970s combine to suggest insufficient local autonomy in making major decisions. While state organizations may have been too disrupted and constrained by nonbureaucratic styles of operation and by power struggles at the top, they preserved a degree of oversurveillance that affected the workings of other organizations.

The Maoist conception of bureaucracy, as Martin King Whyte (1973) has depicted it, interfered with the usual practices of formal bureaucracies. At its extreme, the Maoist model led to conditions whereby: (1) officials were judged more for political purity or zeal than for technical competence; (2) collective leadership with the involvement of untested revolutionary committees replaced a clear hierarchy of communications under professional management; (3) precise rules and procedures with limited contractual obligations were looked upon with suspicion; (4) rewards based on office and performance were deemphasized; and (5) May 7 cadre schools, as well as other restraining devices, reduced job specialization and career orientation. These and other procedures demoralized officials and reduced the effectiveness of state agencies.

State planning agencies, ministerial offices, and local administrative bureaus are essential cogs in the operations of socialist countries. When these organizations work badly, a great deal more may be at stake than in most nonsocialist countries. During the 1950s China's transition to socialism was complicated by the shortage of competent and experienced personnel in state employment. Later the problem of qualified personnel receded before the increasing shortcomings within the organizations themselves. According to criticisms leveled after Mao's death, decisions in the bureaucracy were made too much from the top down. In the era of acute uncertainty that lingered for perhaps as long as two decades, few dared to take responsibility. Minor decisions were tossed up to very high levels of government. Probably more detrimental to the initiative of experts and managers than the effects of collective decision making was the need for approval from above in a demoralized bureaucracy hesitant to be caught on the wrong side of the next shift in policies. Among the proposed solutions at the end of the 1970s were to stabilize the internal decision-making authority of bureaucrats and to make factories and other organizations less dependent on state agencies.

Some bureaucrats continued in their posts; others were reinstated in the late 1970s. Much reorganization was needed to improve the proficiency of China's sizable bureaucracy, to make it capable of responding to the improved incentives and more professional work conditions of the late 1970s. The Chinese did not have a Soviet-style bureaucracy, whose prerogatives would have been difficult to dislodge and would also have been largely incompatible with the overall strategy of modernization. Yet, they also did not have as highly trained state technocrats as those long attracted to state research institutes and leading agencies in Japan and the Soviet Union. The task of improving competence seems within reach, but it will take considerable time, even in a climate of diminishing surveillance, increased incentives, and heightened foreign investment, training, and participation in economic ventures.

In summary, the Chinese communists with little delay, partially resolved the primary organizational requirements for sustained, rapid modernization, but then allowed conditions to degenerate, especially in their third decade of rule. Their policies clashed with the requirements of modern bureaucracies, unduly restricted genuine interest groups, and vacillated on the proper balance between various types of organizations, Beginning in the first half of the 1950s, there had been important changes in the relative balance of the three major levels of organizations. The family remained remarkably strong for a socialist society although it was clearly controlled in ways atypical of prerevolutionary China. Some types of intermediate organizations remained rather undeveloped, but the production team and the factory emerged as important exceptions. And state agencies were increasingly pervasive, especially in the cities, even if they were not well structured for guiding advances in productivity and efficiency. On the whole, organizational restructuring in the PRC responded to the acute challenge to reorient family solidarities and to establish other forms of control useful for modernization. Further adjustments to improve the capabilities of organizations and the fit among them, remain among the highest priorities for continued, rapid modernization.

Redistributive Processes

Communist movements promise equitable distributions—of resources to be invested for economic growth, of wages to be awarded for work performed, of opportunities to rise on the social ladder, and of benefits to meet the elemental needs of the majority. These objectives held out considerable hope for speeding China's modernization. Closely supervised land reform produced increased revenues for investment. Industrial growth and nationalization offered numerous opportunities for social mobility. Educational expansion and state-controlled unionization contributed to early improvements in the urban labor force. In many respects increased equality was realized during the 1950s, and, by and large, it served the immediate needs of socialist modernization. But what started as a positive factor for meeting well-defined needs eventually acquired a more ambiguous significance as equalization continued to be pressed and the leadership groped for new strategies of development.

Premodern China stands out for its legal acceptance of mobility, migration, and marketing as inherent rights of the individual. Success stories applauded the household's diligence in bringing about a status rise from physical laborer on the farm to scholar-official at court or from poor tenant-farmer to large, leisured landowner. Yet, much as these avenues of advancement anticipated the fluid redistribution of wealth and status that prevails in modernized societies, as we argued in Chapter 5 they did not offer the favorable conditions for modernization identified for Japan and Russia. Unlike the more mobilized and centralized elites in those countries, China's elite was primarily oriented to the native village and was largely unhindered by high taxation or by large-scale production for distant markets. Twentieth-century policies wrestled with these deep-seated decentralized life style preferences, with their major consequences for the redistribution of resources.

Under the PRC, a surprising legal turnabout occurred: ascriptive elements became more important as members of "bad classes" were denied opportunities, geographical mobility except for unwelcome deportations from cities became tightly restricted, and private marketing suffered from intermittent crackdowns. In these respects, the legal character of China in the 1970s seems less modern than its premodern counterpart. New restrictive conditions seriously limited access to education, to jobs, and to income derived from private production. Could incentives be satisfactory and resources or manpower efficiently used in this fashion? The leadership after Mao's death seemed to answer this question in the negative, but it lacked the means to rectify fully a situation so long in the making.

At the heart of the Maoist approach that prevailed until the late 1970s was the treatment of urban and rural areas as separate areas that both required greater equality, which was to be achieved through an almost entirely controlled redistribution of material and human resources. Those eager to move from village to city were restrained, while urbanites reluctant to depart for the countryside were coerced. Jobs were more allocated than selected; labor turnover for personal goals was largely denied. Some regulations were widely circumvented, but the system largely succeeded in artificially severing the normal links between city and countryside. While positive consequences no doubt resulted from denying spontaneous forces the opportunity to sidetrack the basic plan for modernization, inefficiencies and disincentives took their toll, particularly in the decade of mass urban-to-rural migration after the Cultural Revolution.

MOBILITY

In the 1950s the Chinese leaders restructured opportunities for social mobility. Intelligent youths competed for high examination scores and admission to prestigious programs, less educated activists threw their energies into successive campaigns hoping to win appointment to leadership posts, workers could aspire to bonuses and promotions for exceeding production norms, and even peasants for a time maintained some traditional channels of ownership and private commerce. But many capable persons were quickly excluded because of family class labels, and such discrimination, especially in admissions, intensified from 1963 on. Before long opportunities declined for others as well. Many managed to hold on to the positions they attained in the 1950s, but there was little hope by the 1960s for further upward mobility based on specialized skills or experience. Attacks against material incentives and careerism buttressed the reality of few desirable urban openings within the occupational hierarchy.

It was not so much a matter of revising the material conditions of the 1950s, but of freezing them. For instance, wages continued to vary by region, sector, job level, and seniority; actual wages were virtually unchanged over twenty years. Even for city youths to secure a lower level job as a factory worker became a real challenge. By the late 1970s it was acknowledged that wages had to be raised and opportunities for meritorious promotions increased if workers were to feel they had adequate incentives.

Traditional means of mobility were viewed with suspicion. The accumulation of household savings to buy land or to invest in commerce and industry was seen as incompatible with state ownership. Educational specialization and career orientation were criticized as too individualistic. The household could do little to distinguish itself and earn rewards superior to those prevailing in its assigned collectivity. In turn, the collectivity was often entrusted with the selection of those who might move on, perhaps to a commune office, to an urban enterprise, or to a post-Cultural Revolution university. This process was subject to abuse and at the same time reduced the incentive effect of mobility opportunities for diligent study and labor.

Both Japan and the Soviet Union have had much success in filling specialized posts with able people through high rates of social mobility based primarily on educational performance. China had the most obvious historical precedent for a similar outcome, but its leaders rejected the substance and later the spirit of the traditional examination system. However, in the late 1970s China shifted abruptly back to a system that makes educational excellence the filter for career access and highlights anew the appeal of scientific knowledge and mastery of foreign languages that make upward mobility possible.

Within collectivities, certain categories of people have seen their status upgraded, a form of upward mobility, while others have lost status by virtue of their class labels. Initial equalization meant gains for poor and lower middle peasants, whose households once had fewer resources at their disposal, and for ordinary workers. At the same time it brought down the status of many who formerly enjoyed considerable wealth or power. As in Japan and the USSR, land reform and other steps toward equality have refocused interest on the educational ladder. But because of the many years in which rungs in the ladder have been missing and the narrowness of the ladder in comparison to the crowds striving to climb aboard, there have been fewer alternatives to the collective settings in which individual talent does not easily stand out.

At the same time, one should not overlook new forms of recruitment of leaders in the PRC. Selection into local cadre posts, into the PLA, and into the CCP are forms of recognition of superior ability and activism. Fear of exposure to criticism in a position of responsibility as well as factionalism and other abuses has meant that the most able have not necessarily been selected, but the tens of millions who have been selected—often by the communities themselves—include many whose leadership skills have proven helpful in pursuing rapid modernization. The record of selection has some bright spots, but on the whole Chinese social mobility is a depressing commentary on missed opportunities. The promotion of incompetents will haunt China for decades.

Migration

Chinese leaders have defied the usual contemporary expressions of popular will in choice of residence in the following ways: (1) by largely prohibiting the movement of rural residents into cities; (2) by coercing large numbers of urban inhabitants to move to the countryside; (3) by resettling long-time residents of Shanghai and other populous East Coast cities in less attractive and smaller inland cities; and (4) by relocating in frontier and minority areas citizens of Han nationality. Have these policies promoted modernization? Have they reallocated scarce labor skills to places where they might more advantageously be employed? Have they curtailed movement that would have increased unemployment or added to the costs of employment? Available evidence suggests that they have produced some positive results, such as holding down the increase in urban consumption, concentrating urban growth in small cities, and more fully exploiting natural resources on the periphery.

The negative effects of China's extraordinarily stringent controls on migration are perhaps of no less consequence. They have divided families, separating couples for little apparent reason except administrative convenience in the assignment of labor, and wresting children of high school age from the close bonds of their households for an uncertain existence in a distant milieu. Migration policies that allocate labor without adequate consultation and approval necessarily reduce incentives for performance at work. PRC policies also do not seem to have done notably well in matching personnel skills and employment needs. The post-Mao leadership has criticized certain of these policies and promised to redress them to the extent that circumstances permit. Nevertheless millions of youths still languish in the countryside without contributing substantially to either village needs or their own career longings. Leaders do not know how to absorb them back into their cities of origin without diverting scarce funds away from modernization goals.

Controls on migration persist. Yet, they are no longer so rigid. Performance now counts for more, and individual preference is of some consequence. The search continues for a satisfactory balance between the planned allocation of labor and the encouragement of individual aspirations.

Marketing

Both collectives and individuals are motivated by incentives for selling produce, often at nearby marketing centers. The success of modernization in

China has been deeply affected by the adequacy of these incentives and by the flexibility of the means available to take advantage of changing opportunities. To some degree, a sizable part of China's economic program is also immune to these factors because goods are channeled directly to state and collective agencies at fixed prices, ensuring a high rate of investment and production in an attempt to meet targets set in successive national plans.

In many ways, marketing has been restricted in China. Policies that prohibit activities smacking of private enterprise include rationing of basic commodities, fixed and uniform prices, and central decisions about what is to be produced. At times even tighter restrictions led to the curtailment of private plots and markets, but more often the rural private sector has been tolerated, as long as it did not exceed prescribed limits. To get around many restrictions, a black market exists, in rationed goods, for example, and in other items generally unavailable and for which demand far outruns supply. To obtain scarce goods and services and to improve their chances for favorable mobility and migration, many have resorted to "going by the back door," that is using influence or money to win illegal or unethical advantages.

In 1978 and 1979 much discussion centered on relaxing restrictions on seeking personal or collective profits. Newly formed street collectives met previously unmet needs for goods and services. Production teams demanded the right to produce the most profitable crops. Both urban and rural collectives complained about their inability to specialize on items in great demand, which would produce a higher income.

On balance, the PRC accomplished much in redistributing resources in a manner consistent with its strategy for economic development. After 1949 it severely reduced conspicuous consumption, greatly increased state revenues and investments, and redistributed property and incomes so that minimal needs were largely met and welfare costs were kept low. The basic steps taken proved adequate for sustained economic growth. However, many, such as college students who had to squat to eat in their cafeteria and apartment dwellers who waited in long lines for access to a toilet, suffered with barely tolerable provisions. Waste was considerable and incentives insufficient. Only in the late 1970s was there an unquestioned commitment to basing rewards closely on one's contribution to production.

Personal Relationships

CONTRACTUAL ORIENTATIONS

The rule of law fell victim in the 1950s and even more in the mid-1960s to the manipulation of political symbols and zealotry. Within a short time after the communist victory, agreements between individuals or households could not be enforced because of legal restrictions against private transactions in land, labor, and interest-bearing loans. Increasingly, public collectives, not individuals or households, entered into agreements. Of course, customary law persisted; with the support of their communities and, where necessary, the formal authorization of officials, parties continued to reach agreement on such matters as the inheritance of property, the exchange of services, and marriage and divorce. On other matters, however, the absence of a secure legal framework led to inertia or to makeshift arrangements. Instead of negotiated labor contracts for a fixed term, China evolved a system of virtual lifetime employment for urban workers known as the "iron rice bowl." When workers retired, their children could often inherit their jobs. The response to uncertainty was inflexibility, often accompanied by ascriptive favoritism that favored the status quo.

Contracts offer some assurance of a stable and predictable environment. They facilitate long-range planning and optimal allocation of household resources. The communist leaders belatedly recognized their utility in the late 1970s after begrudgingly making concessions in earlier periods of duress. Of course, the establishment of a centralized government and of peace under the communists went far toward alleviating the rampant insecurity and instability of several of the preceding decades. Nevertheless, resort to campaign methods and hostility to binding legal precedents did not create an adequate environment for optimal planning. To the extent that during most of the 1960s and 1970s households, production teams, and other collectivities managed to cope with difficult circumstances, they operated under hard-won guarantees that gave some stability to their planning even if the role of material incentives remained quite limited.

LINES OF AUTHORITY

In the decades before 1949, lines of authority were in flux. Within many localities lineages or powerful landowners gained greater control, while household authority also remained undiminished. Communist leaders set out to alter the balance of authority: to increase the direct influence of the state (and the CCP), to eliminate authority based on property and on locally amassed power, to redirect lineage allegiances toward newly developed corporate communities, and, at the same time, to restrain emergent, modern forms of laissez faire individualism.

They moved also against the powerful deference to authority that extended beyond mere kinship (lineage) or property and local power, against that shown, for example, to teachers and religious leaders, indeed against all prestige as defined by the old society. Beginning in the 1950s and intermittently thereafter, the communists seemed to approach the pathological in their efforts to eradicate all such authority lines lingering from the old society, even at times encouraging children to denounce parents—an exception to the usual pattern of allowing the small family to remain strong. Structural reorganizations supported these objectives; so too did attempts at ideological remolding.

China's leaders pursued a strategy to remake popular attitudes pertinent to modernization. Their image of the new socialist personality, in line with the unidimensional positive heroes portrayed in all forms of art, was characterized by dedication to work, selflessness, and lack of interest in individual rewards. The schools, the mass media, small groups at work or residence, and all formally constituted organizations shouldered the responsibility of fostering this new type of individual. Directly inspired by the mass inculcation of altruistic service ideals, the "new socialist man" would, in theory, strive unflaggingly for many goals, among them those of modernization.

If human behavior could have been transformed in accordance with CCP intentions, the implications for all avenues of social change would have been considerable. Above all, existing lines of authority could have been bypassed through essentially direct communications from national leaders espousing ambitious goals to the responsive masses who would have required few material benefits. Mass memorization of the little red book of Mao's sayings was the extreme application of China's experiment in direct socialization. Imbued with the teachings of the ideal proletarian ethic, individuals might be expected to forgo short-term consumption, to require no additional remuneration for extended or specialized work, and to respond without delay to campaigns aimed at meeting various needs of modernization.

In the literature on China, one finds widely divergent interpretations of the motives behind stringent Chinese demands on the individual. Some argue that the drive to create a universal model citizen developed in its own right, even taking precedence in the struggle for modernization over such policies as specialization. Others contend that the heavy reliance on exhortation and normative incentives was primarily a means to carry forward a strategy for modernization dependent on very high rates of savings and labor force participation. It is beyond our scope to attempt to sift through the motivations and even the priorities of Chinese leaders. Nor is it essential to focus on policy objectives when our main interest is on the actual conditions of China's road to modernization; not why policies were adopted but the difference they made. The extent to which Chinese peasants and workers actually accepted the high-sounding pronouncements of their much publicized representatives cannot be determined with any precision. In the absence of public opinion polls and easy access of information, claims for extraordinary changes in consciousness must be treated with skepticism, particularly given the many personal revelations after 1976 about the fear-filled climate that had prevailed.

Limitations on the expression of individual aspirations created a climate that greatly shaped the means available for modernization. The individual had little opportunity for self-expression. At school or work place, career aspirations were suspect. Strict controls ruled out the formation of voluntary associations. The rise of individualism, in one's choice of a marriage partner, employment, residence, leisure, information, and the like, was stifled. This was done both by the pervasive Chinese communist hostility to "bourgeois" individualism and by the consequences of policies that reinforced household and community-centered controls. While there was little prospect that China would develop a widespread laissez faire type of individualism sometimes found in the West, the balance of incentives shifted perceptibly after Mao's death in favor of individual aspirations. Under the new circumstances, moral imperatives far removed from actual conditions assumed a lower profile, while pragmatic approaches based on personal benefits took precedence.

The unsatisfactory experience of the PRC with normative incentives, collectivist orientations, and lofty ideals of selflessness and sacrifice does not perforce demonstrate the superiority for modernization of policies that approach the opposite extreme, that is, remunerative incentives, individual orientation, and crass motives of selfishness and gratification. There are two reasons for not shifting precipitously to this opposite viewpoint. First, the policies of PRC leaders have often been so extreme and so hurriedly imposed that they have not offered a fair test for the basic approach that underlies them. A more balanced and cautiously implemented reliance on persuasion, group interest, and human generosity might have proven more enduring than have many policies of Mao's leadership. Second, the acute need for new forms of control and coordination, as well as for other conditions identified as important to the modernization of Japan and Russia and requiring special attention in China because of its premodern legacy, called for some of the very measures that PRC leaders carried to a counterproductive extreme. Authority vested in rural community organizations is likely to persist as is the need for delayed gratification in order to keep rates of savings high, even if they are not so high as they were at times when immediate consumption was reduced to a bare minimum.

International Comparisons

Between the 1860s and 1950s Japan and Russia modernized, reaching a stage of social transformation we call high modernization. Birth rates, except for some minorities in southern republics of the USSR, had fallen to the levels of the modernized West. Agricultural workers made up less than 50 percent of the work force and were continuing rapidly to decrease in proportional importance. Mass secondary schooling was a reality and a sizable portion of high school graduates continued their formal education. Rural-urban migration continued at a high rate, and cities rapidly grew to house more then 50 percent of the national population. Of course, important differences existed between Japan and Russia, as for example, in the operation of voluntary organizations, in divorce rates, in access to information, and in the availability of consumer goods and services; yet the major indicators associated with modernization largely show two societies similarly moving toward an advanced stage.

The same set of indicators shows China in 1980 still decades away from high modernization. Much of the explanation for China's slower transformation lies in the lack of momentum during the first half of the twentieth century. Before 1950 one can discern neither a demographic transition nor a surge in urbanization, neither the spread of literacy nor the redistribution of resources into savings. The balance between household and lineage on the one hand and community and state on the other lacked the conditions for mobilizing resources already evident in mid-nineteenth-century Japan and Russia. To be sure, there were significant changes within Chinese society, such as the development of new groups associated with the modern urban sector and the transformation of rural life under the impetus of political reforms and militarization. They were important in bringing the communist leadership to power and in making possible radically new policies, but the changes prior to 1949 did not carry China much beyond initial levels of modernization.

The three decades of communist rule that fall within our purview produced a massive social transformation, much of it pertinent to modernization. On some indicators, such as those showing the demographic transition and literacy, enormous headway was made toward modernization. In many areas, Chinese leaders removed longstanding bottlenecks; for example, they reorganized settlements to strengthen village cohesion, and they created large, state bureaucracies that could assert central control and draw together vast amounts of resources. By 1980 China had reached an intermediate stage of modernization, in most matters having made the most spectacular advances in the 1950s while registering in the 1960s and 1970s a mixed record.

The main indicators for China cannot in some cases yet be stated precisely, but as more information is becoming available it is increasingly possible to make informed estimates about some of them. Employment in agriculture appears to have fallen from 85 percent of the labor force in 1957 to 75 to 77 percent in the late 1970s. At the same time, manufacturing employment has risen notably, from 6 percent in 1957 to 11 to 12 percent, and the services, including government and the army, have gained more gradually from 9 percent to roughly 12 percent. This changing labor force deployment suggests a still modest level of modernization. The level of urbanization also indicates how far China remains from high modernization. From an urban population of 11 percent in 1949 and 14 percent in 1957, China reached a level of perhaps 20 percent in the late 1970s. The contrast with the steeply rising indicators of coal and steel production and other products associated with heavy industry attests to uneven development.

A comparative assessment of China's modernization after 1949 points to two periods of extreme measures that could not have been sustained without dire effects. The dramatic modernization gains of the 1950s camouflaged a variety of imbalances and problems that threatened CCP goals. Borrowing heavily from the Soviet approach to modernization, the Chinese overconcentrated on the urban capital-intensive sector. Then for roughly another decade beginning with the Cultural Revolution, extreme measures against professional training and service again unbalanced China's transformation in a manner costly to innovation and efficiency. Together with jerky campaign methods and intermittent policy reversals, these two periods of one-sided approaches skewed the relations between various facets of modernization.

China's recent record affirms the relevance of four comparative perspectives in ascertaining which policies can be used to greatest advantage for modernization. First is China's past: many policies can be understood as reactions to the legacy of premodern social conditions; often leaders have overreacted, not only remedying a circumstance not conducive to modernization but carrying the new policy to an extreme, as in the attempts to endow community organizations with vast powers. A second perspective is of a densely populated, labor-intensive economy. This condition is by no means unique among nonmodernized societies, but the Chinese case is extreme because of the vast numbers of people involved and because of the already very high yields per acre in the agricultural sector. The conclusion that effective policies must use labor-intensive methods to advantage implies that factor productivity will not rise rapidly, that urbanization will be slow, and that in other ways modernization can be most quickly pursued by a combination of indicators different from what was observed in earlier modernizing countries. Third, looking at Japan offers insight into a situation common to East Asian countries: the solidarity of the household as modernization proceeds. Low divorce rates in China are one indicator that can best be understood in this comparative context. Finally, despite the abandonment of many elements of the Soviet model, China has remained a socialist society guided by Marxist-Leninist doctrines. In Chapter 14, the implications of a comparative communist perspective are examined in some detail.

Aspects of social integration in the PRC could be discussed at greater length by applying each of these four perspectives more fully. We would, at the very least, like to draw attention to their interplay in explaining Chinese developments as well as to the more familiar explanations centered on the idiosyncratic decisions of Mao Tse-tung and other leaders guided by goals embracing many features of modernization but extending to other features also.

CHAPTER TWELVE

Knowledge and Education

THE INDIGENOUS EDUCATIONAL INSTITUTIONS described in Chapter 6 had grown out of the needs and resources of an agrarian society in which government control was relatively indirect and chiefly reliant on the internalization of moral values designed to maintain the status quo, rather than direct and reliant on administrative mechanisms designed to extract resources and mobilize the population.

Perception of Problems and Problems of Perception

The end of the nineteenth century saw few endogenous changes that would have dislodged traditional institutions, and yet ten years later these institutions had been practically eradicated. The primary cause of this reversal was external: the encroachment of the western powers and Japan drove the government to the discovery of other needs than the smooth operation of existing structures. Concerned scholars and officials did not identify these needs as being for greater central control of local resources—a preliminary to state-led modernization in Japan and Russia—but rather, in accordance with a long-standing preoccupation with ideological approaches to political problems, diagnosed the fault as lying largely in Chinese educational institutions, and the remedy as the adoption of those of the victor. Consensus did not, however, come easily. As F. W. Mote points out in Chapter 3, the strategic elite was sharply divided, and the turn of the century saw a bitter struggle between reform and reaction over educational policy. Perhaps for this reason, the changeover when it came was absolute. The examination system, reformed in 1902, was abolished in 1905, academies and charity schools were converted into primary and secondary schools on the western model, and attempts were made to proscribe *ssŭ-shu*.

To say that the decision to change to a western-Japanese educational system was taken under duress is not to say that this model was without intrinsic appeal to elements of the Chinese elite. Modern education offered the prospect of transforming powers far exceeding those promised by Confucianism— of both material and spiritual strength, of the tangible "wealth and power" possessed by Japan and the West and the intangible civilizing and uplifting of brutish and backward customs. Confucian scholars and bureaucrats had never been slow to ascribe these customs to the bulk of the unenlightened peasantry and the half-educated pedants who taught them; now the circle of the elite was drawn tighter, the scope of missionary work expanded, as "civilized" came to stand for those who had accepted borrowed institutions and new methods. As possessors of a sense of mission, educators carried forward the commitments of their predecessors. Other elements of the new education were seen as removing deficiencies long perceived in the old: by being universal, it would ensure that no talents were stifled; by being practical, it would do away with the empty formalism for which the examinations were often criticized and enable all its products, rather than only those who became officials, to be usefully employed. That is, it was believed that the new schools would break the link between education and office so that the former could be pursued as a matter of national advantage rather than simply for individual goals. China's territorial losses had aroused lively fears that the whole country would be partitioned and sink to colonial status; the new schools' graduates were charged with the task of saving the nation.

The fact that the new education could be seen as fulfilling time-honored goals—the selection of talent for office, the transformation of the people—and the promise it held of achieving new ones—rapid transition to the strength and wealth of modernized nation-states—meant that the mechanisms by which these goals were to be reached were not carefully scrutinized. The desirable features of the new system, universality and practicality, were assumed to come in the package, along with blackboards and chalk, a ministry of education, universities and primary schools, and physical training. That these features were somehow omitted is evident from the numerous unrealized, unrealistic plans for making schooling free, universal, and compulsory and the rapid succession of societies and tracts designed, unavailingly, to wean Chinese youth from a literary education.

The expectation that the new schooling would be universal and practical ignored political, economic, and other constraints. The Chinese government was in no position to divert resources to education; it could hardly cajole enough out of the provinces to maintain the Ministry of Education and Peking University. Difficulties in the attainment of universal education were exacerbated by the fact that the new schools were far more expensive than the old, requiring—ideally—trained teachers, administrative superstructure, special texts, buildings, uniforms, and equipment. It is conceivable that, by a massive effort, late Ch'ing reformers and their successors could have encouraged the foundation of sufficient charity schools and *ssŭ-shu* to teach perhaps 50 percent of the male population basic literacy; but the old schools were anathema to them, and they devoted themselves to their eradication or conversion rather than expansion. The new schooling retook much ground occupied by *ssŭ-shu* rather than making direct inroads into illiteracy. It flourished chiefly in urban centers—particularly treaty ports—with a concentration of resources and a felt need for such new subjects as English. As David Buck points out in his study of Tsinan (Elvin and Skinner, 1974, pp. 185–186), government subsidies tended to go to the city schools, so that most of the best schools were located in the cities. Rural people tended to regard the new schools as "foreign" in contradistinction to the Chinese *ssŭ-shu*. The gap between rural and urban access to education was thus increased.

Practicality—the acquisition of technical rather than literary skills, and their employment as an end in itself rather than as a step up the social ladder—proved as difficult of achievement as universality. Disillusioned by the discovery that the new crop of talent had the same defect of nonproductive ambition as the old, educators took to referring to the new schools' products as "high-grade layabouts."

These perceptions—on the part of government, educators, the elite, and the populace—of the uses and goals of the new education were established during the last decade of the nineteenth and the first of the twentieth century. What changes occurred in succeeding decades, and how far were these functional, how far dysfunctional, in China's pursuit of modernization? What obstacles lay athwart the acclimatization of western schooling in China, and what achievements can be laid to the credit of educational innovation?

The problem of adapting an alien system to the changing needs, resources, and expectations of Chinese society has plagued all educators in twentieth-century China. Successive foreign models—Japanese, American, Russian—have been adopted in the hope of replicating the achievements of the advanced industrial societies that produced them. The prestige of the foreign model has meant that the transfer has often been made wholesale with little regard for Chinese conditions and sensibilities. This has led on the one hand to waste, anomalies, and unreal expectations as the few familiar with the new system have struggled to implement it among a largely apathetic populace, on the other to a backlash of national pride which has reasserted the superiority of Chinese methods of reaching national goals and has rejected outside tutelage. Even the latter reaction, however, has never contemplated throwing out the basic structure of the modern school system. Critics of twentieth-century education have had, over several decades and on both sides of the political fence, much common ground in their diagnosis of ills and their remedies. They have seen modern schooling as being foreign oriented, impractical, and expensive, and on all counts producing an elite alienated from the rest of society. None, however, wishes to go back to the examinations, the academy, or the *ssu-shu*: rather, their remedies are the raising of national pride through symbolic action, the exercise of common sense and restraint in setting standards and courses, and the closer integration of schooling with the outside world. Thus Chuang Tse-hsuan, writing "How to Sinicize the New Education" in 1927, saw the problems as lying in a Chinese sense of inferiority vis à vis everything foreign, in the cost of the new system, and in the fact that "school lessons can be said to be almost totally unrelated to life in society" (1938, p. 27). His suggested remedies included exhibitions of Chinese-made goods and stress on Chinese strengths and achievements; shorter courses, with their content reduced to essentials; and the discouragement of rote learning and encouragement of observation, manual labor (around the school), and social investigation. Similar objections were made in Tung Wei-chuan's *Condemnation of the Old Education* (1948), in the communist analysis of their educational problems in the Yenan base areas, and during the Great Leap Forward and the Cultural Revolution.

Had China modernized more rapidly, there might have been less to blame education for, and more outside pressure for greater accessibility and practicality. China might, in other words, have grown into an educational system borrowed from modernized nations, have been less constrained by financial limitations, and have found diversity of courses and length of schooling less of a burden. As it was, complaints about education during the republican era reflected objective reality. Few educators had sufficient influence to remold education as they wished. Government parsimony in education, whether caused by simple indifference or the exigencies of military strife, was a continuing source of anxiety. Attempts to simplify and shorten courses were always counteracted by the demand that standards be raised, and that Chinese educational institutions be in no whit inferior to foreign ones.

A test of the accuracy of the critical perceptions outlined above—of elitism, expense, irrelevance, and foreign orientation, the enduring problems of Chinese education—was made during the Cultural Revolution, when for the first time an educator had power to remold the education system to his vision. The Cultural Revolution saw a vigorous attempt to reestablish China's intellectual independence from foreign masters, an assault on the foreign trained and on specialism in general, and the corresponding exaltation of home-grown methods and the homespun wisdom of the worker and peasant. In the strictly educational sphere, earlier prescriptions were carrried out: book learning was downgraded, forays into society—"open-door schooling"—and physical labor encouraged. The link between schooling and office, the bugbear of educators for several centuries, was temporarily eradicated. An attempt was made to do away with formal educational prerequisites for tertiary study, and the authority of teacher and text as a source of wisdom was replaced by practical experience in the commune, factory, or army. Integration of school and society, it appeared, could go no further. The new type of education, however, produced as many unintended consequences as the old. The link between educational achievement and social advancement, so often deplored as being a regrettable survival from the competitiveness of the old examination system, proved to have provided much of the motive force behind young people's pursuit of learning; with the commune as their destination, interest in achievement wilted. Doctrinaire antiintellectualism was more easily implemented than genuine "learning from practice," and students with only a little secondary education found difficulty in coping with tertiary courses. Policy was shaped in a highly radicalized atmosphere, making difficult the trade-offs necessary to arrive at compromise solutions. Tertiary education and research work—those areas most subject to attack for being elitist, costly, and foreign oriented—lost a decade in most fields. Intellectuals worked in a straitjacket or did not work at all. Ironically, many of the goals of the revolution in education have been so discredited by its excesses that they are further out of reach now than they were in 1966.

Writing about education only a few years after the Cultural Revolution decade, one is inevitably impressed by the extraordinary disruptions to which the educational system has been subjected. In republican China, international and civil war, as well as nationalist agitation, caused periodic upheavals. In the People's Republic, to a remarkable extent, education was disrupted mainly on the initiative of the country's leaders: educational policy became the object of political conflict in a manner not seen for seventy years, while educational institutions became the arenas of political strife.

The disruptions were manifestations of policymakers' difficulty in devising a consistent and coherent strategy for education, one compatible with both technological requirements and social goals, and in gaining acceptance for their plans from the bulk of the populace. No simple indices of success or failure can be drawn up. Educators and politicians still face the task of balancing mass and elite education, foreign input and self-reliance, rising expectations and limited opportunities, technocratic expertise and egalitarian rhetoric. How to design an educational system that will meet the complex and differentiated needs of China's modernizing economy, be compatible with meager resources, and minimize or even reshape mobility aspirations continues to be a key issue for the country's leaders.

Inevitably, education in the PRC cannot be assessed in unequivocal terms. On the one hand, 1949 is clearly a watershed in the promotion of education as part of the modernizing transformation in terms of the expansion of education at all levels from adult literacy to scientific research and development. The communist government carried the alignment of the educational system with the needs of economic development much further than its predecessor, by using its much greater capacity for control and coordination. But this same power enabled the communists at times to press for the achievement of unrealistic objectives, leading to unnecessary setbacks, as with the Great Leap Forward and the Cultural Revolution. Given thirty years of peace and uncontested rule, far greater gains could have been made than were in fact achieved.

Mass Education

The school system set up in 1902–1904, in the wake of the allied armies' occupation of Peking, was based on that developed in the modernized West and thence transferred to Japan: state controlled, standardized, professionalized, with knowledge, resources, and manpower compartmentalized into tertiary, secondary, and primary institutions of learning, and within them into classes divided by age and subject. The closeness of the imitation was reflected even in the wording of the Chinese ordinances. Confucian influence was still observable in the exclusion of women from public education and the amount of time devoted to the classics, but these anomalies were removed a few years later with the setting up of a separate stream for female education (up to secondary normal school) and the streamlining of the curriculum.

In the decades that followed, the new system experienced a series of structural reforms. Some, such as the introduction of coeducation at the elementary level in 1912, at Peking University in 1920, and in some middle schools in 1921, remained mainly on paper. Others had greater impact. In 1922, the Japanese system of lower and higher primary, undivided middle school, and preparatory courses before university was replaced by the American 6:3:3 system (six years of primary school followed by three of lower and three of higher middle school leading directly to the university or college). The new system remained in effect until the Cultural Revolution when the length of schooling was drastically cut. It is likely that in the 1980s the pre-Cultural Revolution norms will be restored.

Making primary education universal and eliminating illiteracy among adults are the core tasks of the transformation stage of modernization. Progress in the attainment of these goals was made throughout the twentieth century, but it was only in the era of the People's Republic that a quantitative breakthrough was made in the provision of primary education, and remarkably, on the secondary level as well. Enrollment statistics clearly attest to the difference in scale of the educational effort before and after 1949 (Table 12.1).

Throughout the twentieth century, the expansion of the educational sys-

Table 12.1   Enrollment trends in the twentieth century.

Year	Primary Schools (*in millions*)	General Middle Schools (*in millions*)	Higher Schools (*in thousands*)
1912	2.8	.06	—
1919	—	—	16
1928	8.8	.189	35
1946 (pre-PRC peak)	23.7	1.5	155
1949	24	1.04	117
1965	110	14	695
1972	127	36.5	c. 200
1978	146.24	65.48	850

Sources of Data: For the precommunist period: Glassman, 1978; Edmunds, 1919, p. 19; T. E. Chen, "Education in China," in Sih, ed., 1970. For post-1949: Bernstein, 1977, p. 46; Lewis, 1973; State Statistical Bureau, 1979, p. 41.

tem has been constrained by inadequate funds. Before 1949, the result was fairly slow growth. After 1949, funding improved greatly, but did not keep pace with expansion, resulting in schools of poor quality, especially in the villages. Under the late Ch'ing, educational finance devolved downward, with the Ministry of Education and Peking University the responsibility of the center, secondary and other tertiary institutions in the provincial capital under the provincial government, and primary education under the county. (A similar three-tiered educational administration existed in the republic.) Each level was starved for funds, with the center dependent on unreliable provincial remittances and the provinces and counties raising their educational budget from ad hoc taxes and levies. Educational revenue was no more secure in the republican period: in 1913 schools in one province were simply closed down to save money, and in 1922 Peking teachers led demonstrations against the government over arrears in their pay. Between 1911 and 1926, educational expenditure by the Peking Ministry of Education never amounted to more than 3 percent of total central expenditure, and was in most years less than one-twentieth of the amount spent for military purposes. The gap between military and educational expenditure was even greater in the provinces.

Substantial provincial autonomy led to sharp disparities in the growth of education. Under the Ch'ing, Chihli led the way in expansion of lower primary schooling, with nearly a quarter of a million students in primary school in 1909. In poorer provinces, with fewer resources and less active government promotion, the rate of attendance was much lower: the most backward were Anhwei, Kweichow, and Fukien. During the warlord era, not all military leaders were indifferent to education: weak central control freed Yen Hsishan to carry out his own strategy for universal education in Shansi. By 1923, vigorous promotion of popular education in that province had reportedly resulted in 60 percent attendance of school age boys in primary schools, and approximately 11 percent of girls. Anhwei had more than tripled its absolute number of primary school students, but remained with Kweichow at the bottom of the educational ladder, with only about 6 percent of school age boys enrolled in primary school.

The establishment of the Nationalist government in Nanking in 1927 saw the beginning of a genuine commitment to the expansion of education by the center, but civil wars and military intervention by the Japanese meant that military spending continued to take priority. Provincial expenditure on education did increase severalfold during the first years of Nationalist rule, but funds continued to come mainly from indirect taxes on commodities and services, as well as from the land tax and its surtaxes. The rural people on whom the main burden fell did not gain much of the benefit of expensive urban-centered education, giving rise to the bitter comment that "in foreign countries, the wealthy people pay money to [educate] the poor. Only in China, the poor people pay money to [educate] the wealthy." Educators drew up plans to remedy this imbalance. The financing of schools through an inheritance tax was proposed, and in 1930 a national conference on education decided that the government should increase its contribution to the funding of compulsory education to 45 percent. The next two decades of civil and national war thwarted their intentions, however, and educational funding remained on shaky foundations.

A second major problem, that of teachers, was naturally most acute when the new school system was set up at the turn of the century. No longer was mere literacy a sufficient qualification for the teacher. Within the country, institutions for professional training were set up. Outside it, educational administrators made exhaustive tours of the Japanese school system, and thousands of Chinese students took short-term courses in teacher training in Tokyo. At the same time, previous classical study remained in practice sufficient qualification for such "Chinese" subjects as language, literature, and Chinese history, and for school administration. By 1909, nearly two-thirds of the teachers in higher education were Chinese with modern qualifications. At the elementary level, however, the new teachers tended to be less acceptable to the village community than the old: alongside the formal organization of the new schools, an informal network of *ssŭ-shu* persisted into the first years of the People's Republic. Rural primary schools were often modern in name only, partly by default and partly by deliberate choice on the part of their patrons.

The position of schoolteachers in the eyes of the western-oriented elite was not an exalted one. Many teachers chose their profession as the cheapest way of getting an education for themselves: for the Ch'ing and part of the republican period, students at teachers' colleges were the only ones on scholarships, and came from families who could not afford the tuition fees at regular schools. Chang Po-ling, whose own foundation, Nankai, charged high fees, averred that teacher training did not attract the best class of student. A great many talented, even brilliant men devoted time and effort to raising the standard of education in China—Ts'ai Yuan-p'ei, Hu Shih, Chiang Monlin—but their contributions tended to be confined to university teaching or to planning and theory. As American influence increased in the 1920s, entry to the educational establishment began to require a doctorate from Columbia. There were, of course, men who devoted their lives to building up a single school, and others—T'ao Hsing-chih, Liang Shu-ming, James Yen—who implemented projects and plans for mass education, but their luster did not rub off on the struggling primary teacher in rural areas. In theory, education was a glorious vocation, a means of saving the country. In practice, as reflected in Yeh Sheng-t'ao's novel *Ni Huan-chih* and Mao Tun's *Shih*, those who took it up from idealistic motives were speedily disillusioned. The problem of motivating teachers has persisted under the People's Republic, aggravated during the Cultural Revolution by Maoist political discrimination.

The first major problem of educational expansion, that of finance, was eased under the PRC. Education received unprecedentedly generous funding in the 1950s: the PRC's state budgetary expenditures on education rose from 813 million *yuan* in 1951 to 2.906 billion in 1957. The rate of growth leveled off in the early 1960s and probably decreased during the Cultural Revolution. In 1978, spending on education rose sharply, by 25 percent, but by 1979, the rate of growth had slowed to 7 percent. In 1978, the state budget allocated a total of 11.266 billion *yuan* for education, science, culture, and public health combined, or 10 percent of the total budget. Although significant growth in the financing of education has taken place, allocations have always been inadequate to meet demand, in, for example, higher education, a point readily acknowledged by the government.

Resource limitations required the setting of priorities and a search for low-cost solutions in those sectors not accorded priority. Early on, the state decided to assign priority to the development of secondary and higher education needed for rapid modernization. Thus, the state budget for secondary education rose by a factor of seven between 1951 and 1956 and that for higher education by a factor of five. Allocations for primary education rose marginally and then declined by 1956 below the level of 1951, the money being concentrated on the urban sector and on primary schools in centrally located villages. To be sure, rural primary schools were also financed from locally collected agricultural surtaxes, but the state has not been able to provide basic education for all peasant children. As a substitute the state called for the establishment of *min-pan hsueh-hsiao*, schools financed and operated by collective units, the production brigades and teams. Such schools drew upon the tradition of *ssŭ-shu* schooling and especially on the experience of the Yenan base, where, in 1946, three-fourths of the primary schools had been locally run. The *min-pan* schools have been surrounded by an aura of revolutionary purity—they are said to embody the virtues of self-reliance, control by the masses, and integration with labor. They have in fact grown rapidly during "leftist" periods such as the Great Leap Forward (when primary enrollments rose from 64 million to 90 million) and the Cultural Revolution. But their main advantage, as Mao once put it, is that "they don't cost the state one cent." Actually, some state subsidies have been paid, and since the state grain tax has not risen, increases in grain output have strengthened the local resource base.

Partially financed by the state and partially from local resources, primary education grew rapidly, as shown in Table 12.1. Despite the impressive growth, China has not yet passed the benchmark of universal school attendance. In 1978, the minister of education formulated a cautiously worded goal, saying that by 1981, "over 95 percent of all school age children in most of the counties must attend school." But expansion of primary schooling has sharply narrowed the urban-rural and interprovincial imbalances that the PRC inherited. According to David M. Lampton, in 1949, 4.5 percent of the country's population was enrolled in primary school, but less than 1 percent attended primary school in Kweichow as compared to 10 percent in Tientsin. By 1957, 10 percent of the population attended primary school, and in Kweichow the percentage had risen to 4 (Lampton, 1978, pp. 515 and 518). Since then, disparities have narrowed further, but have not completely disappeared.

In 1972, 98 percent of urban children of primary school age were reportedly in school in Kirin but only 86 percent of their rural counterparts. In the same year, while probably on a national scale around 90 percent of primary-age children attended school, only 80 percent did so in Inner Mongolia, Kwangsi, and Szechwan. Since then, still further gains have been made. The PRC's achievement is impressive especially in an extreme case such as Tibet, where reportedly barely 1 percent of school age children were in school in the 1950s, as compared to 31 percent in 1965 and 85 percent in 1976.

These successes have been purchased at the price of quality. To begin with, there are substantial qualitative differences among the community schools because of differences in local wealth, but on the whole, the *min-pan* schools lag behind the state schools, particularly those in the cities. Often operated on a shoestring, their facilities have necessarily been makeshift and rudimentary. The qualifications and motivation of the teachers have usually been minimal. Rural and resettled urban youths with some secondary education have filled a good many of the teaching posts. In times of economic hardship, as after the Great Leap Forward, the schools have often had to close down. Conversely, the *min-pan* schools have had the advantage of the flexibility and simplicity of the old *ssü-shu*. Unrestricted by bureaucratic regulations fixing minimum standards, community schools have been set up wherever they are needed, as in natural villages difficult of access. Classes can be held to conform to the distinctive local work cycle. The Chinese press has in fact reported all sorts of ingenious ways in which classes have been adapted to local needs to facilitate attendance. These advantages show, however, that the *min-pan* schools represent a form of adaptation to rural backwardness. As modernization advances, the need for qualitatively improved rural schools is likely to grow.

Qualitative deficiencies have afflicted not just the community schools but many state primary schools, urban as well as rural. The supply of trained teachers has not kept up with the actual numbers employed. In 1978, the teaching force for all levels was put at 9 million, or nearly three times the number employed in 1964. Only a fraction of the primary school teachers among them could have attended a secondary normal school. Short-term courses, use of mobile "tutorial teams," and other expedients may have alleviated but certainly did not solve the problem of poorly qualified teachers. Shortages of textbooks and teaching aids have beset all schools, especially during the Cultural Revolution decade, when teaching materials were only prepared locally. The main teaching method has continued to be rote memorization, even though one of the impulses behind the "revolution in education" was dissatisfaction with old-fashioned approaches.

Since 1976, efforts have been underway to upgrade the quality of the entire educational system, primary schooling included. Remedial teacher training has been stepped up, the national supply of textbooks vastly improved, and ambitious goals set. These include the phasing out of substandard community schools and untrained teachers. Attainment of these goals is likely to take a long time. Funding continues to be a major problem, in part because higher and secondary education continue to command high priority. The result of resource constraints is that primary schooling will continue to be characterized by significant disparities in quality for some time to come. Schools founded before 1949, schools affiliated with teacher training institutions, and schools designated for special attention as "keypoints" offer a far richer educational fare than their less privileged counterparts, most of which tend to be concentrated in the rural interior.

Probably because of inadequate funds, the PRC government has not made primary education compulsory. Political and social pressures have partially substituted for legal constraint, but families have in fact had some choice in deciding whether and especially for how long to educate their children, even when primary schools were readily available. Peasant choices have been influenced by economic considerations, which are important especially in the case of poor families. They include work points forgone because of school attendance as well as the direct cost of small payments for tuition and books, primary and secondary education not being free of charge. Persistence of the traditional lack of interest in female education, in part resulting from the valued contribution of girls to the peasant household, has resulted in a substantial sexual differential in school attendance. Restrictions on outward mobility may also have reduced peasant interest in education. When peasants were able to migrate to cities and towns, the educated left in disproportionate numbers. Since the late 1950s, educated young peasants have normally had to remain within their home communes. The resettlement in rural areas of educated urbanites, a distinctive feature of PRC life, may well have reinforced lack of interest in education divorced from valued mobility prospects: "Since graduates of universities and senior middle schools all end up with shovels in their hands, what's the use of children being able to read?"

Political pressures and such practical steps as shortening the school year to align it with the work cycle have served to counteract attitudes and interests inimical to education. Moreover, restrictions on outward mobility have to some extent been offset by mobility opportunities within the collectives. The collective farm structure has led to fairly widespread office holding—Parish and Whyte (1978, p. 101) estimate that one-fourth of the males over sixteen have a chance to serve in some kind of capacity at the team or brigade level—and this acts as an incentive in favor of education. Most important, the modernizing process itself is likely to have a positive effect upon interest in education. As the technological transformation of agriculture has gained momentum in the last fifteen years, the demand for trained manpower has risen, while the excitement of working with modern technology has acted to stimulate interest in the acquisition of knowledge. The effect of these stimuli must not be overestimated, however. Office holding, especially at the team level, is not always very attractive, and the penetration of modern technology has thus far not had a profound impact on most peasants. Schooling, as Parish and Whyte (1978, p. 230) note, is seen as providing "useful knowledge (political as well as academic)" but is not seen as "absolutely indispensable for later life as a farmer." Consequently, to secure universal school attendance for the full five or six years of primary school, China will probably have to follow the experience of other countries and make primary schooling compulsory.

INFORMAL EDUCATION AND ADULT LITERACY

As early as the 1900s, long before the highly publicized mass education movements of the 1920s and 1930s, awareness existed of the need to reach adult illiterates and the poor. As preparations for constitutional government got underway toward the end of the 1900s, official interest in education outside the regular school system was reflected in the setting up of Simple Reading Schools (*ssŭ-shu*-like establishments teaching only reading and arithmetic) as well as in government-sponsored attempts to reform the *ssu-shu* itself. The Ministry of Education, however, took a conservative aproach, rebuffing attempts to introduce the teaching of literacy through a phonetic script first used for this purpose under Yuan Shih-k'ai in Chihli.

Outside of government, a mixture of altruistic and prudential motives—educating the masses in citizenship and preventing unruliness among the poor and the unemployed—inspired many private citizens and a few officials to undertake the foundation of half-day schools for poor children, night schools for illiterate adults, newspaper reading rooms, and public lectures. The impact of these measures was limited by inadequate government support and by considerable lack of interest in schools. Half-day schools, which were usually free, attracted pupils not from the working poor but from those already oriented toward education. Adult illiterates were often not interested in "learning to become citizens" and pleaded their work or their age as an excuse for not attending even those schools devised for their benefit.

At the same time, however, urban interest in literacy did rise since it was reinforced by broader modernizing changes. In Peking, for example, a number of gossipy illustrated vernacular papers appeared, which chronicled exciting street accidents, improper behavior among young women (such as riding in a rickshaw), and so on. Such commercial enterprises served also to spread common concepts and information. In contrast, for uneducated or semieducated rural people, the language of modern journalism was simply unintelligible: they often did not know the meaning of neologisms like "economical" and "historical background," even if they were able to read the popular romances of old China. Insofar as it has occurred, the reunification of popular and elite vocabulary and media has taken place largely since 1949.

The weakness of central government authority in the years after 1911 was a stumbling block in the implementation of mass education. The republican Ministry of Education gave "social education" or extension work among adults parity with the different branches of formal education, drafting ambitious plans in 1916 for reading schools using phonetic script, as well as for a network of popular libraries and lecture centers. Civil wars and shortages of funds, however, meant that these plans remained largely on paper. The Nationalist government established in 1927 evinced a commitment to the extension of education in ordering local authorities to allocate 10 to 20 percent of their educational budget to part-time schooling, popularization of the phonetic script, and other measures designed to extend education to adult illiterates and the poor. This resulted in a sixfold rise in expenditure between 1928 and 1932, but here again the budgetary needs and material ravages of the ensuing years of war prevented these ameliorative efforts from making much headway.

In default of government action for the extension of literacy, private citizens took up the work. The politicized atmosphere of the May Fourth era gave urgency to old fears about China's fate if her millions remained ignorant and disunited. New initiatives came both from those professionally associated with education and from students who set up night schools within their own institutions. One of the most lasting was James Yen's Mass Education Movement, founded on the basis of Yen's experience teaching illiterate Chinese laborers in France during the First World War. His association started part-time "people's schools" for adult students all over China and edited a series of "Thousand Character" textbooks designed to teach simple hygiene and citizenship as well as literacy. The readers were illustrated, but tended to be didactic and patronizing. The movement had less success than expected, especially in rural areas, and in 1925 Yen concentrated his forces on a single county, Ting hsien, in Hopei, intending to use it as an experimental model whose results could later be applied to the rest of China. A similarly limited rural base, Tsouping county in Shantung, was selected by Liang Shu-ming as the center for his rural reconstruction program. Liang's program went further than Yen's, in that it was meant to lead not merely to material but to spiritual regeneration. Unlike Yen, who was American trained, Liang proposed to draw on indigenous Confucian tradition to achieve his ends.

Although these and other experiments in mass education accumulated valuable experience, they were never taken up enthusiastically by the mass of the rural populace, who remained passive recipients rather than active participants in the various schemes. What the long-term results of the projects would have been is hard to say, since they were cut off by the War of Resistance and the civil war; but it appears that such results as were achieved in model counties derived from a concentration of effort and individual dedication that would have been hard to replicate throughout the remainder of China's 1,800-odd counties. In the communist base areas, on the other hand, adult literacy education had a wider impact. In the backward Shen-Kan-Ning base, for instance, not only was an educational network developed to teach cadres, but so were *min-pan* schools, literacy groups, and night schools. The curriculums were simple, related to productive work, and presented in traditional form, as in the case of teaching materials written in the rhyming style of the old classical primers. More economically advanced base areas used a combination of modern and traditional methodology and organization.

Although literacy rose in the cities and in parts of the countryside, a large majority of the population was unquestionably illiterate in 1949. The problem of illiteracy was compounded to some extent by the nature of the communist revolution, since new kinds of competence in political as opposed to commercial terminology were now required. Moreover, the revolution put into positions of power those who had been on the bottom of the social ladder and among whom illiteracy was most pronounced. As of 1956, for instance, two-thirds of 25,000 heads of *hsiang* (townships) or secretaries of *hsiang* party branches in Fukien were either illiterate or "semiliterate."

In the 1950s, adult literacy classes and campaigns naturally focused first on cadres, urban and rural, and on factory workers. It was apparently only during the Great Leap Forward that a major effort was made to set up literacy classes for the peasants at large. Participation in adult spare time literacy classes rose from 657,000 in 1949 to 7.2 million in 1957, and leaped to 40 million in 1958 or even more if other reports are to be believed. The efficacy of such mass literacy campaigns was probably low. Since the Great Leap Forward, evening literacy classes for adults have been carried on more sporadically but on a fairly wide scale, using the *pinyin* phonetic system as a teaching aid.

Retention of characters is the main criterion for assessing the long-term effects of both adult literacy classes and primary education, the latter of which has by now reached more than half of the entire population. The standard for measuring literacy has apparently been reduced in the rural areas from 1,500 to 800 characters, as compared to a standard of 2,000 in the urban sector. Retention is likely to be greatest in the case of those whose jobs require ability to read. Illiteracy is no longer a serious problem among rural cadres, political and technical, and more broadly among those who take part in modernizing activities. As for the mass of the peasantry, interest in reading may not extend much beyond capacity to decipher work-point listings or publicly posted team accounts. But retention of characters is also being encouraged by such stimuli as political posters and the growing availability of reading materials including captioned comic books (*lien-huan hua*).

Has China become a literate nation? The overwhelming majority of urbanites are undoubtedly literate, but as a vice minister of education acknowledged in 1978, China still has a "fair amount of illiteracy, mainly among the peasants." For rural Kwangtung, Parish and Whyte found a literacy rate of 72 percent (83 percent male and 61 percent female) among those fifteen or older (1978, p. 83). A recent estimate for the population as a whole by Eberstadt (1979), based mainly on school attendance, indicates a literacy rate of 60–70 percent. According to other recent appraisals, illiteracy among rural youth actually increased in the 1970s. These findings place China among the more literate nonmodernized countries, far ahead of India, but behind Sri Lanka.

SECONDARY EDUCATION

In the republican era, only a small fraction of primary school graduates entered general secondary schools. In the PRC, secondary schooling has assumed mass proportions. No sector of the educational system had a greater rate of growth than the secondary schools. Enrollment leaped forward especially in the wake of the Cultural Revolution, after schools were reopened in 1968 and 1969 (Table 12.2).

Part of this increased rate is a product of redefinitions rather than genuine growth. As noted earlier, the Cultural Revolution saw the replace-

Table 12.2   Enrollment in secondary schools.

Year	Junior Middle	Senior Middle	Total
1949–50	832,000	207,000	1,039,000
1957–58	4,851,000	835,000	5,686,000
1965–66	11,900,000	2,100,000	14,000,000
1978–79	51,480,000	14,000,000	65,480,000

Sources of Data: Bernstein, 1977, p. 46; State Statistical Bureau, 1979, p. 41; and *Jen-min jih-pao* editorial, May 17, 1979.

ment of the old 6:3:3 system of primary, junior, and senior middle schooling by a 5:2:2 or the current 5:3:2 system, in effect, adding the last year of the old primary school to the secondary level. Still, remarkable growth has taken place. Reportedly, in the largest cities, ten-year schooling (that is, five years of middle school) has already been made universal, and in smaller towns the pattern is eight years, while peasants have had increasing access to one to three years of junior middle school. Continuing urban-rural differences are reflected in a national goal set for 1985, when all cities and towns are to supply universal ten-year schooling, whereas the rural sector is to achieve only eight years of education. For Kwangtung, a relatively advanced province, Parish and Whyte found that 46 percent of male children whose education began after 1959 had attended junior middle school, but only 20 percent of females (1978, p. 83). Junior middle schooling has thus become increasingly available to the peasantry, but relatively few peasants attend senior middle schools, which are often located in the commune center and which require payment for room and board as well as tuition.

The tremendous growth in middle school enrollments necessarily took place at the expense of quality. The decline in quality assumed disastrous proportions in the Cultural Revolution era. Five reasons account for the deterioration of standards. The first is financial. Before the Great Leap Forward, growth in enrollments kept pace with growth in budgetary allocations, the former growing roughly five times and the latter about seven times. Data are not available for the two decades since then, but it is highly unlikely that financing grew at a similarly rapid rate. Part of whatever growth in funding has taken place, moreover, has had to go toward offsetting the widespread destruction of libraries and other school facilities in 1966–1968, when urban middle schools were battlegrounds of contending Red Guard factions. During the Cultural Revolution decade, moreover, state funds that were allocated to education could easily be diverted to other uses, since educational officials, under suspicion for "revisionist" leanings, lacked the power to protect their interests.

As in primary education, part of the growth in middle schooling is accounted for by locally financed, brigade-operated junior middle schools. First promoted during the Great Leap Forward as half–time agricultural middle schools, they were revived in the mid–1960s, largely because of their low cost. According to Jonathan Unger (forthcoming), in one Kwangtung county, it cost 120 *yuan* to maintain a student in a state senior middle school and 76 *yuan* in a junior school, but only 6.8 *yuan* to do so in an agricultural middle school. In such schools, the curriculum necessarily had to be simplified, a general course, ''agricultural knowledge,'' often substituting for courses in chemistry, physics, or biology.

Second, there was a shortage of teachers who had attended tertiary normal or other colleges. The supply of trained teachers already lagged behind demand before the Cultural Revolution. In 1956, 83 percent of senior middle school teachers but only 48 percent of their junior counterparts had attended tertiary normal schools. While the situation improved in the early 1960s, the closing and subsequent underuse of higher schools during the Cultural Revolution decade sharply aggravated the problem, as did dismissals of experienced teachers labeled bourgeois. The shortage of trained teachers necessitated the hiring of underqualified but politically reliable substitutes. It was not rare to find graduates of senior middle schools assigned to teach in junior middle schools, especially in the villages. Some were graduates in name only, their education having been terminated by the Cultural Revolution. Short-term courses offered in the 1970s to upgrade the qualifications of these teachers could only have been inadequate substitutes for proper training, as in the case of primary school teachers.

Third, teachers were afraid to teach basic theory and to insist on high standards of performance during the Cultural Revolution era. Teachers had borne the brunt of the violent 1966 assault on ''bourgeois domination'' of the schools. Even after the resumption of classes, they labored under intense pressure to abide by the prevailing ideological orthodoxy. These pressures were temporarily lifted in 1972–1973 when some policymakers sought to raise the quality of education, but already in late 1973, new radical campaigns were launched to preserve the ''fruits'' of the Cultural Revolution. Fear of political attack prompted teachers to play it safe by emphasizing study of Mao's thoughts, manual labor, and applied knowledge.

Fourth, the ''revolution in education'' aimed at replacing the college-preparatory curriculum with a work-oriented one. This was deemed desirable not only on ideological but also on practical grounds, since only a tiny fraction of middle school graduates would eventually be able to attend a college or university. But in the cities, at least, only the destructive side of the reform was carried out successfully, in that serious academic study was largely done away with. It proved difficult to implement a workable vocational program in the general middle schools; only a few model schools succeeded in meaningfully combining labor with study of school subjects. Industrial enterprises called upon to teach skills to pupils quickly tired of doing so. Middle schools then had to set up their own workshops, but the skills taught were often useless for later life. Rural middle schools were better situated to integrate course work with production than their urban counterparts. Some, especially senior middle schools at commune centers, cooperated with experimental or extension stations, thereby increasing their relevance to agricultural modernization.

Fifth, at the heart of the decline in quality was the poor motivation of students. This applies first and foremost to urban secondary school students. The fundamental reason lay in the divorce of education from prospects of upward mobility, that is, entry into higher schools. Performance in middle school had little bearing upon college admission. The requirement that students go to work either in a factory or on a farm after graduation caused students to feel that their futures were beyond their control and that "it was no use to study." As Jonathan Unger (forthcoming), who interviewed young émigrés in Hong Kong in 1975–1976, notes, "with no other topic of inquiry in my interviewing did I receive interview responses of such uniformity." Unger reports that even courses in industrial skills or agricultural knowledge failed to elicit much interest among students. Often, urban school graduates sent to live in the villages had not been taught usable skills, thereby compounding their problems of adjustment.

Although the changes of the Cultural Revolution decade were aimed at redirecting Chinese secondary education toward the long-sought "universality and practicality," these goals receded before their seekers. Most middle schools of these years failed to transmit the knowledge normally associated with the term "secondary education." If the popular saying, "senior middle schools are like junior middle schools which in turn are like primary schools" is an accurate measure of the situation, then the main accomplishment of the increase in enrollment was to keep young people in school until some kind of employment could be found for them. It is difficult to associate the expansion with a rational strategy of modernization.

Since the death of Mao Tse-tung and the ouster of leftist leaders, the ideal of educational excellence has been revived. Policy now aims at raising the quality of the middle schools and at restoring their central role in the preparation of qualified university entrants. The status and authority of teachers have been raised. In-service training programs under the auspices of rehabilitated experienced teachers seek to upgrade the qualifications of younger teachers. Higher normal schools have expanded their enrollment. Standards in the middle schools have been tightened, entrance examinations at various levels have been restored, and at the tertiary level, a third of admission slots have been reserved for students still in middle school. Elite keypoint schools for the brightest have been designated once more, tracking of students is being introduced, and discrimination against able students from "bad" class backgrounds is being abolished. These changes have already had a significant impact, especially on the motivation of students and teachers, a highly competitive educational system being popular and legitimate. At the same time, the new policies will accentuate qualitative differences between the various categories of middle schools, if only because of the incapacity of the state fully to underwrite the qualitative improvement of so huge a middle school system in its entirety. Urban-rural differences are thus likely to grow. Moreover, there is still the problem of finding employment for the majority of middle school graduates who cannot go on to higher schools. Recent responses to this perennial issue include efforts to provide genuine job training within general education middle schools and to encourage especially rapid growth of secondary technical schools.

Elite Education

The recruitment, composition, allegiance, and legitimacy of a country's elite are of crucial importance to its modernization prospects. Imperial China had defined its elite largely in educational terms. The mastery of classical learning and canons of morality, attested to by an examination degree, was accepted as qualification for governing; conversely, government office lent prestige to book learning. Humiliation by the western powers and Japan meant that the content and structure of the old education were found wanting, but did not change the belief that education was a suitable means of selecting talent for government service and a proper path for upward mobility. To what extent did the new education fulfill these goals? What type of elite did it produce, what was the elite's contribution to modernization, and what was its relation to the bulk of the population?

At the beginning of the century, it was envisaged that schools would coexist with a reformed examination system, purified of the eight-legged essay. The new questions on current topics caught most scholars unprepared and resulted in a decline in the number of candidates; at the same time, sufficient numbers were prepared to stick with the examination track to cause perturbation among proponents of the new schools, who saw even their enrolled students disappear to take the examinations. It was therefore decided, in 1905, to switch over wholly to the schools as a source of talent. But despite the change, the government appears to have seen the schools as performing the same function as the old examination system: the names of the old degrees were retained and awarded to domestic and overseas school graduates who passed a government reexamination. The degrees were in turn tied to the award of office; but with 21,000 students enrolled in 1907, for courses whose completion would entitle them to the *chü-jen* degree, or six times the number of *chü-jen* produced by the examinations, the imbalance between supply and demand for official candidates threatened to become unmanageable. A critic of the system pointed out that once China reached Japan's level of education, it would be producing 66,960 *chü-jen* a year, or forty times the total number of official positions. In 1911 the government bowed to common sense and cut the millennial link between degrees and office holding. The administrative change was easily made, but not so the intellectual one: those who devoted years of their life to study continued to expect the reward of lucrative and prestigious positions and concomitant social status.

Under the old system, candidates had obtained a degree through a combination of luck, talent, and money. Sufficient amounts of the first two were needed to ensure a pass where forty others failed, sufficient amounts of the last to forgo ten or fifteen years of earnings and provide ten or so not necessarily consecutive years of tuition fees. Gaps in formal education could be compensated for by self-study. The new schools of the late Ch'ing changed the proportions of the required ingredients: little luck was required to secure a pass, and not an exceptional amount of talent, but money became important for anyone wishing to go beyond elementary education. Under the Ch'ing, the selection point for more advanced study was the higher primary school, which was usually established in the county seat: that is, all pupils from rural areas had to find not only tuition but boarding fees. Middle schools were in prefectural cities, colleges in provincial capitals. Mission schools, too, were founded chiefly in the cities. This made sense from the point of view of concentration of resources, but imposed a heavy financial burden on prospective students. Nor was self-study or broken attendance any longer a possibility for tiding over hard times: institutional ties were required all the way through, whereas in the past a mature student had normally worked on his own. Nankai Middle School, in Tientsin, charged nine *yuan* a month in the late 1900s—enough to keep a family in modest comfort—and St. John's, an Episcopalian church college in Shanghai, began to be known as a ''rich boys' school.'' Both of these were privately run, but government schools were often equally costly. Education in Japan—the closest source of up-to-date western learning and prestigious qualifications—was dearer yet, with travel costs on top of annual fees ranging from 300 to 600 *yen* per student.

Whereas previously, intense competition was the main restriction on the number of degree holders, family income now became an important determinant. Few students got scholarships. The situation worsened in the republican period, as free teacher training was dropped, and an American, rather than a Japanese, education became the key to open all doors. As Y. C. Wang has pointed out (1968), private firms and the government bureaucracy both gave the highest salaries and positions to graduates of American universities: next came other overseas degrees, finally Chinese university degrees.

The Ch'ing dynasty had produced in the late nineteenth century 30,000 civil *sheng-yuan* twice trienially from a pool of 2 million candidates; only 1 in 600 of the successful had risen to the *chin-shih* degree which guaranteed high office. The disposal of unemployed *sheng-yuan* and unsuccessful candidates had been a problem mitigated only by rural areas' capacity for absorbing them— as persons of status if not means—and their own hopes for success in the next encounter. The school system had been introduced partly to solve this problem, but had exacerbated it. The pool of middle school graduates from whom universities drew their students were urban educated, and not likely to settle for farming or village school teaching as second best; they knew that moving on to higher education was not simply a matter of passing a three-day examination, but of supporting oneself for the next three or four years. For the two-thirds of rural families whose hopes had never extended to producing an educated man, the change in prospects of social mobility was immaterial, as it was for the 1 or 2 percent who could afford the heights of the new system; but many of those in the middle had expectations that had been raised but not fulfilled, and were disgruntled and resentful. Rural families often dropped out of the race for higher education altogether.

Even with the restrictions on mobility imposed by monetary barriers to education, the supply of graduates at each level had outstripped demand by the 1930s. The economy was suffering the effects of the depression, and graduates whose skills would have been competed for ten years earlier found that the market was saturated. This applied even to the highest category, those who had studied overseas: 2,000 unemployed returned students were said to have congregated in Shanghai. The problem of employment for middle school graduates naturally existed on a much wider scale. The new Nationalist government sought a remedy by promoting more practical, industry-oriented education, but its measures did not solve the problem of unemployment among educated urban youth.

The long established interweaving of power and scholarship frayed at the end of the Ch'ing and came asunder during the chaos of the first fifteen years of the republic, when a career in banditry sometimes seemed a better prospect for political success than years of study. The Nationalist period saw a degree of rapprochement between the new-style intellectual and the center: figures collected by Y. C. Wang (1968, pp. 178–182) testify to the prominence of the American trained in the central government and in government industries.

The symbiosis, however, was not a stable one: it did not include a large portion of an equally well trained younger generation, and was still marked by the importance of personal connections rather than having the appearance of a meritocracy. Had industrialization really taken off in China at this time, the narrowness of the government sphere of employment would have been compensated for by openings in the modern commercial and industrial sector, but neither the world economic climate nor the unsettled domestic scene allowed for expansion on a scale sufficient to soak up the urban unemployed.

ELITE EDUCATION IN THE PRC

The commitment of the new state to economic growth and to the broadening of mobility opportunities gave promise that an educated elite would emerge far better integrated into the society and able to serve the needs of rapid modernization effectively. Yet the PRC's record in the promotion of higher education as well as advanced science and technology (see next section) is a remarkably uneven one. The first seventeen years of higher education, though full of troubles, were years of real achievement, especially in comparison with the disastrous decade that followed. Despite the achievements, the country's leaders proved unable satisfactorily to resolve issues of recruitment and status of the educated elite.

After 1949, the new government moved vigorously to establish control over the 200-odd institutions of higher learning. In some respects, the communists carried Nationalist policy to its logical conclusion, as in the case of Christian institutions; their autonomy had been curtailed in the late 1920s, and they were now nationalized altogether. Drawing heavily on Soviet advice, the communists sought to overcome the lack of coordination, geographical imbalance, duplication, and separation from the needs of the economy that characterized much of the old system. Universities and colleges (*hsueh-yuan*) were merged, new ones established, especially in the interior, and financing significantly improved. Enrollment increased from 117,000 in 1949 to 441,000 in 1957 to 695,000 in 1965. Subjects studied shifted sharply in favor of those needed by the economy, a shift that the Nationalists had initiated in the 1930s. Students were trained in narrow specialties in accordance with the Soviet model. Fifty-five hundred undergraduates were sent to the Soviet Union to study. On the negative side, the tertiary system suffered from serious managerial deficiencies. In 1956 and from 1958 to 1960, the orderly intake of students was upset by excessive increases. During the Great Leap Forward, not only did the student population mushroom to 950,000, but the number of institutions grew from 229 to 1,065, of which only 400 survived post-Leap cutbacks. Most of the new schools supported themselves by farming or by the manufacture of industrial products and probably offered little more than middle-level training. Even without the Leap, rapid expansion meant that the percentage of teachers with graduate degrees declined sharply; many college teachers did not even have the equivalent of a college degree. A vast qualitative gap thus separated older, established institutions from new ones. To some extent, the shortage of qualified faculty was alleviated by the presence of up to 700 Soviet scientists who taught in China for one to three years in the 1950s. But the effectiveness of teaching and research programs was further undermined by excessive course loads for students and excessive administrative loads for teachers. An additional difficulty was misallocation of graduates in the 1950s, when manpower planning was still in its infancy. Many of these problems, however, were problems of growth: the orderly implementation of educational expansion along planned lines would in due course have resolved them.

Much more serious than managerial growing pains was the issue of politicization of education, which often encroached upon the necessary minimum of intellectual autonomy. Given the rural nature of the revolution, the relationship between the untutored but powerful "reds," the party secretaries of institutions, and the bourgeois "experts," who had lived in the "white" areas, had frequently been educated in the United States, now an enemy country, and yet possessed vital knowledge and skills, was bound to be a difficult one. The frustrations of the specialists, the "nonpower elite," as Vogel terms them, who felt that their expertise was not being used effectively by ignorant power holders, were well articulated in 1957, during the Hundred Flowers, a brief period of relatively free expression.

The political authorities, however, were determined not simply to control but to transform the intellectuals. The thought reform campaign of 1951 was only one of a long series of efforts to change their "world outlook," to turn them into "reds" or educated proletarians. Thought reform entailed time-consuming political studies and meetings, participation in psychologically stressful criticism sessions, participation in social campaigns, and after 1957, manual labor, often in the form of prolonged stays in rural communes.

In the pre-Cultural Revolution era, periods of intense pressure on the intellectuals were followed by periods of relaxation and relative liberalization. In 1961, for instance, Ch'en I explicitly recognized that scientists needed both time and a measure of autonomy to do their work and that performance should be the key in judging them. Professionals should be able to devote five-sixths of their time to their jobs and should enjoy freedom of scientific debate. One current in the ruling elite thus recognized the need for an accommodation with the specialists, but this current was ultimately overwhelmed by another that saw in professionalization and intellectuals generally a basic threat to the revolution.

The long-term way of solving the problem of bourgeois experts was thought to be the recruitment of a new generation of intellectuals from the workers and peasants. And in fact, even though academic achievement continued to be important in university admissions up to 1966, the percentage of students from these classes reportedly increased from 36 in 1957 to 65 in 1966, though less markedly at elite institutions. Nonetheless, this change meant that students were still being recruited disproportionately from the old upper classes. And besides, radical leaders suspected that elite education as such has a corrupting, "revisionist" influence. Thus, during the Cultural Revolution, even experts from impeccably proletarian backgrounds suffered disgrace as "spiritual aristocrats."

The underlying issue was the growing gap between mass and elite education. Secondary school enrollment had risen rapidly, but college enrollment was restricted, mainly for reasons of cost (higher education is free, in contrast to primary and secondary schooling, which cost the state 1,200 *yuan* per student in 1956). With the curtailment of college enrollment after the Great Leap Forward, the percentage of senior middle school graduates able to continue their education, thereby automatically gaining elite status as "state cadres," declined. Moreover, the gap between those who managed to enter and those who did not widened. In the cities, job opportunities for secondary school graduates shrank, resulting in increasing resettlement of graduates in the countryside. In the villages, the number of university aspirants was restricted by the low quality and limited availability of middle schooling, but the curtailment of opportunities to move to the urban sector eliminated substitute satisfaction of aspirations for many. It is these circumstances that gave impetus to the idea of a "revolution in education," that is, an assault on elite education.

THE CULTURAL REVOLUTION DECADE

During the Cultural Revolution, the gap between mass and elite education was closed by the virtual destruction of the latter. The experiment cost the country a generation of advanced manpower and widened the gap between China and the rest of the world. Colleges and universities were closed for about four years. Some did not reopen at all; those that did enrolled far fewer students than they had prior to 1966. Enrollment rose to about 200,000 in 1972 and 584,000 in 1975, compared to the 695,000 of a decade earlier. The quality of higher education deteriorated sharply and fell to the level of secondary schooling. When 1977 college graduates assigned to Shanghai technical organizations were tested on middle school knowledge, having had time off for review, 68 percent failed mathematics, 70 percent failed physics, 76 percent failed chemistry, and "most astonishingly," some "could not even answer one question on the basic knowledge of their own specialties" (*Jen-min jih-pao,* October 23, 1977). The drop occurred first because entering students were poorly prepared, as a result of lowered middle school standards, the enforced hiatus for almost all between secondary and higher schooling, the elimination of proper entrance examinations, reduced entrance requirements, and absolute preference in the early 1970s for worker-peasant-soldier students. (Actually, "open admission" based on work unit recommendations redounded to the advantage of children of powerful officials.) Second, the drop occurred because many qualified faculty members were purged or forced to stand aside, being replaced by young Cultural Revolution appointees. Curriculums were drastically pruned with extreme emphasis placed on practical application and integration of learning with production. The period of study was shortened, even while political study and manual labor were emphasized. The physical facilities of many colleges and universities, if not already damaged by Red Guard fighting, were often diverted to noneducational use. In the name of coming close to production, some institutions were dispersed among various localities. Shenyang Agricultural College was "ordered to move four times," for "removal means revolution." As a result, "the teaching and research base which we had spent years of painstaking effort to build up" was all but destroyed (*Jen-min jih-pao,* July 6, 1978).

To appraise the decade of the Cultural Revolution in purely negative terms is a slight oversimplification. Not all higher schools were hit equally hard, in part because of extensive decentralization. Moreover, there were major attempts to change Cultural Revolution policy in 1972–1973 and again in 1975, when initiatives were launched to raise standards in the schools, restore entrance examinations, and place greater emphasis on the study of theory. Almost as soon as they were made, however, these reform efforts came under attack, and therefore, they had only limited impact.

Post-Mao Era

In 1977 and 1978, Cultural Revolution policy in higher education was completely reversed, as the country's leaders embraced the cause of achieving the "four modernizations" of industry, agriculture, science and technology, and defense by the end of the century. The leaders recognized the critical role that higher educational institutions would have to play in training the necessary manpower. Ambitious programs were initiated in 1978 for rehabilitating existing institutions, establishing nearly 200 new ones, and expanding enrollment. Enrollment climbed to 1,020,000 in 1979 and is supposed to reach 2.5 or even 3 million by 1985. The courses of study have again been lengthened. Entrance examinations permit selection of the most talented for the top schools. Eighty-eight keypoint institutions have been designated for special support. Class background, political purity, and work performance have faded into the background. Moreover, several thousand students are being sent to western countries and Japan to study.

The change in political climate has entailed a drastic redefinition of intellectuals as part of the "working class." As in 1961, the main criterion measuring political loyalty is to be work performance rather than political thinking or willingness to integrate with the masses. An individual may now be considered loyal unless he manifests open opposition. Teng Hsiao-p'ing has designated political cadres as "assistants" to the professionals. Discriminatory political labels from past campaigns such as the 1957 anti-rightist movement are being removed, and numerous Cultural Revolution victims have been rehabilitated. Professional achievement is being rewarded materially as well as in terms of social status.

A new course has been set, but it will not be easy to attain the goal of a quantitatively much larger, yet qualitatively superior tertiary system. Already in 1979, with the inauguration of a general three-year readjustment period, the leaders had to recognize that there are limits to the speed with which advance can take place. In 1978, for example, enrollment leaped forward by 400,000 students, necessitating a cutback in admissions in 1979. Not only are there funding constraints, but time is required to build up an infrastructure that will support high-quality learning. Tertiary institutions are beset by an acute shortage of teachers—the best academics are in research institutes—and by acutely strained facilities.

Managerial difficulties aside, what are the prospects that higher education and the intellectual enterprise as a whole will not once again suffer political disruption? One possibility is that China will continue to experience cycles of repression and liberalization of intellectual life, as happened in 1957 and again from late 1962 on. The pressure for repression may be strengthened if critical intellectuals take advantage of liberalization to press for greater expansion of individual rights, thereby coming into conflict with the authoritarian essence of communist rule. Repression could then extend to wider intellectual circles, and affect education and scientific inquiry. Forces in the leadership eager to modernize might then press for curtailment of repression and initiate a new phase of liberalization. It is an encouraging sign, however, that the crackdown on the short-lived "democracy movement" of 1978–1979 was not followed by widespread antiintellectual repression.

Another possibility requires more extended discussion; it revolves around the issue of elite-mass education, which, as noted earlier, is a central one in China. The point is that with the reversal of Cultural Revolution policies, a highly elitist tertiary system is being restored, with greatly increased incentives to reward those who succeed in entering. With the restoration of entrance examinations in 1977, observers have become aware of the enormous number of those who aspire to enter universities and colleges as compared to those who actually manage to do this, the ratio being about twenty to one. In 1979, according to a *People's Daily (Jen-min jih-pao)* editorial "about 7 million students will graduate from senior middle school [and] adding the educated young people in society and a part of the workers and staff members on jobs, there will be more people taking entrance examinations this year than last; while college enrollment this year cannot be increased. . . . It is impossible to meet the desire for further education of the vast majority of the young people."

Not only must the vast majority of aspirants be disappointed, significant inequalities will arise in the proportion of applicants from particular social groups who gain entry into the tertiary system. With the phasing out of discrimination against the offspring of intellectuals and former bourgeois, entering classes are likely again disproportionately to come from these groups as well as the official class, since high ranking cadres are able to send their children to the best preparatory schools. Peasants in particular are likely to be underrepresented, if only because few of them attend senior middle schools and because the quality of rural schooling is generally inferior to that in the cities. The undereducated Cultural Revolution generation is also likely to lose out in the competition.

To what extent, then, can the PRC tolerate growing inequality? The problem, of course, is the recent Maoist past. In contrast to other Marxist systems, there is in China a ready-made ideology of social protest against elitism, an ideology that is egalitarian, antibureaucratic, and antitechnocratic in orientation. This ideology played a major role in fueling mass protest during the Cultural Revolution. It could well have an appeal to the losers in the struggle for upward mobility. Their espousal of Cultural Revolution ideology could be fueled by nativistic, xenophobic "victims of modernization," who resent the emerging cosmopolitan elite of scientists and technocrats. Some manifestations of protest have already appeared, including expressions of rural resentment against high rates of college admission in culturally advantaged coastal cities. The most vocal protest has appeared among young urbanites sent to the countryside, whose difficult adaptation had to some extent been facilitated in the past by the Maoist assault on elite education, but who now see themselves deprived of urban educational and work opportunities. It is not inconceivable that leaders may appear who mobilize the grievances of those who failed to get access to elite education and who feel disadvantaged by the post-Mao modernization drive.

At the same time, social tensions over inequality and differential access to elite education and more generally to urban employment need not necessarily get out of hand. The current situation differs from the pre-Cultural Revolution period because college enrollment has in fact been rising rapidly though at varying rates, in contrast to the period after the Great Leap Forward, when it was contracting. Moreover, access to elite education is being based more purely on achievement, in contrast to the important role that class criteria played in previous years. That rewards should go to those who do best on examinations has deep cultural roots in China, and hence may mitigate the resentment of those who fail. Furthermore, the gap between winners and losers in the game of educational access may be narrowing. This gap was widest in the case of those pre-Cultural Revolution graduates who were sent to the countryside even while their classmates enrolled in Peita or Futan. The transfer movement has been scaled down and is being phased out, as more opportunities are being created in the urban sector. Indeed, as China's modernization drive gains momentum, demand for personnel at the middle levels will increase. In other words, the country may in the future be able increasingly to provide substitute satisfactions for educated youth denied access to higher school. This is precisely the prospect the regime is holding out as a way of defusing discontent.

Even if frustrated expectations do become a major social problem, it does not of course follow that outlets for the release of tensions will necessarily be available. Much will depend on the cohesion and skill of the country's leaders as they seek to combine a relatively liberal approach to education and knowledge necessary for modernization with appropriate controls and incentives to manage social frustration.

Science and Technology

An education system modeled on the West's was introduced into China partly because of an awareness that indigenous education was weak in the areas of science and technology, an awareness pointed up by the military and economic success Japan enjoyed after its adoption of western learning. The

Ch'ing government hoped by following in Japan's footsteps to duplicate its achievement: to promote industrialization through adopting the educational institutions of industrialized nations. Its hopes, however, may have been unrealistic. As Herbert Passin (1965, p. 9) points out in his study of modern Japanese education, it is important in considering Japanese modernization to avoid the *post hoc, ergo propter hoc* fallacy: because Japan succeeded in implementing universal compulsory education, therefore it rapidly achieved self-sustaining economic growth. Technical education in Japan, according to recent studies, appears to have developed in small-scale, semitraditional industries in the 1890s rather than being a prerequisite for industrial development; and in England state support for scientific and technological education occurred only after the heyday of British industrialization had passed. Chinese educators, in hoping that education would lead to modernization, may have been putting the cart before the horse.

This is not to say that education does not have an important role to play in the accumulation and dissemination of the scientific and technical knowledge and skills required for modernization. Ideally, however, planing for scientific and technological education should be integrated with the current needs and projected demands of the economy, rather than either lagging behind it or producing personnel so highly trained that they are unemployable within the current structure. This match of education and industrial development has proved difficult to achieve in China, as the previous sections of this chapter have indicated.

The educational system set up in the Ch'ing allowed for the establishment of tertiary and secondary technical schools (in agriculture, commerce, and industry), centers of technical extension work, and apprentice training schools. The higher levels of the technical schools were staffed almost entirely by Japanese teachers, who were cheaper than Westerners and more knowledgeable than Chinese, creating inevitable problems with the comprehension of concepts that were in any case unfamiliar. At the same time, a diligent attempt was made to promote the study of science in the regular school system, with science included in the curriculum from the higher primary school up. Here, too, however, the shortage of trained teachers meant that the subject was often omitted or ill-taught. Some headway had been made by the end of the dynasty: in 1909, only 108 of a total of 1,541 teachers in China's 254 technical schools were foreigners. Not all of the 16,000 pupils at these schools, however, were future technicians: many entered the schools simply to get a diploma, regardless of which specialty it was in, and others spent a few years in technical education before going back to the regular stream. The number of single faculty science and medical colleges in the regular stream reflects the lack of interest in these subjects: there were only 3 of the former and 8 of the latter, with a total enrollment of a little over 500 students. In the vacuum left by the lack of state support, medical education became largely the province of missionary educators. Study in Japan in the early years of the century shows

428

a similar pattern of preference for subjects in the humanities and social sciences, which were not only congruent with the traditional scope of Confucian learning but required less preparation. The Ch'ing government's attempt to upgrade the criteria for and the quality of overseas study in 1906 resulted in a considerable fall in the number of students and the eventual closing of the special schools set up by the Japanese to provide short-term courses for the Chinese. More care was exercised in the allocation of scholarships to America made possible by the return of the Boxer indemnities in 1909, with regulations stipulating that 80 percent of the students had to take courses in agriculture, industry, commerce, or mining.

Perhaps the only new specialization for which there was a genuine popular demand, as opposed to sporadic governmental efforts at intervention, was English. This related less to a desire to obtain at first hand the best that had been thought and written in that language than to employment opportunities in foreign firms and in the customs and postal administration, then under foreign control. Openings for engineers and scientists were limited.

The problem of an inadequate match between future needs for people familiar with science and technology, the existing capacity of the economy, and the preferences of students themselves, was even more marked under the republic. "Science" became a popular catch cry, along with "democracy," during the May Fourth period, but by the word was understood not so much the intricacies of physics or zoology, as a rational, progressive approach to life, in contradistinction to supposed Confucian obscurantism and reaction. In a more technical vein, the movement for vocational education which spread in America in the second decade of the century had a considerable influence on Chinese educators seeking a way of diverting student energies—which tended to be concentrated on reaching the next rung of the educational ladder—into productive work. Their interests meshed with those of the new class of businessmen and industrialists in the large cities who were concerned about the supply of skilled workers for their enterprises, resulting in the establishment in Shanghai in 1917 of the Chinese Vocational Education Association. The influence of the association was evident in the American-based school system promulgated in 1922, which set up separate, specialized vocational middle schools, whose students would go from school to work rather than aiming for higher education. By 1925, 167 schools of this type were in existence, but the political turmoil of the Northern Expedition and the ensuing years of internecine war curbed their growth. Contradictions within the schools also inhibited their effectiveness: nearly 80 percent of agricultural schools, for example, were located within urban areas (an incongruity that persisted into the post-1949 period and led to the Cultural Revolution attempts to relocate agricultural colleges in the countryside); and students still tried to use vocational schools to meet their own aims for upward mobility, rather than contentedly going into the work force in the specialties in which they had been trained. The Nationalist government made a strong commitment to vocational education, ordering that provinces and cities should assign to it 35 percent of their current budget—only 5 percent less than that allotted to regular middle schools, and 10 percent more than went to normal schools. Wartime conditions, however, precluded the realization of the potential benefits of this shift.

Science and technology did register some progress in the 1920s and 1930s: 1922 saw the foundation of the Chinese Science Association and the Astronomical Society, and other scientific bodies followed. Research was taken under the wing of the government in the crowning achievement of that decade, the foundation of the Academia Sinica in 1927–1928 "to promote scientific research and to direct, coordinate, and encourage scientific research." Many distinguished scientists worked in its research institutes for the natural, applied, and social sciences. Whatever the uncertain social consequences of an American-trained elite, it meant the infusion into Chinese scientific research of personnel familiar with the most advanced techniques and theories of the West. In the 1930s, as Theodore H. E. Chen observes (1970, p. 301), the policy of the Nationalist government "was to discourage the study of literature, arts, law, social science, education, and commerce and to lay emphasis on 'practical courses,' namely science, technology, agriculture, and medicine." This goal was largely realized through control of scholarships and subsidies, which went primarily to students in the "practical" subjects, resulting in a shift from a predominantly arts, law, and commerce enrollment to one in which by 1935 51 percent of students took the practical subjects—a 20 percent switch in four years. Budget expenditures reflected the change.

The progress of higher-level education along these lines was disrupted by the War of Resistance, when many universities relocated in the interior behind Nationalist lines. Personnel could be transferred, but not equipment and libraries, and educational work during this period was carried out under great difficulties.

Perhaps the main defect of the Kuomintang effort at redirecting educational energies lay not in higher-level or even middle-level technical and scientific education, but in the fact that they did not for the most part, extend even the most basic modern approach to agriculture, hygiene, and so on, into the rural areas. The Rural Reconstruction Movement and other reformist programs were designed in part to achieve this end, but the bulk of the task was left to the communists in the period after 1949.

SCIENCE AND TECHNOLOGY IN THE PRC

Chinese industry has been growing at the rate of about 10 percent per year, generating a need for technicians and skilled workers. This need has been met only in part by the country's network of technical or vocational schools, whose enrollment increased from 77,000 in 1949 to 482,000 in 1957, leaped forward to over a million in 1958, but was only 680,000 in 1977. These technical middle schools usually serve a particular industrial branch. One such school in Nanking, for instance, trains technicians for the electric power industry of Kiangsu province. Others serve the railway system or maritime industry. Many of these schools were closed for some years during the Cultural Revolution, and since 1976, their neglect has been sharply criticized. By 1979, enrollment in this network had risen to 1,199,000, while enrollment in general middle schools had dropped.

Probably most of the need for skilled labor and technicians has been met by industrial enterprises themselves. Large enterprises have a range of educational facilities, including apprenticeship programs, spare-time and evening classes, vocational middle schools, as well as spare-time or full-time "July 21 worker universities." These last developed from half-work, half-study programs initiated during the Great Leap Foward. They offer courses of up to three years, some of which may in fact be of postsecondary quality. What is particularly significant about enterprise educational programs is that they teach skills used elsewhere. Large enterprises in the developed northeast and in Shanghai have trained thousands of skilled workers and technicians for employment in the industrializing interior, thereby helping to meet a critical need for human resources.

In the agricultural sector, three approaches to the diffusion of technical knowledge have been used: formal educational programs of varying sorts, teaching by rural small-scale industrial enterprises, and the network of "scientific experiment" stations. With regard to the first, "May 7 agricultural colleges"—the counterparts to industrial "July 21" schools—have been set up, mainly at the county level. In 1977, these institutions enrolled perhaps a million students. One such school, in Chiang-ning hsien, Kiangsu, offers full and part-time courses of study ranging from three to six months to two or even three years in duration. The courses are strongly oriented to practical subjects; they include agronomy, machinery maintenance, animal husbandry, paramedical knowledge, and the like. Students are selected from among those already working at tasks requiring some specialized knowledge as well as from among young people with a junior middle school education. Teachers are assigned by regular educational institutions as well as by appropriate technical work units.

Second, the small-scale industrial undertakings that have mushroomed in rural China in the last twenty years not only teach skills to the peasants assigned to work in them, but also disseminate skills to the teams and brigades that use their products. Commune-level enterprises might give short courses on the operation and maintenance of farm machinery, or they might send technicians to purchasing units to give appropriate instruction. Sigurdson (1977, p. 222) regards rural industry as being "part of a communications network" that encourages awareness and knowledge of a new technology throughout the villages.

431

Third, China has built up an impressive network for the testing, adaptation, dissemination, and popularization of agricultural technology and agronomic innovations. Science and technology groups function down to the commune level of the rural administrative hierarchy, as do experimental stations which also extend to many production brigades. Numerous production teams have set up "scientific experiment small groups." Sigurdson estimates that 14 million rural inhabitants take part in "mass scientific activities" (1977, p. 81). These activities have been costly because during the Cultural Revolution decade, research scientists often had to spend their time on what amounted to extension work. But from the point of view of rural modernization, this network has not only facilitated the testing and rapid diffusion of new seeds—the economist Wiens (in *Chinese Economy Post-Mao*, 1978, p. 680) speaks of the "extraordinary speed with which hybrid rice went from breeding to full-scale production"—but must also have significantly increased relevant knowledge and skills among the participating peasants.

The Cultural Revolution had a contradictory effect upon the diffusion of technical knowledge. On the one hand, the Maoist emphasis on the integration of work with learning and on bridging the gap between manual and mental labor gave a boost to work-study. May 7 and July 21 are, in fact, dates of directives given by Mao in 1966 and 1968 on this subject. On the other hand, interest in the acquisition of knowledge and skills was damped by the Cultural Revolution's egalitarian reluctance to provide appropriate material rewards, especially promotions. The Maoist ideal of tapping mass creativity should also be conducive to the diffusion of technical knowledge. In principle, the cooperation between the highly educated and the less educated in "three-in-one" combinations serves to break down status and communications barriers, and raises the self-confidence of the less educated in their ability to learn and to innovate. The many publicized cases of ordinary peasants, workers, or housewives (in cooperative street industries) tackling a technical problem, learning by doing, and ultimately succeeding would seem to attest to the worth of the Maoist ideal. Yet, all too often, such a triumph of mass creativity came at great cost: it came as a "triumph" over the "reactionary specialist" rather than as a triumph of guided and cooperative learning. Mass creativity was extolled even while experts were humiliated, degraded, and purged.

The ideals of the Cultural Revolution should have given a boost to the popularization of all kinds of knowledge in the country at large; yet the pervasive antiintellectualism of the Cultural Revolution decade perceptibly reduced popular enthusiasm for learning. Efforts were made to widen access to knowledge, as in the form of radio and TV programs, inexpensive technical manuals and booklets, or the republication of the series "Shih-wan ke wei-shemma" (100,000 Whys). But class struggle intruded, and the pervasive suspicion of "revisionist poisons" often deprived these initiatives of the impact they might otherwise have had. This emerges clearly when the pre-1976 years are contrasted with the current period. Not only have vigorous steps been taken to widen the scope of popularization—the Science and Technology Association has been revived, TV and radio programs expanded, new popular science magazines issued, and the publication of "how-to" manuals stepped up—but popular interest in learning has perceptibly risen, as visitors report. Learning has once more become legitimate. It appears that the institutions and practices for the diffusion and popularization of knowledge and skills developed in the PRC may now have a chance to come into their own.

ADVANCED SCIENCE AND TECHNOLOGY

In the realm of education and knowledge, the main quantitative effort during the transformation stage of modernization has to be on the primary and middle levels. But this does not mean that advanced education and research can be neglected. China's strategy of "walking on two legs" requires using modern technology even as older methods are adapted for current use. Much of the modern technology has to be imported from abroad—the great technology transfers of the 1950s and 1970s attest to this—and specialists are needed who can understand, evaluate, and adapt this technology to China's needs. Moreover, as a latecomer, China is in a position to profit from the advantage of backwardness: it can skip over the costly initial phases of technological development and adopt the most advanced and efficient versions of a particular technology. But to do this requires experts trained to the most advanced levels of theoretical and applied science. Inevitably, the main emphasis in higher education and advanced research has to be on application. Yet, at the same time, some scientists must be allowed to work on the frontiers of knowledge, if only to prepare for future application and to generate necessary technical competence. Such an approach began to be worked out in the 1950s and early 1960s, but was largely abandoned in favor of extreme emphasis on application; it was restored in the late 1970s.

As noted earlier, tertiary education was restructured in the 1950s to emphasize even more strongly technical and scientific education, while enrollment rose rapidly. However, in part because of poor planning but mainly because graduates were in short supply as industrialization proceeded apace, high-level technical competence in industrial enterprises had still to be acquired largely on the job. According to a survey taken in 1957, only 56 percent of chief engineers, the number two men in enterprises, had graduated from higher schools. Only 13.8 percent of a sample of 800,000 engineers and technicians had higher education, while 22.4 percent had gone through specialized secondary training and 64 percent had learned on the job. The presence of Soviet advisers in key industrial units alleviated the problem.

With regard to research and postgraduate training, a complex structure of over 100 institutes under the Chinese Academy of Sciences emerged in the 1950s, built around the 1,100-odd holders of foreign doctorates who remained in China or returned from abroad. Ministries, including that of defense, set up research units, as did some universities and colleges. With Soviet advice, a twelve-year plan for research and development was adopted in 1956, which called for training of top-level scientists and a large cadre of college-level support personnel. Research priorities were set. Problems to be investigated included atomic energy, electronics, petroleum technology, and several questions in basic natural science, as well as applied problems such as the harnessing of the Yellow and Yangtze Rivers. As these plans began to be implemented, state funding increased sharply from 38 million *yuan* in 1955 to 1.08 billion in 1960. Thirteen hundred scientists went to the Soviet Union, and since cultural relations were not broken off until 1965, 30 Chinese nuclear scientists worked at Dubna until then. Two thousand graduate students studied in the USSR as well, though few apparently received graduate degrees. Within China, a small graduate program was inaugurated in 1955, and in 1958, a University of Science and Technology was established in Peking and Shanghai for the purpose of training advanced researchers. A first class of 1,600 graduated in 1963; it is one of the mainstays of the post-Mao research and development revival.

The progress of research and development was checked by the politicization of the Great Leap Forward and the Socialist Education Movement, but their effects were insignificant compared to the havoc created by the Cultural Revolution. As the sphere of action least easily appraised by the common man, advanced scientific research came in for particularly uncompromising attacks.

The research establishment as a whole was subjected to sweeping decentralization. Only twenty institutes remained fully under central control. Carried out sensibly, decentralization might have freed scientists from excessive bureaucratic control. Under Cultural Revolution conditions, however, the result was a reduction in communication among scientists, as professional societies were disbanded and scientific journals not published. Scientists working in one locale were not aware of work done elsewhere, leading to unnecessary duplication. Reduced funding also led to a sharp decline in the quality of the instrumentation of laboratories and other research facilities.

Research and development were blocked by pervasive hostility to theoretical investigation. In benign forms, this hostility meant that research scientists worked in their fields of expertise but on an elementary level. In plant breeding, as an American delegation observed in 1974, current knowledge was being disseminated, but no new knowledge created: "If the nation is to continue to improve yields and production, a dynamic production-oriented and much more sophisticated fundamental research effort will be required" (*Plant Studies in the People's Republic of China*, 1975, p. 119). In malignant form, the hostility to theoretical research and more broadly to specialists was purely destructive:

Many research projects undertaken by scientific research institutions and agricultural institutes were cancelled. Many valuable seed strains and specimens were destroyed and numerous books, data, and equipment scattered and lost. . . . The agricultural research network established nationwide after liberation was seriously damaged.

Under the reactionary slogan of . . . "dismantling temples to drive away the gods" about 10,000 scientific and technical personnel in Liaoning Province alone were forced to settle down with their families in the countryside to be "absorbed locally" . . . college graduates, who, according to the original plans, were to be assigned to scientific and technical work were instead appointed as buyers, sales workers, custodians, typists, cooks, etc. Some specializing in rocketry were assigned as doorkeepers. Remote control specialists were turned into butchers. Mathematicians and foreign language teachers became fuel sellers and bakers. (*Jen-min jih-pao,* May 6 and 7, 1978)

Pockets of excellence survived or even prospered, as achievements were scored in nuclear research, in the launching of earth satellites, in biological pest control, x-ray diffraction, or the chemical synthesis of insulin. Some of the research units operated by the defense establishment and by economic ministries continued to function or were disrupted only briefly. But on the whole, advanced research and training came to a halt, leaving a ten-year gap.

Since Mao Tse-tung's death, a major effort has been underway to make up for lost time. Science and technology are now viewed as the keys to the other three modernizations. It is now hoped that China will not only adapt the fruits of advanced research from abroad but will itself join those nations in the front ranks of science by the end of the century. To this end, strong central leadership has been restored. The Science and Technology Commission of the State Council has been reestablished; it is now headed by a Politburo member. The Academy of Sciences is being reinvigorated. An Academy of Social Sciences has been established, with a strong focus on the study of foreign industrial management, Chinese industry being deficient in modern managerial expertise. A large-scale graduate program is being launched, science centers in four cities are to be established, and research priorities for various periods up to the year 2000 have been mapped out. The decision to send students abroad is of particular significance for science and technology. The initial group sent abroad includes many who were trained before 1966, but whose knowledge and skills need to be upgraded. Indeed, expanding scientific and technological cooperation with the outside world is one of the most outstanding features of the new policy. At the popular level, too, the prestige of the scientist-intellectual is being restored.

A major bottleneck is the shortage of top level personnel. According to Suttmeier (1980), the "leadership corps" of China's advanced research and instruction is perhaps 30,000 strong. The top leaders of this group are scholars trained before 1949—testimony to the severe disruption in the orderly growth of China's science since then. The bulk of the group was either trained abroad since 1949, mainly in the Soviet Union, or trained within China before 1966. The top stratum is extremely thin. It will take considerable time to increase its number, all the more since the best active scientists are engaged in research rather than in teaching.

It can also be asked to what extent China's research effort is organized to serve the country's needs, which in the near future include both generation and diffusion of innovation for China's agriculture and industry. One of the costs of the sledgehammer approach of the Cultural Revolution was that good ideas, such as bringing research and production together, may have been discredited by association with that upheaval. Thus, despite the continuing importance attached to applied research, China's scientific organization continues to be modeled after the Soviet Union's, and there bureaucratic barriers separating research institutes, universities, and industrial firms have long acted as blocks to innovation. It remains to be seen to what extent such blockages will inhibit the country's progress.

Education and Values

The values acquired from formal education are not easy to define. Are they those explicit or implicit in the curriculum and organization of the school? Are they of primary importance, or merely secondary reinforcement—positive or negative—for values learned at home and from society? Where the values of family and school clash, does either prevail, or does a new type of orientation emerge from conflict between them? These questions are more than academic for twentieth-century China, where a school system predicated on the inculcation in students of constructive values tending to the maintenance and improvement of existing conditions has time and again been rent by student action aimed at destroying the status quo. Under the Ch'ing, the stated aims of education were "loyalty to the ruler, veneration of Confucius, public spirit, martial spirit, and respect for solid learning"—but the Revolution of 1911 was spearheaded by students who had evidently forgotten the first two precepts. Even more striking is the example of the Cultural Revolution, in which many of the young joined in turning against and temporarily paralyzing the party.

As important as the revolt of the privileged is the question of attitudes and habits imbibed by the ordinary school attenders—children who after four or six or eight years of sitting in a classroom take up vocations in their native village or market town. Do they share the discontent that has periodically swept over the student intellectuals of the cities, or do they have personal or local grievances of a different order? Or does their schooling fit them, as it is for the most part intended to do, to a productive life in that station to which they have been called?

In weighing questions of the integrative or disruptive effect of education, one has little concrete data to go on. Analysis of the intentions of educators, observations on their fulfillment or lack of success, and the recorded activities and sentiments of students, may offer some clues to their solution.

The framers of China's new school system in 1904 attempted to lead their nation toward modernization while preserving traditional social values. To this end, the curriculum orginally planned for lower and higher primary schools contained twelve hours of classical study per week, in addition to Chinese and morals. At the same time, approved modern texts were compiled stressing love of country and martial spirit; not an easy task, since the stories of national humiliation that were to inspire these feelings could not be couched in terms suggesting that the dynasty was weak. Many teachers— some returned from Japan, others influenced by the reform and revolutionary movements emanating from there, others caught up in the spirit of Chinese anti-Manchuism—did not stick to the letter of the text, but added their own explanations of China's perilous position; even young children often gained a sense of their country's plight.

In addition to nationalistic lessons conveyed in textbooks or read between the lines, the very establishment of the school system in itself conveyed a powerful message about the relative worth of Chinese and foreign institutions and qualifications. The new education would not have been introduced had the old not been considered a failure, its course of study empty and for-malistic, its degrees a certification in useless knowledge and dead books. The new schools, on the other hand, were seen as the vanguard of civilization, with their students as China's future masters. It is little wonder that students who internalized these lessons were ready to challenge authority, whether their protests were directed against poor food in the school canteen or Man-chu concessions to foreigners. Particularly galling was the fact that the in-fluence that, under the premises of the new school system, should have ac-crued to its graduates, proved elusive: whether in the army, the educational world, or the bureaucracy, those who had acquired modern skills in Japanese or Chinese schools often chafed under the direction of ill-qualified superiors.

The organization of the new schools—of postelementary boarding schools in particular—was supposed to instill in pupils an unaccustomed military discipline. The restraints of the examination system had been removed, but in their place were irksome new requirements of attendance and decorum. Even village schools found discipline a problem.

Allied to resentment of institutional restrictions as a cause of unrest was a new intellectual freedom. Although the number of schools with an organized revolutionary group—often growing around the nucleus of a committed revolutionary returned from Japan—was small in relation to the total, there were many where first reform and later revolutionary periodicals circulated underground. School authorities were powerless to intervene. Even students not politically active were at least exposed to the journalism of the treaty port cities. This was especially true of middle or higher level schools, which were located in the prefectural or provincial capital.

Many students supported, a few played an active part in, the overthrow of the Ch'ing. Their actions did not, however, bring the expected personal or national rewards. Under the rule of Yuan Shih-k'ai and successive warlords, placement most frequently went to old-style leaders and their clients and associates: merit and talent, even if certified by the schools, meant little without the right connections. Nationally, China was still bound by the unequal treaties, and Yuan's accession to the Twenty-One Demands threatened continuing loss of independence. The student movements of the May Fourth period emerged from conditions not unlike those behind the turbulence of Ch'ing schools; poor conditions in the schools themselves, and a school environment usually different from the home; the ambiguous social status of the new learning and its products; contact with radical teachers and the opportunity to organize; consciousness of national humiliation, and inept handling of protest by the government. The Northern Expedition of the Kuomintang offered a new focus for student idealism and new disillusionment. The frustrated hopes of the May Fourth period often degenerated into a habit of defiance. Lao She's bitter novel Cat City (*Mao ch'eng chi*) provides both a satiric *reductio ad absurdum* of the schools of his own time and a tragic prophecy of the turmoil of the mid-sixties in which he lost his life. He describes a society in which education has lost its purpose: students are handed degrees as they come in the school door, and lacking examinations and lessons to occupy themselves, devote their time to carving up unpopular teachers. Given the great issues of the times, however, student idealism flared up again and again, as in the December 9 Movement in 1935 and in the student movements of 1946 and 1947.

After the communists came to power in 1949, they experienced many of the difficulties that had plagued earlier governments intent on persuading highly politicized students that the fate of the nation was now in safe hands, and that their primary duty was the unromantic one of study. Tension was eased in the first years of the People's Republic by the need for cooperation in rebuilding the country after the civil war and by the plentiful supply of jobs awaiting the highly trained: it seemed that education was once again a legitimate route to a good job. At the same time, however, students resented tight bureaucratic control by Youth League and party organizations. When the opportunity came in 1957, some were quick to protest, their complaints poignantly anticipating those voiced in the Cultural Revolution nearly a decade later. By then, Mao had himself turned against the party bureaucracy, and he harnessed students' energies to the attack of the old order, instead of repressing them as in 1957. The students were idealistic. They, too, had been reared on the notion of the corruption of the old society and their purity as representatives of the new. For a while it seemed that the old slogan that students would be the future masters of China was being fulfilled before they

438

were out of their teens, as they traveled and lodged free and sent delegations to the national and provincial leadership. But the imperatives of order took precedence over anarchy, and the "down to the country and up to the mountains" campaign redefined the duties of educated youth as physical labor alongside the peasants. Most emerged from this experience with a conviction of the value of book learning as the legitimate route to a good job.

Description of student unrest stresses the disruptive aspect of modern education, its unintended if not necessarily unproductive consequences. But education, after all, can be used deliberately to foster national integration, patriotism, and new values. With regard to language, the twentieth century has seen protracted efforts to use the schools to teach Mandarin. As classical learning disappeared from the curriculum, so did the dominance of the literary language in which the classics were written. In 1922 all primary and normal schools were ordered to include the teaching of standard Mandarin (*kuo-yü* or the national language, now known as *p'u-t'ung-hua* or the common language, out of sensitivity to the feelings of minorities) and the phonetic script developed to represent its sounds. The schools thus became the vehicle for the transmission of a standard spoken and written colloquial language, a move of potentially great significance for Chinese national integration. In the PRC the teaching of *p'u-t'ung-hua* has been vigorously promoted; yet, paradoxically, the localizing initiatives of the Great Leap Forward and the Cultural Revolution may have dealt this cause a setback. Rural *min-pan* schools, for instance, sometimes adapted to village needs by teaching in the local subdialect, for example, Toishan rather than Cantonese, not to speak of Mandarin. Articles in the Chinese press in the late 1970s stressing the need to teach the common language in all primary schools indicate that the country still has some way to go in this respect.

Education can also be used to instill a government-sponsored ideology providing a standardized morality and focusing on the national symbols, thus minimizing the actual or threatened dislocations arising from rapid change; late Meiji Japan is a prime example of the promulgation of an official state ideology through the school system. Despite their Japanese model, the framers of the Chinese education system of 1904 made little use of the potential of mass education for the inculcation of a nationalist ideology. Chang Chih-tung attempted instead to reinforce the culture-centered values of Confucianism, not because he was unconscious of national sentiment but because he feared it. Yet, Chang's Confucian conservatism was behind the times: new theories of the uses of education to inculcate national consciousness were being imported from Japan through the reform press—Liang Ch'i-ch'ao's *Hsin-min Ts'ung-pao*—and student journals also produced in Tokyo. The new *chun-kuo-min chiao-yü* (education for military citizenship) had as its purpose the ideological and organizational remolding of the population. By 1910, the concept had found its way into the vocabulary of the Ministry of Education, under the impetus of belated preparation for constitutional government.

Later, under the Nationalists, the teaching of the Three People's Principles became a regular feature of the curriculum. Under the communists, education was even more politicized with extensive introduction of ideological, patriotic, and service-to-the-collective themes. At times, the effect was detrimental to substantive learning.

The politicization of education in the PRC raises the question of the extent to which values taught in the school and ancillary organizations conflict with those taught in the family. The evidence on this point is mixed. Direct value clashes have certainly occurred, as when children were mobilized during political campaigns to attack the beliefs of their parents. Moreover, communist textbooks place less emphasis on the family than republican and Taiwanese texts do; they also foster loyalty to the goals of larger collectivities. This shift in focus is congruent with a socialist approach of modernization, but may have made it more difficult for the schools to tap the strong interest in education inherent in the Chinese family. Certainly this was true during the Cultural Revolution years, when education was largely divorced from prospects of personal and therefore family advancement, and when it placed unprecedented stress on self-abnegating service to the people. The extent of conflict must not, however, be exaggerated. In their study of rural schools, Parish and Whyte find that the notion of the schools as the "primary locus of the state's battle with parents for the minds of their children" is erroneous. Rural schools, they write, "are not viewed as Trojan horses, introducing strange new values into the community or the home. Instead they are viewed primarily as institutions where useful knowledge is transmitted. . . . Some of the moral training that is carried out in the school, in fact, reinforces themes stressed in the home—discipline, hard work, cooperativeness, avoidance of fighting. . . . Schools also teach children the basic terms and ideas of Maoist political culture, but these seem to be regarded by parents as 'useful knowledge,' much like the three Rs, since success in later life will require familiarity with the political catechism of contemporary China" (1978, p. 229).

On balance, it seems fair to suggest that the messages transmitted by the PRC educational system have with some important exceptions been congruent with the needs of modernization, certainly more so than was the case in republican times. If in the latter popular education could be criticized for its remoteness, a major effort has been made in the PRC to ensure that the content of education for the ordinary person is relevant, comprehensible, unambiguous, and widely available. Texts emphasize the virtues of loyalty to the nation, courage, initiative, and perseverance. More concrete lessons concern hygiene, medical care, and other improvements in the immediate environment.

In assessing the influence of education, the major communist achievement, that of nearly universal primary education, takes on particular importance. When education is universal, everyone shares certain fixed points of experience, and possibly certain common attitudes and assumptions. When, as under the republic, a large portion of the rural population is illiterate and unschooled, those who attend school are constantly having the message they receive there contradicted by their elders and peers. In principle, the organizational imperatives of schooling impose common orientations: acceptance of the need for punctuality, for the allotment of tasks by time, for coordinated action, for obedience, and for attentiveness. The degree to which the various kinds of schooling in China are in fact inculcating attributes associated with modernity undoubtedly varies, depending on whether the degree of surrounding modernization confirms or negates school experiences, and also depending on the period: the laxity of industrial discipline that characterized the Cultural Revolution had its counterpart in the disarray of schools. Overall, however, it appears that the schools, building on the commitment to study of premodern China, act as an integrative force providing young Chinese with a coherent set of modern concepts, attitudes, and habits.

International Comparisons

For almost eight decades the Chinese have sought to use a western-derived education system as a tool for economic and political modernization. Initial expectations of the results of reform were unrealistically high: a new universality was supposed to lead to political maturity among an enlightened populace, a new praticality to the elimination of underemployment and the growth of industry. But the supposed panacea proved unequal to the demands placed upon it. Even with compulsory enrollment and a technical curriculum, education is a tangential approach to the industrialization that underlies modernity. In Japan, educational policies—for the rapid creation of a cadre of specialists trained by the best European professors, and for the attainment of mass schooling—were planned and implemented under firm government control as one component of the modernization effort. Equal attention was paid to fiscal and administrative reform and to investment in communications and strategic industries. In China, effective central planning was long in coming and much interrupted. An educational system that was in theory highly advanced—allowing by the 1920s for coeducation at all levels and the promulgation through the schools of a national language—was hamstrung by successive governments' lack of interest or funds and by remoteness from the perceived needs of the majority of the rural population. In 1928, less than one child in eight attended primary school. Peasants tended to regard "modern" schooling as irrelevant to their children's needs, and to be content with the *Three Character Classic* of their ancestors. Educationalists' sorties into mass education were probably as instructive for their initiators as their objects, as the communist experience in the wartime base areas demonstrates.

Practicality was perhaps slightly better served than universality by the new system, in that deliberate concentration by the Nationalist government on training—often completed overseas—in science and technology led to the formation in the 1930s and 1940s of an elite of highly qualified specialists in these fields. The majority of graduates, however, had their expectations raised in the schools but dashed in the labor market, and despite the limited number of graduates, "Graduation means unemployment" became a common saying. Personal frustration combined with national humiliation turned a significant minority toward revolution.

The cessation of civil war and the founding of the People's Republic offered the prospect of successfully coordinating educational planning with economic growth. The new government dedicated itself simultaneously to the expansion of a mass educational base and the raising of standards in advanced science and technology. A conflict remained, however, between the proponents of high standards and formal courses—training an elite in the research and management skills appropriate to an advanced economy—and those who believed that education should function primarily as a solvent rather than an agent of existing social stratification, and should be geared to the current level of the rural masses. The Cultural Revolution proved that the wholesale transference of the lessons of wartime Yenan—one of China's most backward and barren areas—was inappropriate as a strategy for the whole country in the 1960s and 1970s, and the pendulum has swung back to regularization and formalization.

Educational advances in Japan and Russia were more cumulative. Major gains were achieved in each period, beginning with the dynamism prior to the reforms of the 1860s and continuing into the contemporary era. Popular education, elite education, science and technology, and the use of education to foster modern attitudes have received very high priority in these countries. These impressive results contrast to the Chinese failures in adapting the premodern educational foundation to modern needs, in promoting mass education before 1949, and in sustaining a commitment to high level education during the 1960s and 1970s.

CHAPTER THIRTEEN

Summary: Twentieth Century

International Context

BY THE EARLY TWENTIETH CENTURY, THE IMPORTANCE OF MODERNIZATION WAS strongly impressed on the Chinese consciousness. The failure of the anti-foreign Boxer Rebellion and the successive Japanese victories over China and Russia provided military and nationalistic justifications for a new course. It had taken long for this lesson to sink in, but foreign influences had at last aroused a consensus on the need to modernize (variously interpreted) quickly.

China had to and did borrow from abroad during this new era of institution building. In many respects, borrowing proved difficult. In some areas, as in educational change, there was a rootless and uncritical shift from classical to foreign standards. In other areas, notably political change, forms were taken from abroad, but the implementation and content remained conservatively Chinese. Not only could change be too rootless or too superficial, it could be too little guided by the central government and existing or stable organizations. Borrowing occurred without much coordination. Into this disarray entered the students who had studied abroad. Their position was ambiguous. They could not easily be integrated into the old system, and a new system that they would have been prepared to support and serve had not been constructed. The attitudes of the returned students proved a major catalyst for nationalism and a preparation for revolution.

A new world view emerged more from below than from above. Popular mood became the moving force of much of Chinese history: nationalism, cultural awakening, boycotts, and resistance to foreign aggression emerged as themes in the first half of the century. The popular perception of a hostile international environment, grounded in reality but varying at some remove from the reality, exerted a major impact on Chinese society. In the 1910s the onerous foreign presence corroded the idealism and naiveté of the 1900s. The Japanese Twenty-One Demands and the Versailles peace treaty in particular worsened the perception of modernized countries. Images of rapacious neighbors and dishonest governments in China were strengthened. In the 1920s, the period in which Chinese unity was least threatened by new acts of imperialism, the mood was more strongly antiimperialist than ever; there was more indignation with less cause. And in the 1930s and the first half of the 1940s, the preoccupation with Japanese aggression nurtured the psychology of endangerment from abroad. This new world view created a national consensus and a feeling of participation, a sense of urgency in all activities and a new form of borrowing—especially from the Soviet Union—centered on the organizational mechanisms and historical interpretations that would promise national relief and ascendancy. In the short run at least, the more negative results were extremist solutions arising out of a heightened sense of frustrations.

Foreign factors shaped the course of China's modernization more directly. The Japanese destroyed the Kuomintang as a viable government that had been moving toward unifying and stabilizing China and eliminating the Communist Party. The war forced expensive military measures that took precedence over internal reform, drove the KMT into western China far from its revenues and the bulk of its supporters, and wiped out the economic base of a new capital-forming set of entrepreneurs who seemed to be the nucleus of a new modernizing elite. The results of the civil war that followed were to a large extent based on the political results and national feelings of the struggle against Japan (and on the opportunity the CCP had to develop and the KMT to show its weaknesses). The international context before 1949 did not so much shape the actual modernization of China's economy or other social conditions as affect politics and the determination of who would lead modernization. External factors, though foremost in popular consciousness, were not decisive in producing China's political disorder. Nevertheless, the chaos and frustrations of internal politics increased the antiimperialist vehemence.

Before 1949 the turbulent internal politics of China greatly limited the potential for drawing on foreign models, trade, or assistance to promote modernization. After 1949, with unity and order restored, it matters more what effect the international environment had on the domestic social structure, on the importation of technology, and on organizational strategies. Since 1949, that environment has been inconsistent and often unfavorable. The Soviet tie had long-lasting consequences and some positive effects, but it proved disappointing to the Chinese and led to near total isolation. Ideological pronouncements in favor of self-reliance bordered for a time on xenophobia.

Indeed, by the mid-1970s the PRC accounted for well under 1 percent of the world's exports. International factors contributed to Chinese isolation, but that isolation was largely self-made. Only at the end of the decade did it appear possible that for the first time the Chinese would harness international forces in a decidedly positive manner to accelerate modernization.

Political Structure

China's fall, that is, the destruction of the traditional integrative system, was especially hard. The longstanding political deterioration during the Ch'ing dynasty and the acute inadequacy of late Ch'ing leadership in responding to crises and challenges were important factors leading to the state's collapse. The Chinese failed to build on traditionally strong solidarities, to convert the strengths of the old system to the tasks of the new era. Following the commitment to transform China made in the reform decade of the 1900s, political disintegration occurred without being followed by centralization. It caused subsequent changes in political structure to be less clearly or quickly modernizing.

Through the first half of the twentieth century, the successors to the Ch'ing government did not have the strength to plan or develop the diverse and scattered elements of modernization that appeared. Disunity, persisting for many decades, diverted attention from many aspects of modernization. China lacked a central leader who could perform the symbolic and integrative roles of the emperor. The government was not in a position to contribute importantly to economic growth or to take advantage of its benefits and was further weakened by the lack of the resources, such as adequate tax revenues, that made other governments stronger at comparable phases of their development. The ideal was still centralization, but divisive regional powers prevailed. The Northern Expedition made a beginning for unification, yet the Japanese occupation set China back again.

Disunity and the absence of vigorous state leadership do not mean that the local political structure was unchanged. In fact, profound changes occurred in local government. The elimination of the old bureaucracy's regularizing role meant that the base from which change took place after 1949 was very different from the base in mid-Ch'ing. The county magistracy ceased to function as the point at which central and local interests joined and were kept in

445

equilibrium. Chinese rural society drifted toward compromises with mostly illegitimate regional and local holders of power. The time-tested procedures for selecting good leaders were replaced with nothing except the ability to muster coercion. China's traditional elite had been held together at the county level by an ideology that was centralist, meritocratic, ethical, and non-national; the changing conditions of national life in modern times challenged it more fundamentally than ever before. The realignment of official career patterns, of the composition of the local elite, and of the elite's role in government had important, and largely destabilizing, consequences for the fabirc of local life.

At times when disunity became a less consuming preoccupation (mainly after 1949), other priorities took precedence over elements of political reform that were in the long run conducive to modernization, such as stability and participation. The campaign approach under the CCP discouraged both low-level autonomous political participation and low-level stable institutions. In the long run at least, China needs more stability in the mechanisms for pursuing modernization than large campaigns permit. Intense social controls also produced some serious negative consequences. Enforced to a varying degree over the past three decades, such controls were efficient only under some economic conditions in urban areas; they aroused frustration among many and failed to encourage stable political institutions or the development of autonomous participation. Although increasingly large and important sectors of the public became better informed and had higher political expectations—mass political participation increased—the Chinese did not participate in decisions about the major campaigns and reforms that played havoc with their livelihoods and had no sense of the means of achieving rights and freedoms. Individual rights, present in the traditions of the old society and widely regarded as a feature of modern politics, were not linked to the new political forms and legal concepts. Stability was also impaired by the lack of moderation and hasty implementation of CCP policies, policies that attempted much more than the infrastructure could bear. In the handling of those with specialized knowledge and skills, communist measures were forceful, usually overwrought, and thus often counterproductive. The leaders misjudged the time and cost required for various changes and instead of encouraging individual drive produced superficial conformity.

The reunification of China has had many favorable consequences for its modernization. The leadership of the CCP has solved many of the pressing problems that hindered modernization, though serious problems remain. It has provided a degree of control and coordination previously missing in China. It has clarified ambiguities about China's sovereignty. It has showed itself capable of bridging local and national areas. The resources available to the state expanded eightfold in the years 1950-1959, and the leadership has increased its ability to manage and plan in many spheres of life, particularly the economic. It has succeeded, at least for the present, in putting conformity, if not loyalty, to the national interest, as it interprets it, above family and local interests to an extent never sought in China before.

Economic Structure and Growth

During the first half of the twentieth century modern economic growth—in the technical sense of substantially rising rates of capital formation and per capita output—was not achieved in China, but there were periods with economic advances that held out promise of accelerated gains. Under the Ch'ing government in the last years of the nineteenth century, important steps were taken to launch industrial development. During World War I and over much of the next two decades, modern industries appeared in Shanghai, in Manchuria, and in cities elsewhere near the coast and the Yangtze River, where foreign and Chinese capital, technologies, and managements mingled freely. In the absence of peace, stability, and active government support, these advances could not go very far. Firms in the city ports had to return their investments quickly. "Commercialization" rather than "industrialization," the episodic quick kill in luxury goods rather than integrated increasing capital formation, was strongly reinforced and rewarded. The rural sector especially was affected by the unfavorable conditions of the 1920s and early 1930s and finally by the crippling effects of the Japanese invasion and subsequent civil war. The Kuomintang managed to increase its claim on gross national product slightly and to divert some resources from the private sector for necessary expenses. For a time in the mid-1930s economic growth accelerated, but KMT efforts were cut short before they could bear much fruit. Apart from the problems of worldwide depression and national disorder, the KMT could not do much because its control over the national economy was limited. Under these circumstances, it was difficult to initiate major reforms whereby conditions for modernization could be strengthened through government management and spending to develop an infrastructure. The considerable industrial growth that did occur, even given the absence of political stability, was centered in coastal and riverine cities linked more closely to each other, and to foreign places, than to most of the Chinese interior.

After 1949 the Chinese economy underwent rapid but uneven growth. The CCP leadership has demonstrated a remarkable capacity to mobilize and increase the supply of resources; growth has resulted primarily from this rapid expansion of resources, especially of labor. Massive mobilization of farm labor has remained the crucial means to increase agricultural production. That mobilization also increased coordination and control by habituation. Cultivated area scarcely increased, as roads and structures took valuable land out of production almost as fast as new land could be developed. Despite the expanded use of fertilizers, irrigation, and better seeds, overall labor productivity in agriculture has remained low.

Summary: Twentieth Century

The leadership has had most success with heavy industry and has usually, despite claims to the contrary after 1961, given highest priority to that urban-based sector. The high rate of industrial growth can best be explained by socialist institutions that forced savings and by added inputs of labor, which make it possible for factory managers to use their capital equipment intensively. Rural small-scale industry using abundant labor and scattered resources has also grown rapidly.

After the CCP's assumption of power in 1949, the state launched vigorous campaigns to alter China's economic structure, in both industry and agriculture. These policies greatly affected performance in some fields, especially manufacturing. The major consumer goods industries bought inputs and sold products at prices set by the state; when these industries were nationalized in the 1950s, their profits quickly became the main source of government revenue and of national savings. This ostensibly nontax mechanism of raising revenue extracted vast funds, which were largely invested in heavy industry. This grew quickly in the first decade of the PRC era.

During the severe recession that followed socialist experiments in rural organization during the Great Leap Forward, this method of accumulation temporarily failed, and China's economic performance faltered in practically all fields. Industrial growth resumed in the mid-1960s and continued through the mid-1970s, at a more moderate pace with stagnation caused by the political turmoil of the Cultural Revolution and the succession conflicts at the death of Mao Tse-tung. China's current rulers have reduced the degree to which resources are spread evenly among more- and less-modernized parts of the country, and greater incentives to labor and even capital have been introduced, in efforts to speed growth and raise productivity. In 1980 the profit motive became an important incentive for enterprises. These current policies, which reverse many aspects of China's official economic strategies during much of the first twenty-five years of communist rule, will probably result in more balanced and higher quality industrial production.

The unevenness of economic transformation is revealed by such anomalies as the tremendous increase in labor resources without a meaningful increase in labor productivity after the mid-1950s, the rapid growth in manufacturing's contribution to gross domestic product without much increase in agriculture beyond that required to keep pace with population growth, and, despite this sectoral imbalance, some curtailment of income inequality and little shift of labor to big cities. Obviously the state's method of mobilizing resources—that is, its awesome ability to save and to draw on previously underused labor—accounts for these unusual conditions. Most of the increased per-person production has gone into savings, producers' goods for later growth, and increased national strength. The portion that has gone into individual consumption and that part of the service sector not oriented to heavy industry is small.

Social Integration

Social change during the early stages of China's transformation did more in the short run to destroy the old order than to build a new one. The elimination of the elite degree holders as a meaningful social category hastened social disintegration. The decline of local governments' integration in a national focus cut families, lineages, and other localisms loose to an extent unseen in recent centuries. As a consequence, rural solidarities that interfered with outside control and influences were reinforced. Chinese society above the family and the lineage became more weakly integrated, exacerbating the already serious problem of drawing together local resources for purposes of modernization.

Even in the urban sector, where there was a greater impact from modernizing forces and increased potential for transcending primary bonds within the community, specialized groupings committed to modernization established themselves slowly. New urban interest groups arose and, in the absence of adequate government sponsorship, groped for organizational forms to help realize their goals of transformation. Only in the 1920s did transformation within the cities come primarily to mean building new organizations rather than undercutting old ones. The gap between urban and rural widened as the countryside was both released from the traditional, respected urban linkages and removed from the emergent developments in the cities.

The victory of the Kuomintang in 1927 represents a turning point in the establishment of new, primarily urban, organizations. Using the modern elites that were expanding in the cities, the new government went a long way toward forging a critical social infrastructure in the regions it controlled. Nevertheless, the results were quickly disrupted by war and were, in any case, tarnished by the pronounced role of the military. Despite their urban advances, Chinese leaders still faced an enormous task in coping with the social structure of the village and in more fully involving the village in the urban-led intensification of economic development.

The changes in urban social stratification, the growth in large cities, and the expansion of modern skills and organizations count among the important contributions of the first half of the twentieth century to the modernization potential of the People's Republic. The communists were particularly skilled in creating organizations that mobilized large numbers of people and unified them under a central leadership. They faced enormous problems for, despite the many assets inherited from the premodern society, China had not advanced very far in modernization during the previous half-century.

The Chinese communists accomplished a great deal in social integration. Much of it they did in obvious ways by providing strong leadership. They seized the levers of society and, through waves of social reorganization, mobilized increasing amounts of resources in the cause of modernization. To some extent they brought population growth under control; the near doubling of the Chinese population over three decades to one billion at the beginning of the 1980s actually reflects considerable success in planning. They greatly expanded the number of skilled white-collar workers and of skilled workers generally. Trained teachers and nonagricultural workers became much more abundant. The communists restricted growth in areas that might have proven costly or wasteful and to an extraordinary degree for a developing society, controlled the flow of population from rural to urban areas. If estimates that in the late 1970s less than 20 percent of the Chinese lived in cities are correct, then China's leaders have had unusual success in holding down an urban total already in excess of 10 percent in the first years of the PRC. On the whole, this was a spartan regime that demanded extraordinary sacrifices, usually in the pursuit of rapid economic growth.

Although the CCP satisfied the most visible necessities for modern development over part or all of its first three decades, some means favored by the party mobilized resources without offering adequate long-range solutions to problems of modernization. Land reform, collectivization, and disciplined urban intervention in the countryside do not signify a transformation of rural social conditions similar to what was accomplished in the cities by building on over a half-century of changes. Modified communization and the establishment of a corps of local activists under the CCP are only a partial substitute for engaging rural residents in a materially rewarding challenge to improve conditions. The Great Leap Forward represented the extreme policy of relying on coercion and exhortation in rural areas, rather than on opportunity and meaningful incentives. Such extreme organizational measures were abandoned—although extremism reappeared in waves of radicalism during the 1960s and 1970s—generally leading to a measure of accommodation based on guarantees and material incentives for households and production teams. The Cultural Revolution brought extreme measures to the cities, undoing many of the gains achieved in education since 1949. The thrust has remained more to demand participation than to motivate it.

Since 1950 the Chinese have achieved rapid rates of modernization, rates above those of most nonmodernized countries, but below those achieved in some neighboring East Asian countries. By the late 1970s it was becoming apparent that continued rapid modernization required major changes in approach. Attacks on expertise and specialization in particular cast doubt on the capacity of leaders to apply modern knowledge and to use resources effectively. The restrictive and often totalitarian means of the previous periods are less appropriate as modernization proceeds and the volume of underused resources diminishes. More attention is now being directed toward increases in productivity and toward creating a stable order in which household and individual aspirations are encouraged and potentially rewarded. By 1980 the Chinese were much further along in the modern transformation, despite the

450

backsliding that accompanied the turbulent phases of the Cultural Revolution, but the new approach remained as much a goal as a reality.

China's actual modernization reflects an uneasy alliance between forces of tradition and imposed forces of transformation. Each seems more pronounced than in other modernizing societies at comparable points in their development. There has been little urbanization but much growth of heavy industry, little consumer benefit but much economic growth, and little individualism but much education and work force participation. Modernization over these thirty years has been rather rapid along some dimensions, but very uneven overall. The leaders are now conscious of important readjustments that are needed to maintain the momentum and, perhaps, to change the course of modernization.

Knowledge and Education

In the first decade of the twentieth century, the premodern educational system was abolished, the long-institutionalized link between education and office holding severed, and a new, western system imported from Japan. Reformers set unrealistic goals, both with respect to the rapid implantation of a new system on a nationwide scale and with respect to the role that the new education would be able to play in the attainment of modernization. The system that emerged in the late Ch'ing and in the republican era was not in fact able to meet these high expectations.

Chief among the deficiencies of republican education was inadequate central direction, coordination, and support. To some extent, localized and private efforts compensated for the lack of an effective national effort—Yen Hsi-shan's promotion of education in Shansi, the advances in higher education under American and European missionary auspices, and the mass education movement of James Yen and others are examples. But the lack of a national impetus meant that progress was uneven and fragmented. Inadequate resources confined educational progress largely to the urban sector, where the educational enterprise was in any event reinforced by concurrent modernizing change. The educational gap between town and country consequently widened. The educational system, moreover, was overly foreign oriented, elitist in its focus on preparation for higher study, accessible mainly to the wealthy, and poorly aligned with social realities, giving rise to educated unemployment.

The Nationalist government sought to enhance state control, to make available more resources for education, and to align schooling more closely with economic development. War and civil war cut short much of this effort. Still, by 1949, a base of modern education and knowledge had been laid, inadequate and incomplete to be sure, but one on which the communist

451

successor could build. This base was of particular importance in higher education and advanced science.

The new state used its much greater power to mobilize resources and to coordinate the advance of education on a national scale. Nineteen forty-nine is indeed a watershed with regard to the modernization of education. The PRC achieved nearly universal primary education, made a breakthrough in adult literacy, and achieved an enormous increase in secondary education. The quality of these gains, however, especially in secondary education, leaves a great deal to be desired. The PRC also scored significant gains in the popularization and diffusion of technical knowledge, not only in the urban-industrial sector but also in rural areas, where significant modernizing changes have been underway since the mid-1960s. Higher education and research, essential to the absorption of advanced foreign technology, made major gains until 1966, when further progress was substantially halted for a decade. Even after several years of renewed and vigorous development, the number of students enrolled in institutions of higher education was barely in excess of one million in 1980.

Even before the Cultural Revolution, the efficient use of intellectuals had been hampered by preoccupation with their loyalty and spiritual transformation. During the Cultural Revolution decade, a wide-ranging assault on intellectuals and on educational excellence as generally conceived took place. This was extremely damaging to the country's modernization, among the costs being a missing generation of trained manpower. One of the mainsprings of that upheaval was dissatisfaction with education along lines reminiscent of criticisms voiced in the 1920s: elitism, urban bias, divorce from practical needs, and foreign (Soviet) orientation. This dissatisfaction is an indicator of the extent to which the PRC too had not been able to devise an educational strategy that could accommodate competing needs, especially those of elite mass education.

Resource constraints forced the PRC government to give priority to college-preparatory and higher education in the 1950s. Relative neglect of rural primary education was offset by promotion of locally financed community schools, albeit at the expense of quality. Resource constraints also prevented expansion of higher education proportionate to the growth of primary and secondary schooling. Hence increasing tension arose over access to the elite status conferred by a college degree and thereby heightened the elitism conferred by higher education. Tension was compounded by a growing problem of unemployment among urban middle school graduates, for whom resettlement in the villages widened the gap with the college-bound elite. The Cultural Revolution can be seen as an effort to resolve these issues largely by doing away with elite education altogether.

Since 1976, the status, legitimacy, and role of elite education, as well as of advanced science and technology have not only been fully restored but greatly enhanced in comparison with the pre-1966 situation. This restoration, however, raises the question of the PRC's capacity to manage the relations between a numerically tiny elite and a numerically huge mass. If the country's leaders can cope with the tensions likely to arise from the growth of inequality in education, then the prospect that knowledge and education will be more effectively harnessed to state-guided modernization would seem to be fairly bright.

Patterns of Twentieth-Century Transformation

This summary of five critical areas of China's evolution in the twentieth century reflects eight decades of domestic and international conflict almost unprecedented in modern times. The duels between emerging nationalists and Ch'ing authority, between the Nationalists and rival warlords and between the various warlords, between the Nationalists and the communists, and finally between contending factions and rival programs within the Communist Party, were carried on during intermittent conflicts with and perceived threats from one or another of China's major foreign rivals. Yet in the course of this prolonged agony one can see the gradual reconstitution of China's heritage in a form that by 1980 offered prospects of a resolution of the controversies over program, institutions, and policies that evaded solution for so long.

Fundamental to this process was the search for a consensus as to a program—the goals toward which the country should strive. In a very general sense, the course of modern development represented by Europe, North America, Russia, and Japan was accepted by China's leaders as a model to be followed. But within this general model there were many specific alternatives that became a source of controversy. The respect accorded today to the revolutionary efforts of Sun Yat-sen and to the role of the May Fourth Movement suggests that underlying these acrimonious political controversies, a process of experimentation was in progress in which such designations as first "nationalist" and eventually "communist" began to lose their significance as the practical issues confronting modernization came to assume a larger importance than doctrines. By 1980 the Chinese tradition of pragmatism appeared to be reasserting itself, and policymakers were being admonished to "seek truth from facts." The facts certainly include the experience of other countries, and leaders now looked abroad not for general models but for specific solutions to the problems confronting China.

The search for appropriate political and economic institutions was handicapped as much by the heritage of decentralized administration and lack of concern for the mobilization of resources as by domestic strife. Apart from these handicaps, it was not until the 1930s that several alternative patterns relating government and economy became credible in the more developed countries, so that foreign models offered little institutional guidance. Since the government established by the Nationalists in the brief period of their dominance (1928-1937) was only partially effective, and the communist governmental experience in the Yenan period (1936-1945) was quite limited, the opportunities for institution building were constrained. It nevertheless seems clear that the main goal after 1911 was the establishment of central governmental institutions with an active role in economic and social policy. Sun Yat-sen's ideology had been rooted in the radical republican tradition, and in the 1920s both Nationalist and communist leaders had sought inspiration and training in the Soviet Union. Even the communist institutions that have emerged since 1949 have been significantly less centralized than those of the Soviet Union, and the twenty-nine provinces retain important functions while the four-fifths of the population living in communes are only indirectly administered by the central government.

The effort to evolve a social policy for China in the twentieth century—in the sense of an equitable program for mobilizing skills and resources and allocating them to investment and consumption—has been constrained both by the disproportion between population and arable land and by the efforts of at least the Maoist tendency in the Communist Party to implement a social policy providing simultaneously for rapid development, egalitarian distribution, manpower allocation, and tight political control. The growth of the population by over 75 percent during the first thirty years of communist rule has called for a most stringent management of resources in the effort to develop industry while making provision for minimally adequate supplies of food and consumer goods.

The victory of the Communist Party in 1949 was the victory of a political organization but not yet of a program, or of institutions, or of social policy. These still had to be worked out, and thirty years later the outlines of a reconstituted China in which the potentialities of historical experience would be matched by policies and organizations relevant to the modern era were still vague. At least in one sphere, the ratio of population to resources, the obstacles to China's development had grown during the thirty years of communist administration. Yet in the course of experimenting with policies and organizations over a period of eighty years much has been learned, and by the ninth decade of the twentieth century the prospects for the reconstitution of China in a modern form were brighter than at any earlier period.

CHAPTER FOURTEEN

The PRC as a Modernizing Society: Appraisal and Implications

THE RECORD OF THE CHINESE PEOPLE SINCE 1949 offers a model of great interest to other peoples. Those seeking national dignity in a world filled with nationalistic resentments can look to the Chinese rise from the degradation of foreign humiliations to a position of autonomy and great power. Leaders striving for firm administrative controls in the face of internal division and endemic disunity can look to the Chinese communists' restoration and general maintenance of order in a country earlier plagued by warlordism and the persistent helplessness of aspiring central governments. Managers and economic planners committed to high rates of economic growth, especially in the prestigious heavy industry sector, can look to the notable annual rate of economic growth—for long periods in excess of 10 percent—sustained by China after it greatly increased investment through the public sector and made fuller use of its labor resources. And, of no less relevance, social planners beset by undiminished rates of urbanization, continuously high birth rates, and increasingly rampant demands for social services, can look to the Chinese as a rare example of massive social reorganization to counteract these complex problems. The Chinese experience in dealing with many of the most difficult challenges stirring the peoples of today's less developed countries— to the above list one could readily add military security, energy self-sufficiency, and checks on the public display of wealth and privilege by officials—is both recent and distinctive. Unlike Japan or Russia, and, even more, unlike the first countries to modernize, China still faces many of the troublesome problems of nonmodernized societies. Understandably, there has been talk of the PRC as a model for contemporary modernization, particularly for large countries that are latecomers.

Nonetheless, there is much confusion over the meaning of China's experience with modernization. Many of the very traits so widely cited in the waning years of Mao's life as integral to the Chinese approach have been repudiated by the succeeding leadership. Abrupt changes in foreign policy and in ideological pronouncements have added to the uncertainty about China's course of modernization. The commitment to self-reliance has been compromised by new foreign ties made to bolster the Chinese in their abiding hostility to Soviet policies and by a dramatic turnabout on foreign trade and assistance from Japan, the United States, and the Common Market. Egalitarian proclamations have lost their priority as new policies favor incentives and pragmatism to achieve the "four modernizations." In the midst of sweeping reversals in policies, it is easy to lose sight of the enduring elements and fundamental features of modernization in China. There is more consistency to the first three decades of communist rule than the sharp leadership clashes might suggest.

What lessons can be learned from this review of China's record by those who might be tempted to consider the PRC as a model for modernization? Our conclusions point to at least three areas that warrant elaboration: (1) the relevance of the historical legacy; (2) the selection of policies by a modernizing leadership; and (3) the implications of a Marxist-Leninist program.

The Heritage of the PRC

Past development is a point of departure for the PRC as for any society. Metaphors about revolutions sweeping aside the past must not be taken literally. Before 1949 the modernization of China had not proceeded far; the policies directed toward that objective were of short duration and had often proven difficult to implement. From the disarray of the late 1930s and 1940s the communists rose to chart a new course for the country. Their victory was a turning point for China. Building on the heritage of the existing society and guided by the socialist model they adopted, the Chinese communists forged policies in large part aimed at achieving economic growth, military might, scientific mastery, and other goals that we and they identify with modernization. Seeking to transform Chinese civilization, they were in turn dependent on that civilization—its human and material resources, its customary practices, and its ideals, grounded in one way or another, in earlier modes of thought and behavior.

Factors Conducive to Modernization

The preceding chapters conclude that for the most part China in the nineteenth century lacked conditions important for modernization and that, on balance, over the first half of the twentieth century it made little progress in establishing those conditions. China's political structure and social integration, especially in comparison with those of Japan and Russia, were missing many of the strategic conditions that appear to have facilitated the modern transformation. Yet, the foregoing discussion offers a different impression as well, that of a society which on the eve of the foreign challenge had much in common with the countries that did manage to modernize rapidly, and which already prior to 1949 had made certain changes useful for rapid growth. On the whole, China in 1949 falls into an intermediate category, possessing many factors favorable to modernization, but lacking various strategic ones Japan and Russia had both possessed a century earlier.

Let us first consider China's assets for modernization. The communists took power with an improved international position, and also with long-standing strengths for interacting with other countries. Not least important was pride in Chinese civilization and its ability to stand in the forefront of world advancement. Recognition in the U.N. Charter that a government representing China merited a place as one of the five permanent members of the Security Council was one form of international support for Chinese pride about their rightful place in the world. The heritage of unified and relatively centralized government and China's vast population and area also shaped the international context; once a strong central government emerged, China could quickly appear as a state that must be reckoned with. Popular pride, vast size, unified state heritage, and international standing could be invoked by the new government.

The communists had other assets to draw on in their quest to reshape the international environment to the advantage of China's modernization: (1) a large, disciplined standing army forged in the 1930s and 1940s; (2) a competent, experienced diplomatic corps, which would be largely replaced, but whose successors would be guided by similar standards of professionalism; (3) an absence of indebtedness, after foreign debts incurred by previous governments were canceled, and of low dependence on imported raw materials; and (4) a group of internationally educated experts with access to a corpus of modern knowledge and practices that eased the task of future borrowing. Although these and other assets may not have been sufficient to guide policies toward the most effective borrowing, the most productive trade and credit relations, and the greatest security without diverting many scarce resources from modernization, the PRC's foundation for drawing effectively on its international environment was considerable. China's experiences over the previous century had heightened its awareness of the need to borrow, its contempt for slavish imitation, and its fear of the consequences of foreign dependence.

Political factors conducive to modernization could also be invoked by China's communist leaders. For the most part, these factors awaited the resolution of regional conflicts and civil war. The demand for setting aside divisions and achieving a strong, unitary central government was a deep-seated force in the historical legacy, especially in the absence of a legacy of

457

competing religious or secular organizations and authority. Once this demand had been met, it had a momentum of its own; many modern governmental features useful for pursuing modernization were accepted aspects of central rule. Proper government meant: (1) a high concentration of power in the center; (2) provincial and local government fully responsive to the center; and (3) dedicated, professional officials capable of inspiring many inside and outside the government with a strong sense that they were serving popular interests. The Chinese knew and accepted many of the ideal qualities of modern government.

By 1949 some other requisites of modernizing states had also become part of the heritage. Nationalism, military reorganization, modern communications, and techniques for mass participation in particular enhanced the state's capacity to offer vigorous leadership and to penetrate local areas. The communist victory owed much to these new elements. They likewise enhanced the means available for reorganizing the country with increased coordination and control.

The economics chapters assert that many factors possessed by China, such as a prevailing market orientation, highly competitive conditions, flexible use of land, labor, and capital, and widespread entrepreneurial aspirations, would ultimately be conducive to modernization. Furthermore, during years of relative stability in the 1910s to 1930s, under foreign impetus the small industrial sector managed to grow quite rapidly. Raw materials began to be exploited by new technologies, and modern means of transportation, especially railroads, greatly added to nonagricultural capabilities. Despite the hard times on which the Chinese economy had fallen by 1949, there were premodern as well as more recent factors that boded well for accelerated rates of economic growth.

There were also aspects of social integration that could prove helpful in meeting the goals of the PRC leadership. Above all, these were qualities visible in local areas: the achievement-oriented aspirations, skills, and interest in education of the labor force, the long and substantial urban tradition, the willingness to sacrifice and plan for the long-term prosperity of one's family, the familiarity with state bureaucracies, the orientation toward social mobility, and the acceptance of contractual relations. In some of these dimensions, not many gains for modernization had been registered prior to 1949, but new currents emanating from the treaty ports associated with the emancipation of women, the lessening of family authority, and the reorganization of urban life could, in a new context, add to the capacity for drawing the population into the modern sector. Although Chinese were primarily rural, poverty stricken, and illiterate in 1949, they had exceptional qualities and outlooks on which a new leadership could capitalize.

Finally, in the educational sphere, China had the extraordinary foundation of respect for learning, initially high premodern rates of literacy, and a presumption of objective competition to advance those who achieved superior performance. The first half of the twentieth century witnessed a reorientation in the content of learning, substantially increasing its relevance for modernization. Despite the still limited impact of the new learning on the majority of the population and on production, at mid-century there were probably few countries among those not modernized that could match China's population in being accustomed to the development, transmission, and implementation of an ordered body of knowledge and techniques.

These examples of preparedness for modernization are only a sampling of the points raised in the preceding chapters. If comparisons had centered less on Japan and Russia and more on latecomers that have been slow to modernize, the Chinese legacy of social conditions would undoubtedly have appeared as a relatively favorable base for modernization. This study concludes that positive features for rapid modernization inhered in premodern China or were added during the transition before 1949, and that they survived into the 1950s when they were invoked by the communists to accelerate the rate of transformation.

FACTORS HINDERING MODERNIZATION

The problems facing the leaders of the PRC in the 1950s were far greater than the immediate needs of international security, centralized government, and economic recovery, in other words, the necessary conditions so clearly wanting over much of the previous half-century. By 1953, with the inauguration of the first five-year plan, these issues, to the extent that they represented serious deterrents to modernization, were basically resolved. But longstanding problems of building a foundation for modernization could not be so quickly disposed of. As the preceding chapters make clear, the communist leadership inherited many factors that impeded its efforts to modernize.

The legacy of international relations in China offered certain obstacles to effective borrowing. Although foreign influences had penetrated widely in the cities before 1949, the Chinese had yet to demonstrate that they could borrow effectively on a vast scale, that is, choose selectively from abundant foreign models what most suited China's needs. Their historical legacy did not include valued experiences of massive borrowing like those that had left such an indelible imprint on the consciousness of Japanese and Russians. Transitional governments of China had not established an adequate base for capitalizing on foreign trade, investments, or expertise to spur modernization. Suspiciousness toward foreign associations and toward foreign intentions threatened to hamper modernizing policies. Moreover, in the era of the Cold War the Chinese faced a divided industrial world with implications of restricted access to markets and technology for those who sided with the Soviet Union. A Sino-Soviet alliance also threatened to undermine Chinese sovereignty under the pretext of Soviet claims to leadership in the international communist movement.

China's political heritage, particularly its internal erosion in the Ch'ing period and its poor performance during the first half of the twentieth century, long posed a more serious barrier to modernization. Even if the disappearing balance between state and familial interests, which had worked well in stabilizing the premodern order, had been maintained, it would not have offered a promising foundation for the higher degree of control and coordination essential to modernization. In addition, the public cause, represented by public-spirited officials and informal extension of governing through degree holders, lost ground during the Ch'ing period and afterward before family and lineage-centered aggrandizement. The erosion of the Chinese bureaucracy and the increased personalization of power relationships further weakened the political base for modernization. Even though the communists could reestablish central control, they did not face an easy task in balancing the interests of diverse groups to allow for the flexibility of decision making and the sustained motivation essential in the long run for modernization.

Another element in China's political and economic legacy was a lack of vigorous government leadership in using the resources available in the society. Government operations had been modest and slow to expand in comparison to the emerging nation-states and Japan and Russia. The state's acceptance of a limited role in management and control of the economy is striking in view of the latecomer's need for an activist state when pursuing economic growth. Over the first half of the twentieth century, warlords and the Kuomintang central government sought to establish a new role for the public sector in building an infrastructure and in leading the way to economic growth. Political fragmentation and weakness, however, restricted these efforts. In 1949, the economic factors that had impeded rapid growth, such as inadequate state management and a low rate of savings, were still much in evidence. The communist promise to alter these conditions might quickly be realized by a vigorous government committed to land reform and nationalization, but finding a viable role for the state conducive to modernization in all sectors remained a serious challenge.

Indicators of social integration provide additional evidence of needs for mobilizing resources. Evaluations of China's network of cities, both in terms of the overall level of urbanization and the distribution of cities by size, suggest that intercommunity dependencies and forces of accumulation had not developed significantly in recent centuries. Population growth in scattered villages reduced the potential for extracting local production without damaging incentives. Furthermore there was only a skeletal network of organizations intermediate between the household or lineage and the state bureaucracy. Despite the establishment of some new organizations in cities between 1900 and 1937, the organizational base for modernization had not greatly improved. Indeed, the elimination of degree holders as a meaningful social category actually enhanced rural solidarities that could stand in the way of central coordination. No quick solutions were likely to be found for the basic problems of restructuring China's system of cities, creating a new balance between organizations, and establishing a framework for motivated individual action that would lead to rapid modernization.

Even in the area of knowledge and education, there were difficult questions of priorities and of coordination with job opportunities and social needs. Large numbers in the population were ready to absorb and apply modern knowledge, but the leadership was divided on the criteria for access to education, type of learning, and application of skills. Long accepted assumptions about the superiority of mental labor clashed with communist claims about the leading role of the workers who are engaged in manual labor.

The list of historical factors that impeded modernization could be greatly enlarged with a thorough scrutiny of the preceding chapters. In any case, China's communist leaders faced many problems that could have been mitigated had their country's legacy been more favorable to modernization. Opportunities for dramatic advances through initial policies would not obviate the need for addressing, sooner or later, other basic problems inherent in the fabric of Chinese society.

The Policies of the PRC

In seeking to appraise the experience of the People's Republic of China as a modernizing society, and to evaluate the implications of this experience for modernization studies, it is important to recognize that we are concerned with a discrete period of three decades in a process of societal transformation that in most other cases has taken a century or more. In the context of the approach to modernization that sees this process as developing in three periods—premodern, transformation, and advanced (high) modernization—we regard China as entering the period of transformation at about the turn of the century and as continuing in this transformation into a future that is likely to extend beyond the end of this century. The development of the PRC in the years 1949–1980 thus represents only a relatively short phase of the much more extensive process of transformation, and this should be taken into account in evaluating its experience with modernization.

Comparison with Japan and Russia suggests a mixture of conditions in China in 1949, some still indicative of the earliest phase of modernization as in the other countries during the 1860s and others already indicative of advances that did not occur there until the end of the nineteenth century. To say that China was more than a half-century behind Japan and Russia—in, for example, urbanization, the spread of modern schooling, and industrial growth—should not imply either that all variables are moving in tandem or that our measurements are exact. China neither would nor could duplicate the modernizing experiences of either Japan or Russia, but it was passing some of the same milestones of development and establishing some of the same sets of conditions. By the criteria we have been using, China remained at an early stage of modernization until well after the founding of the PRC.

China's lack of development before 1949 can also be demonstrated if we compare its progress in terms of many indicators of development to that found in the less developed countries in the 1970s. Foreign trade was small and employment in the state bureaucracy low, as was the per capita distribution of the mass media. The modern sector constituted only a tiny part (perhaps 3 percent) of the economy, and the overall rate of economic growth had not risen appreciably. Only about 10 percent of the population lived in cities, and both birth and death rates remained high, perhaps close to 40 per 1,000. Neither a literacy rate of perhaps 25 percent (well above this level for men and well below it for women) nor meager attendance in institutions of higher education suggested a substantial turn toward modernization. Although, as noted above, China possessed many historical factors conducive to modernization that do not appear on this list, on most available indicators it falls relatively low in the ranking of contemporary less developed countries. China's communist victors faced the task of spurring modernization in a country without many of the advances clearly visible in Russia and Japan in the 1910s, that is at the time of the Bolshevik revolution and in the Taishō period as the first generation of Meiji leaders was passing from the scene.

In Part Two of this volume societal transformation is treated as a single and discrete phase of the modernization of China starting about 1900, but several features of change under the PRC nevertheless distinguish it in significant ways from the longer process of transformation that started half a century earlier. The most important was the unification of China under a single government that possessed the authority to implement policies on a nationwide basis. This represented a marked change from the preceding half-century with its continuing civil and international strife, and also from the longer-term decline of the authority of the central government, which can be traced back to the late eighteenth century. Both the earlier, and the more drastic twentieth-century, weakening of the government resulted more from domestic than foreign influences, and it was precisely in the establishment of a strong central government that the PRC made its most significant break with the past.

A China under a single government did not necessarily mean a China guided by a single policy, and intermittently between 1958 and 1976 profound rifts within the new leadership caused many aspects of the country's development to falter. These periods of disarray did not, however, represent a return to the earlier disunity. The effectiveness of the central government was also limited by the practice of locating many aspects of control and coordination at the regional and local, rather than the national levels.

The most immediate consequence of the establishment of a unified central government was the mobilization of skills and resources for rapid economic growth. Even though economic policy under the PRC took several sharp

462

turns and was the subject of major disagreements within the leadership, by comparison with the first half of the twentieth century the Chinese economy developed rapidly. Growth was most rapid in heavy industry, but in other aspects of manufacturing and also in agriculture the PRC set in motion policies and practices that for the first time in the modern era established a fairly steady pace of economic development for China.

At the same time, the priority given to heavy industry greatly restricted the relative availability of resources for other aspects of development. These latter were largely administered by and drew on the resources of regional and local authorities, in particular the communes within which the vast majority of the population lived and worked. In these areas, which directly affected the livelihood of the majority of the population, the national effort was less concerted and more constrained then in the promotion of heavy industry.

The social impact of the policies of the PRC has nevertheless been considerable. The establishment of communes mobilized and consolidated the rural population to an unprecedented degree and also in some measure narrowed the gap between rural and urban levels of living. The urban population was also organized and rationalized for purposes of economic growth to a degree not possible before 1949.

Great efforts were also made through public campaigns to control population growth by postponing the age of marriage and limiting families to fewer children, to reduce disparities in income distribution within communities and producing organizations, and to improve health care. While the practical results of these measures are not yet entirely clear, Chinese society after 1949 was significantly more purposeful in fostering social integration than it had been in the preceding half-century.

The establishment of a single and authoritative central government is the factor primarily responsible for the economic growth and social integration achieved since 1949. Despite the paucity of reliable indicators, it seems clear that the record of the PRC, seen as the most recent three decades in a process of transformation that has been under way for three-quarters of a century, is one of considerable dynamism after half a century of relative stagnation. For example, the GNP per capita, which underwent little change from 1900 to 1949, has tripled or quadrupled in the last three decades. Steel production, which was under 1 million tons in the 1930s, rose from some 2 million tons in 1949 to 32 million in 1979. Railroad mileage, which stood at about 2,000 km in 1900 and 21,000 in 1949, rose to some 50,000 in 1979, albeit this represents but a slight gain in per capita terms since 1949.

In the realm of health care, to take another example, a great deal has been accomplished by the PRC in controlling infectious diseases, reducing infant mortality, and organizing medical care. One effect of improved health, in China as elsewhere, has been a rapid increase in population. China's estimated population grew relatively slowly from roughly 400 to little more than 550 million in the first half-century, but rose to an estimated 980 million in 1980. The improvement in health therefore had to be counterbalanced by measures to restrict births, and the PRC has succeeded in reducing the natural increase in population from a peak of more than 20 per 1,000 by the end of the 1950s and early 1960s to perhaps as low as 12 per 1,000, a figure reported in 1979. These are only a few of the indicators that could be cited to illustrate the extent to which the dynamism of the PRC experience with modernization stands in sharp contrast to the preceding half-century.

We judge the PRC's international policies to be of relatively slight value in stimulating modernization. Foreign trade and assistance, apart from the Soviet ties in the 1950s and the growing Japanese and western connections in the late 1970s, were remarkably limited. Although the Chinese probably did not divert an unusual amount of resources to military purposes, they fought wars or engaged in skirmishes on nearly all borders: the Korean War, the shelling of Quemoy and Matsu in the struggle for reunification of Taiwan, the border war with India, the border clashes with the Soviet Union, and the punitive foray into Vietnam. In addition, they supported North Vietnam in its long fight against the United States and, to a lesser extent, Afghans battling against the Soviet Union. For a time their dependence on the Soviet Union encouraged nonselective borrowing. Afterward Chinese rejection of most foreign models and learning greatly reduced the possibility of effective borrowing. In the late 1970s China had a severe shortage of specialists who could draw skillfully on the vast stores of modern knowledge abroad. China also had a tremendous, long-unmet need for modern technology. Given these serious acknowledged shortcomings, how can the policies of the PRC over three decades be judged very successful in using international resources? At the same time, there were gains in high priority sectors such as nuclear weapons, in the pursuit of applied methods for increasing production, and in the application of skills learned in the years prior to the Cultural Revolution when education drew heavily on foreign sources.

The political structure of the PRC also exhibits a mixed record in fostering conditions for modernization. Factionalism and purges as well as discrimination against persons with certain class labels meant that the most able individuals often did not fill the most important positions. Restrictions on the performance of duties also hampered modernization. Fearful of punishment, teachers, managers, officials, and others often acted cautiously. In contrast, excessive controls vested at the top enabled Mao Tse-tung to act precipitously, drastically altering the life circumstances of hundreds of millions without allowing time to anticipate the consequences of new policies. After Mao's death, China's leadership decried the lack of a solid legal foundation for regularizing expectations and creating a more predictable environment for modernization, yet it has denied that China's socialist society needs legal guarantees of the individual's human rights. To be sure, the mass media now reach enormous numbers of people, and the population participates in mass meetings. Also, controls from above have kept the population almost continuously employed in the labor essential to modernization. Nonetheless, who can doubt that a system of governance so arbitrary and fitful would be damaging to personal and group incentives important to the improved use of resources for modernization? In 1980 China's leaders were counting on the expanded decision-making power of enterprises and the power of their employees to participate in management to improve motivation.

Whereas in international affairs and in political structure the Chinese barely met minimal needs for sustaining modernization, in economics they went much further. Again there is much evidence of sharp policy reversals, of callous tampering with individual aspirations, and of waves of excess control. But, above all, what saved China's developmental goals was the ability to extract large savings and to employ virtually all able-bodied individuals. High rates of capital accumulation and fairly rapid rates of economic growth, primarily attributable to the heavy industrial sector, persisted with brief interruptions over three decades. These achievements did not occur without painful adjustments in rural organization and necessary compromises in the form of modest material incentives. They represent an economic strategy heavily dependent on state coercion and on organizational balancing. They produce a one-sided pattern of development ultimately difficult to sustain. Thus the considerable economic successes over three decades offer evidence of policies that produce immediate payoffs but, because of the enormous sacrifices and the inflexibility they demand, also produce negative long-term consequences difficult to repair.

Many of the most original policies of the PRC are examples of new forms of social integration. To a great extent, Chinese leaders have redefined the roles of pivotal individuals, groups, and settlements. For example, their interest in altering the position of women has a twofold significance for modernization: it reduces the birth rate and, as a result, consumption, and it draws women into the labor force. Policies in favor of a corporate village within the context of the commune likewise bear on modernization in two ways: they curtail waste and any diversity among households that might lead to nonessential claims on resources, and they maximize community pressures for labor inputs.

By redefining the place of cities in Chinese society, leaders have found another means to achieve the same goals. Through sending youths out of the cities and limiting migration in, China's leaders have curtailed costly urban consumption and worked to increase the ratio of hands at work to mouths to feed. Each of these role redefinitions was for a time, at least, carried to an extraordinary extreme. In the Great Leap Forward, the drive to transform the position of women severely disrupted rural life. At that time and again in some villages in the aftermath of the Cultural Revolution, attempts to transfer activities from the household to the community or from a small to a large community also upset the balance of rural life in ways harmful to human motivation. And it was eventually acknowledged that the transfer of millions

465

of youths to the countryside in the decade before Mao's death caused widespread discontent and had many negative consequences. These elements in the Chinese strategy for modernization all contributed to forced savings and directed labor allocations. When carried to an extreme at times of big campaigns they were counterproductive. At other times they had mixed results, supporting a particular form of economic development that exacted a high toll in popular initiative and satisfaction.

Educational policies and the treatment accorded experts and specialists are now regarded as in many respects having been costly to China's modernization goals. The policies of the so-called Gang of Four set back China's ability to generate and apply modern knowledge severely, affecting the quality of teaching, of management, and of technical guidance. Economic development proceeded as rapidly as it did because of the educational advances and employment of specialists prior to this time and because many of the gains resulted from continued increases in inputs as opposed to increases in productivity. Mass education advanced more steadily over the entire period, but its quality was very uneven.

Over three decades, China's communist leaders made many errors but still managed to guide their country into an intermediate stage of modernization. Various indicators give differing impressions of how modernized China has become. Although inanimate sources of energy are widely used and have been massively applied to heavy industry, most production still is overwhelmingly dependent on human labor power with little mechanical assistance. By the criterion of energy use, one finds parts of the urban sector relatively modernized, but most of the society still overwhelmingly nonmodernized. Foreign trade remains very low; yet this may be in part attributed to the large scale of China and its abundance of many resources as well as to the still limited degree of modernization. A low GNP per capita and spartan patterns of consumption and of most services point to an early stage of modernization, but the fact that industry exceeds agriculture in its contribution suggests greater modernization. The labor force remains heavily concentrated in agriculture, migration rates are slight, and urbanization has only reached approximately 20 percent; yet birth rates are falling below those normally found in countries with these conditions. Levels of mass education are also far above the other indicators usually associated with them, such as the percentage of the population with higher education.

The above measures provide ample testimony of the many contrasts in contemporary China. Some of the contrasts are no doubt remnants of China's distinctive legacy from the precommunist and especially the imperial eras; for instance, a high ratio of population to resources reduces the possibility of raising per capita standards. Some may result from geopolitical factors; the largest countries of the world have relatively low levels of foreign trade. Moreover, some one-sided patterns of modernization must be accounted for in terms of the priorities of the leaders themselves, particularly because Chairman Mao was insistent on implementing his visions for Chinese society. Apart from these explanations, there is the fact that China's leaders have been guided by the model for social change inherent in the Marxist-Leninist tradition. Since this model is widely cited as the basic or primary source for policies and its appeal is evident in nearly all areas of the world, it behooves us to look closely at the PRC's experience with modernization in the context of Marxism-Leninism.

The Socialist Program: Comparisons with the Soviet Union

Since 1949 efforts to modernize China have proceeded under a blueprint for building socialism and then communism. However ambiguous and subject to expedient interpretations that blueprint may be, it persists as a guide to policy decisions. Basic elements of the Marxist-Leninist plan endure even under such varied guises as Stalinism and Khrushchev's utopianism following the Twentieth Party Congress (1956) in the USSR and Maoism and Teng's pragmatism following the Eleventh Party Congress (1977) in the PRC. In this section we seek to isolate from the general discussion of modernization elements that bear the distinctive imprint of socialism of the Marxist-Leninist variety. We seek to answer the question: what is unusual about modernization in large-scale socialist societies? The answer bears importantly on the overall assessment of China's modern transformation.

It is widely assumed that modernization under the leadership of a communist party is different from that in which private enterprise prevails. Without much difficulty one can distinguish in this popular image of promised social change at least five characteristic *claims*: (1) Modernization under communist leadership reduces international dependency of the sort that primarily benefits already modernized societies or their multinational corporations. (2) It relies on a strong central government capable of mobilizing vast amounts of resources to strengthen the national well-being without serious challenge from elites with more selfish or divisive interests. (3) It promotes rapid economic growth in a planned and coordinated manner so that resources can be efficiently channeled into uses that produce the greatest benefit to the population as a whole. (4) It creates a more egalitarian, more community-oriented, and more just society, reducing sources of discontent and social cleavages found elsewhere. (5) It emphasizes education for all and the replacement of local customs and religions with what it holds to be a scientific outlook that lowers barriers to the advancement of knowledge.

Are these benefits to modernization in fact realized? Do the socialist features of China account for a particular pattern or rate of modernization? Drawing on the information in the preceding chapters for post-1949 China, we now consider the consequences of CCP leadership for modernization.

The PRC as a Modernizing Society

The slogan of "self-reliance" resounded during the final decade of Maoism. For an even longer period, roughly two decades out of three, that slogan fairly accurately represented the practices of the PRC. Chinese leaders did not permit foreign ownership or investments. On average, they maintained a remarkably low level of indebtedness to foreign countries; they sought and accepted little assistance. Apart from small amounts of foodstuffs and selected handicrafts, little Chinese production reached markets abroad except for neighboring Hong Kong. Following rejection of the Soviet model in the late 1950s, Chinese leaders while continuing to regard themselves as Marxist-Leninists, acted almost without reference to foreign models, advisers, or interests in addressing problems of modernization. Unfettered by the weight of external pressures that smaller and more dependent communist-led societies have borne, China under Mao resembled the Soviet Union under Stalin (except for the years of World War II and the influx of foreign specialists in the 1930s) in its go-it-alone approach to modernization. While the Soviet Union compensated for its isolation by avid borrowing of foreign technology and (after its armies occupied Eastern Europe) by bringing other countries into its orbit, China was more fully isolated until it abruptly turned to Japan and the major western countries for advanced technology.

After 1949 China's international relations passed through three stages that bear a striking resemblance to Soviet stages through the 1950s. During the first years, expectations that a favorable environment would emerge were fairly high. Then, under the firm direction of Mao and Stalin, these countries slid into isolation (partly self-imposed and partly a result of foreign containment). Finally, after the charismatic leader's death, the new leaders acknowledged certain shortcomings of isolationist policies and loosened some controls on the international environment. The second period predominates as the strategy for transformation; it sets the standard against which subsequent partial openings to the world are measured.

Is there a distinctive pattern of international relations for the USSR and China as large-scale, powerful socialist states? Yes, both tightly limit contacts, including the flow of information and people, with the partial exception of dependent socialist states and communist parties in opposition abroad. Leaders largely cut off their citizens from the outside world; unauthorized contacts with foreign visitors are no less dangerous than correspondence with relatives or friends abroad. Individuals are offered a restricted range of domestic goods, entertainment, and publications. Freedom of choice and quality are sacrificed in the interest of social control and frugality. As modernization proceeds, the most extreme measures are retracted; "peaceful coexistence" with modernized states brings economic and scientific advantages at the same time that it produces pressures, difficult to contain, for breaking down the barriers that seal off the society.

This artificial world of restricted competition and slanted information has many consequences for the pattern of modernization. Borrowing occurs largely in spurts. Techniques, once copied from abroad, are applied ever more intensively rather than adjusted to new international circumstances. Demand is measured neither in terms of competition against other goods nor in terms of a search by domestic consumers for a desired product; the plan guarantees an outlet for any production that meets the minimal standards of utility. Exaggerated patriotism, minimizing the achievements of others and making a virtue out of hostility to others, reduces the capacity for borrowing effectively. In general, this kind of international environment enhances the state's leverage and limits the citizen's opportunities. It reduces the resources available to individuals or groups for either resistance or advocacy of alternatives to state policies.

The fact that China and the Soviet Union managed to accelerate modernization at times of relative isolation may be interpreted by some as evidence that tightly constricted international relations are advantageous at an early or intermediate state of modernization. In our view, the international environment for a large-scale society is not likely to be decisive for accelerating modernization; sharply restricting its impact skews modernization without necessarily changing its pace. Of course, the irony of these socialist examples is that the long-term ideal of proletarian internationalism, a form of international citizenship in the service of all peoples, fades before the immediate reality of national isolation and chauvinistic glorification for purposes of modernization. Continued support of revolutionary forces abroad can be dismissed in this context as of little consequence for transformation at home. Clearly socialism does make a difference; it limits the potentialities for either a positive or negative impact from the outside.

POLITICAL STRUCTURE

The long-term ideal in this area also contrasts sharply with actual conditions. The ideal of the fading away of the coercive, as distinct from the administrative, role of the state recedes before the ubiquitous cult of the ruler. One must follow the concept of state power through a labyrinth of slogans before uncovering its true form, that which can be most readily observed in the historical experiences of the Soviet Union and the PRC. Government by the people as expressed in the name, the People's Republic of China, is interpreted as the dictatorship of the proletariat, which, in turn, vests its authority in the vanguard of the people, that is the Communist Party, and that restricted organization operates through democratic centralism—a catchword that, in practice, supports the virtually unlimited power of the party secretary.

Under Stalin and Mao, legal structures and interest groups placed relatively few checks on the abuse of power by the party leader. Of course, for long periods leaders were careful not to challenge the interests of particular groups, such as in China, regional military officials. The cult of personality, embellishing the leader's personal feats and proclaiming his omniscience, reached enormous proportions. Woe to the person (even a child) overheard making a joke or chance remark or discovered having disfigured (even accidentally) a picture in a manner that might be interpreted as disparaging to the leader! Decisions on a potentially unlimited range of issues came within the leader's purview; policies could be promulgated at his whim or by virtue of certain favorites gaining exclusive access to him. In practice, many socialist programs are decreed by intolerant and vengeful leaders capable of purging large numbers of the experts (and fellow communists) needed to advance modernization.

Parallel stages of leadership appear in the USSR and the PRC. An early stage of collective leadership under the direction of the helmsman who led the revolution to victory gave way to a period of uncertainty over policies and more open disagreements among leaders. In both countries, powerful leaders then asserted their authority as they newly interpreted the ideals for building socialism and the harsh realities of accelerating modernization in the sobering context of roughly a decade of communist rule. Policy excesses, particularly in the rural sector, mounted as Stalin and Mao pushed for massive reorganizations. Subsequently, in response to famine, mass disillusionment, and new leadership fissures (during the early 1930s in the USSR and the early 1960s in the PRC), the leaders suddenly turned to purges and to new demands for ideological conformity as they bolstered their own primacy. After nearly twenty years of communist leadership in their respective countries, Stalin and Mao moved decisively to eliminate rivals (real and imagined) in positions at every level of authority and to consolidate new social programs. They prevailed until their deaths as the chief arbiters in the momentous struggle to find a workable compromise between the country's special requirements for modernization and the lofty goals expressed in the blueprint for socialism. As a result of Stalin's and Mao's immense power, the compromises between these goals inevitably reflected the personal antagonisms and megalomania of these leaders.

China carried even further than the Soviet Union practices of collective responsibility and of administrative, extralegal sanctions. Household members could be punished, at least informally, for the deviant behavior of their relatives. Coworkers bore some responsibility for each other. The community, particularly in the rural areas, acquired increased control over the individual. Extralegal punishments included denial of appropriate housing, required transfer of residence out of a desired urban location, rejection of one's children from higher and even lower levels of schooling, and sanctions against one's spouse. Usually in each country basically apolitical behavior masked by required obeisance on necessary occasions sufficed to get by, but there were times when particular groups experienced terror that had little or nothing to do with their current behavior. Even in the absence of terror, community controls restricted individual initiative and discouraged bold decisions or resistance to the mistakes of others; any overt act of nonconformity might later be used against one. In general, controls penetrated further and it was harder to find an escape from the politicized environment in China.

Despite the mistakes that resulted from the excessive concentration of power and the exercise of that power without adequate awareness of its consequences (as in the three periods—1959–1961, 1966–1968, and 1974–1976— when the Chinese economy stagnated or declined and the morale of large numbers including experts fell to its nadir), the political structures of socialism are in many ways conducive to early and intermediate modernization. Unified and centralized leadership increases the levels of control and coordination—prior to 1949 low levels had hampered China's modernization. State ownership, bureaucratic growth, and central planning provide a strong mechanism for channeling resources into economically productive purposes. Socialism enabled both China and the Soviet Union to perform unusual feats of social engineering—to reorganize rural and urban communities and to vest power in those who would give increased priority to the goals of modernization. As long as this often heavy-handed command structure is on the whole sufficient to increase inputs without increasing incentives and to rely on crude measures of performance, it can produce impressive results. While it creates a climate of surveillance, depresses initiative, and weakens interest groups, socialism also greatly expands the resources available for production. It draws on previously inaccessible or underused resources. As modernization advances and resources are virtually fully employed, however, it becomes necessary to shift gears to find ways of increasing productivity and rewarding initiative. Given China's extreme record of suppressing intellectuals through the mid-1970s, one might anticipate an especially difficult adjustment to the new era, particularly since officials and party members responsible for carrying out earlier repressive policies largely remain in their posts.

ECONOMIC STRUCTURE AND GROWTH

"To each according to his work" is the principle by which rewards are supposed to be assigned in socialist societies. Apart from leaving unresolved the problem of finding measures for the comparative value of all forms of work, this principle does not indicate how much of the available resources should be allocated as rewards or how fast that pool should grow. In fact, socialism has meant a deemphasis on consumption and on the service sector with the exception of education and health. Economic growth takes priority. It benefits from a high rate of investment at the expense of current gratification, a concentration of investments in heavy industry that exacerbates the inability of light industry and agriculture to keep pace with consumer demand, and a rapid expansion in the labor force under circumstances in which few families can make ends meet without having both husband and wife gainfully employed by the state or the collective sector. In short, the welfare of the people is mainly interpreted as the welfare of the country as measured by rapid economic growth in heavy industry.

China resembles the Soviet Union in its high rate of savings and in the mechanisms that ensure savings. Direct taxes on personal income are low or nonexistent. Direct taxes on the incomes of collectives are moderate and stable. Private savings are a minor factor. What primarily accounts for a high rate of savings are revenues from heavy industry and from the turnover tax (a tax common in Western Europe also), a discrepancy between the sale price of goods and their cost to the producer; prices are high on luxury goods in general, on clothing, and on producers goods targeted for sectors with low priority. This situation is made possible by public ownership of the means of production and by controlled prices such that much of virtually any expense that does not go for a necessity (and some that do) ends up as a donation to the state in the form of the turnover tax. These conditions result in the paradox that a sizable number of urban residents find that they have more money than they can easily spend, while their standard of living does not rise much above the minimal level.

The command economies of China and the Soviet Union in various ways reduce the operation of market forces. Housing, which through the transformation fails to increase in proportion to the growth of urban population, is allocated to new families and to authorized migrants whose names are recorded on long waiting lists. Many other goods are also allocated through nonmarket criteria; in China this takes the form of rationing basic commodities. Restrictions also exist in the market for labor. In China, these restrictions have resulted in a very low rate of labor turnover; jobs are assigned with little likelihood that a worker can arrange a transfer. Managers and supervisory cadres rarely dismiss an employee for poor performance. These conditions are not conducive to an efficient matching of qualified or interested personnel with job assignments. In one sector, however, private markets do operate; the cultivation of private plots and the sale of subsidiary products from these plots are strikingly similar in the two countries, despite attempts in both to restrict this potentially nonsocialist element.

Analysis of the vicissitudes in economic structures reveals the same underlying three stages of development noted before. During the early years, primarily devoted to the consolidation of power, economic recovery, and organization building, a mixed economy existed with plans for rather gradual change. Then in the much longer period of Stalinist and Maoist dominance occurred radical rural equalization or reorganization and stringent measures to hold down urban consumption. Finally after the deaths of the charismatic leaders, the strict controls were somewhat relaxed. Wages rose, housing was given a higher priority, and methods to increase labor productivity were discussed. In this third stage leaders give a larger role to experts and to interest groups and eliminate some highly unpopular draconian measures. New policies announced by Chinese leaders in 1980 apparently indicate that they are prepared to give freer rein to market forces than have Stalin's successors.

The socialist economies of the Soviet Union and China are characterized by high rates of growth in heavy industry and in overall measures of national product. They modernize rapidly, but by the standards of modernized societies their modernization is one-sided. As the transformation proceeds, efforts to stimulate labor productivity and to deal with accumulated problems in low priority sectors force them to make difficult adjustments. China largely exhausted its resources of labor and land while its transformation was still decades behind the transition reached in the USSR in the 1950s. As a result, Chinese leaders had to face readjustment problems—initially by giving higher priority to agriculture and later by searching for new incentives—at a much lower level of modernization. These socialist economies share largely positive implications for industrial growth over a long early period, but less positive implications after the first few decades and for other aspects of modernization.

SOCIAL INTEGRATION

Does socialism offer adequate incentives for conscientious work? The Chinese and Soviet leaders have drawn large numbers into the work force, but have they motivated them to take their jobs seriously? Given the absence of private ownership and the relative egalitarianism discussed later in this chapter, one might wonder what kinds of incentives do operate. Obviously the performance of the labor force has major consequences for the modernization of the society.

Motivation to choose an occupation or a specific job and to perform diligently at it may stem from a variety of considerations: (1) the lure of immediate wages and bonuses; (2) family benefits associated with the job, such as housing, medical care, day care, or a pension; (3) opportunities opened by the position to parlay access to scarce goods or information into personal gain; (4) the location of work, reducing travel time or making it possible to live in a desirable community or near close relatives; (5) long-range career opportunities, perhaps including job security and informal prestige from society at large; (6) the creative nature of the work, that is, less tedious and onerous conditions of labor relative to other possibilities; (7) formalized praise and recognition, for example, through honors and public acclaim; (8) positive reinforcement from the work group; (9) collective material benefits to the work group or the entire organization; (10) private profits; (11) coercion. Undoubtedly each of these considerations operates for some individuals in the PRC and the USSR. Do we observe any distinctive features in the prevalence of these factors among large numbers of persons?

Wages and bonuses. The contrast is more striking than the similarity in the use of these direct material incentives to allocate labor. In the Soviet Union, piece rates long rewarded workers who overfulfilled norms, higher wages continue to lure workers to undesirable types of labor, and considerable job turnover in part reflects the search for more money. In China, seniority has played a more determinative role in promotions (on the rare occasions when they have been allowed), while bonuses until the late 1970s represented a slight factor at best, and wage scales have only recently been unfrozen. Despite continuing wage differentials almost as wide as in the USSR, there have been few outlets for Chinese interested in finding more remunerative employment. The recent upgrading in the role of wages and bonuses in motivating performance indicates that the contrast is diminishing. Of course, the two countries are similar in denying workers the legal opportunity to strike or in other ways press claims for better pay and in channeling much of the growth in production into productive investments rather than into wages.

Family benefits. Fringe benefits are a substantial factor in both societies. Access to new housing can mean running water, central heating, electricity, and other improvements. Directly or indirectly much housing has been allocated through job-related criteria. Day care and vacation facilities are among the benefits available in certain jobs, and elite positions bring much richer plums, such as access to special stores. In China, at least three levels of work-related benefits are apparent. The most advantages go to civil servants and workers in state industry in the big cities. They receive health insurance, inexpensive day care, pensions, alternative jobs in case of disability, and sometimes housing. In an intermediate position are workers in the state sector at the county or commune level. At the bottom of the hierarchy with least access to family benefits are workers in smaller collective industries at the commune or brigade level, peasants in production teams, and laborers in urban neighborhood factories. Their benefits depend largely on cooperative savings from earnings, in some cases not those of their immediate work group but those of the production team from which they have been sent. Given the restricted access in China to positions that would improve access to these benefits, it is likely that Soviet citizens have had greater opportunities to strive for these rewards. The similarities among societies in which money may not buy what one needs are considerable; a job with special access can be more lucrative than one with a higher wage. For the most part, however, fringe benefits reinforce wage differentials.

Illegal personal gain. Instances are recorded in the Chinese press of cadres taking advantage of their positions for private gain; during the years of the Cultural Revolution and its aftermath, various checks on elitism seem ironically to have opened the way to new excesses. Personal networks offered protection to the very individuals who claimed to be acting out of revolutionary zeal. Others, according to refugee interviews, reported a widespread reluctance to become an official in the absence of tangible rewards and opportunities.

There seems no doubt that, especially in the USSR, a "second economy" based largely on questionable or illegal use of position greases the wheels of society. In almost all walks of life, individuals use scarce goods diverted from normal channels to barter favors for family and friends. A job with greater access to valued scarce goods or to influence peddling is prized. Collective determination of work points and oversight of decision making along with legal limits on cadre incomes were once thought to curtail the possibility of similar abuse of position in China, although nepotism and personal networks are now understood to have operated as potent forces for misuse of privilege.

Location. Given the sharp difference in living standards, cultural facilities, and life chances among settlements, where one lives matters a great deal. Furthermore, in both countries the desire to remain close to or to rejoin family members operates as a powerful force. Chinese have little opportunity to satisfy this desire, but Soviet citizens make it one of their chief priorities. Women leave jobs in small cities to accompany their spouses or to find day care facilities. Both men and women seek a livelier and better provisioned community. Workers search for jobs that will cut down long commuting times. Since the assignment of housing is relatively inflexible, it is often easier to switch to a new job than to change residence. The same kinds of inflexibilty and motivations appear in China, but there are fewer means to grapple with them; indeed, assigned jobs create serious problems of separated spouses with no right to get back together and of children sent to the countryside in defiance of family desires.

Career. Soviet citizens are much more likely to take into consideration the long-range career prospects of a particular line of work. It is common for them, particularly men, to switch jobs to make better use of their specialty and to choose a career with long-term prospects for advancement. The intense competition for entry into prestigious institutes and departments of universities attests to the crucial role of higher education in the search for the best careers. For the Chinese, careerism is reemerging as a meaningful force, but few until recent years have had alternatives to weigh. With the reinstatement of competitive examinations, there can be no doubt that calculation of long-range opportunities has risen for many to the top of the list of considerations. In both societies this is a powerful incentive. China's neglect of it has proven costly for modernization.

Creativity. While Chinese have sought to glorify onerous labor for its contribution to society, Soviet leaders acknowledge the mounting aversion to tedium among the work force. Large numbers of Soviet people, particularly women, switch jobs because of working conditions. Furthermore, numerous studies show that higher education is seen as a vehicle to research positions and to creative work. Disappointed hopes for those who fail to obtain one of these scarce positions are commonplace, spurring labor turnover and job dissatisfaction. Perhaps this problem becomes more acute as other difficulties are resolved and modernization reaches a high level; when this issue reaches the forefront in China it will be a sign that mental labor is fully secure.

Formalized recognition. Public acclaim represents an ideologically sound and at the same time, a cheap form of motivation. Honorary rewards, titles, publicly displayed photographs, and laudatory newspaper articles are examples of this genre. Each is a form of normative incentive. Both the Chinese and the Soviet leadership have used this type of incentive extensively, the former as a substitute for other incentives and the latter to complement bonuses and other material rewards. They are available to organizations in all walks of life. Their chief drawback appears to be that in the long run, and perhaps even in the short run, their effectiveness is low. Such rewards are subject to manipulation and cynicism, which raise doubts that when widely used they can operate as meaningful incentives.

Work group solidarity. Various studies demonstrate that the individual worker responds to the pressures of the small group at work to increase or decrease output. A cohesive, supportive group can contribute in a major way to realizing production goals. There is little evidence that the Soviet work group achieves the necessary solidarity or operates in any special way as a unit to raise production. The oft-repeated ideal for the Chinese work group was different; evidence has been mounting, however, that group relations have not spurred productivity. While some have claimed that the omnipresence of small study groups and the attention to collective involvement reinforce the individual worker's sense of participation, problems with labor productivity and recent relaxation in collectivist practices cast doubt on that assertion. The overturning of the verdicts of the Cultural Revolution has created a situation in which accuser and accused now work side by side—a source of continued animosity.

Group benefits. Bonuses and discretionary funds awarded to the group rather than to the individual play an integral part in both economies, but in China they assume far greater importance. First, the collective, as distinguished from the state sector, employs a much larger percentage of the Chinese work force. Second, despite stringent limits on how much of the collective's income can be withheld from private disbursement for work points, the Chinese provide for many local services from the collective's funds and, of course, reward the individual farmer from the collective's overall earnings. However, in the state sector, the Soviet leaders probably make greater use of bonuses for a group's success in fulfilling the planned output target. Each country has had some success with these incentives, and the Chinese are experimenting with incentives for smaller groups in order to link individual performance and reward more closely.

Private profits. The role of private plots in the two countries is approximately the same although a far larger percentage of the Chinese population is involved. For households in the countryside and in small cities the private plot, pigs and other small livestock, and subsidiary crafts are a major source of income. Thus the private sector, including regulated private markets, persists. It provides a fairly high level of self-sufficiency for groups often neglected by the state. It brings in much of the household's cash income (grain is awarded for many of the work points earned on the collective), and in China it provides a means for saving to meet the high mutual expectations about the groom's family's contributions to the marriage and to pay the large expenses of housing and household ceremonies.

Coercion. The Chinese have apparently repeated the Stalinist reliance on forced work in labor camps, but not for as substantial a minority. For the majority in both countries there exists a meaningful element of coercion beyond the need to work to make ends meet. Not to put in a full year's work when one is an able-bodied adult below retirement age is to be antisocial—a parasite on society. Some exceptions are made for women with children and for persons in school. For others the penalties can be severe and the pressures overwhelming. This socialist characteristic helps to account for the very high percentage of adults in the labor force.

With respect to incentives in general, Maoist practices were normally neither as blatantly coercive nor as enticingly materialistic as Stalinist ones. In many areas, important differences can be identified. There are also basic socialist similarities, including the predisposition to reduce incentives in ways harmful to long-term modernization. The priority is to increase the number of hands and hours at work. Under these circumstances, motivational problems are serious and damp the prospects for increased labor productivity.

KNOWLEDGE AND EDUCATION

The ability to apply modern knowledge, one of the keys to modernization, is deeply affected by a society's manner of treating the difference between mental and manual labor. This dichotomy, in fact, is one of three major inequalities often singled out in the communist literature as a kind of litmus test for socialism (urban-rural and worker-peasant being the other two).

The mental-manual distinction has both rural and urban significance. In Russia this distinction historically and even into the contemporary period had meaning almost exclusively in the urban setting. In contrast, this dichotomy has operated with much force in the villages of China, in both the old society and the new. Prior to the Cultural Revolution these inequalities were addressed relatively timidly, chiefly through campaigns against erroneous attitudes of officials and technocrats. Subsequently the targets were expanded to incorporate the entire educational system and many aspects of the employment system. Perhaps the most vociferous Chinese attacks against inequality centered on the privileges and attitudes of aspirants to and employees engaged in mental labor. The attacks have now ended.

Schools in China in many ways prepared students to combat the elitism of mental labor. First, teachers and management in general had to accept the active involvement of manual laborers in decision making. Second, segregated training of the best students in cities was replaced with community-based schools serving diverse interests. Third, work was combined with study, just as for officials and many other persons in leading positions it was necessary to engage in physical labor part time or to attend the manually oriented May 7 cadre schools. Fourth, the applied curriculum meant that book learning was transformed into an adjunct of practical problem solving, often involving construction tasks. In addition, procedures for the selection and advancement of students, methods for making the payment of fees more equitable, and reductions in the length of various study programs all worked against an exclusive academic and mental career orientation. Following Mao's death many of these policies were dismantled in an effort to restore quality education.

With respect to the mental-manual dichotomy, China until recently bore little resemblance to the Soviet Union. Avoiding the drudgery of physical labor poses little problem in the Soviet Union for the children of intelligentsia families and for the academically successful. Indeed, many take as evidence of failure an inability to escape from physical labor. They aspire to higher education and the employment that follows from it, but because of tight quotas on educational advancement and on the number of desired mental positions they have to resign themselves to work as laborers or to menial mental labor. In China, the privilege of mental labor begets the same privilege in the next generation to a smaller degree. For practically nobody was total escape from physical labor possible under the system that prevailed until Mao's death. A vigorous Chinese assault on this dichotomy contrasts to muted Soviet lip service to the goal of reducing it. Following recent changes China is becoming more similar to the Soviet Union in this area.

China's inequalities between elite and ordinary worker long appeared minimal in comparison to Soviet elitism. Soviet special stores and other attractive rewards available to a tiny elite symbolize a system of privileges decried in China since the Cultural Revolution (although recent reports show that they were and are present). The tendency for a distinct and privileged elite of mental laborers to form is counteracted in China by at least three preoccupations: (1) with proclaiming the virtues of asceticism; (2) with democratizing decision making and the oversight of organizational actions; (3) with judging job performance according to criteria that promote group solidarity at the expense of elitism, but induce mediocre performance by denying recognition for individual merit. Chinese leaders undoubtedly have not uprooted all elements of elitism, but manifestations of it are less visible to the outside observer and probably actually as well. On looking back, the Chinese now recognize that their antielitist measures endangered modernization plans and are now espousing new rewards and career opportunities for the scientific elite and others.

OTHER EGALITARIAN POLICIES

Countless basic concepts in communist ideology, such as class struggle, land reform, collectivization, and communization refer, at least in part, to the justness of distribution within the society. The state, by establishing the criteria for and the legal forms of ownership, setting relative prices and personal wages, rationing scarce commodities and bonuses, allocating community benefits in the form of a social wage, and assigning quotas and requirements for access to desired rewards and positions, wields powerful levers of control. How it uses these controls is critical in the struggle to balance modernization and other socialist goals.

Sustained pressure to reduce inequalities within urban organizations did not appear in China until the Cultural Revolution, yet even earlier such inequalities had begun to be viewed in an increasingly negative light. The elitism of technocrats and managers, the widespread striving for higher levels of education and a career in mental labor, and the exclusivity of the so-called permanent or secure workers were each perceived as a serious challenge to the principles of equalization, especially during the retrenchment after the Great Leap Forward when upward mobility through urban organizations virtually ceased. Since that time, a variety of measures has made these organizations more egalitarian, exacting a high price in incentives for these groups and, thereby slowing modernization.

Maoist policies directed at equalization cannot be treated as a reverberation of premodern practices. The right of a select few to capitalize within generous limits on the positions they had won as well as the fundamental division between mental and manual labor had emerged as customary features of premodern Chinese society. Communities traditionally did not become actively involved in promoting equality. Communist rule and specifically Maoist initiatives in the 1960s represented a sharp break with the past.

Apart from sincere belief in the socialist ideology, why did China's leaders adopt moderately or, for some disparities between social strata, vigorously egalitarian policies? One factor affecting the Chinese strategy was the early saturation and the stunted rate of continued growth in what had become the privileged sectors in their labor force. This virtual immobility in the job market did not result simply from policy decisions; rather it existed as an inevitable consequence of economic and demographic factors. The combination of a rapid expansion in educational opportunity, an ethic glorifying achievement in socially approved occupations, and lack of opportunities for mental labor and even for other workers posed a dilemma. To release the mounting pressures for access into these privileged strata and to increase motivation for those denied entry, inequalities were narrowed. The responses, however, were so extreme that conditions quickly deteriorated in the opposite direction.

Clearly traditional patterns have not been followed in the narrowing of peasant-peasant differences within a village, of worker-manager differences within an enterprise, and of mental labor-manual labor differences. These partially egalitarian measures are feasible in an environment where a surplus of individuals qualified for desired positions exists, perhaps a temporary condition of the 1960s. A reappraisal of manpower needs for such goals as supplying the army with modern armaments and expanding large-scale industry portends some increases in inequalities.

How do these significant steps at equalization in social strata differentials relate to China's premodern heritage? In some ways they clash with the familism of old by solidifying communities, enterprises, and other organizations. Yet for the most part these policies do not directly challenge the family; instead they accept a limited but, by modern standards, rather considerable sphere of family interest, and strengthen more widely embracing organizations at work. This goal of refocusing solidarities to wider units is a direct response to the absence of such organizations; the contrast with Japan and Russia in this respect has frequently been cited. It remains to be examined how adequate policies preoccupied with fostering equality are for building lasting solidarity.

Both Chinese and Soviet leaders claim enormous progress in improving the status of women, that is, in reducing inequalities with men. The criteria for making this claim include: (1) legal reform assuring certain forms of equality in family relations, employment, and educational opportunity; (2) monolithic expression in the mass media of views favoring greater equality for women; (3) information on marriage, divorce, birth control, and other family practices showing how women have gained; and (4) records on labor force participation indicating the increased percentage of women in leadership posts, in medicine, in other positions requiring above average education, and in the work force in general. Certainly a great deal of evidence supports the conclusion that the lot of women has improved markedly especially in education and in consciousness of inherent abilities—but not in every respect.

With regard to marriage and family life, Soviet women more closely approach full equality. Bride prices still prevail in China even as dowries are disappearing. Chinese women in most cases must reside with their in-laws. Property generally passes only to sons. After divorce, rural women are, in effect, denied child custody or rights to property. And household duties traditionally defined as the wife's work remain her responsibility even more than for her Soviet counterpart, also without much leisure time because of this double burden. Whereas Soviet marriage, family life, and divorce increasingly share the free-wheeling, unstable conditions present in the contemporary United States, China maintains an agrarian framework in which women are much further from equality.

In neither China nor the Soviet Union have women earned equal wages with men. Among the reasons for this difference are: (1) the tendency for "women's" jobs to receive lower wages; for example, textile jobs are lower paid than mining; (2) the substantial involvement of women in heavy physical labor, at which they are outperformed by men and advance in grade more slowly; (3) the weaker professional orientation or the part-time nature of women's work, often the result of competing family responsibilities; and (4) an apparent preference in wages for men in the most prestigious and best-paying professions. All along the Soviet Union has undoubtedly contained a higher percentage of women who outearn their husbands; the nature of the Soviet labor force and of the marriage market makes this possible. With the disproportionate male deaths and male migration to cities during the Stalin years, women entered the labor force in colossal numbers. Also part of a vast labor force expansion, the typical Chinese woman obtains an agricultural job in her husband's village at a wage lower than the going rate for men. Indeed, her wage goes directly to the household head—normally a male.

The shortage of services to ease the lot of the mother and housewife plagues both Chinese and Soviet women. Day care—until recent changes in the Soviet Union—existed in a minority of settlements for a minority of families with children in the relevant age groups. Indeed, one reason for migration in the Soviet Union has been the inadequacy of day care facilities outside of major cities.

Overall, the Soviet Union has moved closer on these tangible measures to equality for the sexes. Yet, China has taken great strides since 1949 along many dimensions. After the first decade following the revolution, neither country's leadership saw fit to move vigorously on this disparity; the goal remains alive, while the means for realizing it, which depend primarily on persuasion, are viewed in a long-term perspective.

COMPARATIVE CONCLUSION

There are many similarities between China and the Soviet Union. Not only are their professed goals essentially the same, their chosen means are also similar, and their forms of private property and personal income bear substantial resemblances. Small garden plots and subsidiary household animal husbandry in each case add an important private dimension to the collective determination of work points and to the state allocation of wages. Neither government has pushed vigorously on all fronts of the battle for equalization. For example, the implementation of changes in a woman's actual standing in the family have largely been left to persuasive means.

Yet, on the whole Chinese leaders have taken more decisive steps, bringing the issue of equalization more to the forefront. On rural-urban and mental-manual differences in particular, they aggressively moved to reduce differentials of the sort that had become pronounced under Stalin's leadership. Some of these actions are explicable in the context of China's historical legacy. Furthermore, it seems that during the 1960s, and in the early 1970s to a lesser degree, many of these inequalities could not have been justified in terms of China's short-run needs for modernization. Thus our overall assessment is that the Chinese have pushed harder for equalization, especially in accord with long-term problems associated with its legacy for modernization and certain short-term needs arising out of new problems that came to the fore in the 1960s and 1970s. Nevertheless, on balance, the priority the Maoists placed on equality has probably been a negative factor in modernization; its lasting impact in delaying the transition from adding more manpower to improving productivity cannot easily be overcome in the foreseeable future.

CHAPTER FIFTEEN

Conclusions: China's Modernization in Historical Perspective

THE PROBLEMS OF MODERNIZATION FOR LATECOMERS are fundamentally different from those for first-comers in four respects: (1) Latecomers must jump gaps and carry out many activities, especially planning and capital formation, on an unprecedented (for them) scale. (2) They are unable to apply their material, assets, and skills directly to new purposes and hence are forced into a special kind of interdependence with others who are already modernized. (3) They have the advantage of the models presented by those who modernized before them, but they are also frustrated by these models being or appearing to be hopelessly far ahead of them. (4) Finally, at the very time they need coordination and control on a scale they have never needed or been able to sustain before, their prevailing forms of coordination and control are likely to be undercut by their very involvement in the process of modernization. The first three of these disadvantages all come to a head in the fourth.

Modernization is always an exercise in exponentially increasing interdependence, and all previous societies have been based on relatively low levels of interdependency and correspondingly high levels of local self-sufficiency. First-comers grew into this gradually over a long period. Latecomers are catapulted into it overnight, and rarely do they have, as did the Russians and Japanese, alternative methods of coordination and control that can be invoked on a previously unprecedented scale. Very few

482

latecomers can "convert" their patterns of governance directly; most must revolutionize them, and first attempts at this are usually not successful.

For many the problem has been complicated by "imperialism" in one form or another, but the basic problem would have been there even in its absence. Most forms of governance for most nonmodern societies rest in the last analysis on family and lineage style solidarities and on high ideals of local self-sufficiency. But localism and family and lineage governance are everywhere vulnerable to modernization. The appeal of modernization is ineluctable. However one may evaluate modernization, its undeniable prowess in material productivity bursts open the horizons of the possible for all who have material interests—and there are few who do not. Subsequent disillusionment is always too late. No Pandora's box can ever be closed, despite frequent fundamentalist attempts to do so.

All these factors operated in China, and not until the leaders of the PRC took power did the national interest—rather than the family, the lineage, or local considerations—become the focal point, ideally and actually, of individual decision making. How one evaluates the CCP's manner of doing this is not under discussion here. These leaders did it; their predecessors did not. They established a new and radically different basis of coordination and control which has so far been largely effective for purposes of modernization.

Yet that it should take so long for this change to occur remains a source of wonder. Premodern China was so spectacular in its scale and effectiveness along so many cultural dimensions in a society large in numbers and in territory and with so many features that seemed to foreshadow modernization—above all meritocratic open class social mobility, bureaucratic organization, and a high emphasis on literacy—that we are surprised by the fact that China lacked the convertibility that characterized Japan and Russia. Both these countries, after all, suffered from the same general vulnerability as China.

One explanation for this puzzle has to do largely with the political aspects and implications of Chinese institutions. Starting in the later imperial era, the effectiveness of coordination and control began to break down, largely as a function of attempts to push administrative centralization beyond a necessary or supportable limit. This process was particularly marked in the Ch'ing dynastic era, when new circumstances hastened its development. The very worries of the Ch'ing rulers as outsiders in China led them to set a watch over the Chinese bureaucrats that induced counterforces, tendencies toward local power alliances at the expense of the center and other degenerative imbalances.

The Chinese basis for modernization was very much affected by another factor—an unusual increase of population dating from the eighteenth and nineteenth centuries. According to our best estimates, the Chinese population increased over barely one century by some 200 million without corresponding additions to the land in cultivation. In terms of rates there was a comparable increase in Russia, but there because of low population density and vast expanses of available land, undue strains were not placed on the effectiveness of either local or national government. During the nineteenth century the enormous loss of life in the Taiping rebellion kept China's population from rising further for perhaps half a century, but the destructiveness of those events with their attendant decline in agricultural productivity more than offset any winnowing effect.

To these factors must be added the fact that the movement of resources from the countryside to the national centers had always been modest in China. China was so populous and so large that even modest achievements along these lines were absolutely impressive in terms of walls, temples, palaces, and governance. This moderation probably had a great deal to do with the stability of the imperial system and the fact that it was so often renovated rather than revolutionized. The increase in state power so characteristic of France and England and Japan and Russia and the accompanying increase in the development of central urban centers did not take place in China, nor did the Chinese republic in the twentieth century markedly improve resource mobilization. Indeed central control may have worsened as various pressures, not the least of which was the Japanese invasion of the 1930s, gave regionalism, the age-old nemesis of Chinese government, a new place to stand.

When the communists established the PRC in 1949, they introduced sweeping changes. One change was immediately clear: the referent for all action was going to be how that action affected the PRC, what it contributed to the state. Family loyalty and all else were to be superseded if any conflict arose. Furthermore, the PRC had a charismatic leader in Chairman Mao: in effect he and he alone assumed the position of final judge of what contributed and what did not. Although for the most part Mao retreated from day-to-day administration, on crucial matters he intervened, and what he called for or was believed to call for often took immediate effect despite entrenched opposition among the leadership. If it turned out to have unanticipated or undesired consequences, so much the worse. Nevertheless, the achievement of coordination and control was real and has so far survived Mao's death.

Premodern Social Change

It is time now to take a more integrated approach to China's premodern foundation for modernization as a latecomer. Did social changes during the Ming dynasty and the early and middle Ch'ing dynasty improve the capacity of the society and its leaders to carry forward a program of modernization? Was the overall structure of social control and integration "balanced" and "efficient" for meeting the increased demands in an era of transformation? Did an appropriate organizational capacity exist for activating modernization? Could Chinese social patterns be readily adapted to the needs of the new age? Have the Chinese leaders and people been motivated to seek modernization in any explicit organized way? With comparisons of Ch'ing China, Tokugawa Japan, and tsarist Russia in mind over a similar span of roughly one to two centuries through the mid-nineteenth century, we have sought answers to these questions.

Implicit in much of our description of China are the conditions present in an earlier era, perhaps the Sung dynasty or the mid-Ming dynasty. Certain capacities existing in China at those times would, it seems, have given it a partial foundation for modernization as a latecomer, if European countries had begun their modernization then and presented the sort of challenge that actually came in the nineteenth century. In other ways those patterns formed a base from which a wide range of conditions conducive to modernization might have evolved. Early social change had endowed this society well; other societies would have to catch up to be equally prepared for the modern transformation. Despite some erosion prior to the Ch'ing dynasty, certain of these capacities remained largely intact. By premodern standards, China exhibited a well-defined state long experienced in carefully observing and responding to shifts in foreign relations; a bureaucracy selected largely on merit possessing extensive information and control mechanisms capable of eliciting a concerted response at all levels of the society; a commercialized, contractually oriented economy involving vigorous competition; a variety of signs of local vitality characterized by families relatively free to pursue long-term strategies for upward mobility and prosperity; and an unrivaled educational system commanding the attention and respect of large masses of the population. Without doubt, prior to the seventeenth century and for some time thereafter, neither Japan nor Russia could match China in these and many other dimensions of premodern development.

Starting from divergent themes, Chapters 2-6 converge in their interpretation of the eighteenth century as decisive for what did and did not happen in China. In terms of international relations, this was a period of withdrawal—a period of ignoring the possibility of an aggressive maritime threat and of tolerating foreign trade only under closely regulated auspices. Imperial expansion and domestic preoccupations drew the Chinese away from preparations to face the inevitable next encounter with the expanding world sea powers. While Japanese leaders took even more extreme steps to seclude themselves, their actions were explicitly defensive, and they never lost sight of the increasing threat that loomed over the horizon from across the seas. Chinese attention was especially focused by continued expansion of Ch'ing rule across Inner Asian frontiers; the bearers of modernization were not to come from that quarter.

Politically, highly contrived control mechanisms premised on an obsessive concern for the dynasty's security bred cynicism, passivity, and administrative decline. Not only did the Manchu ruling caste fail to use the substantial administrative resources developed during previous dynasties, the rulers inhibited the initiative and sense of responsibility of the Chinese elite in both its administrative and nonadministrative roles. Indeed, the Manchu rulers, albeit unintentionally, gradually freed the elite, especially in its out-of-office roles, from the obligation to act in the national interest. By freezing taxes, by not expanding the bureaucracy as the population increased, and by allowing formal and informal mechanisms of governance to slip into decline, the rulers of China were losing the means to pursue major new objectives. Preoccupied with surveillance and intimidation, they squandered conditions conducive to modernization that resided in the well-institutionalized powers of the central government.

For the economy, the eighteenth century apparently signified not so much a loss of existing capacities as a lack of dynamism in expanding them. The degeneration of administration accompanying the obsession with dynastic security did not leave the economy entirely unscathed, as the blatant corruption of top ministers in the late eighteenth century attests. On the whole, however, transactions in the private sector probably did not suffer greatly from the decline of local supervision by the state. The private economy became ever more predominant and at the same time more vulnerable to irregular interference by officials. Nevertheless it normally met the needs of the market. What did not happen was a decisive restructuring of the market through active state intervention as in Japan or Russia or through international trade and other means as in some West European countries. A basis was not established for economic growth to keep up with population growth throughout the late eighteenth and nineteenth centuries, as it generally had for previous centuries.

The lack of dynamism in early and mid-Ch'ing China becomes especially clear through comparisons of social integration. In the wake of accelerated urbanization, Japan and Russia had experienced major transformations in their patterns of social stratification, settlement, social organization, and resource mobilization. By the end of the eighteenth century, these societies had largely built an infrastructure capable of serving the needs of a program of modernization although certainly not engineered for such a purpose. In at least two basic ways the Chinese did not match this record; they did not increasingly tap the assets of separate communities and local areas to draw them into the cities for new forms of elite consumption and state use, and they did not forestall a massive growth in population that reduced the future potential for extracting resources for the countryside. China's peak population growth occurred late in the eighteenth century; thereafter it was more difficult to mobilize local resources for centralized capital formation.

Neither the content nor the availability of education appears to have changed much during the Ch'ing dynasty. A period of literary purges and narrowing scholarly inquiry, the eighteenth century in China did not witness such dramatic innovations as the emergence of national scientific organizations, as in Russia, or the expansion of mass education, as in Japan. Of course, China had previously far surpassed Japan and Russia and, perhaps, all other countries as well, in its level of literacy and reliance on education.

Customarily, writers on China view the eighteenth century as an era of peace and relative prosperity, reserving for the following century the charges of ineffectual government and social decline. While we note much in the eighteenth century that represents a continuation of longstanding trends and also many respects in which a real deterioration gained momentum in the nineteenth century, we find that most of our evidence for missed opportunities and reduced means for vigorous response to new challenges focuses squarely on the eighteenth century. The results of course became apparent only later, but the roots were there.

The latent or, in the short term, relatively inconsequential problems of the eighteenth century became real and serious in the nineteenth. Aggressive foreign powers easily exposed China's vulnerability to expanded military, commercial, and diplomatic contacts with seafaring intruders. Chinese preparations essentially faced west along land frontiers, but new powers and patterns overwhelmed them from the east. As imperial leadership declined, there was further ossification in the form of overly suspicious control techniques and of power structures in general, undermining the performance of the elite in both administrative and nonadministrative capacities. Constraints loosened, leading to politically anomic pursuit of family ends on the one hand, and, in the wake of vast social upheavals, to regionalism and personalized government based on bonds of loyalty among opportunists dependent on military support on the other. Economic dislocations, resulting in part from the drain of silver caused by opium smuggling, meant capital contraction rather than growth and hence unemployment and decreased incomes. Continued population growth until mid-century in the face of economic stagnation or contraction threatened rural prosperity and stability. The sale of scholarly degrees to raise revenue damaged the link between educational achievement and state reward and recognition. As problems became exacerbated, China plunged into a crisis at mid-century from which it only temporarily and marginally emerged in 1911 and in the late 1920s and early 1930s. Only the establishment of the PRC in 1949 removed some of the basic barriers to modernization.

In brief, the critical elements in China's premodern heritage are: (1) the early development of many precociously modern features and certain conditions that seem to be conducive to modernization; (2) the lack of further accretions to this base, especially as a result of missed opportunities in the eighteenth century; (3) a deterioration of this base in some respects, primarily traceable to administrative decline which signified a lack of direction from the top, and to population growth, which caused a drain on local resources from below: and (4) an exacerbation of problems in the nineteenth century that further undermined the previous basis from which modernization might have proceeded more smoothly.

Phases of Modernization

China was clearly more modernized in 1980 than in 1900, but how much more? How far must it still proceed before reaching a stage of high modernization, the stage reached in Japan and Russia during the 1950s? There exist many indicators of modernization, but no agreement as to which combination of them demonstrates precisely the magnitude of these differences, so that we cannot determine whether over the past eight decades China has traversed one-quarter, one-half, or some other fraction of the way to high modernization or whether the rest of that route will, with optimistic (from the point of view of the post-Mao leadership) projections, require another three, four, or more decades. Given this state of the field, reference to Japan and Russia at least serves as a comparative standard throwing China into perspective. In this section material on China at roughly twenty-five-year intervals is summarized, and the rate and pattern of modernizing change are compared to the closest analogues in the other two countries.

1905

Nineteen five, the year the examination system was abolished, is the first date in our sequential review of China's transformation. In the period of initial broad reforms, this year has special significance. Abolition of the examinations based on the Confucian classics cast a long shadow on matters brought up in the preceding chapters. (1) It reoriented the search for answers to social problems to foreign sources of knowledge and thus produced a rush of students abroad, important in precipitating both the 1911 revolution and the May Fourth Movement later in that decade. (2) It cut the already frayed link (via formal appointments as officials and informal performance of elite responsibilities) between localities and the national government and thus helped plunge the country into further governmental deterioriation from which warlordism eventually emerged. (3) It led to the redistribution of local resources away from persons likely to be imbued with a sense of responsibility for public services and a stake in securing outside assistance that benefited the entire community toward persons more interested in serving family or parochial interests and encouraged career patterns irrelevant to national interests. (4) It shattered the existing hierarchy of social status, making the boundaries between urban and rural more fixed, with long-run negative consequences for the capacity to integrate urban and rural sectors. (5) And it greatly altered the place of education in China's development, creating a sharp discontinuity that contributed to the persistent struggle over what forms of education would be appropriate in the new era. With its real and symbolic importance, the reform of the examination system is representative of China's break with the past in roughly the same way as the abolition of serfdom in 1861 and the abolition of domains shortly after the Meiji Restoration in 1868 epitomize the launching of the era of transformation in those countries.

The waves of reforms in each of these three countries have much in common. Each followed a stunning exposure of military weakness, a widespread sensation that fundamental internal shortcomings were at the root of the country's security problems, and a long simmering worry, even among the principal beneficiaries of the old order, that old institutions were not operating in as fair or as smooth a fashion as before. There are many other similarities with Japan and Russia in the 1860s. On the whole, they suggest that China entered the transformation some forty years after the other two countries, but any simple assumption of a forty-year gap requires several qualifications.

In important respects 1905 in China does not evoke 1861 in Russia or 1868 in Japan. With the emergence of considerably more modernized countries (consider, for example, the vast changes in Germany and the United States over these years), the international context had changed. More deeply ingrained imperialist competition now reached all corners of the globe and involved, among other things, more pervasive foreign trade and investment mechanisms. In addition, the rise of Japan and Russia as important Asian powers already achieving notable gains in modernization had special meaning for China's foreign relations. Not only do the problems of latecomers differ from those of first-comers, but the later the latecomer, the more intense those problems are likely to be—quite apart from the internal factors considered in isolation. For these and other reasons, Chinese policies from the beginning of its transformation were less autonomous; the international context pressed more directly and forcibly on decision-making circles than it had in Japan or Russia. Did this different international setting offer models and resources to enhance China's capacity to compress the period before achievement of initial, modern economic growth? Did it complicate the realization of internal controls and coordination, drain financial resources, and in other ways retard modern economic growth? Conclusions here are mixed. Although the international context had far more influence on China in the twentieth century than it had in the eighteenth and nineteenth centuries, as in that earlier period variations in the international setting do not seem to be crucial for explaining differences in modernization among the three countries. We have concluded that China both benefited and lost from its interactions with foreign countries. Although the international setting proved less hospitable for China, the explanation of the differences lies elsewhere, primarily in the internal political structure.

What sets China apart, above all, is its political disorientation in the reform decade. All levels of the previous political hierarchy simultaneously experienced disarray, from the tottering Manchu imperial leadership to the highly proliferated lame duck elite of degree holders scattered from district to district. When Russian serfowners received state bonds as compensation for a portion of their lands, the tsarist government with its sizable bureaucracy remained firmly entrenched. When *daimyo* were compensated in bonds for the loss of the domains, the emperor soon became the center of a cult that, after some interruption, ensured continuity in controls over the population. Village community controls based on earlier solidarities were actually reinforced in Japan and Russia. In China, however, the central government fell without an obvious successor; provincial levels spawned warlord rivalries; local government could not readily replace degree holders either in official capacities or as its primary constituents; and village leadership shifted to more self-serving groups unable to harness powerful divisive forces in lineages and secret societies. In building a centralized polity with emerging capacities for mobilizing resources and coordinating local activities, China was far more than forty years behind Japan and Russia.

The modern economic sectors of the three countries were too minute to justify a comparison of existing data for these early periods. Data on the traditional sectors are not easily obtained or compared. On the basis of the comparisons in Part One there is little to suggest that China in the 1900s was better prepared than Japan and Russia had been four decades earlier. The fact that each of these countries was nonmodernized at the beginning of the transformation should not be taken to mean they had a common starting point. The bulk of evidence suggests that traditional sectors could well have given Japan and Russia a considerable advantage, one reason being that both public and private channels already amassed much of the local surplus in the cities of these two countries. In any case, the three countries' reform periods are similar in being accompanied or followed directly by railroad construction and other forms of stimulus and reorganization that are preparatory to initial, modern economic growth.

The modernizing impact of reforms affected the rural sector of China less visibly and less immediately than in Japan and Russia. In all three countries the urban-rural gap widened; modern attitudes and organizations appeared primarily in cities. In Japan and Russia, however, the reforms specifically included major rural objectives such as emancipation of serfs and systematization of a land tax; governments became involved in reorganizing rural life. In contrast, Chinese leaders did not demonstrate a comparable capacity to reach into the countryside or to alter urban-rural relations. Change occurred indirectly, often by default, and did not contribute to a rural transformation. In Japan, on the other hand, agricultural productivity rose, and in Russia massive quantities of grain were exported. Above all, until after 1949 there was nothing in China that compared in these respects to the repeal of serfdom in Russia or the termination of domains and the system of universal conscription in Japan.

The educational stimulus of the reform era provides an example of profound changes in China with modest short-term results for modernization. As classical studies gave way to modern schools beginning to use the vernacular language, education became geared to new careers in the cities. Yet, China did not experience the explosion in attendance over the following decades that occurred in the other countries.

In short, China's reform period had much the same significance in reorienting social change as the reforms of the 1860s had had in Japan and Russia, bringing massive change and signifying a sharp break from the past. But destabilizing forces were unleashed through reform, and the short-term results were unpromising. Although in some obvious indicators of entry into modernization, China appears about forty years behind, it was most likely even further disadvantaged in other signs of readiness for modernization.

1930

A quarter-century later, China had a new nationalist government and a fledgling modern industrial sector. How far had modernization advanced by 1930? The preceding chapters identify many pertinent achievements including the following: (1) China was in a much improved position to borrow on equal terms from modernized states; the scramble for spheres of influence had subsided although pressure from Japan was mounting. (2) It had reestablished a central government with potential for further centralizing control; warlordism was at least temporarily in retreat. (3) The modern, industrial sector had begun to grow quite rapidly although it only constituted a negligible part of the economy. (4) Changing urban social organization, including the growth of business groups and workers' associations, and changes in family structure reflected an era of intense urban transformation. (5) The educational accomplishments *of small numbers* of Chinese had reached high levels in various areas of modern knowledge. Some of these characteristics, particularly the political conditions, had existed in Japan or Russia during the initial years of transformation. The others appeared there by the 1880s and 1890s. Looked at more closely, however, the evidence for 1930 confirms that in most respects China was not keeping pace with the rates of change in the other countries.

Despite its improved international standing China continued to experience a rather unfavorable world environment, in part because of its domestic disunity. The most serious blow came from the Japanese occupation, which set back China's modernization considerably. Physical damage, death, and dislocation compounded the setback and wiped out the base for promising new leaders, but on the other hand, military and guerrilla mobilization and training in new skills meant that the time was not altogether unproductive. Hostility toward foreign actions reached a higher level in China, strongly affecting domestic politics and permeating parts of China that had previously been barely affected by foreign activities. On the positive side for modernization, the foreign presence exerted a powerful, if initially ineffective, force for political mobilization and national reintegration. On the other hand the areas invaded by Japan were precisely the economic base of the new entrepreneurial elites who were beginning to wield political influence within the Kuomintang. The occupation reduced them to dependency on the Japanese or on the conservative elements of the KMT or threw them into the opposition that was to take over in 1949.

The political arena offers the strongest evidence that basic requirements for a full-scale transformation were still absent in 1930. Of course, significant aspects of political modernization had emerged, including a new government based on a political party that made use of modern communications and organizational devices. Political values had shifted, ideally speaking, with the absorption of western knowledge and thought, but China's borrowing actually remained notably incomplete. Modern elements appeared without the foundation of a strong central government that could guide social change. The establishment of Kuomintang rule did not expunge the warlord legacy of debureaucratization and political fragmentation. Just as during the late Ch'ing dynasty such change as occurred had been rootless through want of guidance and sponsorship by a strong central government, during the 1930s modern elements appeared without the guidance necessary to integrate them into society. In the political sphere, China was falling further and further behind the pace of transformation set by Japan and Russia. At this time China was still unable to create an alternative basis for coordination and control that would be relatively impervious to the disintegrating forces affecting the previous bases. The Japanese occupation was only the last straw. Indeed, by stimulating nationalistic and defensive sentiments, it may even have temporarily strengthened the KMT.

By the early 1930s the modern sector contributed some 3 percent of the national product. Industrial growth continued in peacetime, but it did not yet signify initial, modern economic growth as had begun in Japan and Russia during the late 1880s and early 1890s. The rate of capital formation remained very low, and there was no sustained growth in agricultural productivity. Per capita output stayed at premodern levels and may even have fallen to its lowest level in centuries when civil war engulfed China in the 1940s. An important reason for the slow start is the limited role the Chinese state played in fostering economic growth; it remained fiscally weak while the public sector expanded slowly. Credit, banking, and the long-distance commercial sector in general were less developed than in Japan and Russia a half-century earlier. Thus the advances in modern industry were not yet indicative of a modern infrastructure and robust modern growth.

A considerable rural lag in transformation is common to all three countries, but in China the lag was acute. Two indicators of how cut off villages remained are the persistent low tax rates apart from emergency local military levies and the very slow rate of conversion from scattered periodic markets to modern commerce. Contrast Chinese conditions to the depersonalization of landlord-tenant relations apparent in Japan or to the early stages of a fertility decline in rural Russia between 1897 and 1926 suggested by census data. We have not found evidence of similar modern transformations in rural China; indeed reanalysis of the Buck survey (Barclay, et al., 1976) shows that even by premodern standards mortality rates were at a very high level in 1930.

In education, Japan was moving toward universal primary schooling and Russia toward nearly universal urban education during the early years of the century, whereas China's efforts to extend mass education showed a marked lack of dynamism. Estimates indicate that on the eve of the communist victory the level of literacy, at least for males, was no higher than the 30 to 40 percent estimated for the Ch'ing period. Of course, in all three countries the content of formal education and the meaning of literacy were changing continuously.

In brief, while China in 1930 in some respects resembled Japan and Russia in the 1880s and 1890s, in other respects it had not reached their levels. Some advances were only superficial because they were insufficiently linked to the state as the implementing vehicle and because structural changes (in government and the rural sector) had actually sapped the vitality of activities providing control and coordination. Despite notable gains under Kuomintang rule, the foundation for modernization remained weak and uneven, and the advances in that direction were still quite tentative.

1955

In the 1950s a new leadership brought a different program for social change to bear on China's problems of modernization. Nineteen fifty-five is a good year for taking another look at the state of the long-term transformation because it follows the recovery from prolonged warfare, comes at the midpoint of the first five-year plan, and leads directly to the culmination of collectivization and nationalization at the end of the year and in the following year. Chinese society was marching headlong toward socialism and the promise of modernization. The path ahead seemed to be clearly demarcated.

With their early achievements, how far had the communist leaders of China led their country toward modernization? In the mid-1950s it was already clear that they had overcome at least five longstanding barriers. (1) China had recovered full sovereignty in international relations and was demonstrating that it could make good use of a large number of modern enterprises built with outside (Soviet) assistance. (2) A powerful state directed social change in all sectors and continued to reorganize the society in order to extend its controls. (3) Heavy industry was growing at a very rapid rate as requirements for modern, economic growth were being met. (4) Leaders mobilized resources in urban and rural areas on an ever-expanding scale as they quickly achieved a high level of social integration for a still relatively nonmodernized society. (5) Education and modern knowledge became available to rapidly increasing numbers of people. In a few respects, such as the strength of the central government, only in the 1950s did China reach the levels achieved by the beginning of transformation in Japan and Russia. In other respects, particularly the achievement of initial, modern economic growth, China resembled these countries during the late nineteenth century. And in some characteristics of the urban sector, such as the decline in fertility that became apparent by the late 1950s, China had already reached early twentieth-century levels in Japan and Russia. After falling even further behind the pace set by Japan and Russia in the race to modernize, at last in the 1950s China had begun to gain on its two leading neighbors.

The period just after 1949 is in many ways an oddity in the history of Chinese foreign relations. Initially close alliance with the Soviet Union was the cornerstone of China's international relations. The Chinese received assistance in the form of entire plants and their products, which reinforced the primacy of the heavy industrial sector, and in return they provided foodstuffs, handicrafts, and certain raw materials. Chinese leaders accepted a relationship of economic dependency, but their uneasiness with it was already apparent in the hate with which they sought to accelerate change in the mid-1950s.

At the same time, China was also establishing the groundwork for applying the Soviet model of development to politics. The state, with the aid of Communist Party members, penetrated into local areas and mobilized large amounts of local resources. It undermined old hierarchies centering on lineage and landlord. Loyalties to household heads remained, but by the late 1950s they could be circumscribed through loyalties to new organizations and the presence of external controls. Burgeoning modern bureaucracies filled the cities. The top-heavy political structure had long-run negative consequences for modernization, but the obstacles that had most interfered with modernization in the past had been largely overcome. Accelerated modernization now depended primarily on meeting requirements of economic organization, social integration, and knowledge and education.

China's rapid economic growth in the 1950s mostly resulted from recovery in a period of peace and unity and from the application of methods that were well tested in the Soviet Union. Even though economists find evidence of an excessive emphasis on capital-intensive industrial projects during the 1950s and although the ill-conceived economic policies of the Great Leap Forward were enormously wasteful, the overall economic performance over the decade had left China markedly more modernized. It also should be noted that at an earlier stage of modernization than in the USSR, Chinese leaders were implementing a one-sided strategy that could not be perpetuated. Their strategy shortchanged agriculture and the services, sectors that were already so extended in meeting the minimal needs of a growing rural population that they could not be depended on to continue to satisfy the enormous appetite of the growing urban, heavy industrial sector as well.

Major gains in social integration also resulted from CCP policies in the 1950s. Such gains came faster, more in fits and starts, through more intensive controls and at an earlier stage of modernization than somewhat analogous programs in Japan and Russia. A contrast emerges of forced and perhaps premature integration from above coupled with only modest involvement in modernization of the village populations below. Land reform could be imposed on villages that had until then experienced little change resulting from modernization as such. Collectivization and various types of commune organization did not immediately lead to deep penetration of urban patterns into the countryside. Rather, periodic markets endured, transportation remained largely premodern, and rural to urban migration was too low to suggest a meaningful exchange of residents among settlements. The rural areas proved sufficiently resilient and fluid to absorb the new practices without undergoing much change in the basic way of life. The most direct effect of the communes was to change the precedence of obligations beyond local, familial considerations rather than to alter directly most of the patterns of everyday life. The context of these patterns had been changed much more than the substantive content of the patterns themselves. Indicative of this condition was the still limited per capita improvement in the agricultural sector and the still slight decline in rural fertility to the mid-1960s. In each of the three countries, the urban population at this stage of modernization represented a small minority, and the gap between rural and urban areas had greatly widened. Especially in China a strained situation resulted from the unevenness of modernization and from the premature or excessive seizure of social levers by the state, as in the continued expropriation of property and labor. Transformation had long proceeded slowly, but then accelerated hurriedly beyond the rates attained elsewhere. From that chronology much can be learned about China's distinctive path.

In education and scientific knowledge the 1950s also brought swift advances that partially compensated for the limited improvements of prior decades. At the same time there were early signs of discrimination against many who would likely have risen to the top if unlimited competition had been allowed. Experts were suspect in a manner not conducive to full use of their talents. It is easy to overlook these signs in the face of the great influx of new graduates at all levels of education.

On the whole, the mid-1950s were a period of rapid advances and of optimism that these advances would continue. In retrospect, this period has also come to symbolize what might have been, that is, the gradual building of socialism more in accordance with the Soviet model. The beginning of the 1930s symbolize another alternative, the possibility of modernization without socialism, as occurred in Taiwan. Each of these periods thus lends itself to a specific international comparison—although conditions in the Soviet Union and in Taiwan following Japanese occupation offer important contrasts—and leaves nagging questions about the long-term possibilities of a form of modernization that was abruptly interrupted. Rejecting these alternatives, the Maoist leadership steered China along another path, already beginning to take shape in the mid-1950s, which later emerged more fully in the Great Leap Forward and in the following periods.

1980

At the beginning of 1980 the course of modernization in China remained unsettled. Since the mid-1950s there had been many advances. In some areas there were also serious setbacks. Again the great unevenness characteristic of modern China's development is striking. Five examples of factors that slowed modernization and were later recognized as detrimental are: (1) China for a time made relatively little use of international assistance or trade to further its domestic goals, but in the late 1970s its leaders abruptly sought a massive inflow of credits and technology. (2) Surveillance and controls permeated the society, signifying a political system that provided little security or legal guarantee; however, in the campaign against the Gang of Four major elements of the political system were repudiated as stifling and harmful to modernization. (3) On each of three occasions, for two to three years each, political turmoil and short-lived programs aimed at radical reorganization crippled economic growth. (4) Attacks against privilege and profit, coupled with tight restrictions on individual choice affecting many of life's major decisions, had the effect of virtually destroying personal incentives. (5) Policies that suppressed specialization, professionalism, and higher education led to a deterioration in managerial and technical skills vital to long-term modernization. Not only were developed talents permitted to fall into disuse, but preparation of the young in these fields was brought to a virtual halt. Despite these shortcomings and others, at least some aspects of modernization had made enormous strides by 1980. Heavy industry continued to grow rapidly; in this period manufacturing replaced agriculture as the primary contributor to the national product. Communes, to the extent that they tolerated a mixture of private and collective pursuits and a blend of household-oriented and state-oriented behavior, created a workable system of control and coordination that contributed to gradual rural advances. Mass education for an increased number of years became nearly universal. In most measures China had reached the early twentieth-century levels of Japan and Russia; in some measures it approached levels of the 1920s and 1930s. After roughly eighty years, China still trailed the other two countries much as it had a quarter-century earlier. In areas where the Maoist leadership had blocked advances in the 1960s and 1970s, the gap was especially wide.

496

In the international arena, the critical question for China in the 1980s is how to pay for the foreign factories and equipment that are vital to the new economic plans. Vigorous steps are being taken to expand exports of oil, following the precedent of the Organization of Petroleum Exporting Countries, and of textiles, a proven currency earner for small, booming economies on China's periphery. Without much income from exports, the Chinese will be unable to take full advantage of their external relations. In fact, for almost the entire period of transformation, international relations have not been well exploited for the sake of modernization. For a time, China lacked the necessary unity, later it was partially occupied, and, after an unusual period of looking to the Soviet Union as a model, it was controlled by leaders hostile to international influences. It remains to be seen whether China can now draw beneficially on the resources and experiences of already modernized societies over a prolonged period.

The political problems of the 1980s are primarily a legacy of Maoism. Will there be a fairly high degree of centralization without oversurveillance through dossiers, class labels, and paralyzing campaigns? Will interest groups gain a voice in policy decisions? Are conditions to be regularized so that decisions can be made in an atmosphere of stability and predictability? Will the will of the majority (and the claim to speak on its behalf) in various organizations be more effectively balanced by the authority of managers and experts who give higher priority to the needs of modernization? Some trends apparent in the late 1970s indicate positive answers to these questions, but the problems that have plagued China for much of the past quarter-century are far from resolved.

Economically, the difficult task ahead is to increase labor productivity. The gains of the past twenty-five years were almost entirely associated with increased labor inputs, especially through the inclusion of women and the employment of off-season farm workers. There is little possibility of further expanding the labor force. A shift of the labor force into nonagricultural activities now demands increased agricultural productivity per hectare as well as per worker. To provide more consumer goods and services as part of a renewed emphasis on incentives requires a transfer of labor without a corresponding loss in production in other sectors. Not only must productivity be increased, but much of the increase must be directly given to increased standards of living.

The Chinese have proved themselves fairly successful in using labor-intensive methods, but they face a difficult challenge during the 1980s in keeping the growth rate from falling. High costs can be anticipated in increased per capita rates of consumption, in higher wages for a growing nonagricultural labor force, in higher procurement prices designed to give incentives to rural collectives, and in other devices aimed at motivating workers and managers.

Social indicators also give a mixed impression of China's current level of

497

modernization. On the one hand, we see evidence among the majority ethnic group of a nearly universal decline in fertility which has reached beyond the cities into the villages. The declines are reminiscent of the immediate prewar years in Japan and Russia. On the other hand, most basic indicators put China at an earlier stage of modernization. The percentage of the labor force in nonagricultural activities remains low even if we somehow take into account part-time labor in rural small-scale industries. The estimated 20 percent level of urbanization is less than half the figures Japan (56 percent in 1955) and the USSR (48 percent in 1959) reached as they made their transition to high modernization. Rates of rural-urban migration and intercity migration, per capita rates of consumption, the rate of labor turnover, and the frequency with which married couples set up new, independent residences are also closer to premodern than to modernized levels. For a large part of the unevenness there is an explanation: modernized characteristics appear among the urban population but are rare among the much more numerous rural inhabitants. A pronounced gap between urban and rural has become increasingly evident in the twentieth century. Efforts to reduce the gap, which have been tried in certain periods, may slow economic growth and, yet, in the long run such efforts are unavoidable.

Education, more than any other area, illustrates the detrimental impact on modernization of the policy line in effect for at least a decade during the 1960s and 1970s. The percentage of the population with a higher education, not to mention one that meets international standards, is much lower than it would have been if the earlier course had been maintained. Indicative of the problems that this creates is the comment made in 1979 by Fei Hsiao-t'ung, president of the newly established Chinese Sociological Association, that China may not have anyone well enough trained to benefit from observing the United States census of 1980 before preparing a Chinese census planned for 1981. In the 1970s large numbers of Chinese were exposed to a low level of education that previously would not have been available, but—probably far more important for modernization—the much smaller numbers with the ability to take advantage of specialized and higher-level training were denied the opportunity. At the end of the 1970s educational policies made a sharp turnabout. It appears clear that the Chinese are making great haste to remedy this situation.

In 1980 China was still far from high modernization. If its scaled down, but still optimistic plans can be realized, and if it can avoid war losses and destruction like those experienced by Japan and Russia during the 1940s in the midst of their transformations, one could expect China to regain some of the years it had lost since the 1900s. Perhaps China will emerge into high modernization early in the next century. Before that can happen, however, some difficult problems of transition must be resolved. The challenge of the 1980s requires new policy initiatives in many areas; the results are by no means as easy to extrapolate from past performance as would have been the achievement of high modernization in Japan and Russia. Apart from other considerations, it is difficult to contemplate a society of one billion using the resources necessary to enter high modernization. If China does approach high modernization, we must anticipate a startlingly different look in some indicators such as per capita income levels.

Centralization and Decentralization

On the basis of the precedents supplied by Japan's and Russia's histories, we take the position that "successful" latecomers to modernization must avail themselves of both unusual elements of centralization and a balanced distribution of powers and resources at various levels. The concepts of "centralization," "mobilization," and "balanced" are invoked repeatedly in the preceding chapters, each referring to the spatial distribution of activities, groups, or resources pertinent to the needs of modernization.

Starting at the top of the urban and administrative hierarchy and of the social ladder, we can see the first signs of imbalance in the Ch'ing dynasty in the leadership in Peking. The emperor acquired ever more unlimited control. While new checks were limiting absolutism in other countries, the opposite trend prevailed in China. Simultaneously, the Inner Court gained at the expense of the Outer Court, and the capital also expanded its importance within the bureaucracy at the expense of the provincial and subprovincial levels on which previous Chinese bureaucratic effectiveness had depended. The Manchus, as aliens largely living apart from the Han Chinese, were already remote, and Peking was remote as a capital city near the northeastern frontier of the eighteen provinces and as an economic center far from the rich grain-producing areas and major commercial entrepôts. The Manchu leadership created a top-heavy government rather than extending its grasp outward via the middle and bottom ranks of bureaucracy. By obsessive concern for Manchu control it did much to demoralize the Han Chinese components of its centralized leadership. This center orientation was intended to tighten the leadership's grip over active officials, but it impaired the potential for centralizing control over local resources. Economically China's national captial no longer stood out among urban centers; at the same time the other great regional cities and lesser cities too had probably never been governed with so little administrative flexibility or with so little concern for mobilizing the potential resources of their regions. At the very least, commercialization over the previous millennium had not induced any serious administrative reorganization to expand the center's grip on resources.

The leaders vested little power in those at the second level in the administrative hierarchy, intentionally restricting the coordination of offices and the emergence of strong provincial governments. The equilibrium of the eighteenth century rested on the tightly limited capacities of government at this level. During the following century, in conditions of crisis, the expansion of provincial powers signified the breakdown of the center's hold and the emergence of regionalism. Instead of adjusting to the realities of vast and scattered resources, China's rulers stifled the legitimate development of regional and provincial powers and thus forced those powers to assume an illegitimate personalized form that destroyed the articulation between the center and the county (*hsien*). The Japanese devised a two-tier administrative system with vast powers assigned to the separate units or *han*. The Russians established provincial-level units called *gubernii* to provide direction at a level superior to the local districts. But the Chinese system relegated the levels between the center and the county to a marginal place despite the difficulties of providng active leadership over such a vast population from one national center.

In various ways, the preceding chapters address the problem of leadership at the local level. Why was the bureaucracy so unprepared to govern for new purposes at the county and subcounty levels? What accounts for the relatively low concentration of population in small cities? Why was commercialization in the most immediate marketing areas not matched by a funneling of resources into superior marketing centers? A pattern emerges of deeply entrenched local interests who accepted as social peers officials from outside, but only insofar as they did not intrude actively into local affairs, and assumed, with a decreasing measure of social responsibility, many duties once expected of the government, giving highest priority to family and lineage objectives. The shift from official to unofficial governance may have had many positive consequences for the health of rural society, but it also strengthened localism that would prove to be incompatible with new strategies for vigorous central leadership or for mobilization of scattered resources. The dispersed and relatively unorganized elite, lacking a particularly urban orientation, and the highly competitive small-scale units of production and distribution exacerbated the decentralized character of local society.

Finally, the village stood as a potential basic building block for aggregating power on a nonfamilial basis. The village was after all the territorial governance unit in which more than 90 percent of all Chinese lived. At this level, the contrast with Japan and Russia is even starker than at any of the higher levels. In those societies, village cohesion represented both a deliberate state policy and a longstanding local tradition, while in China a conscious preference was accorded to familial bonds through systems that organized families while bypassing the village. In many varied ways, social customs as well as state policies reinforced the precedence of the family and the vertically integrated lineage. When the government operated effectively and when local resources were adequate, the prevailing conditions were sufficient for local vitality and national stability. As long as the large subadministrative elite remained motivated to act responsibly for the public good, the open society was pervaded by downwardly persuasive models and upwardly imitative aspirations. Lineages could link households with diverse means in a cooperative strategy for long-range upward social mobility; the absence of village cohesion did not impair local prosperity. But even in the eighteenth century, there was little to recommend the rural social structure as a basis for drawing resources from the village level or for enlarging the government's role. In a period of weakening central control and increasing cynicism, the local impact of this social structure could only be to release the family and the lineage from the few constraints that still operated. In addition to the decline emanating from above, new problems from below associated with economic depression, population pressure, and military insecurity further weakened the bonds within the elite, bonds already strained by emerging loyalties among political opportunists and necessary submission to military power.

The Ch'ing hierarchy did not provide a good basis for integrated vigorous regional or local governance or for extracting resources. Again, undue concentration at the center inhibited the initiative and sense of responsibility of the elite in and out of government and set adrift family and lineage interests, in opposition to village or county powers in mobilization of resources. Thus, (1) even at the height of Ch'ing prosperity, spatially Chinese society was balanced in a manner that made local mobilization difficult; (2) the main currents of the eighteenth and nineteenth centuries unbalanced the distribution of power and resources at the top and bottom of the hierarchy; and (3) with the introduction of new forces a spatial reordering occurred that was inimical to the establishment of the more centralized and mobilized society necessary if modern development was to proceed smoothly.

We have talked frequently of problems of balance, referring to shifts in control or in access to resources between the center and the regional units or the localities, the city and the countryside, the village and the household or lineage, and the county officials and the local elite. Over its long history, Chinese society had made stringent demands on its members to maintain a balance of interests and had carefully evolved procedures to reinforce an equilibrium between family and lineage interests on the one hand and central government objectives on the other. Success in these endeavors is rightly acknowledged as one of the extraordinary achievements of that civilization. Yet, during the Ch'ing dynasty the norms that balanced diverging interests were gradually undermined by rulers who tipped the balance in favor of the state and by an ensuing elite cynicism. Quite unintentionally, these forces, when combined with pronounced population growth and massive rebellions, in fact tipped the balance away from the state; they accentuated the priority of family and lineage interests. As the tasks faced by government mounted in the late nineteenth century, the disequilibrium became more marked. We have referred to this process as devolution, degeneration, decentralization, or disintegration. Controlling influences from above diminished. The twentieth

501

century is marked by repeated attempts to restore equilibrium and to establish a viable balance of interests conducive to modernization, but the results were often counterproductive.

Throughout its history, China had had an unusual degree of integration between city and countryside. The elite lived mainly in the countryside, education was widely available in both rural and urban areas, and it was no less prestigious to live outside of urban centers. As F. W. Mote has pointed out (1970), China may be unique in the lack of differentiation between rural and urban architecture and in other aspects of daily life. It is therefore notable that among the strongest signs of the decline of previously centralizing elements and of the concentration of modernizing elements in cities is a widening urban-rural gap.

Over the first quarter of the twentieth century the imbalances in Chinese society became more serious. In particular, the character of rural society altered profoundly. Bureaucratic oversight of local activities, including tax collection, became less effective. Until the examination ethic began to deteriorate during the late Ch'ing, one way in which the balance between the center and the localities was maintained was through a local elite educated in an ideal of public service which restrained it from being wholly self-seeking and encouraged it to govern the countryside unofficially in harmony with the needs and goals of the center. With the end of the examination system and with the appointment of officials no longer determined primarily by its results, rural notables were largely freed from responsibility to a supervising government. This change was symbolized by the abandonment of the requirement that the aspiring degree holder go to the capital to take the examinations, receive appointment, and be integrated into a national elite. In some areas officials even became locked into a fixed status with a secure local dominance. Control shifted from bureaucratic and semibureaucratic structures under central constraints to local bosses under no such constraints. Without the long-nurtured integrative functions of education and bureaucratic centralization, the political norms of the imperial era could not be widely perpetuated; the pursuit of wealth could no longer be counterbalanced by the performance of respected services.

Several of the chapters in Part Two convey an impression of a countryside cast adrift in the era of warlordism and beyond, by both the decline of previously centralizing forces and the heavily urban concentration of emerging modernizing elements. There is evidence of a dual economy, with the rural areas even more removed from modern economic currents than in Japan and Russia at a similar time. How else can one explain the continued proliferation of periodic markets as important channels of exchange in rural China? Agriculture lagged greatly; eventually Chinese leaders would find themselves heavily dependent on industrial sources of savings because of the low productivity of agriculture. The term "dual polity" refers to the political situation that prevailed after the withdrawal of controlling influences. Rural society became closed. Local elites gained autonomy. From the 1920s on separate and distinct modern organizers continuously competed in the countryside and the cities. Yet, not until the last years of resistance against Japan and the following years of civil war did a new elite begin to integrate China and undertake state building.

During the second quarter of the century, especially in the Nanking decade, some measures were taken to constrain localist forces. Of course, the reassertion of central government represented an essential step. The KMT followed this with attempts to recentralize local administration at the level of the county magistrate and to establish intracounty subdivisions with effective controls. But it proved beyond their means to regain a balance of central and local interests; the KMT ended up allied only with some rural elites oriented toward the status quo. The county-level government's loss of prestige and effectiveness persisted even after central government was restored.

Under these circumstances of lessened governmental capacity, new patterns emerged locally. Restraints ordinarily imposed by the local social setting also became vulnerable to changing conditions. Moreover, heightened needs for mid-level organizations, such as the expansive local systems of security, facilitated the growth of organizations that did not provide integration on a broad basis. Part of the vacuum was filled by secret societies and military units in league with the new local bosses. Lineages too became stronger. The persistence of a vast array of moderately well-off landholders further complicated renewed attempts at centralization. The emerging central state could find few easy targets to displace in order to reassert control. Fluid social boundaries and the close ties of powerful individuals to diverse social milieus limited the capacity for identifying or mobilizing homogeneous social strata and the capacity for building alternative social organizations. The fragility of village solidarity, the absence of aristocratic domination, and the lack of convertibility of the old elite's position impaired efforts at renewed centralization. Compromises with illegitimate holders of power—ancient compromises which had lent flexibility to the old society—set back modernization.

Recentralization, realized partially under the KMT but much more thoroughly under the CCP, contributed importantly to economic growth. National unity and control together with new military techniques, modern means of communications, and nationalist political norms enabled new leadership to organize local politics to some extent, but the vastness of the managerial task required for mobilizing this society precluded any easy resolution of the central government's problems. Both before and after 1949 efforts to penetrate the villages were never successful on the scale sought.

The CCP leaders have expended enormous energy in resolving problems of spatial distribution. They have achieved some notable successes and have produced some dismal failures. In many areas related to centralization their policies have been more cyclical than linear—a vivid testimony to the inconsistency that has prevailed. At the root of their difficulties were recurrent attempts to control more than they had the resources to control, to control more, indeed, than was required. They met little direct, organized resistance; local communities could not overtly resist land reform, collectivization, and other programs introduced during waves of social reorganization. The existing intermediate organizations, such as secret societies and even lineages, were quickly eliminated. Drawing on the increasing membership in the new elite of party members, the leaders solidified new organizations. Yet these structures actually relied heavily on local institutions inherited from the past; they were shaped as much by the compromises resulting from attempts to mobilize too much on too fragile an organizational base as by the immediate goals of centralization. The CCP constantly misjudged how long modernization would take and what the cost of its policies would be.

At the top layers of government, we observe striking swings in the authority vested in central, multiprovince, and provincial officials. Efforts to extend greatly the reach of central authorities proved abortive. Contrary to popular impressions, regionalism at the large multiprovince level was generally the most important and effective kind of centralization after 1949. When these units were abolished, the provincial level gained autonomy, and at times, such as during the Great Leap Forward, decentralization went even further. With the reestablishment of multiprovince units in 1962 and again in 1976, centralization again gained impetus. In general, there was less tolerance for localism during the 1970s; a gradual trend toward the centralization important for long-term modernization can be discerned.

Nevertheless, China remained much less centralized than Japan and Russia at similar stages of modernization. Unlike these two countries it was unable to resolve the tensions between centers of power and levels in an administrative and social hierarchy quickly and easily.

Also limiting the state's hold over its localities was the persisting weakness of local government. County-level officials never became the crucial nexus of the national elite's interaction with village society that they had been in the dynastic era. Nor did large or later moderate-sized communes have sufficient initiative to exert a local counterweight to central concerns. Rather it was left to the production team and, to a lesser extent, to the production brigade to balance state and local interests. They were sufficiently autonomous and isolated from all but sporadic administrative communications to guarantee the perpetuation of localism.

Yet, the accommodation that emerged after the Cultural Revolution held hopes of resolving many local spatial imbalances even if central ones continued. Gradual centralization operated as a more consistent principle than in any previous period. This centralization was not based on frantic campaigns, but on clear-cut regulations and increasing scope for market incentives.

The PRC government, recognizing the problems brought on by the failure of the Ch'ing and the KMT governments to integrate a spurt in population and in investment in large coastal cities with broader urban and rural development, adopted policies aimed at redressing this situation. Although large-scale permanent migration to the great urban centers had not been a traditional feature of Chinese society, by the 1950s the desire to live in large cities had become a demographic force to be reckoned with. By limiting the number of people allowed to live in the cities and by pressing birth control and sending youths out of the cities, the PRC averted massive overcrowding. Today rural-urban and intercity migration rates are closer to premodern than modern levels. Small cities gained in population relative to the tightly controlled large ones, improving the efficiency of the urban hierarchy. The urban-rural gap became less pronounced in such fields as health care and education. At the same time, the well integrated village increased as a force for modern change; community-centered family planning policies, for example, could, and in many cases did, facilitate a notable decline in rural fertility. As social mobilization proceeded more cautiously and organizations responded to more guarantees of stability and self-interest, the hierarchy of production teams, brigades, and communes appeared to be a secure foundation for local development.

Strong central governments, tight local controls, and sharp rural-urban discrepancies are usually associated with being a successful latecomer. The Chinese, however, have remained reconciled to regionalism in one form or another. At times, exaggerated attempts to take control of the society and to penetrate local units occurred, but these were too sudden, and often too violent, to give the center a solid foundation for mobilization. Through the 1970s the central government remained relatively weak. The Chinese did not establish firm local controls that reinforced central interests. Indeed, local situations, not national decisions, determined much national policy. Movements to increase the leaders' responsiveness to central concerns actually hampered the goals of centralism. Finally, differences between city and village showed little sign of declining as China modernized. On the contrary, many discrepancies, as in marriage patterns and family practices, appeared to harden as time wore on. Among latecomers, China appears spatially anomalous.

How then has China achieved the degree of success in modernization that we have credited it with? In lieu of a strong central government, we find a combination of central and regional centralizing elements, including charismatic national leadership and nationalism, a fairly centralized Communist Party, powerful political-military cliques at regional levels, and effective use of modern technologies and the mass media. In the Ch'ing period the central government relied on the family and the lineage to control its members while attempting to weaken already tenuous solidarities in the village by dividing the countryside into units that did not coincide with the villages for the purposes of taxation and surveillance. Under the PRC local modernization has again curiously rested on strengthening and balancing two tradition-minded organizations, the village (or neighborhood) in the form of

505

the production team and the rural household. These organizations actually have more meaningful resources at their command than in previous periods. As a result of their renaissance, individualism, even discounting for its limited historical foundation, has not made the usual advances associated with modernization. In fact, two characteristics of the distribution of authority in China that diverge most sharply from the ordinary expectations in treatments of modernization are the survival and prosperity of the community and the household. Both of these primary groups heavily based on kinship ties and residential propinquity contrast with the interest groups normally associated with modernization which have scarcely materialized.

A Global Perspective

In seeking to appraise China's record of modernization in the perspective of the worldwide experience of modernizing societies, it is appropriate to start out by asking two general questions: what levels of development has China achieved in pursuing the goals common to all modernizing societies? In what respect is China's modernizing experience significantly different from that of other countries?

LEVELS OF DEVELOPMENT

Most indicators of modern change lack the degree of accuracy and comparability one might wish, and such indicators are particularly scarce in the case of China. In seeking to evaluate China's development relative to other countries, one must therefore more often than not resort to general appraisals rather than to carefully calibrated comparisons. Indicators of development are based on per capita rates, but the scale of the country is also relevant in cases in which the accumulation of sufficient resources to meet particular goals is a consideration. Thus China has the capacity to develop advanced missiles even though it has a low per capita income.

Acceptance of modern knowledge and of its application to societal problems lies at the heart of development, but it is an aspect that can best be measured in terms of ultimate outcomes. Although not without interruptions, both Nationalist and communist policies have been directed toward making China a full member of the international community of learning. The establishment of the Academia Sinica in 1928 was an important step in the purposeful organization of research, indicative of a desire in the decades of Nationalist rule to make China a center of modern knowledge, and in Taiwan it has become an important research institution. In 1978 the academy in Peking was divided into two autonomous institutions: the Chinese Academy of Sciences, devoted to the natural sciences, and the Chinese Academy of Social Sciences, devoted to social sciences and humanities. This decision brings to an end a long hiatus marked by ambivalence toward foreign learning.

A major effect to bring scientific research up to date was inaugurated in 1978 with the adoption of a national plan for the development of science and technology for the period 1978–1985. Research efforts were centered on twenty-seven specific areas, and the resources devoted to this enterprise have been estimated at 1 percent of China's GNP (Suttmeier, 1980, p. 63). This compares with over 3 percent of GNP devoted to research and development in the Soviet Union and between 2 and 3 percent in most industrialized societies (National Science Foundation, 1977, p. 184). While China's effort does not at present match that of the other major powers, it is nevertheless significant for two reasons: in view of the size of China's GNP, 1 percent represents a considerable investment in research, and probably no other state at China's GNP per capita level is investing nearly as much as 1 percent in this systematic fashion.

At the same time, one should keep in mind that the PRC starts from a relatively low base of trained manpower. The limited size of the higher education establishment it inherited after years of domestic and international strife, combined with some ten years of damage caused by the Cultural Revolution, has left China with a relatively small cohort of students in training and almost an entire generation denied comparable training. One standard by which this may be judged is higher education per 1,000 of population. While this measure says nothing about quality, it does indicate how many are receiving education beyond the secondary school level. In the mid-1970s, for example, this ratio was about 50 per 1,000 for the United States, 20 each for Japan and the Soviet Union, and 5 for India. The comparable ratios for China are 0.3 per 1,000 in 1946, 0.2 in 1949, about 1.0 in 1965, 0.2 in 1972 after universities were reopened, and again about 1.0 in 1980.

Political development is also a sphere in which measurement and comparison are difficult, and what constitutes modernization in this sphere is even more controversial. Of the various possible approaches, the two aspects that seem most appropriate for a brief appraisal are administrative capacity and political participation.

Not much of China's venerable and distinguished tradition of bureaucracy based on merit survived the decline of the empire and the five decades of strife in the twentieth century. Nevertheless this heritage was an important factor in the PRC's ability to reorganize the country within a few years after it gained power in 1949 and to implement major nationwide programs subsequently. The reorganization of agriculture in several stages, the construction of a large industrial and communications base, and the establishment of nearly universal primary and greatly broadened secondary education and of medical and other social services, reflect a significantly greater administrative capacity than that of other countries at the PRC's level of economic development.

At the same time, while the PRC is able in many spheres to assume the responsibilities of a great power, its administrative capacity falls considerably short of that of other major states. The central administrative system follows the tradition of the empire, and even more the practice of the late nineteenth and early twentieth centuries when important functions were assumed by the multiprovincial, provincial, and county levels. The capacity of the central government to assert its authority in day-to-day affairs at the local level is thus relatively limited. The central government does not directly administer the affairs of the four-fifths of the population living in communes, a limitation no doubt resulting from China's nonmodernized state. The central government and the party set policies for the country, but direct administrative functions are restricted to the relatively small urban sector and to the realms of heavy industry and national security. Even so, the bureaucracy that does exist has far to go to overcome the legacy of the 1950s when a large central bureaucracy was hastily formed, and of the late 1960s and the 1970s when its functioning was impaired by leadership struggles and by the hostility toward management aroused by the Cultural Revolution. By 1980 serious doubts were being raised about the qualifications of many of the party members and officials who had been selected in previous periods.

It is more difficult to gauge the level of political participation, defining this term to mean regular and meaningful consultation by policymakers with major governmental and nongovernmental interest groups. The party apparatus plays the principal role in mediating the concerns of various major interest groups and the central authorities. As in the case of the administrative system, the four-fifths of the population in the agrarian sector plays a relatively small role. The most important interests to be taken into account are regional, as represented especially by the twenty-nine provinces; urban, including the needs of the major industries and of labor; science and technology in the broad sense, including higher education as well as the research establishment; and security, with the military in this case playing a much larger role than the police. Over much of the PRC's history, however, not all of these interests have been articulated adequately in making the major decisions that have affected people's lives. There are many avenues of participation within production teams, street committees, and other organizations, and during certain campaigns individuals who claim to follow the approved line may be able to seize the initiative, but regular channels of participation that lead to the center have had an erratic history.

The role of the party apparatus in mediating between interest groups and policymakers was reasserted after the Cultural Revolution, and is related especially to the annual and longer-term formulation of economic plans and to occasional national campaigns. A more formal symbol of political participation is the National People's Congress, which meets irregularly and possesses little real authority. There are, in addition to the Communist Party, eight small democratic parties which are permitted to play a nominal role at the national level.

In considering the economic status of contemporary China, one cannot fail to be impressed by the size of its economy, which in terms of gross national product ranks sixth in the world after the United States, the USSR, Japan, the Federal Republic of Germany, and France. The fact that these other countries have a much smaller population than China, and that for example China's GNP is less than twice that of Canada with a population of 24 million, reflects the relatively low per capita level of China.

China is one of forty-one countries with a GNP per capita of $200-$500, including Indonesia among the larger countries and numerous African and Asian states. This compares with twenty-one countries, including India, in the category below $200; Taiwan and fifty-five countries in the category of $500-$2,000; thirty-one in the category of $2,000-$5,000, including the UK, the USSR, and the socialist states of Eastern Europe; and the twenty-nine in the category above $5,000 (World Bank, 1978, p. 4). Another way of defining China's economic status is that with 23.2 percent of the world's population, it accounts for only 3.2 percent of the world's gross national product (U.S. Department of State, 1979, p. 45).

A more reliable but still not altogether satisfactory indicator of the level of economic development is the share of the labor force employed in manufacturing and services as distinct from agriculture, since these proportions unavoidably reflect most other aspects of modernization. In the advanced industrial societies some 80 percent or more of the labor force is in manufacturing and services (ILO, 1979, pp. 168–200). The comparable shares for China have been estimated at 15 percent in 1957 and 23 percent in 1975 (T. Rawski, 1979, pp. 37–39), which is below the Japanese or Russian levels in 1900. These percentages may not fully reflect the growth of manufacturing and services in China because of the extensive production of industrial goods in the communes.

The rate of growth of the Chinese economy is a matter of some dispute, but the average annual growth rate per capita for the period 1970-1977 is estimated at 4.5 percent. This places China along with Taiwan and 26 countries in a group with a growth rate of between 4 and 6 percent, as compared with 126 below this range and 25 above it (World Bank, 1978, p. 6). This rate encompasses a per capita growth rate for industry of perhaps 10 percent and a very low one for agriculture. In the late 1970s pervasive reforms aimed at birth control and agricultural improvement began to narrow this wide sectoral gap, with the most immediate effects in Szechwan province, which in 1980 was adopted as a model for the nation.

These few basic comparisons reflect an economy still at a low level of development, a condition attributable to many decades of political and social disorder prior to 1949 and the high ratio of population to resources. It is also an economy that in the 1970s had a per capita rate of growth that placed it in the upper third of the countries of the world. If this rate is maintained, the economy will double in some fifteen years, and experience will be gained in the special problems confronting China that may permit more rapid rates of growth in the future.

In the sphere of social integration, an indicator that often reflects accurately the level of development is the stage in the demographic transition—the evolution of societies from high fertility and high mortality, before the modern era, through an extended period of high fertility and low mortality, resulting in rapid population growth, to a phase of low fertility and low mortality, tending toward zero growth. With a growth rate falling to an estimated 16 per 1,000 in the period 1970-1977, China is one of 78 countries below a rate of 20 per 1,000 as is Taiwan at 2 per 1,000, which compares with 100 with a higher rate of growth (World Bank, 1978, p. 8). If at the end of the 1970s this rate was, as recently reported, reduced to 12 per 1,000, China will be entering the final low growth phase of the demographic transition—a phase with many unusual features because of the large number of women still in the child-bearing years. The PRC is making a massive effort to reduce its population growth by a variety of means. Its leaders have set themselves a target of zero growth by the year 2000, but demographers question the feasibility of this goal. Considering the deliberate and coercive features of China's fertility decline, one should not in any case assume that this indicator is a fully reliable index of modernization in its other dimensions.

The predominantly agrarian character of Chinese society is also reflected in the fact that about 20 percent of its population lives in urban areas. This compares with a similar level for African countries, 60 percent for the countries of Latin America, and 75 to 80 percent or more for the highly modernized countries. Government policies, such as household registration, rationing, restricted migration, and forced movement out of cities must be held accountable for a level of urbanization somewhat lower than one would expect. If demographic indicators exaggerate modernization, urban indicators understate it.

DISTINCTIVE FEATURES

The question of how China's modernizing experience differs from that of other countries has been given a great deal of attention in this volume and may be summarized briefly under three headings: the reluctance of intellectual and political leaders to accept modern knowledge; the progressive weakening of the premodern government; and the relations among the size of the population, China's level of technology, and the amount of arable land.

Acceptance of modern knowledge is a first essential step in the process of societal transformation, implying as it does a belief in the possibility of understanding and managing the human environment and of eventually enhancing human welfare through great increases in per capita productivity. Yet it has always been difficult for leaders to relinquish the verities of their age-old heritages and to launch out on new courses based on untried principles. The struggle between the ''ancients'' and the ''moderns,'' in a wide variety of forms, is one of the most characteristic confrontations of the modern era.

For the early modernizing societies this confrontation took place over many generations; some would see it beginning in the renaissance of the twelfth and thirteenth centuries, or at least in the scientific revolution of the seventeenth. For latecomers to modernization, however, the confrontation between tradition and modernity is more often than not intense and dramatic. The forms it takes include the rejection of modernity or of western modernizers or, at the other extreme, of inherited modes of thought and action. This confrontation resembles in some ways the conflict of generations within a family, in the course of which the daughters and sons must establish their identity by revolt before they can accept (and perhaps modify) the norms of maturity.

China represents a case in which the authority of the old regime was so great, both in its substance and in the status it gave to an elite trained exclusively in the classics, that modernity was in effect rejected by the elite until the end of the nineteenth century. Not until the twentieth century did China, under the influence of the commerce and industry of foreign-controlled seaports, of returning students with a western education, of western missionaries and educators, and especially of the example of modern transformation in Japan, begin to undergo rapid change. The first western-style university was not established until 1898, training in the classics remained the basic requirement for the civil service until 1905, and an academy of science was not established until 1928.

The other major latecomer to resist modernity in a somewhat similar fashion was the Ottoman Empire. Although its tradition of classical culture did not match that of China, the Ottoman Turks saw themselves as defenders of Islam and perceived Westerners essentially as Christian infidels and hence enemies of the faith. To adopt western ways thus involved abandonment in significant degree of the Islamic tradition. The Ottoman Empire had much closer ties with Europe than did China, in terms of cultural and commercial relations as well as geographical proximity; and its Christian minorities, representing two-fifths of the population in 1800, and one-quarter a century later, were western in outlook. Westernizing reforms were initiated half a century earlier than in China, and Islam itself underwent a gradual process of secularization. Yet the conservative leadership relying on the Ottoman Islamic tradition remained in power until the First World War, and the modernizing reforms introduced in the 1920s by the Turkish republic were regarded as revolutionary (Black, 1980, pp. 27–28). In China, after initial delays, the inherent rationalism of Confucian thought sowed the seeds for a much quicker rejection of past ways and more complete acceptance of modern knowledge.

Japan and Russia found it much easier to avoid long delays in moving from the outlook of the old regimes to that of modernity represented by the early modernizers. Their elite cultural heritages had been borrowed from China and the Byzantines, and were more varied than those of China and, to a lesser extent, the Ottoman Empire. While conservatives attached to the old values were strongly entrenched in both countries, there also existed a realization that the cultural heritage had come from abroad and could be exchanged for other foreign ways that now demonstrated their effectiveness in the form of military power. These were countries with well-organized premodern political systems, and change took place rapidly once modern-minded leaders came to power.

Similarly, countries that became colonies of the West, typically India but also many others in Asia and Africa, were introduced to western languages and modes of thought and action quite rapidly. The very fact that they became colonies reflected, in most cases, not only the vulnerability to aggression resulting from the relative weakness of their central institutions, but also their openness to foreign influences. More often than not, western languages became the main vehicle of culture and administration, and this gave the educated elite easy access to modernity.

In the late nineteenth century China stood virtually alone in the extent of the neglect by its leaders of modern culture, and this reluctance to adopt a modern outlook was enhanced by political weakness. China entered its era of modern transformation eighty years ago, with a political system that in the nineteenth century had exhibited increasing incapacity to mobilize the skills and resources required to meet the challenge of more modern states. It was another half-century before it acquired a government with the capacity to administer the entire country and to take advantage of the rapidly spreading receptivity to knowledge in the urban sector.

Such a prolonged record of political weakness on the part of a major state is rare in the modern era. Again one must turn for parallel developments to the Ottoman Empire, which resembled China, and also Japan and Russia, in having a long record of relatively effective premodern central government. Starting in the seventeenth century, however, its central authorities began to lose power to the provincial, and as its weakness progressed it came to be known as "the sick man of Europe." In some respects this decline was similar to China's in that it enabled the European states to impose militarily unequal treaties, fiscal controls, capitulations, and territorial infringements. But there were also significant differences. The empire had never achieved the cultural hegemony that in all but a few peripheral areas invariably accompanied Chinese imperial rule. The empire's minority peoples, strongly influenced by European nationalism, gained their independence one by one until the new Turkish republic established in 1921 had a population of only 13 million as compared with 27 million in 1860. The differences between the two empires in their decline—on the one hand, dismemberment with little impetus for reunification, and on the other, paralysis with an intense nationalist mood in favor of unity and centralization—are thus greater than their similarities.

These examples of administrative decline stand out in sharp contrast to the continuity of political authority in Russia and Japan from premodern into modern times. Despite a devastating revolution in Russia after World War I and a no less devastating defeat in Japan in World War II, the two governments in a few years arose from disaster like the mythical phoenix to pursue their modernizing course with renewed vigor.

The relation of China's population to its arable land is also a critical factor. While some other countries have ratios of people to land that are as high or higher than China's, these are in most cases countries where much higher levels of technology permit both more efficient and specialized agriculture and industrial production that can be traded for food. China's problem has been exacerbated by its population growth in premodern times. Between 1750 and 1850 China's population grew from about 200 to over 400 million, and by 1850 it constituted about one-third of the world's population. Thenceforth it grew somewhat more slowly to roughly 540 million in 1949, only to explode again to about 1 billion by 1980. In the eighteenth and early nineteenth centuries the population growth was not accompanied by a comparable increase in the country's administrative apparatus, and this was an important factor contributing to the political decline; the even more rapid growth after 1949 has been a major handicap confronting China's leaders in their efforts to stimulate economic growth and social integration.

CHINA'S PLACE IN THE MODERN WORLD

Our appraisal of China's level of modern development and of certain distinctive features in a world of modernizing societies suggests that it is sufficiently different from other countries in the correlations among the factors making up its modernizing experience as to constitute a case of exceptional interest. In studying China, one is impressed more than ever with the decisive role played by the premodern heritage. On the one hand, in the tradition of a culture that has recorded some of mankind's most notable achievements in the humanities and the sciences, and in the authority of a political system that can trace its lineage back some twenty centuries during many of which it had exhibited an almost unequaled capacity to mobilize skills and resources for particular challenges, China is probably comparable only to Japan and Russia among latecomers in the potentials it has brought to the tasks of modernization.

On the other hand, in the aloof lack of interest of its nineteenth-century leaders in the changes taking place in the world around them, in the weakness of its government when confronted with the challenge of more modern societies, and in the failure of its reform movements in the first half of the twentieth century to establish a stable national government with the capacity to promote science and technology, economic growth, and social integration, it resembles in one degree or another countries that are still at an early stage of modern development.

In other respects, especially its economic vitality at the local level, its urban heritage, and its institutions for promoting initiative, China shows signs of being intermediate between Japan and Russia at one extreme and other premodern countries at the other. Although for most purposes, following the conclusions of *The Modernization of Japan and Russia,* these two countries are judged to be similar in this discussion, a more extensive comparison would no doubt show many ways in which China more closely resembles Japan, for example, in literacy and respect for learning and in the freer status of the rural population, and other ways in which it is closer to Russia.

It would appear that the dilemmas confronting China today were predestined in the sense that the qualities that made China great before the nineteenth century were among those that also proved to be the main obstacles to its modern transformation. The very prestige of China as a "middle country" unchallenged for so long in its orbit as a political and cultural force, led to an unawareness of the changing relative status of that orbit and a failure to recognize the nature of the modern challenge until it appeared unavoidably at China's doorstep. Among the consequences of this failure were delays in making the reforms that might have permitted the government to cope with the new international environment, postponement until the twentieth century of the preparation of a new generation of leaders attuned to the modern world, and political and ideological disunity when faced by the crises provoked by the two world wars.

Both Nationalists and communists in China, like their peers in India and elsewhere, have been inclined to blame their difficulties on imperialism. We recognize the important role played by the foreign challenge and military threat, but we are also impressed by the examples of Russia and Japan which were stimulated by challenge to take charge of their modern destinies. In China's case in particular, where the potentialities for a vigorous national policy were so great, we find the weakness of the response rather than the strength of the challenge to be the main explanatory factor for delayed modernization.

China entered the modern world with an unusual combination of assets and liabilities, and these are reflected in the pattern of its contemporary level of development. In some respects, the PRC is, in comparison to other Asian and African countries, today close to the forefront of modernizing countries—a distinction that, not coincidentally, it shares with its much more modernized neighbors Korea, Taiwan, Hong Kong, and Singapore, all deeply influenced by the legacy that inheres in China. The capacity of its political system to mobilize skills and resources for specific goals, reflecting its bureaucratic heritage as well as the organizing ability of the Communist Party, is relatively rare among the latecomers to modernization. The average annual rate of growth of its economy in the 1970s was above the norm for countries at a comparable stage of development. In the rate of growth of its population, China is leaving the phase of rapid growth and achieving rates approaching those characteristic of highly modernized societies. Likewise, in the intensity of learning and the depth of commitment by individuals to achieving a superior education, few countries can rival China today.

In other respects, China remains a country at a low level of development and the portion of its population living in urban areas is also relatively small. Enrollment in higher education in proportion to the population is quite low, and its universities have not yet recovered from the ravages of the Cultural Revolution. Its GNP per capita is matched by many countries in Africa and Asia. The small share of its labor force in manufacturing and services is a further indication of underdevelopment.

These areas of low performance may be attributed in some measure to the high ratio of population to resources, a fundamental problem that has been intensified in the twentieth century. Neglect during a century or more of domestic turmoil has likewise played a role, as has also in the case of higher education deliberate destruction for ideological reasons. The areas of high performance, on the other hand, can be attributed to the careful planned mobilization of skills and resources by state and party for specific ends. It is also important to recognize that both types of indicators are affected to a greater degree than in other countries by restrictive state policies, such as those discouraging population growth and migration to cities.

If there is one characteristic that particularly sets China's pattern of modernization apart from that of other countries today, it is its organizational capacity. No country has adequately resolved the dilemma of the appropriate relative emphases that should be placed on investment for economic growth and distribution for consumption. In practice, which interests should bear the burden of contributing to the mobilization of resources in taxes and profits, and which should benefit from the allocation of these resources? It is not a question of one or the other, but of how much one should be sacrificed to the other. Most countries, especially including socialist countries with centrally planned economies, have opted to give priority to economic growth; and even the wealthiest countries today have pockets of poverty that reflect a limited concern for human values.

It is still too early to determine to what extent the vigorous programmatic and organizational initiatives taken since 1949 by the Chinese leadership will endure as a distinctive pattern of modernization. Since the death of Mao Tse-tung, the test of pragmatism has swept aside some earlier features of the system, but left others virtually intact. Basic elements typical of modernization under communist leadership persist. Their relevance for the future course of modernization is considerable, and it is essential to continue to examine their impact on China's development.

Only since the late 1970s have more or less reliable statistics and candid discussions of actual social conditions become available for China. To date much remains unknown or difficult to document. The census planned for 1981 promises to be an important source of information both to Chinese planners and to observers everywhere. No less important is the resurgence of the social sciences with their demands for survey data and objective analyses of social problems. The rush of new journals, new professional associations, and new international contacts should lead to an enhanced understanding of contemporary China. Nonetheless, both the shortage of trained personnel and the uncertainity of the leadership's commitment to freedom of information continue to curtail the availability of adequate materials for investigating conditions in China.

Now that a new generation of leaders is rising to power, it is appropriate to conclude this study with several questions arising from the choice of priorities during the first three decades of the PRC. Will the rural and urban working populations in the years ahead be relieved of the heavy burdens placed on them in the interest of economic growth? Will new military burdens stand in the way of such relief? Will the emphasis on equal or seniority-based rewards in work units give way to an achievement-oriented system of incentives in an effort to improve productivity?

How will leaders cope with the reality of, in effect, three, or perhaps, four, distinct populations, with unequal burdens and benefits: the 800 million peasants in more or less self-sufficient communes with little prospect of emigrating to the cities; the urban population of workers and nonspecialists, who also are normally not free to change jobs or place of residence, but who cling tightly to their urban registration; the recently upgraded specialists including those with higher education, whose skills are scarce and coveted by millions of youths readying themselves for the annual entrance exams to schools on successive levels of the educational ladder; and perhaps the small elite including party leaders, officials, and managers whose positions have been buffeted by the egalitarian and capricious assaults of the Cultural Revolution, yet who have also wielded substantial power in a system that has denigrated legal and institutional checks and balances?

One may also ask whether a greater effort will be made in the years ahead to establish a more equitable system of political participation. Will the new bureaucratic establishment, somewhat weighed down by size and by appointments and promotions based on politics rather than merit and affected by ideological factionalism, become capable of vigorous performance under the newly pragmatic leadership? Will expanding economic cooperation with modernized societies lead to a greater recognition of personal freedoms? Will the achievement by the PRC of a basic level of nutrition, security, health, and other services not easily provided in a nonmodernized society be maintained and developed in accord with the expanded economic capacity of the past decades and with future growth as well, despite other pressing claims for resources?

The answers to questions such as these depend not only on the outcome of the leadership succession and on the ability of world leaders to avert a major war involving East Asia, but also on the effectiveness of old organizations and new policies in meeting realistic goals for the "four modernizations."

Bibliography

This list consists primarily of works cited in the text and is not intended to be a complete listing of relevant scholarship.

ADSHEAD, S. A. M. *The End of the Chinese Empire.* London: Heinemann, 1973.
———. "An Energy Crisis in Early Modern China." *Ch'ing-shih wen-t'i,* 3:2 (December 1974), 20–28.

AIRD, JOHN S. *Population Estimates for the Provinces of the People's Republic of China: 1953–1974.* Washington, D.C.: U.S. Department of Commerce, 1974.

ALITTO, GUY S. *The Last Confucian: Liang Shu-ming and the Chinese Dilemma of Modernity.* Berkeley: University of California Press, 1979.

ASH, ROBERT. "Economic Aspects of Land Reform in Kiangsu, 1949–52." *China Quarterly,* 66 (June 1976), 261–292; 67 (September 1976), 519–545.

ATWELL, WILLIAM S. "Notes on Silver, Foreign Trade, and the Late Ming Economy." *Ch'ing-shih wen-t'i,* 3:8 (December 1977), 1–33.

AYERS, WILLIAM. *Chang Chih-tung and Educational Reform in China.* Cambridge, Mass.: Harvard University Press, 1971.

BARCLAY, GEORGE W., ANSLEY J. COALE, MICHAEL A. STOTO, and T. JAMES TRUSSELL. "A Reassessment of the Demography of Traditional Rural China." *Population Index,* 42 (October 1976), 606–635.

BARNETT, A. DOAK. *China on the Eve of Communist Takeover.* New York: Praeger, 1963.

BAUM, RICHARD, ed. *China's Four Modernizations: The Technological Imperative.* Boulder, Col.: Westview Press, 1980.

———. *Prelude to Revolution.* New York: Columbia University Press, 1975.

BERNSTEIN, THOMAS P. *Up to the Mountains and Down to the Villages: The Transfer of Youth from Urban to Rural China.* New Haven, Conn.: Yale University Press, 1977.

BIGGERSTAFF, KNIGHT, *The Earliest Modern Government Schools in China.* Ithaca: Cornell University Press, 1961.

———. "Modernization—and Early Modern China." *Journal of Asian Studies,* 25 (August 1966), 607–619

BLACK, CYRIL E. "A Comparative Approach to the Preconditions of Ottoman Modernization." *International Journal of Turkish Studies,* 1 (1980), 25–37.

———. *The Dynamics of Modernization.* New York: Harper and Row, 1967.

BLACK, CYRIL E., MARIUS B. JANSEN, HERBERT S. LEVINE, MARION J. LEVY, JR., HENRY ROSOVSKY, GILBERT ROZMAN, HENRY D. SMITH II, and S. FREDERICK STARR. *The Modernization of Japan and Russia.* New York: Free Press, 1975.

BLEACHER, MARK. "Income Distribution in Small Rural Chinese Communities." *China Quarterly,* 68 (December 1976), 797–816.

BORTHWICK, SALLY. "Schooling and Society in Late Qing China." Ph.D. dissertation, Australian National University, 1978.

BRUGGER, WILLIAM. *Democracy and Organization in the Chinese Industrial Enterprise 1948–1953.* Cambridge: Cambridge University Press, 1976.

BUCK, DAVID D. *Urban Change in China: Politics and Development in Tsinan, Shantung, 1890–1949.* Madison: University of Wisconsin Press, 1978.

BUCK JOHN L. *Land Utilization in China.* 3 vols. Nanking: University of Nanking Press, 1937.

The Cambridge History of China. Vol. 10, pt. 1 and vol. 11, pt. 2, *Late Ch'ing 1800–1911.* New York: Cambridge University Press, 1978 and 1980.

CARLSON, ELLSWORTH C. *The Foochow Missionaries, 1847–1880.* Cambridge, Mass.: Harvard East Asian Monographs, 1974.

———. "The Kailan Mines, 1878–1912." *Papers on China,* 3 (1949), 24–77.

CASSOU, PIERRE-HENRI. "The Chinese Monetary System." *China Quarterly,* 59 (July-September 1974), 559–566.

CENTRAL INTELLIGENCE AGENCY. *China: Economic Indicators.* Washington, D.C.: Central Intelligence Agency, 1977 and 1978.

CHANG, CHUNG-LI. *The Chinese Gentry: Studies on Their Role in the Nineteenth Century.* Seattle: University of Washington Press, 1955.

———. *The Income of the Chinese Gentry.* Seattle: University of Washington Press, 1962.

CHANG, HSIN-I. *An Estimate of China's Farms and Crops.* Nanking, 1932.

CHANG, HSIN-PAO. *Commissioner Lin and the Opium War.* Cambridge, Mass.: Harvard University Press, 1964.

CHANG, JOHN K. *Industrial Development in Pre-Communist China.* Chicago: Aldine, 1969.

CHANG NAI-WEN. *Shih-chieh nien-chien* (World Yearbook). Shanghai: Lo-hua ch'u-pan she, 1936.

CHANG, PARRIS H. *Power and Policy in China.* University Park: Pennsylvania State University Press, 1975.

Bibliography

CHANG TE-CH'ANG. *Ch'ing-chi i-ko ching-kuan te sheng-huo* (The Life of a Capital Official in Late Ch'ing Times). Hong Kong: Hsiang-kang Chung-wen ta-hsueh, 1970.

CH'EN CHEN, ed., *Chung-kuo chin-tai kung-yeh-shih tzu-liao* (Materials on China's Modern Industrial History). Vol. 4. Peking: San-lien shu-tien, 1961.

CHEN, FU-MEI CHANG and RAMON H. MYERS. "Customary Law and the Economic Growth of China during the Ch'ing Period." *Ch'ing-shih wen-t'i*, 3:5 (November 1976), 1–32.

CH'EN, JEROME. *Great Lives Observed: Mao.* Englewood Cliffs, N.J.: Prentice-Hall, 1969.

——. *Mao and the Chinese Revolution.* New York: Oxford University Press, 1967.

CHEN, NAI-RUENN, ed. *Chinese Economic Statistics: A Handbook for Mainland China.* Chicago: Aldine, 1967.

CHEN, THEODORE H. E., ed. *The Chinese Communist Regime: Documents and Commentary.* New York: Praeger, 1967.

CH'EN TUNG-YUAN. *Chung-kuo chiao-yü-shih* (History of Chinese Education). Shanghai: Shang-wu yin-shu-kuan, 1937.

CHENG CHU-YUAN. *Chung-kung ts'ai-ching cheng-ts'e hsin tung-hsiang* (New Trends in Chinese Communist Fiscal and Economic Policies). Hong Kong: Tzu-yu ch'u-pan she, 1953.

CHESNEAUX, JEAN. *China: The People's Republic, 1949–1976.* Hassocks: Harvester Press, 1978.

——, ed. *Popular Movements and Secret Societies in China, 1840–1950.* Stanford: Stanford University Press, 1972.

CH'I, HSI-SHENG. *Warlord Politics in China. 1916–1928.* Stanford: Stanford University Press, 1976

CH'IEN, TUAN-SHENG. *The Government and Politics of China.* Cambridge, Mass.: Harvard University Press, 1950.

China and the Chinese. Joint Economic Committee, U.S. Congress, Washington, D.C., 1976.

China Handbook, 1937–1944. Chungking: Chinese Ministry of Information, 1944.

China Mission Handbook. 1896.

Chinese Economy Post-Mao. Joint Economic Committee, U.S. Congress. Washington, D.C., 1978.

CHOU HSIU-LUAN. *Ti-i-tz'u shih-chieh ta-chan shih-ch'i Chung-kuo min-tsu kung-yeh ti fa-chan.* Shanghai: Jen-min ch'u-pan she, 1958.

CHU HSIEN-FANG. "San-shih nien-lai Chung-kuo chih fang-chih kung-ch'eng" (Engineering in China's Textile Manufacturing during the Past Thirty Years). In Chung-kuo kung-ch'eng-shih hsueh-hui, ed., *San-shih nien-lai chih Chung-kuo kung-ch'eng.* Nanking, 1936, pp. 1–6.

CH'Ü, T'UNG-TSU. *Local Government under the Ch'ing.* Stanford: Stanford University Press, 1962.

CH'UAN, HAN-SHENG and RICHARD A. KRAUS. *Mid-Ch'ing Rice Markets and Trade: An Essay in Price History.* Cambridge, Mass.: Harvard University Press, 1975.

Bibliography

CHUANG TSE-HSUAN. *Ju-he shih hsin chiao-yü Chung-kuo-hua* (How Can the New Education Be Made Chinese). Hong Kong: Chung-hua shu-chü, 1938.

Chung-hua nien-pao (China Yearbook). Taipei: Chung-kuo hsin-wen ch'u-pan she, 1957.

Chung-kung yen-chiu yueh-k'an (Research Monthly on Chinese Communism). Taipei.

Chung-kuo ching-chi (China's Economy). Peking.

CLIFFORD, NICHOLAS. *Shanghai, 1925: Urban Nationalism and the Defense of Foreign Privilege.* Ann Arbor: University of Michigan Press, 1979.

COHEN, JEROME A. "China's Changing Constitution." *China Quarterly,* 76 (December 1978), 794–841.

Conference on Modern Chinese Economic History. Taipei: The Institute of Economics, Academia Sinica, 1978.

DERNBERGER, ROBERT F. "Economic Development and Modernization in Contemporary China: The Attempt to Limit Dependence on the Transfer of Modern Industrial Technology from Abroad and to Control Its Corruption of the Maoist Social Revolution." In Frederic J. Fleron, Jr., ed., *Technology and Communist Culture.* New York: Praeger, 1977, pp. 224–264.

DERNBERGER, ROBERT F. and JEROME COHEN. *China Trade Prospects and U.S. Trade Policy.* New York: Praeger, 1971.

DOMES, J. *China after the Cultural Revolution: Politics between Two Party Congresses.* Berkeley: University of California Press, 1977.

DONNITHORNE, AUDREY. *China's Economic System,* New York: Praeger, 1967.

DORRILL, WILLIAM F. "The Transfer of Legitimacy in the Chinese Comunist Party: Origins of the Maoist Myth." *China Quarterly,* 36 (October–December 1968), 46–60.

DULLES, FOSTER RHEA. *China and America: The Story of Their Relations since 1784.* Princeton: Princeton University Press, 1946.

EBERSTADT, NICK. *Poverty in China.* Bloomington: International Development Institute, Indiana University, 1979.

ECKLUND, GEORGE N. *Financing the Chinese Government Budget: Mainland China, 1950–1959.* Chicago: Aldine, 1966.

ECKSTEIN, ALEXANDER. *China's Economic Revolution.* Cambridge: Cambridge University Press, 1977.

EDMUNDS, C. K. "Modern Education in China." U.S. Department of the Interior Bulletin no. 44, 1919.

ELVIN, MARK. *The Pattern of the Chinese Past: A Social and Economic Interpretation.* Stanford: Stanford University Press, 1972.

ELVIN, MARK and G. WILLIAM SKINNER. *The Chinese City between Two Worlds.* Stanford: Stanford University Press, 1974.

EMERSON, JOHN P. *Administrative and Technical Manpower in the People's Republic of China.* International Population Reports, Series, p. 95, no. 72. Washington, D.C.: U.S. Department of Commerce, 1973.

ESHERICK, JOSEPH W. *Reform and Revolution in China: The 1911 Revolution in Hunan and Hubei.* Berkeley: University of California Press, 1975.

Bibliography

FAIRBANK, JOHN K., ed. *The Chinese World Order: Traditional China's Foreign Relations.* Cambridge, Mass.: Harvard University Press, 1968.

——. *Trade and Diplomacy on the China Coast: The Opening of the Treaty Ports.* 2 vols. Cambridge, Mass.: Harvard University Press, 1953.

FEUERWERKER, ALBERT. *China's Early Industrialization: Sheng Hsuan-huai and Mandarin Enterprise.* Cambridge, Mass.: Harvard University Press, 1958.

——. *The Chinese Economy, ca. 1870–1911.* Michigan Papers in Chinese Studies no. 1. Ann Arbor: University of Michigan Center for Chinese Studies, 1969.

——. *Economic Trends in the Republic of China, 1912–1949.* Ann Arbor: University of Michigan Center for Chinese Studies, 1977.

——, ed. *History in Communist China.* Cambridge, Mass.: MIT Press, 1968.

FONG, H. D., *The Growth and Decline of Rural Industrial Enterprise in North China.* Tientsin: Chihli Press, 1936.

FRANKE, HERBERT. "Treaties between Sung and Chin." In Françoise Aubin, ed., *Etudes Song: Sung Studies in Memoriam Etienne Balazs.* The Hague: Mouton, 1970.

FRANKE, WOLFGANG. *The Reform and Abolition of the Traditional Chinese Examination System.* Cambridge, Mass.: Harvard University Press, 1960.

FU CHIA-LIN, ed. *Fu-chien-sheng nung-ts'un ching-chi ts'an-k'ao tzu-liao hui-pien* (Materials on the Village Economy of Fukien Province). Yung-an, Fukien: Fu-chien-sheng yin-hang ching-chi yen-chiu-shih, 1941.

FU PING-HSIUNG. *Code Civil de la République de la Chine.* Paris: Recueil Sirey, 1930–1931.

——. *Tsui hsin liu-fa ch'uan-shu* (New Compendium on the Six Laws). Taipei: Hsin-lu shu-chü, 1954.

FUJIWARA SADAO. "Kindai Chugoku ni okeru toshi zandaka no suikei" (An Estimate of Net Foreign Investment in Modern China). *Tōa keizai kenkyū,* 45:4 (November 1976), 15–55.

GALLIN, BERNARD, "Land Reform in Taiwan: Its Effects on Rural Social Organization and Leadership." *Human Organization,* 22:2 (Summer 1963), 109–112.

GAMBLE, SIDNEY D. *Ting Hsien, A North China Rural Community.* New York: International Secretariat, Institute of Pacific Relations, 1954.

GERSCHENKRON, ALEXANDER. *Economic Backwardness in Historical Perspective.* New York: Praeger, 1962.

GITTINGS, JOHN. *The Role of the Chinese Army.* New York: Oxford University Press, 1967.

GLASSMAN, J. "Change and Continuity in Chinese Communist Education Policy: 'Two-line Struggle' versus Incremental Trends." *Contemporary China,* 2:2 (Summer 1978), 51–70.

GRAY, JACK, ed. *Modern China's Search for a Political Form.* London: Oxford University Press, 1969.

HABOUSH, JA HYUN KIM. "The Fall of the Ming Dynasty and the Korean Legitimacy Crisis of the Seventeenth Century." Ms.

HARRISON, JAMES PINCKNEY. *The Long March to Power: A History of the Chinese Communist Party, 1917–72.* New York: Praeger, 1972.

HO, PING-TI. *Studies on the Population of China.* Cambridge, Mass.: Harvard University Press, 1959.

Bibliography

Ho, Samuel P. S. *The Economic Development of Taiwan, 1860–1970.* New Haven: Yale University Press, 1978.

Hofheinz, Roy, Jr. *The Broken Wave: The Chinese Communist Peasant Movement, 1922–1928.* Cambridge, Mass.: Harvard University Press, 1977.

———. "The Ecology of Chinese Communist Success: Rural Influence Patterns, 1923–45." In A. Doak Barnett, ed., *Chinese Communist Politics in Action.* Seattle: University of Washington Press, 1969, pp. 3–77.

Howe, Christopher. *China's Economy: A Basic Guide.* London: Paul Elek, 1978.

Hsiao, Chi-jung. *Revenue and Disbursement of Communist China.* Hong Kong: Union Research Institute, 1954.

Hsiao, Kung-chuan (K. C.). *A History of Chinese Political Thought.* Vol 1. Translated by F. W. Mote. Princeton: Princeton University Press, 1979.

———. *A Modern China and a New World.* Seattle: University of Washington Press, 1975.

———. *Rural China: Imperial Control in the Nineteenth Century.* Seattle: University of Washington Press, 1960.

Hsiao, Liang-lin. *China's Foreign Trade Statistics, 1864–1949.* Cambridge, Mass.: Harvard University Press, 1974.

Hsin-wen jih-pao (News Daily). Shanghai.

Hsu, Immanuel. *The Rise of Modern China.* New York: Oxford University Press, 1970.

Huang, Ray. "Institutions." In "The State of Ming Studies: A Symposium." *Ming Studies,* 2 (1976), 6–12.

Hucker, Charles O. "Government Organization of the Ming Dynasty." *Harvard Journal of Asiatic Studies,* 21 (1958), 1–66 and 23 (1960–1961), 127–151.

International Labour Office. *Year Book of Labour Statistics 1979.* Geneva, 1979.

Iriye, Akira. *After Imperialism: The Search for a New Order in the Far East, 1921–1931.* Cambridge, Mass.: Harvard University Press, 1965.

Jansen, Marius B. *Japan and China: From War to Peace 1894–1972.* Chicago: Rand McNally, 1975.

Jen-min jih-pao (People's Daily). Peking.

Jing Su and Luo Lun. *Landlord and Labor in Late Imperial China: Case Studies from Shandong.* Translated by Endymion Wilkinson. Cambridge, Mass.: Harvard University Press, 1978.

Johnson, Chalmers A. *Ideology and Politics in Contemporary China.* Seattle: University of Washington Press, 1973.

———. *Peasant Nationalism and Communist Power: The Emergence of Revolutionary China, 1937–1945.* Stanford: Stanford University Press, 1962.

Jones, Susan Mann. "Scholasticism and Politics in Late Eighteenth Century China." *Ch'ing-shih wen-t'i,* 3:4 (1974), 28–49.

Juan Hsiang. *Chung-kuo nien-chien* (China Yearbook). Shanghai: Shang-wu yin-shu kuan, 1924.

Kapp, Robert A. *Szechuan and the Chinese Republic: Provincial Militarism and Central Power, 1911–1938.* New Haven: Yale University Press, 1973.

Kau, Ying-mao. "Urban and Rural Strategies in the Chinese Communist Revolution." In John Wilson Lewis, ed., *Peasant Rebellion & Communist Revolution in Asia.* Stanford: Stanford University Press, 1974, pp. 253–270.

KLATT, W. "Cost of Food Basket in Urban Areas of the People's Republic of China." *China Quarterly,* 70 (June 1977), 407–408.

KRAUS, RICHARD CURT. "Withdrawing from the World-System: Self-Reliance and Class Structure in China." In Walter F. Goldfrank, ed., *The World System of Capitalism Past and Present.* Beverly Hills, Cal.: Sage Publications, 1979, pp. 237–259.

Kuang-ming jih-pao. Peking.

KUHN, PHILIP. *Rebellion and Its Enemies in Late Imperial China: Militarization and Social Structure, 1796–1864.* Cambridge, Mass.: Harvard University Press, 1970.

K'UNG HSIANG-HSI [H. H. KUNG], ed. *Ts'ai-cheng nien-chien* (Finance Yearbook). Nanking: Ts'ai-cheng pu, 1935.

LAMPTON, DAVID M. *Health, Conflict and the Chinese Political System.* Ann Arbor: University of Michigan Press, 1974.

———. "Performance and the Chinese Political System: A Preliminary Assessment of Education and Health Policies." *China Quarterly,* 75 (September 1978), 509–539.

Lao-tung pao (Labor News). Shanghai.

LARDY, NICHOLAS R. "Central Control and Redistribution in China: Central-Provincial Fiscal Relations since 1949." Ph.D dissertation, University of Michigan, 1975a.

———. "Centralization and Decentralization in China's Fiscal Management." *China Quarterly,* 61 (March 1975b), 25–60.

LEVENSON, JOSEPH. *Confucian China and Its Modern Fate.* Combined ed. Berkeley: University of California Press, 1968.

LEVY, MARION J., JR. *Modernization and the Structure of Societies.* Princeton: Princeton University Press, 1966.

LEWIS, JOHN WILSON. *Communist China, Crisis and Challenge.* New York: Foreign Policy Association, 1966.

———. *Leadership in Communist China.* Ithaca: Cornell University Press, 1963.

———. "Political Aspects of Mobility in China's Urban Development." *American Political Science Review,* 60:4 (December 1966), 899–912.

LEYS, SIMON (PIERRE RYCKMANS). *Chinese Shadows.* New York: Viking Press, 1977.

LI, CHIEN-NUNG. *The Political History of China, 1840–1928.* Translated by Teng Ssu-yü. Princeton: Van Nostrand, 1956.

LI, CHOH-MING. *Economic Development of Communist China.* Berkeley: University of California Press, 1959.

LIANG CH'I-CH'AO. "Hsin-min shuo" (On The Renovation of the People) (Part Two), *Hsin-min ts'ung-pao hui-pien: hsu-k'an,* 1903.

———. *Intellectual Trends in the Ch'ing Period.* Translated by IMMANUEL C. Y. HSU. Cambridge, Mass.: Harvard University Press, 1959.

———. "Lun hsueh-hsiao: tsung-lun" (On Schools: General Discussion). *Shih-wu pao,* 5 (1896).

LIAO, T'AI-CH'U. "Rural Education in Transition: A Study of the Old-fashioned

Chinese Schools (Szu Shu) in Shantung and Szechuan.'' *Yenching Journal of Social Studies,* 412 (1949), 19-67.

LIEBERTHAL, KENNETH (with JAMES TONG and SAI-CHEUNG YEUNG). *Central Documents and Politburo Politics in China.* Ann Arbor: University of Michigan Center for Chinese Studies, 1978.

LIPPIT, VICTOR D. *Land Reform and Economic Development in China.* White Plains, N.Y.: International Arts and Sciences Press, 1974.

LIU, ALAN P. L. *Communications and National Integration in Communist China.* Berkeley: University of California Press, 1971.

LIU MU and CH'EN SHOU-CH'U. *Shih-chieh t'ung-chien* (World Informer). Hong Kong: Shih-chieh ch'u-pan she, 1956.

LIU, TA-CHUNG and K. C. YEH. *The Economy of the Chinese Mainland.* Princeton: Princeton University Press, 1965.

MACDOUGALL, COLINA. ''The Chinese Economy in 1976.'' *China Quarterly,* 70 (June 1977), 355-370.

MARTIN, W. A. P. *Hanlin Papers, or Essays on the Intellectual Life of the Chinese.* London: Trubner & Co., 1880.

MAO TSE-TUNG. *A Critique of Soviet Economics.* New York: Monthly Review Press, 1977.

―――. *Selected Works of Mao Tse-tung.* Vols. 1-4. Peking: Foreign Languages Press, 1961-1965.

MEADOWS, THOMAS TAYLOR. *The Chinese and Their Rebellions.* London: Smith Elder and Co., 1856.

MENCIUS. Translated by James Legge. New York: Hurd and Houghton, 1870.

METZGER, THOMAS A. *The Internal Organization of Ch'ing Bureaucracy: Legal, Normative, and Communication Aspects.* Cambridge, Mass.: Harvard University Press, 1973.

―――. *Escape from Predicament: Neo-Confucianism and China's Evolving Political Culture.* New York: Columbia University Press, 1977.

MICHAEL, FRANZ and GEORGE E. TAYLOR. *The Far East in the Modern World.* 3rd ed. Hinsdale, Ill.: Dryden Press, 1975.

MILAM, AVA B. ''Standards of Living among Intermediate Income Groups in China.'' *Journal of Home Economics,* 19:8 (August 1927), 427-438.

MIYAZAKI, ICHISADA. *China's Examination Hell.* New York and Tokyo: Weatherhill, 1976.

MORSE, HOSEA BALLOU. *The International Relations of the Chinese Empire.* 3 vols. London: Longmans, Green, 1910-1918.

MOSER, CHARLES K. *Where China Buys and Sells.* Washington, D.C.: U.S. Government Printing Office, 1935.

MOTE, F. W. ''The City in Traditional Chinese Civilization.'' In James T. C. Liu and Wei-ming Tu, eds., *Traditional China.* Englewood Cliffs, N.J.: Prentice-Hall, 1970, pp. 42-49.

―――. ''Yuan and Ming.'' In K. C. Chang, ed., *Food in Chinese Culture.* New Haven: Yale University Press. 1977, pp. 195-252.

MOULDER, FRANCIS V. *Japan, China and the World Economy.* Cambridge: Cambridge University Press, 1977.

MUHUA, CHEN, "Birth Planning in China." *International Family Planning Perspectives,* 5 (September 1979), 92–101.

MURPHEY, RHOADS. *The Outsiders: The Western Experience in China and India.* Ann Arbor: University of Michigan Press, 1977.

——. *Shanghai, Key to Modern China.* Cambridge, Mass.: Harvard University Press, 1953.

——. *The Treaty Ports and China's Modernization: What Went Wrong.* Ann Arbor: University of Michigan Press, 1970.

MYERS, RAMON H. *The Chinese Economy, Past and Present.* Belmont, Cal.: Wadsworth, 1980.

——. *The Chinese Peasant Economy: Agricultural Development in Hopei and Shantung, 1890–1949.* Cambridge, Mass.: Harvard University Press, 1970.

MYERS, RAMON H. and ULIE, THOMAS R. "Foreign Influence and Agricultural Development in Northeast China: A Case Study of the Liaotung Peninsula, 1907–45." *Journal of Asian Studies,* 31 (February 1972), 325–350.

NATIONAL SCIENCE FOUNDATION, NATIONAL SCIENCE BOARD. *Science Indicators 1976.* Washington, D.C., 1977.

NEEDHAM, JOSEPH. *The Grand Titration: Science and Society in East and West.* London: George Allen & Unwin, 1969.

NELSON, HARVEY W. *The Chinese Military System.* Boulder, Col.: Westview Press, 1977.

OKITA, SABURO. "Japan, China and the United States." *Foreign Affairs,* 57:5 (Summer 1979), 1040–1110.

PA CHIN (LI FEI-KAN). *Shang-hai wen-hsueh* (Shanghai Literature).

PARISH, WILLIAM L. "Factions in Chinese Military Politics." *China Quarterly,* 56 (October–December 1973), 667–699.

PARISH, WILLIAM L. and MARTIN KING WHYTE. *Village and Family in Contemporary China.* Chicago: University of Chicago Press, 1978.

PASSIN, HERBERT. *Society and Education in Japan.* New York: Teachers College, Columbia University, 1965.

PEPPER, SUZANNE. "Education and Revolution: The 'Chinese Model' Revisited." *Asian Survey,* 18:9 (September 1978), 847–890.

PERKINS, DWIGHT H. *Agricultural Development in China, 1368–1968,* Chicago: Aldine, 1969.

——, ed. *China's Modern Economy in Historical Perspective.* Stanford: Stanford University Press, 1975.

Plant Studies in the People's Republic of China. Washington, D.C.: National Academy of Sciences, 1975.

PRINGSHEIM, KLAUS H. "The Functions of the Chinese Communist Youth Leagues (1920–1949)." *China Quarterly,* 12 (October–December 1962), 75–91.

PRYBYLA, JAN S. "A Note on Incomes and Prices in China." *Asian Survey,* 15:3 (March 1975), 266–278.

RAWSKI, EVELYN SAKAKIDA. *Education and Popular Literacy in Ch'ing China.* Ann Arbor: University of Michigan Press, 1979.

RAWSKI, THOMAS G. *Economic Growth and Employment in China.* New York: Oxford University Press, 1979.

Bibliography

RAY, J. FRANKLIN, JR. *UNRRA in China*. New York: International Secretariat, Institute of Pacific Relations, 1947.

RIDLEY, CHARLES P. *China's Scientific Policies: Implications for International Cooperation.* Washington, D.C.: American Enterprise Institute for Public Policy Research, 1976.

————. "Educational Theory and Practice in Late Imperial China: The Teaching of Writing as a Specific Case." Ph.D. dissertation, Stanford University, 1973.

ROLL, CHARLES ROBERT, JR. *The Distribution of Rural Income in China: A Comparison of the 1930s and the 1950s.* New York: Garland, 1980.

ROZMAN, GILBERT. *Population and Markets in Ch'ing China: Studies of Aggregate Data from North China.* New York: Cambridge University Press, 1982.

————. *Urban Networks in Ch'ing China and Tokugawa Japan.* Princeton: Princeton University Press, 1973.

————. *Urban Networks in Russia, 1750–1800, and Premodern Periodization.* Princeton: Princeton University Press, 1976.

RUSSETT, BRUCE, M., et al. *World Handbook of Political and Social Indicators.* New Haven: Yale University Press, 1964.

SCALAPINO, ROBERT A., ed. *Elites in the People's Republic of China.* Seattle: University of Washington Press, 1972.

SCALAPINO, ROBERT A. and GEORGE YU. *The Chinese Anarchist Movement.* Berkeley: University of California Press, 1961.

SCHRAN, PETER. "China's Demographic Evolution Reconsidered." *China Quarterly,* 75 (September 1978), 639–648.

————. *Guerrilla Economy: The Development of the Shensi-Kansu-Ninghsia Border Region, 1937–1945.* Albany: State University of New York Press, 1976.

SCHRECKER, JOHN E. *Imperialism and Chinese Nationalism: Germany in Shantung.* Cambridge, Mass.: Harvard University Press, 1971.

SCHURMANN, FRANZ. *Ideology and Organization in Communist China.* Berkeley: University of California Press, 1966.

SCHWARTZ, BENJAMIN. *In Search of Wealth and Power.* Cambridge, Mass.: Harvard University Press, 1964.

Shan-hsi nung-ts'un ching-chi tiao-ch'a (A Survey of the Shansi Rural Economy). Vol. 1. T'ai-yuan: Shan-hsi jen-min ch'u-pan she, 1958.

SHANG, YEN-LIU. *Ch'ing-tai k'e-chü k'ao-shih shu-lu* (A Descriptive Account of the Civil Service Examination under the Ch'ing). Peking: San-lien shu-tien, 1958.

SHEN, SUNG-FANG. Jen-min nien-chien (People's Yearbook). Hong Kong: Ta-kung shu-chü, 1950.

SHERIDAN, JAMES E. *China in Disintegration: The Republican Era in Chinese History 1912–1949.* New York: Free Press, 1975.

Shih-chieh chih-shih nien-chien (Yearbook of World Knowledge). Peking: Shih-chieh chih-shih ch'u-pan she, 1958.

SIGURDSON, JON. *Rural Industrialization in China.* Cambridge, Mass.: Harvard East Asian Monographs, 1977.

SIH, PAUL K. T., ed. *Strenuous Decade: China's Nation Building Efforts, 1927–37.* Jamaica, N.Y.: St. John's University Press, 1970.

Bibliography

SKINNER, G. WILLIAM, ed. *The City in Late Imperial China.* Stanford: Stanford University Press, 1977.

———. "Marketing and Social Structure in Rural China." *Journal of Asian Studies,* 24: 1–3 (1964–1965).

SMIL, VACLAV. *China's Energy: Achievements, Problems, Prospects.* New York: Praeger, 1976a.

———. "Energy in China: Achievements and Prospects." *China Quarterly,* 65 (March 1976b), 54–81.

SPENCE, JONATHAN. *To Change China: Western Advisers in China, 1620–1960.* Boston: Little, Brown and Co., 1969.

STATE STATISTICAL BUREAU. "Communique on Fulfilment of China's 1978 National Economic Plan." *Peking Review,* 27 (July 6, 1979).

SUTTMEIER, RICHARD. *Science, Technology and China's Drive for Modernization.* Stanford: Stanford University Press, 1980.

SWAMY, SUBRAMANIAM. "Economic Growth in China and India, 1952–1970: A Comparative Appraisal." *Economic Development and Cultural Change,* 21:4, Part 2 (July 1973), 1–85.

———. "The Response to Economic Challenge: A Comparative Economic History of China and India, 1870–1952." *Quarterly Journal of Economics,* 93:1 (February 1979), 25–46.

SWISHER, EARL. *China's Management of the American Barbarians: A Study in the Relations between the United States and China from 1840 to 1860, with Documents.* New Haven: Far Eastern Publications, 1953.

TANG, ANTHONY. "Input-Output Relations in the Agriculture of Communist China, 1952–1965." In W. A. Douglass Jackson, ed., *American Policies and Problems in Communist and Non-Communist Countries.* Seattle: University of Washington Press, 1971, pp. 280–301.

TAWNEY, RICHARD HENRY. *Land and Labor in China.* New York: Harcourt & Brace, 1932

TEIWES, FREDERICK C. *Provincial Leadership in China: The Cultural Revolution and Its Aftermath.* Ithaca: Cornell University China-Japan Program, 1974.

———. *Provincial Party Personnel in Mainland China, 1945–1966.* New York: Columbia University East Asian Institute, 1967.

TENG, SSU-YÜ and JOHN K. FAIRBANK. *China's Response to the West: A Documentary Survey.* Cambridge, Mass.: Harvard University Press, 1954; New York: Atheneum, 1963.

TIEN, HUNG-MAO. *Government and Politics in Kuomintang China, 1927–1937.* Stanford: Stanford University Press, 1972.

———. "Taiwan in Transition: Prospects for Socio-Political Change." *China Quarterly,* 65 (December 1975), 615–644.

TOWNSEND, JAMES R. *Political Participation in Communist China.* Berkeley: University of California Press, 1967.

———. *Politics in China.* Boston: Little, Brown and Co., 1974.

UNGER, JONATHAN. *Education under Mao.* New York: Columbia University Press, forthcoming.

Bibliography

United Nations. *Statistical Yearbook 1978.* New York, 1979.

United States Department of State. *The Planetary Product.* Special Report no. 58, Washington, D.C., 1979.

Vogel, Ezra. *Canton under Communism: Programs and Politics in a Provincial Capital 1949-1968.* Cambridge, Mass.: Harvard University Press, 1969.

―――. "Early Meiji 1868-1890 and Mao's China 1949-1971." In Albert Craig, ed., *Japan, A Comparative View.* Princeton: Princeton University Press, 1979, pp. 130-153.

Wakeman, Frederic, Jr. *The Fall of Imperial China.* New York: Free Press, 1975.

―――. *History and Will: Philosophical Perspectives on Mao Tse-tung's Thought.* Berkeley: University of California Press, 1973.

Wakeman, Frederic, Jr. and Carolyn Grant, eds. *Conflict and Control in Late Imperial China.* Berkeley: University of California Press, 1975.

Wang, Foh-shen. "China's Industrial Production 1931-1946." *Social Sciences Study Papers,* 2 (1948), 1-17.

Wang, Y. C. *Chinese Intellectuals and the West, 1872-1949.* Chapel Hill: University of North Carolina Press, 1968.

Wang, Yeh-chien. *Land Taxation in Imperial China, 1750-1911.* Cambridge, Mass.: Harvard University Press, 1973.

Watson, James L. "Hereditary Tenancy and Corporate Landlordism in Traditional China: A Case Study." *Modern Asian Studies,* 11 (1977), 161-182.

Weber, Max. *The Religion of China.* Glencoe, Ill.: Free Press, 1951.

Weng, Chih-yung. *Min-kuo ts'ai-cheng chien-lun* (An Examination of the National Finance). Taipei: Hua-kuo ch'u-pan she, 1952.

White, Lynn T. III. *Careers in Shanghai: The Social Guidance of Personal Energies in a Developing Chinese City, 1949-1966.* Berkeley: University of California Press, 1978.

Whitson, William W. (with Chen-hsia Huang). *The Chinese High Command: A History of Military Politics, 1927-71.* New York: Praeger, 1973.

Whyte, Martin King. *Small Groups and Political Rituals in China.* Berkeley: University of California Press, 1974.

―――. "The Ta-chai Brigade and Incentives for the Peasant." *Current Scene,* 17:6 (August 15, 1969), 1-17.

Williams, Bobby A. *China: Grain Output Growth and Productivity, 1957-72.* Washington, D.C.: Central Intelligence Agency, 1974.

Willmott, W. E., ed. *Economic Organization in Chinese Society.* Stanford: Stanford University Press, 1972.

Woodard, Kim. *The International Energy Relations of China.* Stanford: Stanford University Press, 1980.

World Bank. *Atlas 1978.* Washington, D.C., 1978.

Wright, Mary, ed. *China in Revolution: The First Phase, 1900-1913.* New Haven: Yale University Press, 1968.

Wu, Silas. *Communication and Imperial Control in China: Evolution of the Palace Memorial System, 1693-1735.* Cambridge, Mass.: Harvard University Press, 1970.

Bibliography

WU, YUAN-LI. *Income Distribution in the Process of Economic Growth in the Republic of China.* Baltimore: University of Maryland School of Law, 1977.

YAMANE, YUKIO. " 'Shantung sheng Tzu-yang hsien hu-ts'e' ni tsuite" (Concerning the Household Register of Tzu-yang County in Shantung Province). *Tokyo Jōshi daigaku fuzoku hikaku bunka kenkyūjō kiyō,* (June 1963), 23–111.

YEH, K. C. "Capital Formation in Mainland China: 1931–36 and 1952–57." Ph.D. dissertation, Columbia University, 1965.

YEN CHUNG-P'ING, comp. *Chung-kuo chin-tai ching-chi-shih t'ung-chi tzu-liao hsuan-chi* (Selected Statistical Materials on Modern Chinese Economic History). Peking: K'o-hsueh ch'u-pan she, 1955.

YOUNG, ARTHUR N. *China's Nation-building Effort, 1927–1937: The Financial and Economic Record.* Stanford: Hoover Institution Press, 1971.

———. *China's Wartime Finance and Inflation, 1937–1945.* Cambridge, Mass.: Harvard University Press, 1965.

Notes on the Authors

THOMAS P. BERNSTEIN is associate professor of political science at Columbia University. His teaching and research interests include Chinese politics and comparative communism.

CYRIL E. BLACK is Shelby Cullom Davis Professor of European History and director of the Center of International Studies at Princeton University. His teaching and research interests include Russia and Eastern Europe, modernization, and comparative communism.

SALLY BORTHWICK received her Ph.D. from the Australian National University in 1978 and currently is in Singapore pursuing research on Chinese education.

MARIUS B. JANSEN is professor of history and East Asian studies at Princeton University. He is a specialist in Japanese history and in Sino-Japanese relations.

MARION J. LEVY, JR. is Musgrave Professor of Sociology and International Affairs in the Woodrow Wilson School and chairman of the Department of East Asian Studies at Princeton University. His teaching and research interests include modernization and social change in China and Japan.

F.W. MOTE is professor of East Asian studies at Princeton University. He is a specialist in Chinese history.

Notes on the Authors

RAMON H. MYERS is scholar-curator of the East Asian collection at the Hoover Institution, Stanford, California. He is a specialist in Chinese economic history.

GILBERT ROZMAN is professor of sociology at Princeton University. His teaching and research interests include China, Japan, and Russia and modernization and comparative communism.

LYNN T. WHITE III is associate professor of politics at the Woodrow Wilson School, Princeton University. He is a specialist on modern Chinese politics.

Bibliography of C.I.S. Books

BOOKS WRITTEN UNDER THE AUSPICES OF THE CENTER OF
INTERNATIONAL STUDIES, PRINCETON UNIVERSITY

GABRIEL A. ALMOND, *The Appeals of Communism* (Princeton University Press, 1954)

WILLIAM W. KAUFMANN, ed., *Military Policy and National Security* (Princeton University Press, 1956)

KLAUS KNORR, *The War Potential of Nations* (Princeton University Press, 1956)

LUCIAN W. PYE, *Guerrilla Communism in Malaya* (Princeton University Press, 1956)

CHARLES DE VISSCHER, *Theory and Reality in Public International Law,* trans. by P. E. Corbett (Princeton University Press, 1957; rev. ed., 1968)

BERNARD C. COHEN, *The Political Process and Foreign Policy: The Making of the Japanese Peace Settlement* (Princeton University Press, 1957)

MYRON WEINER, *Party Politics in India: The Development of a Multi-Party System (Princeton University Press, 1957)*

PERCY E. CORBETT, *Law in Diplomacy* (Princeton University Press, 1959)

ROLF SANNWALD and JACQUES STOHLER, *Economic Integrations: Theoretical Assumptions and Consequences of European Unification,* trans. by Herman Karreman (Princeton University Press, 1959)

KLAUS KNORR, ed., *NATO and American Security* (Princeton University Press, 1959)

GABRIEL A. ALMOND and JAMES S. COLEMAN, eds., *The Politics of the Developing Areas* (Princeton University Press, 1960)

HERMAN KAHN, *On Thermonuclear War* (Princeton University Press, 1960)

SIDNEY VERBA, *Small Groups and Political Behavior: A Study of Leadership* (Princeton University Press, 1961)

ROBERT J. C. BUTOW, *Tojo and the Coming of the War* (Princeton University Press, 1961)

GLENN H. SNYDER, *Deterrence and Defense: Toward a Theory of National Security* (Princeton University Press, 1961)

Bibliography of C. I. S. Books

KLAUS KNORR and SIDNEY VERBA, eds., *The International System: Theoretical Essays* (Princeton University Press, 1961)

PETER PARET and JOHN W. SHY, *Guerrillas in the 1960s* (Praeger, 1962)

GEORGE MODELSKI, *A Theory of Foreign Policy* (Praeger, 1962)

KLAUS KNORR and THORNTON READ, eds., *Limited Strategic War* (Praeger, 1963)

FREDERICK S. DUNN, *Peace-Making and the Settlement with Japan* (Princeton University Press, 1963)

ARTHUR L. BURNS and NINA HEATHCOTE, *Peace-Keeping by United Nations Forces* (Praeger, 1963)

RICHARD A. FALK, *Law, Morality, and War in the Contemporary World* (Praeger, 1963)

JAMES N. ROSENAU, *National Leadership and Foreign Policy: A Case Study in the Mobilization of Public Support.* (Princeton University Press, 1963)

GABRIEL A. ALMOND and SIDNEY VERBA, *The Civic Culture: Political Attitudes and Democracy in Five Nations* (Princeton University Press, 1963)

BERNARD C. COHEN, *The Press and Foreign Policy* (Princeton University Press, 1963)

RICHARD L. SKLAR, *Nigerian Political Parties: Power in an Emergent African Nation* (Princeton University Press, 1963)

PETER PARET, *French Revolutionary Warfare from Indochina to Algeria: The Analysis of a Political and Military Doctrine* (Praeger, 1964)

HARRY ECKSTEIN, ed., *Internal War: Problems and Approaches* (Free Press, 1964)

CYRIL E. BLACK and THOMAS P. THORNTON, eds., *Communism and Revolution: The Strategic Uses of Political Violence* (Princeton University Press, 1964)

MIRIAM CAMPS, *Britain and the European Community 1955–1963* (Princeton University Press, 1964)

THOMAS P. THORNTON, ed., *The Third World in Soviet Perspective: Studies by Soviet Writers on the Developing Areas* (Princeton University Press, 1964)

JAMES N. ROSENAU, ed., *International Aspects of Civil Strife* (Princeton University Press, 1964)

SIDNEY I. PLOSS, *Conflict and Decision-Making in Soviet Russia: A Case Study of Agricultural Policy, 1953–1963* (Princeton University Press, 1965)

RICHARD A. FALK and RICHARD J. BARNET, eds., *Security in Disarmament* (Princeton University Press, 1965)

KARL VON VORYS, *Political Development in Pakistan* (Princeton University Press, 1965)

HAROLD and MARGARET SPROUT, *The Ecological Perspective on Human Affairs, With Special Reference to International Politics* (Princeton University Press, 1965)

KLAUS KNORR, *On the Uses of Military Power in the Nuclear Age* (Princeton University Press, 1966)

HARRY ECKSTEIN, *Division and Cohesion in Democracy: A Study of Norway* (Princeton University Press, 1966)

CYRIL E. BLACK, *The Dynamics of Modernization: A Study in Comparative History* (Harper & Row, 1966)

PETER KUNSTADTER, ed., *Southeast Asian Tribes, Minorities, and Nations* (Princeton University Press, 1967)

Bibliography of C. I. S. Books

E. VICTOR WOLFENSTEIN, *The Revolutionary Personality: Lenin, Trotsky, Gandhi* (Princeton University Press, 1967)

LEON GORDENKER, *The UN Secretary-General and the Maintenance of Peace* (Columbia University Press, 1967)

ORAN R. YOUNG, *The Intermediaries: Third Parties in International Crises* (Princeton University Press, 1967)

JAMES N. ROSENAU, ed., *Domestic Sources of Foreign Policy* (Free Press, 1967)

RICHARD F. HAMILTON, *Affluence and the French Worker in the Fourth Republic* (Princeton University Press, 1967)

LINDA B. MILLER, *World Order and Local Disorder: The United Nations and Internal Conflicts* (Princeton University Press, 1967)

HENRY BIENEN, *Tanzania: Party Transformation and Economic Development* (Princeton University Press, 1967)

WOLFRAM F. HANRIEDER, *West German Foreign Policy, 1949–1963: International Pressures and Domestic Response* (Stanford University Press, 1967)

RICHARD H. ULLMAN, *Britain and the Russian Civil War: November 1918–February 1920* (Princeton University Press, 1968)

ROBERT GILPIN, *France in the Age of the Scientific State* (Princeton University Press, 1968)

WILLIAM B. BADER, *The United States and the Spread of Nuclear Weapons* (Pegasus, 1968)

RICHARD A. FALK, *Legal Order in a Violent World* (Princeton University Press, 1968)

CYRIL E. BLACK, RICHARD A. FALK, KLAUS KNORR and ORAN R. YOUNG, *Neutralization and World Politics* (Princeton University Press, 1968)

ORAN R. YOUNG, *The Politics of Force: Bargaining During International Crises* (Princeton University Press, 1969)

KLAUS KNORR and JAMES N. ROSENAU, eds., *Contending Approaches to International Politics* (Princeton University Press, 1969)

JAMES N. ROSENAU, ed., *Linkage Politics: Essays on the Convergence of National and International Systems* (Free Press, 1969)

JOHN T. MCALISTER, JR., *Viet Nam: The Origins of Revolution* (Knopf, 1969)

JEAN EDWARD SMITH, *Germany Beyond the Wall: People, Politics and Prosperity* (Little, Brown, 1969)

JAMES BARROS, *Betrayal from Within: Joseph Avenol, Secretary-General of the League of Nations, 1933–1940* (Yale University Press, 1969)

CHARLES HERMANN, *Crises in Foreign Policy: A Simulation Analysis* (Bobbs-Merrill, 1969)

ROBERT C. TUCKER, *The Marxian Revolutionary Idea: Essays on Marxist Thought and Its Impact on Radical Movements* (Norton, 1969)

HARVEY WATERMAN, *Political Change in Contemporary France: The Politics of an Industrial Democracy* (Charles E. Merrill, 1969)

CYRIL E. BLACK and RICHARD A. FALK, eds., *The Future of the International Legal Order.* Vol. I: *Trends and Patterns* (Princeton University Press, 1969)

TED ROBERT GURR, *Why Men Rebel* (Princeton University Press, 1969)

C. SYLVESTER WHITAKER, *The Politics of Tradition: Continuity and Change in Northern Nigeria 1946–1966* (Princeton University Press, 1970)

Bibliography of C. I. S. Books

RICHARD A. FALK, *The Status of Law in International Society* (Princeton University Press, 1970)

JOHN T. MCALISTER, JR. and PAUL MUS, *The Vietnamese and Their Revolution* (Harper & Row, 1970)

KLAUS KNORR, *Military Power and Potential* (D. C. Heath, 1970)

CYRIL E. BLACK and RICHARD A. FALK, eds., *The Future of the International Legal Order*. Vol. II: *Wealth and Resources* (Princeton University Press, 1970)

LEON GORDENKER, ed., *The United Nations in International Politics* (Princeton University Press, 1971)

CYRIL E. BLACK and RICHARD A. FALK, eds., *The Future of the International Legal Order*. Vol. III: *Conflict Management* (Princeton University Press, 1971)

FRANCINE R. FRANKEL, *India's Green Revolution: Economic Gains and Political Costs* (Princeton University Press, 1971)

HAROLD and MARGARET SPROUT, *Toward a Politics of the Planet Earth* (Van Nostrand Reinhold Co., 1971)

CYRIL E. BLACK and RICHARD A. FALK, eds., *The Future of the International Legal Order*. Vol. IV: *The Structure of the International Environment* (Princeton University Press, 1972)

GERALD GARVEY, *Energy, Ecology, Economy* (Norton, 1972)

RICHARD H. ULLMAN, *The Anglo-Soviet Accord* (Princeton University Press, 1973)

KLAUS KNORR, *Power and Wealth: The Political Economy of International Power* (Basic Books, 1973)

ANTON BEBLER, *Military Rule in Africa: Dahomey, Ghana, Sierra Leone, and Mali* (Praeger, 1973)

ROBERT C. TUCKER, *Stalin as Revolutionary 1879–1929: A Study in History and Personality* (Norton, 1973)

EDWARD L. MORSE, *Foreign Policy and Interdependence in Gaullist France* (Princeton University Press, 1973)

HENRY BIENEN, *Kenya: The Politics of Participation and Control* (Princeton University Press, 1974)

GREGORY J. MASSELL, *The Surrogate Proletariat: Moslem Women and Revolutionary Strategies in Soviet Central Asia, 1919–1929* (Princeton University Press, 1974)

JAMES N. ROSENAU, *Citizenship Between Elections: An Inquiry Into The Mobilizable American* (Free Press, 1974)

ERVIN LASZLO, *A Strategy For The Future: The Systems Approach to World Order* (Braziller, 1974)

JOHN R. VINCENT, *Nonintervention and International Order* (Princeton University Press, 1974)

JAN H. KALICKI, *The Pattern of Sino-American Crises: Political-Military Interactions in the 1950s* (Cambridge University Press, 1975)

KLAUS KNORR, *The Power of Nations: The Political Economy of International Relations* (Basic Books, 1975)

JAMES P. SEWELL, *UNESCO and World Politics: Engaging in International Relations* (Princeton University Press, 1975)

Bibliography of C. I. S. Books

RICHARD A. FALK, *A Global Approach to National Policy* (Harvard University Press, 1975)

HARRY ECKSTEIN and TED ROBERT GURR, *Patterns of Authority: A Structural Basis for Political Inquiry* (Wiley, 1975)

CYRIL E. BLACK, MARIUS B. JANSEN, HERBERT S. LEVINE, MARION J. LEVY, JR., HENRY ROSOVSKY, GILBERT ROZMAN, HENRY D. SMITH, II, and S. FREDERICK STARR, *The Modernization of Japan and Russia* (Free Press, 1975)

LEON GORDENKER, *International Aid and National Decisions: Development Programs in Malawi, Tanzania, and Zambia* (Princeton University Press, 1976)

CARL VON CLAUSEWITZ, *On War,* ed. and trans. by Michael Howard and Peter Paret (Princeton University Press, 1976)

GERALD GARVEY and LOU ANN GARVEY, eds., *International Resource Flows* (Lexington Books/D. C. Heath, 1977)

WALTER F. MURPHY and JOSEPH TANENHAUS, *Comparative Constitutional Law Cases and Commentaries* (St. Martin's, 1977)

GERALD GARVEY, *Nuclear Power and Social Planning: The City of the Second Sun* (Lexington Books/D. C. Heath, 1977)

RICHARD E. BISSELL, *Apartheid and International Organizations* (Westview Press, 1977)

DAVID P. FORSYTHE, *Humanitarian Politics: The International Committee of the Red Cross* (Johns Hopkins University Press, 1977)

PAUL E. SIGMUND, *The Overthrow of Allende and the Politics of Chile, 1964–1976* (University of Pittsburgh Press, 1977)

HENRY S. BIENEN, *Armies and Parties in Africa* (Holmes and Meier, 1978)

HAROLD and MARGARET SPROUT, *The Context of Environmental Politics* (The University Press of Kentucky, 1978)

SAMUEL S. KIM, *China, the United Nations, and World Order* (Princeton University Press, 1979)

S. BASHEER AHMED, *Nuclear Fuel and Energy Policy,* (Lexington Books D. C. Heath, 1979)

ROBERT C. JOHANSEN, *The National Interest and the Human Interest: An Analysis of U.S. Foreign Policy,* (Princeton University Press, 1980)

RICHARD A. FALK and SAMUEL S. KIM, eds., *The War System: An Interdisciplinary Approach* (Westview Press, 1980)

JAMES H. BILLINGTON, *Fire in the Minds of Men: Origins of the Revolutionary Faith* (Basic Books, 1980)

BENNETT RAMBERG, *Destruction of Nuclear Energy Facilities in War: The Problem and the Implications* (Lexington Books, 1980)

GREGORY T. KRUGLAK, *The Politics of United States Decision-Making in United Nations Specialized Agencies: The Case of the International Labor Organization* (University Press of America, 1980)

JAMES C. HSIUNG and SAMUEL S. KIM, eds., *China in the Global Community* (Praeger, 1980)

DOUGLAS KINNARD, *The Secretary of Defense* (The University Press of Kentucky, 1980)

NICHOLAS G. ONUF, ed., *Law-Making in the Global Community* (Carolina Academic Press, 1981)

Index

Index

Index

Index

dynastic cycle, 52-53, 294-295; decline, 231, 257, 259, 445, 485-487, 499; legitimacy, 51-60, 100, 206-208, 215, 231, 256, 264, 357; *see also* Mandate of Heaven

E

Eastern Europe, 349, 468, 509
Eberstadt, N., 415
economic growth rates, 111, 318-321, 350-351, 450, 455, 465, 467, 492, 509, 514; *see also* agriculture and industry
Edo, 42-43, 171; *see also* Tokyo
education adult, 405, 412-415, 452; classical learning, 190-195, 197, 213-215, 228-229, 262-263, 355, 406, 408, 419, 437, 439, 443, 488, 491, 511; coeducation, 406, 411, 416, 441; discipline, 199-202, 437, 440-441; entrance examinations, 249, 392, 418, 424-426, 475, 516; financing, 407-411, 413, 416-417, 420, 422, 430, 434, 441, 478, 507; impact on social integration, 201-202, 322, 354-355, 359, 485; *min-pan* schools, 409-411, 414, 439, 452; practicality, 402-405, 417-418, 421, 424, 430-431, 441, 452, 459, 478; reform, 228-231, 262, 270, 296, 311, 357, 361, 405; rote learning, 199, 404, 411; school enrollments, 398, 406-408, 410, 412, 415-416, 422-425, 427, 431, 441, 452, 491, 498, 507; *see also* literacy
egalitarianism, 247-249, 251, 336-338, 369, 371, 376, 386, 391, 392-393, 405, 426-427, 432, 454, 456, 467, 473, 478-481, 516
Eight Powers, 260, 269
electricity, 318, 323-324, 328, 431; *see also* energy
Eleventh Party Congress (CCP), 285, 467
elite privileges, 140, 153, 390, 455, 474-475, 478
emigration, 39, 143
employment, 108, 121, 132, 331, 359, 372-373, 399, 438, 461, 465, 480; *see also* labor *and* unemployment
energy, 107, 113, 127, 318, 327-328, 455, 466
entrepreneurs, 67, 90, 152, 214, 311, 324-325, 330, 334, 342-343, 347, 358, 444, 458, 492
examination system (*k'e-chü*), 11, 38, 83-85, 90, 105, 123, 125, 184, 190-195, 226;

abolition, 228-229, 261-263, 270, 285, 355, 359, 402, 404, 419, 488-489, 502; *chien-sheng* degree, 90; *chin-shih* degree, 80, 124, 420; *chü-jen* degree, 124, 419 eight-legged essay, 192, 197, 419; impact on government, 184, 190-195, 202, 214, 257, 419, 487, 502; impact on social integration, 142, 149, 154, 165, 168-169, 170, 174, 183, 296, 393, 475, 502; *sheng-yuan* degree, 90, 230, 420
exchange rates, 113-115, 132, 134, 139, 325; *see also* currency *and* money
extraterritoriality, 101, 204, 241, 313, 379

F

factories, 322-325, 327, 332, 336-338, 347, 360, 363, 380, 383, 497
Fainsod, Merle, 105
Fairbank, John K., 22, 23, 26, 35, 43
family, 92-97, 100, 104-106, 121, 123, 156-157, 163-169, 173-174, 180-182, 185, 205-207, 211-212, 215, 251, 278, 301, 353, 355-356, 358-359, 368, 380, 382-386, 394, 449, 460, 474, 491, 500-501; loyalties, 94, 166, 180, 301, 378, 440, 447, 475, 480, 483, 484, 487-488, 495, 500, 506; practices, 363, 377, 505; strategies, 108, 110, 125, 165, 208, 363, 458, 485
family planning, 363-366, 380, 385, 463-464, 480, 505, 509, 510
famine, 133, 145, 175, 321-322, 331, 335, 339-340, 470; relief, 109, 113, 126, 129, 139, 238
Fei Hsiao-t'ung (Fei Xiaotong), 339, 498
fertilizers, 116, 127, 339-341, 447
feudalism, 105
Feuerwerker, Albert, 39, 101
first-comers to modernization, 1, 4, 47, 177, 383, 482, 489
fishing, 112, 151, 338
Five-Anti movement, 288, 301, 311
five-year plans, 246, 292, 459, 493
Fletcher, Joseph, 30, 35, 40
Foochow, 28
footbinding, 337, 356
foreign influence 391, 459, 468-469; and economic growth, 109, 133, 140, 204, 321, 324-326, 447, 458, 511; and education, 197-199, 201-202, 228-231, 262, 279, 402-406, 419-420, 430, 441, 443,

Index

Index

Index

J

Japanese invasion (War of Resistance), 239–243, 258, 260, 279–280, 288, 306, 322, 332, 344, 346–347, 359, 365, 379, 408, 414, 430, 443–445, 447, 451, 484, 491–492, 503
Japanese-American Security Treaty, 246
Jardine, Matheson and Co., 41
Jehol province, 241
Jenks, Jeremiah, 133
Jing Su, 296
Johnson, Chalmers A., 273
Jones, Susan Mann, 194, 196
July 21 schools, 431–432
Jurchen, 78

K

Kagoshima, 41
Kaiping Mining Bureau, 200
K'ang-hsi emperor, 25, 28, 184, 209
K'ang Yu-wei, 228, 260, 262, 269–270
Kansu province, 136
Kao Kang, 292
Karakhan Declaration, 260
Kazakhs, 267–268
Khrushchev, Nikita, 247, 266, 467
Kiangnan Arsenal, 134
Kiangsi province, 80, 130, 241, 252, 262, 265, 273–274, 283, 344
Kiangsu province, 80, 112, 118, 120, 130, 193, 229, 262, 264, 285, 322–323, 332, 334, 339, 344, 431
King, Frank H., 340
kinship, 9, 62, 93–95, 157, 163, 166, 168–169, 178–182, 212, 358, 369, 382, 386, 396, 506; see also family and lineage
Kirin province, 410
Kiukiang, 239
Kobe, 41
Koo, Wellington, 343
Korea, 28–29, 31, 36–37, 104, 203, 227, 277, 285, 303, 514
Korean minority, 267
Korean War, 245–247, 303, 306–307, 311, 464
Ku Yen-wu, 193
Kuang-hsu emperor, 199, 260, 271
Kuhn, Philip, 71
Kung Tzu-chen, 194

Kuo-tzu-chien, 192
Kuomintang 2, 238, 240–241, 243, 260, 264–265, 267, 272, 278–282, 291, 298–299, 306–307, 310, 313, 332, 346, 357–358, 383, 444, 449, 460, 492–493, 503; see also Nationalist China
Kwangsi province, 283, 410
Kwangtung province, 114, 118–119, 129, 133, 136, 170, 193, 229, 241, 272–273, 283, 285, 294, 304, 330, 345, 415–417
Kweichow province, 126, 131, 136–137, 290, 407–408, 410
Kyoto, 42

L

labor, 73–75, 108, 114–115, 151, 178–179, 181, 234, 237, 325–327, 329, 335, 341, 347, 370, 472, 477; discipline, 110, 200–201, 358, 363, 370, 441; distribution of, 398, 498, 509, 515; division of, 148, 152–153, 155, 191, 197–198, 320, 338–339, 359, 361, 363, 404, 450, 458, 466, 478–481, 496; education, 404, 410, 414–418, 423, 425–429, 439, 458, 477–478; intensification, 116, 119, 126–128, 208, 332, 380, 400, 447–448, 497; mental vs. manual, 477–480; productivity, 110, 125, 190, 320, 334, 337, 341, 346, 447–448, 450, 472–473, 476–477, 480–481, 497; riots, 121; skilled, 121, 153–156, 160–161, 196, 358, 372–374, 431, 450, 507; turnover, 371, 379, 472, 474–475, 498, 516; unskilled, 121; see also guilds and unions
labor camps, 308, 477
laissez-faire philosophy, 210, 398
Lampton, David M., 410
land: distribution, 105, 119–121, 128–129, 164, 178–179, 181, 319, 330–331, 334, 359, 458; investments, 124–125, 149–151, 170;-labor ratio, 121–122, 125, 133, 138; ownership, 150, 153, 157, 159, 161, 208, 211, 242, 358, 367, 393, 396, 503;-person ratio, 111, 145, 454, 483–484, 509–510, 513, 515; reform, 273, 287, 300–301, 306, 320, 333–334, 338–339, 358–360, 369–370, 377, 391, 393, 450, 460, 478, 495, 504; survey, 110, 128, 331
landlords, 124, 131, 148–150, 152–153, 156–158, 164, 178–179, 238, 295–297,

Index

Index

marriage, 147, 157, 164–165, 168, 179, 359, 363, 365–367, 375, 384–385, 396, 463, 477, 480, 505; *see also* bride price *and* dowries

Marshall, George, 243

Marxism (Marxism–Leninism), 11–14, 264, 372, 382, 400, 456, 467–468

Mass Education Movement, 414

mass media, 102, 278, 281, 290–291, 293–294, 307, 356, 413, 437–439, 462, 464, 480

mass organizations, 307, 310, 370, 386, 388, 458

Matsu, 464

May Fourth movement, 234–235, 258, 355, 413, 429, 438, 453, 488

May 7 cadre schools, 390, 431–432, 478

May 30 Incident (1925), 237

mechanization, 127, 135–137, 322, 337–339, 346, 466; *see also* technology

medicine, 37, 103, 195, 200, 348, 362, 365, 428, 430, 440, 463, 471, 473, 474, 480, 507, 516

Mencius, 31, 52, 184

merchants, 108, 124, 148–153, 158, 161, 167, 169–170, 175, 179, 208–209, 355, 358; *see also* entrepreneurs

Metzger, Thomas, A., 129, 186

Mexico, 312

migration, 10, 65, 143–145, 156–160, 175–177, 227, 330–331, 353, 363, 365, 371, 375, 379, 391–392, 394, 411, 465–466, 498, 510; rural–urban, 375, 398, 412, 450, 481, 495, 498, 509, 515, 516; urban–rural, 248, 363, 371, 387, 412, 424, 427, 439, 452, 465–466, 475, 505, 510

militarism, 72, 81–82, 103–104, 235, 240, 263, 276–285, 291, 302, 316, 330, 390

military, 25–26, 30, 53–54, 63–65, 67–77, 79–81, 99, 103–104, 151–152, 204–208, 238–240, 242, 245–247, 255, 263–266, 276–285, 296, 331, 346, 354–355, 449, 455, 457–458, 491, 501, 503, 508; education, 195–197, 263, 280–281; Field Armies, 283, 291–292; Fourth Route Army, 243; Green Standard Army, 68–71; Hunan Braves, 69, 71, 80, 277; Kwantung Army, 240; manpower, 479; Nan-yang Armies, 277; New Army, 103–104; Newly Established Army, 277; Nineteenth Route Army, 240; Pei-yang Army, 277–278; People's Liberation Army

(PLA), 246, 386, 393; Self-strengthening Army, 276–277; spending, 140–143, 148, 166–167, 282–283, 343–344, 354–355, 407, 408, 449, 516

Mill, John Stuart, 312

Ming dynasty, 6–7, 25–26, 29–30, 45, 184, 259, 348; economic growth, 120, 129–132; education, 184, 192, 194, 196; political structure, 51, 62–63, 65, 67–74, 78–79, 88, 110, 206; social integration, 142, 144, 148–149, 158, 169, 171, 212, 484–485

mining, 65, 126–127, 197, 429

Ministry of Agriculture, Industry, and Commerce, 135

Ministry of Education, 402, 407, 412–413, 439

minority nationalities, 24, 61, 69, 257–259, 267–268, 316, 360, 394, 439, 511–512

missionaries, 24–25, 35, 37, 41, 44, 103, 188–189, 198, 202, 402, 420, 422, 429, 451, 511; *see also* Christianity

modernization; definition of, 3–6; literature, 1, 3, 13

money, 26–27, 65, 107, 113–114, 124, 129, 131–134, 139, 200, 210, 287–288; fiscal system, 57, 130–132, 135, 139–140, 285–290; *see also* copper, currency, *and* silver

money lending, 126, 149–150, 174, 355–356, 358

Mongolia, 227, 316

Mongols, 25, 28, 30, 67, 69, 78, 85, 148, 259, 267, 316

monopolies, 73, 128–129, 151, 167, 209, 226

morality, 184–185, 199–202, 257–258, 264, 419, 436–441

Morse, Hosea Ballou, 22, 37–38

Moscow, 235, 246

most favored nation treatment, 34–35, 41–42, 204

Murphey, Rhoads, 133

N

Nagasaki, 28–29, 202

Nankai, 408, 420

Nanking, 80, 238–242, 270–273, 279–283, 291, 323–332, 340, 346, 408, 431

national assembly, 228–229, 270

National Central Military Academy, 281

National Humiliation Day, 233

National Humiliation Society, 230

545

Index

Index

Index

seniority, 334, 474, 516

serfdom, 110, 115, 140, 150, 153, 161, 211, 368, 489–490

services, 85, 111, 113, 122, 124, 151, 176, 306, 324, 336, 348, 362, 371, 376, 380, 471, 481, 488, 495, 497, 502, 507, 509, 515, 516

sex ratio, 147–148, 164–165, 174, 331

Shan people, 267

Shanghai, 37–41, 70, 101–102, 112, 133, 136, 159, 162, 197–198, 232, 237–238, 240, 260, 265, 286, 306, 323–324, 327, 331–332, 334, 394, 421, 424, 429, 434, 447

Shanghai Communiqué, 249

Shanghai International Settlement, 34

Shanhaikuan, 226

Shansi province, 80, 131, 133, 136, 170, 294, 311, 341, 407, 451

Shantung province, 38, 128, 130 133, 136, 138, 147, 151, 232–237, 240, 263, 274, 277, 296, 306, 336, 340, 414

Shao-hsing, 84, 124

Shaoshan, 266

Shensi province, 136, 265

Shenyang Agricultural College, 424

Shiba Yoshinobu, 112

Shidehara Kijūrō, 239

Shihchiachuang, 340

Shikan Gakko Military Academy, 280

shrines, 166, 176, 266

Shu Hsin-ch'eng, 187

Shun-te county, 136, 323

Sian Incident of 1936, 241, 291

Sigurdson, Jon, 431–432

silk, 28, 112, 114–115, 117–119, 127, 132, 136–137, 323; see also textiles

silver, 26–27, 33, 42, 50, 65, 109, 113–114, 118, 124, 131–132, 134–135, 178, 210, 241, 295, 325, 331–332, 487

Singapore, 514

Sinkiang, 36, 59, 267, 268

Sino-Japanese War (1894–1895), 36–38, 45, 199, 346, 443

Sino-Russian relations, 14, 24, 28, 30, 33, 36–38, 40–41, 47, 226–230. 268, 276

Sino-Soviet relations 2, 238–254, 260–261, 265, 267, 272, 310, 314, 327, 336, 342, 346, 349–351, 362, 365, 383, 389–390, 393, 399–400, 444–445, 454, 456, 459, 464, 468–469, 481, 493–494, 497; see also Soviet advisors and Soviet Union, as model

Smith, Adam, 210

social mobility, 95, 108, 141–142, 149, 152–156, 165–166, 170, 173–175, 178–181, 189–195, 208–209, 296, 356, 392–394, 405, 411–412, 418–419, 429, 483, 501, 505; decline of, 206–207, 261, 300–301, 305; impact on social integration, 211, 213, 295–297, 356–358, 368, 372–374, 391–394, 458, 485

social sciences, 193–194, 196, 230, 429–430, 515

Socialist Education Movement, 361, 434

Soochow, 114, 117, 241

South Asia, 26, 30, 137

Southeast Asia, 26, 29–32, 203, 246, 249

Soviet advisors, 247, 280–281, 433; see also Sino-Soviet relations

Soviet Union, as model, 2, 247, 399–400, 403, 422, 433, 444, 464, 468, 494–495, 497

Spain, 26–27

spheres of influence, 37–40, 226–227, 236, 379, 491

Sputnik, 246–247

Sri Lanka, 137, 415

ssŭ-shu (private schools), 185, 187, 197, 214, 402–404, 408–410, 412

Stalin, Joseph, 238, 244, 246–247, 253, 266, 268, 310, 314, 341, 346, 362, 467–470, 472, 481

state budget, 76–77, 132, 288–289, 293–294, 331, 333, 343–345

steel, 328, 346, 463

Sterling, Admiral, 42

Stilwell, Joseph, 35, 243

storytelling, 185, 188

street committees, 380, 508

strikes, 230–231, 237–238, 291, 319, 474

student activities, 229–231, 234–235, 242, 248, 356, 418, 438–439; see also foreign study

Sui dynasty, 184

suicides, 230, 292

Sun Yat-sen, 2, 44, 95, 199, 231–232, 238, 252, 259, 272, 280, 294, 310, 312, 453, 454

Sung dynasty, 25, 30, 62, 78, 85, 158, 184, 188, 190, 192–193, 195–196, 261, 291, 485

surpluses, 108, 132, 158, 163, 174, 181–182, 210, 212, 379, 490

surveillance, 66, 84, 88, 105, 357, 388–389, 391, 471, 483, 485–487, 496–497, 505

Index

Index